Stage Manager: The Professional Experience

LARRY FAZIO

Focal Press

Boston   Oxford   Auckland   Johannesburg   Melbourne   New Delhi

Focal Press is an imprint of Butterworth–Heinemann.

Ɒ Butterworth–Heinemann is a member of the Reed Elsevier group

∞   Recognizing the importance of preserving what has been written, Butterworth–Heinemann prints its books on acid-free paper whenever possible.

Butterworth–Heinemann supports the efforts of American Forests and the Global ReLeaf program in its campaign for the betterment of trees, forests, and our environment.

Library of Congress Cataloging-in-Publication Data

Fazio, Larry
   Stage manager : the professional experience / Larry Fazio.
      p. cm.
   Includes index.
   ISBN 0-240-80410-4 (pbk. : alk. paper)
   1. Stage management. I. Title.
   PN2085.F39 2000
   792'.023—dc21   00-022768

British Library Cataloguing-in-Publication Data
A catalogue record for this book is available from the British Library.

The publisher offers special discounts on bulk orders of this book.
For information, please contact:

Manager of Special Sales
Butterworth–Heinemann
225 Wildwood Avenue
Woburn, MA 01801-2041
Tel: 781-904-2500
Fax: 781-904-2620

For information on all Butterworth–Heinemann publications available, contact our World Wide Web home page at: http://www.focalpress.com

10 9 8 7 6 5 4 3 2 1

Printed in the United States of America

In dedicating this book, a list of names comes immediately to mind—people I want to acknowledge and honor. People who opened doors for me, gave me my first breaks, supported me in my career. One person however, stands above the others. I don't think they will mind taking second place to her.

I dedicate this book to my wife,

Toby,

who shares my life in all my endeavors.

I would also like to acknowledge the following people for their help in my career and in the writing of this book:

SKIPPY LYNN, who saw potential early in my career, opened doors, and let me explore and exercise my talents.

THE PASADENA PLAYHOUSE, for my scholarship, formal training, and early professional experience.

EDWIN LESTER and the LOS ANGELES CIVIC LIGHT OPERA, for giving me my first "big-time" shows.

LARRY DEAN, for showing me the ropes in stage managing, and demanding that as his assistant, I do nothing but my best work.

PAUL BLAKE, for long-term experience and employment.

BILL HOLLAND, who fired me, then later became my buddy and working associate.

JOHN, JACK, and BILL, friends and working associates who have passed on to another plain of existence, but whose spirits have sat with me in the writing of this book.

Special thanks to SHEILA ROMAN, friend and neighbor, whose editorial skills shaped and molded the manuscript of this book into a presentable form to be submitted to publishers.

DEDICATION TO THE READER

THE BRIDGE BUILDER

An old man traveling a lonely highway,
Came at evening time, cold and gray,
To a chasm, vast and wide and steep,
With waters running cold and deep.

The old man crossed in the twilight dim,
for the sullen stream held no fears for him.
Yet, he turned when he reached the other side,
And he built a bridge to span the tide.

"Old man!" cried a fellow pilgrim near.
"You're wasting your strength with building here.
Your journey will end with the ending day,
And you never again will pass this way.
You've crossed this chasm deep and wide,
Why build a bridge at the eventide?"

The builder lifted his old grey head.
"Good friend, on the pathe I've trod," he said,
"There follows after me this day,
A youth whose feet must pass this way.
This stream which has been as nothing to me,
To-that fair-haired youth might a pitfall be.
He too must cross in the twilight dim.
Good friend, I build this bridge for him."

Dromgoole

This book is my bridge for those who will follow the path of being a stage manager.
Larry Fazio

Contents

7. Profiles and Working Relationships 75

8. Running Auditions 104

11. The Rehearsal Script   145

12. The Last Week of Rehearsals   167

13. The Cueing Script   176

14. Technical Rehearsals   202

1

Introduction

At the beginning of most books, there is a group of pages set aside for a preface, a forward, an introduction, or all three. I remember in the early days of my studies, especially when in college, I would skip over those pages and turn to the first chapter. For me this was where the important information started—the material on which I would be tested. It wasn't until much later that I discovered the importance of those first pages and the information they contained. Reflecting back on this practice and thinking that there may be others like me, I have once again cut directly to Chapter 1. I will not, however, spare you an introduction.

THE PROFESSIONAL GAP

You are about to journey into professional stage managing as it has never before been traveled. Many good books have been written on this subject, so why another? To my knowledge, there is no one book that deals with the *total experience* of a professional stage manager. Some books direct their information toward academic studies and community theatre, segueing into the professional experience. Often there is a difference between what a stage manager does in college and community theatre and what a stage manager can or cannot do in professional theatre. There are some very clear and distinct boundaries for the professional stage manager to follow. These differences are what I have labeled the *professional gap*.

LEARNING THE HARD WAY

When I started stage managing professionally, some of the charts, plots, plans, and lists I had learned to create in school were filled with excellent information for working in an academic or community theatre. In the professional world, however, much of that same information was part of someone else's job. Believing I had been taught the definitive way, I had a rude awakening. I was like a floppy, enthusiastic puppy and I was told (sometimes with a smile, sometimes in a patronizing way) to save myself the work and leave that part for the person who was hired to do the job. I quickly had to learn what things I should and should not do as a professional stage manager.

THE HUMAN AND PSYCHOLOGICAL SIDE

In addition, there was little to no discussion in school about the *people* side of stage managing. There was no talk about working relationships, human behavior, managing people, the psychology of working with people in the theatre, stars, and egos. Just as important, nothing was said about a stage manager's personal beliefs, behavior, conflicts, struggles, or biases and how they might get in the way of the work. I had to experience and learn these things as I worked through the various jobs and situations. I did not want to be saved from my experiences, for they were what made me learn and grow. However, had I been introduced to some of these things, I might not have wandered into as many mine fields or left myself open as a target.

Personal Side Bar: I was an idealist. I went into the professional world and did battle with windmills. I believed right triumphed and truth prevailed. I thought rusted shaving pots could be buffed into golden helmets and I refused to see the truth when people held a mirror up to me. I believed everyone in theatre lived and embraced the same work ethics and professional code as I did.

OBJECTIVE AND INTENTION OF THIS BOOK

In writing this book, it is my intention to bridge the professional gap, sweep some of those mine fields, flag danger zones, point out pitfalls, and talk about the people with whom the stage manager works and must have a working relationship. I have made a great effort to describe the total experience and not just the academic view. In many places I will share experiences, make observations, and present how it has worked for me and for other stage managers. I will write with a positive pen, but from time to time I will relate things that will be neither encouraging nor inspiring. Your experience as a stage manager will be your own. However, all stage managers experience similar things. My way of doing things may not be your way. Take what you like. Feel free to change and adjust things to suit yourself and the situation in which you are working.

It is in my nature to be detailed and thorough, sometimes to a fault. I am also highly visual and write to create a comprehensive picture. Although most books on stage managing are handbook size, with my propensity for detail and my quest to describe the entire professional experience, this book has grown in size. Never having had to commit my job to paper, by the end of the first rough draft I was quite surprised and somewhat overwhelmed by the enormity and responsibility of being a stage manager. Up to that point, my lack of awareness had been bliss. Writing each chapter was easy. Stepping back and looking at the entire job can be frightening.

The reader too must approach this book one chapter at a time. My intention is not to make you a stage manager, but rather to help you become a stage manager. The stage manager's position is unique. People working in the same show do not see and experience what the stage manager sees and experiences, including the producer and director. This book is written strictly from the stage manager's point of view.

The Chapters

The chapters are arranged in the order in which the stage manager experiences the job and lives a personal life while working on a show. The chapters take the reader through the various stages and development of the production, including rehearsals, opening night, the touring show, and closing the show. The earlier chapters deal with practical and factual things like charts, plots, plans, lists, tools, supplies, and the power structure of a theatrical company—the *chain of command*. Then there are the chapters that make this book unique—the exploration of what makes a good stage manager, creating a resume, interviewing for the job, getting the job (or *not* getting the job), creating the cueing script and calling the cues for the show, and the all important study of people working in theatre—their behavior and the stage manager's working relationship with them. Again, each chapter will give a comprehensive picture of the total professional experience.

The last chapter in this book is a story based on one stage manager's experience. It is a compilation of incidents and experiences that reveals what can sometimes happen to a stage manager.

End of Chapter Features

At the end of some chapters, I may include a feature called "The Total Experience." This will consist of short stories or accounts of experiences I or some other SMs have had while working.

Another feature that may be found at the end of some chapters is entitled "Interviews." This will be excerpts from interviews conducted with producers, directors, and other SMs who may corroborate what has already been said in a particular chapter, or bring in another point of view. Let me introduce you to these people:

- **John Bowab**, director/producer/writer from Broadway (Associate Producer on *Mame* and *Sweet Charity*) to productions in regional theatre. Over one hundred twenty in all, most of them star packages. His equally impressive credits in television include: *The Cosby Show, Benson, The Facts of Life,* and *Soap.*
- **Paul Blake**, producer/director of award-winning regional theatre and all-star national tours, is based in New York and California. He has just completed his tenth year as Executive Producer of the St. Louis Muny, where he has produced and directed over 60 productions.
- **Bill Holland**, producer/PSM. For twelve years producer, associate producer, and PSM for the Los Angeles and San Francisco Civic Light Operas. He has worked over one hundred productions including the original production of *Gigi*

on Broadway and has worked with the who's who of stars.

- **Lara Teeter**, actor/singer/dancer/director/choreographer and now full professor with a tenure-track position in the theatre and dance department at California State University, Fullerton. Lara has performed on Broadway, received a Tony Award nomination for his performance in *On Your Toes*, and has toured the country several times over in national touring shows. Peppered throughout his illustrious career, Lara has staged, directed, and choreographed star package shows, full-scale musicals, yearly fundraising events, and is a favorite to play the lead in the musical, *My One and Only*. I have had the good fortune to work with him in all of the above capacities. A man who follows his spirit, Lara was pulled away from his teaching position to return to the stage as the Scarecrow in the most recent touring production of *The Wizard Of Oz*, staring Mickey Rooney and Eartha Kitt. Lara is presently in Evanston, Illinois working as the artistic director of the Light Opera Works. His talents are diverse, his energy boundless, and his destiny . . . great!

A Glossary of Words, Terms, Expressions, and Phrases

For a book on stage managing to be complete, there must be a list of words and terms that are defined as they are used in theatre. This list traditionally appears at the back of the book in the form of a glossary. What makes the glossary in this book stand out from others is that there are nearly 600 words, terms, expressions, and phrases, and each is defined for the stage manager—from his point of view, for his use, and what they mean to him. It is the stage manager's working vocabulary. In many of the terms, additional information is given to create a greater picture and understanding for the beginning stage manager. In some definitions, technical details have been simplified or left out. When a stage manager is first starting out, a general working knowledge and understanding of things is more important. Later, with experience, the stage manager's knowledge will become more enriched, and the definitions more sophisticated.

Side Bar: At the beginning of this chapter I shared with you the bad habit I practiced by passing over the preface, foreword, or introduction. I confess I was just as delinquent when it came to the glossary. I went

to it only when it was absolutely necessary. As a person who has learned some things the hard way, I strongly recommend that at some point in reading this book you bookmark your place and turn to the glossary. In keeping with the order in which the information in this book is delivered, that should happen upon the conclusion of reading Chapter 4. I will remind you at that time.

A DEFINITION OF *PROFESSIONAL*

The operative word throughout this book is *professional. The World Book Encyclopedia Dictionary* has several definitions:

1. *"The professional makes a business or trade of something that others might do for pleasure."* There is no question that theatre is a business—*show business*. Also, there is a very thin, almost nonexistent line between what professional people in show business do for pay and what many others do for pleasure.
2. *"A professional is a person who belongs to a recognized and organized profession."* As far back as the Greek theatre we see how performers and theatre productions have been organized and considered a profession. Anyone who has worked in a play, from high school to Broadway, knows the organization required to produce a show.
3. *"A professional does a job to a high degree and quality."* There is no doubt as to the degree and quality that all people in theatre put into their work and into the productions they present.

For stage managers and people in the theatre, I would add to this definition:

Being professional means following an honorable code of ethics, practices, and standards, being responsible to give the best to yourself, to fellow workers, the employer, to the production, and ultimately, to the people who come to see the show.

THE DISTINGUISHING LINE

The previous definitions are all workable, but they apply equally to any group of thespians who work to do their best. Where do we go then to find that distinguishing line between professional and nonprofessional? Definition #2 brings us closest: *A person who belongs to a recognized and organized profession.*

This leads us directly to the unions and the guilds to which the artists, creators, and technicians belong. In the professional world, it is the unions and guilds that people use to distinguish between what is professional and what is nonprofessional. For the actor this would be the Actor's Equity Association (AEA), more commonly called Equity. For the technicians this would be the International Alliance of Theatrical Stage Employees, I.A.T.S.E. (pronounced *Eye-aht-see*). *For our purposes in this book, people and productions in association with the unions and guilds will be the distinguishing line between what is professional and what is nonprofessional.* For a stage manager, the highest attainment in professional work in theatre is to get an Equity show.

THE MOST IMPORTANT WORK

In many places throughout this book, I have found myself singling out a particular part of the stage manager's job as being the most important. After a while the statement began to lose its effectiveness. How many parts can be the most important? I considered striking the phrase, but realized that the part of the job the stage manager is doing at any one time is the most important: *Each part of a stage manager's job has an effect on what is happening at the moment and more than likely will affect another important part later.* This is what makes a stage manager's job intense. This is what makes it exciting, exhilarating, rewarding, energizing, and high powered. This is what also makes the stage manager's job stress filled and exhausting.

THE MUSICAL PLAY

The musical show is the ultimate experience for any stage manager. There are more charts, plots, plans, lists, sets, scene changes, costumes, cues, and people. With a musical, there is more of everything.

STANDARD STAGE MANAGER TITLES AND THEIR ABBREVIATIONS

The title of *stage manager* is a general term that can be applied to any person who works in that position.

Usually on small shows where one person is hired to do the job, that person is referred to simply as the stage manager. On musicals and large shows where more than one stage manager is needed, the head or lead stage manager becomes known as the *production stage manager* while the other stage manager becomes an *assistant stage manager*. The more elaborate and impressive title of production stage manager was invented by producers who wanted to give their favorite, longtime stage managers credit on posters and on the program's title page. On shows where a third stage manager is needed, the third manager is also called the assistant stage manager, but in the program credits the titles among the three stage managers may read:

Production Stage Manager (the first or head stage manager)

Stage Manager (the second stage manager)

Assistant Stage Manager (the third stage manager)

The common abbreviations for these titles used by the members of a theatrical company are:

PSM = Production Stage Manager

SM = Stage Manager(s)

ASM = Assistant Stage Manager(s)

From this point on, I will use these abbreviations. I will further manipulate the English language by using these shorthand notes:

SMs = plural for stage manager

SM's = possessive (belonging to a stage manager)

SMing = the act of working as a stage manager

THE ASM

The ASM must be capable of doing all that the PSM does. The ASM must be ready to take over the lead position should the PSM become unable to do the job. Throughout this book the term SM will be used in the singular form, and all of the information/work duties, though seemingly directed to the head SM (the PSM), should be understood to include the ASM as well. Only when there is a clear separation of work will the terms PSM and ASM be used. Generally, the only difference between a good ASM and PSM is sometimes age and often the amount of experience.

WOMEN SMs

It is my intention throughout this book to speak to both men and women. This book is as much for women who are interested in becoming a professional SM as it is for men. In the first half of the twentieth century, men dominated this field. Cheryl Crawford was one of the first exceptions in the 1930s. It wasn't until World War II that women were given the opportunity, and in some cases were better than their male counterparts. By the 1950s, women had taken their place and it was not uncommon to find women SMs on major Broadway shows. In Chapter 17, The Touring Show, we will meet one such person, Anne Sullivan. She will share with us her experience with a day in the life of an SM on a musical show.

A HISTORY OF SMing

In the final stages of putting this book together, I realized that I wanted to include a section on the history of SMing. In my research, I found only one SMing book that briefly described the evolution of the SM, which started in the seventeenth century during Shakespeare's and Molière's time.

In my heart and in the wilds of my imagination, I know SMs existed long before the 1600s. I am convinced that SMs existed at least as far back as the days of the cave man. There is no documentation to substantiate this, but I am certain that during the time when humans sat around camp fires to reenact the thrill of the hunt and to tell of the glory of the kill, there was someone in the group who built the fire, cleared the ground for seating, and during the event handed out, at the most dramatic moment, the spear or rock that killed the beast.

The history of theatre starts with the Egyptians, Greeks, and Romans. Back then productions were simple. There was no scenery. The props were limited to a crown, a chalice, or a mask on a stick. Aside from the basic costume for the character, there might be a cloak and a pair of twelve-inch Cathernis boot-shoes to give the character greater stature. The actors managed all things having to do with the production. They had free range over direction and style, which

was usually loud, bombastic, exaggerated, and melo-dramatic—often including wailing and bellowing. Pantomime was the art of communicating action, and the only movement that might have required organizing and coordinating (not yet called choreography) was the unison movement of the Greek chorus.

In medieval time (give or take a hundred years), there was still no hint of an SM. The actors took over directing, often padding their parts. Rehearsals were argumentative and chaotic. Egos were large and fiery.

By Shakespeare's and Molière's time, the actor and/or playwright was well established as the director of the show and putting together a production had become more civilized and organized. More props were used and special costumes were needed to portray the characters. It wasn't until the eighteenth century in England that the term stage manager was used instead of director. This was the first time a person, separate from the actors and playwright, was hired to direct or manage the stage. With the advent of elaborate sets, multiple costume changes, mechanical scenery and devices, gas lighting, and the lime-light spotlight, the SM's job split into the two positions as we know them today—the director and the SM.

THE PROFESSIONAL EXPERIENCE

This is a good time to give you some background on how I became an SM. In this account I minimize the use of names and places and have focused more on the progression, evolution, and experience of becoming an SM.

There was never a time when I did not want to be in show business. The feeling was fostered and kept alive throughout my childhood and teen years by going to the movies. Even back then I was interested in the "behind the scenes" activities. I knew about directors, producers, and the work they did. Back then my dream was to some day go to Hollywood.

I did not have the opportunity to express my theatrical inclinations until I joined the U.S. Army. I first became a motion picture photographer. As fate would have it, I came across a touring musical variety show comprised of all military personnel, and was extremely fortunate to become a part of that group. The people in charge saw my potential both as a performer and as a person who could work behind the scenes. Almost immediately I was made assistant to the SM, and by the end of the year I was given full SMing duties. When my time was finished with the military, I was given the Golden Key award for my work and contributions to the army entertainment program. With the key came a three-year scholarship to study theatre at the world-famous Pasadena Playhouse in California. This was all too good to be true. Not only was I going to study that which I loved most, but I was one step closer to Hollywood.

While at the Playhouse, there wasn't an area I didn't explore as a performer, director, and stage manager. The school and the professional theatre attached to the school recognized my stage managing abilities early and within my first year of study, I was brought in as a student-assistant stage manager, a position usually reserved for second- and third-year students. Upon completion of my studies at the Playhouse, I was given a scholarship to California State University where I finished studies for my bachelor's degree in theatre arts. It was during that time that I focused my studies on directing. In my final year, I was awarded the Best Director Award for my final project.

After my graduation, my wife and I moved to a suburb just north of Hollywood. Hollywood was not impressed with my degree or awards and it took almost three years to get a foot in anyone's door. The opportunity came when a former teacher from the Playhouse recommended me to a civic light opera group to be the second ASM on a musical version of *Gone With The Wind*.

I had arrived. I was working with a major Broadway director, with star name performers, and after a tour across the country, the show was scheduled to open on Broadway. I excelled in my work. Before we finished our run in Los Angeles, I was calling cues for the show and performing many of the first ASM's duties. Unfortunately, the "wind" blew itself out by the time we got to San Francisco, and I never got to Broadway. I did, however, continue to work for the same producing company for the next seven years, working on star name shows and building an impressive resume. In between seasons, I worked for two television producers, moving easily between stage, film, and TV. I worked practically the year round with very little downtime.

Good things come to an end, and sometimes quickly. Within the space of a few years, the light opera group closed its doors, the TV producers split up their partnership, and I was fired from a major production having to do with a major star in a major conflict. Shortly afterwards, another producer moved to the Midwest to produce shows there, and a director who hired me for all his shows died of an aneurysm. In one sweep of fate, my network of employment disintegrated and I remained an unemployed SM for a long time. But I did not remain idle. During this time I directed shows for civic light opera groups. I tried getting work on Broadway, but Broadway was not impressed with my LA credits. I was not too distressed over this fact, because my family and roots were now planted in Los Angeles, and I had been lulled into the comfortable Southern California living.

Throughout these years of SMing and directing I was also associated with a magician friend. My wife was one of his assistants and together we traveled throughout the United States, Canada, and many foreign countries.

Eventually I became associated with another producer who did touring shows, and for the next five years I spent most of my time SMing on the road. Touring shows are a hard gig, and after five years my wife and I made a collective decision that I would no longer take shows that took me out of town. I went through another period of unemployment and it was during this time that I started writing this book. However, bills must be paid. This time I combined my directing and SMing skills and got a job at a world-class theme park just a few miles from my home.

After completing this book, the next logical thing to do is teach a course on SMing at a college or university. I still hope to work a show on Broadway someday. In any event, it has been, and continues to be, a full life. The memories, experiences, and friends remain my reward and treasure. I would change very little in my experience, except perhaps to have made some of those unemployment periods shorter.

INTERVIEWS

Being a longtime-veteran of theatre and having had the Broadway experience, John Bowab had a lot to say on "how it was" with SMs back in the 1960s and 70s

John Bowab: Sammy was the first big-time professional SM I worked with. He was a working SM. Back then he wore a suit and tie. What made Sammy special was that he was extremely professional and he demanded that from everyone else. He was organized and worked well with people, although he had a temper and wouldn't tolerate a whole lot of bull.

Back then they first started calling SMs "Production Stage Managers." These were highly sought-after SMs. Every producer on Broadway had their special favorite and to keep them they started giving them billing on the title page, on posters, and in front of the theatre.

In those days, SMs were also very much part of the casting system, which is not done much today. Today we have casting directors. Casting directors came about in the 70s. Back in the 40s, 50s, and 60s, SMs could control very much who was seen or not seen for an audition. The producing companies sent out "Character Breakdowns" and then the SM would get to sort through all the pictures and resumes to save the producer's and director's time. Today the SM's job leans more towards the technical, what with electronics, computers, and high tech. Even understudy rehearsals and cast replacements, which the SM always did, is now done by the director or assistant director.

For an SM to stay on Broadway, he has to be extremely good because the job is a lot more demanding than in theatre anywhere else. Only the good ones last. You can't work for big-time Broadway producers, directors, and stars and not come under a strain. The talent around is big and the show is important. If an SM can't deliver, he's out! It certainly can't be easy on the home life and the personal life, because so much has to be given to the show.

Interviewer: What is your definition of a stage manager?

John Bowab: The title says it all—the person who manages the stage, and that covers a lot of territory. I believe that an SM is responsible for everything that happens on the stage—that is, everything that makes the show function the way the director chooses. As a director and producer, I want to know that my cast is being taken care of and is happy and the SM has great influence on that by how he does the job. I want to know that if the toilets won't work or if it's freezing because of too much air-conditioning in the mid of winter, the SM is there doing something about it, talking to the right people, and at the same time, keeping the show at performance peak the way that it was set.

Bill Holland offered this observation about SMs:

An interesting fact about SMs: have you noticed at our level of stage managing that there are only a few good young ones and a lot more older ones? That's because the not-so-good ones fall by the wayside quickly, sometimes in one or two shows, while the real good ones keep getting work and stay around for a long time. I imagine that there's burnout too.

2

The Anatomy of a Good Stage Manager

In the exploration or analysis of what makes a good SM there are three areas or levels of understanding to discuss. Each layer goes deeper into the individual:

1. **The Practical Application.** This is the outermost layer. This is the way in which the SM works and does things when on the job. On the surface, this means doing the paperwork. Just under the surface and beginning the journey into the anatomy of an SM, *practical application* means being organized, disciplined, focused, and concentrated; having the ability to follow through on things; and working efficiently and effectively.
2. **The Qualities.** These are the personal qualities of an SM—personality, demeanor, attitude, and approach. This is the SM working with people—knowing human behavior and knowing the psychology of working with people in the theatre. These are qualities that can be studied, developed, and acquired.
3. **The Spirit.** This is the innermost part of the SM, the part that drives and motivates an individual to want to be an SM. This is the part of which most SMs are least aware—the *soul* of being an SM.

THE PRACTICAL APPLICATION

This is the part of an SM's job that is included in all books on SMing: charts, plots, plans, and lists. These things are discussed in detail in a later chapter. In addition to all of those things, practical application includes having the ability to administrate, coordinate, schedule, run the show, and know when to lead and when to follow.

A good SM begins by preparing, planning, and reviewing. Each day the SM prioritizes the things that need to be done, makes good notes, creates working lists, and then works from them. A good SM learns to set into motion those things that must be done now and hold at bay those things that can wait a moment longer.

While working within the structure of being organized, having things planned out, and being prepared, a good SM also has the ability to *work spontaneously,* handling things as they come up. There is always some detail that demands immediate attention. The SM learns to deal with things on-the-spot and at the same time keep the priority list moving forward.

A good SM is *thorough* and *completes things,* leaving nothing out and covering all areas. The smallest detail is included, no loose ends remain, and the SM works until the day's work is complete. There is no downtime for an SM during the workday. While everyone is on a break or out at meal time, the SM is catching up, rewriting lists, reprioritizing, and setting up for the next portion of the day. An SM's break time comes in sleep, maybe on a day off, and surely when unemployed.

An SM learns to work at a rapid pace, with high energy and with multiple things going at one time. An SM cannot, however, be seen running around frantically. Moving swiftly with efficiency is impressive. Even complaining about not having enough time is acceptable. But being frantic, displaying panic, or being out of control is unnerving to everyone around.

An SM must not get pulled into drama or hysteria. While everyone around may be loosing their heads, the SM must maintain enough distance to remain calm and objective, ready to steer the ship through turbulent waters, and keep the show and the company afloat. As soon as an SM shows anything less than complete confidence and control, directors become nervous, producers fearful, and performers insecure. The company would rather live under a delusion of strength and security than see their SM display anything less.

SMs must never get pulled into a mindset of "it can't be done." The word "impossible" should not exist in an SM's vocabulary. Looking for a solution or an alternative is the order and practice of the day. A good SM is:

- **Organized.** Seldom, if ever, is a successful SM disorganized. Those who are not highly organized get weeded out before they hit the professional boards.
- **Detailed.** An SM cannot casually pass over a thing or do a thumbnail sketch. Missing a detail today can cause loss of time and unnecessary money spent later. With enough time lost and extra money spent, a less-detailed SM will find fewer jobs in the future.
- **Visual.** An SM must learn to create vivid mind pictures. This is an art that needs to be cultivated and applied throughout the workday. From the first reading of the play, to descriptions of set design and costumes, to imagining how the scenery will move, to making and changing schedules, the SM must see things from different angles and various points of view. The SM must see how things fit into the overall picture, how they affect each other, and the positive contributions or the negative distractions of each element.
- **A planner.** A good SM thinks ahead and anticipates. These things are practiced and become perfected while on the job. Fortunately, SMs usually work first as assistants, which allows them to practice and flex this muscle before taking on the responsibility of the lead position, the PSM.
- **A timekeeper.** An SM watches the time throughout the day, monitoring how the time is being used and if people are working according to the schedule. The good SM has an excellent sense of "realistic" time and knows how long it takes for things to be done. Many of the people with whom the SM works will work in "theoretical" time or "wishful thinking" time, or time that is manipulated to suit their needs.
- **A good scheduler.** With a good sense of realistic time, an SM learns how to get the most out of a period of time and is able to schedule two or more things at one time and yet have neither be in conflict or disrupt the other. The good SM learns to keep everyone working efficiently and effectively.
- **Punctual.** The SM always arrives on time, if not early, starts things on time, and learns how to deal with people who have a tendency or a great affinity for being late.
- **A person who does it now!** Now is the only choice. Later is too late. Later will be filled with too many things that need to be done now! No matter how small, trivial, or inconsequential a thing may be, if something must be postponed or momentarily set aside, the SM must put it on the work list and get back to it as soon as possible.
- **A person who follows through and completes things.** SMs make copious work notes on every matter that crosses their desk or is brought to their attention. No matter is too small or unimportant. The SM sets nothing aside, tending to everything in the order of its importance, is thorough, and brings all things to completion.
- **Focused.** Being concentrated and "working in the moment" is being focused. This may seem a contradiction to planning and thinking ahead, but it is not. The two are separate yet complementary to each other. A good SM knows when to stay focused, concentrated, and work in the moment, and when to step back to think ahead or reflect on the past. An SM's work is based in the present. Problems arise when the SM remains stuck in the past or is too concerned with the future.
- **Centered.** Being centered is being at ease and comfortable with oneself. It is liking and loving yourself and at the same time not making yourself the center of the universe. Being centered is not personalizing all that happens. It is living in the positive and being alert to the negative. It is knowing and applying your strengths, admitting your weaknesses and faults, and being ready to make changes or improvements. It is not being driven by your needs. It is not having to be right all the time. It is knowing when to relinquish, when to win, and when to accept loss or defeat. Being centered is having the ability to take suggestion, accept criticism, stand in adversity, and at the same time, know you are still a good and worthy person as well as an SM.
- **Confident.** Confidence comes with experience in doing the job. It is the result of success and failure, compliments and complaints, criticism and

strokes. Being confident allows the SM to be assertive, take the lead, stand alone when necessary, maintain personal inspiration and motivation, and inspire and motivate others.

- **A communicator.** An SM does not have to be an orator, a debater, or a manipulator of the spoken language. A good SM is direct and to the point, has a clear picture in mind and is able to convey it to others in simple, clear, and understandable terms. An SM cannot be preachy, teachy, pedantic, or long-winded.

- **A jack-of-all-trades.** A good SM is the master at stage managing and is the jack of all other trades within the company. The SM knows a little about all things. This includes management and administration, as well as the artistic and technical parts. The SM needs to have enough information to communicate effectively, appreciate the work a person must do, and know the difficult parts of each person's job.

- **A person who knows the boundaries and limitations of all things, including the SM's job.** Good SMs learn not only their own boundaries, limitations, and job description, but also the boundaries, limitations, and description of other people's jobs. From time to time, people will attempt to deposit some of their work on the SM. An SM must become vigilant in requiring all people to keep the responsibility of their own jobs.

- **Alert, observant and highly aware.** Throughout the work day an SM hears and see things both directly and indirectly. The SM is aware of each person as they do their work, and is observant of all situations and events. The important things—the things that may affect the show or the company, the SM tends to immediately. The rest is filed away for future reference.

- **Able to evaluate, assess, and make *on-the-spot* decisions.** Often, in matters large and small, there is no time for the SM to go into deliberation. The SM must draw from personal experience, knowledge of human behavior, and past experience of working with people in the theatre, to make quick decisions and give immediate responses.

THE QUALITIES OF A GOOD SM

This next area of exploration and understanding takes us further into the person of the SM. To varying degrees, people who are drawn to being a SM already have the qualities that make up a good SM. These are qualities that can be cultivated, built upon, and made part of an SM's character and way of working. People are not always conscious of these qualities, unless they stop to analyze them. These are the qualities that make producers, directors, fellow workers, and peers feel comfortable and secure in having a particular person as their SM.

- **A love for working with people.** SMing is more than the business of putting on a show. At least one-third of the job is having to deal with people. Through the course of working on a show, the SM crosses paths with all people in the company, experiencing the good and not so good of their actions and behavior. Without a genuine love, interest, and understanding of human nature and human behavior, and without knowing the psychology of working with people in theatre, the job of being an SM can be a confusing, frustrating, and highly negative experience.

- **Understanding and compassion.** The foundation of understanding and compassion is knowledge of human nature, human behavior, and the psychology of people. The SM learns quickly the coloring and shading of the individuals in the company and allows them the space to express their individuality, but not at the expense of professional and social improprieties. Good SMs use understanding and compassion to better lead and direct the people left in their charge and under their care.

- **More communication skills.** Communication involves not only being able to convey thoughts and words, but also being a good listener and observer. A good SM creates an environment for people to express their feelings and to speak freely and candidly without fear of recourse. As the person speaks, the SM hears the choice of words, reads between the lines, watches body language, listens to the tone of voice, and feels the intensity and the energy being used. In addition, an SM learns the subtle differences between the various groups involved in the production and learns to speak in their terms without sounding out of place or being patronizing.

- **Arbitration skills.** A good SM remains clear, unattached, unbiased, fair, and just. Do not get pulled into the feelings of situations. Whenever possible, bring quick resolution and closure, trying to turn a negative encounter into a win-win situation for all.

- **Serves.** An SM learns early that the job is one of service and does not mind giving service. On the other hand, a good SM knows the difference between giving service and being a servant. The line between the two is very fine and at times people easily step over it. An SM learns which services must be provided as part of the job, and selectively chooses to perform extra services that are beyond the call of the job.

- **Neither rescues nor caretakes.** An SM is caring and has concern for all the people in the company, is ever present to lend an ear, provide a shoulder, and offer assistance. The SM steps forward in a preventative capacity to oversee and resolve anything having to do with the show or the company. The SM gives guidance and counsel, but does not become a rescuer or a caretaker. All individuals should maintain the choice and responsibility of their acts/actions. Some people want a caretaker in their lives and in the absence of a director or producer may turn to the SM. The SM must guard against being pulled into such situations. *A good SM knows when to say no and when to say yes.*

- **A quick study of people.** A good SM is able to size up people on first encounter and trusts that instinct, but is willing to change any wrong first impressions.

- **Discrete and confidential.** An SM is privy to personal information and learns things about people that are not generally known nor are for publication. They should remain that way.

- **Know the art and craft of delivering a message.** An SM never delivers an angry message from one person to another. The *art* is to edit the message, soften the blows, minimize the intensity, and yet still get the point across. The *craft* is to convey the sender's anger to a lesser degree, perhaps conveying it as annoyance or frustration. The craft is also not to fall victim to the "Off with the Messenger's Head Syndrome." In medieval times the king cut off the messenger's head if he did not like the contents of the message. Today, when a director sends the SM to deliver an angry message to the star, the reaction is not as deadly, but the results can be almost as volatile.

- **Delegate work—keep multiple areas of operation going.** An SM does not get tied up in doing the work, but learns what work can be delegated. As much as possible, an SM tries to stay free to move about, going from area to area in a supervisory capacity, overseeing and keeping people working productively.

- **Work quietly, efficiently, and effectively.** An SM works without fanfare, reward, or having to be at center stage. In fact, an SM keeps the attention focused on others.

- **Work under pressure.** There are few parts of the workday in which there isn't pressure. Pressure comes from all directions and from all people. Each part of the production demands attention and detail, and needs it NOW! Also, there is the pressure self-imposed by the SM to do the job perfectly at all times.

- **Take direction.** A good SM is able to take direction as well as give it.

- **Acknowledge.** Good SMs acknowledge their good work and strengths, and graciously accept compliments and rewards. On the other hand, when SMs are wrong, they must openly admit to it, face their shortcomings, state their inabilities, and whenever needed and appropriate, apologize publicly as well as personally. A good SM acknowledges others too, recognizing their good work and deeds, and whenever possible, acknowledging them in public and personally. The SM gives as much encouragement, compliments, and words of praise as complaints, criticisms, or orders.

- **Truth and myth.** An SM knows the truth and myth of the SM's power and position within the chain of command and also learns how to use it effectively.

There are other qualities that could be listed in the anatomy of a good SM, but the preceding list is a good start. Each SM develops a unique combination of qualities. Take what you like and add it to what you already have. However, before we move on to the next level of understanding, there are two more qualities that I have saved for last—leadership and humor.

- **Leadership.** For an SM, leadership is knowing the job well and putting all its parts into practical application. Leadership is working with people: knowing and loving them, guiding and directing them. Leadership is standing at the front, knowing when to step forward and command, and when to remain subordinate and follow. It is learning from mistakes and using success to build assurance and confidence. Leadership is being strongly motivated and focused to achieve, getting the job done well, and being responsible to coworkers. Leadership for an SM is the sum total of all the things listed in this chapter and throughout this book.

- **Humor.** This is a quality seldom considered, yet an SM with humor is a joy to have in the good times as well as during the stress-filled times. In his interview for this book, Bill Holland said, "I like an SM with a good sense of humor." Paul Blake agreed, and the others interviewed made it unanimous. They liked having an SM who could generate fun as well as participate in it. They were careful to add, "As long as the humor is done at the right time, appropriately, is not disruptive, not harmful to the show, mean-spirited, or at the expense of someone else."

THE SPIRIT OF AN SM

Most people today working as professional SMs did not start out wanting to be an SM. Has anyone ever heard a child express the desire to grow up to be a stage manager? A performer, yes, or maybe a director, but not an SM. Most students in theatre arts will major in acting, directing, stage craft, design, and maybe take an SMing course as an easy technical elective, or as part of their required curriculum. For the most part, becoming an SM just happens. One day a person simply begins helping out backstage, maybe assisting the director, or coordinating, organizing, making some lists, prompting from the side lines, or calling some cues during a performance. Maybe there's a chance to be in a show as an actor if the person will also assist the SM in some duties. Maybe a person has a good working knowledge of the technical part of theatre and a producer is comfortable in putting this person in the SM's position.

The Right Stuff

The elements of leadership and the qualities of being an SM can be learned and acquired, but there also must be an internal drive, desire, and perhaps need to be an SM. An SM's life is extreme, the intensity and pressure is great, and without that internal push the desired success of being an SM may remain elusive. This last level in the anatomy of an SM is the least explored or talked about, probably because of its highly subjective and private nature. Generalities can be drawn, but the reader may easily discount them, saying, "Such things do not apply to me."

This level of understanding takes us deeper into the psyche of what makes a good SM and why a person may want to become an SM. This is the heart, the soul of the SM. It is the spirit, the internal drives and motivations of SMs, that makes them want to stand at the front and lead, that makes them stay during times of adversity, abuse, punishment, and extreme intensity of the job.

Many SMs never go to this place of exploration within themselves, and yet they are successful. They have the right internal stuff and their drive is strong enough to carry them through. There are perhaps as many SMs who have failed, with disastrous experience and results. Had they explored this area within themselves, they might have learned early that being an SM was not the work for them, that perhaps it was not in their nature.

Like every other kind of job, SMing requires a certain kind of a person. Those who remain all seem to have similar qualities in spirit, behavior, way of working, attitude, and mindset. Many SMs get great satisfaction out of being, given a task, following through on the task, and bringing the task to completion. SMs also like being in charge, being the leader, and being in a position of power and authority. SMs get gratification from being involved with all parts of the production, and I would venture to say their need for attention, recognition, and feeling important is as great as that of any other person in the theatre.

Core of the Spirit

To take this journey into oneself is not easy. Some are afraid to go there. Some don't know how to get there. It is not always a journey to be taken alone. A friend, a confidant, or a person with professional experience may be needed.

Let us cut deeply and directly to three core qualities that can make an SM successful. Note that these same qualities, when used inappropriately, obsessively, compulsively, or without control, are also the things that bring SMs down and cause them to fail in their job.

Ego

Whenever ego is present, it has tremendous presence, power, control, and influence over people and situations. It is believed that people in the entertainment industry have greater egos than people in other industries, but it only appears that way because people in entertainment seem to be more tolerant of ego. They seem to allow their peers to express it more freely—especially if that person's work makes the show successful and brings in lots of money.

There is only a small part of ego that is good and healthy, and that is the part that makes people stand up for themselves, allows them to step forward and be counted, and makes people want to do their jobs well. A little ego goes a long way. For an SM, less ego is more desirable and beneficial. Too much ego gets in the way of the job. Ego will cloud thinking, confuse issues, cause loss of good judgment, twist decision making, toss fairness out the window, and leave the SM self-centered.

The members of a company want their SM to be ego-less. This, of course, is not humanly possible. Whatever size ego an SM might have, a concerted effort must be made to shrink it down while on the job. A good SM does not spend time on self-promotion. A good SM does not need to be right every time or win every argument. In fact, it is more ingratiating when an SM admits errors and apologizes for any wrongdoings. A good SM makes others feel like a winner too.

SMs will be confronted and challenged by both their own egos and the egos of others—from the producer on down to a production assistant, to some vendor who might come by to drop off a prop or costume. Large and inflated egos do not come only in "star" packages. An SM needs to learn to recognize ego each time it rears its head. Ego comes in many disguises. Egos can be voracious and damaging and often need stroking and feedings at every opportunity. Ego is also a high-maintenance item, one that people go to great measures to keep in shape. Ego can consume people and be the thing that drives and motivates them.

A Need for Perfection

Generally speaking, mixed in to most SM's spirit is a strong sense of perfection. *Perfection* is the difference between doing a good job and doing an excellent job. Perfection is going beyond the bounds of expectations and doing something as flawlessly as possible. Perfection is very helpful and useful to an SM. When used at the appropriate times and in healthy portions, it catapults the SM to excellence.

Perfection, however, can be carried over the line of sanity and into obsession and compulsion. Perfec-

tion can be addictive. When perfection reaches this intensity in a person, perfection loses its usefulness. Doing things perfectly every time is not humanly possible. People in the company expect the SM to be perfect and mistake-free. They have very little tolerance or patience for errors the SM might make. However, these same people readily accept their own mistakes and lack of perfection without acknowledgment or apology.

The *art* of perfection is to strive for it—not live for it. The *craft* of perfection is to benefit from the imperfections, the mistakes made. Try not to make the same mistakes in the same way, but if you do, learn the lesson again and move on without judgment or self-recrimination.

Control

Control works hand in hand with perfection. Perfection is a person's way of being in control. This is doubly true for SMs, whose work requires that they *control* and be *in control*. SMs make a mistake when they let control (and for that matter, perfection) be the master and motivating force in their work.

Control (and perfection) is a great tool for an SM. It must, however, be used as an aid, just as an SM uses paper, pencil, and an eraser to get the job done. An SM remains in control not by tight-fisted rule and dictatorship, but by doing the job well and applying the qualities discussed in this chapter and throughout this book.

ANATOMY OF THE ASM

The information in this chapter applies equally to the ASM. There is, however, something more for the ASM. The ASM must learn how to *assist*. An ASM must learn when to lead—when to take the ball and run—and when to step back and let the PSM be the boss. A part of the ASM's job is to support and be of service to the PSM. The ASM also learns to take up the slack where there might be slack. If necessary, the ASM saves the PSM from mistakes, failure, or embarrassment, without expectation of recognition or reward. The ASM does this job within the company with complete power and authority, and at the same time stays within the boundaries, not threatening the PSM's pride, position, or ego.

The working relationship between the PSM and the ASM is in many ways like a marriage. There is a relationship to be cultivated and maintained. To help make this relationship work, it is the ASM's job to learn the ways in which the PSM likes to work—the things the PSM expects from an assistant. Learning the PSM's perfection level is important, as is learning the PSM's ego factor. Most PSMs will not stop to think about their assistants in these terms. All they know is that they are comfortable with the person and feel assured. They will continue to work with this assistant show after show, and will be reluctant to work with anyone else.

SHOW BUSINESS: A GLAMOROUS BUSINESS

It is all true! Being in show business is every bit as glamorous, exciting, and thrilling as everyone imagines. There are parties and gala affairs. You meet the rich and famous, travel, and perform for dignitaries, politicians, and other very important people. You get to ride in limousines, have people wait on you, live in grand hotels, and maybe even have your own fifteen minutes of fame. As an SM you may work directly with the leaders in the industry, working at a high level of intensity. Your position is important, respected, and often held in esteem. Your work contributes to the performance each night, and you'll have your ego stroked. In short, you get to live on the outer edge and send postcards to all your relatives and unemployed friends.

This is the part the general public and some young aspiring SMs focus on. It is intoxicating to the spirit and draws people in. The rewards and victories of being an SM are rich and sweet. The defeats can be great, lonely, and agonizing. The glamorous part is less than one-fifth of the total experience of being in show business and being an SM. The other four-fifths is what this book is about—read on and be informed!

INTERVIEWS

Interviewer: As a producer or director how do you choose an SM?

Lara Teeter: I go with somebody I have a certain chemistry with. Somebody who has a love for theatre. I like an SM who is a "people person." Someone who knows how to work with people. Someone who can deal with people in all positions and at all levels—from the executive producer to the man or woman who provides the janitorial services. Someone who likes being part of a family.

Interviewer: What are some of the qualities you look for in an SM?

Bill Holland: I want to know if this SM can work under pressure! While everyone is losing their heads and into a state, does this SM remain cool, clearheaded, calm? Also, can this person bend, go with the flow, work under adverse conditions? Can this SM get along with all kinds of people? I look for someone who is assertive, who is up front, present, and clear in thought and conversation. Someone who is too sharp, too Mr. Cool and Mr. Experience, is a turn-off. This is a warning to me because he's got something more to prove. He's not putting his time into the job but into himself. I look for balance.

Interviewer: As a PSM, what do you expect from an assistant?

Bill Holland:

- Healthy assertiveness
- Ability to change
- Knows the job well, the craft
- Can function in all the areas that I as the PSM function
- Can take over for me when I have to be somewhere else
- Know how to work with performers/stars
- Have an ability to handle all things as I would
- Perhaps most of all, a sense of humor helps a lot!
- In short, my assistant must *know* my job without having my job.

Interviewer: What about a good sense of humor in an SM?

Lara Teeter: Oh god, thank you for that! I forgot all about sense of humor. YES, and that should be at the top of the list for any SM.

Interviewer: Will you hire someone off the street?

John Bowab: Not as a rule, but this one time I did. I liked him the moment he walked in. The unpretentious way he greeted me, sat down, and presented his resume. It was clean, simple, easy to read. Then on the first day of rehearsals I was really shocked when he had newly sharpened pencils at my table, a clean script if I wanted it, and he knew that I liked working with a tape recorder so there were fresh batteries. The man was a quiet and understated type of person, but he was a DYNAMO, getting the job done with a lot of extra considerations.

Interviewer: Why do you think people become SMs—why is a person *attracted* to becoming an SM?

John Bowab: Most of the SMs I have known started out with another intent—to act, to direct, to produce—

and then somewhere they got to be an SM, maybe on a show, or as part of their studies in college. Then there are those people who love it. Why they love it, I don't know; for the most part it is a thankless job. I'm thankful that they do it. Why does someone work on a building, eighty stories up? Some just like putting the show together. Maybe they like the regimentation, the power, the control, the challenge, being at the center of something. I don't think it's because they can't do anything else.

Interviewer: What about ego in an SM?

John Bowab: A good SM must almost always have to eliminate ego, because with ego you have to pay a price. People become actors or performers because they need attention, acclaim, confirmation, praise. People behind the scenes don't get that and if that is a driving force in them, then they shouldn't be there. The SM's praise and recognition come from knowing that the show worked, it comes from himself. An SM executes someone else's dream, someone else's vision.

Interviewer: Why do you think people become SMs?

Lara Teeter: I think it's someone who LOOOOOVVVVES being organized. Who likes to get things done. Who loves to compartmentalize—making sure things are together and doing things well. You can see it in the tools they carry: their colored tape, a pencil sharpener, rubber bands in little containers, paper clips, aspirin, band-aids. They are ready to do the job and they get gratification.

Interviewer: What are some of the qualities you look for in an SM?

Paul Blake: Aside form all the things an SM must do in the job, I like an SM who is also caring, nurturing, and encouraging.

3

The Stage Manager's Chain of Command List

The SM's *chain of command list* is the first of several important lists an SM needs to have. Throughout the life of a production, the SM will refer to this list for any number of reasons: keeping departments informed, providing a list of program credits to the publicity department, assuring no one is forgotten, or creating a guest roster for a social event. The chain of command list created in this chapter is complete and comprehensive. It is ordered and structured from the SM's point of view. However, as the SM moves from show to show, production company to production company, some of the positions may be excluded or combined, depending on the size of the company and/or financial structure of the show. As a fail-safe measure, the chain of command list in this book includes people and organizations that are seldom, if ever, part of the chain of command. They are nonetheless important to the SM as a reminder of their presence so they too can be informed or dealt with at the proper times.

Do not try to memorize this list; that will come in time. Familiarize yourself with the various sections and positions, read over the introductory paragraphs on each position, and then make a copy of the list and put it at the beginning of your production notebook, using it as a reference.

1. **The Production Executives**
   Founder
   Board of Trustees
   General Manager
   Executive Producer
   Producer
   Associate Producer
   Company Manager/Tour Manager
   Assistants to the above positions

2. **The Production Office Staff**
   Production Secretary
   Casting Director
   Publicity/Programs/Press/Photography
   Accounting
   Office Staff

3. **The Creators**
   Book/Script
   Music/Score
   Lyrics/Words

4. **The Production Staff**
   Director
   Assistant Director
   Musical Director
   Assistant Music Director
   Conductor
   Rehearsal Pianist
   Arrangers (vocal, dance, orchestrations, copyist)
   Musician's Union
   Choreographer
   Assistant Choreographer
   Dance Captain
   Production Stage Manager (PSM)
       Assistant Stage Managers (ASMs)
       Production Assistant (PA)

5. **The Performing Artists and Actor's Equity**
   Star(s); the Star's Staff and/or Entourage
   Principal Performers
   Supporting Roles
   Children's Roles; Parents, Teachers, Social Workers (required when children performers are in the show)

Ensemble Performers: Singers, Dancers, Chorus,
Pit Singers, Swing Dancers
Equity Deputies for:
    Principal and Supporting Actors
    Singers/Chorus
    Dancers
Walk-on Roles and/or Extras

6. The Technical Staff
Designers for:
    Sets
    Lights
    Costumes
    Props
    Sound
    Hair
    Makeup
Special Designers, Trainers and Coaches
Vocal, Speech, Dialects
Films, Slides, Video
Stunts, Animals
Effects, Illusions, Magic
Firearms, Pyrotechnics
Technical Director (TD)
Department Heads for:
    Carpentry
    Rail (Flys)
    Electrics
    Props
    Sound
    Costumes/Wardrobe
    Hair
    Makeup
    Effects
Crew / Stage Hands
Stage Hand's Union (I.A.T.S.E.)

7. Shops and Vendors
Costumes (construction/rentals)
Set (construction/rentals)
Electrical (supply/rentals)
Prop Houses (purchase/rental)
Hair and Supplies
Recording Studios
Makeup and Supplies
Shoes and Boots

8. The Theatre, Performance Site, or Venue
Backstage:
    Tech Dept. Heads

    Local Crew
    Dressers
    Doorman/Security
    Janitorial Staff
Front-of-the-house:
    Box office
    House Manager
    Ushering Staff
    Parking

9. The Fire Marshall

As an introduction and to create a more comprehensive picture, let us review each position in the chain of command list as seen by the SM.

THE PRODUCTION EXECUTIVES

In a large Broadway show each of the production executive positions most likely will be filled by an individual. With other shows, depending on the size of the company and its financial structure, a person might fill one or more of the production executive positions at one time. As you read about the various positions, note the crossover and similarity in job descriptions.

The **founder**, if still actively working, usually is at the helm running the entire company. This person may fill one or all of the executive positions, possibly also being a director. Other times, the founder may have become an inactive figurehead represented only by a life-size portrait hanging in a lobby. The founder's greatest contribution is, of course, having started the organization. Often the founder is the inspiration and guiding force, bringing an artistic vision to light. Usually this person is also good at rallying financial supporters to subsidize the company through the beginning years. Sometimes the SM never meets the founder or just sees him or her in passing. Other times the SM will work as closely with this person as with the director.

In addition to the founder, some production companies may also have a **board of trustees**. Other times the production company is led and guided solely by the board. Whatever the setup, the SM has little to no dealings with this group. At most the SM may come to know some of the board members from opening night affairs, in social times, or during a publicity event.

The **general manager** is both the overseer and keeper of the production company. This person is the keeper of the purse and is concerned more with the finances and running the entire company than with the individual shows. The general manager leaves the care of the shows to the producers, who in turn are accountable to the general manager. If the general manager is the top figurehead of the company, it is also part of the job to see that the artistic vision, direction, and integrity of the company/shows are maintained. When in the position of top person, the general manager may exercise the right to offer artistic and creative suggestions. However, for the most part that work falls to the producer and the producer's staff. The general manager is responsible only to the founder and/or board of trustees. As with the founder, the SM may or may not work directly with the general manager.

In the past, the position of **executive producer** was more prominent in film and TV, but the production executives of theatre saw its worth and value and have made it more and more a part of the chain of command. The executive producer may be administrating and budgeting several shows at one time, depending on the workload and structure of the production office. In many ways the executive producer's position is similar to the general manager, but the executive producer has more control over the creation and artistic values of the shows. The executive producer can spend a lot of business time socializing and getting backers and investors interested in the company or in a particular show. Like the figureheads already mentioned, the SM may or may not work directly with this person.

On many occasions the SM will find that the **producer** of the show is the highest executive position in the production company. While the creators of a show give the show birth, the producer is usually the first to have faith in the project, seeing its artistic merit and financial potential. The producer becomes a surrogate parent and primary caretaker who turns the show over to the director and actors for day-care, development, and growth to maturity.

The producer often sets the tone and presentation style of the show. This is the person who hires the artists, craftsmen, and talent best suited for the product—those who will bring the artistic vision to light, improving upon what the producer has already imagined.

With any show, the "buck" starts and stops at the producer's desk—literally as well as metaphorically. The producer has the ultimate power over the show and company. There is a general belief that the producer is the money person—the person who invests money into the show. Most times the producer is merely the custodian of the purse, and just gives the illusion that the money is personally coming from the producer's own pocket.

In many working situations, the SM has greater contact with this person than with the other executive figureheads. In some cases, the relationship may grow and extend into social interaction. For the most part, however, the SM communicates with the producer through the director, or has the director's consent and knowledge of what information is passed between the producer and SM.

The position of **associate producer** also has its roots in film and TV. The associate producer's work is an extension of what the producer would do. In small production companies, a person might be hired as an associate producer, but is often called the assistant to the producer and is paid much less money. With a big show and/or production company, when the producer's work becomes too much for one person, the more responsible position of associate producer is adopted.

Primarily, the associate producer transposes the entire production into dollars and cents. The associate producer breaks the budget down into the various departments, and must have excellent knowledge of what things truly cost for each department. The associate producer also has detailed knowledge of the working rules for the different unions associated with a production, especially when it comes to pay scales and anything having to do with overtime, penalties, fines, or fees. In many respects the associate producer's and SM's position run parallel courses. However, the SM may not be as knowledgeable in budgetary matters, and except for Equity, usually has only a general working knowledge of the rules and regulations of the other unions. In the absence of an associate producer, a producer might require the SM do some of this work.

For a show whose daily business requires full-time attention, a producer may hire a **company manager** to do that part of the job. It is the company manager's job to handle all the business that has to do directly with the company, both administratively and financially. If the show is a touring show, the company manager also sees that the transitions from one city to another go safely and smoothly, dealing with housing, transportation, reservations, and the logistics of moving the company. The company manager will also act as the advance person, going to the next town several days early in preparation for the arrival of the cast, crew, and technical setup of the show. When a show becomes a touring show, the terms company manager and tour manager sometimes become interchangeable. On a big show with a large cast, another person may be hired and the work of the two positions be divided. On small touring shows, when there is no company or tour manager, the work of these two positions is done by the producer's office and the PSM.

THE PRODUCTION OFFICE STAFF

The production office staff includes all the people who administrate, coordinate, and provide great support to the company and production. Heading this sector in the production company is the **production secretary**. Nearly always, this is the producer's secretary, but in a large organization or on a big-budget show, the two positions are kept separate and are filled by different people.

The production secretary is the person who starts the wheels of organization turning on a show before the director or SM begin their jobs. In many ways, the production secretary's work is like that of an SM: creating lists, making phone calls, organizing, providing service, and just generally pulling the production together. Seldom will an SM meet a production secretary who is not good at the job. Production secretaries are dedicated to their jobs and can be a great source of information to the SM. It is the wise SM who befriends all production secretaries.

The position of **casting director** most definitely started in films, carried over into TV, and by the early 70s, became more commonplace in theatre. Casting directors are most often found working on big-budget shows or new shows that are heading to Broadway. The casting director is usually an independent outsider, contracted by the production company for a particular show. The casting director's responsibility is to gather the talents best suited for the roles in the play. A good casting director has an excellent eye for talent and has a knack for placing actors in roles. The casting director saves the producer and director from having to sit through hundreds of auditions with people who are not right for the show. Prior to the casting director being used in theatre, the SM prescreened the talent—a job that made the SM's

position more prestigious and important. The SM's work with the casting director is limited and brief, taking place mostly during the audition period.

Depending on the size and budget of the show and producing company, the **publicity** sector of the office staff may consist of an entire department with several people, or it may be one desk with one person working on programs, creating press and media exposure, doing photography, and sometimes designing graphic artwork. It is the publicist's job to get the word out on the show, create interest, and draw in a paying audience. The ways of doing this can be as extreme as the publicist, producer, and stars choose. More traditionally, getting the word out is done mostly by advertising, interviews with news and entertainment media, doing special appearances by the stars and selected cast members, and participating in benefits and/or charity affairs. The SM's most important work with the publicity department comes in giving them correct information on the cast and show, which will be printed in the program, and in working closely with them during photo shoots.

Accounting, too, may consist of several people, or be a one-desk, one-person operation. This position on the chain of command list needs no further introduction other than to say that this is the place from which the paychecks are generated, the bills are paid, and the petty cash is handed out.

The size and number of the office staff is dictated by the support and administration the producing company and/or show needs. The SM usually gets to meet and work briefly with some or all of the office staff.

THE CREATORS

In the book of Genesis, the Creator of heaven and earth was first and foremost. So it is with the creators in theatre, the **writers, composers,** and **lyricist** (the script, music, and words). We know from history that during Egyptian, Greek, and Roman times the author (the playwright) was preeminent, then came all the other parts of theatre. Today the creators in theatre remain first and foremost. They are still revered and held in high esteem.

The writers, composers, and lyricists begin their work alone, sometimes in pairs, sometimes in small groups. The creators conceive the child, give it birth, but they must relinquish the child to others in this chain of command for it to be nurtured and grow.

Sometimes the union between the creators and the others is a happy, rewarding, and highly successful experience, with each person making contributions greater than anyone's expectations. Other times, the child is short-lived and the creators return to their quiet place, first to recover and then perhaps to start the creative process over again.

The SM's work with this group of people is usually limited to being a "host" during the rehearsal period, seeing that they are included in the loop of daily information and, if needed, have a place for them set up in the rehearsal hall where they can continue their work.

THE PRODUCTION STAFF

Heading this illustrious group, the largest portion of the chain of command, is the **director**. People in all walks of life know the importance and power of the director's work. Films are probably most responsible for bringing the director's work to public attention. Television helps keep it there.

In theatre, directors and their work have always had a place of importance and prominence among their peers and theatre-goers. Today, the general public gives as much recognition and acknowledgment to the directors of a stage production as they do the performers: Jerome Robbins, Bob Fosse, Gower Champion, Joshua Logan, Michael Bennett, George Abbott, Abe Burrow, Tommy Tune, Harold Prince, Moss Hart, Michael Kidd, Ron Field, and Noel Coward are among the well-known names in this category.

The writers conceive the idea and bring it to term, the producer nurtures the piece, giving it a healthy home and environment, but it is the director who molds and shapes the work, giving it character, personality, and style. It is the director who breathes energy and movement into the piece, giving it greater values and coloring.

The director's and SM's work together is like a marriage; however, the relationship is not a fifty-fifty proposition; the SM is there to serve, honor, and obey (lots more to come on this subject).

In theatre, the **assistant director** moves and lives within the shadow of the director. The assistant director is there to assist and serve. Whatever creative or artistic input the assistant director might bring to the production, it is always made through the director. The director often gives the assistant due credit, but ultimately the assistant's contributions are absorbed into the production, and full credit is given to the director. The assistant director's duties are as simple or as involved as the director chooses. Sometimes the director will turn over a whole scene to the assistant, giving the assistant full range for artistic and creative expression. At other times the assistant is allowed to work with the actor only in running the scene and drilling the performers in their parts. At still other times the assistant director is kept more as a personal assistant or secretary to the director, taking notes and giving reminders. If there are many script changes and/or rewrites, the assistant usually works closely with the director, then sees that new pages are typed and copies are made for the next rehearsal. Sometimes the typing and copying is given over to the SM. The assistant director is usually a good friend to the director, and/or a longtime working associate. In his own right, the assistant director may also be an accomplished actor, director, choreographer, or even an SM. The SM and assistant director will work closely together in serving the director.

When doing musicals, the **musical director** is next in a chain of command list. This person brings to the music what the director brings to the overall show. However, although the director may take liberties with the author's words, intentions, and interpretation, the musical director remains truer to what the composer has written. In smaller productions, the musical director may also be the rehearsal pianist, vocal coach, copyist, and almost certainly the conductor. On larger shows, especially those heading to Broadway, each of these positions may be filled by different qualified individuals. The SM does not work as closely with the musical director as with the director. Nonetheless, the musical director is usually present for each rehearsal, and needs to be kept in the loop of information and have workspace in the rehearsal hall.

If the **conductor** is hired simply to conduct the music for the performances, the SM may meet this person only one or two times during the latter part of rehearsals. Otherwise, the conductor will appear in the orchestra pit when the orchestra starts working with the cast. Whatever business needs to be done with the conductor is usually done through the musical director. By performance time, the SM makes certain the conductor has a dressing room. Throughout the run of the show, the SM checks regularly with the conductor to offer assistance, and receives any performance notes the conductor may want the SM to give to cast members.

The **rehearsal pianist** seems to have the most tedious job; the pianist must remain at the piano throughout the entire rehearsal day, waiting and ready to play over and over just a few bars or whole sections of the score. During rehearsals, the rehearsal pianist becomes the orchestra, playing special parts or effects that will be played by other instruments when the full orchestra is together. For the SM, the rehearsal pianist is a low-maintenance person. As long as the rehearsal pianist is informed of each day's schedule, the piano is in tune and placed so that the pianist can see the performers, the rehearsal pianist requires little else throughout the day.

If the show is a new musical or the revival of a musical that is getting a makeover or update, the SM may get to meet and deal with the **arrangers**, the people who put on paper the arrangements of the vocals, orchestra instrumentation, and dance as created or recreated rehearsals. These arrangers do most of their work outside the rehearsal hall and may come to the rehearsal hall one or two times in the last week:

- The **vocal arranger** creates the harmony, blend, and overall sound that the performers recreate for each performance.
- The **dance arranger** carefully counts out each measure of music to fit the different sections of the dance being performed on the stage. Then the special rhythms, dance times, tempos, beats, accents, and musical effects are noted.
- The information from the vocal and dance arrangers is given to the **orchestra arranger,** who transposes everything into the musical instrumentation of the orchestra—the *orchestrations*. It is during this time that the sound of the orchestra and the number of instruments to be used is finalized, and the overture, incidental music, and underscoring are completed.
- Included within this group of musicians is the **copyist**. After the arrangers have completed their work, the copyist painstakingly transcribes to manuscript paper every note for every instrument in the orchestra, for the entire score. At one time this was done tediously by hand and by many copyists; with the advent of copy machines the job was made easier and less expensive. Now with computer programs, the job has become a one-person operation.

It is important the unions and/or guilds for the different groups within the production also be listed on the SM's chain of command list. Each union with its rules and regulations has an effect on the SM's work and must be kept in the SM's loop of information to be distributed.

The SM has little to no dealings with the **musicians' union**, or for that matter, the musicians themselves. Any business the SM might have with either group is done through the musical director or conductor. They see to it that the union rules are followed by both the musicians and the producer. The SM need be aware only of break times and prevent situations that could lead to overtime or penalty fees being paid to the musicians.

The **choreographer** completes the musical portion of the chain of command list. The choreographer brings the same kind of creative artistry to the show as does the director and musical director, but the choreographer's job may be a bit more difficult; the director has the script and the musical director has the score, but most of the text for the dances must be created from the choreographer's head. Even for shows that have already been choreographed for Broadway, many times the choreographer will reinvent some or all of the dance, while the other parts of the musical remain the same.

Under the choreographer is the **dance captain**. This person is a dancer in the show who has been chosen by the choreographer to oversee and maintain the dances after the choreographer is gone.

At last we come to the SMs, the **PSM** and the **ASM(s)**. The SMs are the bonding agents that keep all departments connected. However, the SMs' work is neither technical nor artistic. There is no part of the job that requires the SMs to make a contribution in either area. In fact, in most professional situations, the artists prefer that the SMs stay out of their areas, and technicians and their unions echo the sentiment. The SMs' greatest artistic contribution to the show comes during each performance as they call the cues for the show.

The **production assistant (PA)**, is also known as the *runner* or *gofer*. The person filling this position is usually young, filled with ambition, and is excited to be working in show business. PAs are willing to put in the time and effort to prove themselves and get that proverbial foot in the door. With that kind of energy, willingness, and enthusiasm, the PA gets to do many things for all people in the production who may need those services. However, the PA works directly with the SM, the director, and producer. The PA is eternally on the run, with a list of things that must be done within the hour. PAs put in extremely long hours and the pay is usually below scale and at poverty range; they are assured by everyone that the experience more than makes up for the lack in pay.

THE PERFORMING ARTISTS AND ACTOR'S EQUITY

It is difficult to place the **performing artists** and their union, **Equity**. They are an entity that stands alone, and when following a natural order of placement for this SM's chain of command list, the actors and their union end up at the bottom. Their importance certainly demands a higher placement. Because they work closest with the director, stage manager, music director, and choreographer, they are being placed at this point, though certainly they are not part of the production staff. This particular group needs no further introduction here. In Chapter 7, Profiles and Working Relationships, you will meet each of them and learn more about their working relationships with the SM.

For a professional SM, performers cannot be discussed without also talking about **Actor's Equity**. In professional theatre, wherever the actor goes, so goes Equity. Membership in Equity has already been established as the dividing line between being a professional and nonprofessional actor. Equity's purpose is, of course, to work for and protect the performers (including SMs) from substandard working conditions and unscrupulous producers. It is the SM's job to act as "watchdog," seeing that the performers, as well as management, abide by contractual agreements between Equity and the producers.

The **Equity deputy** is a cast member chosen by the cast whose job it is to represent the Equity members to management in all union matters, keep the Equity office informed on all business matters, and like the SM, act as watchdog to ensure that the performers, as well as management, abide by contractual agreements. In a musical or in a show with a large number of cast members, separate deputies are chosen: one to represent the principal performers, others to represent all or various groups of the ensemble performers.

THE TECHNICAL STAFF: DESIGNERS, DEPARTMENT HEADS, THEIR ASSISTANTS, AND CREWMEMBERS

Last on the production staff portion of the SM's chain of command list is this illustrious group of individuals. Do not let the placement distract you from their importance. Collectively, this sector is to the show as a voice is to a singer or fingers are to a pianist. Without them, the illusion of theatre, as we experience it today, would be relegated to Greek and Roman times, when some masks, a few props, and suggested pieces of clothing were used as costumes.

The **designers** are the bridge between the artistic and technical aspects of the show. In doing their work, not only must the designers know the creative and artistic design of their particular specialty, but they must also have a good technical and working knowledge of the medium in which they are working. Designers bring to the show the same intense artistry, design, and style that are brought by all the others on the creative staff. Their work sets the physical and visual look. They dress up the show, giving it color and its particular look. The look and style for the show is created between the producer and designer, and sometimes may include the director. It is the designer's job to create the illusion of reality and/or lull the audience into acceptance of theatrical time, place, and space.

The technical staff members are the practical applicators, the nuts and bolts people, the backstage laborers. After the designers in each technical area have done their work and the shops and vendors have provided what is needed, the department heads and crew take over. It is their job to assemble the physical elements of the production and technically support the show during the performance. No matter how automated or computerized things may become backstage, department heads and crewmembers are needed to execute the technical effects that help create the environment of the play and the illusion and magic of theatre. The SM does none of the crew's work, nor does the crew do any of the SM's, yet their jobs are complementary, each needing the other to do their best for a smooth running performance.

The **technical director** (**TD**) has a good working knowledge of all things technical, and coordinates all technical departments, is the leader of the crew, and sees that all the technical elements of the show get into place and become operational. The TD leads the stagehands to make repairs, adjustments, or changes. Once the show opens, the TD makes certain that the technical elements are maintained and remain operational throughout the run. The TD is the final word in technical matters backstage.

The **head carpenter** is in charge of the scenery. This person, with an assistant and a portion of the crew, is responsible for putting up the set and taking it down, as well as maintaining the scenery and making all repairs. The head carpenter, along with the crew, is in charge of the scenery moves, and executes the scene changes during the performance. Often, the head carpenter's position and the TD's position are combined.

In the early days of theatre, when the flying in and out of painted drops and pieces of scenery became part of theatre, sailors were the first **flymen** or **railmen**. They were hired to work this part of the crew because they already had experience in hoisting and letting down sails on ships. To tie off the ropes after a sail had been hoisted or lowered on a ship, there was a log or railing with pegs or pins driven through, projecting out on both sides. By winding the rope around both parts of the pins, the sail could be tied off and secured into place. This operation was also applied in theatre. The place or space above the stage where the drops were stored became known as the flys, the place where the sailors stood to tie off the ropes became known as the rail or pin rail, and the sailors became known as flymen or railmen. The head of the rail is often the assistant to the head carpenter. Together they work in setting up and striking the set/scenery.

The titles of the remaining technical heads and crewmembers—**electric, props, sound, costumes/ wardrobe, hair,** and **makeup**—describe quite well the work they do. We will get to know them in greater detail in Chapter 7, Profiles and Working Relationships.

The stagehand's union is the **International Alliance of Theatrical Stage Employees (I.A.T.S.E.).** This union is to the stagehands what Actor's Equity is to the performers—caring for and protecting its membership. The SM must be sure to learn the rules and regulations of this group that deal with work times, breaks, overtime, fees, and penalty payments. The SM must also learn not to do any technical work that has been designated as union stage crew's work, even if it is something as innocuous as picking up a broom and sweeping.

THE SHOPS AND VENDORS

The **shops** and **vendors** are seldom, if ever, included in the chain of command. However, these are places and people with whom the SM must deal and/or keep informed (especially during the rehearsal period). The shops and vendors provide the sets, costumes, props, sound, lights, hair, makeup, and anything else needed for the show that is made, constructed, assembled, rented, hired, bought, borrowed, or begged.

THE THEATRE, PERFORMANCE SITE, OR VENUE

An SM will work in as many different places as there are different places in which to present theatre: concert halls, arenas, hotels, ballrooms, lobbies, theme parks, trailer beds, ice rinks, domes, bowls, forums, coliseums, amphitheatres, convention centers, converted storefronts, shopping centers, auditoriums, VFW halls, and theatres—famous theatres in major cities, theatres holding 5,000 people, theatres with 99 seats or less, theatres with severely raked stages built in 1886, or a modern civic center theatre designed by Frank Lloyd Wright.

At each performance site, there are people both backstage and at the front of the theatre to staff and maintain the venue. Backstage, the SM meets a second group of technical heads, the **house crew**. These are people hired by the theatre to operate the various technical areas backstage and to support each product that comes to that particular venue. The house crew joins with the show's technical heads in assembling the show in the theatre, and then during performance becomes part of the crew in running and supporting the show. Some house crews may also include a doorman or security people, a janitorial staff, and if needed for the show, dressers. To distinguish more clearly between the people hired by the venue and the technicians who come with the show, the house crew is often called the *local crew* and the terms become interchangeable, used sometimes in the same sentence.

The **front-of-the-house staff** may consist of one or two people doing all the jobs needed to run the front of the house, or it may be broken up into the theatre manager, box office workers, administrating staff, ushering staff, concession stand operators, parking attendants, and additional security. The people who work the front of the house are the first to meet and greet the audience. In providing quick and courteous service, they help in making the audience receptive to the entertainment and begin the experience of going to the theatre. The SM has a very limited working relationship with this group, but it is good for the SM to make introductions and social contact with them.

The **fire marshal** seldom, if ever, is included in the chain of command list. This is the forgotten person who shows up one or two days before the show opens to inspect all flammable items, to see if permits have been obtained, to see if all flammable items have been made fire retardant, and to see if any open flames are being used in the show, such as matches or candles. It is important that the SM keep this per-son in mind and, once the show gets into technical rehearsals, reminds the various technical heads to be prepared for the fire marshal's last-minute inspection.

IN REVIEW

It might be worth going over this chapter once again, reviewing and getting to know these positions better. These are the people with whom every SM works throughout an entire career. With the information from this chapter and Chapter 7, Profiles and Working Relationships, you have a well of valuable information. Take it and use it to move forward into the professional experience.

4

Stage Manager for Hire: Seeking Work, Getting the Job, and Being Hired Again and Again

Being unemployed and looking for work is a fact of life for every SM. It is the nature of SMing work to move from show to show, working for different production companies. Only a few SMs are fortunate enough to become associated with a company that produces shows regularly and keeps the SM employed the year round. This book is dedicated to the working SM and the things the SM does while employed; in this chapter, we will explore the things an SM can do while unemployed and seeking work.

The conventional ways of seeking work in theatre are limited for an SM. There will be ads in the trade papers that are good for beginning SMs to respond to, but the better jobs are filled before an ad is needed. There are no agents or agencies to go to, nor can SMs present their abilities and skills in an audition. How then does an SM get jobs? There are some distinct actions, when performed in combination, that make the task of looking for SMing work easier: networking, building a resume, establishing a good reputation, and having good word-of-mouth.

NETWORKING

Networking is making telephone calls, socializing, doing benefit shows, staying in touch with friends, business associates, producers, directors, performers, other SMs, and sending out resumes or little reminder notes that you are available and looking for work. SMs need to create a network of people who can either give them a job, lead them to a job, or who can personally recommend them to others.

BUILDING A RESUME

The resume is the door opener—the passport and entry into the minds of prospective employers. While performers can also use pictures, videotapes, and auditions, an SM has only a resume in which to make an introduction and create interest.

Presentation of the Resume

Even before it is read, the overall look of the resume sets the first impression. With computer programs being as understandable and accessible as they are these days, there is no reason for having anything less than a printshop quality resume, perhaps even with a few fonts and graphics added for division of information and appeal. Also important to the presentation is the type and quality of the paper and the choice of color. These, of course, will be personal choices that suit you best, but choices that nonetheless must be made.

The Layout

Next is the form of the resume—how things are laid out on the page. Even the order in which the information appears can have a psychological effect on the reader. Keep the resume simple, neat, and easy to read. Readers of resumes do not want to study the resume, but rather extract from it in a single glance the type and caliber of shows, where the shows were done, for whom, and whether any star performers were involved. From this quick glance, the readers will determine if you are what they want for their shows, and if you are worth their time for further consideration.

The Credits

If you have come this far in your interest in theatre and SMing, more than likely you already have some credits, even if they happen to be high school, college, or community theatre credits. We all start somewhere, and in the beginning no credit is too small or insignificant to list. As your credits get more impressive, place the most impressive at the top and start eliminating the less impressive from the bottom.

One-Page Resumes

Make it a standing rule to have your resume no longer than one page. It is a natural inclination to want to list every credit, but if the reader must turn the page you run the risk of losing the reader's attention. List only those credits that you believe are impressive and best sell your abilities. An SM might consider having several resumes, slanting each toward a certain type of show, and then presenting the resume that features the credits similar to the show for which the SM is applying. Separate resumes could be prepared for:

Musicals, Opera

Dramas, Comedies, Classical

Concerts, Magic Shows, Showrooms, Variety Acts

Slanting the Resume and Additional Credit Headings

Before continuing our discussion on building a resume, let's look at a sample resume (Fig 4-1). As you can see, Sarah has slanted her resume toward musicals. She also has extensive experience in straight dramas and comedies and has listed those credits under a second heading. Under a third heading, "Variety, Clubs, etc.," Sarah chose to list still other musical credits to show the versatility of her experience. Sometimes in a show for which you are applying, a *secondary element* such as magic, vaudeville, or variety is important to the play. If the SM happens to have a credit listed that is similar to what is needed in the show being applied for, this could become a factor in being chosen for the job.

Repetitive Credits

It is also impressive and reassuring to the reader to see the names of directors, producers, or production companies listed two or more times. Sarah has disregarded chronological order and listed her repetitive credits together. This is an eye catcher and quickly points out that this particular SM not only gets hired by different companies and people, but is hired again and again by the same companies/people.

Absence of Dates

Notice that dates have been omitted from Sarah's resume. For the sake of simplicity and the limited space on the page, dates can be eliminated. In fact, it is best to leave this information out entirely. When dates are included, people start counting, calculating, and passing judgment. Any credit older than five years has less impact. Although people hiring for a show refuse to believe it of themselves, it is a well-established axiom in entertainment that you are only as good as your last or most-recent credits. Producers and directors want to be assured that the SM they are choosing is a currently working SM, highly regarded, and is in great demand. Only in the interview does an SM talk about dates and, even then, only after being asked a specific question.

Further Experience

Notice also that at the bottom of the resume, in smaller print, credits are listed for television, film, and directing. These seemingly unrelated credits further guide the reader into knowing Sarah's experience and versatility. Some directors and producers like their SMs to know about directing. They are then assured that their SM can communicate with actors, keep the show at performance level, and work closely with the director during rehearsals. They do not, however, want an SM who wants to be a director. If directing credits are listed, they should be placed in a subordinate position.

References

Including references on a resume is a strong feature. Listing three or four names is enough. Whenever possible, it is good to list various types of people in the industry: a director, a producer, perhaps a star name, and even another SM. This list invites prospective

SARAH JOHNSTON
Stage Manager
341 Oakridge Dr. Glenn Oaks, Ca 90014 (818) 555-1234

MUSICALS

GONE WITH THE WIND	Leslie A.Warren/Pernell Roberts	Dir:Joe Layton, LA-CLO/SF-Tour
KING AND I	Ricardo Montalban/Sally A.Howes	Dir:Joseph Hardy, LA-CLO/SF Tour
ANNIE GET YOUR GUN	Debbie Reynolds/Gavin MacLeod	Dir: Gower Chanpion,LA-CLO/SF Tour
KISMET	Rhonda Flemming/John Reardon	Dir: Albert Marr, LA-CLO/SF-Tour
FIDDLER ON THE ROOF	Robert Merrill	Dir: Steven H. Bohm, LA-CLO/SF-Tour
SUCCEED IN BUSINESS	Robert Morse/Rudy Vallee	Dir: Robert Morse, LA-CLO/SF-Tour
SHE LOVES ME	Pam Dawber/Joel Higgens	Dir/Prdcr: Paul Blake, Ahmanson,LA
GOOD MAN CHARLIE BROWN	Jo Anne Worley/Marcia Wallace	Dir/Prdcr: Paul Blake, Snta.Barb/SF
THE BOY FRIEND	Gretchen Wyler	Dir/Prdcr: Paul Blake, Snta.Barb/SF
MEET ME IN ST.LOUIS	Debbie Boone	Dir/Prdcr: Paul Blake, National Tour
MY ONE AND ONLY	Cynthia Ferrer/Dirk Lumbard	Dir: Jack Bunch, San Bernardino-CLO
THEY'RE PLAYING OUR SONG	Nancy Dussault/Dick Gautier	Dir: Glenn Casale, San Bernardino-CLO
GUYS AND DOLLS	Jack Jones/Nancy Ringham	Dir: Jack Bunch, San Bernardino-CLO
BIG RIVER	Jym Diabis	Dir: Jack Bunch, San Bernardino-CLO
SINGING IN THE RAIN	Cynthia Ferrer/Kirby Ward	Dir: Dan Mojica, San Bernardino-CLO
MAN OF LA MANCHA	Jon Cypher/Marilyn McCoo	Dir: Gary Davis, Calif.Music Thtr./Pasad.Civic
IOLANTHE	Noel Harrison/Lu Leonard	Dir: Tom Blank, Caif.Music Thtr./Pasad.Civic

DRAMA/COMEDY

IT HAD TO BE YOU	Jean Smart/Richard Gilliland	Dir/Prdcr: Paul Blake, GFI Productions, Tour
SAME TIME NEXT YEAR	Marriett Hartley/Earl Holliman	Dir: Tom Troupe, Empire Productions, LA
HAMLET	Jamie Jameison	L.A. Olympic Art Festvl.
DRACULA	Michael Ansara/Werner Klemperer	Dir: Ezra Stone, National Tour
BALLAD OF A CITY	Steve Allen/Diane Ladd	Dir: John Mac Donald, Pasadena Playhouse
DEATHTRAP	Robert Reed	Dir: Harvey Medlinsky, Empire Productions, LA
ODD COUPLE, (Female)	Lee Meriweather/Marcia Wallace	Dir: Jack Bunch, Empire Productions, LA
SOCIAL SECURITY	Bernie Kopel/Deborah Raffin	Dir: Jack Bunch, Empire Productions, LA

VARIETY, CLUBS, INDUSTRIALS, AWARDS, BENEFITS

BURLESQUE - USA	Red Buttons/Eddie Bracken	Dir: Barry Ashton, Las Vegas, Tahoe, Reno
AM. STOCK EXCHANGE	Mus.Rev.Shw/Lounge Show	Sahara Htl-Las Vegas, Reno
HOLIDAY MAGIC	Blackstone/Burton/Jones/etc.	Canada, Austrl, NZ, Englnd
WORDS AND MUSIC	Sammy Cahn	Dir/Prdcr: Paul Blake, National Tour
FORD INDUSTRIALS	Hal Linden/Barbara Mandrell	Las Vegas, Canada
HEALTH CARE-COMIC RELIEF	Chevy Chase/JoAnne Worley	Peter Rank Prdns., Bev.Hls.
UNI-HEALTH AWARDS SHOW	Bonnie Franklin/Christine Ebersole	Dir: Jeff Calhoun, Peter Rank Prdns., Bev.Hls.
AIDS BENEFIT	Joel Gray, Twiggy, Gene Kelly	Dir: Tommy Tune, Peter Rank Prdns., Bev.Hls.

ABC-TV & FILMS	DIRECTING	REFERENCES
(6) Pilots	Industry Actor's Showcase	Paul Blake, 213-555-1234
MacNamara's Band, Mini-Series	Holiday Magic Tour	Peter Rank, 310-5551234
(3)Midnght Spcls. "L.V. Showgirl Contest"	Gypsy,Fiddler, Music Man	Bill Holland, 818-5551234
Movie o/t Week, "MacNamara's Band"	West Side Story	Earl Holliman, 818-555-1234

Figure 4-1   Sarah Johnston's SM Resume.

employers to call the references, and shows that the SM is confident enough about past work to have it checked out. It also directs the prospective employer to people whom the SM knows will give a good reference.

Optional Information

As a professional SM, it is not necessary to list Equity as your union. The shows listed in the credits reflect that information. Also, it is not necessary for an SM to list personal physical statistics as actors do. Including a business address is optional, but a telephone number is absolutely necessary. If there is space at the bottom of the page, you may choose to list hobbies or special interests as long as they don't appear sophomoric. On some occasions during interviews this information can spark interest or conversation with the interviewer.

ESTABLISHING A GOOD REPUTATION

Building a *circle of fame* is among the things an SM must do to help in finding and getting work. This is not the fame a performer or director might achieve, but is rather the reputation among peers and associates as being a good and reliable SM. Establishing a good reputation begins on the first day of the first job with the first employer, and continues with every job thereafter. A good SM is judged by character as well as by excellence in work. Achieving a good reputation is not something for which an SM works directly, but is the natural result of providing good work and all the things discussed in Chapter 2, The Anatomy of a Good Stage Manager.

GOOD WORD-OF-MOUTH

An SM has a resume and good reputation to help in job searches, but that does not complete the circle of getting the job. The SM also needs *good word-of-mouth*. Remember that SMs have limited ways in which to present their talent, craft, and skills. There is no way to display organizational and administrative skills, show how well they work with people, or show their excellence in calling cues, so SMs need other people to help sell them. Producers and directors will call references or others listed on the SM's resume. Job openings for an SM spring up quietly and often behind closed doors. Hiring an SM is as difficult for producers and directors as it sometimes is for an SM to get the job. Most producers and directors will turn first to an SM with whom they have worked and have had a positive experience. If that person is not available, the producer or director will turn to friends, business associates, and even performers for a recommendation. SMs want their names to be first on those people's lists.

INTERVIEWING FOR THE JOB

An SM spends a good amount of time meeting and interviewing with prospective employers. There are some excellent books written on this subject and, although they are not geared to the SM or other people in the entertainment industry, they have some very good suggestions on how to dress, how to handle yourself, and how to get the job. It is worth your time to read one or two of these books or to take a seminar or workshop on the subject.

Gut Feeling

Interviews for SMs are conducted by the producer or director or both. Usually these interviews are casual and informal; after reviewing the credits, the conversation may go in any direction. The credits have played a major part in getting the SM to the interview and they are what assure the producer and/or director that the SM is qualified. The conversation during the interview and the SM's self-presentation further directs the interviewer(s) into making a decision. However, even with impressive credits and high recommendations, the producer and/or director often choose an SM on their *gut feeling*—how good or how comfortable they feel with this particular person.

Controlling the Interview and the Outcome

It is not a good idea to go into the interview with preconceived ideas as to how it should go. Let the interviewer lead. Let the interviewer set the style and pace. Each interview will be as different as are the people doing the interviewing. The best thing that SMs can do is to go into the interview with resume in hand, feeling good about their credits, knowing they are good at the job, and present themselves in the best light possible. Often, there is no rhyme or reason to the outcome. Sometimes you get the job when you feel the interview was disastrous. Other times the interview goes very well, you are certain you have the job, but you don't. Don't even try to figure it out— half of the time getting or not getting the job has nothing to do with you or your credits.

If you don't get the job, you might want to review how the interview went. Look to see if there was anything with which you were uncomfortable. Evaluate your contribution to those moments. Learn from those things to prepare you for the next interview. As certain as there is air to breathe, there will be more interviews.

Wanting the Job

The SM's job market is limited and the competition is stiff. Although there are several possible roles for performers with each show, there are only two positions for the SM—the PSM and the ASM. When interviewing for a job, the SM usually is out of work and may have been so for an extended time. The need and want for the job is great, but if this kind of desperation is taken into the interview, it will get in the way. It is perfectly acceptable to express your interest in the job and state your desire to have it, but do not sound desperate for work. Interviews should remain clear and focused in the present, and you should display confidence, asserting that you are good at your work and would be an asset to the show.

First Impressions

As much as people try not to let a first impression affect their judgment and decision making, it is a wise SM who knows that the first impression is important and lasting. The first impression is probably the only part of an interview over which an SM has some control.

When entering the room for an interview, the SM should appear confident and self-assured. Also important is the kind of energy the SM exudes—which should be genuine and not put on—how the SM greets the people present, and how the SM proceeds with the interview. First impressions are built on how the SM answers questions, offers information, makes conversation, and allows his or her personality to come through.

Dressing the Part

How the SM dresses is probably the most important part of the first impression. It is the jacket cover to the book, the billboard or marquee poster that catches the eye and draws a person's interest. Gone are the days when an SM is expected to wear a business suit, although on some interviews a business suit might be appropriate, especially if the production company is large and set up in a corporate-like structure. SMs should dress to satisfy their own personality and style, but must keep in mind that they are applying for a very responsible position and being chosen to lead an entire company of people. Dress that is too stylish, too trendy, or too funky can be a deterrent in getting the job, even if the producer or director dresses in an extreme fashion. On the other hand, dressing without style or awareness of the trend of the day can also have an adverse effect. There is a middle road to be traveled in the SM's fashion and style of dress: neither too far "in" nor too far "out."

The Chit-Chat Part of the Interview

Once past the introductory stage and review of credits, there comes a time when the conversation becomes more informal and the interviewer wants to settle in for a little chit-chat. Sometimes this takes the form of shoptalk or becomes an exchange of theatre stories. Other times the conversation may turn toward gossip. The interviewer may be very direct or ask leading questions. Regardless of the conversation, the SM should be careful not to give more information than is necessary to keep the conversation alive. The SM should never become involved in political, religious, or opinionated conversation. On occasion, an interviewer will see a name on the resume and ask, "I see you've worked with so-and-so. How did you find him? I hear he's very difficult?" Beware! Whether this is a test or just time to gossip, keep it brief and simple. If, in your experience you found the person named to be difficult, you can say so, leaving out the tabloid-like details. On the other hand, if your experience was contrary to popular belief, state that too. You may have some juicy stories to tell but you should resist the impulse; they will do more harm than good, impairing whatever first impression and credibility you have built.

The Other Side of Interviewing

Keep in mind that as you are being interviewed, you are also doing some interviewing yourself—deciding if this is a company, group of people, or a situation in which you would like to work. You might think that wanting and needing jobs means an SM does not have the luxury to pick and choose, but you do and should. There will be times in interviews when all indications are that this is not the job for you. Follow your instincts, no matter how badly you may need the job.

The Most Difficult Parts of Interviewing

The two most difficult parts to an interview come after the interview: waiting for the decision, and hearing that you did not get the job—rejection. Waiting for an answer and being rejected are a fact in anyone's life, but for people in show business they happen more often and sometimes feel more personal. All SMs share this with their show business brothers and sisters. The only protection against such feelings is to be strong and confident in yourself, have the desire and drive to remain working in the entertainment field, and know that what you have to offer is good. As for the rest, just keep networking, sending out resumes, and going on interviews, and the jobs will come.

GETTING AN EQUITY CARD

In Chapter 1, I said that being a member of Equity makes the difference between being professional and nonprofessional. To get an Equity card an SM must first be hired by a producer or director who is doing an Equity production. However, most producers and directors doing an Equity production are not willing to hire an SM who is not already Equity—the classic "Catch 22." Remember that producers and directors need the security and assurance of knowing that the SM they choose is experienced and qualified. So how does an SM get an Equity card?

Persistence, Paying Dues, Doing Your Best

To get pulled into this circle and become a member of Equity, a beginning SM must be persistent. Aside from continuing to build credits by working on shows regardless of their nonprofessional status, the aspiring SM also needs to ease into more professional situations, perhaps by working as a gofer, a production assistant, or as an assistant to a star, a director, or producer. A person aspiring to become a professional SM needs to meet people, at appropriate times express the passion to be working as an SM, and take advantage of opportunities that come up by doing the best job possible. Yes, luck and being in the right place at the right time play an important part in success, but it will be the person's patience, persistence, putting in time, and paying those proverbial dues that will make the difference and lead to that first job as an SM. This, of course, is predicated on the fact that the person has talent and can deliver.

Getting an Equity card is an important event in an SM's life and should be celebrated. The SM, however, should not be lulled into a false belief that this is the end of job worries. Getting an Equity card is a giant step, a quantum leap into the professional world, but the SM is still faced with all the things we have discussed in this chapter.

THE TERMS OF THE CONTRACT

Once the director or producer decides to hire the SM, the final phase in getting the job is signing the contract. First and foremost, each professional contract with an SM comes under the auspices of Equity, with terms that have already been established and agreed on between Equity and the producer—namely minimum salary, benefits, and working conditions.

Negotiating

Producers would prefer that everyone worked at union minimum salaries. Performers usually have agents or managers to help them get more, but SMs have only themselves. There are only a few SMs who have the power to walk in and ask for a sum of money substantially above union minimum. For the rest, an SM must go in with self-confidence, self-assurance, and experience, and then go through the negotiating process. Producers will haggle, bargain, barter, and ping-pong terms back and forth with star performers, but they have little tolerance or patience in playing the same game with SMs. This leaves a very small window of negotiation for the SM.

Before going into the meeting, the SM must decide on the lowest acceptable amount of salary. If the producer is unwilling to meet even the lowest price and insists on paying union minimum, the SM might suggest some perks instead, asking for title page credit in the program and on posters, a biographical write-up in the program, or complementary tickets for several performances. For the producer these things are not an out-of-pocket expense, and it costs them nothing to give these things. Even if a producer meets the SM's asking price, it is worth a try to get the perks too. At times an experienced SM with an impressive list of credits may accept minimum terms just to get established with a particular producing company or director. Whatever the case, once the terms have been agreed on and the contract is signed, the SM must set aside all thoughts of compensation, plunge into the work, and do the million dollar job that is expected of a good SM.

PERSONAL FINANCIAL PLANNING, BUDGETING, AND SUPPORT FOR THE SM

It is very important that the working SM plan ahead and budget money for the time when the show ends and the job search begins again. The time between jobs can be joyfully short or excruciatingly long. An SM needs to have a backup, a reserve of money to use during these times of unemployment.

The key to financial planning and budgeting is to live and spend moderately at all times. A wise SM's lifestyle and spending don't increase during the times the paychecks are rolling in. Charge things on credit only if absolutely necessary and if you know you can continue to pay off the charge once the job ends and the paychecks stop. Most important, each week you must take from your paycheck a set amount, putting it into a reserve account. This will be money you might need to draw from if your unemployment becomes extended. If you should get a job before it is necessary to dip into this money, you should take the money and sock it away into investments for your retirement.

With this kind of planning and budgeting you will not have to live on the outer edges. You will not dread the closing of a show; you will live with ease, enjoy the time off, and get caught up on personal things. More important, you can continue to network, interview, and look for work without having to take just any job or do some other kind of work while you wait.

UNEMPLOYMENT INSURANCE BENEFITS

This section on unemployment benefits (UIB) is neither an endorsement nor encouragement to collect unemployment benefits, but applying for UIB is another fact of life in show business work. Within the first week of a show closing at least half of the company, if not more, will apply for such benefits. Being unemployed is not an easy or comfortable feeling, but the unemployment system is set up for unemployed people's benefit and is of great financial assistance during the times an SM is seeking work. UIB is a financial assistance, an aid, a subsidy—not a way of life and a source of income.

THE SM's SURVIVAL KIT

Being unemployed and looking for work is a way of life for SMs and many other people in theatre. Despite a resume full of impressive credits, there often comes a time when all SMs wonder if they will ever find another job. If you are the type who needs security, sanity, continuity, and continued employment, then close this book and run to some other profession. Being in show business, and in particular being an SM, is not going to provide such things. To survive, an SM needs persistence, perseverance, fortitude, and lots of confidence. The SM will need to continue the quest for employment, watch personal cash flow, and be regimented in personal budgeting. However, while doing all this, it is also important to retreat, take some days off, collect your thoughts, review priorities, and renew your physical and spiritual energies, so that you can once more go out and fight the dragons and windmills you will encounter in the next job.

THE PROFESSIONAL EXPERIENCE

Proud to Join the Ranks

When I finally moved into PSM status, I proudly wrote at the top of my resume PRODUCTION STAGE MANAGER. While this was impressive and assuring to producers and directors who were considering hiring me as a PSM, it stopped others from offering me work on major shows as an ASM because they didn't want to insult me and offer me a lesser position. Being a person who likes working regularly, I set my pride and ego aside and chose merely to put at the top of the resume, STAGE MANAGER. My readers were more comfortable in offering me ASM work and I was happy to receive those offers too.

The Terminator Negotiator

I interviewed with a producer with whom I had immediate rapport. This was one of those interviews that, after I left, I felt certain I had the job. Several days later, the producer's secretary called and confirmed my feelings. She requested I come in to sign the contract. I told her I had not yet talked terms of the contract or salary and she assured me I could do this at the time of signing.

When I arrived for my meeting with the producer, he was changed. He was annoyed and said abruptly, "My secretary tells me that you want to talk about the contract?" "Well yes. We have not talked about salary and then there are a couple of things I always like to include in my contracts." "I don't know what those things are, but I can tell you off the top, I pay only Equity minimum." I was not deterred from my objective because I had heard this many times before. "I understand that, and when I first started stage managing, I used to work for Equity minimum, but today I feel I come with a lot more experience—"

Before I could finish, the producer cut in, " I don't think you heard me. I don't pay above Equity minimum!" I laughed, thinking he was joking, but from the stony expression on his face I could see he was dead serious. A painful and awkward silence filled the room.

"Well," I sputtered, "is there no room for negotiation?" The producer said nothing. The silence became more painful. I stammered and sputtered, "Well, I guess this leaves us at a standstill." By this time I had decided I did not want to work for this person even if he offered me three times the salary. "Yes it does! Take it or leave it." I was taken back by his approach. I thought to myself, "Whatever happened to negotiating and making counter-offers?" For a short period of time I thought perhaps I was responsible for such an adverse reaction. Several years later I told this story to a fellow SM and he asked, "Was the producer's name, so-and-so?" "Yes!" I replied in surprise. "Well I was the SM who ended up getting that job. It was a job from hell! This guy was

a megalomaniac. It was the worst job I ever had. I should have known from the interview not to take it but I needed it at the time. You were lucky."

That Gut Feeling

One day a producer of a well-known and established dinner theatre called and asked if I'd be interested in coming in for an interview. The theatre was forty minutes from my home. I had been out on the road doing shows for several years and by this time I was ready to do some work at home base. In addition, the dinner theatre was operational year round. Can you imagine, a job near home and working the year round? This would be too good to be true. I fantasized about it and by the time I arrived for the interview, I wanted this job badly.

The producer was an agreeable sort of person, warm and welcoming. She was highly complimentary, saying she had heard of my work, I came highly recommended, and that she was anxious to have someone like me come aboard and take over the operation as the PSM. I was of course flattered and I'm sure filled with pride and ego. "Let me show you around," she said.

As we strolled through the facility, the producer explained, "I've made a few changes this past year. The biggest move is to do fewer star shows and give some of the younger performers a chance to perform in lead roles. Also, Equity has agreed that as long as I hire X number of Equity performers, I can also use non-Equity performers. This will give these nonunion people credits toward getting their cards!"

As we got into the backstage area, the producer said, "I've made a big change here too which will really be cost effective. No more union stage hands." "That'll save a lot of money," I joked. We laughed and she continued, "I've made deals with some of the local colleges and their drama departments to let their tech students work backstage for the run of a show and get college credits." "But you'll have professionals as heads of the different technical departments?" I asked with terror in my heart. "Oh sure!" she assured me and added, "But we'll always be here to take care of things."

That worried me. By this time I had learned to be wary of producers and directors who were vague or left dangling alternatives. "I am a bit concerned about the setup backstage. I worked in a theatre where college kids were brought in to do the backstage work and I can tell you that at the drop of a date, a party, or cram-study night, some of these kids will not show up for the performance. I know! I've had it happen! What do we do then?" "I've got that all figured out too," she assured me again, "I've already started a roster of people we can call and get into the theatre in five minutes." For me this was not a workable plan, especially when I would be the person confronted with the problem ten minutes before a performance, but I did not express further my feeling or concerns.

We went up into the technical booth at the back of the house. It was an excellent setup, but I noticed there was only one chair at the lighting console and a place for the spotlight operator. "Where does the SM sit to call the cues for the show?" I asked. The producer proudly pointed to the chair. "But where does the light board operator and sound person sit?" "This is the beauty of the new setup," she boasted. "You'll be operating the lights and the sound and for that I will pay you extra. It won't be difficult. The SM who's doing our current show is less experienced and is doing it with no problems. Besides, we've made the shows much simpler. We don't have as many lights cues and once the sound levels are set, you just leave them and operate the few sound effects we might have."

Another wave of fear and panic came over me. Despite all the rules I had created for myself about not being negative, challenging, or controversial in interviews, I said, "This worries me. In the past I have been told by producers that things would be easy, but once a director gets working, he wants everything full-scale and at production value. I know the quality of the shows this theatre produces, and a few light cues and setting some sound levels is not going to be enough, especially when doing musicals."

"Don't worry about that! Any director who works for me will know my operation and budget. Besides, you'll be my right-hand man and I'll back you all the way. If we get a show that's busy, or really technically involved, then we'll bring in people to help." Jokingly I said, "I think my assistant is going to be one busy person." "That's another point . . ." The producer informed me that since making the changes, the theatre now came under a different contract with Equity and although she had to use some Equity performers, she was no longer required to hire an Equity ASM. Instead, I would have a new apprentice for each show. In that moment my desire for the

job tarnished, crashed, and crumbled. I felt sick and empty in my gut.

All the way home I agonized over taking or not taking the job. Each time I decided to take the job I got that sick feeling again. By bedtime I had talked myself into accepting the job. I could not sleep. Finally, around three o'clock, I decided to follow my gut feeling and not take the job. As soon as I made the decision, I felt better and fell asleep. Next morning I reversed my decision, deciding again to take the job. By ten o'clock I was driven to call the producer before I changed my mind again. The producer was thrilled to hear from me so soon and saw this as a good sign. Before she could say another word, I blurted out, "I just called to say that I will not be taking the job." I was shocked to hear the words come out of my mouth, for I had not intended to say them.

"Oh!" the producer responded with what I thought was hurt in her voice. She asked, "May I ask why not?" Every excuse or reason I gave she assured me my concerns were unfounded. Finally I said, "I'm just not comfortable with the working setup. I came to you with one expectation and after we talked, I found your set up was different." She became somewhat defensive, "I know it's not Broadway! Don't you think my plan will work?" "I'm sure it will," I said. "I just want to work in a more professional situation." With that statement the conversation ended. I felt I closed a door, maybe burned a bridge. I had learned not to do that. One day a person is producing dinner theatre, next year he is headed to Broadway and looking for an SM. A month later I got another show more to my liking, but which took me out on the road again. As far as I know, this producer never went to Broadway, so the bridge burned was not something to come back to haunt me.

INTERVIEWS

The people interviewed were asked a series of the same questions.

Question #1

Interviewer: How do you go about finding an SM?

Lara Teeter: First I think back to the people I've worked with, or I call people in the business—other producers, directors. People whose opinions I respect.

Bill Holland: This is a small business. In some way we are all connected. I know somebody who knows somebody.

Paul Blake: I'll tell you, the best people to call are the technical people. The costume people. The sound people. They get everywhere. Nobody sees them as a threat, so a lot of stuff is said and done in front of them that maybe a person would not say or do in front of a director or producer.

Question #2

Interviewer: When you look at a resume, what impresses you? What things do you look for?

Lara Teeter: First I am impressed with how it's written, how clean and clear it is to read. If I can look at it and in two seconds know this person, then this is a good resume and right there, that tells me something about the SM. If it's printed on nice paper and if it looks like they gave it some thought, then I'm impressed. Presentation of the resume is very important to me.

John Bowab: I check to see if the SM has done the kind of show I'm doing. I look to see where the SM has worked and with whom. I like to have the director's names listed as well. This also shows me that the SM is not afraid to have me call people about him.

Bill Holland: I look at the experience—the caliber of shows, the type of shows, the stars. I look to see if the person is a seasoned SM, capable of doing my shows or if he is a newcomer.

Paul Blake: You can get a very good idea of what an SM is like and what he is capable of, just by the shows listed and more importantly, the people he's worked with. I usually know how these people work, the kinds of shows they do, and the kinds of people they like to work with! This then tells me a lot about the SM.

Question #3

Interviewer: What about the way an SM dresses?

Lara Teeter: It's not about style or fashion! Clean, neat, comfortable, casual. How a person dresses tells me who they are and how they are feeling that day.

Paul Blake: I work on instinct. As soon as the person walks into the room, I know if I'm going to like that person. Sometimes they change my mind but usually, I'm right the first time.

John Bowab: I have a firm belief that how you dress is how you want to present yourself, and, is how people will respond to you! When I first started, SMs always wore a jacket, shirt and tie. Today that's not necessary, but I do think it is important for an SM to dress up!

Question #4

Interviewer: Do you call and check references?

Lara Teeter: ABSOLUTELY!!!

Bill Holland: It's like getting a history of the SM. How he works under fire, his attitude, work habits, temperament. How he gets along with people, stars, or deals with the temperamental artist.

John Bowab: It's risky not to do some checking. I've had SMs who are good at giving interviews but then don't deliver—that's why it's important to call people.

Question #5

Interviewer: How do you judge a good SM from an interview?

Bill Holland: With the actors you can see pictures or videotapes, audition them or go see them in a show, but with an SM you only get to see them in the interview, and that's a one-shot deal. I've never needed to have a second interview with an SM. In the first interview, I see how the person carries himself, how he dresses, the total package. My final decision on an SM, after everything else, is gut feeling. If I feel that he is going to serve me, take care of the show and look out for my best interest, including my best financial interest, then he gets hired.

Paul Blake: The most important elements in hiring an SM are the interview, the face-to-face meeting, and the references and recommendations.

ATTENTION READER!

In Chapter 1, we talked about the glossary—the SM's working vocabulary—and how the definitions are written for the beginning SM. Now is the time to bookmark your place and turn to the glossary at the back.

It is important at this point in your study of becoming a professional SM that you spend some time with this list of words, terms, expressions, and phrases. You will meet them time and time again throughout this book and certainly as you work on the job. An SM must communicate with all departments and people throughout the production. To do this effectively, the SM needs to talk to each department in their terms. If a director is vague or esoteric in the use of some terms, people will overlook it. For an SM, the same people will be less tolerant.

Is your bookmark in place? Turn to the Glossary.

5

Tools, Supplies, and Equipment

Whether working in academic theatre, community theatre, or in a professional situation, the SM must be ready and equipped to do the job with efficiency and expediency. Like any other profession, there are tools and supplies required. Essentially, an SM needs an office accessible at all times. However, an SM is highly mobile. In the course of a day the SM might work at home, at the production office, at the rehearsal hall, in a business luncheon, and at a production meeting. When on the road with a touring show, the SM becomes even more mobile and must have the office along at the hotel, on a bus or plane, at the theatre, or in the ballroom of some hotel during understudy rehearsals. It should be no surprise to see an SM entering a rehearsal hall or the backstage of a theatre carrying in one hand a briefcase bulging with supplies and hard copy, and in the other hand a laptop computer. Tucked under the SM's arm might be rolls of blueprint drawings and slung over the SM's shoulder could be a tote bag with lunch, some personal items, and more than likely, more supplies.

THE SM's PORTABLE OFFICE

All SMs come up with a portable office that works for them. The least mobile office some SMs create for themselves is the *stage manager's box*. The SM's box is discussed below. First, we will review the other elements of the portable office, the SM's bag and the SM's console.

The SM's Console

For the SM who moves frequently from show to show or travels with touring shows, the SM's box may be made into an upright, podium-style unit on wheels. It will have built into it drawers and com-

partments for the SM to keep the necessary tools, office supplies, a filing system, and personal items. In addition, there is space at the top for the electronic equipment the SM needs when calling cues during a performance. This unit is moved by the prop department, easily wheeled into the rehearsal hall or any backstage area, plugged in to an electric power source, connected to the theatre's communication system, and the SM is ready to work back stage. Stagehands may continue to call this unit the stage manager's box or they may more appropriately call it the *stage manager's console*.

The SM's Bag

The SM's box and the SM's console are excellent tools to be used as part of the job, but they cannot be quickly moved to a production meeting, business luncheon, or a rehearsal somewhere other than the rehearsal hall. SMs need still greater mobility. They need to have an office at their side, something they can pick up, take along at a moment's notice, and have everything they need with them. This type of office conveyance often takes shape in the form of a briefcase, attache case, or a shoulder bag filled with all that the SM needs. For our purposes throughout this book, we will devote our conversation to a large, sturdy, shoulder carrying bag, with at least three main sections or divisions to hold scripts, a three-ring binder, and a limited filing system. In addition, this bag must have other sections and side pockets for holding the smaller office supplies needed.

The Contents

As much as possible, the things put in this bag should be lightweight and/or scaled down. This bag will be slung over the SM's shoulder and can become quite heavy when being schlepped from place to place. The items listed below are essential in this bag, the bare necessities, and are complete for the SM's use in any situation.

1. **A hardcover three-ring binder** (for the rehearsal/blocking script). The pages to an SM's rehearsal script should never be bound in any way. The pages must be easily removable so they can be changed or rearranged at any time. For convenience, the cover should be hard. At times in rehearsals, the SM will fill in for a missing actor, reading the actor's lines and doing the blocking. The hard cover allows the SM to hold the script in one hand while using a prop in the other. The hard cover also gives the SM a backing against which to write blocking notations or changes in the script while still standing and filling in.

   Once technical rehearsals begin the SM will be creating an additional script, a *cueing script*. This script can be put in a lightweight, softcover, three-ring binder. For convenience, it is best to keep the rehearsal/blocking script and the cueing script separate. Be certain these binders are clearly marked as belonging to the SM.

2. **Another three-ring binder** (the production notebook). This binder will hold all the charts, plots, plans, and lists that will be created or collected for the production. The information in this binder is fingertip information for the SM. It needs to be highly accessible and attainable in a moment's notice. It will not be convenient to have this information placed in a filing system, especially when on the phone or in a production meeting. For many reasons, it is best to keep the production notebook separate from the rehearsal/blocking script.

3. **Full-page dividers and stick-on tabs.** Both the production notebook and the rehearsal/blocking script should be divided with full-page dividers and each divider should be tabbed. This allows for greater organization and easy access to whatever information the SM might need at any moment. There is nothing more impressive than to see an SM deliver information in no more time than it took to ask for it. For durability, the full-page dividers should be made of a thick paper or card stock. They might also be a color other than white. It is better to use tabbed, full-page dividers rather than to just tab the first

page of information in each section because the pages of information will more than likely change, and when they do the SM will have to take the time to tab the new page.

Some of the tabbed divisions should include:

- **Sched.** (schedule): Placed in this section is the block calendar, the scene/character breakdown chart, the schedule reminder list, and a copy of the daily schedule (these charts and lists will be discussed in Chapter 6, Hard Copy: Charts, Plots, Plans, and Lists.)
- **Staff** (the staff address list): In this section are placed the names and addresses and phone, fax, cell phone or pager numbers of the production people—both the creative and technical. As a reference and in times of need, it is a good idea also to keep copies of staff lists from previous shows.
- **Cast** (the cast address list): Like the staff list, this list too contains the names, addresses, and various phone numbers of all the cast members. For greater organization and quicker access it is best to keep this list separate from the staff list. It is also a good idea to include in this section cast lists from previous shows.
- **Prod.#s** (production phone numbers): This section will contain the names, addresses, and phone numbers for all shops, vendors, rental houses, coaches, trainers, artisans, and craftsmen having to do with the current production. Keeping a list of these people from past productions can be more valuable than gold in times of need or emergency.
- **Props** (the prop list)
- **Sets** (scenery): The SM's personal 8½-by-11-inch floor plans (which will be discussed in Chapter 6), and all notations concerning the scenery.
- **Lights** (lighting/electric)
- **Snd.** (sound): This section primarily includes the list of sound effects (SFX) for the show and possibly information having to do with recording.
- **Cstms.** (costumes/wardrobe): A copy of the scene/character tracking chart, quick change information, and dressing room assignments.
- **Hair:** Information on wigs, hairstyles, and special supplies.

- **Run. Tm.** (running times): Keep notations on the timings taken for scenes, acts, and the entire show.

4. **Notepad or clipboard** (letter size). This is an item that should be at the SM's side every moment of every workday. Anything and everything that needs to be done or remembered is noted here. Nothing is too small or unimportant to write down. Leave nothing to memory. There is too much in the course of a day to think about. Forget one thing and it could have serious consequences later. The SM's mind should be free to deal with things happening at the moment while the notepad becomes the reminder for things that need to be done later.

5. **Three-hole punch.** Script changes and information that needs to be placed into the SM's binders often come on pages that have not been punched with three holes. Instead of having these pages loose until the SM can get to a three-hole punch, a wise and organized SM owns a punch and gets these pages placed into the script as soon as possible. The SM also sees that the actors punch their script change pages and get them securely into their scripts before they lose them.

6. **Pencil sharpener.** A dull or broken pencil tip may seem small and inconsequential, but in a rehearsal during moments of creativity and fast-paced work, a nonfunctional pencil can become a crisis.

7. **Ruler.** A ruler is not only good for getting measurements from blueprint drawings, but is also good as a straight edge for hand printing.

8. **Stapler** (with refill staples). Staples keep things bonded together more permanently and prevent pages of information from getting separated as they can with a paper clip.

9. **Dictionary** (paperback edition).

10. **Log book.** Traditionally this book can be as simple as a 5-by-7-inch, loose-leaf notebook, or a hardcover, permanently bound book with blank pages. Today, SMs can make the log book a file in their laptop computers. The SM writes in the log book every day, keeping a journal of the day's events, especially those that were unscheduled or unexpected. The SM's log book can become a legal record in an Equity arbitration or be subpoenaed in a court of law.

11. **Actor's Equity rulebook.** The SM's guide and bible to seeing that the actors, as well as the producer, follow the union rules and agreements. A new rulebook is given to the SM with each Equity show worked on. The SM needs to have this book accessible to refer to on all matters between the actors, Equity, and the producer.

12. **Personal address book.** With each show an SM makes new friends and working associates. Networking with these people is an important part of being in show business. At times, situations arise in a show on which an SM is working. A personal address book enables the SM to contact the people who might be able to resolve a problem at hand. Today, there are some hi-tech computer devices that are no bigger than a credit card, in which such personal information can be stored.

13. **Petty cash envelope** (accordion pleated with several pockets, about 6 by 12 inches). This particular item is important because there are several aspects to handling the producer's money. The SM will receive advance money or petty cash. As the money is spent receipts need to be kept to account for the petty cash spent.

    SMs will also pay for things out of their own pockets. These receipts should be kept in another part of the petty cash envelope for later reimbursement.

    Other people in the company will also spend money out of their own pockets, and will turn in receipts to the SM for reimbursement. The SM needs to keep these receipts organized and separate from the other transactions.

    Finally, the SM may give people in the company *advance money* out of the petty cash fund. With each advancement the SM needs to have the individual sign a piece of paper, a *chit*. The SM dates the chit, notes the amount of money, and has the person sign it, then keeps this chit in the petty cash envelope. When the person either pays back the money, or gives the SM a sales receipt for whatever has been purchased, the SM either tears up the chit in front of the person or gives the chit to the person, first noting payment, dating it, and signing it.

14. **Pocket-size calculator.** Needed mostly in totaling up petty cash expenses and double-checking other people's petty cash receipts turned in to the SM.

15. **Postage stamps.** Keep these in a concealed place—they are as good as money.

16. **Tape measure** (carpenter's cloth or metal, 30 to 50 feet). This tool is used mainly for measuring the dimensions of the set on the rehearsal room floor. When traveling with a show, the SM will use the tape measure at each new performance site in laying out the spike marks.

17. **Stopwatch.** Used for timing scenes, acts, or the entire show. A wristwatch with a second hand is workable, but a stopwatch allows the SM to continue doing other parts of the job while timing. Then at the moment of completion, the watch can be stopped and an accurate account of the minutes as well as the seconds is displayed. The stopwatch should have a lace or chain attached to it to place around the SM's neck while the watch is being used. When not in use, the watch should be put away in a safe place.

18. **Small flashlight.** The flashlight is used mostly backstage, during the performance. ASMs have greater need for a flashlight because they are free to aid or assist actors and technicians during the performance. The PSM uses a flashlight on occasion to light the way for an actor as the actor passes the SM's console, or to aid the stagehands as they move props on and off stage through the wings. The flashlight should be small and not project too bright a beam, because the light can spill onto the stage and be seen by the audience.

19. **Extra batteries** (for all battery-operated items).

20. **Extra pair of eyeglasses** (if needed).

21. **Permanent ink, felt-tip pens, and markers.** An SM needs a variety of these pens and markers, ranging from razor-thin line, to bold wide tip. Having the different primary colors along with black is useful and practical. The pens should be in permanent ink so the writing will not become smudged or water marked.

22. **Extra pencils, #2 lead.** An SM can never have too many pencils; however, a box of twelve should be enough. Do not keep these pencils out and in view or the box will be emptied before the day is over. Throughout the work day the SM should have a pencil in hand at all times. Most performers and directors have yet to adopt this practice and look to the SM to supply them with a pencil during each rehearsal. For them the SM keeps a bundle of used pencils, along with a pencil sharpener.

23. **A variety of colored pencils.** These pencils will be used in creating the cueing script.

24. **Ballpoint pens.** As a rule, SMs do not write with anything that cannot easily be erased. There are times, however, when the SM needs to document in ink, such as in the log book if it is not a file in a laptop. One or two pens are good to have as part of the supplies in this portable office.

25. **Erasers.** Change is constant throughout the day and an SM needs a good smudge-proof eraser that won't tear the page or wear holes in it.

26. **Scissors** (medium or large size).

27. **Artists' Exacto knife.** Used for fine cutting when the scissors won't do the job.

28. **Cellophane tape** ¾-inch and ½-inch) with dispensers. It is important to get the frosted or the invisible kind of tape, which is easily written on. This becomes very important when cutting and pasting in the cueing script. Also, the copy machine does not reproduce the image of the frosted tape on copies.

29. **Masking tape.** A roll of ½-inch, and if there is room in the portable office, a roll of 2-inch.

30. **White glue, cement glue,** and quick-dry bonding glue.

31. **Paper clips.** Large and small clips. Have also on hand a few of the squeeze, clamp-on kind to hold a script or a large amount of paper together.

32. **Script binding brads.** These brads have round tops with a stem, which is placed through the holes of the script and then spread apart to hold the script together.

33. **Push pins.** Used mostly for the callboard, but also useful for putting blueprint drawings and

sketches of the set and costume design up on the rehearsal room walls.

34. **Rubber bands** (various sizes).

35. **Blank address labels or package labels.** These should be address size, 4 by 2 inches, and self-adhesive. Also, when touring with a show, the large 5-by-3-inch labels in bright colors are great for labeling the SM's boxes for quick identification.

36. **Hole reinforcements** (self-adhesive). An important item, especially when the pages of an actor's script are falling out or the pages in the SM's binders wear loose.

37. **Wite-out or Liquid paper.** This item needs to be fast drying and made to use on photocopies. It is also excellent for making small script changes or corrections on floor plans.

38. **Post-its** (a couple of sizes). Great for pasting notes on scripts, marking things that need to be copied, writing notes to the director, or as reminder notes at the top of the SM's notepad.

39. **Antiseptic spray or cream, and bandages.**

40. **Aspirin, buffered aspirin, and menstrual pain reliever pills.**

41. **Instant ice pack.**

42. **Blackboard chalk.** When taping the outline of the set onto the rehearsal room floor, the chalk is used to mark the measuring points in preparation for laying in the tape. Chalk is also good to make quick and temporary spike marks on stage during technical rehearsals, until the ASM or prop person can make them more permanent with colored tape or paint.

43. **Sturdy string** (about 25 feet). With chalk tied at one end, this string is used as a compass for drawing on the rehearsal room floor circles or parts of circles that might be part of the set design, such as a turntable. Once the circle is drawn with chalk, the cloth tape is laid over it, which can withstand the wear and tear of the actors walking on it during rehearsals.

44. **Sturdy, heavy-duty, zip-lock bags** (12-by-6-inch or 8-inch square; the kind found at stationary stores, not grocery stores). These bags are perfect for holding small office supplies. Each bag can have its own category of items. They can easily be retrieved from the SM's office bag and will save the SM from having to search for things buried at the bottom.

This list of items and supplies for the SM's office bag comes with a guarantee. Any SM, beginner or old-timer, who has these items as part of a portable office will be ready and able to do the job effectively and efficiently, on-the-spot and at every moment.

THE SM's BOX

The PSM cannot live by office bag alone; there are additional tools and supplies the PSM must keep for the show, things that are either not practical to carry all the time or are not needed at a moment's notice to do the job swiftly and effectively, and these are kept in the SM's box. This is often a shipping crate or a sturdy trunk that holds everything the SM needs. Often these boxes are improved upon simply by adding casters for easy moving. With each show, the SM ships this box first to the rehearsal hall, then later to the theatre.

Within the SM's box, a neat, organized, and information-packed filing system must be maintained. The ASM can make the show filing system part of the office bag, but the PSM usually needs the larger box for these materials. A few PSMs choose to have the filing system at their side at all times, so they put it in a briefcase and carry it along with the office they have in their bag. In most working situations this is not necessary and the filing system, along with the remaining list of things an SM needs, is better kept in a container that the SM can keep at the rehearsal hall, then later at the theatre.

The SM's Filing System

First, foremost, and most important is the SM's filing system. The different folders/sections of the files must be clearly labeled and organized at all times. The division of files can be arranged either in alphabetical order, or put in the order most frequently used. For our use in this book, we have chosen the latter. The files should include the following items.

1. **Daily schedules.** It is important to the producer, Equity, and the actors to keep the daily schedule

on file should there be any questions in scheduling, work hours, or attendance.

2. **Sign-in sheets.** For the same reasons, the SM keeps the sign-in sheets.

3. **Original copies.** Each time a copy of a document is made on a copy machine some of the print quality is lost from the original. If the SM makes it a practice to make copies from copies, eventually the print on the page will become difficult to read. To maintain quality, the SM keeps the originals on file and uses them only to make copies.

4. **Extra copies.** In most working situations there is a copying machine available for the SM's use, so it is not necessary for the SM to keep a stockpile of copies, but only enough to last until the SM is able to get to a copy machine and make more.

5. **Technical departments.** Next in the SM's filing system are the technical departments. Each department should have its own folder. The SM keeps copies of some of this information in the production notebook carried in the office bag, but for the most part this information goes into the filing system. The SM also keeps copies of all correspondence with each department.

   - **Props.**
   - **Set.** In addition to the technical information on the scenery, the SM keeps extra copies of the personal 8½-by-11-inch floor plans.
   - **Lights.**
   - **Sound.**
   - **Costumes.**
   - **Hair/Makeup.**
   - **Vendors.**
   - **Misc.** (miscellaneous).

6. **Equity.** A section for Equity business is needed. From time to time, Equity will send official notices that the SM must post. After a while, old notices are taken down to make room for new ones. The old notices should be kept on file for future reference.

   - **Med. Insur.** (Equity medical insurance forms). The SM must keep these forms on file and give them to any actor on request.
   - **Callboard.** All notices or information taken down from the callboard should be kept on file for future reference until the end of the run. This file is most used when touring with a show. By Equity rule, a callboard is set up at each performance site. When leaving one location, the information on the callboard is taken down and filed away. On arrival at the new location, the information is put up on the new callboard set up by the SM.
   - **W-2 forms** (payroll tax deduction forms).

7. **Scripts.** This next section in the SM's filing system contains copies of the script. If the production is an original show or a show with a lot of rewrites, this section of filing can become large and used daily.

   - **Original script copy.** Once again, for the sake of quality reproduction, the SM should set aside an updated copy of the script and use it as an original for making all other copies. In addition, the SM keeps in this file a copy of the script as it was originally written, before any changes or rewrites were made.
   - **Script copies.** For numerous reasons, the SM should have on hand at least two updated copies of the script.
   - **Latest script changes.** After distribution of the latest script changes, the SM needs to have on file at least two copies.
   - **Old script changes.** The pages in the script that are replaced by the new script changes need to be kept on file. The SM keeps a copy of old script changes as a matter of record, for future reference, or should the producer or director want to go back to them.
   - **Show reports and show timings.** Once the show goes into performances with an audience, the SM begins making out show reports. Copies of this report should be kept on file.

8. **Music.** Music is placed at this point. It is the least used by the SM, except to store chorus parts and perhaps an extra copy of the conductor's score.

9. **Envelopes** (letter, business, and script-size).

10. **Paper.** For photocopies and computer printouts.

11. **File Folders** (letter size).

The preceding list of files is a good beginning for any SM and guarantees success. SMs eventually create their own file names and arrangement.

Other Items in the SM's Box

1. **Rolls of colored cloth tape.** This tape will be used for taping on the rehearsal room floor the floor plan of the set. Do not use paper or plastic

tape, because it cannot withstand the traffic and abuse it will get in the rehearsal room. Also, at the end of the rehearsal period, the SM must take up this tape, and paper or plastic tape will require the SM to spend three times the amount of time on hands and knees scraping. The cloth tape, even if torn and tattered, will easily pull up.

If doing a musical or a multiset show, each set taped on the floor needs to be in a different color. The choice of colors should be bright and quite distinguishable from each other, because the different settings will be laid over each other.

Save the ends of the rolls. Rope or chain them together, using this tape to make spike marks on the stage or rehearsal room floor for the placement of furniture, props, and important places where the actors must stand.

2. **First-aid kit.** By Equity rule, the producer must provide a first-aid kit. It is the SM's responsibility to keep it nearby and well supplied with:

Gauze roll and/or pads
Antiseptic spray and/or cream
Spray for burns
Cold packs and hot packs
Cleaning pads/towelettes
Smelling salts
Band-aids
Roll of medical tape
Eye drops/eye wash
Aspirin, buffered aspirin, and menstrual pain reliever
Antiseptic wash
Cotton—rolls and balls
Small scissors

Aside from having some basic first-aid knowledge, it is important that the SM take some classes in performing CPR and the Heimlich maneuver.

3. **Extra office supplies.** The SM should make an effort to keep just enough extra supplies on hand so that each item is always available. The job of being an SM is fast-paced and intensive. Things need to be done expediently and with efficiency. Even a small thing like not having paper clips or pencils can slow down the work process and be annoying to everyone involved.

4. **Workman's tools.** A hammer, combination wire cutter and pliers, bullnose pliers, combination wrench, and screw driver with a changeable head to accommodate different screws and sizes are good as a starter collection.

5. **Electrical extension cord.** This is not a priority item, but convenient to have when needed.

6. **Clip-on lamp with a dimmer control switch.** Inexpensive utility lamps can be found in hardware stores, along with a dimmer switch, which can be spliced into the wire to control the amount of power going to the bulb. More stylish ones, with the dimmer control built in, may be found in stationary or office supply stores.

This item is important once the SM gets in the theatre and begins calling cues during technical rehearsals and performances. All SM's consoles in theatres have a light for the SM to read the script during the performance, but they are usually too bright. The SM may not be aware of the brightness until a blackout is called and the SM looks at the stage only to see colored spots instead of the darkened stage. With the dimmer control, the SM can adjust the light reflecting on the cueing script to a lower intensity at the start of the show. The SM's eyes get used to that intensity, and when a blackout comes they can quickly adjust to the darkness.

TODAY'S STAGE MANAGER

Electronic Equipment

There was a time when the only remaining item to name on the list of things an SM needs was a portable, electric typewriter. With today's SM, there are five additional items. They are costly, but are extremely useful and effective. They also add to the load of equipment the SM must carry to the rehearsal hall and theatre.

1. A laptop computer
2. A small and portable printer
3. Combination fax machine, copying machine, scanning device
4. Combination pager and cellular (mobile) phone

Fortunately, an ASM can slowly purchase these items as the need and desire to have them arises. Until then, the SM can use what the production company or PSM provide.

Shoulder carrying cases/bags are already designed and made for the computer, printer, and scanner, which makes it easier to transport these things. However, with the SM's office bag, the large blueprint drawings, perhaps a tote-bag for personal items, and now the addition of this electronic equipment, the SM has quite a load to carry each day. Some SMs have consolidated these items into a small traveling suitcase on wheels with a pull-out extension handle, or have had made for themselves a custom fiberglass case on wheels with straps and handles. These cases are easily lifted in and out of cars, maneuvered up and down stairs, wheeled down halls and corridors, and each day are quickly set up in the rehearsal room. In addition, such cases can also become carry-on luggage when traveling by plane.

Software

Along with the hardware comes the software. Most important are the following:

1. A *word processing program* which will be primarily used for making changes in the script.
2. A program that enables the SM to create the *forms* and *lists* needed to organize and administrate the show.
3. A *drafting program* for the SM to make reduced, personal-size, 8½-by-11-inch floor plans.
4. A *scanning program*, which enables the computer to accept handwritten text as well as printed/typed text.
5. A setup for receiving and sending *e-mail*.

In Transition

At present these electronic items are standing at the threshold, waiting to take their place permanently on the SM's list of things required for the job. There are, however, still plenty of SMs who continue to do their work well and effectively without them. Some producers lag behind in seeing the value and worth of this state-of-the-art equipment for their SMs, especially when they are asked to provide them. As we move further into the twenty-first century these things will become less expensive and more commonplace in their use. Perhaps at that time producers will begin providing some or all of this equipment as they have with typewriters and copying machines. Until then, SMs who want to use these things in their work will have to purchase them for themselves.

THE PROFESSIONAL EXPERIENCE

The Well-Supplied SM

On the first day of my first professional job, I showed up with a slim-line attaché case. Inside I had the show script placed into a three-ring binder, a clipboard with a notepad, some pencils, a ruler, an eraser, a small flashlight, scotch tape, paper clips, a pair of scissors, and a pocket-size dictionary. I felt proud, confident, ready to do the job, and I knew I would impress my new boss, the PSM.

On that particular day it was only myself and the PSM at the rehearsal hall. We were there to tape the set on the floor. The PSM, too, was ready to do the job. He showed up with an attaché twice the thickness of mine and it bulged from its contents. In addition, he carried a briefcase just as full. He had the blueprint floor plans rolled under his arm, a brown paper bag lunch gripped in the hand that held the attaché case, and rolls of colored tape chained together, swinging from the handle of the briefcase.

Our first task was to round up and set up tables to work on. We found a banquet-type table on which the PSM spread the blueprints and the items we needed to do the job. I settled in at the far end. As the PSM laid out the blueprints, he suggested I get out my tape measure. I did not have one. "That's okay, we'll use mine," he said, "but you'll need to get yourself one." I wrote myself a note on my clipboard pad. I felt redeemed because the PSM complimented me on having a notepad and expressed the importance of making notes to myself. I felt further redeemed when the PSM asked me to get out my ruler to take the measurements of the set from the blueprints as he measured them out on the floor. I noticed the PSM reaching into the corner of his briefcase and pulling out a box of children's blackboard chalk, which he used to mark the floor as I gave him the measurements. When he wasn't looking, I quickly added chalk to my notepad. The show was a musical. We had six different sets to lay on the floor. At one point we used up the PSM's red quarter-inch tape. He asked, "You wouldn't by chance have some red tape?" Apologetically, I said no.

The morning passed quickly. For lunch the PSM opened his brown bag lunch, placed his cup of yogurt and fruit next to the blueprints, took a spoonful of food, and continued working. There was no time to stop for a lunch. Fortunately, a catering truck appeared outside the rehearsal hall, as it did every day, and I was able to get a sandwich and return to continue my work.

We also had a second rehearsal room in which the choreographer would do most of his work. In this room we had to lay out on the floor only the dimensions of the stage. It was my job to start this work and the PSM would join me after he finished putting in the dance numbers at the foot of the stage in the first rehearsal room. He loaned me his tape measure and gave me the half-inch white tape that he always used to tape out the parameters of the stage. I had to ask for some chalk, to which he gave no reaction or comment. For that I was thankful. I worked diligently by myself and when the PSM joined me, he was once again complimentary. As an added touch to help the choreographer know the amount of space he had for each dance number, the PSM decided to indicate on the floor the places where each drop was placed on stage. At each point, we placed a strip of white tape, about eighteen inches long. The PSM then asked me to write on each strip, in bold letters, with a wide-tip marking pen, the names of the different drops. I was quite capable of doing this except for one thing—I had no marking pen. Once again I had to borrow from the PSM, and once again I added to my list.

By the end of the day I had quite a list of things to buy. They were small things. Things that I had previously given little consideration or importance. Nonetheless, they were tools or supplies I needed with me regardless of their limited use in doing my job. What I realized that day and in the days to follow, was the SM needs to have many things with him at all times. Producers, directors, and actors are not willing to wait for the SM to run off to the production office to get supplies. They expect the SM to have the necessary tools and supplies, and to be ready to service the job and their needs.

Halfway through the rehearsal period on that first job, I retired my slim-line attaché case for a much wider one, and in addition purchased a sturdy leather shoulder bag with several divisions, zippered sections, and side pockets. This bag did not bulge as fiercely as the PSM's, but I was on my way.

Log Book: Star Witness

This next story was told to me by an associate SM. It shows the importance and effect the SM's log book can have. I have excluded names to protect myself, my associate, and the two star performers involved. The stars of the show were husband and wife. Both were renowned for their work in some very classic and now famous Broadway shows. They made a wonderful starring team and when they performed together, they filled the theatre each night.

They were wonderful to work with. The rehearsal period was a joy and pleasure. However, once the show went into performance, the working relationships between the husband and wife and SMs took a turn. We could hear the husband and wife arguing behind closed dressing room doors, and they were continually late getting into places for the top of the show. One time we had to hold the curtain for twenty minutes. It seems the husband started drinking again. We had been warned of his drinking problem, but it escaped our minds because there had been no indication of it during rehearsals. For a while the wife was able to cover for him.

At first I entered each incident into the stage manager's log book and left it at that. But when the incidents became more frequent and severe, I started sending copies of my entries to the producer and to Equity. Toward the end of the run the husband was drunk practically every performance. It was like a bad movie with all the classic symptoms of an alcoholic performer. The wife's performance suffered, as did the rest of the cast. We were glad to have the show complete its run. Several weeks later we heard the couple had separated and then one day I was subpoenaed along with my log book to give deposition and eventually testify in divorce court. The log book had some pretty damaging evidence against the husband and played a very important part in the judge's decision to grant the wife the divorce.

6

Hard Copy: Charts, Plots, Plans, and Lists

An important and major portion of the SM's job, especially in the first two weeks of working on a show, is to gather, compile, and note information. The SM must put this information in comprehensible form and distribute when it is needed. Failure in any part of this job leaves giant holes in the organization and communication of putting together a show.

There are no standard forms from which an SM works. Each SM learns what forms to use through academic studies and through working with other SMs. With time, all SMs make these forms their own by changing them or reinventing them to suit the show or their own working needs. An SM must learn what makes good and workable charts, plots, plans, and lists. You can create some pretty impressive looking hard copy, but if the information is incomplete, poorly laid out, difficult to understand, or requires study to extract, then the form does not stand and deliver. A guide to seeing if your paperwork is serving its purpose is to see the people to whom the hard copy is given. If you find people seeking information you've already distributed, then it is time to go back to the drawing board and redesign.

FORMS DEFINED

Among the thirty definitions given in the *World Book Dictionary* for *form*, the best elements to include in an SM's definition are:

- appearance, neatness, shape
- order and arrangement of parts
- content
- to bring from a scattered state into organization
- inner structure and composition

I would add:

- clarity
- conciseness
- thoroughness
- ease in reading
- ease in extracting information quickly without having to study
- understandability

THE SCENE/CHARACTER TRACKING CHART

We will talk about layout and design as we create our first chart—the *Scene/Character Tracking Chart*, henceforth abbreviated as Sc./Chctr.Track.Chrt.

Sidebar: I was introduced to this chart on the first day of my first professional job. The PSM handed me a copy from a previous show and instructed me to create a similar chart for the show on which we were presently working. Since that time I have used the Sc./Chctr.Track.Chrt. for every show. Back then, the Sc./Chtr.Track.Chrt. was printed by hand. Today it is generated completely by computer. Through the years, I have changed it enough to call it my own. This is a versatile chart and, as you will see, will be used in many ways.

OUR IMAGINARY PLAY

The Sc./Chctr.Track.Chrt. is designed to *track the scenes* in the play, *list the characters* in the play, and display in block form *which characters appear in which scenes*. To begin construction of this chart I have created a simple two act, one set, comedy play entitled, *John and Mary*. This play will serve us well here and with other documents we will create in this chapter. If this play were in published form, the SM would first read it through for its entertainment value. On the second read through, the SM would begin to create the Sc./Chctr.Track.Chrt. Here are the characters in the play:

JOHN and MARY: husband and wife (the lead characters)

GEORGE: John and Mary's best friend, financial adviser, and attorney

ALICE: George's zany girlfriend

FRIEDA: Mary's nurturing but overbearing mother

FLORENCE: the maid, who acts as if John and Mary's home is her own

The smaller or cameo roles are:

POSTMAN

SUPERINTENDENT of the apartment

DELIVERY MAN

FIRE MARSHAL

REPAIR SERVICE MAN

A GIRL SCOUT, a seven-year-old child selling cookies

DELIVERY MAN HELPER is a 10-second walk-on part that will be played by the ASM

BEGINNING THE SCENE/CHARACTER TRACKING CHART

We start by listing the character's names across the top of the top of the page (see Figure 6-1).

Note the design and layout. The order of characters starts with the starring and leading roles and ends with the 10-second, walk-on part of the delivery man helper. To be complete and thorough, all characters who appear on stage or whose voices are performed live (not recorded) must be listed. The SM cannot depend totally on the list of characters printed at the front of the script. It is not always complete, especially when it comes to the small, walk-on parts. The SM must read through the entire play.

Note: In laying out the form and for the sake of space on the printed page, SMs may abbreviate words as they choose, as long as the readers of this chart can understand the abbreviations.

A Refinement

Before developing this chart further, let's refine the work already done, giving the readers of this chart more clarity, greater understanding, and the ability to extract information at a single glance. In this production of *John and Mary*, the producer and director have signed a comedian-actor who is well known from television and plays many different characters on his show. Our play is a perfect vehicle for this actor and he is signed to play the roles of the Postman, Superin-

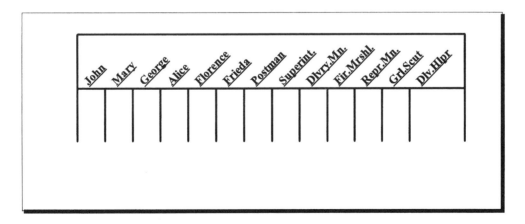

Figure 6-1   First step in creating the Sc./Chctr.Track.Chrt: the layout of character names across the top of the chart.

tendent, Delivery Man, Fire Marshal, and Repair Man. The script calls for a child between seven and ten years old to play the Girl Scout. However, there are state laws governing child actors that require a social worker present at rehearsals and performances. The producer is not willing to pay those weekly expenses. He and the director decide the TV comedian will also play the role of the Girl Scout. To convey this information, we can refine and modify the chart as shown in Figure 6-2.

Any person reading this chart can see in a single glance the working situation of this particular production. Note also the use of bold lines, thin lines, and shading to group or separate information. It is this kind of tailoring, refinement, and modification that helps make this chart easy to read and makes the chart stand and deliver.

THE HEADING

Every chart, plot, plan, or list should be headed at the top of the page with a name identifying the document and have with it information concerning the particular production. In the layout of our Sc./Chctr.Track.Chrt., this information is placed in the left-hand corner, before the character names (see Figure 6-3).

BREAKING DOWN THE PLAY BY SCENES

Under the heading and along the left side of the page, the acts along with their scene numbers are listed. In addition, either in parenthesis or in quotes, the scenes are *tagged* with a name, location, or title that further identifies the scene. In our imaginary play, the first part of Scene One has no strong identification other than it being in the apartment and establishing John and Mary's characters and relationship. The tag for this part of Scene One is noted simply as, *Apartment*.

With each scene written in the left-hand column, a grid of boxes forms across the rest of the page connecting the names of the characters with the scenes. An X is put in each box that corresponds to the characters who appear in the scene (see Figure 6-4).

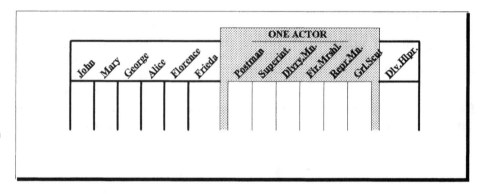

Figure 6-2 Refining the chart to suit the particular production, using bold and fine lines along with shadow areas to separate information and make it easier to extract information in a single glance.

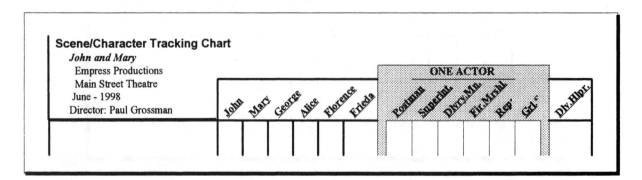

Figure 6-3 Adding the heading to the Sc./Chctr.Track.Chrt. with identifying information about the production.

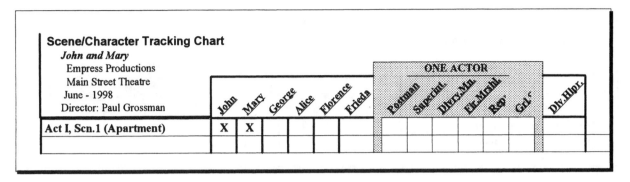

Figure 6-4 Listing the first part of the first scene in the play, the "Apartment". Mark an X in the boxes under the names of the characters who appear in the scene.

SUBDIVISION OF SCENES, OR FRENCH SCENES

This first scene in our imaginary play has many parts. Somewhere on page six, the character George enters. According to the script, we are still in Scene One until page thirty-two. Within those thirty-two pages, all the main characters in the play make an entrance. If we were to merely list Scene One as the apartment and put an X in the characters' corresponding boxes, the chart would be too general. To be complete and thorough and to make this chart highly usable, the entrances of each character must be noted and their portions of the scene identified with a tag. These divisions within a scene are called *French scenes*. French scenes begin when a character enters the stage or when a character on stage exits. French scenes end in the same way. In the case of our play, the next portion of Scene One, or the first French scene, begins when George enters on page six. This is how we would note it on the chart (see Fig.6-5):

> *Note:* In addition to tagging George's entrance, the page number is included. This is extremely helpful to the SM, director, and actors in leading them to the correct part of the script without their having to flip through the pages.

NAMING OR TAGGING A SCENE

George has come to talk business. The scene is named or tagged accordingly, "Talk Business." This identifies the scene, gives the reader of this chart an idea of what the scene is about, and at the same time gives the SM, director, and actors an identifying mark.

When making up the Sc./Chtr.Track.Chrt., most times the SM creates the name or tag for a scene. Sometimes the director tags a scene. The director of the musical play *Man of La Mancha* might say to the SM and actors, "Let's rehearse the missive scene." This is the scene in which Sancho reads to Aldonza the love note (or missive) from his master, Don Quixote, then sings the song, "I Like Him." There are scenes in some shows with a notoriety all their own: the balcony scene in *Romeo and Juliet*; the spaghetti scene or the twins scene from *The Odd Couple*; or the washroom scene and boardroom scene from *How to Succeed in Business*. . . .

Using the French scenes, we can now list and tag the entrances of all the characters in Scene One (see Figure 6-6).

The first scene of *John and Mary* is plotted. In a single glance we know which characters are involved, approximately how long they remain on stage, and have some idea of what the various portions of Scene One are about. We can also see that Scene One is over thirty pages long, which means it runs between twenty and thirty minutes. (As a general rule, allow one minute for each page of dialogue.)

Notice that Frieda's phone call is part of the list of French scenes. This means that in some way the audience can hear, and maybe even see, Frieda as she talks. If the audience saw and heard only Mary's part of the conversation, Frieda and the call would not be noted. We are now ready to note the rest of Act I and begin Act II (see Figure 6-7).

> *Note:* Once again bold lines and spacing are used to group and separate information.

The Sc./Chctr.Track.Chrt. is most effective when all the information appears on one page. Sometimes in

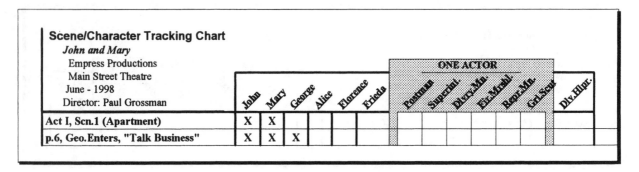

Scene/Character Tracking Chart *John and Mary* Empress Productions Main Street Theatre June - 1998 Director: Paul Grossman	John	Mary	George	Alice	Florence	Frieda	Postman	Suprint.	Dlvry.Mn.	Ext.Mrshl	Repr.Mn.	Grk.Scpt	Dlv.Hlpr.
							ONE ACTOR						
Act I, Scn.1 (Apartment)	X	X											
p.6, Geo.Enters, "Talk Business"	X	X	X										

Figure 6-5 Writing in the next part of Scene One, "Talk Business," and noting with X's the characters appearing in this part of the scene.

musicals where the cast of characters is greater, the SM lays out the page horizontally, choosing "landscape" on the computer page layout screen so that all the names will fit across the top.

This chart is an invaluable piece of hard copy. Copies should be kept at the beginning of the SM's rehearsal script, cueing script, and in the SM's production notebook under the tabbed heading, "Schedule." This chart aids the SM and director in creating the daily schedule. It is also useful to the SM on those days when in the middle of the rehearsal, the director decides to abandon the daily schedule and wants to rehearse a scene that has not been scheduled. At those times the director expects the SM to make

the change in as little time as possible. With the Sc./Chctr.Track.Chrt., the SM merely runs a finger down the left-hand column to find the selected scene and page number, then across to see which characters/actors must be gathered for that scene.

Copies of this chart are given to the director and actors, with the suggestion that they too place it at the front of their scripts. The costume/wardrobe department is glad to receive a copy, which they use to check against the charts they have created for themselves. The Sc./Chctr.Track.Chrt. is also a useful tool to the sound department for tracking body mics which might be used in each scene. Likewise, the publicity department finds it extremely helpful in decid-

Scene/Character Tracking Chart *John and Mary* Empress Productions Main Street Theatre June - 1998 Director: Paul Grossman	John	Mary	George	Alice	Florence	Frieda	Postman	Suprint.	Dlvry.Mn.	Ext.Mrshl	Repr.Mn.	Grk.Scpt	Dlv.Hlpr.
							ONE ACTOR						
Act I, Scn.1. (Apartment)	X	X											
p.6, Geo. Enters, "Talk Business"	X	X	X		X								
p.7, Interuptions, "Frieda Phone Call"	X	X	X		X	X							
p.10, Florence, "Mi Casa, Su Casa"	X	X	X		X								
p.13, Geo., "Down To Brass Taxes"	X	X	X										
p.21, Alice, "Whirlwind Entrance" "Shopping Spree"	X	X	X	X	X								
p.23, Geo., "Doomsday Speach"	X	X	X										
p.30, Postman, "Letter from IRS"	X	X	X		X		X						

Figure 6-6 Writing in the remaining parts of Scene One and marking X's for the characters appearing in each part.

Scene/Character Tracking Chart
John and Mary
Empress Productions
Main Street Theatre
June - 1998
Director: Paul Grossman

	John	Mary	George	Alice	Florence	Frieda	Postman	Superint.	Dlvry.Ma	Ele.Mrshl	Renr.Mn	Grl.Scut	Dlv.Hlpr.
							ONE ACTOR						
Act I, Scn.1. (Apartment)	X	X											
p.6, Geo. Enters, "Talk Business"	X	X	X		X								
p.7, Interuptions, "Frieda Phone Call"	X	X	X		X	X							
p.10, Florence, "Mi Casa, Su Casa"	X	X	X		X								
p.13, Geo., "Down To Brass Taxes"	X	X	X										
p.21, Alice, "Whirlwind Entrance" "Shopping Spree"	X	X	X	X	X								
p.23, Geo., "Doomsday Speach"	X	X	X										
p.30, Postman, "Letter from IRS"	X	X	X		X		X						
p.32, SCN. 2., "Guy Talk"	X		X										
p.41, Girls Enter, "Girl Talk"		X		X									
p.44, "Girls Against The Guys"	X	X	X	X									
p.47, Superintendent, "The Lease"	X	X	X	X				X					
p.50, SCN.3., "Women's Lib"		X		X	X	X							
p.59, Dlvry.Man, "The Package"		X		X	X	X			X				X
ACT II													
p.61, Scn.1., "Trial Separation"	X	X	X	X	X	X					X		
etc.													
etc., to end of play													

Figure 6-7   Writing in the information for all of Act I and beginning to note the information for Act II.

ing which shots they will want to take when scheduling for production photos.

THE CHARACTER/ACTOR–ACTOR/CHARACTER LIST

In the musical *Big River* there are fifteen principal roles and sixty-five smaller roles to be played. Depending on the size of the cast, actors in the company may each play three and four roles. The situation is similar in the two-part epic *Nicholas Nickelby*. When working a show of such proportions, the SM needs to have a list that lists the characters and the names of the actors playing the characters. This is the *character/actor list*. This list will be of great service to the SM when the director asks in the middle of a re-

hearsal or in some meeting, "Who have I assigned to the role of so and so?" The SM has only to run a finger down the list to the character and give the actor's name, "John Jones." Directors expect the SM to have such information readily available and deliver it within seconds.

This, however, is only half the information the SM needs to have at hand. The director may reverse the question and ask, "What roles are John Jones playing?" Instead of having to go down the list of characters to find each time John Jones' name appears, the SM needs to have assembled a corresponding list naming the actors in the company and the characters they are playing. This is the *actor/character* list. With shows like *Big River* and *Nicholas Nickelby*, it is almost certain the department creating the program will be looking to the SM to provide such a list. Thus, the character/actor–actor/character list is ready to do service, no matter how the director or anyone in the company asks for this information.

THE SIGN-IN SHEET

The sign-in sheet is a simple form to create. Once it becomes a file on the computer, the same form can be used for each show, tailoring only the text to suit the current production. The sign-in sheet is designed for the actors to sign each time they come to rehearsals or performances. It is to be posted in a place where it is easily seen and accessible, which usually is on the callboard. Originally the sign-in sheet was a sheet of paper the SM posted daily. It has since evolved into a weekly form on which the actors are required to enter their initials in the boxes that correspond to their names and the day on which they are signing in. At first the sign-in sheet was for payroll purposes; however, it quickly found its place in helping the SM to keep track of the presence or absence of actors and became a record for tardiness.

The Rehearsal Sign-In Sheet and Performance Sign-In Sheet

There are two different forms for the sign-in sheets, one for rehearsals and one for performances. It must be clearly noted at the top of the form as to which is which. After the heading, which contains the name of the document and has the information pertaining to the particular production, noted across the top are the days of the week, starting with Monday.

> *Note:* Equity and management have agreed the workweek starts on Monday and ends on Sunday.

In a column along the left side of the page the actors names are listed. With each name written, a grid of boxes is created across the rest of the page, similar to the grid of boxes created when making the Sc./Chctr.Track.Chrt. The lines of boxes connect the actors' names to the days of the week. It is in these boxes the actors enter their initials (see Figure 6-8).

Each day is divided into two parts. Each part is headed by the abbreviations "morn." and "brk."

REHEARSAL
Sign-in Sheet

Show: Date:
Producer: Place:
Director:
SM:

CAST *Please initial*	MON		TUES		WED		THUR		FRI		SAT		SUN	
	morn.	brk.	morn.	brk.	morn.	brk.	morn.	brk.	morn.	brk.	morn.	brk.	morn.	brk.

Figure 6-8 The rehearsal sign-in sheet, designed for the actors to note their initials in the correct boxes when they first arrive for rehearsals and when they return from their midday break.

which stand for morning and break. This being a professional production, the workday is eight and a half hours long. When the actors arrive for the first part of their day, which usually is sometime in the morning hours, they are required to enter their initials in the "morn." block. By no later than the fifth hour of each actor's call to rehearsal, the actor must be given an hour and a half for a meal break. Upon return from the break, the actor is required to sign in once again, this time in the "brk." block.

Listing the Actors' Names on the Sign-In Sheet

There are two approaches to listing the actors on the sign-in sheet: listing the entire cast in alphabetical order, or listing the actor's names in categories according to the roles they play—starring roles first, principal roles next, with supporting roles following. Listing the actor's names according to the roles they play is more in keeping with the SM's sense of order. In most situations when having to deal with the cast, such as in making out the daily schedule, sending actors to costume fittings, setting up the program, assigning dressing rooms, and even when arranging for social events, the SM divides the cast into playing categories. In musical shows, there are even more categories of cast members for the SM to list: singers, dancers, and sometimes extras. Also, the list of names within each category in musicals will be longer. It is within each category that the SM lists the actor's names in alphabetical order.

The Day Off While in Rehearsals

By Equity regulation, after six consecutive working days, the actor must be given a day off or be paid overtime. During rehearsals, the day off may be the same for everyone or it may be different for each person, depending on how the director likes to work. Whatever the day off, the SM hand writes this information, either in the column on the day everyone had off, or in each box corresponding to the day each person had off.

The Performance Sign-In Sheet

In the performance sign-in sheet the "morning" and "break" sections are gone and the shaded areas indicate matinee days (see Figure 6-9). The shading distinguishes the *rehearsal* sign-in sheet from the *performance* sign-in sheet with just a glance. In addition,

the shaded areas remind the actors as the matinee days approach during the week.

Matinee Performances

By Equity agreement with producers, actors are required to perform eight shows a week, which means two of the shows are performed in matinee. Traditionally, matinee days were on Wednesday and Saturday. In recent times, producers on Broadway and throughout the country have found matinee performances are better attended on other days of the week. Each theatre or city has found which days are best at its location and works accordingly. It is the SM's job to find the correct information for each theatre or city and reflect that information on the sign-in sheet before it is posted on the callboard.

The Day Off When in Performance

A tradition that has remained pretty constant is having the theatre dark on Monday, which becomes the cast's day off, but this too can vary depending on the theatre and the type of Equity contract under which the actors are working. Before posting the performance sign-in sheet for the week, the SM can indicate the day off by writing this information within the column on the day the cast has off.

ADDRESS LISTS AND CONTACT SHEET

One of the first lists the SM creates when starting work on a production is to assemble an address list. This information is available initially from the production office/production secretary; however, the SM is obligated to call each person, both in the cast and on the production staff to get:

- The correct spelling and professional name of each person as it will appear in the program
- A home address and/or business address
- Social security number
- Home phone, pager/cell phone, fax, and manager's and/or agent's numbers

The Cast Address List and Staff Address List

The address list is divided into two separate parts: the cast address list and the staff address list. For the cast address list the SM must once again decide whether

PERFORMANCE
Sign-in Sheet

Show: _____   Date: _____
Producer: _____   Place: _____
Director: _____   _____
SM: _____   _____

CAST *Please initial*	MON	TUES.	WED MAT	WED EVE	THUR.	FRI.	SAT MAT	SAT EVE	SUN.

Figure 6-9 The performance sign-in sheet on which the actors place their initials when they first arrive at the performance site for a performance.

to arrange the names alphabetically or in categories according to the roles played. To be consistent, we will continue using the categories/roles played (see Figure 6-10). On the staff address list, the names are in the same order as they appear in the chain of command, starting with the producer and production secretary, the director and assistant, creative staff members, SMs, and production heads and their assistants.

The address lists contain a lot of personal information that is not for general publication and distribution. The address lists are distributed only to those people who need to have it, namely the production office, director, and SMs.

The Contact Sheet

The contact sheet, on the other hand, is designed for general distribution. It is quite different from the address lists in that it is in alphabetical order and lists only those people who choose to be on the list and gives only the numbers they choose to have noted. The contact sheet is not a workable document for the

SM, but is generated and distributed as a service to the company and to enhance the general communication.

SCHEDULES

The Block Calendar

This form is the backbone for the SM in organizing and getting the entire company to work in the same time frame. It is the first step in keeping all departments informed. The block calendar is designed to give an overall view of the rehearsal period, the technical rehearsals, pre-opening performances, and the run of the show. For a detailed breakdown of each day's work, the daily schedule, which we will discuss next, is published and distributed each day.

Massive Coordination

In putting together the block calendar, SMs are pushed to the maximum of their coordinating abilities. The SM must first talk with the production office/producer, extracting from that department the

CAST ADDRESS LIST

John and Mary

Empress Productions - Broadway Celeberity Series

Producer: Glenn Jorden   Date: June - 1998
Director: Paul Grossman   Place: Main Street Theatre
                                                                                     Los Angeles, CA

KAREN GREY		555 Gateway Place	(H)	(310) 555-1212
(Mary)		Beverly Hills	(cell)	(213) 555-1212
		CA 90210	(fax)	(310) 555-1213
			(Mgr.)	(818) 555-0987
HAL LINDSLEY	NY (H)	237 Central Park, We	(H)	(212) 555-7890
(John)		New York	(fax)	(212) 555-6000
ss# 666-66-6666		NY 10024	(NY Agent)	(212) 555-8574
	LA (H)	10023 Sunset Hills	(H)	(818) 555-3412
		Glenn Oaks	(pgr)	(213) 555- 1092
		CA 91108	(LA Agent)	(310) 555-9283
DAVID FRANK	(H)	7450 Dantes View Dr	(H)	(805) 555-5341
(George)		Westlake Village	(pgr)	(805) 555-5341
ss# 333-33-3333		Westlake, CA 91360	(fax)	(805) 555-5342
			(Agnt.)	(310) 555-4334
	(Hlywd Ofc)	3450 Vineland Ave.	(O)	(818) 555-0010
		CA 91608	(fax)	(818) 555-6650
LUCEILE BAKER				
(Alice)	**etc., etc.**			

Figure 6-10   A sample cast address list identifying all cast members and listing their business/home addresses and all phone numbers where they can be easily reached. The staff list is similarly prepared.

time frame and schedule for the different phases of the production. The information from the producer's office becomes the foundation and framework for the calendar. With the information from the production office, the SM then meets with the director, who provides more details for the rehearsals and in putting together the show. If the show is a musical, the SM meets with the musical director and choreographer, getting their input. It is important that the SM also talk with the publicity department to see what interviews have been scheduled and if and when publicity photos are to be taken.

The SM then meets with the technical director (TD). In most working situations, the TD has already gotten the schedule information from the production office and has created a schedule for the crew. During this meeting the SM gets from the TD any information not already noted on the block calendar, and checks to see that the TD is working in the same time frame. Having all the information from the TD, the SM still meets or talks with the heads of the different technical departments, just to make contact, get additional input, and be assured they too are working in the same time frame. The SM also meets or talks with the designers of the different departments, once again, just to make contact, get additional input, and be assured they are working in the same time frame.

Publication and Distribution

With the information gathered, the block calendar has pretty much created itself. As the SM assembles the information on the block calendar, each day's entry must be checked to assure that there are no conflicts in times, dates, or places. The SM is also vigilant in judging the time frames, making sure they are reasonable for the work that needs to be done. Most of all, the SM is expected to know the union rules governing the actors' and technicians' work days, call times, breaks, and days off. The SM must never schedule a working situation where the producer must pay overtime or penalties, unless approved by the producer.

On completion of the block calendar, but before publication and distribution, it is imperative that the SM return to the key people from whom the information came, have them read over the calendar, and get their approval. This calendar should be given out liberally to everyone in the company, including those who are in any way associated with the production. With the use of a computer, there is no reason why the layout and presentation of this form should be less than printshop perfect. Whenever possible, the information in the block calendar should appear on one page. Each PSM has a preferred form in presentation. Ours is shown in Figure 6-11.

This is an involved and complicated calendar to produce. Beginning SMs take heart. This is PSM work. You will get your knowledge and experience during your time as an ASM, before you will be called upon to make one yourself.

The Daily Schedule

This schedule is the soul mate and partner to the block calendar. The daily schedule gives the details the block calendar does not provide. In most working situations, the director and SM create the daily schedule each day for the next day. In it they detail the entire work day, sometimes down to the minute, specifying the scenes to be worked on, the actors needed for the scenes, the actors' call times, meal breaks, and dismissal time. A copy of the next day's schedule must be posted on the callboard before the actors leave at the end of the day, otherwise the SM is required to call all of the actors to give them the schedule.

There is no particular form to follow in laying out the information for the daily schedule. For the SM the objective is, as with all paperwork, to be simple, clear, straightforward, informative, neat, easy to read, and easy to understand. With this piece of hard copy, more so than some of the others, there is no room for interpretation or misunderstanding of information by the reader, who might mistakenly come to rehearsal at the wrong time or not be prepared for the work to be done on that day. Whenever possible, this schedule should be published on one piece of paper, even if the SM must print it out on legal-size (8½-by-14-inch paper). Whatever form the SM uses in creating the daily schedule should be the same for each day. Once the company members become familiar with the format and layout of information there is less chance for mistakes.

In addition to the copy of this schedule being posted on the callboard, copies need to be distributed to the producer, director, and all staff members who are directly involved with each day's rehearsals. The SM is responsible for seeing that everyone on the schedule is informed (see Figure 6-12).

When working a musical show, the daily schedule becomes more involved because the choreographer and musical director must also have their work days scheduled. If there is an assistant director with the show, there can be as many as four rehearsal rooms to schedule at one time. The logistics of moving performers and not double-scheduling become a lot more intense. Once again, it is the job of the SM to see that there are no conflicts in scheduling. Once again the layout and information on this form must be easily read and understood (see Figure 6-13).

Each day the SM is pressed to get the daily schedule published, posted, and distributed before the actors leave. If at any time the SM is unable to create this schedule by computer, it will have to be hand-printed. The same rules of neatness, order, layout, and comprehensibility apply. Using different felt-tip pens helps get the thin-line and bold-line effect in both the printing and separation of information.

THE SM's PERSONAL FLOOR PLANS

In many professional working situations, by the time an SM is hired for a show, the set has been designed and the SM is handed a set of blueprints with the *floor plans* and *elevations*. If the SM is hired early enough, the SM may sit in on meetings where the set designer presents to the producer and director the

BLOCK CALENDAR
GENERAL SCHEDULE

John and Mary
Empress Productions
Producer: Glenn Jorden
Director: Paul Grossman

(See Daily Schedule for detailed breakdown)
June - July, 1999

Main Street Theatre, L.A.
PSM: Sara Johnston
Moreland Rehearsal Studios
Main Street Theatre, L.A.

SUNDAY	MONDAY	TUESDAY	WEDNESDAY	THURSDAY	FRIDAY	SATURDAY
June -1999	**1** 10:a-11:a -EQUITY BIZ. 11:a - 7:30p -CAST READ THRU play & begin setting Act I, Scn.1.	**2** 10:a-6:30p-CASTcont.REH. Cont. setting scns. in Act I ⋯ Costume measurements at reh. hall	**3** 10:a-12:30 p -PROD. MEET. all depts. 1:p-9:30p -CAST cont. RE Cont. setting scns. in Act I	**4** 10:a-6:30p-CAST cont.REH. 11:a - 1:p -John and Mary tape interv. at NBC for *Today Show*	**5** 10:a-6:30p-CAST cont.REH. Finish setting Act I	**6** 9:a-5:30p -CAST cont. REH. Work & run all scns. in Act II
7 Cast DAY OFF	**8** 10:a-6:30p-CAST cont.REH. Begin setting scns. in Act II ⋯ Begin costume fittings at costume shop	**9** 10:a-6:30p-CAST cont.REH. Cont. setting Act II ⋯ Cont. costume fittings	**10** 10:a-12:30 p-PROD. MEET. all depts. 1:p-9:30p-CAST cont. REH. Cont. setting Act II ⋯ Cont. costume fittings	**11** 10:a-6:30p-CAST cont.REH. Cont. setting Act II ⋯ Finish costume fittings	**12** 10:a-6:30p-CAST cont.REH. Finish setting Act II & run Act I	**13** 9:a-1:p -CAST cont. REH. Work and run all scns.Act II 2:30p-5:30p Run Acts I & II w/ photog. taking reh.shots
14 Cast DAY OFF	**15** 10:a-6:30p-CAST cont.REH. Begin clean scns., Act I & run Act I	**16** 10:a-6:30 -CAST cont.REH. Finish clean scns., Act I & run Act II	**17** 10:a-12:30 p -PROD MEET. all depts. 1:p-9:30 -Begin clean scns. in Act II & run Act I	**18** 10:a-1:p -CAST cont.REH. Finish clean scns. Act II 2:30p-6:30p -Run show & notes 8:a -CREW Load-in theat.	**19** 10:a-6:30 -CAST cont.REH. Clean & work problem areas 2:30p-6:30p -Run show for Light Dsgnr. & notes after 8:a -CREW cont . in theat.	**20** 9:a-1:p -CAST cont. REH. Run show & notes 2:p-5:30p - Run show for invited guests & notes after 7:30p-Set light. cues w/Light. Dsgnr., Dir., SMs, & Crew
21 Begin 10 hr. day out of 12 hrs. 12:30p-12:30a CAST and CREW BEGIN TECH	**22** 12:30p-12:30a CAST and CREW cont. TECH and add Act I costumes	**23** 12:30p-12:30a CAST and CREW cont. TECH All cstms. in afternoon reh. Add makeup in evening reh.	**24** 12:30p - 5:30p CAST and CREW finish TECH 5:30 p-7:p -MEAL BREAK 7:p -Half-hour call 7:30p -DRESS REH	**25** 12:P-1:30p -CAST notes 1:30-2:p -Half-Hour call 2:p -Perf. for Unified Schools. Notes after perf. 5:30p-7:p -Meal BREAK 7:p -Half-hour call 7:30p -PREVIEW PERF.	**26** 2:30p -CAST and CREW Notes & run parts of show 5:p -MEAL BREAK 7:30p -Half-hour call 8:p -OPENING Perf.	**27** 2:p -MAT. PERF. 8:p -EVE. PERF.
28 2:p -MAT. PERF. 7:30p -EVE. PERF.	**29** Theatre Dark Cast DAY OFF	**30** 8:p -EVE. PERF.	**JULY 1** 8:p -EVE. PERF.	**2** 8:p -EVE. PERF.	**3** 8:p -EVE. PERF.	**4** 2:p -MAT. PERF. 8:p -EVE. PERF.

IMPORTANT PHONE NUMBERS:
Production Office: (213) 555-6421
Office Fax Machine: (213) 555-2938
Director: (310) 555-7239
SM: (818) 555-1217

Rehearsal Hall: (818) 555-6398
Backstage phone: (213) 555-9631
Box office: (213) 555-1000

Figure 6-11   An overall view of the work to be done in the first weeks of putting together a show, starting with the first day of rehearsals and into the first week of performances. Subject to minor changes or a major rewrite.

drawings, sketches, color renderings, or even a three-dimensional scale model set. Otherwise, the SM learns about the set from the blueprints. The blueprints give the layout, measurements, and dimensions of the scenery. They also give the placement of any backdrops that might be part of the set design.

Starting with the Blueprints

Blueprints are not difficult to read. Just keep in mind that the various drawings are all viewed from the audience's point of view. In addition, the floor plan drawings of the scenery are viewed from above looking down on the stage to a flat perspective. On the other hand, the elevation drawings are drawn to give the heights of the various parts of the set and are viewed from the same audience perspective, but from eye level, head on.

SMs' Knowledge of the Set

Like the script, the SM must study the blueprints. Anything that the SM doesn't understand in the blueprints must be clarified before rehearsals begin. In the absence of the designer, everyone will turn to the SM for information about the set, and will expect the SM to know as much as the designer. To aid the SM in this effort and to make it easier for the rest of the

Daily REHEARSAL Schedule
FRIDAY, June 5, 1999
John and Mary

10:00a - 11:30 Director, in Reh.rm #1, Clean & run......

        Act I, Scn. 1.,   "Down to Brass Taxes" (p.13)

        Mary, John, George

11:30a - 1:30 Director, in Reh.rm. #1, Clean & run......

        Act I, Scn. 2.,   "Girl Talk" (p.41)

        Mary & Alice

        w/ Asst.Director in Reh.rm. #2, Work & run ......

        Act I, Scn. 1.,   "Guy Talk" (p.33)

        John & George

    1:30 LUNCH

3:00p - 4:30p Director, Reh.rm. #1, Set ....

        Act I, Scn.1.,   Alice's "Whirlwind Entrance" (p.21)

        John, Mary, Geo., Alice, Flo.

4:30 - 5:30   Director, Reh.rm. #1, Work......

        Act I, Scn. 1.,   Frieda's "Phone Call" (p.7)

        Frieda

4:30p - 6:30p Asst.Director, Reh.rm. #2, Run......

        Act I, Scn.1., Alice's "Whirlwind Entrance" (p.21)

        Act I, Scn. 1., "Guy Talk" (p.33)

        Act I, Scn. 2., "Girl Talk" (p.41)

        Act I, Scn. 3., "Woman's Lib" (p.52)

        John, Mary, Geo., Alice, Flo., Frieda

5:30p   Director, Reh.rm. #1, Work.....

        Act I, Scn.1.,   Postman's Entrance (p32)

        Act I, Scn.2.,   Superintendent (p.51)

        Act I, Scn.3.,   Delivery Man w/ assistant (p.59)

6:30p   **DISMISSED**

        Mary, John, George, Alice, Florence, Frieda

7:00p   **DISMISSED**

        Actor playing multi roles

        Postman, Superintendent, Delivery Man

7:00p   Director, Asst. Director, & SMs

        Short PROD. MEET. w/ Costume Designer

Figure 6-12 The daily rehearsal schedule, broken down into hour increments and detailing the work to be done for a particular day.

Daily REHEARSAL Schedule
FRIDAY, JUNE 5, 1999
John & Mary - The Musical

	DIRECTOR		CHOREOGRAPHY		MUSIC DIRECTOR
10:00a	Reh.rm. #1, clean & run...... Act I, Scn. 1., "Apartment" (p.1) John & Mary	10:00a	Reh.rm. #2, clean & run...... Act I "Closing" (p.59) & set...... "Grl.Talk-BoyTalk" sng.(p.32) w/ Dancers only	10:00a	Music rm., rehearse...... "Doomsday" song (p.23) w/ George
				10:30a	Music rm., rehearse...... "Girl Talk -Boy Talk" song (p.32) w/ Ensemble Singers
11:00a	Reh.rm. #1., add...... Act I, Scn.1.,"Geo.Entrance"(p.6) John, Mary, George	1100:a	Reh.rm. #2, add to...... "Grl.Talk-BoyTalk" sng.(p.32) Ensemble singers	11:00a	Music rm., rehearse...... "Girl Talk -Boy Talk" Song (p.32) w/ Frieda
	DIRECTOR & CHOREOGR.			12:noon	Music rm., rehearse...... Act II, Scn. 5., "Grl.Sct. Cookie" sng. (p.87) w/ multi-character actor
12:noon	Reh.rm. #1., work, run & clean...... "Girl Talk -Boy Talk" song (p.32), w/o John & Mary Geo., Alice, Flo., Frieda, Ensmbl. Sngrs. & Dncrs.				
12:noon	**John & Mary, luncheon & interview at Century City Plaza Hotel**				

1:00P - 2:30P   LUNCH

2:30p	Costume fitting at Western Costume...... Dexter, Mary Ann, Susan J. & Sue-Ellen			2:30p	Reh.rm. #2, work and run...... "Girl Talk -Boy Talk" Song (p.32)
2:30p	**DIRECTOR & CHOREOGR.**				Geo., Alice, Flo. Frieda, Ensmbl. Sngrs & Dncrs...... **add John, Mary, & people at costume fittings, as they arrive**
	Reh.rm. #1, set...... Act II, Scn. 5., "The Girl Scout Cookie" song (p.87) Multi-character actor				
3:30p	Reh.rm. #1., set...... Act I,Scn.3. "Woman's Lib",(p.50) Mary, Alice, Flo., Frieda	3:30p	Reh.rm. #2, clean-work-run...... "Opening" sng. & "Boy Talk- Grl.Talk" sng.w/Sngrs.& Dncrs.	3:30p	Music rm., rehearse...... Act II, Scn. 2, "Pleasure Fare", (p.72) w/ John
3:30p	George DISMISSED, doctor's appointment				**** When finished DISMISS**

BY 6:30P - REST OF CAST DISMISSED OR EARLIER, WHEN FINISHED

7:00p	**STAFF MEETING w/Producer** Conference rm., third floor Director, Choreographer, Music Director, SMs, Prod. Sec., Prod. Assists.

Figure 6-13   The daily rehearsal schedule for a musical show, listing the work to be done by the director, choreographer, and music director.

company to picture the set, the SM gathers and puts up on the rehearsal room walls whatever artist renderings the designer has made, the blueprint drawings, and arranges to have a scale model (if there is one) at the rehearsal hall at least for the first week of rehearsals.

From Blueprints to the Personal Floor Plans

The floor plan and layout of the set on the blueprint drawings are drawn to scale—usually one inch or a half-inch for every foot of real space on the stage. Even with this reduction in size, the pages of the blueprint drawings are large. Traditionally, they come rolled up and do not fit in the SM's files, briefcases, or notebooks unless they are folded several times. SMs have found that reducing the blueprint floor plans down to personal size, ¼-inch or ⅜-inch scale, and

putting them on 8½-by-11-inch letter-size paper is a tremendous convenience. They can be placed in the rehearsal script at the beginning of each scene. The placement of actors at the beginning of the scene can be noted, props listed, the placement of furniture drawn in, and when called on to set up a particular scene in rehearsals, the SM can refer to the personal floor plan without having to roll out the original blueprint drawings or go to the wall on which they are hanging. In addition, they are a helpful piece of hard copy for people in other departments.

Computer-Generated Floor Plans

Most designers and draftsmen working in professional theatre today create the blueprint drawings by computer. However, SMs, in creating their personal floor plans, lag somewhat behind. The programs are costly and complicated to work with.

Sidebar: This book was written entirely on computer along with the generation of all the hard copy forms you see. However, at the time of publication, I had not yet acquired a program to do the personal floor plans. On my last major production, the technical director had such a program on his laptop. He generously supplied me with whatever personal-size copies of floor plans I needed, thus delaying my need to purchase a program for myself. The personal floor plans entered in this chapter were drawn by the SMs freehand.

The SM's Personal Floor Plans for *Annie Get Your Gun*

In the musical *Annie Get Your Gun* there can be several different setups of scenery within the first scene of Act I, depending on the design of the set and the choices of the director. In the production represented in Figures 6-14 and 6-15, the designer started with a basic set:

- The Boarding House Drop (a painting of distant hills and sky)
- The Tree Cutout Drop (cutouts of tree trunks, spaced out across the stage)
- A Leaf-Teaser (a lacy arrangement of leaves and branches hung high across the top of the stage and placed just down stage of the tree trunks to give the illusion of full vegetation of the trees)

The show begins with this setup. Then, as the performers bring on props and furniture and set units are flown in or wheeled on, the audience is transported from one place to the other: for example, from a meadow (Figure 6-14) to the front lawn of Mr. Wilson's hotel (Figure 6-15).

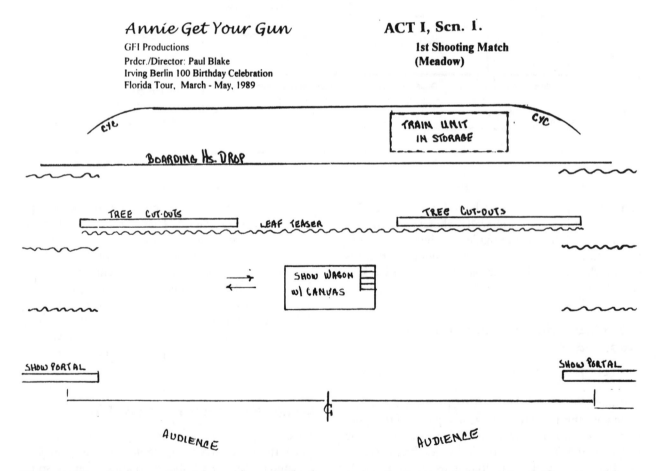

Figure 6-14 Stage manager's personal floor plan for the musical *Annie Get Your Gun,* depicting the first setup of the show (the meadow scene), with the scenery/drops in place and the show wagon at center stage.

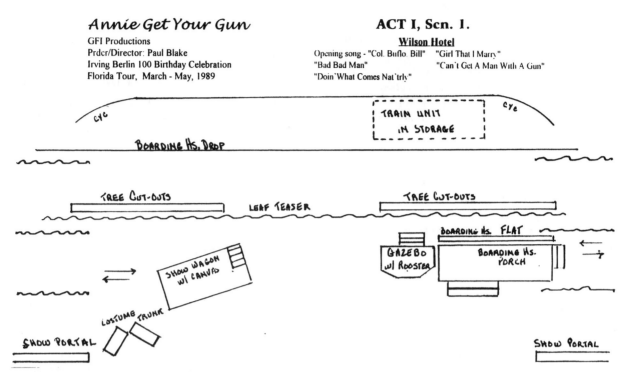

Annie Get Your Gun
GFI Productions
Prdcr/Director: Paul Blake
Irving Berlin 100 Birthday Celebration
Florida Tour, March - May, 1989

ACT I, Scn. 1.
Wilson Hotel
Opening song - "Col. Buflo. Bill"   "Girl That I Marry"
"Bad Bad Man"   "Can't Get A Man With A Gun"
"Doin' What Comes Nat'rly"

Figure 6-15   Stage manager's personal floor plan for the Wilson Hotel scene in the musical *Annie Get Your Gun*. The floor plan depicting the new placement of the show wagon with the added set pieces for the gazebo, boarding house porch, and the costume trunk.

Note: Direct your attention to the heading. Each page in the SM's personal floor plans is clearly headed to the left of the page with the show's name and information concerning the particular production. To the right is the more immediate information pertaining to the scene represented on that particular drawing.

Some SMs prefer noting the act and scene numbers as I-1, I-2, II-1, II-2, and so on, and circling the figures. This is standard notation on blueprint drawings. However, the SM's personal floor plans are also used by people who are not familiar with reading blueprint drawings, such as actors and some directors. In addition, the act and scene number is the first bit of information a person needs when viewing the page of the SM's personal floor plans. This information needs to be bold and stand out. Writing out the words creates a definitive and visible heading that gives the reader the information at a glance, without them having to know that I-1 means Act I, Scene 1.

The drawing of the floor plan for this production includes some basic parts (the stage) that will remain the same in every drawing:

- The audience
- The downstage edge of the stage (which in this case is also the proscenium line)
- The show portals (just behind the ends of the proscenium on each side of the stage)
- The soft wings on each side of the stage (represented by short wavy lines)
- The cyc (the cyclorama that is permanently placed at the back of the stage)

When the boarding house drop is added along with the tree cutouts and the leaf teaser, the Meadow Scene is complete. The performers roll on the show wagon. The arrows drawn next to the wagon indicate the direction in which the wagon travels on stage and then off. Notice that the train unit is just in front of the cyc, but hidden from the audience's view by the Boarding House Drop. It is in storage and is standing by to be rolled in place for Scene 2.

The SM's personal floor plans are void of all measurements and figures. At times the SM will include the figures of some important measurements such as steps, risers, or platforms. If the SM needs to have more than just a few numbers noted on the personal floor plans and does not want to go to the blueprint drawings each time, it is easiest to create another page of the same drawing, and on this drawing note all the technical information needed.

The SM does not note the scale used to create the personal drawings. The SM's personal floor plans are not meant to have the accuracy and precision of blueprint drawings, although with computer-generated personal floor plans, the scale is quite accurate to the page. However, in making copies from a copying machine, that accuracy is sometimes lost. It is best for the SM not to note the scale and if anyone wants to know that information, the SM either gives them the information or directs them to the blueprint drawings.

Let us now view a busier, more complicated floor plan drawing (see Figure 6-15). We are still in Act I, Scene 1 from *Annie Get Your Gun*, but the scenery has changed, more props have been brought on stage, and we are now standing on the front lawn of the Wilson Hotel.

Direct your attention to the changed information just below the heading, Act I, Scene 1. Note that the location is changed and now reads "Wilson Hotel." Below this information is a list of songs or events that take place within this setting. This is extremely helpful information for all who use these personal floor plans.

The SM has meticulously noted the placement of every piece on stage. With this kind of information these floor plans will be useful not only to the SMs, actors, and director, but to the crew in setting props or changing the scenery.

- The wagon unit has been moved to stage right center.
- The gazebo is just off left center, and a stair unit at the back has been added. Also, the rooster on top of the gazebo is noted because this is an important prop to the scene. It must be mechanically rigged for each performance so when Annie takes a pop shot at it to prove her marksmanship, the rooster's head pops off.
- The boarding house porch unit with stairs was rolled in from stage left.
- The boarding house flat that depicts the front of the Wilson house has been flown in and sits just behind the porch unit to give a three-dimensional illusion of the Wilson Hotel and Boarding House.

- The costume trunk at the extreme right side of the stage is either rolled on or carried on by actors.

Judging from the list of songs noted at the top of this page, this particular setup of scenery will remain on stage for a good amount of time. Also, there will be times when the Buffalo Bill troop and the Wilson family and townspeople will be on stage at the same time. During those moments the SM can note on additional copies of this floor plan the blocking and placement of the actors. This is valuable information that the SM will use later during the run of the show.

The *Hello Jerry* Personal Floor Plans

Here is the SM's personal floor plan for the tribute to Jerry Herman and his music, *Hello Jerry* (Figure 6-16). Before we discuss this floor plan, look over the drawing and see what information you can extract for yourself. See if you can get a picture in your mind about the show, the design of the scenery, and what is taking place in this particular stage setting.

From the information in the heading:

- We are first introduced to the production staff. People in entertainment continually read the credits to see if they recognize any of the names. The name Jeff Calhoun might be recognizable—director of the most recent production of *Grease*, which continues its long run on Broadway. The SM's name may also ring a bell—author of this book.
- From the title of the show and the notation below the title, we know this is a tribute to Jerry Herman and his music.
- From the information to the right, we learn the date of the presentation, that it is performed at the Century Plaza Hotel in Century City, Los Angeles, the name of the song/show is "Hello Dolly," and the setting is the Harmonia Gardens.

From the body of the floor plan we learn:

- The primary feature of the set is a turntable with three-tier risers placed on each side of the table to seat the musicians. We see the turntable is divided in half with the Jerry Herman side and the Hello Dolly side (which is presently showing to the audience). From the lines and

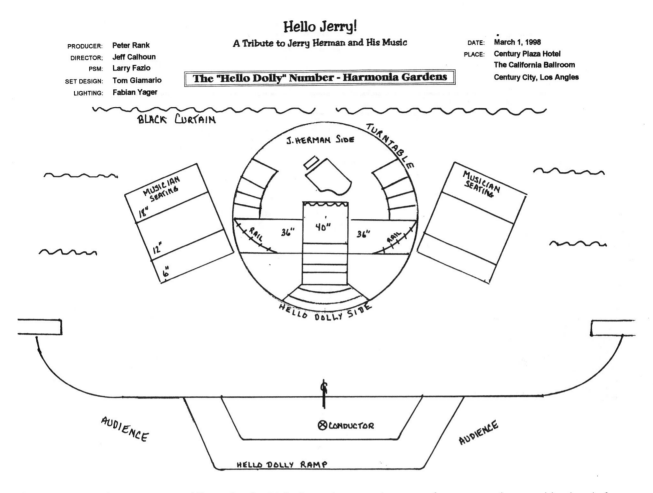

Figure 6-16   The SM's personal floor plan for *Hello Jerry*, depicting the setup of scenery on the turntable, the platforms on which the musicians sit, and the *Hello Dolly* ramp projecting out into the audience.

configurations drawn within the circle of the turntable, we get some idea of the set design: stairs go up to a 40-inch high platform at the center, but there are 36-inch high platforms on each side, which means there is a step down to those areas. On the back side of the turntable there are more stairs leading down to a piano placed center.

• Turning our attention to the musicians' platforms we see that the height or rise of the different tiers is in 6-inch increments.

• The rest of the stage is simply set with a black curtain across the back and black curtain legs to create entrances and exits for the performers.

• A last feature that stands out in this drawing is the Hello Dolly ramp, a signature feature of the Harmonia Gardens set and in the presentation

of the "Hello Dolly" song. Note the conductor is placed at the foot of the stage surrounded by the ramp, while the musicians play seated on the platforms on stage.

You can almost see the legendary Carol Channing descending the stairs, gliding across the stage, and strutting over the ramp (and she did on the night of the performance of this show).

Personal Floor Plans for the One-Set Comedy, *John and Mary*

In this last example (Figure 6-17) we see the personal floor plan the SM might draw from the blueprints of the set that might have been designed for our imaginary play, *John and Mary.*

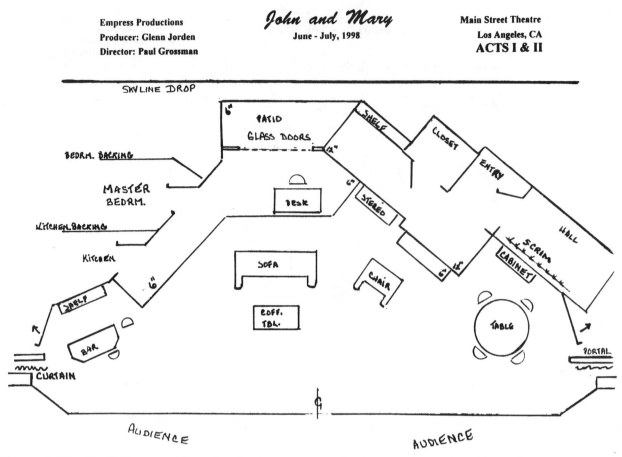

Empress Productions
Producer: Glenn Jorden
Director: Paul Grossman

John and Mary
June - July, 1998

Main Street Theatre
Los Angeles, CA
ACTS I & II

Figure 6-17   The SM's personal floor plans for the one-set comedy of our imaginary play, *John and Mary*.

This includes a three-level set:

1. The stage floor level with the placement of the primary furniture.
2. The 6-inch rise level that leads to the kitchen, master bedroom, patio, and to the desk and chair placed at center.
3. The 12-inch rise which is primarily the entry, the hallway with a scrim through which the characters can be seen as they enter, a closet, shelf, and acting area that the director can use for visual variety in blocking the show. Note the two steps leading back down to the stage level.

Note also the skyline drop, backing the entire set.

This is a simple *one-set*, *box-set* design; however, it looks busy and complicated from all the lines of detail drawn in. For measurements and more specific technical information about the set, the SM will use the blueprint drawings and will meet with the designer to see sketches, drawings, or possibly a scale model.

Tip: I have found the SM's personal floor plans to be a popular item. When I first started, they were strictly for the SM's use, but eventually various members of the production staff asked for a set of their own. Choreographers and directors liked having them to aid them in making blocking notes and to create stage pictures with the placement of actors. Lighting designers liked using them to rough out light cues. Head carpenters made copies and distributed them to their workers to use for the scene changes. Similarly, prop people found them a great help in prop placement. For each show on which I work, making the SM's personal floor plans is required work. They are as necessary as having a script, a producer, a director, a cast of actors, technicians, an SM, and an audience.

LISTS

A good SM is a good list maker and cannot work without making lists. Making lists and having them at hand for quick and easy reference relieves the SM from having to remember. No SM can be expected to remember everything about the production. Blessed are those who can. It is the SM's job to commit information to paper for others to use and perhaps look back on at a later time. Making lists frees the SM's mind and preserves energy to work on matters at hand.

The Schedule Reminder List

This list is strictly for the SM's use. The SM simply creates on a computer the heading *Schedule Reminder List* and prints it out, leaving the rest of the page blank. This is then placed in the production notebook at the beginning of the tabbed section "Schedule." On it the SM notes anything that affects the schedule, be it something for the next day, next week, or next month, then refers to this list each time a schedule must be created.

People in the company will give the SM information for the schedule in advance, sometimes to relieve themselves of having to remember, other times to assure they are included or excluded from the schedule, depending on their needs. The SM is highly responsible for seeing that all of this information is entered into the schedule at the prescribed times. This information should never be committed to memory. Failure in this area is of grave concern to the people involved and to the organization and coordination of running the company, and may result in loss of time and money.

Industry Phone Numbers List

This list also is mainly for the SM's use. It is started on the first day of an SM's first professional show and is kept in the production notebook as the SM moves from show to show. This list is a collection of phone numbers and addresses of people who were involved with the production in some way, but not enough to be placed on the staff or cast list. Primarily, these are people who may have provided a service, a specialty, or product: shops, vendors, supply houses, rental places, magic, music, vocal coaching, dialects, script typing, publishing, publicity, videos, recording studios, still photography, props, food, hair supply, printer, fabric, shoes, repairs, and so on.

This list can be organized in categories and in alphabetical order, or it can be a series of handwritten notes and taped-in business cards, entered on the list as they were received. The information collected on this list can be a treasure and a life-saver to both the SM and the show when a problem or need arises.

The Correct Spelling of Names List

It is important to all people that their names are spelled correctly in print and pronounced correctly when spoken. With people in the entertainment business, fame is the name of the game and the correct spelling of that name is very important. People in entertainment spend a great amount of time and effort to get their names known both to the people in the industry and to the public at large.

Although no one has ever lost work or fame because their name was misspelled in the program, most actors' reaction to a misspelled name might lead you to believe that their career was in jeopardy. In fact, having a performer's name spelled correctly in the program is important enough to the actors that Equity found it necessary to create a rule with management that if and when misspelling happens, management must correct the problem by reprinting the program or placing an insert sheet in each program giving the correct spelling.

Part of doing the SM job well, and saving the producer from the embarrassment and expense of printing program corrections, includes creating the *Correct Spelling of Names* list. This too is an easy list to create. The basic form is already in the computer in the design of the sign-in sheet. All the SM needs to do is change the heading to "Correct Spelling of Names." The cast members' names are listed in the left-hand column. Then change the many columns on the right side of the page to two large columns. If the actor's name on this list is misspelled or is incorrect in any way, the first large column is for the actor to print in clear letters the correct spelling of his or her name. The second large column is for the actor to initial. If everything about the actor's name in the left column was correct from the start, the actor still initials the second large column to show that the list has been checked and the information is correct.

This list should be circulated throughout the cast on the first day of rehearsals. For thoroughness and greater efficiency, the SM may also want to include on the correct spelling of names list the names of the director, choreographer, musical director, rehearsal pianist, SMs, and assistants of these individuals. The production office will be responsible for getting the correct spelling of the designers, technical head, their assistants, and crewmembers. Copies of the correct spelling list should be given to the producer, to the department creating the program, put into the SM's files, and placed in the production notebook at the beginning of the tabbed section "Cast." In addition, the SM should go through the files and correct all names that may have been misspelled on other hard copy. Whenever possible, the information gathered on the correct spelling of names list should be distributed to the proper places within the first week of rehearsals and well in advance of the first draft of the program or playbill.

The Prop List

Of all the technical departments within the production of a show, the SM is most involved with the internal work of the prop department. While the other technical departments create their own charts, plots, plans, and lists, it is the SM's job to begin during rehearsals and keep up-to-date the prop list. In actuality, the ASM usually is assigned this job and responsibility, while the PSM sees that the job is done accurately, making contributions to the list as information is received.

The prop list starts with the ASM's second reading of the play. In that reading, the ASM hand-writes on separate sheets of paper for each scene, the props that are directly or indirectly indicated in the script. Each day in rehearsals the SMs add to or subtract from the prop sheets as the director and actors work on each scene and make their choices. With each prop noted, the SMs also note the character who uses the prop, how it is used, where the prop starts in the show, and any special needs or descriptions which the actors or director may request.

In many productions, the union prop person will not join the rehearsals on a regular basis until the last week of rehearsals. By that time the ASM must have created and organized a detailed prop list from which both the ASM and the prop department can work. The information on this list must be laid out so the props can be set in the same place and in the same way for each rehearsal and subsequently for each performance. There is no particular form to follow in making a prop list, although prop lists from different SMs look similar. On new shows, shows heading to Broadway, heavy prop shows, or shows with big budgets, the prop person may be hired to gather rehearsal props before rehearsals start. Once rehearsals begin, the prop person or assistant may be required to be at the rehearsals to set up props for each scene. The SMs continue to work closely with the prop department, providing information and seeing that an organized and up-to-date prop list is created and maintained, either by the prop department or by the SMs.

A Working Prop List

About ten minutes before each performance, after the props have been set by the prop department, it is the SM's job to double-check, seeing that all props are in place. For this, both the prop department and the SM need a *working* prop list (see Figure 6-18). This is what an SM works toward creating. A working prop list contains some very specific notes detailing the placement of the props, along with instructions necessary to ensure that the prop is set exactly as it should be.

The more academic prop list for the archives or for publication at the back of the play book leaves out such details and instructions. In this list, the props are listed by the scenes in which they appear, and if any instructions or details are included, they are intended more for amateur productions. The director and actors of the next professional production will create their own placement and set of instructions.

The props listed in Figure 6-18 are noted according to their placement on stage. This arrangement allows the prop department to set the props in an organized fashion with as little error as possible. It also allows the SM to check the list with the same proficiency and accuracy.

Note: Set dressing—items the actors do not use or handle, which are present to decorate the stage—are not listed on the prop list. Once set dressing items are set, they remain in place. If they are accidentally moved or not present during the performance, it will have no effect on the actors or the play in general. Only the artistic integrity of the set designer is interrupted, which the SM corrects as soon as possible.

Note: Items marked as personal are things the actors are responsible for either placing on stage themselves or keeping with them in their dressing rooms and tak-

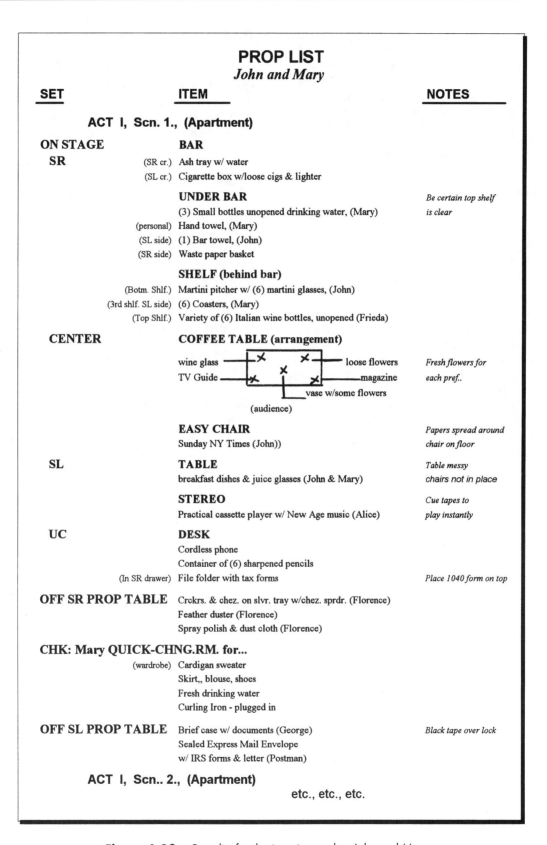

Figure 6-18   Prop list for the imaginary play *John and Mary*.

ing on stage when needed. If an actor forgets a personal prop in a performance, the actor has no recourse to the SMs or prop department. In the same vein, items noted as wardrobe items on the prop list are the responsibility of the wardrobe department. Although personal props and items marked wardrobe are not the SMs responsibility, the wise and efficient SM adds them to the prop list anyway and checks to see that these props too are in place.

Sound Lists

On a large and big-budget show, the sound department may consist of three separate parts: the equipment/rental company, the recording studio, and the person hired to set up the sound at the theatre(s) and run the cues during the performances. On smaller shows, one person or sound company may provide all three services. In most working situations, the SM works primarily with the person running the sound during the performances. This person usually is responsible for creating and having recorded the sound effects (SFX) tape or CD. On occasion and to varying degrees, the SM may be asked to oversee and participate in getting some of this work done.

Whatever the working situation, throughout the rehearsals, and especially during the first days, the SM and sound person are in close communication, creating an SFX list. As the rehearsals continue, this list may change radically or remain as it was originally written, depending on the director, actors, and designers as they work in putting together the show. It is the SM's job to keep the sound person informed on a daily basis so the changes can be implemented and the SFX tape or CD can be made and be ready for the first day of technical rehearsals, if not for the last week of rehearsals in the rehearsal hall.

The Sound Effects and Recording List

Within each production there are several lists for sound that the SM may be required to produce. The first and most common is laid out in Figure 6-19, an example from the play *It Had To Be You,* a comedy in two acts, with two characters—Theda and Vito. This list is designed to guide the sound person/sound recorder through the show, scene by scene, assuring that each SFX and piece of music gets recorded on tape or CD. In addition, the SM includes on this list information that guides the person in making the recordings, to ensure the director gets the *timing* and *type* of effect or music wanted.

The Sound Requirements List

The SM is not responsible for providing to the sound department lists containing the technical equipment that will be used in the sound design for the show. That list is created by the sound designer and agreed on by the producer and director. There are, however, times when the SM needs to make a sound requirements list of another kind. As for example, when the play *It Had To Be You* became a touring show, the producer chose not to travel a sound department with the show. Instead, the producer made arrangements with each theatre at which the show performed, to use their sound person and system. The SFX tape/CD was already made as laid out in Figure 6-19 and traveled with the show. The sound SFX and recording list made up to create the tape/CD was not a workable document for the sound people at the different performance sites. They needed information so they could assemble the equipment and have it set up and ready to use when the show arrived at their theatre. The SM had to create the list shown in Figure 6-20 for this purpose.

The Sound Cues List

With each show that travels, there is seldom adequate time at each new performance site for the sound person to learn the sound cues for the first performances. When the show *It Had To Be You* became a touring show, the SM created the sound cue list in Figure 6-21 to aid the sound person at each new site until they became familiar with the show and cues. The stage manager was responsible for calling all sound cues for every performance, but this list aided the sound technician during the technical rehearsals and first performances.

Many academic studies and some of the SM handbooks published say the SM must prepare this list for each show and hand it over to the sound person. In most professional situations where the sound person is hired to be with the show from the start of rehearsals, a list with cues or a cue sheet is not necessary and becomes extra work for the SM. The sound person has been working with the SM from the start of rehearsals, has been given the sound SFX and recording list, the tape or CD has been made, and just before technical rehearsals begin, the sound person and the SM get together, each noting the cues in their scripts. In most professional situations the sound person needs nothing more. A sound cue list such as the one shown in Figure 6-21 is good for the archives.

It Had To Be You

SOUND   So. West & West Coast Tour-1996
SFX and Recording   GFI Productions
Reel to Reel & CD   Producer & Director: Paul Blake

ACT I   Scn. 1 (Limbo - on apron, front of house curtain)

| 1. | p.7 | Played during opening monologue
On SM's cues | Record w/pianist, (3) versions of "Had 2 B U" theme
- FULL version (16 bars)
- CUT-OFF version (8 bars)
- MULTIPLE version
  a. Fast tempo (4 bars)
  b. Jazzy (4 bars)
  c. Sweet (4 bars) |
| 2. | p.7 | End of opening monologue | TAG Music
(See director, he has music on CD) |

Scn. 1a (TV audition studio)

| 3. | p.12 | Theda meets Vito | "Had 2 B U" piano theme
FULL version (16 bars), same as above |
| 4. | p.14 | Transition music from TV studio
into Theda's apartment | "Had 2 B U" piano theme (4 bars), blending into....
Busy N.Y.C. Street (traffic, horns, etc.) dissolve into....
"Deck The Halls w/Holly" (See SM, has on vinyl album) |

Scn. 2 (Theda's apartment)

| 5. | p.36 | Theda's Russian dance | RUSSIAN DANCE MUSIC (20-30 seconds)
(Bring choice to director for approval) |
| 6. | p.36 | End of scene music.
Same as Russian dance music or
different music to take us out of Act I
and into intermission | RUSSIAN MUSIC
Complete song (2-3 minutes)
(Bring choice to director for approval) |

ACT II   Scn. 1 (Theda's apartment)

7.	p.37	Music to open Act II and continue as underscoring for Theda's "Mother Russia" speech	LYRICAL RUSSIAN MUSIC (2-3 minutes, to fade-out on SM's cue) (Bring choice to director for approval)
8.	p.45	Dogs barking down the hall (To fade out on SM's cue)	DOGS BARKING Series - first one dog barking (3 or 4 times) - add one or two more dogs barking - add more dogs barking Entire segment, 45 sec.
9.	p.50	Radio SFX and Christmas song	SFX of RADIO STATIC and STATION CHANGING blending into Johnny Mathis, "Have Yourself a Merry Little Christmas" (90 sec.) (To be cut off on SM's cue)
10.	p.55	Phone ring	SFX PHONE RING (6 rings)
11.	p.56	Car horn	SFX CAR HORN BLASTS Annoying, impatient, (3 blasts)
12.	p.59	Ending kiss	"Had 2 B U" theme (cut off at 3-1/2 bars) **Leave 13 SEC. LEADER SPACE for live dialogue...** Follow with "Looney Tunes" TAG
13.	p.59	Curtain Bow Music	Benny Goodman version of "Had 2 B U" (full cut from CD)

Figure 6-19   A sound effects (SFX) and recording list for the play, *It Had to Be You*. This list is submitted to the person who will be recording the sound and in many cases will also be running the sound for each performance.

SOUND   **It Had To Be You**   So. West &
REQUIREMENTS   West Coast Tour
LIST   1997

GFI Production

Producer/Director: Paul Blake (213) 555-1212   PSM: Sarah Johnston (818) 555 -4321

(2) BODY MICS Mics & (1) SPARE - There are only two actors in the show

REEL to REEL TAPE PLAYER or CD PLAYER - For playback of sound cues. We have cues recorded on both mediums.

"Hot" MIC at SM's Consol.. w/ "ON" and "OFF" SWITCH (To be controlled by SM). As part of the play, the SM does dialogue with the actress on stage.

SPEAKERS -The house speakers you use in your theatre. In addition:

    -ON STAGE SPEAKERS

        (1) speaker off stage left for dog barking cue.

        (1) speaker up stage right, behind set.

        (1) small speaker placed on set, stage right, for radio SFX and music cue.

    All speakers must work separate of each other, but must also be able to work in combination. In addition, sound played through house speakers must have ability to cross fade or dissolve into speakers on stage.

PHONE RINGS through PHONE ON STAGE - There will be two phones on stage. The one placed on the desk at stage right will be the phone which rings. (See set floor plan included with this packet of information.)

STAGE MANAGER'S COMMUNICATION from CONSOLE. - SM must have two-way communication with all technical departments and/or people executing cues.

IN ADDITION: -SM's headset, LEFT ear cup ONLY

            -Show monitor speaker w/volume control at SM's console

COMMUNICATION SETUP in AUDIENCE for director or SM during technical rehearsals: - Hot mic to communicate with actors on stage

                - Headset to communicate with all technical departments

                - Desk light

THANKS -- If you have any questions please call director or SM listed above.

Figure 6-20   Sound requirements list, detailing the sound needs for the play *It Had To Be You* as it travels to each new theatre/performance site.

It Had To Be You

SOUND CUES
LIST

So. West & West Coast
Tour - 1991

GFI Productions

Producer /Director: Paul Blake, (213) 555 -1212   PSM: Sarah Johnston, (818) 555-4321

All CUES listed below are called by Stage Manager. Sound man responsible for
z   *controlling "on", "off", and "gain" for actor's mics and mics on stage.*

			NOTES
	ACT I,	**Scn. 1 (Limbo), Opening Monologue**	
p.7	SQ 1	(3) Versions of PIANO THEME, "It Had 2 B U"	*(Continuous Play) !! NO STOPS !!*
p.7	SQ 2	TAG MUSIC at the end of monologue	*Short (15. sec.)*
		Scn. 1a (TV Audition Studio), Theda meets Vito	
p.12	SQ 3	"It Had To B U" piano theme	*Full version, (16 bars)*
		Scn. 2 (Transition into Theda's Apartment)	
p.14	SQ 4	(4 bars) of piano theme, "It Had To B U", blending into...	*Continuous play of cue, but on SM's*
		NYC traffic SFX, dissolving into...	*cue, sound from house speakers*
		"Deck The Halls w/Holly"	*X-fade to on stage speakers*
p.36	SQ 5	RUSSIAN DANCE (22 sec.)	***Next cue !! VERY QUICK !!***
p.36	SQ 5a	TAG and FULL VERSION of Russian Dance Music going into intermission	*Play to end of music (3min., 11sec.)*

INTERMISSION (15-20 min.)

	ACT II,	**Scn. 1 (Theda's Apartment)**	
p.37	SQ 6	"MOTHER RUSSIA" MUSIC	*FADE-OUT on SM's cue.*
p.45	SQ 7	DOGS BARKING series	*Continuous play* *FADE-OUT on SM's cue.*
p.50	SQ 8	RADIO SFX	
		Radio static, station changing, into Johnny Mathis, "Have Yourself A Merry Little Christmas"	*CUT-SOUND, on SM's Cue*
p.56	SQ 9	CAR HORN SFX	*(6 sec.)*
p.59	SQ 10	Ending kiss...	
		PIANO THEME "It Had To B U" (cut off at 3 1/2 bars)	*CONTINUOUS PLAY*
		leader space for live dialogue....	***!! NEXT CUE QUICK !!***
		into LOONEY TUNES tag	
p.59	SQ 11	CURTAIN BOW MUSIC, Benny Goodman version of "It Had 2 B U"	*Play to end of cut (3min., 25 sec.). This music is used also as audience exits.*

Figure 6-21   The sound cue list for *It Had To Be You*, which was sent or given to the person who would be running the sound during performance, as the show traveled to each new theatre/performance site.

Some SMs may make up one after the show is in its run, and when the show closes, the SM includes it in the production book that is turned in to the production company.

Body Mic Tracking Chart

If three or more actors in a show use body mics, the sound person may ask the SM for a mic tracking plot—that is, a chart listing each scene in which the actors appear wearing body mics. Fortunately, the SM has already noted this information in the form of the Sc./Chtr.Track.Chrt and needs only to pull out a copy of this chart, give it to the sound person, and let the sound person make any necessary notes.

Dressing Room Assignments List

This list must be published and posted on the callboard by the first day the cast comes to the theatre. This can be simply a list with the actors' names and the dressing rooms to which they are assigned, or it can be a simple schematic drawing of the layout of the dressing rooms on each floor, with the actors' names written within the space on the drawing that makes up the dressing room.

A great amount of thought, consideration, and conferencing with the producer, wardrobe department, and director needs to happen before the information on this list is revealed to the cast. The SM goes first to the producer to see if there are any contractual agreements concerning dressing rooms that must be fulfilled. With the producer's input, the SM creates a hand-written draft of the assignments. The SM then takes this list of assignments to the head of wardrobe to see if there will be any logistical problems between the dressing rooms assigned and the costumes the performers will be wearing. Resolving any problems in this area, the SM revises the list. The SM then goes to the director. This meeting is usually a formality. The list is pretty well established, but the SM looks for any point that might have been overlooked and to get the director's approval. If there is a conflict of ideas between any of the departments, the SM works it out and gets everyone to agree before going to the laptop to publish and post the assignments.

Egos sometimes become involved in dressing room assignments. Some performers may feel they should get a preferred dressing room over other performers. It is important to the SM that the dressing room assignments are made with good reasoning, practical forethought, and have the support of the SM's superiors. In some cases the SM will need this information to sooth an angry performer and create a win-win situation.

Show Rundown or Running Order

During technical rehearsals, no later than a day or two before the dress rehearsals begin, it is very helpful to everyone working backstage if the SM puts up throughout the entire backstage area show rundown lists or running orders. They are strategically placed where the cast and crew can easily read them: in the hallways, on staircases, in dressing rooms, rest rooms, on the back of permanent set pieces and curtains, and in the immediate work areas where the crew members are set up to work the show. The show rundown list notes the running order of the acts and scenes. It is printed from the SM's laptop in large, bold letters that can be read in the partial darkness of the backstage during a performance, and can be read from two or three feet away.

By dress rehearsal time the crew's workstations have become defined. The scenery and props have been placed where they work best for the performance. The wardrobe/costume dressers have found their little niches for quick changes. The show rundown or running order is an aid to the cast and crewmembers who may want to judge their time or who might have a momentary lapse of memory.

The show rundown or running order is an easy list to create. Once again, the SM returns to the Sc./Chtr.Track.Chrt. to get the information. However, in creating the show rundown list, the information is simplified and does not list every French scene as noted in the Sc./Chtr.Track.Chrt. List only the important or most identifiable moments, which when read by the crew or cast members, reminds them of the scene and order of the show. Figure 6-22 shows an example of a show rundown list from our imaginary play, *John and Mary*.

For most shows, especially musicals, the SM must print out the show rundown on two pages. Before going to a third page, the SM should make every effort to keep the information confined to two pages (by using legal-size paper, etc.), but not at the expense of clarity or ease of reading. Remember, this list is often read under adverse conditions. People need to extract information from this list at a glance or they may miss a cue or be late for an entrance.

SHOW RUNDOWN

John and Mary

Act I, Scn. 1

- John & Mary's Apartment
- Geo. Entr. / Talks Business
- Frieda Phone Call
- Alice Entr. / Shopping Spree
- Postman Entr. / Letter from IRS

Scn.2

- Guy Talk
- Girl Talk
- Girls against the Guys
- Superintendent w/the lease

Scn. 3

-etc., etc.

Figure 6-22 The show rundown list for our imaginary play, *John and Mary*. This list is strategically placed throughout the backstage areas to remind the actors and technicians of the order of the show, should they have a lapse of memory at any time during the performance.

An excellent example of how an SM must sometimes be inventive and creative to service the cast and crew is seen in the show rundown list or running order from the musical *Man of La Mancha* (Figure 6-23). As originally produced on Broadway, the set consists of a raked platform stage and a drawbridge that is lowered and raised many times throughout the play. There are no major changes of scenery to help the cast and crew easily identify where they are in the show. There is no intermission and designated Act Two, and the scenes are not numbered. The show just flows from one moment to the next. During performance, in a moment of distraction, cast and crewmembers backstage can become momentarily disoriented, sometimes at a crucial moment in the show. Posting running orders everywhere becomes very important.

Performance Running-Time Chart

This chart is created purely for the SM's use and efficiency in documenting the running time of the show and having it available upon request. There are any number of reasons and occasions when someone needs to know the timing of the whole show, portions of the show, or just a particular scene. The only person to turn to is the SM. During rehearsals when the director runs a scene or the entire show nonstop, the SM is expected to get the running time. The SM does not have to do a timing each time the director runs something, but should have two or more timings to refer to and make comparisons. For each performance of the show, the SM is required to note the starting and ending times of each act, and the amount

RUNNING ORDER
Man of La Mancha

1. 1st VAULT SCN.	- Cervante's Play "Man Of La Mancha"
2. ROAD TO LA MANCHA	Fight Windmill Sc.
3. 2nd VAULT & The INN SCN.	"It's All The Same" "Dulcinea"
4. 3rd VAULT & CONFESSIONAL & ALONSO HOME	Create Alonso Family Sc. Qrtet: "I'm Only Thinking Of Him"
5. 4th VAULT & INN KITCHEN	Letter Reading Sc. "I Really Like Him"
6. The INN STABLE	"What Do You Want Of Me"
7. 5th VAULT & COURTYARD SCNS.	"Little Bird" "I'm Only Thinking Of Him" "Barber Song" & "Golden Helmet" "To Each Is Dulcinea" My-Lady Sc. &"Impossible Dream" - Farce Fight Sc. - Dubbing Sc.
8. RAPE SCN.	etc., etc.

Figure 6-23   An example of the running order an SM might create for the musical *Man of La Mancha*. The play is continuous and not divided into scene numbers. The SM had to create a list of dividing points and identifying marks.

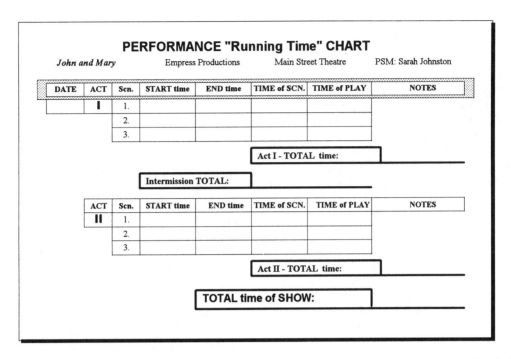

Figure 6-24   The performance running-time chart an SM might create and use to note and document detailed timing for the show in general or for a particular performance.

of time taken for intermission. From time to time throughout the run, the SM may be more detailed and get the running time for each scene. The chart in Figure 6-24 is designed to allow the SM to note detailed timings, or just fill in the starting and ending times of the acts and intermission.

Unless specifically requested for some special reason, the SM seldom, if ever, needs to have on record the timing of each French scene. Timing French scenes requires the SM's attention and concentration and often, especially when doing a musical, the SM is too busy calling cues to pay such close attention. If the SM must time French scenes, it is best done by the SM who is not calling the show for that performance.

Show Reports

There is one more piece of hard copy an SM might be required to create. When a show gets to dress rehearsals and in performances, some producers require that the SM fill out and submit a show report for each and every performance. Some production companies will provide the SM with a form they have already created.

Primarily, the producer wants noted on the show report the starting and ending times of the acts and intermission. If timings run short or long, the producer wants an explanation. The producer also wants the SM's commentary on the actor's performance, the audience's reaction, and an estimated percent of the size of the audience; in essence, anything that happens which is out of the ordinary and not part of the show or the normal routine in running and performing the show.

When the creation of the show report is left to the SM, the SM is free to be either simple or detailed in laying out the form. This report is also a good opportunity for the SM to make some positive and complimentary comments about the show, cast, crew, or anyone working backstage.

CHANGES AND REVISIONS

Change and revision is the only certainty in an SM's life. Some hard copy will go through many changes and revisions, sometimes in form, but most assuredly in noting information, especially if the show is being produced for the first time. With each revision, the SM must distribute the change to all the people it may affect. To eliminate confusion and assure everyone is working from the same paperwork and from the correct and updated information, the SM must document this revised paperwork in some way. Some SMs choose to numerically number their revisions (Revision #1, etc.) and some choose to use different colored paper for each revision. The best form of documentation in any working situation is to simply place at the top of the page, in the left-hand corner, in bold print: **REVISED (6-28-99) sj.** The numbers in parenthesis are the date of the revision. Placing the date not only gives the chronological order of the revision, but provides further information by giving a timeline. The lowercase letters following the date are the SM's initials (Sara Johnston, in this example), which provides further information and leads the reader to the correct person if there are questions to be asked, praise to be given, or blame to be placed.

HARD COPY FOR WHICH THE SM IS NOT RESPONSIBLE

There are other charts, plots, plans, and lists with which the SM should be familiar, but is not responsible for creating: light plots, light cues, set moves or scene changes, costume plots, or technical design of the sound system. This hard copy may be learned in the academic environment or from practical experience, as the SM works each show and has the opportunity to see them and ask questions. The paperwork in these different areas is done either by the designers or by the heads of the different departments. If the information contained in these charts, plots, plans, or lists is needed by the SM, it comes from the designers and the SM works with it as designed and laid out by those individuals.

IN CLOSING

Some charts, plots, plans, and lists will remain the same throughout the SM's career. Others will change radically, and still others will have to be invented to suit the needs of the show. It is the SM's job to document information and present it where it is needed. Creating or inventing new hard copy is relatively simple. First there is the information that needs to be documented. Next is the organization and form in which the information is laid out. Last is to see if the document does its job—see if it stands and delivers. Is the chart, plot, plan, or list thorough, complete, concise, informative, understandable, and easy to read, and can the information be extracted in a single glance?

An SM quickly learns to commit information to paper and not try to commit it to memory or word of mouth. Memory is fleeting—it fades, gets mixed up. Word of mouth can be just as troublesome. For any number of reasons, information in a person's mind can easily be changed or get mixed up. When errors occur, a less-responsible person will claim that the information was conveyed incorrectly by the SM. Having hard copy in hand leaves no doubt as to what the SM said, and it keeps the lines of communication open and clean. Good hard copy helps people do their jobs and keeps the business of putting on a show running smoothly, efficiently, effectively, and with less chance of error—errors which in the production of a show can be costly in time and money lost. Finally, with the use of a computer and the software available, there is no reason why an SM's hard copy should be any less than printshop perfect.

7

Profiles and Working Relationships

This is the chapter I wish would have been included in some of the books I read during my formative years when becoming an SM; I might not have led so easily with my chin and so often. We have met most of the people with whom the SM works in the chapter on the chain of the command. To give a total and comprehensive view of being a professional SM we will now go into more detail. Once again, our discussion is from the SM's perspective. Other members of the company dealing with the same people may have a different experience.

People come to work on a show not only with their talent and sense of artistry, but with their drives, ambitions, issues, behavior, thinking, and ways of working. Throughout the workday the SM deals with any number of these people. For success in doing the SM job and in running a smooth and agreeable company, the SM must have a very good understanding not only of human nature and behavior, but also of the behavior and temperament of the artist.

FIRST AND FOREMOST

Heading the list of people with whom an SM must work over and over is someone who keeps showing up at every job, bringing the same issues, behavior, way of thinking, and way of working. It is YOUR-SELF. You must be your greatest and strongest ally. There will be times when you will be the only person on whom you can depend. When you find yourself standing alone, you need to have confidence in yourself and your ability to do the job. Not only must you be loving and caring for the show and to the company of people left in your charge, but you must also be loving and caring to yourself. In order to know

and understand other people, you must first know and understand yourself.

The SM job is intense and consuming—there is no time to be guarded, showing only your best side. The job brings out the best in an SM and, at times, the worst. An SM must be centered from within and work from that center. It helps if you know your strengths and weaknesses, your likes and dislikes, what triggers your feelings and emotions, and what your contributions are as a person and SM. You must have a sense of reality of yourself and the SM job. If at all possible, the SM must work free of all prejudices and personal needs and drives.

This is a tall order for anyone. To say a person needs to reach such perfection and self-knowledge to become a successful SM is unreasonable. However, if you start this process of understanding early in your career, you will come to know things about yourself and other people which SMs of more senior experience learned later in their careers. The SM's self-discovery and self-exploration can proceed while the job is being done. In fact, the process is accelerated by doing both at the same time.

A Starting Point

The process of self-discovery and exploration cannot be done justice in the few pages devoted to it in this chapter. Self-discovery is an ongoing work in progress. Sometimes it needs to be done with the aid of a therapist. Other times it can be done simply, by reading self-help books. Each person's journey is highly individual, like fingerprints; there are, however, some basic truths and common characteristics that all people share in their feelings and ways of behaving. These are the points from which we will start.

Turning Inward

It is a natural inclination for all people to look outside themselves to get validation, confidence, esteem, and worth. There is nothing wrong with getting these things from outside, but the truth is that SMs, and for that matter all people, must first get these things from themselves by knowing they do a good job, by seeing the results of their work, and by the fact that they get hired again and again. People working on a show cannot meet the SM's needs and wants at all times. People have their own issues and agendas. Sometimes they become so centered on themselves they forget or cannot give to others. However, each person, each SM can give all they need to themselves 100 percent of the time.

THE THREE PARTS OF THE INNER SELF

As an aid and working platform in understanding some of the things that go on inside a person, transactional analysis presents an interpretation which is easy to understand and is a good foundation for SMs to understand themselves and others. Simply stated, transactional analysis talks about the *adult*, the *parent*, and the *child* in all of us.

The adult in each of us is clear, factual, and can tap into all the information necessary to live life normally and sanely. Most important, the adult does not let feelings or emotions get in the way of *thinking, acting, reacting, believing,* or *behaving*. The adult is resourceful, continually seeks to learn more, solicits help when it is necessary, and is good at resolving problems, coming up with solutions, making decisions, and doing business. This sounds like the ideal SM. We could stop here, but people and SMs are not so one-dimensional.

The parent in each person is nurturing. It is instructive, understands with compassion, has empathy, is caring, soothing, has great concern, and most of all, gives unconditional love. Once again the ideal SM comes to mind, especially when dealing with various dispositions and personalities in the chain of command.

There remains however, the third part of each person. The child in each of us is joyous, carefree, happy, fun-loving, playful, imaginative, creative, artistic, intuitive, inventive, instinctive, sensitive, and lives and reacts from feelings and emotions.

Each of these three personas is present at every moment in every person. When in balance, they work within a person as overlapping circles, each having equal influence, each taking the lead or becoming a dominant force, depending on the event taking place. For example, during negotiations for a contract, though all parts of the person are present and working for the best results, it is best for the adult part to dominate. To have the child lead and negotiate terms could be disastrous for the person negotiating. Yet, when an actor is creating a role or a director is directing, they each need to allow the child part of themselves to dominate for the most creative and best results. On the other hand, when dealing with friends, family, and in maintaining working relationships, the parent more than likely takes the lead. There are many times within the course of a workday when each of these parts of an SM comes into play. At one moment the SM may need to be all business. At another moment the SM may be called on to be creative or socially interactive, and in still another moment, will need to be understanding and nurturing to a cast member or someone in the company who needs help or a shoulder to cry on. In each instance, while one part of the SM dominates, the others remain close at hand ready to express themselves.

Life, however, is not always so perfect and balanced. For any number of reasons, experiences, and circumstances in a person's life, these parts of a person can become unbalanced or distorted. One may dominate no matter what event is taking place at the moment. An SM who understands these parts of a person gains greater understanding and compassion. An SM who develops these parts of himself or herself and uses them at appropriate times works freely, moving from one to the other without having to think about it.

PERSONAL BELIEF SYSTEMS

There is still another part within each person that SMs must take a look at, especially within themselves. There is a core in everyone that controls the way they think and feel, act and react, believe and behave. It is called the *belief system*. The belief system is the words and thoughts that play over and over in a person's head. This system of belief begins at birth and is formulated from the experiences a person has in the first years of life.

Unfortunately, belief systems are formulated when a person is a baby and mere child—at a time when we each believe we are at the center of the universe and the universe revolves around us. As babies we are incapable of making true evaluations of ourselves, life in general, and the things that happen in this world. If all goes well in those first years, our beliefs develop and mature but, once again, life is not always perfect. When adverse events take place, the baby/child in us takes it personally, perhaps blaming ourselves. Even more unfortunate is the fact that these beliefs are taken into adult life and adversely affect the way we live, think, feel, and work.

In SMing work things happen quickly and with great intensity. The SM does not have time to be guarded or protective. Old and distorted beliefs easily creep in and tarnish the love and luster we may have for our work. At the end of this chapter in the section "The Professional Experience", there is a revealing and personal account of an SM depicting this very thing.

Making Personal Change

There is hope. If your belief system is adversely affecting your work and life in general, you can make a change. Knowing about the problem is the first step. That, however, is not enough. You must also want to make a change, and more important, must actively work at making the change. Once again, this can be done with professional help or with a good self-help book.

The biggest mistake an SM, and for that matter anyone, can make is in believing we need to change other people's behavior to feel better. We think if we change the world around us, our ill feelings will go away. But we cannot make people change. We can establish rules, set boundaries, create policy, and lead by example, but the people around us will continue to think and behave as they believe and choose. If change is to be made, it must be made inside oneself. Changing someone else does nothing for you; those same feelings will pop up again with the next person or incident.

There is a side effect or bonus for the person who makes personal change: the people around you also seem to change. In a very subtle way people react to you differently. They no longer push the buttons that led to your old way of thinking or feeling, and if they

do, it doesn't matter, because you have changed your way of thinking and believing.

THE SPIRITUAL SELF

None of us can feel whole and at one with ourself until we explore and find the spiritual part of ourselves. The spiritual self is the foundation on which each of us finds our strength. It is the part that makes us feel supported and not alone. The spiritual self is the inner place where there is calm, peace, unity, and harmony. It is where creativeness, imagination, intuitiveness, artistry, and spontaneity live freely. In it is serenity, security, and renewed energy where we can work without fear or worry. When this part of an SM is developed, the SM can do all parts of the job without concern or being driven to do them and can succeed or fail without taking his or her thoughts and feelings to the extremes. We can trust and have faith without having to control and make things happen according to our will.

Some people like to call this part of themselves God. Others see it as being the universal flow of positive energy. Some sit calmly in meditation and become one with this part of themselves. Others practice it in ritual or religious service. Still others discount the idea entirely, embracing only an agnostic or atheistic point of view. Whatever perspective, it is important for SMs to be in touch with this part of themselves, to come to terms in choosing what is right for them. The job of being an SM ranges from great joy, success, and satisfaction, to moments of frustration, despair, and sometimes loneliness. An SM needs good support from within to live and work.

ANGER AND FEAR

It is a known fact in the world of psychology and therapy that behind every anger there is fear. SMs will experience many incidents of anger, from others as well as from within. It will not be easy to understand other people's anger, but we can stop to see what fears are behind our own angers.

The deeper and further we go into self-discovery and exploration, the closer we get to our fears. Often it is at this point that people will stop the process of self-discovery, because the feelings are too great. *Fear is always greater in the mind than it is in reality.* If we were to continue just a little further, we would probably find the child part of the self hurting in some way. This is when the nurturing, parent part of the self needs to step forward to give comfort and assurance.

A LIFETIME WORK-IN-PROGRESS

This process of self-discovery, exploration, and change will appear never ending. Do not step back to take an overall view of the work that must be done. The task will appear monumental and impossible. Just jump in and start working. This will be a lifetime *work-in-progress*. The more SMs explore, the better equipped they become in dealing with the more rigorous aspects of being an SM: knowing and understanding people; dealing with adversities both large and small and resolving matters, hopefully to win-win solutions. Most of all, you will have a better sense of what is needed for yourself and the job.

EGO

It is highly important for SMs to know and understand ego in both themselves and in others. Ego is centered within the child part of each person. Regardless of maturation in other parts of a person, the ego never develops past the primal state of believing it is the center of the universe. Ego is designed to make a person feel good. It puts the person first, above all others. When it chooses, it has little regard for social standards, and sometimes it will join forces with the *willfulness* part of a person, disregarding moral and ethical standards too. Ego expresses itself as it feels, without concern for the consequences of its actions. If used injudiciously, ego can be harmful and highly destructive to the person it serves. When used appropriately and in good measure, ego can be part of what makes people in theatre highly successful.

The SM's Ego

Performers and artists are more free to express their egos than what might be tolerated in other professions. On the other hand, SMs are expected to show little to no ego. They are to be even-tempered and levelheaded, the pillars on which the security of the company rests. Displaying ego can be seen as being weak, out of control, being self-serving, and can be

the cause of an SM not being hired again. To ask a person not to express ego is going beyond human possibility. Many people, including SMs, came to show business to nurture and satisfy their egos. SMs must find ways to do this without letting their ego intrude upon their work, the job, or working relationships.

Working with Ego

Ego is not restricted to performers or artists alone. Every day an SM must deal with ego from stagehands, department heads, dressers, front-of-the-house people—anyone and everyone. Ego comes in all sizes and in varying degrees of inflation. Ego is delicate and fragile. It is easily hurt and each person has a threshold or fuse for setting it off. An SM should never try to fight ego. An SM must learn to recognize the different faces of ego and see when it is the foundation of a situation or problem. Sometimes ego disguises itself under a banner of righteousness or justice. When minor events of ego break out within the company, the SM deals with it like any other conflict, disagreement, or confrontation. However, a good SM takes greater care in seeing the ego is bruised or hurt as little as possible, or the SM may not get a quick and speedy resolve. With major events of ego, such as what might come from a star, the SM should get support and reinforcement by calling upon the producer, director, or Equity for help.

THE ISSUE OF CONTROL AND PERFECTION

A great part of the SM's job is to be in control—to make things happen and make people do things on schedule. Everyone in the company expects this from their SM. Furthermore, the SM is expected to do all things perfectly. For the SM, control and perfection often go hand and hand. An SM can become obsessed and driven by them. The SM who misuses either one of these things can expect only negative reactions and possibly disaster.

It is the SM's job to oversee and be ever watchful of all aspects of the production, walking a fine line between being directly involved in or staying out of every person's business. To get the job done as expected, SMs can easily fall into the trap of ruling with an iron fist and dictating their own will. The people who must work with the SM will resent this approach. They want the freedom to work as they choose, even if it is wrong or less productive. SMs must learn when to step in and take control and when to exert their will. They must learn what degree of perfection they can expect or demand at each moment.

SMs who work from a strong and healthy center from within themselves will instinctively know what to do and when to do it: when to relinquish control and perfection and not be adversely affected when things do not happen their way. It is important that beginning SMs start learning this, for this knowledge and way of working can be applied to themselves and their work, as well as when working with others.

DEALING WITH DISAGREEMENT, CONFLICT, CONFRONTATION

Disagreement, conflict, and confrontation are present in any relationship, be it personal or in a working situation. Within a community of creators and artists they can take place more frequently and sometimes with greater intensity. Throughout the run of a show, the SM will be placed in situations of disagreement with peers, superiors, or people left in the SM's charge. Sometimes the SM's involvement is direct and personal, and other times it will be as a mediator or arbitrator as others fall into disagreement and confrontation.

"You" Versus "I"

When SMs sit in mediation or arbitration of a conflict, it is their job to resolve the matter. To do so, the SM must first set up safe grounds on which the participants can interact and express their differences. Next, see that the word "you" is eliminated from the conversation and "I" put in its place. Get the people involved to express what they felt and experienced, rather than allowing each person to accuse and tell the other person what they did wrong.

When a person speaks from the "I" position, it leaves no room for the other person to argue, because the feelings expressed, whether right or wrong, belong to the individual. When the term "you" is used and directed at the other person, that person may feel attacked and become defensive, which is often a direct path to activating ego.

The Art of Listening

In a confrontation, the parties also need to be instructed to listen as the other person speaks and not interrupt or argue back. The listeners must be assured they will have their chance to speak and express what they experienced and felt.

To bring resolution, the SM too must listen. The SM must hear the words being used, the feelings, intensity, or passion of expression and learn to read between the lines. Never assume anything. If something is not clear, get it clarified. The SM must also watch to see that the participants stay on track, sticking to the points of contention that brought about the conflict, and not bringing in issues that can cloud or confuse.

After the SM has allowed all of the participants to express themselves, each person is asked to restate in abbreviated terms what they heard the other people say. This technique is multilayered. It clears any misunderstandings, it forces each party to step into the shoes of the other, it makes each party feel they have been heard, and at the same time, the parties get to hear the sense or nonsense of their own words.

Bringing Closure

When the SM thinks all participants have had their say and have heard the other people involved, the SM then leads the participants towards closure by getting the parties to talk *to* each other and not *at* each other. The SM has each person express what he or she can do to resolve the situation—how the person can change to make things different. The SM leads the parties to a mutual ground, a place where they might come to some understanding, make compromise, or offer terms for a resolution. If at a stalemate or impasse, the SM reviews each person's rights to their feelings and points of view and asks if they can at least agree to disagree.

SETTING LIMITS, BOUNDARIES, AND EXPECTATIONS

By the time SMs reach PSM status they know the way they like to work, the way they want to be treated, and the way in which they expect people to be professional. In the first meeting with the cast, the PSM establishes the preferred professional working environment. The PSM goes over ground rules that experience has taught are easily broken by any company of actors, and sets the limits, boundaries, and expectations. It is not appropriate for the SM to gather superiors and those not under the SM's supervision in a group to express these preferences. However, SMs should send a clear message about their expectations by the way they work, their efficiency, their preparedness, and in their way of treating and dealing with people. Then when an individual works or behaves in a way that is not agreeable to the SM, the SM can at that time express the preferred working style and expectations.

People want to know their limits, the boundaries, and what is expected of them. For some it provides an environment of security and harmony. For others it becomes a line up to which they can step. With others, it becomes a line over which they can step to challenge or break the rules. These people can be frustrating for the SM, especially when one of them is the producer, director, or star.

The Power and Position of an SM

A theme stated from time to time in this book is the position and power of an SM, and the fact that it is more of an illusion than a point of reality. The SM is third in the position of leadership within a company, but the power ranks below that of the producer, director, star, creators, designers, and heads of departments. The SM's power comes more as influence. The SM is in a position to make suggestions, express an opinion, and to try and influence, but does not have the power to make the final decree, declaration, or decision. The power an SM shows to the world is borrowed from the producer and director. SMs are not free to exercise their own will in this part of their job. Whatever decisions they appear to make on their own are what they have learned would be choices the producer or director might make.

In this matter of position and power the SM works in a paradox. The SM knows the truth and reality of the situation, but perpetuates the illusion anyway. The SM works decisively, with authority, and with conviction, giving the appearance of power. The SM uses this illusion to get the job done, however, it is the wise SM who knows the truth. To believe differently is destructive and can feed the SM's vanity, fire the ego, and have a negative effect on the way the job gets done.

PROFILES: SUPERIORS, PEERS, AND ASSOCIATES

Producer

This is the boss—the person who signs the checks. The producer usually is the person who hires the SM

(although whenever possible, the director also has a voice in the selection). It is the SM's job to always work in the best interest of the producer, however, not at the expense or detriment of the actors or Equity. The producer is the person to whom the SM ultimately is responsible and to whom the SM must give loyalty. Producers expect their SMs to be their eyes and ears and report back to them anything that concerns the show and the company. SMs who are hired again and again by the same producers may work with only a handful of producers throughout their careers. For the SMs who move from show to show, the list of producers will grow and chances of working with various types will increase. Some producers will be very classy, honorable, talented, generous, and considerate. Some will be none of the above. Sometimes the SM is in direct contact and relationship with the producer on a daily basis. Other times the SM may see the producer only in passing.

A Conflict of Loyalty

SMs are often put in a position of having to serve two masters. As a member of Actor's Equity, the SM is expected to be responsible, loyal, and work in the best interest of the union and its members while also serving the best interest of the producer. Some producers do not always work in the best interest of the performer. It is the SM's job to monitor such situations, reminding the producer of any infractions. If the producer does not comply, the SM is required to report the matter to Equity. It is the small and minor infractions that cause the most problems for the SM. It is during these times some producers expect the SM to overlook things. Where then does the SM draw the line? When does the SM step over the line to serve one over the other? There is no answer and it becomes a conflict for each SM to resolve as each situation arises.

Money and the Producer

It is the SM's job to be prudent with the producer's money. While overseeing the workings and operation of the company as prescribed by the job, the SM is obligated to see that the producer does not lose money, or that money is not spent without the producer first knowing about it.

It is the producer's job to control and spend money. An SM may not always appreciate a producer's priority on how money is spent; the producer may manipulate expenses and the budget in one area, then go out and purchase expensive props from abroad instead of purchasing props from a local discount store that could have looked just as effective and authentic from the stage. There will be in every SM's career one or two producers who lack ethics and scruples, having no qualms about writing checks with insufficient funds in their accounts. It is because of these few that Equity requires all producers and productions to put up a bond to protect its members.

User of People

To produce a show, a producer needs people. It is the producer's job to use people for their talent and to get the best from them while they are in the producer's employ. Most producers are quite adept in getting people to do what they want. Some producers do it honorably, with consideration and generosity—others act with less regard. By the nature of the SM's position and work, the SM is most susceptible to being used and sometimes abused. When starting out, SMs may allow themselves to be used just to get the job, or have another credit on their resumes. It is called "paying dues." However, after a while, SMs learn to pick and choose the people by whom they wish to be used.

Salesmanship and the Art of Schmoozing

A good producer is highly persuasive and knows the value of being extremely persistent. Some work like car salesmen while others have learned the art of *schmoozing*—pleasant talk, charming talk, or manipulative talk. Producers come in all packages—from different educational and social backgrounds. Some have refined their art to a class act, others can be more street savvy. No SM is exempt from working with the latter at least once in a career. Somewhere between the extremes, SMs will find most producers working very hard to put on a show and to bring to the world of theatre a highly successful, artistic, critically acclaimed, and financially rewarding product.

Founder, General Manager, Executive Producer

The profile and SM's working relationship with a producer also applies, with some variation, to the founder of the company, the general manager, or the executive producer. Their jobs are all similar, their work greatly overlaps each other, and the people filling those jobs seem to be cast from the same dye.

Associate Producer

Associate producers seem less intense. They work at a driven pace but are quieter in their approach. Associate producers are just as effective in their work as producers, but are more like accountants as they concentrate on budgets, schedules, unions, and working out the technical logistics of the production. Associate producers deal with the nuts and bolts of a production. They do much of their work with the technical staff, the crew, the artisans and craftsmen—the people who put together the physical part of the show.

In many ways associate producers are like the SM. They are thorough, detailed, concentrated, focused, good at completing things, work in real time, and are good at making lists, plans, and schedules. The SM's working relationship with the associate producer may be limited to discussing, comparing, and combining schedules. Their jobs have very little crossover. The associate producer spends most of the time on the phone, in the office, or at the various technical shops, while the SM remains at the rehearsal hall or backstage at the theatre.

Company Manager

The company manager's job description is broad and is often what the producer chooses it to be. For the most part, the company manager's job is to deal with business that directly concerns the company—the daily expenses and operational budget of the show. The company manager does the administrative work for the cast and crew and handles many of the problems they might have which directly concern the show and the company. If the show is a touring show, the company manager organizes, arranges, and coordinates the travel, lodging, and moving of the show from place to place. When there is no associate producer on the show, the company manager's work may include some or all of that work, too. To get the day's work done, company managers are often seen working with great concentration, at a quick and intense pace, and with a good amount of energy. The job requires company managers to work on many parts of the production at the same time, which means they must be organized and focused, although from the various piles of papers scattered about their offices, one would get a different impression. Company managers need telephones, fax machines, pagers, copiers, computer equipment, and any timesaving devices which help them do the job effectively. Company managers are very comfortable in delegating work to others, especially to SMs. In many ways the associate producer, company manager, and SM are very similar in personality traits, ways of working, and maybe even in temperament.

When touring with a show, the company manager is pictured best with a bulging attaché or briefcase and traveling with a large number of boxes, crates, and cases which when opened, convert any empty dressing room, nook, or cranny into an office, complete with files, vaulted cash box, communication system, computer setup, and copying service. Company managers are needed most out on the road with large touring shows. In the absence of a company manager, much of the work may fall to the SM. The company manager's work and the SM's work are clearly defined and overlap very little. However, the two work hand in hand by staying in communication with each other and by the SM assisting or aiding the company manager whenever possible.

The company manager is not always a very popular position. Like the SM, there are times when the company manager must make decisions for the company that may not be popular with some or all of the people. The person filling the position of company manager usually is a seasoned veteran who knows what is required to get the job done and knows the temperament and behavior of working with a theatrical group of people. The company manager's work seems impossible for the amount of time available in each day. Often to expedite things, the company manager works with a no-nonsense approach, cutting quickly to the core or bottom line of a matter. This often makes the manager appear impatient and abrupt. Some company managers are remembered as being loving, benevolent, or parent-like. Others are remembered by the company as being stern, manipulative, indirect, secretive, and seemingly uncaring for those who have been left in their charge.

Production Secretary

The production secretary and the producer's secretary are often one and the same. When it comes to organizing, administrating, making lists, and getting the job done, the production secretary's work equals that of the SM. The greatest amount of work and contact the SM has with the production secretary is during the week before rehearsals begin. This is the week mandated by Equity when the SM officially begins to work on the show—the SM's *production week*. Before the SM begins working on the show, the production secretary is responsible for gathering the information the SM will use in creating some of the charts, plots, plans, and lists.

Once rehearsals begin, and if the office is located away from the rehearsal hall, the SM and the pro-

duction secretary can become passing ships, maybe talking on the phone, exchanging notes, or having packets of information delivered to each other. The production secretary knows as much about the company as does the producer. The production secretary often has the producer's confidence, can make suggestions or recommendations, and often can get the producer to take action on matters that might take others longer. It is wise and advantageous for the SM to have a friendly and amicable working relationship with the production secretary.

Casting Director

The SM's working relationship with the casting director usually is limited to audition time, which can be as long as ten days or as short as just a few hours on one particular day. Once the roles in the show have been cast and the show goes into rehearsals, the casting director is off to other projects.

Publicity: Press, Programs, and Photography

The SM's working relationship with one or more of these people is often limited to the rehearsal period in working out schedules for photo shoots, interviews, appearances, and in providing information for the program or playbill. Otherwise, much of this group's work is done at their offices. After the opening of the show, these people usually fade from view and only the effects of their work are felt in the advertisement of the show and the number of people who come to see the show.

The SM can sometimes be confronted with a conflict in scheduling between the director and the publicity department; the director needs the actors for rehearsals, while publicity needs the same people for an interview, appearance, or photo shoot. The performer's rehearsal time each day is regulated by union rules, so when the publicity department has no choice but to cut into that time, the director can become quite unhappy. Directors want all the rehearsal time they can get. When such times arise, the SM needs to be as creative and inventive as possible, working out a schedule that services all parties.

Office Staff

These are the people who sit at their desks in the production office, hour after hour, day after day, doing the detailed work all organizations need to be productive and remain solvent—creating schedules, budgeting, payroll, designing and laying out artwork for advertisements and the program, doing customer service for season tickets, putting together receptions, making opening night performances gala events, and fund raising. Their work is highly beneficial to the show and to the company, but sometimes it goes unrecognized or is taken for granted. Often, key personnel of the office staff have been with the production company for a long time—some since its inception.

The SM's greatest contact with the staff comes during the first week on the job (production week), because much of this beginning work is done at the office. They are usually generous in their help and welcome the SM to their working space, providing a desk, a phone, their office supplies, and office equipment. Their interest and enthusiasm for the show usually is high and at times, during the rehearsal period or during the run, they know as much about what is going on backstage as does the SM. This group can be easily forgotten. At every opportunity, the SM should express to them thanks and appreciation.

Author, Composer, and Lyricist

Only when working a new show does the SM meet and work with some or all of these individuals. They may also take part in the revival or makeover of an old show. The SM's work and relationship with these people is more as a host in welcoming and accommodating them. When any of the creators are part of the rehearsal, the SM sees that a place is set where they can do their work and watch the rehearsal. The author usually is placed at the director's table or at a separate table near the director. The composer and lyricist are placed with or near the music director and rehearsal pianist. Most times these creators sit quietly and patiently throughout the day, letting everyone do their work while they make notes. From time to time they may have a conference with the director or go off to a private area with the producer and director. The results of those meetings usually are seen the next morning in the form of rewrites or changes. On occasion, the SM may have the opportunity to sit in on such meetings and witness their creative process. It can be quite rewarding, educational, and very exciting.

Director

For better or for worse, the working relationship between the director and the SM is like a marriage. The honeymoon can last forever, with the two working on many shows, or the honeymoon can be over in just a few days, each waiting for the *death do us part* of the relationship. To best work with a director, the SM must zero in on the individual and not make generalizations from having worked with other directors. Also, the SM must keep in mind that this marriage/working relationship is not a fifty-fifty proposition; the director always takes the lead and the SM follows. The SM can be the power behind the throne, but the director is always the king.

For the most part, directors are keyed-in and focused individuals. They seem to be no-nonsense people who like to work at bottom line with the SM. Most directors love their work, and some are driven and obsessed by it. By the time the SM and the director begin working together, the director usually knows the show and what he or she wants. It then becomes a matter of the director passing that information on to the SM.

A Pledge of Allegiance, or More Conflict in Loyalty

We have already established Equity's and the producer's expectations of loyalty from the SM. Now enters the director, who also wants a pledge of allegiance. When all is going well in the rehearsal and all are working happily together, the SM straddles the fence of loyalty and allegiance with ease. However if working conditions become less harmonious, the SM is again faced with the conflict of which master to serve. When in such a situation, the best SMs go immediately to neutral ground and place themselves firmly into the adult part of their personality where neither fears, feelings, emotions, nor ego get in the way of their thinking and actions. The position of the SM puts them in the middle of any conflict between people, but they must be careful not to get pulled in. SMs may offer their expertise to help resolve some of the conflict, but must remain free to guide the ship while the captains do battle.

The Pivotal Point

From the SM's point of view, the director is the pivotal point of the production, the leading force creatively, artistically, and in expressing technical requirements. The producer has hired the director because the producer knows the director's work and ability. The producer allows the director the freedom to do that work, but remains overseer and controller, artistically and financially. If there are differences of opinions between the producer and director, they usually work it out privately. The director's words should not be taken lightly or disregarded, and the SM must follow through on every suggestion and direction the director gives. As long as the director remains on the scene, the SM relinquishes all control to the director. A good SM learns with each director when to lead and when to work in the director's shadow.

Service Versus Servant

The SM's job and working relationship with the director is to be of *service* and not be a *servant*. The difference between giving service and being a servant is a theme that will be repeated throughout this book. Directors sometimes forget and easily step over the line, expecting the SM to do things that are not in the line of service or part of the job. An SM must first know the job description well, decide what is service and what is being a servant, then work firmly within those guidelines. The SM establishes these boundaries and limits early in the working relationship with the director. The SM expresses them first by the way he or she works. If or when the director behaves in a way that is not acceptable to the SM, the SM at that time expresses a preference. Directors have learned the world must revolve around them to get the job done. An SM must be highly accessible and available to the director, working by the director's side, anticipating the director's needs. An SM who chooses to get a cup of coffee for the director is being of service. Being expected to get the director a cup of coffee every time is being a servant and not part of the SM's job!

The Winging-It Director

No matter how fully prepared a director may be, they all work in rehearsals spontaneously or improvisationally, to some degree. From time to time, an SM may work with a director who gives the illusion of working spontaneously but who is in fact winging it, doing the creative work on the spot, while blocking the show with the actors. Some directors' genius lays in working this way. Others do it because they have not done their homework. A director who is good at working this way inspires the cast and everyone else at the rehearsal hall. Those who are not so good at it make the day long, the work tedious, and leave everyone tired and uninspired. An SM must learn to recognize the difference, and when the latter prevails it is the SM's job to talk with the producer and have the producer come to the rehearsals to make an evaluation.

Breaking the Director's Creative Flow

The task of directing a show is monumental, with many things to be thought about, created, designed, and detailed. Throughout the day the director is pulled in all directions, with people demanding his or her attention. During the rehearsal period, the main part of the director's day is to work with the cast in blocking and getting the show on its feet. This is highly creative and focused time. For some directors, this is sacred time. The SM must be sensitive to this and make every effort not to have this time disturbed or interrupted. Some directors can have their creative flow broken, change hats for a moment, then return to their work with the cast. Others find interruptions highly intrusive and hold the SM responsible each time their creative process is broken.

It is also part of the SM's job to, whenever possible, keep the work process of other parts of the production flowing. There will be many times during the rehearsal period when someone needs to have the director's attention for information that only the director can supply. The SM must learn with each director the best window of opportunity to interrupt. Otherwise, the SM can be targeted and blamed for the interruption and become the target of the director's anger and frustration.

A Breech in Allegiance

Directors can also be indulgent, forgetting time, schedules, breaks, even the budget. The SM must be a watchdog, holding rein on the director in these areas, while looking out for the producer's best interest. This can become an even greater danger area for the SM, because directors expect freedom to do as they choose. A director may feel attacked, betrayed, and spied on by the SM. Most of all, the director may feel the SM's activities as a breech in the SM's allegiance. The SM must learn the tolerance and temperament levels of each director, then tailor the approach in getting the director to work in the best interest of the show, the company, and the producer.

The Director's Patience Factor

The director's patience factor can vary with different groups or individuals. Directors most often allow the performers a greater amount of time and patience to assimilate, process, and do their jobs. With technical things, directors in general have less patience and expect quicker understanding, execution, and results. With the SM, the director's patience factor can be even less. Directors expect their SMs to be all-knowing about the production, anticipate their needs (if not their thoughts), have on-the-spot information, and just generally stand and deliver whatever is called for or needed at the moment.

SM: In the Directorial Arena

As SMs work on each show, they witness firsthand the creative and artistic process that each director goes through. Eventually, having worked enough shows, many SMs acquire a director's sense of their own. They come to know what works and what doesn't. Many times as the director works on the show, the SM is able to anticipate the director's next choice before the director makes it. Some SMs become skilled enough to go out and direct shows of their own.

Having a good working knowledge of directing is excellent information and skill for an SM, especially when it comes to working with the understudies or putting replacement actors in the show. However, producers, directors, and cast members do not want their SMs to be directors. They do want their SMs to be knowledgeable of directing so they can maintain the level of performance, anticipate the director's needs and problems, and communicate with the actors in their terms. They don't want the SM's unsolicited opinion, but from time to time they will ask for it. Generally, an SM learns to stay out of the director's arena and when invited in, expresses an opinion with care, keeping in mind that all artistic and creative work comes from a very personal place within each person. When an SM gives an opinion that might be contrary or critical, that SM is stepping into an ego zone where anything can be and will be taken personally.

Each Director

These few paragraphs written on the working relationship between an SM and the director is a good overview, but the SM does not go into the relationship with book in hand and expect things to be as they are written here. The relationship will be much more complicated, with some of the things we have discussed being practically nonexistent while others might be even more pronounced or outrageous. The best an SM can do is go into the relationship with each director being open and alert, ready to serve, doing the best job possible, and allow the relationship to grow professionally and naturally. Every SM does not click with every director. Some SMs and directors will bond and work together on many shows. Others will work together once and, in some of those situations, both will be glad when it is over.

Assistant Director

People who take on the role of an assistant director seem to take on the classical, textbook definition of what is expected from an assistant director: being helpful, assisting, giving service, knowing their place, and never outshining or rising above the director. Assistant directors are usually quiet, ever watchful, do not openly disagree, criticize, contradict, and give all suggestions and ideas in private. It is uncertain if these qualities and behaviors come automatically when a person agrees to be an assistant, or if they are acquired through experience. Perhaps directors choose assistants who already have these qualities. Whatever the case, most assistant directors are often quite capable of directing their own show, but when working as an assistant, choose to remain in the shadow of the director. Many times, only the director knows the assistant's true talent and capability. The SM's job and working relationship with the assistant director run parallel courses. Both are present to help, assist, and serve the director, but the work they do seldom overlaps or crosses over.

Music Director

When working on a musical show, the SM will always work with a music director. Music directors seem to be the quieter members of the creative staff. In the rehearsal hall, they usually sit near the rehearsal pianist, waiting for their time to work with the performers. In their working relationship with SMs, music directors are the least demanding, requiring only a workspace in the rehearsal hall and time on the schedule to work with the cast. Most music directors are amicable and agreeable, bending and working around whatever schedule the director might choose for them. Once the music director is set up to work, it is not necessary for the SM to be there at every moment. Most music directors prefer to be the keeper of the score and orchestrations and remain responsible to distribute them to the cast and orchestra members. With such independence, the SM may at times inadvertently forget the music director. It is the SM's job to remember and give to the music director the same attention, services, and considerations given to the other members of the creative staff. On many shows, the music director will also be the conductor, and may also be the rehearsal pianist.

Rehearsal Pianist

This artist does not require a lot of the SM's time and attention. All the rehearsal pianist needs is the piano where the performers can be easily seen and heard, and each day have a copy of the schedule. On most musical shows there is one rehearsal pianist with the music director filling in when needed. On a large show, a new show, or a show heading for Broadway, there can be as many as three: one working the main rehearsal room with the director; one with the choreographer, and a floater pianist who fills in wherever needed. Most rehearsal pianists dislike being referred to as the "piano player." *Pianist* is the operative word.

During rehearsals each day, a good rehearsal pianist knows to stay at the piano and be ready at any moment to play. Sometimes a rehearsal pianist can sit at the piano for as long as an hour without having to play, but must remain there, ready. During these waiting periods, many of them read, do crossword puzzles, note music, or do personal business with a laptop computer. The use of a cellular phone is disturbing and the SM must request that it not be used in the rehearsal room. Rehearsal pianists take their breaks whenever they can, which usually is when the actors take theirs. However, the SM should not forget the rehearsal pianist entirely. The SM should ask the rehearsal pianists if they have had a break, or thank them for taking breaks on their own and when it is convenient for everyone else.

The biggest problem an SM may have with a rehearsal pianist is a pianist who wanders off without first informing the SM. We know in certain instances and with some people the director's patience and tolerance level is low, and this is especially true for a rehearsal pianist who is not present. The director will turn to the SM and hold the SM responsible for the pianist not being there.

Music Arrangers: Vocal, Dance, Orchestration, and Copyist

Only when working on a new show or the revival of an old show with new orchestrations and maybe some new songs, does the SM get to work with these people, and even then the SM's working relationship will be limited. The music director usually takes care of the business having to do with this group. From time to time, one or two of them may stop by the rehearsal to observe. It is during those times the SM extends the usual courtesies given to other staff members or visiting guests. For the most part, this group's work is done outside the rehearsal hall and the results of their work are only heard in the final stages of rehearsals or in performance.

Choreographer

During rehearsals, when it comes time for scheduling and providing rehearsal rooms, the choreographer requires from the SM as much care and attention as does the director. The director's and choreographer's work are similar in that they both need time to create, experiment, improvise, teach, and clean up. When putting together the daily schedule, the SM must confer with the director and choreographer, then carefully coordinate their schedules so there is no overlap or loss of time. Choreographers are agreeable in yielding to the director's will in setting up the rehearsal schedule, and like the director, display a strong dislike in giving up any rehearsal time.

The Choreographer's Needs from the SM

The choreographer needs music, which requires a piano and rehearsal pianist. It is the SM's job to see that these things are provided and set up in the rehearsal room. On small budget shows with only one pianist, the director and choreographer will work out schedules to share. Some choreographers will work from a cassette audiotape, but may ask for an SM to be with them to start and stop the music and to wind and rewind the tape to a particular spot in the music.

The choreographer likes to work in a room with mirrors. This works out well, because directors do not like working with mirrors; they feel it distracts the actors, who will watch their performances, sometimes sacrificing their best work in lieu of presenting their best image. The choreographer, on the other hand, wants the dancers to see the physical image they are presenting.

The choreographer also needs to have the outline of the stage taped on the rehearsal room floor, along with the floor plans of the different sets in which the dances take place. In addition, they like the dance numbers to be placed along the edge of the stage. These numbers enable the dancers to spot their positions and find their spacing as they move about in the dances.

The SM is also responsible for having at the rehearsal hall any props that are important to the dance. In most situations, once the choreographer is set up, the SM does not have to remain present at every moment. However, from time to time, either the PSM or the ASM should stop in to see if there is anything the choreographer needs.

Most choreographers bring to rehearsals a high level of energy that is positive and uplifting. Their enthusiasm is catchy. They are themselves dancers (or gypsies, as they affectionately call each other) and know how to work with their peers. Seldom do you hear the dancers complain that the choreographer is working them too hard.

Dance Captain and Swing Dancer

These can be two separate positions or one person performing both jobs, depending on the number of dancers in the show and how complicated the choreography might be. In most cases the dance captain is hired as a dancer in the show and is paid extra to be dance captain. The work of the dance captain and swing dancer is very similar, but has different functions. The dance captain is responsible for learning all the choreography in the show. Like the SM, who is responsible for maintaining the blocking and artistic integrity of the show in the absence of the director, the dance captain is responsible for maintaining the staging and integrity of the dances in the absence of the choreographer. If at any time the choreography gets sloppy or needs to be changed, the dance captain can call a rehearsal to make the necessary adjustment.

The swing dancer also learns the choreography—more specifically, the choreography each dancer performs in the show. Then, if a dancer is unable to perform at any time, the swing dancer is put into that position.

In shows with a lot of dancing or a large number of dancers, a male and female swing dancer are hired, sometimes two or more of each. With shows where there is no swing dancer, the dance captain may fill in for a dancer who is missing, or adjust the choreography, cutting out the part for that performance. In situations where there is no dance captain or swing dancer, the dancers themselves will make the changes, with the SM overseeing the work.

The SM's work and association with the dance captain and swing dancer is mostly as it is with the rest of the performers in the company. When it is necessary for the dance captain or swing dancer to do their jobs, the SM acts more in an accommodating manner, organizing and coordinating, seeing that rehearsal time and space is made available and that the cast members involved are scheduled and informed. As the changes are made, the SM sees how the changes affect the different parts of the show, and then informs the rest of the cast and crew. The SM is grateful to have a dance captain and swing dancers with the show. Many times changes that need to be made in the choreography are a last-minute affair due to some emergency. During such times, as the dance captain or swing dancers do their work, the SM continues to keep the company organized, informed, and gets the show started with the least delay and trauma to the company.

Performers

The terms *performer*, *actor*, and *player* are used interchangeably, depending on a person's training in theatre and geographical location. The terms are all-encompassing, including stars, principal players, supporting characters, ensemble singers and dancers, walk-on roles, and extras—anyone who appears on the stage during a performance.

With the performer comes the SM's ultimate experience in working relationships. Performers require at all times the best an SM has to give—the best in business and in doing the job, being loving, caring, understanding, compassionate, and nurturing. Just as important, performers want their SM to be playful, fun-loving, and socially active.

Performers are a highly diverse group of individuals who have many similar characteristics, which makes it easy to group them together and generalize. The performers are the breath and character of the show and company. They are often childlike souls in adult bodies. To do their work well, performers must be in close contact with the child inside of them. Sometimes, however, they continue to live at that center, letting the child also dictate and rule in their business, behavior, and personal lives.

For the most part, working with the performers will be a rewarding experience for the SM, filled with fond memories, great stories, and some very good friends. The performers can sometimes be to the SM as a child is to a parent: the source of great love, fun, and pleasure, and at the same time a reservoir of annoyance, anger, aggravation, and frustration.

An Illusion of Being the Center

When the company of a show is assembled, performers seem to stand out as being the center around which everything revolves. The primary focus for the rehearsal period seems all about the performers. The director appears to give more time and consideration to the performers. Without the performers, the script would not come alive. The costumes are made for the performers, and in most situations they can approve or disapprove a prop they must use. The audience sees the performers as the central figures. The reviews are mostly about the performers and the more prestigious awards are given to the performers. With so much being directed toward this group of individuals in the company, it is easy to see how performers, to varying degrees, buy into the illusion that they are the center of the production.

The SM, who sees all parts of the production, of course has a wider view. It is important for the SM to be aware of the illusions of the performers and keep a proper perspective and balance in working with the entire company. The truth is, everyone in the company feels their work is central, and each is hoping to have their star shine. In a small way the SM is partially at fault for perpetuating feelings of importance, because in dealing with each person, the SM expresses the importance of their work and is generous with compliments, thanks, and appreciation when they do a good job.

A Double-Edged Life

The performer's life is probably the hardest, most double-edged of all within the company. For the most part, performers have the least power and control over the show and yet they have placed upon them the greatest demands for its success. Their work is highly visible and each day they must do it with perfection. Here is where the double edge becomes sharper: performers can receive great acclaim for their work and have their careers accelerated to great heights, or, with severe judgment and critical review for one or two shows, their careers can plummet to oblivion. No one else in the company is subject to such scrutiny and loss for the work they do. Producers, directors, creators, or designers who create a theatrical disaster one season, can one or two seasons later emerge from the rubble with another product, be acclaimed, and make theatre history.

Continuous Work for the Performer

The performers' feelings and emotions are the tools by which they work. Their bodies are the instruments through which they deliver. At the end of each workday, most members of the company can close their scripts, set aside their tools, and go home. Performers take home with them everything, including their scripts, which they must study to be ready for the next day's rehearsal. For a star, the work and responsibility can be greater and more intense.

Magnification of Feelings

Given the dramatic nature of many performers, some performers in their everyday professional life will allow their feelings and emotions to become magnified, blowing up issues or situations to greater proportion. When reacting as a group, the performers' feelings can be even more dramatic. An SM needs to know this about performers and during times when feelings are running high, the SM must evaluate the situation for its true nature, then carefully and lovingly bring the performers back to a base of reality. By knowing that some performers have this tendency, the SM can head off situations as they develop. To keep a finger on the pulse of the performers and on the pulse of the company, the SM must establish and maintain open communication where the performers can feel free to express themselves without judgment or recrimination.

Putting the SM to the Test

It is in the performer's nature to please, be professional, and do the right thing. There will be some, however, who will put the SM to the test to see how far they can go in bending or breaking the rules. The SM will need to be fair, honest, understanding, and display compassion, but at the same time hold firm by the rules and be consistent in their execution, making them effective for all.

Giving Performance/Acting Notes

It is the SM's job to keep the show intact and at the level of performance set by the director. For the most part, performers do not intentionally change their performances but work to improve them. In their search for perfection, some may take direction from most anyone who offers it: the SM, another cast member, a member of the family, a fan, or even a maid at the hotel. Sometimes the changes become a departure from what was originally set and intended by the director. Enter the SM to give a performance note.

Most performers are quite receptive to receiving performance notes from the SM. They like having someone watching over the show. However, receiving a performance note is a very personal matter for a performer. Each performance comes from within. Sometimes a judgment or criticism of their work is received and filtered through their feelings or ego. From the start, the SM give acting notes with great care and concern, being selective in the approach and choice of words. The SM is clear and specific, stating what has been observed and not what the performer did wrong. The SM allows the performer to speak and is careful not to get into a confrontation, even if the performer is heading in that direction. As part of the closure, the SM reminds the performer of how things were originally set by the director and asks if the performer can return to that way. Under no circumstances does the SM try to direct or redirect an actor. If an acting note requires directing, the SM must first confer with the producer and director, then give the note as if it came from the producer or director.

For those performers who receive a performance note from the SM and make a change, be it right or wrong, the SM should acknowledge the performer's efforts, express thanks and appreciation, and take the opportunity to correct anything that is still not right. For those who persist in doing as they choose, it is time for the SM to talk with the director and get a final decision.

Star Performers

All that has been said about the nature of performers applies to star performers as well, but with more of everything. Most star performers live and work at extremes. It seems that everything in their lives is larger, has more importance, and is done with greater intensity.

Stars are very important people to the show. Their power and attraction often is what keeps the show alive. Sometimes even a show that should have failed and become part of obscurity is successful because of the star performer. If it were not for this power, producers would not pay star performers the amounts of money they do, nor would they tolerate some of the things that can sometimes come with a star.

Stars, however, do not always make the show. There have been many cases where the show has made the star. The star of a show could also be the writer, composer, director, choreographer, or producer. On one or two occasions, even the sets and costumes have become the stars. However, it is the *performing* star in whom we are most interested.

No two stars are the same. Their backgrounds, personalities, and motivating forces can be extremely varied. The reasons for a star performer's success and rise to stardom can range from being a brilliant, multitalented genius, to a complete mystery as to how they became a star in the first place.

Every SM who works "star shows" will come upon a unique combination of star personalities along with a few interesting stories to tell. For the most part, star performers have gotten a bad rap. The few outrageous ones have left a legacy that most other stars must live down. It is for those outrageous few that an SM must go into training and be prepared. When a star is all the wonderful things a star should be, the SM cannot help but want to treat that person with special consideration, sometimes going beyond the line of service. On the other hand, when a star is all the horror stories that have been told, the working situation can become a nightmare for both the SM and the company. Stars often set the tone and atmosphere of the company, in both the performance and backstage. Some stars will keep their dressing room doors open for all to come and visit and chat, while others will create fear and tension, having people walk and talk in whispers, staying mostly behind closed dressing room doors.

A Star's Need for Support

All stars are hardworking individuals who have great demands put on them. The roles they play are usually large, complicated, and sometimes rigorously demanding. Their work often goes beyond the rehearsal hall and stage. The demand for star publicity is never ending. A star's business obligations (which often look social) can take up a good portion of his or her personal time. Ultimately the success or failure of the show rests upon the star's shoulders. To accomplish and succeed in all parts of their life, star performers need a strong and highly dependable support system both in personal matters and professionally. To ensure their support and success while working in a show, they will often have with them an entourage of people. In addition, everyone in the company must work toward their star's success.

The SM champions star support by first redefining the line between giving service and being a servant. For the star, the SM broadens this scope, providing the star with a little more service. The idea of treating all performers equally does not apply when it comes to star treatment. However, the SM, as well as other people in the company, may overdo this star treatment and extend themselves beyond the call of duty. SMs will have greater success with star performers if they keep their attention and work focused on providing strong support and consideration to the stars, continue to do their job in the professional manner expected by all, and let their relationships with the stars develop naturally.

The Power and Control of the Star

Stars have more power and control over the show, their performance, and their professional lives than do any of the other performers in the show. Some stars use their power with grace and ease, working it to its maximum effectiveness for themselves, for the benefit of the show, and many times for the people around them. Other stars wield their power and control like a terrible, swift sword to satisfy themselves, get what they want, or maintain what they are fearful of loosing. Stars have learned what works for them and what keeps them stars. If ego, some dysfunction, fear, and possibly a diminishing career are added into the star's life, an SM may be working with a star who is out of control and abusing power. If the picture painted appears bleak, it is because sometimes it can be.

> *Note:* I have seen a star performer rip a costume because she disliked the design. I have seen a star performer fling a prop into the audience during a dress rehearsal with little regard for who was seated in the theatre. I have seen holes being cut in sets for new doorways, because the side on which the star was entering was not his most flattering side. I have seen beaming lights being placed at the foot of the stage, much to the lighting and set designer's horror, so an aging star could maintain some illusion of youth. Much to my surprise, I have witnessed a star performer come off stage in the middle of performance and beat on the SM, calling him some very descriptive and profane names, because she thought he missed a light cue.
>
> Star performers can often get away with things for which another performer would be fired on the spot or at least highly reprimanded, and maybe not hired again. No matter how difficult star performers might be, if they can draw in an audience and make lots of money for the show, they will be hired again and again.

Giving Stars Performance/Acting Notes

There will come a time in every SM's life when a performance note must be given to the star. Most stars are receptive and appreciative of the SM's work, care, and concern for the show. On occasion they may even ask the SM to pay particular attention to a scene so the SM can give an opinion or make a suggestion. Other times, a star's response to a performance note from the SM is met with coldness or deadly silence—sometimes both. There is, of course, not much an SM can do about a star's response to receiving a performance note, except continue to do the job in maintaining the performance. However, an SM can deflect or lessen an adverse reaction by first following the same rules as when giving notes to other performers and, second, by staying out of directing or redirecting. In addition, the SM must build with the star performer a performance note–giving relationship.

In creating a note-giving relationship with a star, the SM starts with notes concerning technical things in the show and at the same time makes complimentary comments on a particular scene, an acting moment, or an audience reaction. The SM lets the star see that these observations are from a professional standard and are not personal or ego related. Most of all, in giving a star a performance note, the SM must keep in mind at all times that star performers have built their fame and success on who and what they are, what they do in a performance, and what the audience expects when they come to see a particular star. The SM must be intrinsically aware of the persona and style of the star and guard against giving notes that criticize or try to change that part of the performance, even if it seems wrong for the show or the character. The SM can express observations and thoughts to the director or producer, but then leaves whatever changes need to be made to either of them. For the most part, star performers stay pretty much within the framework of what was set and agreed on by the director and themselves during rehearsals. During performance, they will refine, improve on, or embellish, but not enough to cause the SM concern.

Delivering Messages to Stars

Delivering messages to the star is a common occurrence for the SM. There will be times when the SM must deliver messages that are from someone else, are of a negative nature, and may illicit an adverse reaction from the star. These kinds of messages often come from the producer or director, who choose not to deliver the message themselves and make it the responsibility of the SM. For anyone else in the company who wants such a message delivered to the star, the SM would merely ask them to deliver their own message. Sometimes a message filled with anger and expletives is given to the SM. SMs who deliver these messages as dictated will surely find themselves victims of "Cut Off The Messenger's Head" syndrome. To protect yourself and lessen an adverse reaction, clean up these messages. Deliver the bottom-line words without the feelings and descriptive adjectives. Before presenting the message, clearly establish who is sending the message and that you are only the messenger.

Each star performer has a unique combination of sanity or madness. An SM's experience with star performers will be two-fold. Some will be warm, loving, memorable, maybe even become a friend. With others, the SM will be glad to have the show close and hope that their paths never cross again.

Children Performers

With shows like *Oliver, The Children's Hour, Sound of Music*, and *The King and I*, the SM is faced with an additional and unique group of performers—the children performers. This is a highly selective group of people. They usually are brighter and more knowledgeable than other children of the same age, and usually are more adult in their manner, speech, and social interactions. At the same time, they remain children.

In dealing with this particular group, the SM must always keep in mind that these are children as well as professional actors. Establish an adult professional working relationship with them, but during times of play, fun, and creativity, allow them to meet the child within yourself. With this group, the SM walks a fine line between the two worlds and is clear when it is time to be adult and work and when it is time to be a kid and play. At times, other members of the company, including the director or producer, may forget these performers are still children and expect immediate and adult-like results. The SM watches for these moments and, if expectations are too high, reminds the adults that they are dealing with children and asks them for a little more tolerance.

The Parents

With the children come parents. This too is a unique group. Some may be professional stage parents knowing all the rules, regulations, and professional standards governing children, and others will be experiencing their first time of being with their child in a production. In theatre, it is required that children performers have with them each day a parent or guardian to care for them.

From the start, the SM establishes a caring and respectful working relationship with the parents. In addition, the SM not only displays a loving, caring, and professional attitude toward their children, but allows the parent to see the child within the SM by playing and having fun with their kids.

As a rule, parents are not allowed to sit in the rehearsal room to watch as their children work, unless the child is an infant or under the age of three or four. When parents are present, children work differently. Directors want the child's full attention and they want to be in control without the child looking to the parent for approval. With this in mind, it is the SM's job to set up a room in which the parents can stay each day. If at all possible, this should be a place with some comfort and amenities, even if it is as simple as providing them each day with fresh drinking water.

There are many stories to be told of the doting stage parent. Most have been blown up and exaggerated. However, sometime during a career an SM may work with one or two of these stage parents and end up having a few stories of his or her own to tell. In dealing with this kind of a parent, the SM remains neutral, maintaining a civil and professional relationship, keeping the parent out of the rehearsal room, and directing all problems or complaints the SM cannot handle to the producer.

The Teacher/Social Worker

On the days the children are required to be at rehearsals, there are laws in each state that require a teacher and social worker to be present. It is the teacher's job to keep the children up on the studies they would ordinarily be having if they were attending their regular school. The social worker is required to assure that living and working conditions are suitable for children. In many cases, one person is trained and qualified to perform both jobs, a feature producers prefer (it saves them from paying two salaries). With the presence of a teacher/social worker, the SM must set up still another room—a room conducive to study and doing school work. Again, the SM is accommodating and considerate of the needs for this particular part of the production.

Actor's Equity

An SM's working relationship with Actor's Equity can be as extensive as each SM chooses. SMs can take an active part on some of Equity's service boards or panels, or can limit contact to the times they are working on shows that come under Equity contracts.

Equity has created with producers, many different types of contracts to financially accommodate the producers, depending on the type of show, the venue in which the show is playing, its location, and the number of people the theatre is capable of seating. These contracts have many different names, including LORT, HAT, Waiver, Special, Dinner Theatre, Regional, Stock, Touring, National, Production, and the granddaddy of them all, the one performers and SMs dream of having, a Broadway Production Contract. Each of these contracts has a different pay scale, with the production and Broadway contract paying the highest salaries.

Unlike most of the technical or craft unions in theatre, Equity, like most other performer's unions in entertainment, does not make it part of its business to help its members find work. Equity's function is to negotiate, administrate, mediate, watch over each production seeing that the rules and regulations are followed, and generally guard its members against poor working conditions and unscrupulous producers.

The Equity Deputy

To aid Equity in the monumental task of watching over each company of performers and to keep the performers in direct contact with the Equity office, the performers of each company elect from within their ranks an Equity deputy. In large casts, such as in musicals, two or three deputies may be elected. The deputy is responsible to the cast and Equity, and keeps Equity informed by weekly reports. If a problem among the performers or with the producer arises, the Equity deputy usually is the first to step in to try and resolve the problem before bringing in representatives or officials from the Equity office.

As we know, the SM also works on behalf of Equity and the performers. The SM's greatest contact with the Equity office usually comes during the week before the first rehearsal (the SM's production week). At that time the SM is in contact with the Equity field representative assigned to the show, confirming cast members' names and social security numbers. Then on the first day of rehearsals, the first hour is devoted to Equity business with the field representative present at the rehearsal hall. The field rep is there to see that all the performers' contracts are signed before they begin rehearsing, and to bring all actors up to date on their membership dues. After the first week of rehearsals, the SM deals with Equity on an as-needed basis. If, for the run of the show, things go smoothly and whatever small problems arise are resolved by the Equity deputy, the SM may never need to talk with the Equity office. On the other hand, some productions will require the SM to be on the phone with Equity daily, sometimes two and three times in a day.

Designers

Designers are to the SM a bridge to understanding the technical parts of the show during the rehearsal period, before the sets, props, costumes, or any of the other technical elements are assembled. In return, the SM becomes the technical bridge to the cast. It is the SM's job to extract from the designers information about their work and bring this information to the rehearsal hall in the form of pictures, plans, scale models, recordings, or verbal descriptions. In addition, the SM keeps the designers informed of meetings, schedules, and relays all changes the director might make that affect the designers' work.

Technicians

The technicians' job is more in assembling the technical elements of the show and to execute cues than in creating and designing. However, within the scope and range of their work, technicians need to be creative and artistic to provide what is needed for the show. Technicians are very practical, nuts and bolts, bottom-line type people. They want it said plainly and simply, in terms that leave no room for misunderstanding or interpretation. For example, to explain to a technical department head or to the stagehands that in a particular scene change, "the set pieces and backdrop are to glide off stage as if in a dreamlike state, and are to subconsciously disappear from view without the audience being aware," is futile dialogue and possible death in the SM's working relationship with the crew. However, if the SM says the set pieces and backdrop should move off stage slowly, on the SM's cue, in a ten-count, and asks that the drop and set pieces travel off at the same time, the SM will get the desired results. The SM takes responsibility for the artistic look while the technicians remain responsible for executing the work.

SM—Leader of the Crew?

In all professional situations, the SM is not the leader of the technical departments and crew. Only in some community and academic situations does the SM take on some or all of the leadership of the crew and technical elements of the show. In professional theatre there is a definite separation between the SM's job and what the technicians do. There is no crossover or overlap of work. The stagehands' union, I.A.T.S.E., has clearly defined the work stagehands do. An SM who crosses over this line in any way will be quickly reminded and asked to stop. If the SM continues to overstep the boundaries, the SM will be reported to the producer and I.A.T.S.E and censured for this behavior. The only working relationship the SM has with the technical departments and crew is to get assurance from the department heads that the technical work will be completed according to schedule and the obligation to provide them with the information they need to do their work. They want the SM to be organized, coordinate their work with the work of the director and actors, see that there are no conflicts or delays, answer their questions, and during the performance call the cues with perfect timing.

The Union Brotherhood: Protective and Defensive

The SM will find the brotherhood of stagehands strong, protective of its members, and sometimes defensive. The SM will find most department heads and stagehands extremely professional and proficient in their jobs. There will be, however, some who are less professional, appearing discontented with their jobs. Some will be negative or argumentative while others will seem to question and challenge every request the SM makes. Some would rather spend an hour telling the SM why a thing cannot be done, than spend twenty minutes in doing the job. Some crewmembers have learned the art of stretching twenty minutes worth of work into an hour. Others have learned the craft of disappearance. This sort of behavior and way of working can be frustrating to the SM, especially when working on a tight schedule or facing a director or producer who is questioning why the work backstage is taking so long to get done.

If the SM finds a stagehand's poor work is having an effect on any part of the production, the SM never deals directly with the individual, but goes to the individual's supervisor or department head. However, the SM must be prepared. Sometimes in a line of defense for the union brother, the supervisor or some of the other stagehands will discount the SM's complaint, perhaps even suggesting the SM's observation is incorrect. For the SM to stand and argue is useless and unproductive. The SM gets best results by doing

a turnaround, perhaps offering to take a second look. In this retreat, the SM moves into a strong position. The brothers see that the SM is alert, not afraid to stand up for what is needed for the show, and at the same time, they are reminded of the standard and professional quality of work the SM expects. In addition, the brothers usually clean up the deficiency brought to their attention—the SM's original goal.

Using Psychology

Maintaining a working relationship with the crew and technical department heads sometimes requires psychology. The SM can be assertive, but never show aggression or exert power or control. The SM knows when to pull back and not let ego get in the way, when to ask questions, how to point out mistakes, and when and where to tell people they are wrong. The SM is observant as the crew goes about their work, saying very little, and steps in only when a grievous mistake is about to happen that could cost time, money, or damage. The SM gives an opinion when it is important and knows when it is important to have the other person's opinions be the last word. The SM also knows when to apologize, when to admit to a lack of knowledge, or when the SM is wrong or has made a mistake. In taking this approach, the SM often gets the wanted results without feeling compromised.

Gaining Respect from the Crew

Once the show gets into technical rehearsals and performance, the SM spends most of the working time backstage. The SM and the crew work in parallel positions, each observing the other at work. From the start, department heads and crewmembers honor the SM's position. With each SM with whom the crew has not previously worked, there is a period of time during which they observe the SM's every move. They want to see if the SM knows the job and does it well. They want to see the SM's temperament, way of working with people, and just generally the kind of a person the SM is. When an SM meets with the crew's approval and gains their respect, that SM gains an army of support who will aid and assist in all technical matters and problems. They will save the SM who calls a poorly timed cue, or maybe misses a cue entirely. They will back him and defend a well-liked SM whose work is being disputed or judged and they will carry the message of good work to the SM's superiors. On the other hand, if their respect for the SM is less than 100 percent, they will continue to respect the position, continue to do their jobs to the highest professional degree, never do anything to hurt the show, but they will not lend their aid, support, or backing during the times when the SM might need it most.

Technicians and Artists: Sometimes a Gulf or Separation

Both the cast members and members of the crew are highly social and enjoy having a good time. It is rewarding for the SM to see the cast and crew mixing and socializing. Sometimes, however, there seems to exist an unspoken separation or hidden gulf between the two. The feelings may arise when the SM least expects it. It may occur between two people or one group against the other.

A major cause for this gulf or separation lies in the appearance that the performers seem to get preferential treatment. Perhaps from the crew's point of view, the cast appears to be pampered and gets more time to do their work, receives more credit for the success of the show, and is rewarded in more demonstrative ways. The technicians get a moment of thanks, but then seem to be forgotten for their continuous work, and sometimes taken for granted. The gap is widened further when the cast members act and behave as if they are privileged and are the center of the production. There is not much an SM can do to change this interaction, except to be watchful, heading off potential situations, or sooth over moments before they have time to fester and grow. The SM can also create good relations by continually extending to the crew praise and thanks, both personally and publicly. The SM might also suggest the director and producer to do the same.

Saving Face

In the world of relationships, the terms *caretaking* and *rescuing* are in most cases negative, especially when they enable another person to continue a behavior that is harmful or destructive. SMs are continually warned against such interaction in their working relationships. It is strongly and wisely suggested that the SM keep all workers responsible for their work, behaviors, and actions. There are times, however, when it is beneficial to the show, the company, the working relationships, or just to an individual, when the SM breaks this rule and does a little rescuing or caretaking.

Steeped in tradition from Asian cultures, the SM will discover the art of *saving face* is an excellent tool in working with the technical crew and, for that matter, with all people in the company. There will be times when people have made a bad judgment, worked in error, or just plain forgotten to do a particular thing and, for whatever reasons, are unable to accept the responsibility for their actions, perhaps they are unable to face the pain of shame and embarrassment. The SM who is observant of all things sees the inner turmoil and quickly determines the severity and importance of the incident. If a little rescuing or caretaking seems beneficial, the SM can step in to help a person save face by diminishing the severity of the incident, offering resolutions or alternatives, or taking on the responsibility for the situation. Sometimes those involved are not the least bit aware of the SM's manipulation. Other times, all parties see clearly what is happening and go along, doing a little rescuing and caretaking themselves. There are times when the SM works in unorthodox ways to bring positive results that are beneficial to the show and the members of the company.

Technical Director (TD)

The TD is the lead technical position backstage, overseeing all the technical aspects of the show. The TD is in charge of the crew, has the final word on all technical matters, works out the crew's schedules, handles all the crew's business, and is responsible for technically setting up the show and taking it down at the end of its run. The TD, along with the head carpenter and head of the rail, works out the logistics of the scenery changes. During the performance the TD oversees, while the carpenter and railhead work with their crews to execute the cues for the scene changes. Most always, the SM defers to the TD's word or decision on technical matters.

However, any decisions that affect the artistic integrity of the show, and in the absence of the producer and director, the SM has the final say. Whenever possible, the artistic integrity of the show should prevail and the TD should defer to the SM. In theory this is an ideal approach. In reality the SM may run into times when the TD feels a technical decision is greater or more important than the artistic integrity and will resist deferment. If a compromise cannot be reached, the matter may have to be brought to the producer. At the end of this chapter there is a story entitled "Maintaining Artistic Integrity" that truly happened and demonstrates such a situation.

Head Carpenter

This is the technician who is in charge of the set/scenery and the stagehands who work this department. This department is responsible for putting up the set, taking it down, and keeping it in repair. Depending on the size of the show and the amount of scenery, the head carpenter may also have an assistant. On touring shows, the head carpenter travels with the show, but picks up a crew in each town, which is called the *local crew*. During the performance the head carpenter and crew execute all the scene changes, moving the scenery on and off the stage. The SM's greatest work and association with this department comes during technical rehearsals when setting cues for the scene changes. During this time, the head carpenter, the TD, and the head of the rail tell the SM the order of the cues for the movement of the scenery. The SM combines this information with the other technical cues. If there is a conflict between the scenery moves and the other technical elements, the SM offers suggestions and contributions; otherwise, the technicians lead and dictate.

TD/Head Carpenter Position Combined
On small shows or shows where the producer is working on a limited budget, the positions of TD and head carpenter may be rolled into one. The producer may pay the individual filling both positions a little more money, but still saves, especially with a touring show where travel and living expenses must be paid to each person traveling.

Head Flyman or Head of the Rail

The TD, the head carpenter, and the head of the rail all work in close association, especially when setting up the show in the theatre and when taking it down— the *drag-in* and *drag-out*. Sometimes the head flyman is also the assistant to either the TD or the head carpenter. The head of the rail is in charge of the drops, curtains, pieces of scenery, or things that hang from above the stage and fly in and out during the performance. During the drag-in, because the things that hang in the flys require the entire stage to be empty to be hung, the rail is the first department to set up.

The SM's greatest amount of work and association with this department comes during performance when calling cues. The crew members working the rail are often highly dependent on the SM for calling an impeccably well-timed show, because in the execu-

tion of many of their cues they are working *blind*— that is, they cannot see when the actors or scenery on the stage are clear and it is safe for them to pull the ropes to execute their cues. On the other hand, the SM is often in a better position to see. If the SM makes a mistake and nearly causes an accident, the head flyman and crew can be very hard on the SM. They are highly concerned about the safety of the people on stage and concerned with protecting the scenery from damage. They allow or accept very little space for error.

Head of Props (Propman, Prop Master, or Property Master)

From conversations in this book thus far, it is an established fact that there is a close working relationship between the SM and the prop department. The SM creates the prop list, is responsible during rehearsals to set up the props for the day's work, keeps both the prop master and the prop list up to date, and before each performance the SM checks to see that all props are in place after the propman has set them. Once the prop master and crew take over, the SM relinquishes control and authority over the props, but continues to keep the prop master informed of all changes. During the technical rehearsals and sometimes in the first week of performance, the prop department is often bombarded with changes or gathering more props. In addition, this department is asked to provide personal services to the star, producer, director, and even the SM—services that are not always part of the propman's job description. A good SM is aware of this, and at every opportunity offers assistance and is free in expressing thanks and appreciation to the prop department.

The Electrical Department (Lighting)

Lighting Designer
The SM's work with this department starts with the lighting designer. In the last week of rehearsals, the SM sets a time for the designer and the designer's assistant to come to the rehearsal hall to see a run-through of the show so they can begin to create the light cues. In professional shows, the SM is not responsible for anything that has to do with the light design, the light plot, the hanging of lights, or the creation of light cues; the SM's only job is to note the light cues in the calling script, as dictated by the designer, then during the performance, call the cues

with impeccable timing. Once the show opens, the designer and the designer's assistant's work is done.

Head Electrician

The SM may meet the head electrician and crew for the first time during the drag-in when the lights are being hung for the show. To hang the lights for a show, the electrical department, like the fly department, needs to have an empty stage. The electrical department is also first in setting up, sharing the empty stage and time with the fly department.

Light Board Operator

Before computers were used to execute the light cues during the performance, the light boards were large and bulky and required several light board operators. The light board operators would include the head electrician, an assistant, and a number of crewmembers, depending on the size of the show and the number of cues to be executed. Today, the head electrician or assistant are the only individuals needed to operate the lights for the show.

The lighting and movement of lights during a performance is a highly visible thing to the audience and can have a great effect on them emotionally and psychologically. The timing and execution of light cues become very important to the show and mistakes in this area can take away from the performance. When the old light boards were used, the operators manually worked the levers that faded the lights in and out. Their timing was just as important as was the SM's in calling the cues. It was very important that the SM and the head light board operator not only have a good working relationship, but also be connected to each other's timing.

Today, with the computer having programmed into it the timing for the movement of the lights, this simpatico relationship between SM and light board operator is not as important and has become more one-sided, with the light board operator merely punching a key on the SM's cue. It is the light board operator's job and responsibility to follow the SM's lead. At the end of this chapter there is another story entitled "Electrical Storm," which shows what can sometimes happen in the working relationship between the SM and the light board operator.

Spotlight Operators

Spotlights are almost always used in musical shows. The operators usually are brought in during the last few days of technical rehearsals, once most of the light cues and scene-change cues for the show have been set. The lighting designer and director set the spotlight cues with the operators. Sometimes they will make the spotlight operators responsible for executing their cues on their own during the performance. Other times the lighting designer or director wants the SM to call all spotlight cues. Calling spotlight cues adds considerably to the SM's workload during a performance. In a show with many cues to call, the SM welcomes the times when the spotlight operators execute their own cues, but when the lighting designer or director decides the SM must call them, the SM is professionally bound to do as they choose.

The SM Assisting the Electrical Department

On some touring shows where the time between one city to the next is short and the setup of the show must be done within a limited number of hours, the SMs may be asked to assist the electrical department in focusing the lights—that is, help in setting the lights so they shine down on the stage in the proper place, lighting the areas they were designed to cover. The SM's job is to stand on the stage in the center of each area where the light is to shine, and tell the stagehand above who is adjusting the light when the hot spot or most intense part of the light is shining into the SM's eyes.

The SM's Working Knowledge of Lighting

Every SM, whether calling light cues for a simple, one-set comedy or for a major musical, should have a good artistic sense of the design of the lights and execution of the light cues. Knowing the technical setup is helpful, but not imperative to the SM's work. While in the academic environment, a person considering becoming an SM should take one or two lighting courses. While in the professional arena, the SM should ask as many questions as necessary to learn more. The lighting designer, head electrician, or any crewmember in this department is more than willing to share knowledge and expertise with someone who expresses interest in this department.

The Sound Department and Head of Sound

As documented in Chapter 6, Hard Copy, the SM's working relationship with the sound department begins early in rehearsals by providing a list of sound effects for the show and keeping the sound department informed of additional sound effects, the timing of the effects, or any changes the director might make. The head of this department may also be the designer, the person who does the recording, and the person who operates the sound during the show, or there may be a different person for each job. During performance, the SM works closely with the person operating the sound. This is the person who executes the sound effect cues the SM calls. In addition, the sound operator *mixes* the sound, controlling the levels of the various mics being used on the stage.

During the setup of a show, the sound department often waits until most of the other technical equipment is set on stage before they lay in their own. Being nearly the last to set up, sometimes when the other departments run into a problem they cut into the sound department's setup time. By this time, according to the schedule, the show should be ready to rehearse or even go into performance. It is the SM's job to be watchful, pushing to bring the work back on schedule, regardless of the problems that have existed. During this time, the SM must approach the sound department with caution and diplomacy. They know they are behind and the SM's presence is an added pressure. An SM who is not careful may bear the brunt of the frustration and anger of the head of sound or the crew.

I.A.T.S.E.: The Stagehand's Union

We cannot talk about technicians, stagehands, or the crew members, without having a word about their union. Actor's Equity is to the performers as I.A.T.S.E. is to the stagehands. This union is strong, tolerating little to no bending or infractions of its rules and agreements made with the producers.

An SM's dealings with this union are limited to knowing rules and regulations governing work hours, breaks, mealtime, overtime, golden hours (which means double pay, sometimes triple), and knowing when penalty payments go into effect. A young SM just out of academic or community theatre learns quickly not to do any technical work, even if it's simply to pick up a broom to help sweep. The union's thinking is that if someone other than a union member needs to lend a hand, then the producer needs to hire another union member to handle the workload.

Costume/Wardrobe Department

The costumes for a show are either created by a designer and made from scratch or they are chosen from racks at a costume shop/house and rented. While in this stage, these garments are referred to as *costumes* and seldom as *wardrobe*. It is not until they have been assembled, tailored to fit the various performers, and are at the theatre ready to be used, that the term *wardrobe* is more commonly used. The wardrobe department on a small show may consist of a party of one. On a large musical, there may also be an assistant along with dressers.

Designer and Head of Wardrobe

During rehearsals, the SM works in close association with the costume designer and costume shop. The SM schedules the performers, first for measurements, then for fittings as the costumes are ready for the performers to try on.

The SM's working relationship with the head of wardrobe begins once the costumes are at the theatre. This relationship goes into full swing at the start of technical rehearsals, continuing until either the show closes or the SM leaves the job. During technical rehearsals the SM and head of wardrobe will be in continuous communication, discussing dressing rooms, placement of costumes backstage during the performance, and quick changes areas. Once the show opens and is in its run, cleaning and repair of the wardrobe is a high priority, along with assembling costumes for the understudies.

Dressers

The SM has very little business with the dressers. The head of wardrobe handles all their assignments and business. The dressers are almost always local people who do this work professionally. If a dresser travels with a show it more than likely is the *star dresser*. The dressers usually are brought in a day or two before dress rehearsal and remain until the show closes or leaves town.

Wardrobe Department: A Personal Service

The wardrobe department's primary work is to provide service, a personal service which gives the appearance of being servant's work especially when dressing another person, washing, ironing, sewing clothes, or having drinks of water waiting in the wings or in quick change rooms. Sometimes the members of the company forget and step over that illusive line between what is providing service and what is being a servant. A good SM is ever watchful of this and is ready to rectify any incidents that might occur in this area.

In theatres where there is no permanent area set up for wardrobe, the wardrobe department may occupy an extra dressing room, be shuffled off into some corner backstage, or be placed down in the basement of the theatre. If sometimes there is a shortage of thanks and appreciation for the work being done by the technical departments, this department appears to receive even less. Again, the SM makes an effort to express thanks and appreciation at every opportunity. Besides, this department is often a good source of home-baked goodies and snack foods, which can be supplied during most performances and intermissions.

The Hair Department

Wherever wardrobe is set backstage, usually the hair department is nearby, some times sharing the same space. This department too may be a party of one. Only on shows that use many wigs and require period hairstyles is an assistant brought in.

The SM may meet the head of this department once or twice during the rehearsal period, depending on the hair needs of the show. The hair department does most of its work before the cast comes in for each performance. At the half-hour point before each performance, the hair person must be available to fit wigs on the performers, do whatever personal hairstyles need to be done on individuals, and tend to the star's needs. During performance, the lead hair person usually works with the star, especially during quick changes, touching-up hair, pinning on hats, and offering a hand to the dressers, if needed.

For the SM, the hair department can be quiet, unassuming, and the least demanding of all technical departments. This department can be easily forgotten and, once again, the SM should be generous with thanks and appreciation.

Shops and Vendors

Each technical department deals with its own shops and vendors and handles all the business that needs to take place with them. The SM works most with the costume shop. The SM and the director may visit the shop where the set is being constructed one or two times. The SM's primary function with the other shops and vendors is to keep in the production book their addresses, phone numbers, and directions on how to get to their locations.

The Performance Site and Their Personnel

At any of these places, the SM will find a staff of some kind, ranging from one person, to a full complement of people. The staff may include a backstage crew, as well as front-of-the-house staff, security, parking, and janitorial services.

Backstage: The House Crew

The group of stagehands who are hired full-time by a particular theatre or performance site is called the *house crew*. Their job is to head and maintain the various technical departments of the theatre, and to work in association with the technical heads of the shows that come to their theatre.

The SM's working relationship with the house crew is the same as it is with all technical people we have discussed in this chapter. There is, however, one difference; the SM and the rest of the company must keep in mind that they are guests of the theatre and house crew. The house crew welcomes shows into their theatre. This is how their jobs are maintained. They are used to having shows take over their facility while they remain watchful and protective of their home. Sometimes the house crew is overprotective, keeping things under lock and key. However, the SM and TD of the show keep in mind that the producer of their show has paid for the privilege of being at that theatre and has made arrangements to use some or all of their equipment. If a certain item or piece of equipment is withheld and there is doubt or uncertainty as to its use, or if the house crew says there will be an extra charge for a particular item, either the SM or TD should be on the phone with the producer.

Front-of-the-House Staff
The Box Office. If a company manager is with the show, the SM has little to no dealings with the box office. If not, the SM's working relationship with this group is still limited, perhaps only setting up or approving *comps* (complimentary tickets), making reservations for house seats for the cast and crew, and sometimes cashing personal checks, either the SM's or other cast members'.

On a touring show and in the absence of the producer or company manager, the SM becomes the producer's representative and liaison with the box office. On occasion the SM may have to deal with receipts of the day or the week. The action of this business is highly regulated by law and is usually a matter of receiving certified paperwork or a cashier's check.

The House Manager.   There are two things with which the SM must be concerned when working with the house manager. First is to post the Equity *casting board.* This board lists the performers' names and the roles they are playing in the show. It is an Equity rule that the casting board be placed somewhere in the lobby in clear view of the audience as they enter the theatre. Most times the ASM is responsible for seeing that this board is properly placed. To do this, the SM talks with the house manager, who usually provides a stand or easel and already has a perfect spot picked out that meets all Equity requirements.

The second thing the SM must do in working with the house manager is to establish a communication at the half-hour point, before the performance is to start. Each theatre and house manager has its own procedure in communicating with the SM to get the house opened, and each SM has a preferred way of working during this time. The SM and house manager must get together and work out what is best. Both the SM and house manager make a great effort to start the show on time or at least to be no more than five minutes late. The house manager also works to seat everyone before the rise of the curtain. For those patrons who arrive after the curtain is up, the house manager establishes with the SM the best time to seat these people without disturbing the performance.

At the beginning of the half-hour before the show is to begin, the SM needs to inform the house manager that all is ready backstage, and the audience can now be seated. If there is some problem backstage, the SM asks the house manager to delay opening the house, either for a certain amount of time or until the SM calls the house manager again. Once the house is opened, usually the SM does not communicate with the house manager again until the five-minute call before the performance is to start. At this time both parties agree that all can run according to schedule, or either can ask for a delay, should there be a last-minute problem backstage or if the audience is late in arriving and being seated. Some SMs like to know the approximate size or percentage of the audience attending. They will ask for this information at this time and enter it into their show report and/or log book.

A very large percentage of house managers are good at their work and diligent in communicating with the SM at the prescribed times. A few will be less responsible. The SM learns within two or three performances which kind of house manager is in charge. When working with the lesser kind, the SM reestablishes the calling procedure. If the house manager remains delinquent and does not communicate, especially at the five-minute call, the SM must then inform the house manager that, if a call is not received, the show will start as scheduled.

In Closing

To varying degrees and in different ways, everyone in the company and associated with the production is important and needed, or you can be sure the producer would not have them there, paying that particular salary. People need to receive recognition and validation for their work and want their stars to shine. In seeking out ways to have these needs met, some people's behavior becomes filtered through their feelings, fears, and beliefs, making them act in ways that are not always professional and acceptable. The SM, more than the producer or director, is confronted each day with the different behaviors people bring to their work. It is therefore important for SMs to understand the general profile of the people with whom they must work. The more knowledgeable and aware SMs are in the psychology and behavior of people working in the theatre and of themselves, the more prepared and equipped they are to deal with whatever arises within the company. SMs who are healthily centered within themselves will find the job less stressful, things will run more smoothly, and they will have longevity as SMs.

THE PROFESSIONAL EXPERIENCE

Throughout a career, each SM collects a number of stories about colleagues. A collection of these could easily fill a volume. Here are only a few.

This first entry is a personal account of how an SM's old belief system, which got established in the first years of his life, got in the way of his work, dictated his actions, shaded his behaviors, and clouded his way of thinking. In addition, his old belief system had great effects on his working relationships, left him with ill feelings, and in general, tarnished the love he had for his work.

Personal Beliefs

For the first three years of my life I was raised in a Catholic orphanage. It was a time when the good nuns believed if the child was picked up and responded to each time he cried, he would be spoiled. Consequently, I spent many hours each day feeling lonely and crying out for attention. It felt as if no one ever responded to me. During those years I formulated in my mind that no matter how long or how loud I cried out, people did not hear me. Even worse, I took it personally. For sure, I did not feel the universe revolved around me.

These things became a truth in my mind and an indelible part of my belief system. Unwittingly, I carried them into adulthood. As an SM, it affected the way I worked and reacted. I became irate when people kept me waiting or showed up late for a rehearsal, even when it was the director or producer. It felt personal and I was compelled to confront them as I spoke from a center of anger. I could get away with this kind of behavior as I worked with late actors, but producers, directors, and stars were not as accepting. Most did not fight back or call me down for my behavior, but I eventually saw that they just didn't hire me again.

My beliefs manifested themselves in other ways, too. When members in the company failed to follow instructions, I felt unheard, misunderstood, even ignored. These feelings did not make sense, but I felt them anyway. To distance myself from these feelings and to ensure relief, I became pedantic in my words and nagging in my approach. I did not allow people to do their jobs without my watching over them every moment. It was tiring working this way and it certainly did not help me in my relationships. I was of the mind and attitude that I could not trust anyone to do their jobs. That angered me, because as an SM I had enough to do with my own work.

My beliefs carried over into my life during the times I was unemployed. I'd send out many resumes. If I didn't get a response quickly, my old belief system would kick in and the words would ring out clearly in my head that people do not respond to me. The feelings were just as strong as they had been back in the orphanage. I'd become despondent, give up, and withdraw. Here I was an adult, a professional SM acting, behaving, and believing like a child. I was unhappy with myself and with being a SM. I blamed everyone and everything around me. It wasn't until I journeyed into myself to explore and discover the things that made me feel bad that I came to know why I thought and acted as I did. It wasn't until I found the spiritual center inside of me that I found peace, contentment, and acceptance. I continue to work as an SM. I relish the good times even more now, and during the not-so-good times I remain centered and healthy. I have made changes in my life, and my love for theatre and the work I do is renewed.

A Central Dance Figure

When profiling choreographers in this chapter, I was about to begin this section by borrowing from Will Rogers to say there wasn't a choreographer I met who I didn't like. Then I remembered one particular choreographer and changed my mind. However, of all the rest, "There isn't a choreographer with whom I have worked, I didn't like."

Each day this choreographer brought with him a cloud of doom, and a field of negative energy. He had none of the gypsy spirit other choreographers brought to rehearsals. Nothing was ever good enough for him, including his dancers. He demanded from the SMs more attention, service, and more time on the schedule than was afforded the director. He had danced on Broadway and at the peak of his career danced in a famous show in which the dancers in the show were as much stars as were the lead roles. He remained with the show for its run on Broadway, moving into the lead dance position and also becoming dance captain. He spent many more years doing national and regional tours of the show, often recreating the choreography and sometimes directing the show himself. On our production, he was the choreographer while another person was hired to direct.

This choreographer had an air of importance, which he made no effort to disguise. He was painstakingly indulgent in recreating the dances and drilled his dancers, demanding perfection before he'd move on to the next section. It was evident from the first day of rehearsals the director and this choreographer would not get along. They let their annoyances and disagreements build without confrontation. Instead, they placed the SM in the middle, each making demands on the schedule and for preferential treatment. As the SM, I went to the producer to apprise him of the situation and the effect it was having on the rehearsals and the company. He already knew. Many of the dancers had come to him to complain. The producer assured me he'd take action on the matter. A week went by, I saw no change. By this time we had only a few more days in the rehearsal hall before we moved into technical rehearsals at the theatre. By the final dress rehearsal, the choreographer was still setting dance. It was a hardship and nightmare for all, it caused tension within the company, and it took the joy and excitement out of the opening night. The show opened and the choreographer, above all others, got great reviews.

Star Power

This is the story of a star with whom I regretfully never worked. This story was told to me by a producer in whose theatre the show performed in Los Angeles. It was one of those shows that would have never played on Broadway nor toured the country if it hadn't been for its star performer.

Through the years this renowned star suffered many ailments and afflictions that were debilitating if not cared for and attended to daily. She had done most of her work in films, where she could stop working throughout the day when she felt ill. To work in theatre, the temperature backstage had to be sixty-five degrees—at seventy degrees she was unable to perform. At this particular theatre in Los Angeles, the temperature of the air conditioning backstage could not be turned down without the temperature in the audience also being turned down. Sixty-five degrees was, of course, too cold for the audience. This put the producers in a disabling bind: no audience, no show; no sixty-five degrees backstage, no star performer; no star performer, still no show; no show, no box office receipts. With the possibility of no box office receipts, the producers were quick to put the mother of invention to work. They had a special refrigeration truck parked outside at the back of the theatre and had pumped into the backstage area all the frigid air that was needed. I was told, "It was like a meat storage locker."

It was summer in Los Angeles, but the cast and crew backstage were wearing their winter clothes. People were continually coming down with colds. Paranoid of catching the cold herself, the star insisted the people with colds not come to work until they were better. The dancers seemed to suffer the most. No matter how warmly they dressed or how much they moved and stretched, they could not keep their bodies warm enough to prevent injury. The performers complained individually, in pairs, in groups, and as a company—first to the SM and then to the producers. The producers expressed their sympathy but confessed there was nothing they could do without losing the star. The performers took the matter to Equity. They argued the working conditions were unbearable, injurious to their health, and beyond what was acceptable to Equity in any other situation. They were right. However, in Equity's research they heard testimony from both the star's physicians as well as independent physicians who all said the star could not perform if the temperature was raised. Equity agreed and stated to its members that the temperature backstage must remain. In fairness to everyone, the performers who felt they could not work under these conditions were offered to be released from their contracts with two weeks' pay. Only two dancers left—they had another show to go to. The star and her power continued to make the show a financial success and when she left the show it fell into obscurity.

Baby June's Mom: Mamma Rose

It was a regional production of the musical *Gypsy*. The role of Baby June is cast with two actresses—one playing a young Baby June and the other playing a Baby June in her teen years. Both actresses need to know how to sing, dance, and do high kicks. The actress hired to play the younger Baby June had performed the role many times before and was expert in the part. Her only problem was that she was slick in her movement and robotic in her acting. She performed the part with physical perfection, but had no heart or sole. Directors in other productions accepted what she had to offer, but our director wanted more. In trying to bring her to a more human level of character and performance, the director continually gave the child acting notes in this direction. The parents of the children were allowed to come into the rehearsal room to watch a run-through of the show and then stay for notes from the director. Each time the director gave young Baby June a note, the child looked to her mother. This stage mother was similar in drive and abrasiveness as was Baby June's mother in the play, Mamma Rose. However, this mother had none of the charm and fun of Mamma Rose. When the director gave her daughter an acting note, she would roll her eyes in annoyance or shift her body in disapproval. For a while the director pretended not see this. Finally he spoke to her. As he spoke, she remained cold, silent, and distant. From then on, whenever the director gave Baby June a note, the actress stared straight ahead while the mother stiffened in her chair. Finally one day the mother cracked. "STOP IT!!!!!" she shouted. "How dare you give this child these notes? She has done over one thousand performances of this role. She has tried to give you what you want, but you keep attacking her. Your notes are senseless and unfounded! Could you not feel the electricity in this room this afternoon when she performed. Every eye was on this child as she performed! What is it that you want?????"

At first the director was taken back by the outburst, then he laughed. "I have this feeling that our production of *Gypsy* is only a play within a play, and that you are the real Mamma Rose and that this is the real show." Then as he walked out, he turned to the SM and ordered for all to hear, "Have her out of here before I return."

The director left, but the woman did not budge. By this time her daughter was crying. The SM finally approached the mother saying nothing, but indicating that she leave. "I'm not going. If I go, she goes!" The SM didn't want or need any more fallout from this incident. "Look, you're upset right now. This is a matter better handled up in the producer's office. Why don't we go up there and you can work things out with him. As for your daughter, I think it is better she stays here so we can finish our work." The mother would not go unless her daughter went with her. You could see the daughter was terribly embarrassed and did not want to go, but she obeyed. Neither was seen again. Two days later a new young Baby June was brought in. This Baby June had also performed the role may times before, and yes, she too came with a stage mother. However, this mother was more reasonable, realistic, and less driven. She took acting notes with grace and worked toward getting a better performance from her daughter.

Maintaining Artistic Integrity

In the musical stage version of *Meet Me in St. Louis* there is a famous scene and song where Esther Smith sings about and talks with "The Boy Next Door," John Truitt. In this particular touring production, John's house is stored off stage right and rolled on to the stage from the number one wing. Similarly, Esther's house is stored off stage left and rolled on from the number one stage left wing. John's house was the smaller unit and covered one-third of the stage, while Esther's house covered the rest. As each unit came together in view of the audience, it covered the interior set of Esther's house. It was an artistic and effective transition from one scene to the next.

With Esther's house being the larger unit, this meant more space off stage left was needed to store the unit and to move it on and off stage. At some theatres the backstage area was very limited. The first time we encountered such a situation, the technical director creatively altered the set by not putting together all the pieces of Esther's house. He left off a good portion of the porch, putting in its place some lattice work and greenery. Artistically, the alteration left something to be desired, but for small theatres it was the best we could do.

The TD also found that setting up only half of Esther's house made the crew's setup time shorter and workload easier. This was especially beneficial when moving into a new theatre where the scenery arrived late or when the setup time was cut down considerably. As we progressed through the tour, the TD took advantage of this fact more and more, even in situations where the space off stage left was ample and we had plenty of time to set up the whole house.

I preferred using the full set. It looked better and maintained the artistic design and integrity of the designer and the show. As the SM, I spoke with the TD using a textbook approach and expressed my preference. I could tell from the start the TD disagreed with me. He argued with many points, but none were strong enough to convince me differently. Before ending the conversation, I recapped my feelings and desire to have the full house set up in every situation where it could be set up. I was left with the feeling that the TD was going to do as he chose, and he did! I approached him again on this matter. He told me to "lighten up" and stop being such a "stickler." At the next theatre where there was plenty of space and time and still he set up only half of the house, I approached the TD for the third and last time. "As the stage manager I am responsible for maintaining the artistic integrity of the show. That includes the work the creators have done, the designers, the director, and the work the actors do each performance. I want the full house set up before this evening's performance and in every other theatre where the whole house can be used. If you disagree, I suggest you call the producer so we can get this straightened out." The TD looked at me for a moment then walked away. I was not sure what he was going to do. I watched and waited. All that afternoon he had the crew work on everything but the house. At fifteen minutes before the crew was to break for dinner, I heard the TD ask two of the carpenters to stay over during their meal break to put up the rest of the house.

A week or so later, I got a call from the producer. He wanted to know why he had to pay meal penalty and overtime for two carpenters to put up the house. He had been told by the TD that I had ordered it. It is during these moments the SM's metal is put to the test. I was able to stay in the adult part of myself, but the child within me was kicking and screaming, wanting to express how I truly felt. With adult composure, I presented my side of the story. The producer agreed with me. He said he would talk with the TD and in the future would never work with this person again. I felt vindicated and appeased. The TD and I remained in a strained relationship for the rest of the tour. Oddly enough, personally and socially, I liked the man. Professionally, he was very good at his work. A year later we worked together again and for the same producer. This time the show played in one theatre. There was less opportunity for our opinions and wills to clash and we did fine.

Electrical Storm

In having light cues called during a performance, the light board operator is obligated to execute the cues as the SM calls them, even if the SM's timing is wrong. In all the shows I have worked and with all the light board operators whom I have called cues to, there have been three who broke this rule.

With the first light board operator, when I called the cue, and then looked up to see the transition of light on the stage, the lights did not change where I expected. "Ooops!" I thought to myself, "I better change my timing," and I did. Next performance, the lights still did not change where I expected. I questioned the operator. In this case, the operator was forthright and said he had changed both the placement of the cue and the timing. My first reaction was to be angry for having my position and authority usurped, but it was early in the run of the show and I wanted to maintain the working relationship. Instead, I asked the operator to execute the cues where I called them, and that if he had any suggestions for change, to talk it over with me, or at least inform me. He was quick to apologize and admit he was wrong.

At the next performance, as we approached this cue, I was curious to see the change the operator had made. I asked him to execute the cue where he thought it should happen. He did, and he was absolutely right! It was the perfect placement and timing. I thanked him and asked if he had any other suggestions.

The second light board operator was not as forthright. He just flatly denied he was executing a light at his own timing, even after I read him my notes from my log book detailing the three incidents I experienced. He simply told me I was wrong. His words became a personal assault and I was ready to do battle. Instead I did a turn around. I told him that I doubted I could be wrong on the three different oc-

casions, but that I would go back to see if he was right. From that point and for the run of the show, the cue and all other cues were executed as I called them, even when I mistakenly called a cue with the wrong timing and the light board operator knew it was wrong.

The third experience was the worst of all. I had been brought in on a show that had been touring Europe. The show was a rock musical and, coincidentally, the light board operator was a would-be rock musician. Though the SM before me called the cues for the performance, she didn't seem to mind having the light board operator do as he chose. I, on the other hand, want to remain responsible for the timing, be it right or wrong. In the six months before I came to the show, the light board operator changed the timing of many of the cues, especially in the musical numbers. In addition, in some performances he would add cues or leave cues out. I was appalled at such unprofessional behavior. I didn't think this was the way they worked in Europe. In fact, I was impressed with how similarly the European and American stagehands worked. I worked in textbook fashion in approaching this operator, but to no avail. He told me not to worry. I then decided to learn the operator's timing. As soon as I learned to call a cue where he was executing it, he would change it. He just didn't want me invading his musical and artistic expression. The producer and lighting director were not moved by my complaint of him—in fact, they saw me as an unhappy, discontented SM. I decided to live with the situation, but found it extremely difficult to sit backstage and call light cues and have that part of my job usurped from under me. Calling cues was the only artistic contribution I made to the show. I enjoyed calling an impeccable, well-timed show. I lost interest, my mind would wander, and at times I would forget to call a cue, knowing it would happen anyway. However, through the headset I would hear in a very stern and Germanic voice, "Mr. Stage Manager, you didn't call the cue." For that reason and many other reasons with that show, I soon became the unhappy and discontented SM, and eventually I was asked to leave.

8

Running Auditions

Auditions are the forum for actors to present their talent to get jobs, a way for producers to find talent to fit their productions, and a part of the SM's job which at first glance appears simple. Like most of the work an SM does, auditions require a great deal of organization and detail, otherwise the audition can become an embarrassment for the SM, the director, and most of all for the producing company. Equity and the actors often get their first impression of a producing company from what they experience at the audition. Auditions are created and tailored to suite the producing company's needs. They are also set up for the actor. It is the SM's job to service both, each in their own way, meeting each of their needs. With most auditions, the time, date, and place is set well in advance and the SM is brought in a week before—sometimes in less time. An SM who works for a producing company on a regular basis may be asked to take on some of the responsibility of placing the ads and finding audition space.

THE EQUITY FIELD REPRESENTATIVE

An audition for a professional show will usually have an Equity field representative present. This representative is there primarily to see that the Equity rules governing auditions are followed. The rules are fairly simple and are stated in detail in the Equity rulebook. If the audition is *open*, which means no appointment times are set, the field rep has the actors sign in, keeps them gathered in the reception area, and sees that they are taken in to the audition room in the order in which they signed in on the list. If the auditions are set by appointment, the rep still has the actors sign in, but sees that they are taken in according to the order of their appointments. In having the actors sign as they arrive, the rep sees that all Equity members are auditioned first, putting the non-Equity members on

another list, telling them they must wait. The rep is also there to see that the Equity members auditioning are in good standing with the union.

The SM welcomes having the Equity field rep at the auditions. In the absence of the field rep, the SM is required to do the field rep's work, following the same procedure and rules. With the presence of the field rep, the SM is free to lead the actors in and out of the audition room and can also sit in on the audition to watch. Otherwise, as one actor is auditioning, the SM needs to be out in the reception area signing up arriving actors and having the next actor ready to enter the audition room.

THE AUDITIONING STAFF

In some cases, the auditioning staff may be comprised of the SM and one other person which could be the producer, director, or a casting director. In other situations, it can be a party of many, consisting of people from the producer's office, the director and an assistant, the casting office, the writers, and if the show is a musical, the choreographer, music director, composer, and rehearsal pianist. The SM needs to know who will be viewing the auditions so tables can be set up in the audition room where the auditioning staff can sit, spread out their papers, and make notes as each actor auditions.

TYPES OF AUDITION CALLS

The Open Call or Cattle Call

For any show being produced under the Equity umbrella, producers are required to have an Equity open call. Equity open calls are designed to give all Equity members the opportunity to audition for all roles in the show. Advertisements for these auditions inform the actors of the day, time, and place. With the number of actors looking for work, this means the SM needs to be organized and prepared, ready to handle and process a large number of actors. Within the time advertised, the actors come at their convenience. At an open call the SM should also be prepared to have a number of non-Equity actors wanting to audition. Some will become annoyed or upset when they are asked to wait until all the Equity actors have auditioned first. Open calls for musicals and shows that are popular and promise long employment often turn into what actors call cattle calls. The term is derived in part from the number of actors who show up, but gets its name mostly from the way the actors feel as they are herded through the audition. At such auditions, the audition staff quickens the audition process by shortening the amount of time the actors can spend auditioning and interviewing. Sometimes the actors may not even get into the audition room because someone from the auditioning staff may first weed out a good number of actors by keeping only those who physically fit the roles being cast.

Auditions by Appointment

In addition to the open call, producing companies will also have auditions that are set by appointments. Most of the time, the actors coming to these auditions are coming with a certain role in mind. The appointments usually are set up by agents, managers, casting directors, or by the producer who knows an actor's work and asks that person to audition. The SM still needs to be organized and ready to handle the actors as they arrive. However, the pace is slower and the SM, along with the audition staff, spends more personal and social time with each actor. Seldom do these auditions run on schedule, according to the appointed times. At the beginning of the day the audition staff is more cavalier with the amount of time they spend with each actor. Only after some reminders from the SM will they quicken their pace.

Auditions for Musicals

For the actors auditioning for a musical, the procedure is the same as described above. For the SM, some audition calls for a musical become a test of skills. With musicals there is more of everything—more actors, more roles to be cast, more auditioning staff, more audition rooms, more coordinating, and more traffic flow.

Singing Auditions for a Role

Actors auditioning for a musical must, of course, be able to sing. Before any actors audition with an acting scene, they must first pass as singers. If the audition staff thinks the actor's singing is what they want for the show, the SM is asked to take the actor out to the reception room, hand out a copy of a particular scene, have the actor look it over, and return in a few minutes to audition with the scene. Meanwhile, the SM continues the auditioning process by bringing in and out of the room more actors to sing, some of whom will also be asked to audition with a scene.

Ensemble Auditions

At one time, most auditions for the ensemble performers (chorus singers and dancers) were two separate auditions—the singing auditions and the dance auditions. Singers did not have to know how to dance, just move about the stage with grace and ease, and dancers did not have to know how to sing, just have an ability to carry a tune. Shows having a choral or legitimate/operatic sound are more apt to have separate auditions and not require singers to dance and dancers to sing. This includes shows like *Oklahoma*, *Brigadoon*, *Kismet*, *Kiss Me Kate*, or *Phantom of the Opera*. However, shows with more contemporary themes like *West Side Story*, *Cabaret*, *Chicago*, *Grease*, or *A Chorus Line* make it imperative that the ensemble performers know how to sing *and* dance extremely well.

Today, despite the type of show being produced, many producers around the country, in both large and small productions, find it financially agreeable to their budget to hire singers who can dance and dancers who can sing. Those who don't do both are finding it harder to get regular employment.

For the SM, ensemble auditions can be very simple, with the dancers and singers having separate auditions on different days. In other situations, where the ensemble auditions are all in one day, the SM may end up moving and shuffling people from one part of the audition to the other. During those times, the SM will need help, either from an ASM or from a knowledgeable and experienced production assistant.

Dance auditions are easiest for the SM. The SM needs only a room with a floor that meets Equity approval, a piano, and a pianist. Sometimes the choreographer will have the music on tape or CD. The dancers come at one time. After the SM has signed them in, gathered their pictures and resumes, and has herded them into the audition room to learn the dance combination, the SM can rest. During this time the SM often watches the audition and aids the choreographer in sorting out the pictures and resumes as each dancer performs the combination. Singing auditions for the ensemble performers are the same as for other singers in the show.

STAR AND LEAD ROLE AUDITIONS

Stars seldom go through auditions. If they do, the SM is not needed. Only on rare occasions does the SM get to sit in on a star audition. The audition more than likely is held privately with the producer and/or director. If the show is a musical, the session may be more informal, with the star coming to listen to the score and sing some of the songs. However, when auditioning the other lead roles in the show, the SM is needed to perform the same duties as with other auditions. The only difference is that some of these actors may be of semi-star status and actors known for their excellent work. These auditions are often scheduled allowing a lot more time between each actor. The interview portion is more social, and the actor is given preferential and star-like treatment.

ACTORS' REPRESENTATIVES

Actors will sometimes show up with their representative such as an agent, manager, or if a child/teenager under legal age, a parent. Representatives show up mostly at auditions that are set by appointments. The reps are, of course, there in the interest of their client or child and go through measures large and small to see that their person gets preferential treatment and strong consideration. The SM is gracious to all and tries to accommodate all requests these reps might make, but is careful to remain within the rules of Equity and the structure of the procedure being followed for that day. In all cases, the reps want entry into the audition room where they can schmooze and sell their client in the way they know best. Before such auditions begin, the SM should ask the audition staff how they want the reps to be handled. Some audition staffs prefer the rep, especially a parent, to

wait outside during the audition, then invite the rep in to talk afterwards.

AUDITIONS FOR THE NON-EQUITY ACTOR

At practically every audition, actors who are not members of Equity will show up wanting to audition. Some will be highly professional, perhaps belonging to some other actor's union. Others will be young and inexperienced, hoping to be discovered. Equity regulations require that all Equity members be auditioned first. If during the day there is a lull and there are no Equity actors waiting, the SM informs the auditioning staff and starts bringing in some of the non-Equity actors until more Equity actors arrive. In consideration for those who are members of another actor's union, the SM might put those individuals at the head of the non-Equity list.

PREPARING FOR THE AUDITIONS

An SM's work begins as soon as the SM is brought in to work the auditions. More than likely, the ads have already been placed and the time, date, and location of the audition have been set. The SM's first point of business is to talk with the person heading or leading the auditions to see how the auditions should be set up and conducted.

Becoming Familiar with the Script

The SM needs to become familiar with the script as part of the preparation for auditions. The SM needs to read the script over several times, learning the storyline, becoming familiar with the characters, listing on paper their particular traits and making a list of possible audition scenes.

Communicating with the Audition Site

The SM needs to call the audition site to talk with the people in charge. After introductions the SM confirms or establishes the following things:

- Time(s), date(s), and type and amount of space.

If the auditions are being held in a theatre:

- Time the theatre will be opened (hopefully an hour before the auditions begin so the SM can set up).
- Is an I.A.T.S.E. electrician required to put on the lights, and if so, has it been arranged for the electrician to be there at least twenty minutes before the auditions are to begin?
- Parking for the audition staff.
- Have arrangements been made to set up an audition table in the audience with electrical power, a light (on and off switch), and a microphone (also with an on and off switch)? Will it be set up and operational at least twenty to thirty minutes before the audition staff arrives?
- Access stairs from the stage to the audience.

If the audition is taking place somewhere other than in a theatre:

- Are there three or four banquet-type tables available along with chairs which can be set up in the reception room and audition room?
- Is there a copy machine on the premises available for use? In asking this question the SM assures that all copies will be paid for and also finds out the charge for each copy.
- Is there a time, prior to the day of the auditions, when the SM can come to look over the audition site?
- Can the SM come the day before to set up? If not, on the day of the audition it is imperative the SM be allowed in at least an hour before auditions begin.
- Heating in the winter, air-conditioning or air-flow fans in the summer.
- Bathroom facilities and fresh drinking water.

When doing auditions for a musical show:

- Is there a piano in the audition room, and has it been tuned?
- If on the day of auditions, the producer decides an additional room is needed, would there be one available at the last minute? If not, the SM needs to ask the producer what will be needed and if the producer thinks a second room should be reserved in advance.

If dancing is part of the audition:

- In meeting up with Equity regulations, are the floors in the audition room made of wood, and not slick tile, or cement?
- If the dancing audition room is separate from the room in which the actors are auditioning

songs or scenes, is there also a piano (tuned) in that room?

Office Supplies

The list of supplies is short and seems almost not worth mentioning, but in the middle of the auditions, a paper clip or rubber band becomes very important:

Pencils: For the actors to fill out the producer's required paperwork and for the audition staff to use at the audition table.

Pencil sharpener: The SM either has many sharpened pencils in supply or has a pencil sharpener available.

Stapler and paper clips: The resume gets stapled to the back side of the actor's picture, while the producer's information sheets get clipped to the resume and picture.

Rubber bands: At the end of the day there will be packets or piles of pictures and resumes—the rejects, the callbacks, various roles, and so on. At the end of the day they will need to be held together for transporting or filing.

8½ x 11 writing tablets/pads: Placed on the audition table for the audition staff to use if they choose.

Blank typing paper: For the SM to make last-minute signs that were not thought of in advance.

Marking pens: Wide and medium tips for correcting signs or making additional signs.

White tape: To mark the spot on the floor where the actors will stand during their audition.

The producer's paperwork: Most producing companies have an audition form which the actors are asked to fill out with personal information which is not available on the resumes.

Large manilla envelopes: To hold the various piles or packets of resumes and pictures, marking clearly on the outside the name of the packet.

If you recall from Chapter 5, Tools, Supplies, and Equipment, the SM has most of these items in the SM's bag, which is with the SM on every part of the job. However, whenever possible, the SM gets these supplies from the production office, keeping the supplies in the SM's bag as backup.

Directional Signs

Signs are easily made on the computer. They should be done simply, on 8½-by-11-inch paper, with large, bold print that can be read from several feet away, giving the name of the show, and clearly directing the actors to the reception area (see Figure 8-1). This sign can be made in advance. On the day of the auditions, if the elevator has been repaired the SM can change the directions with the use of a felt-tip marking pen.

Posting Signs

Posting no-smoking signs and designating a smoking area is good practice. It relieves the tensions surrounding this matter, giving the smokers a place to calm whatever nerves they may have about auditioning, and gives the tense nonsmokers assurance of a smokeless environment.

It is important the SM place the directional signs and the instructions sign as discussed above. The directional signs should start outside of the audition site, directing the actors to the reception area. The easier the location of the reception area is to find, the fewer the signs. The harder it is, the more signs with arrows the SM must post. If the SM is working the auditions alone, the instructions sign leaves the SM free to deal with the other things that must be done to keep the audition running smoothly.

Audition Instruction Sheet

Whether or not the SM has an assistant or expects to have the Equity rep at the audition, it is helpful to post instructions asking the actors to sign in and fill out the producer's paperwork, and giving any special instructions which need to be followed. This information

should appear on one page and the print should be larger than normal for easier reading. These instructions should be placed where the actors can see and read them as soon as they enter the reception area. If possible, the instruction sheet should be posted near the reception table, but far enough away so the actors will not crowd around the table and slow down the SM's work in processing the actors. Do not leave the instructions sheet unattached or it will be moved and misplaced in a very short time.

The Audition Sign-In Sheet

Rather than having a pad with lines, it is more professional looking and efficient to create a sign-in sheet on the computer, numbering each sign-in space, having a column for the arrival time, and a place where the actors print their names.

> *Tip:* It is important to have the actors print their names. Some signatures have become scribbles or scrawls beyond recognition and the SM does not have time to decipher the name or seek out the person.

Choosing Scenes for the Audition

Most times the scenes for the audition have already been chosen by the director or producer. In those cases, the SM makes enough copies to pass out to actors and keeps at least one copy. It is better in many ways to make copies of the scenes rather than having the actors work from full scripts. Also, if the play is new and the characters are unfamiliar, it is extremely helpful to pass out copies of a character breakdown sheet to the actors as they arrive, detailing the different characters and roles being cast.

Figure 8-1 A sign an SM might create and put up to direct the people coming to the audition, especially if the place is difficult to find within the building.

John and Mary
AUDITIONS

Rehearsal Hall #3 - 3rd FLOOR

By Appointment ONLY

Elevator OUT of ORDER.... USE STAIRWELL

John and Mary
Equity Auditions
WELCOME

PLEASE READ -- Sign-In Instructions

----

1. SIGN-IN SHEET at reception table
(Equity List and Non-Equity List)
(PLEASE PRINT)

2. Fill out AUDITION CARDS
and producer's information sheet
(PLEASE PRINT)

3. TURN IN at reception table
  - Pict. & Resume
  - Producer's audition information
  - Have Equity Membership Card ready to show.

You will be taken in the order you have signed in.
All Equity members will be auditioned first

Thank You

Figure 8-2 An instruction sheet an SM might create and put up as the actors enter the waiting area for an audition. This sign aids the SM in doing work without having to be present to monitor and lead each person through each step.

Figure 8-3 The audition sign-in sheet is designed to audition each person in the order in which they arrived. It prevents people from trying to get ahead of others, or reassures people who might feel they are being left behind while others are being taken ahead of them.

| | | | | | | **PAGE 1** |

Equity Members ONLY
Audition SIGN-IN SHEET
John and Mary

Producer:
Director:
Date:

PLEASE PRINT

#	TIME	NAME	#	TIME	NAME
1			29		
2			30		
3			31		
4			32		
5			33		
6			34		
7			35		
8			36		
9			37		
10			38		
11			39		
12			40		
ETC., ETC.			ETC., ETC.		

On occasion, when an SM has worked with a producer or director on many shows and they have come to respect the SM's artistic choices, they may ask the SM to select the scenes and do the character breakdown. These are the times when the SM must know the script and put into application some knowledge about directing. The scenes need to be simple and an exchange between two characters. The scene should run no longer than three minutes. It should feature the character who is being auditioned, and have dialogue that shows relationships, expresses feelings, and gives some range and color of the character. Scenes with exposition, action, or the use of props are poor choices.

THE AUDITION SPACE

Auditions will take place in any space the producer finds and feels is suitable to do the job. This can range from the traditional bare stage in a theatre, to a rehearsal hall, a gymnasium, a loft, an office, conference room, ballroom, hotel room, restaurant, or basement of a church. Wherever the place, whatever the situation, the SM should check out the location before the day of auditions to plan the layout of the different audition areas and think about the logistics for crowd control and efficient movement of actors. On the day of the auditions the SM should arrive at least an hour earlier to set up and be ready for the first arrivals.

Dividing the Audition Space

The audition space must be divided into separate areas—the reception area and the area(s) in which the audition takes place. The audition area(s) must be private, closed off from view of the other people auditioning, and free from the noise that might emanate from the reception area. The reception area should be nearby and can be any space in which the actors can report and wait for their turn. This could be the green room of the theatre, hallways, another rehearsal room, an alley adjacent to the theatre, or a stairwell with the actors seated on the stairs and different landings.

SETTING UP THE RECEPTION AREA

The Sign-In Table

In the reception area the SM sets up a table at the entrance that is highly visible to the act\ors as they arrive. Here they can sign in, turn in their pictures and resumes, fill out whatever paperwork the producing company requires, and get whatever instructions might be needed for the audition. This is also where the Equity rep, if there is one, sets up to work. Having a supply of pencils at this table is very helpful.

Seating

Next in the set-up of the reception area, the SM should set up chairs for as many people as will be there, or set up as many chairs as are available if a large crowd is expected, or as many chairs as the space will hold. For some auditions the reception area can become crowded and very noisy. It will be a full-time job keeping things organized and quiet. Hopefully the Equity rep will be there to help, or the SM will have an assistant; however, don't count on it! The SM should be prepared to do it all.

Toilet Facilities and Drinking Water

In consideration of the actors, bathroom facilities and drinking water is important. Most places that rent space for auditions are equipped with both. If not, the SM needs to seek out a toilet facility and have drinking water brought in.

SETTING UP THE AUDITION AREA

Whether the audition takes place in a theatre or in a room, producers, directors, and casting people who have conducted many auditions develop certain needs and preferences on how they want the room set up and how the audition should be run. Before the day of the audition, the SM should talk with the person leading the auditions to see what is needed.

The Setup in a Theatre

For auditions being held in a theatre, the actors will, of course, stand on the stage while the audition staff will sit in the audience. In this case the SM sees to it that the area in which the actors are to stand is lit sufficiently, so the auditioning staff can clearly see the actors. The stage should also be clearly marked with white tape where the actors should stand.

The Auditioning Staff's Table
The SM makes arrangements with the theatre to have placed out in the audience, midway in the orchestra

seating, a production table around which the auditioning staff can sit. In addition, the theatre needs to provide power at this table, with a light that can be made brighter or dimmer (or turn on and off) and a microphone with an on and off switch.

Access Stairs

Another detail which is often overlooked is to make sure there are stairs for easy access to the stage from the audience so pictures and resumes can be delivered to the audition staff, or any member from the audition staff can come up on the stage to personally talk with an actor.

The Setup in an Audition Room

Placement of the Staff's Audition Table

If the audition takes place in a room, the SM looks over the layout of the room. The first consideration is its length and width. If the room is long and rectangular, the audition table will be placed at one end or the other—preferably at the opposite end from where the actors will enter the room, unless otherwise directed by the leader of the audition. If the room is more square, the table can be placed on any side, taking into consideration the other factors an SM must think about in setting up the audition room.

Lighting

The next consideration is the lighting in the room. Does it come from windows? If so, it is best to place the audition table along the wall with the windows so the glare of the light will not shine into the audition staff's eyes, and at the same time will shine on the actors, for better viewing. If there are no windows, as in most rehearsal halls, the SM puts the performers in the best lighting available in relationship to the audition table. In some situations, the SM might set up some lighting with the use of clip-on spotlights or flood lamps, as long as the equipment is not intrusive or hazardous to anyone.

A Room with Mirrors

If there are mirrors in the room and they cannot be covered, the SM should make every effort not to have either the audition staff or the actors facing the mirrors. If left with no choice, and in consideration of the actors, the SM might ask the audition staff if they mind facing the mirrors as they view the actor's audition. Most times they do not mind. However, if they do mind, the SM's priority is to service the staff.

X Marks the Spot

The SM should always tape on the floor of the audition room a highly visible mark where the actors should stand to do their auditions. This mark needs to be placed just far enough away so the auditioning staff can see the actors' body movements and yet close enough to see the actors' faces and eyes.

Without this mark, the actors may stand or wander too close to the auditioning staff or stand too far back. Placing this mark relieves most of this problem. Without the mark, and with enough times of having an actor audition too close or too far back, the auditioning staff will become annoyed and more than likely ask the SM to lay in a tape mark.

The SM's Table

The SM will also need a worktable. If the SM is aided by an assistant or has the Equity rep present, the table is best placed in the audition room. From this vantage point, the SM sees both the actors and audition staff at their work and can better judge and control the time being used, and can also keep information and supplies on the desk, away from prying eyes and borrowing hands. This table is set off to the side so the SM is not intrusive or distracting to either the actor auditioning or the audition staff. The table should also be placed on the same side of the room as is the door through which the SM leads the actors in and out. This way the SM is not constantly crossing in front of the auditioning staff or the actor.

The SM might also set up a chair or small table near the door in the auditioning room or near the SM's table for the actors to place their personal belongings before they begin their auditions. If this is not available, the SM more than likely will find these things on the SM's table anyway.

If the SM is running the audition without help, the SM's worktable will be most useful if it is set up in the reception room, near the door leading into the audition room.

QUIET PLEASE! AUDITION IN PROGRESS

First and foremost, the SM's job on the day of the audition is to facilitate. The SM is expected to process each performer before entering the audition room, keep the actors flowing in and out, protect the auditioning staff from outside distractions or intrusions, and maintain quiet and order at all times. The audition staff does not want to have to wait for the SM. The SM should do all this at an accelerated and efficient rate and allow the audition staff to work at their own pace.

THE SM's ART AND CRAFT IN WORKING THE AUDITION ROOM

With each of the first few actors at the start of an audition, the SM leads the actor into the audition room, introduces the actor by name to the audition staff, and watches the audition staff's approach in greeting and beginning the audition. Performers like to have a moment of introduction, conversation, and personal contact to perhaps impress or help relieve some of the uneasiness they may be experiencing. If this is also the way in which the audition staff likes to work, the SM goes with the flow, keeping close watch on the time.

This social approach can change at any time. The SM may be told directly to cut short the social time, or may hear it indirectly by someone on the audition staff who might say, "We need to move things along." This is when the SM takes control to accelerate the process. To make the initial moment of meeting highly abbreviated and at the same time make it a smooth transition from introduction to doing the audition:

- If the SM has not already given the auditioning staff the actor's picture and resume, it is in hand as the SM enters the room with the actor. Along with the picture and resume, the SM also has a copy of the scene that will be performed.
- As the SM and actor enter the room, the SM directs the actor to place all personal belongings on the chair or table that has been set up for that purpose. As the actor is doing this, the SM takes the picture and resume to the leader of the auditioning staff, then walks to the taped spot on the floor. The SM watches the actor, and as the actor turns from placing the personal items, the SM gestures for the actor to come to the taped spot. As the actor approaches, the SM announces the actor's name and possibly the role for which the actor is auditioning. In announcing the actor's name, the SM is careful not to make this sound like an introduction that requires response from the actor, but rather a mat-

ter of protocol and information to be given to the staff.
- The SM is not abrupt and rude, but through demeanor and businesslike formality leaves no room for the actor to do something other than the actor is instructed.

If the audition is for a musical and the actor is coming in to sing:

- As the SM leads the actor in, the actor is directed to set personal items aside, and then to take the music to the pianist. The actor and pianist will need a moment or two together.
- While the actor is with the pianist, the SM gives the picture and resume to the leader of the audition and stands off to the side, usually near the SM's worktable. As soon as the pianist is ready, the SM directs the actor to stand at the taped mark and announces the actor's name.
- If the actor and pianist are taking too much time, and if the SM sees the auditioning staff becoming impatient, the SM moves things along by saying in a friendly and pleasant manner, "Folks, we need to begin the audition."

Whatever approach an SM takes in working an audition, it is important to remember that the SM is there to facilitate, keep the audition running smoothly and efficiently, service both the actor and audition staff, and at the same time be a host who is working on behalf of the producer and director. As much as possible, the SM needs to keep the auditions moving along with ease, grace, and protocol appropriate for the occasion.

SERVING THE ACTORS

In taking the host approach to the work at an audition, the SM should also see the actors as guests. As much as possible, the SM needs to greet the actors, making them feel welcome, and give them a moment or two of individual attention. To varying degrees, auditions can be stressful to actors and filled with nervousness and anxiety. It is not the SM's job to relieve the performers of their feelings, but rather, through both work and personal contact, to set up a process that is organized and easy to follow, and creates an environment that is pleasant, comfortable, and considerate of the actor.

READING THE SCENES WITH ACTORS

In most cases the SM will be reading the scene with the actors auditioning, reading both male and female roles. Most audition staffs prefer it this way. It allows them to concentrate and stay focused on the actor auditioning. The SM aids the auditioning staff by standing one or two steps further away from the actor than what is normal. The SM also stands facing away from the audition staff, and is positioned a step further downstage of the actor. This keeps the actor facing toward the audition staff.

When reading a scene, the SM should always read from a separate copy of the script and not share a copy with the actor. The SM's script should be clearly marked at the top of the first page, "SM's COPY," and should never be given out. It is annoying and frustrating to all if an SM must stop the audition process to search for another copy of the scene.

Whenever possible the SM should have the first line in the scene. Through the reading of the first line, the SM helps set the tone and energy of the scene. If the actor is nervous or inexperienced, it gives the actor the chance to respond or react first, and not have to start acting right away. If the actor is comfortable and experienced, no matter what the SM does, the actor will take the scene and run with it. Throughout the audition, the SM reads the lines with intelligence, making sense of the words, and delivers them with some of the feeling and intensity that might come from the character. As the actor auditioning responds to the SM's lines, the SM must listen and respond back, accordingly, and not just do line readings. However, the SM must at all times remember that the audition is for the actor to shine, not the SM. This is not his moment to shine as an actor. The SM must let the auditioning actor lead and take the scene in the direction in which the actor chooses, even if the SM knows it is not right for the scene.

While reading a scene in which the SM is playing a character of the opposite gender, the SM makes no effort to change his or her voice or physical style. If the moment calls for a feminine or masculine quality, the SM stays away from stereotypical affectations and simply draws from whatever masculinity or femininity we all have within.

BRINGING CLOSURE TO THE AUDITION

After the audition, the SM must continue by gracefully leading the actor out of the room. With the last line of the scene, the SM turns to the audition staff and asks if there will be anything else. If not, the SM turns to and thanks the actor for coming, leads the actor to his or her personal effects, and then to the door. As they leave the room, the SM might give the actor some kind of timeline as to when the actor might hear about a callback.

During the time the SM is leading the actor out, the audition staff goes into brief conference, evaluating the audition they have just seen and deciding if this person is to be called back. For the actors being considered for a callback, their pictures and resumes are placed in a pile for further discussion at the end of the day after all the actors have been seen. Meanwhile, the SM has the next actor ready but does not bring that actor into the audition room until the audition staff is through conferring and is ready.

YOUR BEST SIXTEEN BARS

During singing auditions when time is getting short in the day and there are still many actors waiting to audition, the audition staff may ask the SM to announce to the people waiting that when they come in, they should sing their "best sixteen bars" of music. Singers who attend many auditions have heard this phrase before. They usually are unhappy about it because they feel they are not being given a full opportunity to display their range, ability, and talent. Some will complain bitterly to the SM. What the SM needs to know is that in most auditions, sixteen bars of singing is ample time for the audition staff to make a judgment. Often within the first minute of an audition, whether singing or acting, the audition staff knows if this is a performer they want for their show.

A SECOND TIME AROUND

For most actors, auditions are fragile and delicate. The least little thing can throw them off and prevent them from giving what they feel is their best audition. It is important the SM does not contribute to this by insensitive or rude treatment. On occasion an actor may approach the SM wanting to audition again. This can become a difficult moment of judgment and decision for the SM who is sensitive to the actor's plight. If the SM has seen the individual's audition and feels the audition was unfair in some way, the SM might approach the audition staff and ask on the actor's behalf. If the actor was not right for the part, or did not meet up to the standard of the other actors auditioning, the SM will try to discourage the actor with any number of reasonable excuses. If the actor is persistent, the SM takes the issue to the audition staff and lets them decide.

> *A Standing Rule:* An SM never critiques or comments to actors on their performance in an audition—even when solicited by the actor. The SM offers an excuse about not being in a good place to judge.

SM AS TIME KEEPER

An Equity rule states if an actor is kept waiting three or more hours at an audition, the actor will be paid for that time. This rule was established because at some auditions, due to either the large number of people showing up or due to the audition staff's indulgence in taking a long time with each person, actors could be left waiting four and five hours, sometimes more. The sign-in sheet with the arrival time noted becomes the SM's guideline by which to judge the time during the audition, and it can become the actor's proof for staking a claim.

It is the SM's job to see that the actors do not wait too long or the producer has to pay the actors. All auditions run behind. Actors expect to wait a reasonable period of time. Auditions scheduled by appointment are easier for the SM to judge. At an open call audition, the SM needs to keep an eye on the number of people gathered in the audition room and the arrival times noted on the sign-in sheet, and then needs to report this information to the audition staff.

From the start the SM is watchful of the time and should begin reporting to the staff before there are too many actors waiting and there is no chance of getting caught up. The SM must be careful in the approach to the auditioning staff. These reports should be offered not as a warning, but as a statement of fact—as part of the job in keeping the staff informed: "Just to let you know we have about ten people wait-

ing." Otherwise, the SM will become an annoying intrusion, bringing news the staff does not want to hear.

With the first few warnings, the audition staff may be less responsive because it is early in the day, or they may make an effort to speed up their process, but fall back into working at a slower pace. By the third warning, the SM needs to be more impressive— something that will catch their attention; "Ladies and gentlemen I'd say we are about an hour behind. The natives are becoming restless out there and if we fall much further behind, we may have to start paying the actors for their time." If nothing else, the SM has caught the producer's attention.

Before the SM starts any of these warnings, it would be wise to know that the hold-up was not due to the SM. The SM must be working at an efficient and accelerated pace, moving actors in and out of the audition room with no time lost by keeping the audition staff waiting. Otherwise, upon the second or third report, someone on the staff will snap back, "We're only waiting on you!"

CALLBACK AUDITIONS

Actors Getting a Callback

One of the sweeter sounds an actor can hear after having done an audition is, "Are you available to return for a callback audition?" Some audition staffs can decide whether they want an actor to return as soon as they are finished seeing the initial audition. Other audition staffs prefer waiting until they have seen everyone and then at the end of the day they can be more selective.

For those actors who are told on the spot, the SM is organized, getting the actor's name on the callback list and seeing that the correct picture and resume gets put into the callback pile. Before the actor leaves the reception room, the SM gives the actor all the information necessary for the callback. For the actors who must wait until a later time, the SM tries to give a timeline as to when they can expect to hear.

All actors wish they could get a call, even if they were not chosen. With most actors this time of waiting can be filled with anxiety and the feeling that their lives have been put on hold. The SM is aware of this. The textbook choice is for the SM to call everyone. In reality and in most working situations this is not possible. Whenever there is a short list of actors who have auditioned, the SM should make an effort to call everyone.

The Spirit of Callback Auditions

At the callback auditions, the ambiance of the reception room is joyful, spirited, exciting, and filled with hopefulness. For the actors who end up getting the job, the feelings are accelerated and magnified. For those actors who don't, the feelings can plummet as low as they were high. The SM needs to be aware of both ends of this spectrum. At the beginning of the day the SM joins in the good feelings, but remains detached enough to keep the actors grounded to focus in on the work to be done and possibly use their spirit and good feelings to spur them on to doing their best. At the end of the day, the SM cannot save from their feelings those actors who did not get the part. The SM can, however, offer a good word by thanking them for their good work, and maybe even reminding them of the nature of the business.

Working the Callback Auditions

For the SM, callback auditions are set up and conducted in the same way as the initial audition. In most situations, the audition staff sees the actors individually as they did the first time. If the actor is a strong possibility, they will ask that actor to wait until they are finished with seeing all the others, possibly giving the actor a scene to study as they wait. After all the callbacks have been seen, and only the selected individuals remain, the audition process will change as the audition staff chooses. This requires the SM to be alert and ready to facilitate, implement, work out logistically, and make successful whatever it is the audition staff sets out to do. For the most part, actors will be paired off, doing scenes together or singing and dancing together.

SMs CONDUCTING THE FIRST AUDITIONS

In situations where the SM has worked on several or many shows with a producer and/or director, and has their confidence and respect for any artistic choices and judgment, the SM may be asked to hold the first auditions. Then for the callback auditions the producer and/or director will be there to see the talent.

To do this job effectively, the SM must know the show and the characters very well and should have conversations with the producer and director to see what their vision of the show is—what they are looking for and what they want. Then in holding the auditions, the SM makes choices based on their ideas and concepts. The SM is doing this job to save the producer and director time by weeding out the talent that is absolutely not right for the show. However, in the process of doing so, the SM is careful not to be too severe or critical in these choices, but instead allows a greater range of talent to give the producer and director a greater range of choice.

In the process of auditioning an actor, the SM looks for:

- **Physical qualities:** Is the performer physically right for the part? If not, would it be interesting to put this person in the role anyway?
- **Natural qualities of the actor:** The qualities the actor displays before beginning the scene and the qualities projected during the scene.
- **Truthfulness and honesty:** Does the actor work from a center within his or her own feelings?
- **Working in the moment:** Does the actor deliver the lines in response to what comes from the other character, whether it is right or wrong for the scene, or does the actor go off in a different direction, perhaps saying the lines according to a personal plan?
- **Establish a relationship:** Does the actor connect to the other character?
- **Create a character:** Does the actor start with his or her own personality, then layer on the qualities, coloring, or shading of the character? If so, how much and to what degree?

If the audition is a singing audition, chances are the music director will be present, in which case the SM lets the music director make the music judgments and the SM continues judging the acting part of the audition. If the music director is not present and if the SM is not technically knowledgeable of voices or music, the pianist helps greatly in judging the technical elements of the singer. All the qualities suggested above to the SM when auditioning an actor for a role can be applied to a singer when auditioning with a song. In addition the SM looks for:

- **The sound of the voice:** The quality and tone. Does it fit a particular character and generally fit into the show?
- **Pitch:** Does the singer stay on pitch or tend to go sharp or flat?

- **Range:** Is the singer comfortable working in several octaves or limited to one or two?
- **Endurance:** Can the singer sustain high and low notes and appear to be capable of doing eight performances a week?
- **Characterization:** Does the singer create character, interest or evoke feelings? Does the singer marry the music to the text, or just offer a technically good performance and is a candidate for ensemble work?

A good SM is a good judge of good talent, having worked with and seen enough good talent to choose the best. As part of this selection, the SM also uses intuition and gut feeling.

When the SM is leading the audition, very little direction should be given to the actors when they are reading their scene for the first time. The SM needs to see what the actor brings to the scene and character. If the actor shows promise, the SM may ask the actor to read the scene again, this time giving the actor some direction. During this second reading the SM can see if the actor is also good in taking direction. When giving directions, the SM keeps in mind that actors can best act out feelings and not storyline. Giving behaviors or mannerisms of a character are also things an actor can use.

If the actor shows a great amount of nervousness, the SM might take a moment to put the actor at ease by diminishing some of the importance of the moment, and by directing the actor to a calmer internal center.

YOU GOT THE JOB!

On occasion the SM is afforded the joy and pleasure of telling actors either by phone or in person, that they got the job. The SM shares in their joy, congratulates them, and welcomes them to the company. On the occasions when the SM must tell actors they did not get the job, the SM needs to remember the let down and disappointment actors experience. The SM might help to relieve some of their disappointment by acknowledging the disappointment and maybe even sharing feelings on jobs the SM failed to get. It is also accurate to point out that for the actors to have gotten that far in the audition should be a strong confirmation of their ability and that maybe their not getting the job had nothing to do with lack of talent. The actors may ask why they weren't chosen. It is not the SM's place to give this information, even if he or she knows. An SM never makes commentary to an actor about a performance in an audition, but turns that responsibility over to the producer or director, suggesting the actor talk with them.

THE SM's EXPRESSED OPINION

Among peers and the auditioning staff, it is important for the SM to know when to offer an opinion and when to keep it quiet. After an actor has left the audition room, it is not the SM's job to comment or express an opinion on the audition. SMs cannot help but form opinions. With time and experience, they become as adept in recognizing good talent as any person experienced in casting a show. Only when directly invited does an SM express an opinion, at that time speaking freely and honestly, but briefly and to the point. Producers and directors want their SMs to have an opinion, but they want it expressed when they want to hear it.

IN CLOSING

As an SM, you may find yourself working almost as many auditions as you do shows. With some auditions, you will be free to be creative and inventive in setting up the day and running things as you choose. You may even take part in the selection of callbacks or in casting actors in the parts. With other auditions, you may be relegated to being a traffic cop moving actors in and out of the audition room. At some auditions you will meet stars or respected actors whose work you have admired. Other times you will meet actors who want to be stars, or actors who are stars in their own mind—all wanting to be specially treated and accommodated.

Most of all the SM meets and works with the actors who are the foundation of the show and the spirit of any company—the supporting actors, the ensemble performers, the singers, and dancers. Each in their own right, *stars*—each needing individual treatment, consideration, and care during the stressful and anxiety-ridden time of auditions. During some auditions the SM will have hundreds of people clamoring for their moment in the audition room. During other auditions, the SM may have enough time to play the gracious host, meeting and greeting each actor, providing some of the star treatment. Auditions may take place in the best theatre in town, or they may be done in some back room, cold and dank, while the performers wait in an alley.

Whatever situations and events the SM encounters when running an audition, it is the SM's job to facilitate and serve. You must have a sense of logistics and move people with efficiency. You must remain focused and not be swept into the social climate that can prevail when actors in the same town join together. You must remain a timekeeper and see that all is done in fairness according to the procedure set up for the day and the Equity regulations. You must remain flexible and inventive as the audition staff creates new ways to find the best talent for their show.

There is no one way to working and running auditions. The ideas and suggestions made in this chapter are a starting point. Each SM finds and develops a preferred approach. Some of the things you read in this chapter you may readily use, lifting them directly from the written page. Some you will change, altering them beyond recognition, and still others, you will throw out.

THE PROFESSIONAL EXPERIENCE

An Epic Audition

Part One

My first big-time professional job was also my first experience working an epic audition. Since then I've had others, but it's the first that remains the most memorable. I had already been hired as an ASM for the musical version of *Gone With The Wind*. It was an open call audition. The producing company had not anticipated the number of people who would show up, so the PSM was the only SM brought in for the day. The auditions began at 9:00 A.M. By 9:30 I received a frantic call from the production office asking if I could come to the audition immediately. It seems over a hundred actors had shown up and more were arriving every minute. Except for the two starring roles of Scarlet and Rhett, all roles were open. For the actors this was the hottest audition in town. Getting a part in this show meant at least a year's employment as the show traveled across the country and then an open-end run on Broadway. Actors from as far as Athens, Greece, came to audition.

When I arrived, actors filled the reception room and overflowed into the hallway. I had to assertively excuse my way to the reception table. The PSM looked as if he had already put in a full day's work. He was madly juggling his time between processing the actors and getting them into the audition room. For some reason there was no Equity field representative. Perhaps the idea of having a field rep at auditions had not yet been instated. "Am I glad to see you!" the PSM said as he snatched up the next picture and resume and hurriedly led the actor off into the audition room. Before closing the door behind him, he said, "Do something to get things organized out here!"

My first order of business was to get another audition room. I did not seek producer's approval. Fortunately there was a room nearby. We called it the holding pen. I quickly hand-printed signs directing all arriving actors down another hall and into the holding-pen room. This changed the flow of traffic and kept the hallway closest to us clear for our immediate use. I ushered whatever actors remained in the reception room to the holding-pen room.

I then quickly processed the next ten actors listed on the sign-in sheet. I gathered their pictures and resumes along with the producer's information sheets, led them into the reception room, sat them in a row of chairs, and told them they would be going into the audition room in the order in which they were seated. When the PSM came out of the audition room, I handed him the ten sets of pictures and resumes. I explained that these were the next ten actors and that their pictures and resumes were in the order in which they were seated.

The person holding the auditions was the director's wife, and she was accompanied by two associates. The director was in New York and his wife knew as much about the show as he did. She was there to seek out the best talent available for the director to see at a later date in callback auditions. Having been a performer herself, the director's wife was sympathetic to the actor's needs. She wanted to give each a fair chance to present themselves. Consequently, she took a good amount of time with each person. These auditions were held at a time when producers did not have to pay actors after being at an audition for three hours, so the director's wife was free to take her time. Periodically throughout the day, she would come out to the holding-pen room to tell the actors that if they were willing to wait, they would all be seen and have a chance to read for a role. This woman was relentless in her pursuit and held true to her word. We finished auditioning the last actor by 11:35 P.M. In all, we had seen over 450 performers that day. While everyone fell back in their seats exhausted and in relief, I was energized. I thought every professional audition would be as exciting. Today I am thankful that most turned out to be less stimulating. I am, however, thankful for this first experience. It prepared me for the others that came along in my career as a stage manager.

Part Two: A Kiss For Melanie

The auditions for *Gone With The Wind* continued for several days more. The next day was set up by appointments and there were many. Knowing how the director's wife worked, the time allowed for each appointment was not enough. The PSM decided he would need help. He told me to be at the auditions for the next day by 8:30 A.M. to prepare for the day.

Auditions that day were not as frantic. There was always a good number of actors waiting. Many of them showed up with their agents or managers. This made the reception room more congested. We quickly reestablished the holding-pen room. The PSM and I told each actor and rep the way in which the director's wife worked and warned they would wait well beyond their scheduled times. What helped relieve some of the pain or annoyance for having to wait was the fact that the director's wife invited each actor's rep to sit with her at the audition table as their client auditioned.

The PSM and I took turns working the audition room. During the times I worked inside the room, I of course had to also read scenes with the actors auditioning. I read both male and female roles. Most actors are used to having an SM read with them in an audition, regardless of the opposite gender. Only two complained that day. They said it "threw" them to have a man reading a woman's part. The director's wife auditioned them again, this time reading the scenes with them herself. They did no better.

There was one actor, above all others, who from the start was able to look past my gender as I read the role of Melanie to his Ashley Wilkes. This actor had done his homework. He was prepared and his portrayal was full. He was focused, concentrated, and worked every moment. At one point in the scene he crossed to me and took my hand. I became a little self-conscious. He smiled and still in character ad-libbed, "It's okay Melanie." A chuckle came from those in the room, and he continued. At the end of the scene, as per the directions in the script, he drew me close to him and he kissed me on the forehead.

There was a long moment of silence in the audition room. I remained frozen in his embrace—no, paralyzed—hoping the director's wife would yell "cut" or something, anything to break the awkwardness I felt. The director's wife, however, was enjoying the moment. She knew this was my first professional job, and she wanted me to get the total experience. Finally she called out "Alright boys, break it up!" Everyone burst out laughing. The actor nearly got the part. He was, however, too short. Perhaps it was destiny, because a while later he got a series on TV.

Serving the Director's Audition Needs

Part One

Another audition which stands out in my mind is one in which I was hired just to work the auditions. It was for the Los Angeles premier production of a Tony Award–winning musical that had been playing on Broadway for almost two years, and eventually went on to make theatre history. Like the *Gone With The Wind* auditions, every musical actor in town wanted to be in this show. Anticipating the turnout, the open call auditions were set on three days and were held in a theatre. Each day the number of actors showing up did not reach the epic proportions of *Gone With The Wind*, but the line did go outside the back door of the theatre, down the alley, and around the building onto Sunset Boulevard.

The director, the one person most responsible for conceiving, creating, and developing this show, was there to personally audition everyone. It was exciting for me to be part of such a prestigious show and work with the director. I was also hoping to be in the right place at the right time and maybe get hired on as one of the SMs.

The director knew exactly what he wanted. He was quick in releasing actors he felt were not right for the show, but with those actors whom he considered a good possibility, he took painstaking time in working with each of them.

This director also had some very specific demands and restrictions upon the people who worked the audition. He arrived promptly every morning at 9:00 A.M., with an entourage of assistants and associates who surrounded him as if to protect him. Upon his arrival he wanted the first actor ready in the wings waiting to begin, although it always took him fifteen to twenty minutes to get started. I was instructed not to talk to the director, even to say good morning, and if I had any questions, I was to talk to one of his assistants. I could understand and appreciate this. The man was intense, concentrated, detailed, and did not want anything to disturb his creative time. He was devoted to his show and nothing came above that. I did, however, find the "good morning" part a strange request.

The director liked staying in the darkened theatre, remaining just a voice. There were, however, many times when he came on to the stage to work with the actor. He was sullen in his approach, working intimately and speaking almost in whispers. Being in such admiration of the show and this man's work, each time he came on the stage, I'd draw closer, standing in the wings. At one point one of the assistants saw me. In a panic, he pulled me off into the backstage area, telling me never to stand where the director could see me. It seems the sight of a stranger's face while the director worked was distracting and upsetting.

I was in the spring of my career and had not yet come to know and understand some of the behaviors of people. I believed that the director's behavior was due to something I was doing. After about an hour of feeling bad, I asked the assistant if the director was displeased with me or my work. The assistant laughed and assured me that if the director was dissatisfied with either one, I would not be there having this conversation with him. I took this as a compliment and continued working the auditions until the end. I did not, however, get a job on the run of the show as an SM.

Part Two: An Audition Phobia

During the auditions for another show, the director called me to the audition table and asked privately and confidentially, "I would appreciate it if you wouldn't let the actors shake my hand when they come in. Just have them take their place and begin the audition." I must have looked surprised or perplexed, maybe both, as I left the audition room, because the production secretary came running after me, being apologetic and explaining that the director was afraid of catching germs. Up to that time, I had not heard of Howard Hughes's phobia about germs and Michael Jackson's phobia was not yet generally known.

I was not sure how I was going to accomplish this task. I could not tell the actors of the director's phobia. I tried several approaches and each failed miserably. I was apologetic to the director and, despite his affliction, he understood.

My first step was to mark the audition room floor with a large white strip of tape, then as I led each actor into the room, I'd say we were running short of time, and ask the actor to take a place at the taped line, and that we would begin the audition as soon as the director was through looking over their resume. Most times this worked. There were, however, those actors who were more assertive and wanted the time to meet and chat with the director. The director had a humor about himself and his request, because when this happened, he'd look over at me, smile, and shrug his shoulders. To ensure that no actor would slip through, I soon learned that once the actor took a place at the taped line, that if I cut in front of the actor to deliver the picture and resume to the director, the opportunity for approaching was blocked. The director helped by turning his attention to the picture and resume. This approach became foolproof, but it felt abrupt and did not transition comfortably into the audition. Going with my intuition, I started announcing the actor's name, and as I moved into place to do the scene with the actor, I gave the name of the scene. It worked well for the rest of the audition and the director complimented me on my tactics. I worked with the director many more times afterwards and followed this procedure each time I worked one of his auditions. I found this process to also work well when the auditions were running late and I needed to move actors in and out of the audition room quickly. With refinement and variations, I use this procedure in some way with every audition I work.

9

The SM's Production Week

Up to now we have discussed the things that make a good SM, have met the different members of the chain of command, talked about getting the job, gone over nearly 600 definitions, named the tools and supplies an SM needs, discussed in detail the charts, plots, plans, and lists an SM must create, profiled all the people with whom the SM must work and maintain a working relationship, and have talked through the art of running an audition. Now it is time to put all these things together for the SM to begin the work in the SM's production week!

The SM's production week is the first official time the SM goes into full-time action and work on the show. In most working situations in the past, the SM did not start getting paid for work until the first day of rehearsals when the actors started. However, many producers expected the SM to have ready whatever things were necessary to launch the first day of rehearsals and begin work on the production. Equity negotiated and got ratified with producers that the SM must be put on the payroll no later than the week before rehearsals to begin production work on the show.

HOMEWORK

Even with the SM's production week, the SM must still do some work prior to being put on the payroll. Before arrival at the production office on the first day of production week, the SM needs to be *script-smart*, having read over the script several times becoming very familiar with the characters, plot, and storyline. If the SM waits until the first day of the production week to get script-smart, valuable time will be lost and the SM will be working half-blind, because a portion of the work is based on knowledge of the script.

During the first readings of the play, the smart SM will use time economically. The SM begins creating hand-written drafts for the Scene/Character Tracking Chart, props, and sound effects, and notes the necessary light cues in the right-hand margin of the rehearsal script. Reading the script and doing this work is best done in a place where the SM cannot be disturbed. The production office during production week is not the place. Most often, home is the best place.

During this period of homework, the SM might also contact the set designer and begin marrying the set to the script. Doing this work before production week seems to be the only way, unless the SM is ready to put in twelve or fourteen hours, and a full seven days during production week.

AT THE PRODUCTION OFFICE

Going into the production office on the first day of production week is no different than going to the first day of any other job. There will be a mixture of good feelings and excitement along with a measure or two of anticipation and anxiousness. Will this be another one of those glorious experiences where things come together in love, friendship, artistry, and financial success—or will this be the show in which everyone cannot wait for the end?

The production week is when the SM meets and establishes a working relationship with the office staff. In most situations, the office staff is very accommodating. They welcome the SM, providing workspace, a telephone, office equipment, supplies, and gladly share their expertise and advice. After this week and once the show gets into rehearsals, the SM's visits to the office will be brief and the business done quickly.

On the First Day

Having a workspace and telephone are the two most important things an SM needs from the production office on that first day to begin business. More than likely the workspace given will be makeshift, created on the SM's arrival, with maybe an office staff member giving up some or all of their own workspace. The SM must be very flexible and work with whatever is provided. Even with the most ill-equipped office, the SM with an office-in-a-bag can begin the work and do the job effectively.

The business on the first day will feel scattered, unfocused, unproductive, and perhaps a bit overwhelming. A good part of the day will be spent setting up the office space, gathering information, meeting people, and starting the week-long task of making telephone calls. At this early stage in the production, people will have many questions and concerns that they expect the SM to address. More than likely the SM will not have the information or answers. This is when the SM needs to take good notes and promise to get back to them with the answers. Different piles of paper with important information will begin to build and fill the workspace. This information is mostly from the production secretary and the producer's secretary, who gladly release it and are no longer responsible for it. Within a short time, a disabling feeling can consume the SM, a feeling that this load of work is insurmountable. It is at this time the SM must become bipolar, ambidextrous, or whatever it takes to zero in on one thing and yet continue working and dealing with all the other things that will pour in on this day.

THE BLOCK CALENDAR

One of the first piles of information the SM creates and zeros in on is the block calendar, as presented in Chapter 6, Hard Copy. Without the information contained in this calendar, the SM is unable to answer many questions that will be asked by the people the SM contacts. In creating the block calendar, the SM starts by gathering information from the production/producer's secretary, or the producer. More than likely the secretary has already created some sort of a document with this information. The SM takes the information, transposing it to a penciled draft of the block calendar, and then calls or meets with the director to gather and pencil in rehearsal information. If the show is a musical, the SM might also talk with the choreographer and music director.

The information the SM has gathered thus far becomes the basis for the schedule. The SM now talks with the technical director, mostly to verify time frames and to get any additional information the TD might have. The work the lighting designer must do during the technical rehearsals is also important to this schedule, so the SM calls and confers with the lighting designer, making sure any needs expressed are sufficiently met on the schedule. In being thorough, the SM also talks with the costume designer and costume shop to coordinate measurements of the actors, discuss a possible time frame for costume fittings, and give a tentative date as to when the costumes need to be finished and in the theatre. Last, the SM talks with the publicity department to note any publicity events or photo sessions that require time during the rehearsal period.

If any of the information gathered from these various places is in conflict with anything else on the schedule, the SM is quick to see it and work it out. If the SM is unable to resolve any differences, the matter goes to the producer. The producer will dictate the course of action and what is to be the final information on the block calendar.

With all the information penciled in on the handwritten draft, the SM now enters it into the laptop computer to create the block calendar (as a review, this might be a good time to return to the sample of the block calendar in Chapter 6). Upon completion of the block calendar, the SM gets final approval from the producer, director, and TD before publishing and distributing it. This copy of the block calendar may be the last draft for the entire time of the production, or there may be as many drafts as there are changes. Upon completion of this first major project and piece of hard copy, the SM has taken the first step in getting the company organized and working in the same direction.

Key Information

- The rehearsal period dates and times
- The technical rehearsal periods, to include the load-in, invited guests dress rehearsals, preview performances, and opening performance
- Costume measurements and fittings
- Publicity events scheduled at the same time as the rehearsals

- The run of the show, including dates and times for all evening and matinee performances
- Name and address of the rehearsal hall and theatre
- Key telephone, fax, and pager numbers

Under the SM's Watchful Eyes

The SM watches for the following things on the block schedule:

- Time frames must be reasonable amounts of time for the work to be done
- Conflicts or overlaps in schedule
- Events interfering with each other
- Union rules governing the actors' and stagehands' work days, call times, days off, and what constitutes overtime or penalties

PRODUCTION MEETING

While the SM talks with the producer, director, and TD about the block calendar, the SM also finds out if they want to have a production meeting. At this early stage in putting together the show, a meeting where all technical and artistic departments come together is beneficial for organizing and getting everyone working in the same direction and time frame. The right hand gets to see what the left hand is doing. Every department gets a chance to present what work has been done thus far, what things must be done, and whatever problems they think they might encounter. The best time for the SM to have this meeting is at the end of the production week, after all the charts, plots, plans, and lists are completed and can be distributed to the people in attendance. Because of the short notice in having this production meeting, the SM needs to work swiftly in calling everyone to get everyone scheduled. With the producer's and director's approval, the SM shoots for some time on Friday or Saturday. The objective is to have 100 percent attendance at the meeting, even if it means scheduling on Sunday or early some morning in the early part of the following week. It is preferable to have this meeting over no later than Sunday, because on Monday of the following week, rehearsals usually begin. The writers and composers are seldom asked to this meeting unless the show has never been produced before, and if the director or producer specifies they be there. If the show is a musical, the music director and choreographer are often asked to attend.

MAKING PHONE CALLS AND CREATING THE ADDRESS LISTS

The next piece of important business for the SM is to create a comprehensive address list of everyone in the company. The production/producer's secretary more than likely has begun a list with perhaps only phone numbers. The SM needs more information than this to make the list complete and workable (See the Cast and Staff Address Lists in Chapter 6). If there is to be a production meeting, the SM gathers the necessary address information while on the phone scheduling the various individuals.

As the SM is being dictated the information for the address lists, it is immediately hand-written on pieces of paper with appropriate headings: Cast List, Staff List, Technical Departments, and Creative Staff. At this point in time, the SM is more intent on gathering and keeping the information. It can be entered into the laptop and formatted later in the production week when time is less pressing.

Making telephone calls is a time-consuming job. This task can take up a good part of one day's work and will linger into the next several days, depending on how lucky the SM is in reaching everyone or how quickly they return the calls. When leaving a message with a relative, significant other, or agent, the SM must not depend on that person to deliver the message. If the SM does not receive a return call from an individual within a reasonable time, more calls must be made. The address lists cannot afford to wait until the last day or two of the production week to be completed.

Personal Contact

The time used in making these calls is well spent. In most cases, this is the SM's first personal contact with the different members of the company. By the way the SM approaches this task, each person formulates not only their first impression of the SM but of the production company and possibly what their working situation may be like. During these conversations, the SM does not need to do anything more than be natural: gracious, pleasant, fun loving, and work in a businesslike and organized manner. From this first contact, the SM sets a tone that reflects upon the producer and director.

Information Needed

When gathering information from the performers for the cast address list, the SM looks for:

1. The performer's *professional name*—the name as listed with Equity and as it will appear in the program (They should be the same. If they are not, refer the actor to Equity). Also get the correct spelling.
2. Performer's *home address* (assuring them this is confidential information for the producer, director, and SM only).
3. *Personal phone number(s):* home phone and/or a number attached to an answering machine; a pager/cell phone number; a fax number, if separate from any of the other numbers. These are all numbers at which the performer can be easily reached.
4. *Additional phone numbers* (agent, manager, parents).
5. *Social security number.*
6. Confirm *role(s)* contracted to play (and/or understudy).
7. *Union status* (Equity, non-Equity). Up to date on dues? In good standing with the union? If the answer is no to any of these question, refer them to Equity, asking the actor to get this business cleared before the first day of rehearsals. The SM makes a note of this on a piece of paper headed "Equity Rep." This will be one of the things to discuss with the Equity office.
8. Finally, the SM asks if the person wants the name and a telephone number put on the contact sheet, which will be generally distributed to all members of the company. If they do, ask which number they prefer having listed, and assure them that no other information, such as an address, will be noted.

In gathering information for the *staff* address list, the SM needs less information; this requires only their names and correct spelling, addresses, Social Security numbers, positions, and any numbers where they can be easily reached. The SM knows their union affiliation is with I.A.T.S.E., but their status and standing is a matter between the individual and I.A.T.S.E. The SM also asks each person on this list if they want to be included on the contact sheet, giving them the same explanation and assurances as with the cast members.

When talking with each cast and staff member, the SM gives:

1. Time and date of the first rehearsal
2. Generally, the hours the cast will be rehearsing throughout the rehearsal period (i.e., morning-afternoon or afternoon-evening)
3. Place of rehearsals (address, phone number, directions)
4. Parking information (facilities and/or accommodations)
5. Roughly, what the cast will be doing on the first day (anything specific they need to have prepared and the kind of clothing to wear or bring to work)
6. Give them important phone numbers (production office, director, SM, rehearsal hall)
7. Time frame of technical rehearsals (load-in, actors begin rehearsing with crew, dress rehearsals, previews, opening performance)
8. Costume measurements taken on first day or within the first week of rehearsals
9. Performers must sign contracts before they can begin rehearsing (sign contract before first day of rehearsal or on the first day of rehearsals during the Equity business hour)
10. Informs all they will be receiving a packet of information containing important and useful information on the first day of rehearsals

In short, the SM delivers in abbreviated terms the information already published on the block calendar.

APPLYING THE ART OF LISTENING

In most situations, by the time the SM makes the calls to the cast and staff, the beginning of rehearsals is less than a week away. With some of the performers this may be the first official contact since the auditions and being told they have the job. From these phone conversations with each person, the SM too cannot help but get first impressions. For the SM, first impressions should not count too much, but rather be information to be used later, once the SM sees the person in work and action.

In these phone conversations with the different people, the SM listens carefully, paying attention to the positive and negative parts of the conversation. Mentally note the questions they ask, the approach they take, and the attitude they present. Listen to the tone of voice, the tempo in which they speak, and their choice of words. Read between the lines, seeing if there are personal agendas.

Despite humanity's many imperfections, an SM must have a genuine interest in and love for all people. The people in the company needing special attention and care, or the people who will be the most problematic, will reveal themselves early. There is a story at the end of this chapter in the Professional Experience section, under the title of "Fritzie—A Lasting Impression," which exemplifies how listening, getting a first impression, and learning about the individuals pays off.

THE CONTACT SHEET

Once the SM enters the information for the address lists into the laptop, information needed to create the contact sheet can be easily extracted. Remember, the contact sheet lists only those people who elect to be on the list. Also, the phone numbers published are the numbers the individuals have approved to be given out.

CONTACTING THE EQUITY FIELD REPRESENTATIVE

Upon completion of the cast address list is a good time for the SM to talk with the Equity field rep. The rep is interested in having a complete list of all cast members, both union and nonunion, along with their Social Security numbers. The SM informs the rep of the time and place of the first rehearsal and assures the rep that the first hour of the day has been set aside to do Equity business. In the final part of this phone conversation with the rep, the SM goes over any other notes having to do with anything that concerns Equity.

SETTLING IN TO A CALMER PACE

The first two days of production week usually are frantic and maddening. People who have already begun their work, or are anxious to begin their work,

are asking or demanding from the SM information about the production, which the SM is just now assembling or beginning to comprehend. The things discussed above are the most immediate the SM must do on the first two days. As you can see, many of them overlap, tugging and pulling the SM in different directions. By the third day, things usually settle in to a calmer pace. This, however, does not mean there is time for water-cooler talks, extended coffee breaks, or going out to lunch. The SM continues to work at an accelerated pace doing the things that must get done. Otherwise, the SM will run out of time and not be prepared for the first day of rehearsals in the following week.

THE SCENE/CHARACTER TRACKING CHART

Assuming the SM has done the necessary homework and begun work on the Sc./Chctr.Track.Chrt., the SM can now enter into the laptop the hand-written information compiled earlier (see Chapter 6).

CHARACTER/ACTOR– ACTOR/CHARACTER LIST

Now that the SM has a complete list of the actors and the roles they play, the actor/character list can also be created. If the show has many characters and the actors in the company are assigned multiple roles, it is wise to create a character/actor list too.

THE SM's PERSONAL FLOOR PLANS

The next major project to complete is the SM's personal floor plans. This project too can be time consuming, especially if the show is a multiset musical. If the show is a one- or two-set comedy or drama, making the personal floor plans during production week will not eat up a lot of time. However, when working on a musical, the SM is better off doing some or most of this work at home during off hours, when there is less interruption. By the time the SM is ready to do this work, the design of the set usually is complete and there is a set of blueprint floor plans from which the SM can work.

COMPLETING THE LIST OF HARD COPY WORK

Once the personal floor plans are completed, the remainder of the charts, plots, plans, or lists will not take up as much time.

- Rehearsal and Performance Sign-in Sheets
- Correct Name-Spelling List
- Sound Recording and Effects List
- The beginning draft of the Prop List
- Schedule Reminder List
- Daily Schedule for the first day of rehearsals

ASSEMBLING AND DISTRIBUTING PACKETS OF INFORMATION

The only time the office staff may feel inconvenienced with having the SM invade their territory during the production week is when it is time for the SM to monopolize the copy machine to make copies of the gathered and assembled information. In consideration for those in the office, the SM must offer to step aside when someone else needs to use the machine.

The SM assembles and distributes the packets of information to the cast, technical staff, producer, director, and if a musical, to the music director and choreographer. Each packet contains:

- Block calendar
- Daily schedule
- Contact sheet
- Sc./Chctr.Track.Chrt.
- Character/Actor–Actor/Character List
- SM's personal floor plans

The packets will also have additional materials for different people. Variations in the different packets are:

- In addition to the above list, the SM includes in the producer's and director's packets the Cast and Staff Address Lists (remember, this list is not given to anyone else). At this point in time the director already has a script, but the SM may also include in the director's packet an unmarked copy.
- The SM includes in the cast's packets scripts for those who are playing roles but have not yet received a script. Also, payroll deduction forms, medial insurance forms, and any other forms Equity requires from each member.
- Included in the choreographer's packet is also a script.
- Unless the music director specifically asks for a script, the SM does not include one, nor a set of the SM's personal floor plans.
- For the different technical departments, each packet has in it information suited to the particular department and needs. The person who will run the sound during the performance most times will need a clean copy of the script to write in the cues.
- The designers' packets also have information added or deleted that is pertinent to their department. The lighting designer definitely needs a clean copy of the script. The SM might also include a set of the personal floor plans.

The SM needs to also go through the chain-of-command list and distribute to those not receiving a packet, a block calendar and whatever other information is important or pertinent to their position/department.

REVISIONS OF INFORMATION

Any changes or revisions made after distribution of information must be noted at the top of the new page as follows: REVISION, the revision date, the SM's initials (use the bold font, e.g., **REVISED (6-28-2000)sj**).

SCRIPTS

While doing all that must be done on the first day and second day of production week, the SM must also begin work on gathering scripts. To start this work toward the end of production week is too late, especially if the production office has been delinquent in this area. Also, there is some preparatory work to be done: there are always additional copies to be made; each script needs to be numbered; and the SM needs to create and insert a page into the front of the script.

Distribution of Scripts

Whenever possible, all actors playing a role should receive a full script, and not just a copy of the page of the dialogue their character speaks (*sides*). If the show is a revival of a show that has already been produced on Broadway, more than likely the scripts are rented from the publishing company, the company that holds the rights to the play. In this case there will be enough scripts for only the principal and supporting players, and sides for the actors playing smaller roles.

Scripts come from two primary sources: manuscript copies from the publisher, or paperback play books from a local bookstore. The scripts that come from the publisher usually are manuscript size (8½ by 11). They must be kept in good condition and returned at the end of the production. Otherwise, the production company pays a steep price for each script not reusable or returned. To ensure that all scripts are returned and remain in reasonably good condition, the SM numbers each script. In addition, slipped into the front part of each script is a page the SM creates, informing each actor of his or her responsibility:

- Write your blocking notes in pencil, which can be erased.
- Keep the script bound with each page intact and in the order they should be.
- At the end of the run, return script.
- Before turning in the script, all notes, blocking notes, and marks made by the actor must be erased.

This page further states:

- That if any of these conditions are not met, the actor will be required to pay for the script.
- The price of the script.

At the bottom of the page, the SM leaves a space to enter the script number and for the actors to sign their names. The SM distributes the scripts on the first day of rehearsals and collects the signed pages from everyone who has a script, including the people who were given a script prior to the SM coming on the job. The SM keeps these signed pages on file, returning them to the individuals as they turn in their scripts at the end of the run.

Script Copying

It is illegal for any published material to be copied on a copying machine. Many of the actors will take it upon themselves to make a copy for themselves. This gives them the freedom to mark up the copied scripts as they choose or tear them apart into scenes as they work on each scene. An SM seems to have no choice but to make copies of the script; more copies are always needed than are sent by the publisher or bought by the producer. When doing a musical show, the SM may need at least eleven more copies:

- 1 copy for the SM's rehearsal script
- 2 copies to be used for the SM's cueing scripts
- 1 copy to use for final blocking notes
- 1 copy to use as an original for making other copies
- 4 copies to give a copy to the director, choreographer, lighting designer, and head of sound
- 1 copy to the star or lead performer who has the most involved part, so they can mark it up and tear it apart as they choose
- 1 extra copy to keep on file

The Paperback Play Book

Scripts that come in five-by-seven-inch booklet size are highly impractical for professional use, especially for the SM. These pages of the script must be enlarged to manuscript size so the SM can make clear blocking notes and write in the cues for the performance. Copies may also need to be made for the SM's assistant, the director, lighting designer, and possibly the star or actor playing the lead role.

FINISHING THE PRODUCTION WEEK

The SM tries to keep the production week down to five days. When doing a musical, that is nearly impossible; musicals will require the sixth day to get work completed and sometimes will unofficially go into a seventh day without the SM asking for additional pay.

REHEARSAL ROOMS

With the paperwork out of the way, the SM now turns to the more physical aspects in preparing for rehearsals, namely the rehearsal hall. If the production company has its own rehearsal halls or rooms, and if they are in the same building or complex as the production office, the SM's job is made easier—more than likely the rooms are already equipped with all that is needed to set up for rehearsals. If the rehearsal rooms are in another location and are being rented, the SM needs to start early in the production week, perhaps on the second day, to make contact with the managers of the rehearsal space and begin a working relationship with them. The first step is to visit the rehearsal location, checking:

- Size of the room(s)
- Type and condition of the floor(s)
- Availability of banquet-type tables and chairs
- Telephones, fax machine. The SM is interested in having a phone line available for the production staff. If the production company has a cell phone service that can be used, the problem is solved. Otherwise, the SM needs to inform the production office and they usually make arrangements to have a phone line brought in or use an already existing one that belongs to the rehearsal hall.
- Use of a copy machine on the premises
- Bathroom and clothes-changing facilities
- Drinking water
- Refrigerator, kitchenette, or an area to make coffee and have snacks
- Lighting in the room(s)
- Heating or air-conditioning
- Parking
- An area in which the actors can rest and socialize when not in the rehearsal, which is out of view and ear shot of the director
- Keys to the rehearsal room or a place to lock up rehearsal props and other items
- A list of eating places in the surrounding area

In addition, if the show is a musical, the SM should check:

- If the producer has reserved enough rooms to accommodate the various parts of the rehearsals
- If piano(s) are available and in tune
- If a dance/choreographer's room with mirrors is available

When the space for rehearsals is being rented, the SM must determine the earliest day, within the production week, that the SM can get into the rehearsal space to bring in props, set up tables and chairs, tape the floor plan of the set on the floor, and just generally make the space home for the company. Ninety-

nine percent of the time producers will schedule and start paying for the rehearsal space on the first day of rehearsals. If the rehearsal space is not booked by some other party, the SM will have no problem getting in by Thursday or Friday of the production week. However, on occasion the space is booked solid and the SM is not able to get in until late Sunday. It is the SM's job to be ready on Monday for the first day of rehearsals, even if this requires working into the night on Sunday or going in very early on Monday.

Taping the Rehearsal Room Floor

Once the SM is able to get into the rehearsal space, the first big task is to tape the floor plan of the set on the rehearsal room floor. In most cases, taping the set is a two-person job, especially when doing a musical. This is a good time for the PSM to bring in the ASM. If the producer is not willing to pay for the extra person, the PSM must become creative in getting someone to help. The SM may use the production assistant, an apprentice, the wardrobe mistress's daughter who wants to become an SM, or coerce the ASM into helping without getting paid, but with the promise of a great lunch or time off later in the production. The job can be done by the PSM alone, but then it will take twice the time—valuable time that is needed to do other things in this production week. Most ASMs are as willing to please the PSM as the PSM is willing to please the producer. ASMs also want to show they are team players and be hired again and again.

The Layout of the Rehearsal Room

Placement of the performing area in the rehearsal room and where the staff's production tables will be set is dictated by:

- **The width of the room.** The room needs to be at least wide enough to tape in the entire width of the performance area as it will be in the theatre. Ideally, there is also space on each side of the room to simulate the wings and off-stage areas. The depth is less important in that the back part of the floor plan of the set and scenery does not have to be taped on the floor.
- **Lighting/windows.** The greatest amount of light should fall on the performing area. If there are windows in the room, the director's back should be placed against that light so the director is not blinded by the glare. If the room is poorly lit

and if the director or producer gives approval, the SM may set up some scoop flood lamps, which can be purchased at any hardware store. These lights should be set up high, at ceiling level if possible. Actors dislike having the light shining in their eyes as they rehearse.

- **Mirrors.** If there are mirrors in the main rehearsal room, the room in which the director works most, a great effort should be made to have them covered. They become distracting for both the director and the actors. Mirrors in the room in which the choreographer works are an asset. The room should be set up so the dancers can see themselves as they work.
- **The entrance and exit to the room.** The room should be set up so as people enter and exit, they do not cross the performing area or the director's line of vision. For the same reason, the SM's production table is placed on the same side of the room as the entrance so the SM can freely slip in and out of the room without causing a distraction, greet guests and vendors, or intercept people who should not be in the room.

Tools for Taping
To do the job right when taping the set on the rehearsal room floor, the SM needs to have:

- Blueprint floor plans
- Tape measure (25–50 ft.)
- Chalk
- Ruler
- Various bright colors of ¼-inch cloth tape
- One-inch and two-inch white cloth tape
- Wide-tip, permanent-ink marking pen
- If there are round or circular parts of the set design to be taped on the floor, the SM will also need sturdy string (15–20 ft.) to use as a drafting compass

Cloth Tape
In purchasing the tape for the floor, it is important the SM get *cloth* tape and not vinyl or paper. Cloth tape is more expensive, but can better withstand the wear and tear of the actors, dancers, and rehearsal furniture. At the end of the rehearsal period, the cloth tape is easily pulled up from the floor, while vinyl and paper tape need to be scraped and take double the time. The SM buys bright colors which are easy to see and distinguishable from each other, and also saves all receipts to turn in to the production office as miscellaneous expenses.

Laying in the Floor Plan
With ruler in hand and the blueprints laid out, the SM is now ready to start laying the tape on the floor. First the SM marks with white tape, the center of the *performing area*—the area the actors use as they move about the stage in their performance. The SM then lays in with one-inch white tape the parameters of the stage (the outline of the stage), defining the apron and edge of the stage, the proscenium line, and the show portals. If the show is a musical, the SM should also lay tape defining the wings, which are used for entrances and exits by the actors and movement of scenery.

This being done, the SM lays in the floor plan or outline of the scenery. If the show is a one-set drama or comedy, the SM lays in the details and is finished. If the show is a multiset musical, the SM lays in the biggest, most used, or most important set first, and then overlays, with other colored tapes, the other sets.

Indicating the Backdrops
In musicals, backdrops and curtains which fly in from above are often a major part of the set design. These drops and curtains are placed at various depths on the stage, which in turn dictates the depth of the performance space for the scene. Instead of adding more tape lines across the rehearsal room floor, the SM notes this information off on the stage right side of the performance area. Wherever a drop or curtain hangs, the SM lays in white tape, 2 inches wide, and about 18 inches long. On these strips is printed, with a permanent-ink marking pen, the name of the drop and scene number. During rehearsals, when doing a scene with a particular drop or curtain, the SM places chairs or objects across the performance area indicating where the drop or curtain hangs, which reminds the actors of the performance space they will have once they are on the stage with the real drop.

Dance/Blocking Numbers
In all musicals, the director and choreographer want dance/blocking numbers placed at the edge of the stage on the apron. There was a time when these numbers were placed strictly for the choreographer's and dancers' use. Today, more and more, directors of straight plays are requesting to have these numbers to help in blocking of the show. These numbers are guide points for the performers in the dances and scenes to maintain placement and stage picture.

The SM can either purchase these numbers at a stationary store, or can lay them in by placing 4-inch patches of white tape along the edge of the stage and writing in the number with a bold, permanent-ink marking pen.

Whatever approach is used, the SM starts at the downstage, center edge of the stage, laying in the number "0." From that point, and traveling toward stage right, the SM measures off 2 feet and lays in the number "1." Two feet away from number 1 and continuing towards stage right, the SM lays the number "2," and continues laying in the numbers in consecutive order until reaching the farthest point stage right of the performing area. Returning to center stage and zero, the SM starts the process over, this time traveling off toward stage left.

Once the main rehearsal room is taped, the SM repeats the process in the room in which the choreographer will be working. In this room, too, the SM lays out the parameters of the stage, but only needs to tape on the floor the plans of those sets in which the big dance numbers take place.

REHEARSAL PROPS AND FURNITURE

Before production week, when first reading the play, the SM begins creating a prop list. From this list the SM makes a rehearsal props and furniture list. If the SM has the luxury of a prop person at the beginning of rehearsals, the SM gives this list to the prop person who is responsible for gathering the props and getting them to the rehearsal hall by the latter part of the production week, preferably after the SM has taped in the floor plans. If the prop person is not being brought in until the last week of rehearsals, the SM makes either the ASM or production assistant responsible for these props. Gathering rehearsal props and furniture is time-consuming work and the PSM should not take on this job. Be aware that on smaller productions, to avoid having to pay an additional person, some producers will minimize the PSM's work during the production week and try to get the PSM to do this job. The PSM must evaluate carefully to see if indeed this is something that can be done in addition to everything else.

If certain props or pieces of furniture are important to the play or intricately used in the blocking, the SM arranges to have brought in to the rehearsal hall items that are close to the real thing. Otherwise, props can be representational, such as paper plates and plastic cups representing fine chinaware and crystal glasses. If asked or given a choice, the director and actors will opt for the real thing. The SM must check with the producer to see how much the producer is willing to spend on rehearsal props. The decision usually is to work cheaply and generically, with the hope that maybe in the last week, the prop person will bring in specialized items.

There are certain generic rehearsal props and pieces of furniture that can be used as different things. In the barest and poorest situations, folding chairs or different-sized wooden boxes or crates can be used to simulate almost anything needed. In rehearsal situations with larger budgets, the following list of items are a good beginning, depending on the needs of the script:

- 6-foot benches
- 3-foot benches
- Chairs (folding ok)
- End table, coffee table, or piano bench
- Small kitchen table
- Card table
- Stools (tall and short)
- Wooden boxes (strong enough to sit, stand, or jump on)
- A multishelf rolling cart

As for the hand props:

- All things plastic (to represent cups, glasses, dishes, etc.)
- Sticks, broom handles, rope
- Items from thrift shops and garage sales
- An old sheet or blanket

When doing a period play pieces of costumes, such as long skirts and jackets, may be required to aid the performers in working with such items. Confer with the director on this matter.

THE EQUITY CALLBOARD

Most important of all, the SM must set up and establish an Equity callboard in the rehearsal space where the daily schedule, sign-in sheet, company notices, official Equity information, blank company accident reports, and blank Equity medical insurance forms are posted. Whenever possible, it should be placed inside or just outside the main rehearsal room, near the entrance. It should also be placed so it is the first thing the actors see as they come in for rehearsals. In the process of keeping this board neat, orderly, and up to date, the SM can create, from a laptop, headings in large, bold letters under which the different information is posted. The SM establishes from the first day that this is an official Equity/Company callboard and that nothing can be added, removed, or changed without the SM's knowledge and approval. For greater separation and control, the SM might set up next to this callboard an area in which the members of the company can post their own notices and information.

THE FINISHING TOUCHES ON THE REHEARSAL ROOM

The rehearsal room should be complete and ready to use before the first day of rehearsals. The SM should not save anything for the first day that can be done beforehand. There will be no time on the first day for adding and putting in the finishing touches.

- Set up the production tables and areas for the director, SMs, music director, and rehearsal pianist.
- Create an area or space for the actors to sit, place their personal items, have coffee and food items, and just generally congregate when they are to remain in the rehearsal room, but are not being used by the director. This place needs to be off to the side and, whenever possible, out of the director's line of vision.
- Create places on both sides of the room to set up prop tables and store rehearsal furniture needed for the day, but momentarily unused.
- Hang on the wall blueprints and whatever drawings are available of the set and costumes. If a scale model of the set is available, make arrangements to have it at the rehearsal hall at least on the first day if not for the entire first week.
- Have in the main rehearsal room enough chairs for the performers, staff, and guests.
- Cover mirrors if they are a distraction.
- Double-check to see if pianos have been tuned.
- By Equity rule, have a first aid kit.
- Check to see bathrooms are clean.
- Bring in bottled drinking water, if needed.
- Give a block calendar and daily schedule to the rehearsal hall managers, securing keys (if available) or making arrangements for the rehearsal rooms to be open each day before the rehearsals are to begin.
- Place signs directing people to the rehearsal rooms if they are difficult to find once a person is in the building, and signs on all doors entering the rehearsal room, saying "QUIET PLEASE! REHEARSAL IN PROGRESS." Also place signs designating the different areas such as the prop areas/tables and the cast's personal area.
- See that floors in rehearsal rooms are clean and possibly wet mopped each day.

IN CLOSING

Sometime toward the end of the production week, the SM might ask the producer or director if they want food goodies brought in on the first day as a welcoming gesture and social amenity. If so, the prop person, production assistant, or ASM can spearhead this project. When the SM has everything in order and under control, he or she should make contact with the producer and director, giving confirmation of that readiness and getting from them any last-minute instructions.

As described in this chapter, the work the SM does in production week sets the stage for a smooth beginning to a time of hard work where everyone needs to be focused, working in the same direction, and on the same schedule. From the start, the SM lets the left hand know what the right hand is doing and vice versa. It is the SM's job to get the wheels of action and industry moving and keep them moving toward the first day of rehearsals, toward the first day of technical rehearsals, into the opening of the show, and ultimately throughout the run. If the SM lets up in any way or at any point, the results can have a grave effect on the remaining parts of the production, possibly causing delay, inconvenience, or loss of money. It all starts in this first week—the SM's production week!

THE PROFESSIONAL EXPERIENCE

It was suggested early in this chapter that in the first phone conversations with the different members of the company, the SM should listen carefully to what the person says, the person's attitude, tone of voice, and the choice of words. It was suggested that first impressions should not count. However, in the following story of Fritzie, none of the above points mattered. What you got from Fritzie on the first encounter was what you got thereafter.

Fritzie: A Lasting Impression

As one of the supporting performers in the show, Fritzie's name was included on the cast list given to me during my production week. I didn't remember him from the auditions. He must have auditioned privately or was brought in by the producer or director who already knew his work. From his picture, I could see he was an older, character man. From his resume, he had an impressive list of credits dating as far back as vaudeville, burlesque, and the Ziegfeld Follies. I was looking forward to meeting and working with him. I just knew he had a million theatre stories to tell.

Fritzie was pleasant enough when he answered the phone. I introduced myself. Normally the person is really glad to hear from someone from the show. More than likely their last contact was when they got the job or when they signed the contract. In Fritzie's case, after I introduced myself, there was silence. A red flag went up in my mind and my audio sense became more alert. As I spoke, Fritzie grunted in acknowledgment. I started getting a very dark feeling about this man. When I asked him for his address, he spit out in annoyance, "Kid, don't you have it there? I put it on the papers your producer made me fill out." Another red flag went up. It was the way he called me "kid" and said "your producers" that put me on my guard. "You're right!" I laughed, making light of the moment, "I have it right here in front of me. I just want to check to see if it's correct." "Of course it's correct!" he snapped back. "Would I give the wrong address?" "No, you're absolutely right," I said. "Let me read it off to you to make sure I put the correct information into my computer." The word computer set off another grunt.

Our conversation continued as a group of skirmishes. The word cantankerous came to mind and my first impression was well established. I asked him for his Social Security number. He couldn't understand why I needed to have it. He said that back in the old days only his accountant got the number, ". . . now today you have to give it to go to the toilet" (actually, his terminology was more explicit than what I choose to write here).

I must admit Fritzie pushed me to the limits of my patience and tolerance. I wanted to establish a relationship with this man, but not on the terms he was presenting at the moment. I asked, "Fritzie, is there something wrong? Have I called at a bad time?" I was just about to establish some boundaries when Fritzie interrupted. It was as if a Pandora's box had opened. His anger was great and it poured out. "It's about time someone called me!" Then he went directly to the youth of the producer and director, complaining about how young people do things these days. The producer and director were not so young, but I guess in Fritzie's eyes they were. It didn't take much reading between the lines to know where Fritzie was coming from and where he was headed. All I had to do was listen as he talked. In a very strange way, he worked his way into my heart. I could see his hurt and feel his pain. Here was a man who must have been Mr. Big-Time once, and now he was being asked for his address and Social Security number, something I imagine lesser people in his employ did for him in the past.

Fritzie asked how old I was. Knowing his view on this subject, I was compelled to take whatever curse of youth I might have had and said I was older. It wasn't old enough for him; he still called me kid. I tried reassuring Fritzie that despite the ages of the producer, director, and myself, we would do things professionally and had a good many years of experience. "Aaah!" Fritzie expelled, revealing more of his New York accent, "I been in the business over seventy years." "Seventy years!" I said in great surprise and appreciation. "I can't believe that! Were you born in a trunk?" It was at that moment Fritzie blossomed into a human being. He was surprised to hear a kid so young using the term "born in a trunk." He wondered if I knew what I was talking about. I told him, but he proceeded to give me the history and definition anyway. Fritzie's parents were vaudevillians and he began performing at the old age of three. "Wow! Three years old," I said. "At that age, I was still doing potty in my pants!" If I recall, the term "potty" was not my choice of terminology. I chose to use the same explicit terminology Fritzie had used earlier. He laughed. We bonded and became buddies. This, however, did not excuse me from his attacks and outbursts.

When I hung up, I was drained of energy. This was going to be a high-maintenance person—and he was. He drained the energy out of every rehearsal he attended. He could create conflict from the smallest matter or incident. As a performer, he was no longer as sharp in his craft as he may have been earlier in his career. It took a great amount of time and work from the director, and support from his fellow actors, to get him to performance level.

At one point halfway through the rehearsals, I asked the director why he chose Fritzie. He said that in the '30s, '40s and early '50s Fritzie was a major player on Broadway—he even went to Hollywood to make some films. The director said Fritzie had always been a character man. He never reached name recognition with the public, but producers and directors sought him out for the particular roles he could play.

By the mid-1950s his career died out. The director said he chose Fritzie for the part in our show because "his name was written all over it," but admitted confidentially, "Now all I have to do is get him to do it."

The life of Fritzie is the stuff stories are made of. In some ways, actors like Fritzie are easier to deal with than others. Fritzie was not subtle, polished, or crafty in his approach. What Fritzie said and what Fritzie did is what was on Fritzie's mind at the time. The SM's first impression is only the beginning of discovery in getting to know the cast and the rest of the members of the company.

10

Rehearsals

The writers give birth to the show. The producer becomes the caretaker. As godparents and day-care workers, the artists—the designers, director, and actors—take the show into their care, nurturing and developing it into a mature and highly interesting piece of entertainment. The time set aside to do this is rehearsals. During this period the artists give the show character, color, design, style, personality, and an identity of its own.

THE FIRST DAY OF REHEARSALS

This day is often a unique mixture of feelings and experiences for all involved. For the producer, it is the beginning to making a dream and vision come true. It is the culmination of endless planning, gathering artists, negotiations, and phone conversations. Now the producer stands to the side watching carefully, hoping the artists will take the show beyond all those dreams and expectations.

To varying degrees, for the director, musical director, and choreographer, no matter how skilled, successful, and experienced they might be, the first day of rehearsals is the time when they must once again step up to their creative and artistic ability and prove themselves. For the performers, too, rehearsals are a time to step up to their creative and artistic abilities, but in the first few hours on this first day, their feelings are more immediate. There is excitement in the air and a party atmosphere prevails. For the performers, this day is a birth, a marriage, and a celebration rolled into one. There is great expectation and anticipation, followed by some anxiety for the things to come. There is hope for success, the thrill of having the job, relief to be working again, and a very childlike revelry in being the center of attention, for this rehearsal period is intensely focused on them and their work.

The SM is also filled with many of the same feelings. This is a time when SMs, too, step up and prove their abilities. The work the SM has done during production week will seem like child's play when compared to what is to come. Rehearsals are a time when the SM must remain focused, concentrated, devoted to the job, to the show, and work at an accelerated pace to get things done. There will be little to no time for personal life, and the SM must work as many hours as are necessary to do the job. There will be no let up from this pace and intensity, at least until the show opens, and even then the release is minimal.

On the first day of rehearsals the SM also joins in the celebration, but is only a part-time participant, for work began for the SM with the arrival of the first person. While everyone is meeting and greeting, making new acquaintances, and renewing old ones, the SM stays focused and concentrated on the business at hand. The work in the first few hours on this first day launches the ship, steers it out of port, and into the open seas where the director takes over. If the SM has worked well previous to this first day and continues doing so throughout the rehearsals, the launching, departure, and sailing should be calm, smooth, easy, and go unnoticed.

THE FIRST DAY REHEARSAL HALL SETUP

It is strongly advisable that the SM get to the rehearsal hall at least an hour, if not two hours, before everyone else. Most of the work in setting up the rehearsal hall was done during production week, but on this morning the SM must arrange and set up the rooms for the work to be done on this day.

Setting Up for Equity

For the first hour, the Equity field representative will come to get union business completed. To do this, the SM sets up in the middle of the room two or more banquet-type tables with chairs where the actors will sit. At each place should be the packets of information prepared during production week with each actor's name on a packet. Included with the packets are whatever Equity forms need to be filled out. In placing the actors at the tables, the SM is conscious of their placement, putting the star and principal performers at the head, followed by the supporting roles and ensemble performers. The SM might also put a pencil at each place, or hold in reserve a box of pencils and distribute them as needed.

Setting Up the Social Amenities

Whether elaborate or simple, whether paid for by the producer or personally supplied by the SM, it is effective and a gracious start to the working relationships to have some coffee brewing, a tea setup, and possibly some food goodies—preferably healthy items. The layout and presentation of these items is also important, perhaps decorating the table with a tablecloth and some flowers. Having background music playing as people enter is an excellent added feature, as long as it is not intrusive.

Additional Setup

Having set up for the Equity hour, the SM checks to see that the work tables and work areas for the director, music director, choreographer, rehearsal pianist, and any other members of the staff such as the writers or composers, are set up and supplied with whatever things they might need, even if it is to simply supply them with pencils and a writing tablet.

The SM next turns to the signs which need to be in place—signs that lead people to the rehearsal room and define different areas such as prop tables, cast lounging areas, and so on. After the Equity business, the SM will conduct final business and formal greeting with the cast. More than likely the producer and director, too, will want to formally greet the cast and have a word or two.

After all of this business, the director will more than likely have the cast do a read-through of the play. For this read-through the SM has already seen to it that everyone has received a script whether it has been given to them before this day or is now included with the packet of information given to them when they first arrived. For any number of reasons, the wise and prepared SM also has available several extra copies to assign or pass out in a moment's notice. Sometimes the reading takes place around the tables that are already set up—a table read. Other times the director wants the actors to sit in a circle of chairs. The SM will make that setup at the appropriate time.

ARRIVAL OF THE CAST

The arrival of the cast on this first day opens the floodgates of work, action, and intensity which will not let up until the show closes or the SM leaves the show. From this point on, every minute will be filled applying all that the SM knows. With some shows, there will be smooth sailing, but never can the SM operate on automatic pilot and be there just for the ride. With other shows, the rehearsals and even the run of the show can be like a war zone. The SM's ability and character will be tried and tested at every turn of events. Most SMs will rise to the occasion, but in the process of learning and gaining experience there will be an occasional failure. After a failure the SM must quickly dress any wounds and recover, for there will not be time to revel in victory or retreat in defeat. As soon as one campaign is won or lost there is another waiting. With the arrival of the cast, the SM must now put in a great amount of time and energy in serving them in addition to all the other work.

Upon the casts' arrival on this first day, the SM meets and greets the cast members. For the moment, the SM acts as a host, welcoming them as if to a party. Some of them will have been met briefly at the auditions. Others the SM has talked with over the phone. Almost always there will be one or more performers with whom the SM has worked in other shows.

Even as the SM plays host and socializes, focus must remain on the business of the moment, which is to introduce the performers as they arrive, lead them to their places at the table, orient them to the schedule for the day, and start them on the paperwork that needs to be filled out for Equity and the production company. Meanwhile, the ASM is also playing host and doing the same as the PSM. At this point in time, the producer, director, and star are often noticeably absent from the Equity hour. The producer and director usually arrive before the hour ends, and if the star is prone to making an entrance, he or she will arrive fashionably late.

The Equity Business Hour

The Equity business is simple. If the SM has done the work well, if the production office has had signed most of the contracts in advance and now has prepared the ones that need to be signed on this day, and if the field rep is organized, the Equity business will go smoothly and quickly and can be completed within the hour set aside. The Equity hour is an additional hour to the actors' normal workday. If the production office is delinquent in having the contracts prepared and the signing is delayed, at the end of the Equity hour the SM starts the *rehearsal clock*, which puts everyone on the producer's time. If the Equity business takes longer than an hour through no fault of the producer or production company, the Equity hour will be extended until the work is completed. The SM informs the cast that the rehearsal time will start when the Equity business is finished, and apprises the producer, director, and the rest of the rehearsal staff of the change in schedule.

The Equity Business to Be Done

Following is a list of all the Equity business that must be accomplished.

1. Sign contracts. No Equity member is allowed to start rehearsals until there is a signed contract.
2. Bring all Equity members up to date in their membership. Finalize the induction of new members, and make arrangement for payment of dues and fees.
3. Fill out all Equity forms for medical insurance benefits, pension and welfare, and for updating Equity records.
4. Elect Equity deputies for:
   • Principal and supporting performers
   • Ensemble/chorus performers

Attendance at the Equity Hour

The entire cast is required to be present for the Equity hour. This includes non-Equity performers, if any. In situations where some of the cast members cannot be present, the rep needs to be informed before this day, and will take care of business with those individuals at an earlier or later time. The star performer may or may not be present for this meeting. The star's Equity business may be handled separately and at a time convenient to the star.

THE SM's FORMAL WELCOME

If time allows at the end of the Equity hour, the SM formally welcomes everyone and lays out some basic ground rules and expectations. If there is no time at the end of the Equity hour, the SM gives the cast members a break and then, upon their return, gives a speech that:

• Welcomes everyone, expressing the SM's joy and excitement for the project, and extending wishes for success
• Extends to the cast an open-door policy for communication with the SMs
• Asks everyone for professional concentration in their work, professional dedication to the show, and consideration toward their fellow workers
• Assures the cast that the SMs are present to do service for them and will often work beyond the call of duty, but reminds them that everyone is responsible and accountable for their own conduct and professional behavior
• Quickly goes over whatever charts, plots, plans, or lists were included in the actors' packets of information to ensure that the actors know how to use them, understand the information, and answer any questions they may have. The SM also reminds them of their responsibility for the rented scripts.
• Reminds the company of their responsibility to check the callboard on arrival each day and before leaving at the end of the day. Special note should be made that no performers should leave the rehearsal area without first informing the SM, and that they do not leave at the end of the day without first getting the schedule for the next day.
• Takes a moment to review the importance of all actors being on time and signing their own initials on the sign-in sheet, and details how latecomers will be dealt with.

Sidebar: It is at this point I give the "Little Red Box" speech. I express my lack of forgiveness and tolerance for people being late. I tell them that I will outline, in red, the box in which late performers or performers who forgot to sign in were to write their initials. With a tone of humor, I add that excuses short of disaster will not deter me from following through on this procedure. On the third such marking, that person will be reported to the producer and to Actor's Equity, with a recommendation of penalty in some way.

There are more things that can be covered with the cast at this time, but they are better left for the time when they are appropriate and fit the occasion. Having this talk with the cast reminds them not only of their professional responsibilities, but reestablishes the SM as a caring and loving leader, but also as a force to be reckoned with in times of misbehavior or unprofessional behavior.

COSTUME MEASUREMENTS

In many working situations, the costume people are anxious to get the measurements of the actors so they can begin construction or alterations. Sometimes the actors are instructed to go to the costume shop on their own time, which is acceptable within the Equity agreement. However, the time performers can do this on their own time is limited before the performer must either be sent during rehearsal time or get paid for going. Directors dislike losing actors from rehearsals, and producers dislike having to pay to have this task done. Knowing this of the director and producer, in the first two weeks the SM tries to save the number of times performers must go on their own by sending them during rehearsal time when they are not needed. Later on, in the third and fourth weeks, when the director needs practically everyone at the rehearsals at all times, the SM has the actors go on their own time.

Getting costume measurements from the actors is fairly simple work. To accommodate the costume people and at the same time not use up the times the SM can send the actors to the costume shop on their own time, the SM asks the costume people if they can come to the rehearsal hall on the first day of rehearsals to get the actors' measurements. More times than not, the costume people are quite agreeable to this request. The SM arranges for the costume people to set up either in another room or in some private corner of the rehearsal room, instructing the actors to have their measurements taken when they are momentarily free.

EIGHT-BY-TEN GLOSSIES AND BRIEF BIOGRAPHIES

In thinking ahead on this matter of pictures and biographies (bios) for the program, the SM, during production week, in the first phone conversations with the performers, asks each of them to bring in a picture and bio of themselves on the first day of rehearsals. When the actors arrive on this first day, the SM collects these materials. If some of the actors have forgotten or if the SM has not yet made this request, the SM asks the actors to bring them in within the next two days.

Asking that these pictures and bios be turned in so early may seem premature. However, the people putting together the program have already begun their work and this will be one of the first things they will be requesting from the SM. While dealing with the pictures and bios, this would also be a good time for the SM to pass around the Correct Spelling of Names List, and then turn it in along with the pictures and bios.

ENTER THE PRODUCER, DIRECTOR, AND STAR

These people may make their entrances individually or as a group, spectacularly with great fanfare and panache, or quietly and understated. Regardless of the nature of their entrance, the business of the moment becomes suspended while the time turns into a social event. There is no preventing it. The SM joins in, but monitors the time. When sufficient time has been given, the SM suggests to the director that they begin work. The director will either take the lead, perhaps addressing the cast, or give approval to the SM to direct everyone to the next order of business, which usually is a reading of the play. The SM goes into quick action and sets up the room according to the director's instructions.

READING THE PLAY

Reading the play for the first time is another moment of excitement on this first day. This is when the script is given a voice and speaks through this particular group of actors. Each person experiences this reading from a different perspective. For the SM it is the play, which up to this point has been mostly about charts, plots, plans, and lists, coming alive.

From the start, it is important that the SM establish with the cast and director a presence during the rehearsals—as a voice they will hear during their creative time, as well as during the times when they must do business. During this reading, the SM usually reads the author's descriptions or calls out special cues and effects that are important to the action or storyline at that moment. On occasion, the director may choose to do this. As the reading is about to take place, the SM might ask the director's preference on this. At the end of reading the first act, the SM gives the cast a break. After the break, the reading resumes with Act Two.

BREAKS FOR THE CAST

Equity has some very specific rules governing breaks. *Within every hour of work, the actors must be given a five-minute break.* This means the SM must be ever watchful of the time and at the fifty-five minute mark of rehearsing, needs to stop the rehearsal to give the actors a break. For working situations where it is more beneficial to continue working longer, Equity allows *for every hour and thirty minutes worth of work (ninety minutes), the actors are to be given a ten-minute break. No other variations or manipulations of these time periods are permissible.*

The SM comes under all Equity rules and is also entitled to a break at these times. However, the SM needs to be watchful of break times, and also uses the few minutes of a break to regroup thoughts and priorities, check the list of notes, attend to matters that need immediate attention, or set up the room for the next hour of rehearsals. In theory the SM takes breaks at a different time. In reality, the SM seldom takes breaks.

THE DIRECTOR AND BREAKS

For the director, breaks are often an intrusion. They stop the work and creative process, which usually is flowing at a peak rate of intensity. As soon as the break is called, that peak diminishes, and on return from the break, it takes time and effort to get it back—sometimes it is lost completely. Directors would rather give breaks when they choose. If they must be restricted to giving breaks at a prescribed time, they prefer giving them every ninety minutes. However, in this matter it is the SM's job to consider the actors first. Breaks every fifty-five minutes is often more beneficial in preserving and pacing the actors' energy for the day's rehearsal. Most directors know of the ninety-minute option, but the SM does not offer it. The SM calls the breaks at the fifty-five minute mark and lets the director ask for the ninety minutes. Ultimately, the cast makes the choice.

THE STOPWATCH

This is a highly important tool for the SM. There are many instances when accurate timings must be made for scenes, sound effect cues, or just a general timing for a scene, an act, or the entire show. Just as important, the stopwatch needs to be used for timing breaks. For the cast members, breaks are never long enough and often they question the SM, believing their time is being cut short. To directors, the breaks seem to be longer than five minutes and they too question the SM. To eliminate any doubts, the SM calls a break and makes a point of starting the watch for all to see. This psychological gesture reminds everyone that five minutes is a short period of time, and they must use their time wisely and economically. If they are not back by the end of the five minutes, they are late.

Stopwatches are often attached to a ribbon or strap, so the SM can carry them around. This leaves the SM free to move about the rehearsal space and still monitor the time. Also, stopwatches are attractive items, and if left lying around can be stolen or misplaced

THE MID-DAY MEAL BREAK

Equity rule provides that *by the fifth hour of the actors' workday, the actors must receive an hour-and-thirty-minute break for the mid-day meal.* However, if the director is agreeable, the Equity members can vote to have the mid-day meal break cut to one hour, with the remaining thirty minutes being given to them at the end of the day, allowing them to be released from rehearsals thirty minutes earlier. This vote must be unanimous. To ensure that all people vote their true choice without feeling peer pressure or being swayed by majority rule, the SM sees to it the vote is done by secret ballot.

During rehearsals, especially in the first week or two, the mid-day break becomes a welcomed time for the SM, a time to regroup, reorganize, prioritize, check notes, and at the same time grab a quick lunch. At this stage in rehearsals, there is no time to go out for lunch and maybe bond with some of the cast members. However, SMs should not forego some kind of a break, even if it is simply to go into another room where they cannot be found or behind some prop or scenery flat where they cannot be seen. They need this short period of time just to relax, restoring their energy, mentally and physically.

AFTER MID-DAY BREAK

On the first day when returning from the mid-day break, the detailed work in bringing the play to life begins. If the show is a musical, often the ensemble performers will go off into another room with the music director to work on music, the choreographer may work with a principal on dance, and the director will remain in the main rehearsal room working with some of the principal performers to begin blocking a dialogue scene. If the show is a drama or comedy, the SM sets the rehearsal room for one of the scenes in the play, usually the first scene, and work begins on blocking the show. For the rest of the rehearsal days, after the mid-day break, rehearsal continues according to the daily schedule.

MORE ON THE DIRECTOR AND SM's WORKING RELATIONSHIP

By the end of the first day the marriage between the SM and director has taken place and the honeymoon has begun. There is much the SM must do to learn about the director to make this union a workable and successful one. This will not be a fifty-fifty proposition. The SM does not look to see what the director is doing to make this relationship a success, but rather forges ahead, doing the SM's part.

The SM must be a quick study of the director, observing everything, picking up clues on the director's temperament, personality, energy, pace, demeanor,

likes, and dislikes—the director's acceptance level, patience threshold, tolerance factor, causes of anger, or triggers of ego. If the director acts, behaves, or works in ways that are different or out of the ordinary, or if the director seems to have some hidden agendas or issues, the SM tries to understand them and work with them.

If the SM is uncertain about anything in this working relationship with the director, the SM initiates open conversation. The SM must be direct, making no assumptions nor letting things slide for another time. As the SM and director work together in these first days, they establish between them the working rules. In all situations, the SM lets the director set the rules. The SM is free to express opinions, and see if the director is agreeable. Within professional reason, the director is to be served in the way the director chooses, not in the way the SM wants. A good and compatible working situation between the director and SM in rehearsals is when the SM is in charge while the director leads and remains in control.

A Nightmare SM–Director Relationship

An incompatible director–SM relationship can be one of those nightmare stories theatre people tell as they sit around to socialize and unwind after a show. The nightmare part is that the SM and director are stuck with each other. If the relationship between a director and SM needs to be broken up, almost always it is the SM who is removed from the equation. However, the rehearsal period is not an easy time to remove the PSM from the show. Rehearsals can last from ten days to four weeks. By the time it becomes evident that the PSM–director relationship is not working and is having an adverse effect on the show, the rehearsal period is at least half over. If the ASM is capable of taking over and the producer is confident, a change may be made, but most producers are not willing to do so during such a crucial time in the development of the show. Instead, the producer talks with each party, trying to keep the status quo, knowing that the show will soon be opened and the PSM and director will naturally be separated. Thus, the director and SM usually are stuck with each other, just waiting for the time when they will not have to work together daily.

What Directors Expect from Their SMs

In Chapter 7, Profiles and Working Relationships, the apparent double standard of work and expectations directors practice when working with the cast and when working with the SM was noted. With the actors, the director appears benevolent, understanding, and patient. The director appears to allow greater time for learning and experimenting, seems to be more accepting of the actors' shortcomings, will apply greater effort in helping the actors to do their job, and is tolerant of a difference in opinion or a display of their ego. On the other hand, the director expects the SM to do the job quickly, calmly, quietly, smoothly, proficiently, efficiently, effectively, and perfectly. The director has little tolerance for personality or individuality in the SM and wants no ego displayed. The director expects the SM to be a step ahead, anticipating all needs and wants. When the director asks a question or wants a bit of information, the SM is expected to have the response ready to be delivered within seconds. The director who finds such an SM finds a personal treasure. As much as possible the director holds on to this SM, hiring him or her again and again.

Some directors are not above abusing their SMs, taking out their angers, annoyances, or frustrations on them. There is a fine line every SM travels in accepting this kind of behavior. It is up to the individual SM to know what is acceptable and what is not, and to communicate this to a director who works in this way. If the director is unable to change and the situation is intolerable, the SM needs to take steps in getting out of the job. Conditions will never change and often get worse.

The Director's Rehearsal Time

Directors hate having their creative time in rehearsals with the cast disturbed. We have touched on the director's feelings and reactions for having to stop to give breaks. When it comes to being disturbed with matters or business other than the immediate work with the cast, some directors can be even less tolerant or become even more annoyed.

It seems to be a general quality of directors that no matter how much time they have to rehearse, they complain it's not enough. Some directors become guarded and protective, resisting those times when other business must be done during rehearsal hours, such as when actors have to go to costume fittings or publicity events, or take time out of the rehearsal day to do personal business.

Every SM must know this of directors. It then becomes the SM's job not to save the director from these feelings or to change the director's way of behaving, but rather to be creative and manipulative in scheduling so such infringements or disturbances to the director are kept to a minimum.

Breaking into the Director's Creative Process

Throughout the rehearsal day, it is the SM's job to handle all business and answer all questions that come into the rehearsal room. It is the SM's job to keep information flowing and keep the wheels of progress and industry turning. From the information the SM gives out on any given day, other departments are often able to continue their work without having to disturb the director. This is why it is so important for the SM to know as much as possible about the entire production. This is also what makes an SM invaluable to a director.

There will be times, however, when the SM is absolutely unable to answer a question or give information which only the director can deliver, times when the information needed or question to be answered needs to be delivered right now! If the SM cannot persuade the person demanding the information or asking the question to wait until later, the SM has no choice but to disturb the director in the middle of rehearsal. In working with any director, the SM learns the right window of time to step in saying, "Forgive me for breaking in, but this matter cannot wait and you are the only one who can provide the information." The SM needs to be concise and brief in asking for what is needed. Get all the information surrounding the subject and make sure it is understood, because once the director returns to his work with the cast, it will be even more of a disturbance to the director to be interrupted on the same matter.

This conversation about the working relationship between a director and the SM is not over. There is more to come as we work through the process of putting a show together.

THE SM's NOTEPAD

The SM's notepad is a tablet of paper or clipboard on which the SM jots every single thing to do or remember. This pad is carried on meal breaks, to answer the phone, at meetings, to greet a visitor in the hallway—wherever the SM goes throughout the day. During rehearsals, and in fact during any point in a production, people throughout the company and throughout the day will be making requests or passing on information to the SM and the SM will need to follow through on seeing that these things are handled and the information is deciphered and distributed. Only foolish and unwise SMs think their memory is so great that they do not need the use of this notepad. The number of things an SM will jot down on this pad in a day or even in an hour is sometimes too numerous to try and commit to memory. Unless an SM has an absolutely photographic memory, no SM should use energy for such work. There are places in a day's work where that energy is better applied. There are too many little things that can slip through the cracks and be forgotten. Making a note to purchase herbal tea for the cast is just as important as jotting down the flight number and arrival time of the star and passing that information on to the limousine service. As we know by now, the SM is expected to be thorough, detailed, highly organized, and keep the operation running smoothly and with ease. To aid the SM in accomplishing all that is expected, the notepad is an invaluable tool.

MAKING THE DAILY SCHEDULE

A major task each day is for the SM to get from the director a schedule for the next day. Some directors can create a daily schedule for the entire week at the beginning of each week and follow it to the letter. However, in most instances directors prefer creating the daily schedule day by day. In such cases, the SM needs to get this information from the director sometime during the day. Most directors want to make up the next day's schedule at the end of the day after the day's work has been done and the cast has gone home. This, however, is not the best working situation for the SM. By Equity rule, the SM is required to have the next day's schedule posted on the callboard before the cast leaves at the end of their day. If not, the SM is required to call all cast members that night to give them their schedule. For a play with five or six

characters, this is no monumental task and certainly not a hardship for the SM. However, with musical shows having thirty or more cast and staff members, this can become a chore taking two or three hours by the time everyone is reached and the SM is certain all have been informed.

With this in mind, the SM makes a great effort to get the director to create the schedule earlier in the day. The best time to get the director do this work is at the mid-day meal break just before the director goes to lunch. However, by meal time most directors are ready for a break themselves. Many will suggest this work be done on their return from lunch. Some will follow through and return in enough time. Some will forget or return late, then suggest that the schedule be made up during one of the actors' breaks. If the director and SM attempt to make up the schedule during one of the actors' breaks, five minutes is not enough time. The schedule will be nearly completed, but then the rest will be put off until the end of the day.

Sidebar: It is my choice and quest as an SM to get the director to give me the information for the next day's schedule at mid-day, just before the director takes a meal break. There are many areas in which I bend and relinquish my preferred way of working to accommodate the director's way of working. However, on the matter of creating the daily schedule, I become assertive and go for what I want, especially when working a musical. I begin my endeavor on the very first day, telling the director that Equity requires I get the schedule out before the cast leaves at the end of the day. Sometimes this in itself is enough to get the director to do the schedule at mid-day. If the director suggests we make the schedule later in the afternoon, I point out the limitation of time between rehearsing, the time it takes to assemble the information, then get the schedule printed up and posted. It is at this point I must step back to see the director's reaction and response to all of this. Some directors will be very clear in saying no and telling me what they want. Others will reluctantly accommodate me, but eventually return to their preferred way. Still others will comply, compromise, adjust, and be very happy to have this work done and out of the way.

Creation of the Daily Schedule

The general belief that the SM makes up the daily schedule is true in every part except for the actual creation of the schedule—the events that appear on the schedule. The SM facilitates the making of the schedule by getting the director (choreographer and music director) to meet to decide on what they want. At this meeting the SM takes copious notes, then goes off to put those notes in clear and understandable form. The SM publishes the document, makes copies, distributes the copies to all who are involved, and posts a copy on the callboard for the actors.

While creating the daily schedule, the SM has at hand the Block Calendar, the Schedule Reminder List, and the Scene/Character Tracking Chart. From the Schedule Reminder List, the SM presents the things that must be included on the schedule for the next day and then steps aside, listening as the others discuss and dictate what they want. The SM uses the Scn./Chctr.Track.Chrt. to see that there are no parts of the show being missed or neglected and uses the Block Calendar to see if the work being done and the work to be done will fit within the time frame of the overall schedule. The SM watches to see that there are no conflicts of schedule, overlapping time frames, or times when one actor is expected in two places at the same time.

Distribution of the Daily Schedule

The daily schedule should be distributed as follows:

- Producer, production office, production secretary
- Director, choreographer, assistants
- Musical director, rehearsal pianist, assistants
- PSM, ASM, production assistant/runners, SM's production notebook
- Callboard
- Star(s)
- Technical departments or people who might need to know the schedule for that particular day
- All extra copies conveniently and accessibly placed for immediate handout to anyone who asks for one

Working in Realistic Time

In all matters having to do with the company, the SM must have a *realistic* sense of time—the time it truly takes to perform a task or complete an event. Many people in the company will have their own version of how much time it takes to do things, sometimes minimizing or inflating the time to suit their particular needs or purpose. In times when it matters, as in mak-

ing the daily schedule, if the staff members are working in fantasy time or wishful-thinking time, it is the SM's job to step in and guide them to realistic time.

Poor Use of Time

SMs must also be watchful of people in the company who use their time poorly—people who become indulgent in their work, forgetting the overall picture and time schedule. Directors in particular can be negligent in this area. It then becomes the SM's job to step in, reminding the director of the overall time frame and schedule. This can become a strain on the relationship between the director and the SM, especially when the director is having a problem in rehearsals and is not getting the desired results. This is another one of those times when the SM must find the right window of opportunity to remind the director of the fleeting time. If a director continues to work in poor time, and the SM has reminded the director over and over, the SM must then apprise the producer and see if the producer can have an effect on the director. If even the producer's words have no effect, all the SM can do is continue to keep the producer informed.

Considering the Actors in the Schedule

Instead of putting the daily schedule in time frames and having the actors come only at the times when they are needed, some directors choose to have the entire cast come to rehearsals each day. This leaves the director free to work on whatever he or she chooses. Whether the cast is small or large, this is not a good working situation. It is tiring and boring to the actors who must sit and wait for their time to work. It also puts the SM in a babysitting situation. No matter how disciplined and professional the actors might be, little coffee clutches and discussion groups develop which become annoying to the director and the other actors working. After a while some of the actors will wander and just when the director wants to rehearse with a person, that person will be off to the bathroom or on the phone with an agent. In annoyance, the director may turn to the SM demanding the person's presence immediately, and may even remind the SM that it is the SM's job to keep the actors standing by.

When working with such directors, it is advisable that the SM try to get the director to set time frames for the actors to rehearse. However, as is the case with all things concerning directors, some will graciously comply while others will resist and continue to work in the way they choose.

DEALING WITH PEOPLE BEING LATE

Late Actors

Being prompt and on time starts with the SM, who is always early enough to have the rehearsal room set up and ready for work and starts the rehearsal promptly when the actors arrive, even if the director has not yet arrived. On the first day of rehearsals the SM gives the "little red box speech" and from that point on follows through on what has been set up. When actors are late, the SM asks about their well-being. Most times they answer with their excuse for being late. The SM listens, lets the person know the SM has heard them and understands their circumstances. However, in the next breath, the SM reminds the actors of their professional obligation and reviews with the actors the action the SM will be taking in marking the red box on the sign-in sheet.

Ninety-nine percent of the time the actors within the company will be on time and ready to work. It is the remaining percent that, if left unchecked, can send the message it is acceptable to arrive late. Being late is like a highly infectious disease. It can spread throughout the company like influenza, infecting the promptest of individuals.

All offenders are sorrowful and offer powerful excuses. Those who are late for the first time will ask for consideration to not have this offense counted against them. With love and care, the SM explains to the individuals that if being late is not a problem with them, this one red mark will not mean much and the matter will be closed. However, if the individual has a tendency to be late, this will be the beginning of keeping a record.

With individuals who establish themselves as latecomers and are about to receive their third red box, the SM must counsel the individual, expressing concern. The SM may try to get the person to see what things contribute to the regular lateness, or maybe the reason why the person is choosing to be late. The SM may offer suggestions as to how the person might better schedule time. As a final gesture, the SM might offer to overlook this third offense, assuring that with the next incident punitive action will be taken. In addition to this consultation, the SM should record in the log book an accurate and detailed account of each incident and what was said in meeting with the individual. On the next and final offense, the SM has no recourse but to report the individual to Actor's Equity and to the producer.

Late Director or Stars

Rank has its privileges and if the director or star chooses to be late, the SM has no course of action as with the cast members. The SM may express to them in private the SM's efforts in making the cast members be on time and might appeal to them to set the same standard, but should not let their arriving late stop the rehearsals and keep everyone else waiting. In times when the director is late, the SM needs to hold the schedule at bay and have the actors run a scene, or if the show is a musical, have them work on dance or music. In taking this course of action, the SM must make sure the work is worthwhile and productive, and not just busy work.

THE EQUITY RULEBOOK

This is the bible of agreements, rules, laws, and by-laws that have been made and agreed on between Equity and producers. This book provides all the details governing the employment and treatment of all Equity members. On the first day of rehearsals, the Equity field rep brings the SM a copy of this book, and the SM must keep it accessible at all times for quick reference. Sometimes it provides answers and information within seconds, but at other times a master's degree is still not enough to understand what is written. Some rules are simple and straightforward. Others are complex, detailed, involved, cross-referenced and have exceptions, variations, or special circumstances. Also, the same rules may vary according to the type of contract under which the show is working. Every SM should have this book nearby, and at every opportunity read and study it, sometimes underlining, highlighting, or dog-earring pages. Some SMs are most adept and studied in knowing all the rules. Others generally read over the book, then as each situation arises, they refer to the book, which is indexed at the front, making it easy to find a particular subject.

THE DAY'S END

By the end of the first day of rehearsals the SM has begun a working relationship with both the cast and director, set the ground rules, and just generally established the professional way in which the SM will work and the way in which the SM expects the cast members to work and behave. No matter how thrilled people are to be working in theatre and dedicated to their profession, by day's end everyone is looking forward to going home. As the rehearsal draws to a close, in the final hour the SM checks the schedule to see what work remains. If some actors are not going to be used for the rest of the day, the SM does these actors a great service by dismissing them early. The SM, however, does not make this decision alone, but rather confers with the director to get approval.

The last hour in the day can also become an hour lost. The creative level has dropped and most thoughts are being directed toward going home. Most assuredly, the SM too is looking toward this time. However, it is the SM's job to keep everyone focused and use the time remaining. When things are beginning to lag or the director and actors seem to be wandering aimlessly, the SM might suggest reviewing a scene, working on a song, or running a dance before everyone is dismissed.

The End of the Day for the SM

The day's end is indeed a welcome time for the SM, but there is still work to be done. The actors have gone home but the director remains. This is a good time for the SM and director to go over notes, do business that could not have been done while the director worked with the actors, tie up loose ends, possibly decide on a production meeting with the technical staff, or maybe confirm the work to be done on the next day—sort of a mini production meeting between the SM and director. This also becomes a good time for the SM and director to connect and further refine their working relationship.

As the SM and director meet, the ASM and possibly the production assistant (PA) are putting the rehearsal room in order, generally cleaning up, arranging the callboard, or locking up props and other important rehearsal items. If the rehearsal room can be secured for the evening, the ASM and PA might set the props and furniture for the first work to be done on the next day.

Once the director has gone, the SMs and the PA meet to complete their business for the day, organize their notes, prioritize, make calls, plan for the next day, and just generally tie up all loose ends. By this time in the day, the temptation will be to put off some things for the next day. Under no circumstance should the PSM make this part of the regular way of working or allow an assistant to do the same. The SM must make it a working rule to complete all of the day's business. Tomorrow will be filled with its own notes and list of things to do. There will be no room or time to do things left over from the day before.

At last the SM comes to the end of the day. Sometimes there is no choice but to take work home and finish the business there. Most assuredly, during the first week or two of rehearsals the SM's social life is tremendously curtailed. Having dinner, taking a shower, and possibly falling asleep in front of the TV is about as social or eventful as an SM can be.

PRODUCTION MEETINGS

Production meetings throughout the rehearsal period are very important. If the director is not prone to making this a part of the work schedule, it is the SM's job to suggest having production meetings, making time in the schedule, whether they are held before rehearsal hours or afterwards.

The purpose of the initial production meeting during the SM's production week is to bring together all of the artistic and technical elements of the show, allowing each department to present its design, plan, and needs, and confirming to the producer and director that all departments are working toward the same artistic intent and integrity. Subsequent production meetings throughout the rehearsal period are held for some or all of the departments to present their progress, reveal any particular problems they might have, and once again assure artistic integrity, time frame, and schedule. In short, production meetings are designed to let the right hand know what the left hand is doing.

There is no formula as to how a production meeting is conducted. The simplicity or complexity of the show will dictate the number of meetings to have. A brand new production or the remake of a show may require some sort of production meeting every day. The revival of a show that is to be a copy of what has already been designed and produced may require an initial meeting and perhaps one just before technical rehearsals.

The initial production meeting or a major production meeting should include the following people (key figures are indicated by an asterisk).

- *Producers
- Production secretary
- Writers and composers
- *Director
- Choreographer
- Musical director
- *Designers
- *SMs
- *All technical department heads
- Assistants to the various departments if the heads choose to have them present

Smaller production meetings may include only some of the key figures along with one or two of the creative or technical departments.

The SM gets the production meetings established and initially gets them started, but then steps aside and lets someone else take the lead, usually the producer or director. The SM becomes an observer and makes notes on anything that affects the schedule or is significant to the production. The SM might ask questions to probe, clarify information, keep the meeting focused, or just generally play the devil's advocate to open the conversation or to bring in another point of view. Anything more from the SM can become intrusive and perhaps self-serving.

THE WORK CONTINUES

The SM's work in rehearsal is continuous and endless. An SM must have the ability to keep the business at hand going, while attending to and dealing with whatever other matters come up moment to moment, including:

- Answering phone calls
- Answering questions and passing on information
- Meeting the actors' needs and dealing with the problems they may present
- Keeping actors busy at productive things whenever they are not working with the director
- Following script
- Taking down blocking
- Writing in cues
- Noting all changes
- Making notes on the notepad
- Tracking props and adding new props to the list
- Standing in and reading roles of actors who are not present
- Checking in with the production office from time to time
- Keeping the ASM and the PA busy and productive
- Dealing with people who come into the rehearsal room
- Keeping everyone quiet and focused
- Changing rehearsal furniture and setting up other scenes to be rehearsed
- And the ever-constant service and attention that must be given to the director

The information in this chapter is only part of the work the SM must do during rehearsals. There are still three more chapters of work to be done at the rehearsal hall before the rehearsals transition to the theatre and technical rehearsals.

11

The Rehearsal Script

The rehearsal script is the script the SM creates during the rehearsal period at the rehearsal hall. It is the SM's bible and lifeline to the production. In it are noted the actors' blocking, technical cues, and prop placement, preliminary notes on some of the scene change moves, characterization and motivation notes prescribed by the director, all changes the director might make in the dialogue or script, and a copy of the SM's personal floor plans.

LEARNING THE SHOW AND GATHERING INFORMATION

Before work can begin on the rehearsal script, the SM must become knowledgeable of all parts of the show. This is accomplished first by reading the script, then by gathering whatever information can be gathered from the producer, director, designers, and heads of the different technical departments. This information may come in giant chunks or dribbles. A good amount of information comes from the SM's first readings: the plot development, the sequences of events, the action, the characters, and the journey the characters take. From this reading, the SM creates beginning drafts of the prop list, character list, and the Scene/Character Tracking Chart. During these first readings, the SM notes in the script, in the right-hand margin, all technical cues inherent to the script, such as a doorbell ring, telephone ring, off-stage sound effect cue, lightning effect, blackouts, and so on. With the first note the SM makes in the script, it becomes the rehearsal script.

Set Design

Before rehearsals begin, the SM must know as much about the design and layout of the set as does the set designer. The SM must mentally marry the design of the set to the script and be ready to answer any question that might come up in the rehearsal hall. From the set designer, the SM gets blueprint drawings, the floor plans, and whatever sketches or scale models the designer might have made. From this information, the SM creates personal floor plans, which are entered into the rehearsal script.

Costumes

The more knowledge the SM has about the production before going into rehearsals, the better. If possible (although it is not necessary), the SM should also meet with the costume designer, going over sketches or renderings, noting the style, period, material, and colors used.

Music

If the show is a new musical, the SM needs to become as familiar with the music in the show as with the other parts of the script. If the musical has already been produced, more than likely there is an original cast album or CD that the SM might already own or can purchase. If the show is being produced for the first time, the SM might meet with the music director or rehearsal pianist and record on tape or disk the music to the songs and dances in the show.

The SM's quest for knowledge and information on the show is endless, but with just this suggested amount of information and work done, and with the rehearsal script in hand, the SM is ready to begin rehearsals.

BLOCKING

The greatest amount of information gathered and entered in the rehearsal script is the blocking of the show: so much so that the rehearsal script is also called the blocking script. *Blocking* is the noting and recording of all the movement, action, and business in the show, as set and agreed on by the director and actors. Blocking is noted on the rehearsal script, first to aid the director and actors, should they happen to forget it at a later time; second, to aid the SM in preparing the understudies and for putting in replacement actors; and third, for a new play, noting blocking becomes a record of the director's creation and invention. It is the historical account kept for the archives, prosperity, and in part, for the publication of the play (the blocking notes included in the published script are never as detailed and extensive as the SM's notes are in the blocking/rehearsal script). The actors write their own blocking on their personal scripts, while the SM's rehearsal script has the blocking for every actor or character.

In professional situations and in most academic and community theatre, when a director directs a show that has been previously produced the blocking that is printed in the published script is seldom if ever used. If a director refers to the blocking done in another production, it is merely to see how another director handled a particular moment or difficult piece of business.

A DEFINITION OF BLOCKING

The *World Book Dictionary* has no definition for the word *blocking* as it is used in theatre. Under the term "block," this definition is given in reference to blocking a hat: to give form and shape; to mount, mold, and shape. For an SM's definition, this is a good beginning. Perhaps if we list some of the theatrical terms used around blocking we can come to a closer definition:

- staging
- stage directions
- stage business
- stage movement
- stage action
- stage picture
- timing
- traffic pattern
- shtick (comic business)

Blocking is the *visual design of movement* in the play. It is the moving pictures and composition on the stage that enhance the play, the storyline, the action, the characters, the actors' performances, and the entertainment value for the audience. Blocking is movement, action, and business deliberately set for each actor/character who appears on the stage. Blocking is set by the director, and implemented, enhanced, and embellished by the actors. Blocking is the traffic pattern or floor plan of movement that takes place on the stage and within the scenery or stage setting. Blocking is handling props or moving furniture and set pieces during the performance, as seen by the audience. Blocking is doing *bits of business*, be it comic or dramatic.

Personal Blocking

There is also *personal blocking*—bits of business or action an actor does such as making a hand gesture or taking one or two steps. The SM might note this blocking in the script, but would not try to impose it on another actor performing the same part.

Famous Blocking

Throughout the history of theatre, there are many famous scenes and bits of blocking or staging:

- The classic *Romeo and Juliet* balcony scene
- The *Fiddler on the Roof*
- *A Chorus Line*
- Hedda Gabbler burning the Lovborg manuscript
- The "head higher than king" scene between Anna and the King of Siam
- Finch's scaffolding entrance at the beginning of *How to Succeed in Business*

It is important for the SM to know and understand blocking. It is an important part of the job that the SM must deal with throughout the rehearsal period and watch over during the run of the show.

THE SM's RESPONSIBILITY FOR NOTING BLOCKING

The actors are responsible for noting their blocking in their own scripts. From the first blocking rehearsal, the SM establishes that the blocking will be noted in the rehearsal script, but reminds the actors of their responsibility for doing the same. If an SM should happen to work with a performer who insists the SM take down his or her blocking, and if the director approves of this way of working, the SM complies. However, as soon as possible, the SM sees that this information is also entered into the performer's personal script. Even when the actors write in their own blocking, the director and actors are highly dependent on the SM for blocking information, especially when first running scenes without use of their scripts. They expect the SM to do this job thoroughly, accurately, completely, and have the correct, most recent and updated changes.

THE SPEED REQUIRED FOR MAKING BLOCKING NOTES

Noting blocking during rehearsals is one of the more challenging jobs an SM must do. When doing this job, the SM must be totally focused and concentrated, watching and listening to everything the director and actors say and do as they work in the rehearsal. Neither the actors nor the director will stop their work to allow the SM time to take notes. The SM is expected to take notes without infringement or distraction on the actors' and director's time. All notes of blocking are done on the run, which means that anything missed by the SM must be gotten when the scene is run again on that day, in the next rehearsal days later, or by getting together with the actor at some other time when the actor is not rehearsing.

The SM's Shorthand

With this kind of pace, the SM needs to have a quick method of noting—a shorthand. In addition to the limited time, the space on each page of the script for making the blocking notes is limited. To get the blocking noted, the SM must be brief and concise in the notes and at the same time provide the most detailed information, so that it can be read and understood at a later time. Noting blocking is a world of abbreviations, symbols, and hand-written diagrams. There is no standard written language or form to follow. There are some basic symbols or abbreviations used in theatre, but for the most part SMs develop their own. They learn from many sources: from their academic studies, from books such as this, from working with other SMs, and by making up their own.

The first and most basic knowledge every SM must have, is the area breakdown of the stage and the

abbreviations noting each area. Most people in theatre already know this information. However, lets review, starting simply, then becoming more detailed.

KNOWING YOUR RIGHT FROM YOUR LEFT

Above all things in the world of blocking, the SM must know which is stage right (SR) and which is stage left (SL). It must be firmly implanted in every SM's head that *SR is always the actor's right as the actor stands on the stage facing the audience. Conversely lies SL*. This can become confusing to the beginning SM because when viewing the stage to read blueprints, looking at artist's renderings, viewing a scale model, or making blocking notes, the SM is seeing the stage from the audience's point-of-view (POV). This puts SR on the SM's left, and SL on the right. Confusing? Yes!

To complicate this matter further, when talking about the placement of things in the audience (the *house*), the right side of the house is as a person sits in the audience to view the stage. Conversely lies the left side of the house. It is especially important that the SM have this difference firmly in mind because the SM, above most others, will be dealing with both areas.

To distinguish between what is right and left on stage and what is right and left in the audience, and to be clear in communication, whether it be in noting blocking or having conversation, when the SM talks about the placement of things on the stage they are always described as *stage right* (SR) or *stage left* (SL). When talking about things in the audience, the SM always says *house right* (hs.R) or *house left* (hs.L).

THE STAGE BREAKDOWN

Between defining some of the terms in the Glossary and having drawn out the SM's personal floor plans in Chapter 6, we already have a working knowledge of the layout of the stage and some of the terms and abbreviations the SM will use in noting blocking. The basic stage is shown in Figure 11-1.

The Center Stage Line

The imaginary vertical line that travels from the audience up to the back of the stage and cuts the

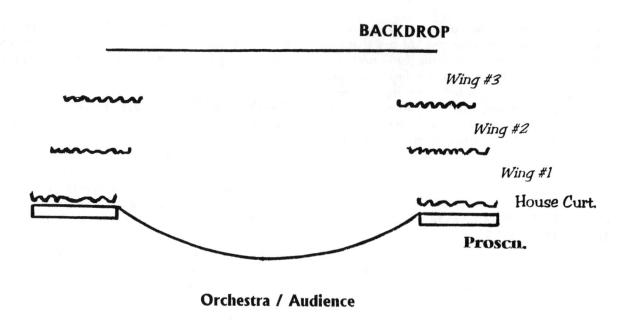

Figure 11-1   The basic parts of a stage.

stage in half is the center stage line (see Figure 11-2). If an actor were to stand at any point on this line facing out to the audience, everything to the actor's right would be SR and anything to the left is SL. Note the symbol or letter "C" at the bottom of the divid-

ing line. This is the abbreviation the SM uses in blocking notes to note the center position on the stage. The symbol for this center position is often written in one of three ways, as shown in Figure 11-3.

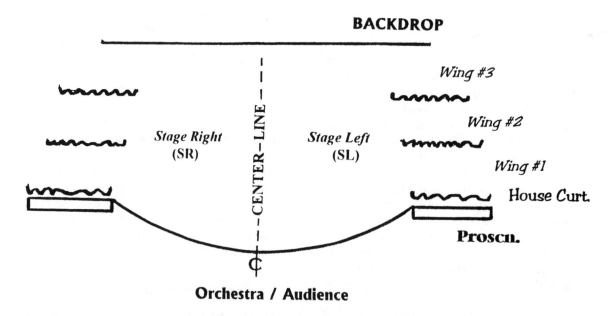

Figure 11-2   The center line vertically dividing the stage in half and creating stage right and stage left.

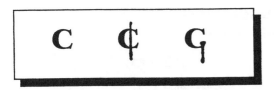

Figure 11-3   The three different ways the center position of the stage is written.

Up Stage and Down Stage

If the stage is divided in half horizontally, anything above the dividing line is up stage (US) and anything below is down stage (DS) (see Figure 11-4). In addition to being areas on the stage, the terms *upstage* (US) and *downstage* (DS) are also used to describe the direction in which anything travels on the stage. Anything on stage that moves away from the audience is traveling US. Conversely, anything that moves toward the audience is traveling DS.

When the stage is divided with the vertical line and the horizontal line, four major playing/performing areas are created, as shown in Figure 11-5.

The abbreviations used thus far are the beginning of the SM's shorthand for making blocking notations. They need to be remembered and become part of the written language when noting blocking.

The Apron

The apron (aprn) of the stage is the part closest to the audience. It is the part that projects past the proscenium arch out into the audience (see Figure 11-6). When the house curtain is drawn across the proscenium opening, the apron is that part of the stage floor that remains in view of the audience. It can be several feet deep, or be as narrow as a few inches. It can arch out into the audience (as in our diagrams), it can be straight across, or it can be constructed to suit the imagination of a designer. On traditionally constructed stages, this part of the stage is seldom used in dramas and comedies. Broadway musical shows may use this area more, while variety art and vaudeville shows put this space to greatest use.

Greater Division of the Stage

The stage as it is divided thus far does not give enough reference points for the SM to take down detailed and accurate blocking. The stage needs to be divided in two more ways. First horizontally, creating three specific areas across the stage—*down stage areas, center stage areas, upstage areas* as in Figure 11-7, and then vertically, creating the *stage right areas*, the *right of center* areas, the *left of center* areas, and the *stage left* areas, as in Figure 11-8.

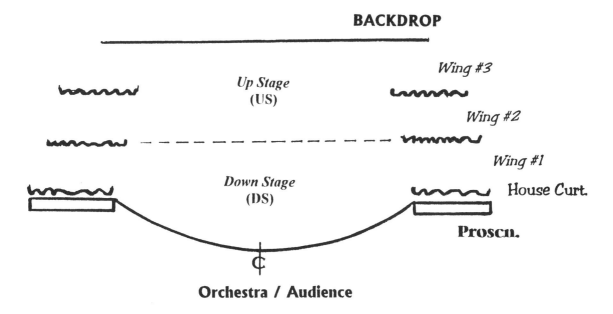

Figure 11-4   Horizontally dividing the stage in half, creating the upstage area and the downstage area.

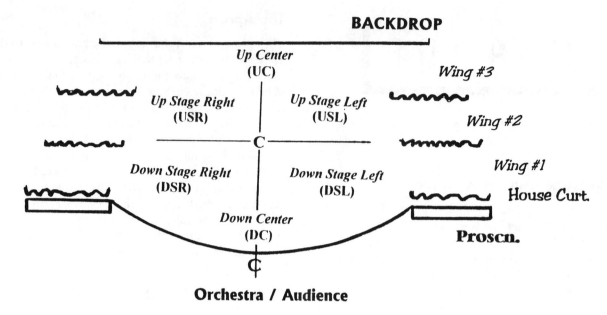

Figure 11-5 Dividing the stage with the vertical and horizontal lines, creating four major performing areas on the stage. Where the two dividing lines meet, that point becomes the center of the stage. Anything above this center point is called *up center* (UC), anything below is *down center* (DC).

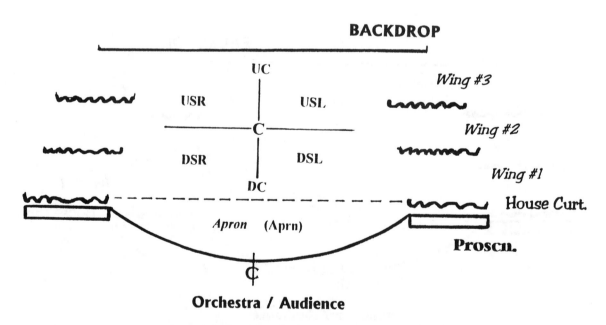

Figure 11-6 Creating the apron part of the stage.

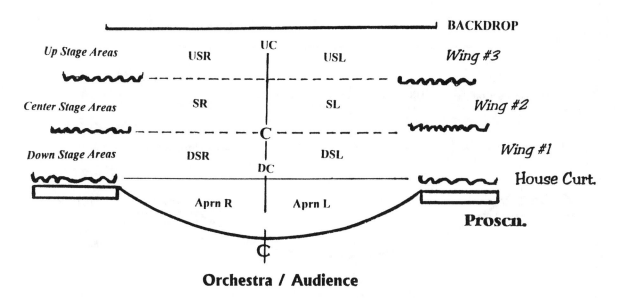

Figure 11-7   Greater horizontal division of the stage, breaking it down into smaller playing areas.

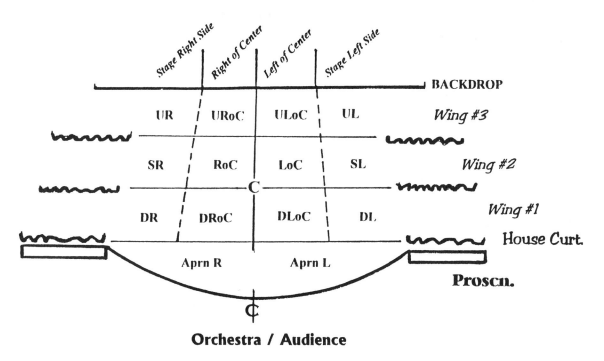

Figure 11-8   Greater vertical division of the stage, breaking it down into even smaller playing areas.

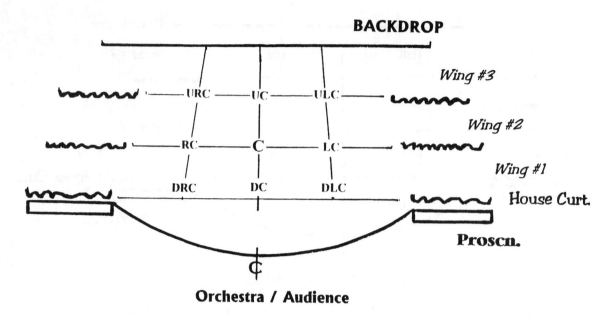

Figure 11-9 Labeling the points at which the various dividing lines intersect.

There is no need to divide the stage any further. The areas and reference points created are more than enough. In addition, take note of all the center points created where the different division lines intersect (see Figure 11-9).

Additional Reference Points

When scenery is added to the stage, the SM's reference points for noting blocking increase and allow even more specificity and detail. In most musical shows, the SM also has the wings SR & SL as reference points, along with the dance numbers that are put along the apron line or at the foot of the stage.

The Complete Stage Breakdown Picture

With the stage divided into areas, the SM now has a large number of reference points to note in great detail the movement and placement of the actors, furniture, props, set pieces, or anything else that appears on stage (see Figure 11-10). For the beginning SM, the diagram presented in Figure 11-9 should be enlarged and copied onto card stock and placed at the front of the rehearsal/blocking script. Each time the SM is noting blocking this card can be placed off to the side and used as a reference. The best test given to determine good blocking notes is when a SM, a di-

rector, or an actor, can go back to the notes a day later or years later, read them, understand them, and recreate the blocking as originally directed.

ARENA STAGING

Some SMs just master the art of *proscenium* blocking when they get a show that is performed in *arena staging* (be it a round or square stage), where the audience either surrounds the stage or is seated on three sides of the stage. The abbreviations and symbols for noting the blocking won't change, but the reference points can at first appear less distinguishable until the SM gets some very specific and identifiable points and areas in mind.

First the SM must decide on a *front viewing* position of the stage, as if the audience was seated in a conventional theatre with a proscenium. This front viewing position can be based on a combination of things:

- The place in the house where the director sits most often to block the show
- The main entrance to the theatre
- Sometimes there is a main aisle with smaller or secondary aisles leading up to the stage
- The placement of the technical booth from which the lights and sound are run, and from where the SM calls the cues for the show

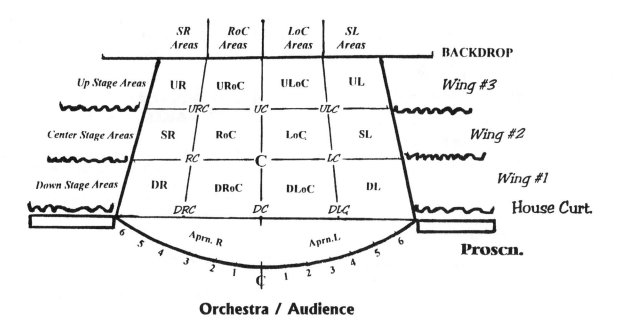

Figure 11-10   The complete stage breakdown, with all its reference points and performing areas.

• If the show is a musical, the placement of the orchestra pit might be a deciding factor

Having established a front viewing position of the stage, the SM has automatically established SR and SL and has created US and DS, and can now divide the stage into areas as with the proscenium stage (see Figure 11-11).

Next, around the edge of the arena stage, be it round or square, the SM might lay out the numbers of a clock, as in Figure 11-12. This breakdown alone is enough for the SM to make clear and detailed blocking notes. The placement of the aisles and orchestra pit allow still greater reference points.

It would be very helpful to the actors, director, crew, and perhaps to the technical designers if the SM makes copies of this breakdown and passes them out. It is important that everyone is working with the same picture in mind and using the same terms of reference.

ADDITIONAL ABBREVIATIONS FOR NOTING BLOCKING

In addition to the area breakdown of the stage floor, other parts of the stage can be used as reference points in noting the blocking:

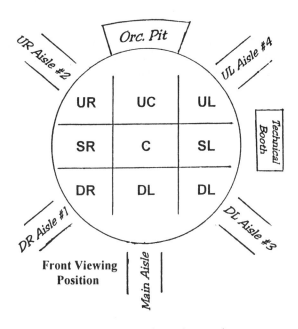

Figure 11-11   Breaking down the circular arena stage into performing areas and using other points of reference to note blocking. Note that the aisles can be identified either by their stage position (DR, UR, etc.), by number (1, 2, etc.), or as demonstrated in the example (a combination of both the position and number). It is the SM's choice, as long as everyone is working with the same information.

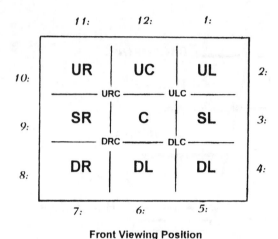

11:
12:
1:
UR
UC
UL
2:
10:
URC
ULC
SR
C
SL
3:
9:
DRC
DLC
DR
DL
DL
4:
8:
7:
6:
5:
Front Viewing Position

Figure 11-12 The square arena stage with the numbers of a clock surrounding the stage to further aid the SM in noting blocking.

- proscenium line = prosc.ln
- curtain line = curt.ln.
- apron line = aprn.ln.
- show portals:shwport
- wings #1, 2, 3, right or left stage = #1Wng R, etc.
- footlights, right, left or center = Foots R, etc.
- dance numbers 1 through ?? = dnc. #1, etc.
- numbers of the clock = @12:, @3:, etc.

With the addition of the scenery, set units, or big props like furniture the SM has even greater reference points to use in taking down blocking.

ABBREVIATIONS FOR CHARACTER NAMES

When having to note in the blocking script a character's name, a good method of abbreviation is to shorten the name as much as possible and then circle it. Figure 11-13 shows abbreviations for the names of the characters for our imaginary play, *John and Mary.*

MOVING SYMBOLS

Symbols that show movement or direction include:

- X = cross (an actor moves or travels on stage from one point to another)
- Xing = crossing
- Xes = crosses

An example of a blocking note in long hand might read "Crossing in front of John, Mary goes to stage right, sits on the left side of the sofa, takes out a cigarette and lights it." Figure 11-14 shows the same

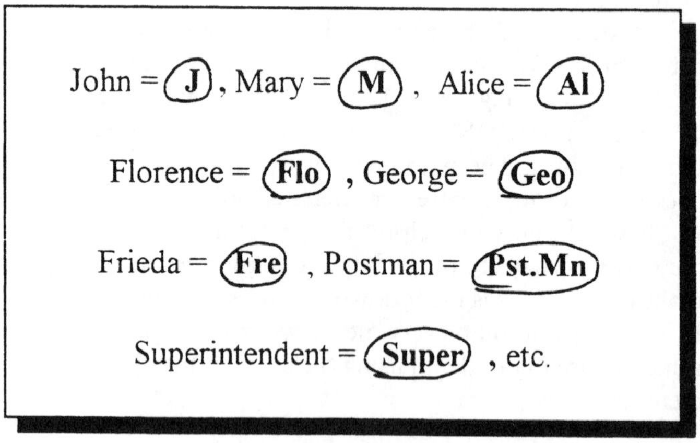

John = J, Mary = M, Alice = Al
Florence = Flo, George = Geo
Frieda = Fre, Postman = Pst.Mn
Superintendent = Super, etc.

Figure 11-13 Abbreviating the characters' names and circling them for quick and easy identification.

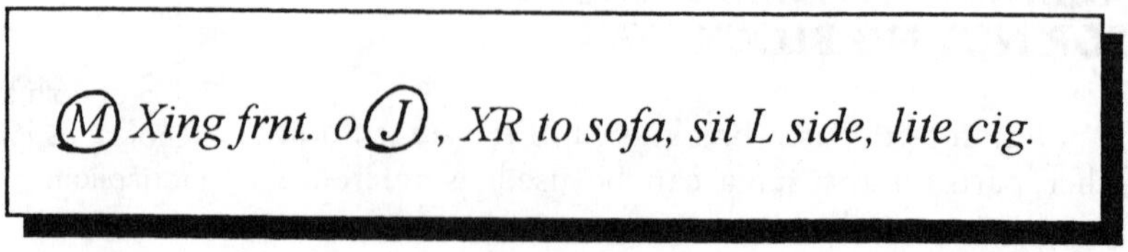

M Xing frnt. o J, XR to sofa, sit L side, lite cig.

Figure 11-14 An example of how an SM might note blocking in shorthand.

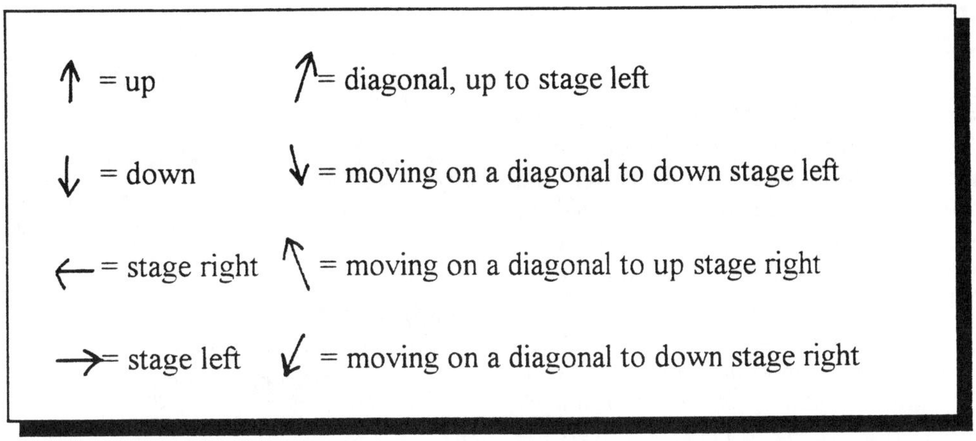

↑ = up   ↗ = diagonal, up to stage left

↓ = down   ↙ = moving on a diagonal to down stage left

← = stage right   ↖ = moving on a diagonal to up stage right

→ = stage left   ↘ = moving on a diagonal to down stage right

Figure 11-15   Arrows of direction an SM can use when noting blocking.

blocking note written in the SM's shorthand, using abbreviations and symbols.

Arrows

Arrows can be used to indicate direction as well as movement (see Figure 11-15). Blocking noted in long hand as "Intoxicated from drink, George stumbles up the stairs, tripping on the third step. When he gets to the top, he burps, smiles, and in his confusion, heads back down the stairs" could be written in the SM's shorthand as in Figure 11-16.

Figure 11-17 shows the uses of squiggly and arched arrows in noting blocking.

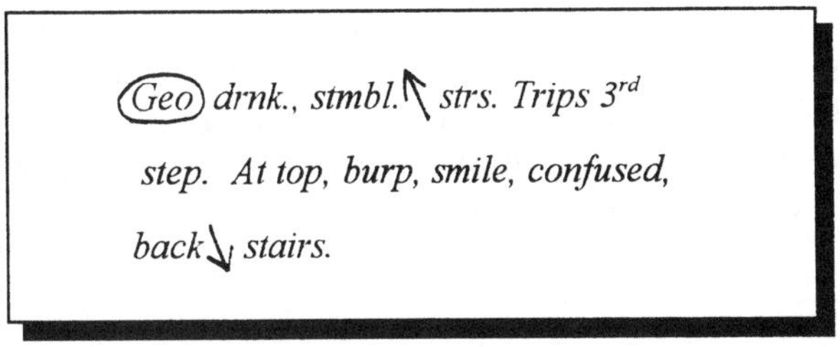

(Geo) *drnk., stmbl.*↖ *strs. Trips 3rd step. At top, burp, smile, confused, back*↘ *stairs.*

Figure 11-16   The SM's abbreviated words, arrows, and symbols to note blocking.

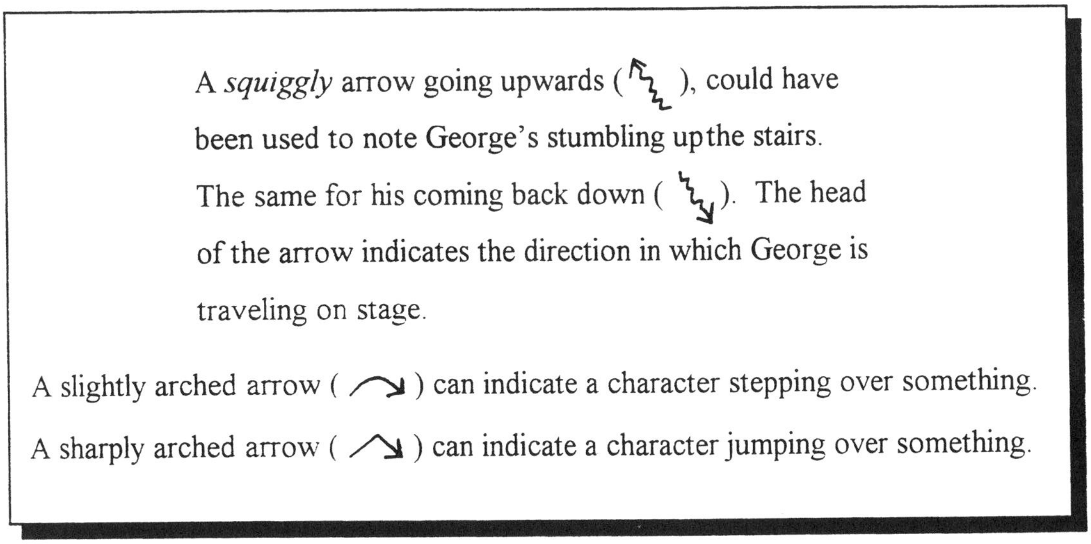

A *squiggly* arrow going upwards (↖), could have been used to note George's stumbling up the stairs. The same for his coming back down (↘). The head of the arrow indicates the direction in which George is traveling on stage.

A slightly arched arrow (⤳) can indicate a character stepping over something.

A sharply arched arrow (⤳) can indicate a character jumping over something.

Figure 11-17   Examples of squiggly and arched arrows and what they mean to further aid an SM in noting blocking.

SOME GENERAL SM ABBREVIATIONS

In writing blocking notes, the SM abbreviates words as much as possible. In doing so the SM follows no standard abbreviated form for the words written; the goal is to write as much detail as is needed in the smallest amount of space. The notes must be clear and understandable. Abbreviations must stand alone—they should not be mistaken or confused with another word. As an example, the abbreviation for *bedroom* and *boardroom* could be the same, *Bd.rm.* However, if the SM abbreviates boardroom as *Brd.rm.* there is no chance of it being mistaken for bedroom. Figure 11-18 shows some typical abbreviations for noting blocking.

The adage "a picture is worth a thousand words" holds very true for the SM when making blocking notes. However, the SM's pictures or diagrams are very basic and primitive (see Figure 11-19). They don't need to be anything more, as long as they convey the blocking information.

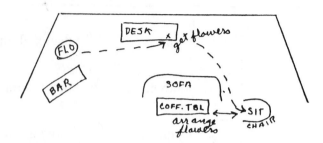

Figure 11-19 A small, primitive diagram the SM might draw when noting the blocking of the character Florence from the imaginary play, *John and Mary*.

NOTING BLOCKING FOR BUSY SCENES

There is a scene on a train in the musical *Annie Get Your Gun* that is confined to the space of a sleeper car with a double berth for sleeping. The scene involves the character Annie, three children, and four of the lead principal performers. There are times during this

adjust = **adj.** (or) **adjst.**	desk = **dsk.**	mirror = **mirr.**
answer = **ans.**	dining room = **din.rm.**	music = **mus.**
at = **@**	door = dr.	near = **nr.**
	down = **dwn.**	newspaper = **nws.ppr.**
bathroom = **bth.rm**	drink = **drnk.**	
bed = **bd.**		of = **of**
bedroom = **bd.rm.**	enter = **entr.**	open door = **opn.dr.**
begin = **bgn.**	*Exit = **EXIT**	overture = **ovrt.**
bench = **bnch.**		
blackout = **BO**	fade = **Fd.** or **FD.**	picture = **pict.**
bottle = **btl.**	follow = **folw.**	platform = **platf.**
bottom = **btm.**	front = **frnt.**	point of view = **POV**
	furniture = **furnit.**	room = **rm.**
chair = **chr.**		
check = **chk.** or ✓	immediately = **immed.**	sound effect = **SFX**
circle = ○		
close door = **cls.dr.**		table = **tbl.**
coffee = **coff.**	kitchen = **kit**	with = **w/**
continue = **cont.**		without = **w/o**
corner = **cr.**	light = **lite**	

* **EXIT** - Noting this word in upper case letters helps single out in the rehearsal script all EXITS. For any number of reasons, the SM will be asked for this information and will need to extract it from his blocking script as quickly as possible.

Figure 11-18 A list of words and their abbreviations an SM might use in noting blocking.

scene when all the characters are on stage at the same time, and the blocking can be fast paced and played for as much comedy as the director and actors choose. It is the SM's job to capture in the blocking notes the movement, the action, and as much as possible, the comic values of the scene. The long version of the blocking notes for this scene might be written as follows: "As the lights come up, Annie's two sisters are already on stage, playing in the upper berth, which is placed left of center. Annie and her brother Jake enter stage right. They cross to the berth. Annie tucks Jake in the lower bed of the berth with his head going toward stage left. Annie then sits on the stage right corner of the bed, takes Jake's primer-reader, and reads. The sisters hang over the edge of the upper berth to listen." This is translated into SM's shorthand as shown in Figure 11-20.

Figure 11-21 shows the shorthand version of the following blocking from the continuation of the same scene: "As Annie reads, Buffalo Bill and the show manager, Charlie, enter from stage right. They stop stage right center to talk. They do not see Annie and she does not see them. She continues to read. Just as Buffalo Bill and Charlie get into place, Frank enters from stage left. He sees Buffalo Bill and Charlie. Not wanting them to see him, Frank does a comic circle around himself and starts to exit the same way he came in."

Figure 11-22 shows the shorthand version of what happens next in the same scene: "Just as Frank is leaving, Dolly enters left at the same time. They bump into each other, each spinning off the other, and end up going in the opposite direction in which they were heading. Thus Dolly exits back out the door and Frank heads straight for Buffalo Bill and Charlie."

(BB & Charl) entr.R - xing to RC.

Stop, mime-talk, do not see (A)

(A) not see them, cont. read

As (BB & Charl) get in place, (Fr) entr.L, sees

(BB & Charl) (Fr) does

comic ⊙ around-self & starts exit L

Figure 11-21   Continuing the same train scene from *Annie Get Your Gun*, with the SM's blocking notes for the entrance of Buffalo Bill (BB), Charlie (Charl), and Frank (Fr).

While the longhand description for this section of blocking and comic stage business, reads like a novel, the SM's notes are concise, highly abbreviated, and to the point.

THE ABSENCE OF SOME BLOCKING DETAILS

Although the SM is required to be detailed in the blocking notes, they should not include things that actors bring to the part, such as feelings, emotions, attitude, gestures, or reactions, unless they have direct importance to the storyline or play in some way. If the SM does make these notes, it is for the SM's information only, and when a director or an actor asks for blocking from the SM's script, the SM does not deliver this additional information. The actors and director want only the basic blocking information—

(Sisters) O.S. in upr.brth, LoC.

(A & Jk) entr. SR, X to lowr. brth

(A) tuck in (J) w/head twrd. SL

(A) sit on bed, read primer.

(Sisters) above hng.ovr.& listn.

Figure 11-20   The SM's way of noting busy or complicated blocking for a train scene in the musical *Annie Get Your Gun*.

As (Fr) Exiting - (Dol) entr L.

They bump into each other & spin.

(Dol) EXITing L

(Fr) Xing R to (BB & Chrl)

Figure 11-22   The same train scene from *Annie Get Your Gun*. The SM notes the blocking for the comic business between Frank (Fr) and Dolly (Dol).

the moves and placement. They will provide the things that fill in their parts. No SM, director, or anyone else for that matter, should expect one actor to do what some other actor has done in the part previously. In the same light, the SM does not always note timing such as the number of beats or seconds the actor takes in a dramatic pause, or the number of steps an actor takes to complete a movement or action unless, of course, the information is important for comic value or dramatic effect to the scene or the play.

NEAT BLOCKING NOTES

It is very important for the SM to be neat in penmanship when noting the blocking. It must be clear, orderly, and highly comprehensible so the SM or anyone else can read it at a later time. There is no time for a quick scribble with the intention of going back to the script at a later time to rewrite the information, unless the SM wants to spend hours of what could be time for doing something else. Learn to be neat and clear on the spot while making the notations. Furthermore, *the SM uses only pencil when making blocking notes.* Change is for certain—it is the rule and not the exception.

The example in Figure 11-23 is an edited scene from the musical *Annie Get Your Gun*, with the SM's hand-written blocking notes. This is the scene where the scrubby and gawky Annie Oakley meets for the first time the handsome and egotistical Frank Butler. Take note of the detail in the blocking notes. Both the director and actors wanted the action done at specific times and on certain words.

THE NUMERICAL WAY TO NOTE BLOCKING

Sometimes when the blocking of a scene is intricate or complicated, or the interplay between characters is involved, or when there are a large number of people in the scene, the SM might want to use the numerical way of noting the blocking. With this method, the SM merely jots numbers on the page of dialogue where the blocking notes are to take place, then on the blank page to the left (which is the backside of the previous page) writes out the notes.

Figure 11-24 shows Scene 1 from Act I of our imaginary play *John and Mary*—the scene in which Mary's mother, Frieda, calls. The director chooses to have Frieda seen by the audience as she makes the call, rather than having her backstage talking over a mic. The director's objective is to show how mother and daughter are so alike even if they seem to be at odds with each other when they speak. In noting the blocking for this scene, the SM is required to note in detail the actions of all the characters.

Note in Figure 11-24 the amount of numbers listed in the small paragraph of stage directions at the beginning of the scene. The numerical way of noting blocking has allowed the SM to make copious notes on seven different directions and their details. Note also that the numbers are not all in numerical order as you read down the page. Notes 9 and 11 come before notes 6 and 7. This is because the director added these directions/details later in the rehearsal. When this happens, the SM just notes the numbers on the page of dialogue and then makes detailed notes on the page to the left. Later, perhaps in understudy rehearsals, the SM sees numbers 9 and 11 on the dialogue page, then refers to the same numbers on the left-hand page.

The numerical approach, however, has its drawbacks. It is not recommended when working on a new play because there will likely be script changes. New pages will replace old ones, and when the old pages are removed, so are the blocking notes on the backsides of those pages. In a new show, if the SM chooses to note blocking using the numerical method, it is safer and wiser to insert blank pages to make the blocking notes.

THE PUBLISHER'S PRINTED STAGE DIRECTIONS AND TECHNICAL EFFECTS

Any manuscript, whether published or unpublished, has written into it stage directions that the author or some director has created. The script will also have noted into it technical effects inherent to the script. For the most part, directors read the stage directions once and then ignore them, doing as they choose. In the second or third reading of the play, the SM should write in pencil in the right margin all the effects that are cues in the show. Using our imaginary play, *John*

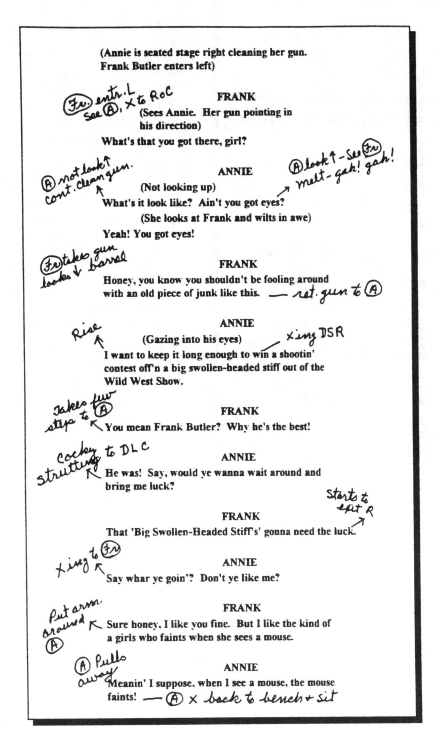

Figure 11-23   The SM's hand-written blocking notes for the first meeting scene between Annie Oakley and Frank Butler from the musical *Annie Get Your Gun*. (©1949, 1952, 1967 by Herbert Fields, Dorothy Fields, and Irving Berlin. Copyright renewed. International copyright secured. All rights reserved. Used by permission.)

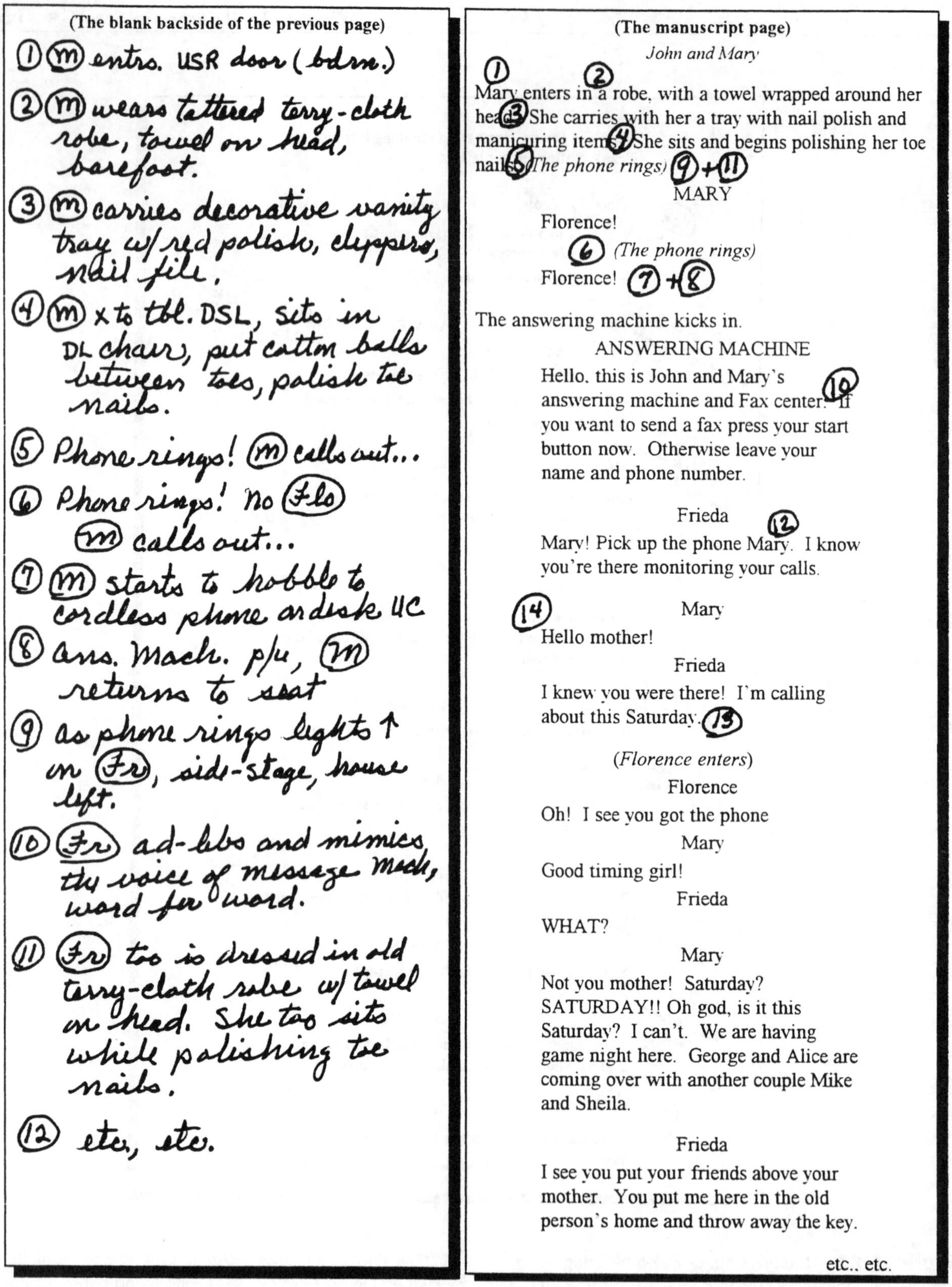

(The blank backside of the previous page)

① Ⓜ entrs. USR door (bdrm.)

② Ⓜ wears tattered terry-cloth robe, towel on head, barefoot.

③ Ⓜ carries decorative vanity tray w/ red polish, clippers, nail file.

④ Ⓜ x to tbl. DSL, sits in DL chair, put cotton balls between toes, polish toe nails.

⑤ Phone rings! Ⓜ calls out...

⑥ Phone rings! No Ⓕⓛⓞ Ⓜ calls out...

⑦ Ⓜ starts to hobble to cordless phone on desk UC

⑧ ans. mach. p/u, Ⓜ returns to seat

⑨ as phone rings lights ↑ in Ⓕⓡ, side-stage, house left.

⑩ Ⓕⓡ ad-libs and mimics the voice of message mach, word for word.

⑪ Ⓕⓡ too is dressed in old terry-cloth robe w/ towel on head. She too sits while polishing toe nails.

⑫ etc, etc.

(The manuscript page)

John and Mary

Mary enters in a robe, with a towel wrapped around her head. She carries with her a tray with nail polish and manicuring items. She sits and begins polishing her toe nails. (The phone rings) ⑨+⑪

MARY

Florence!

⑥ (The phone rings)
Florence! ⑦+⑧

The answering machine kicks in.

ANSWERING MACHINE

Hello, this is John and Mary's answering machine and Fax center. ⑩ If you want to send a fax press your start button now. Otherwise leave your name and phone number.

Frieda

Mary! Pick up the phone Mary. ⑫ I know you're there monitoring your calls.

Mary ⑭

Hello mother!

Frieda

I knew you were there! I'm calling about this Saturday. ⑬

(Florence enters)

Florence

Oh! I see you got the phone

Mary

Good timing girl!

Frieda

WHAT?

Mary

Not you mother! Saturday? SATURDAY!! Oh god, is it this Saturday? I can't. We are having game night here. George and Alice are coming over with another couple Mike and Sheila.

Frieda

I see you put your friends above your mother. You put me here in the old person's home and throw away the key.

etc., etc.

Figure 11-24 The SM's numerical way of noting blocking. Numbers are placed on the dialogue page, while details of the blocking are noted on the blank page to the left (the backside of the previous page of dialogue).

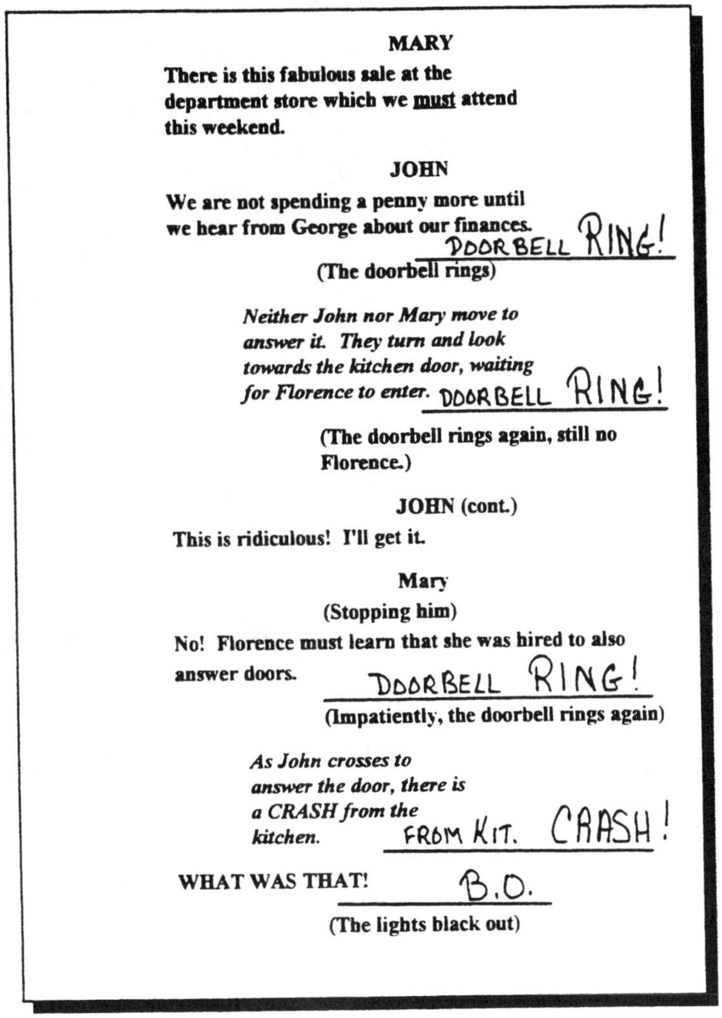

MARY

There is this fabulous sale at the department store which we <u>must</u> attend this weekend.

JOHN

We are not spending a penny more until we hear from George about our finances.

DOORBELL RING!

(The doorbell rings)

Neither John nor Mary move to answer it. They turn and look towards the kitchen door, waiting for Florence to enter.

DOORBELL RING!

(The doorbell rings again, still no Florence.)

JOHN (cont.)

This is ridiculous! I'll get it.

Mary

(Stopping him)

No! Florence must learn that she was hired to also answer doors.

DOORBELL RING!

(Impatiently, the doorbell rings again)

As John crosses to answer the door, there is a CRASH from the kitchen.

FROM KIT. CRASH!

WHAT WAS THAT!

B.O.

(The lights black out)

Figure 11-25 An example from the imaginary play *John and Mary* of what the SM's rehearsal script might look like going into rehearsals. The SM notes the technical cues inherent to the script. Later the SM will be more specific about their placement and when to call these cues.

and Mary, Figure 11-25 shows how the SM's script would look after the second or third reading.

Some SMs prefer highlighting the technical effects that are printed on the page. This is a workable idea, but it becomes a wasted step. From the start the SM should note the cues in the rehearsal script as they will eventually be noted in the cueing script—the script created and used for calling all the cues in the show during the performance. Once the SM makes the blocking notes and writes into the rehearsal script the cues inherent to the script, the rehearsal script will look something like Figure 11-26.

ORGANIZING THE REHEARSAL/BLOCKING SCRIPT

Tabbing the Scenes

During rehearsals it is extremely helpful for the SM to tab the pages of the rehearsal/blocking script. The SM places the tabs at the beginning of each scene. When working on a show in which there will be script changes, it is wise for the SM to insert between each scene a card-stock page and attach the tab to that page. Then when the changes are made, the SM

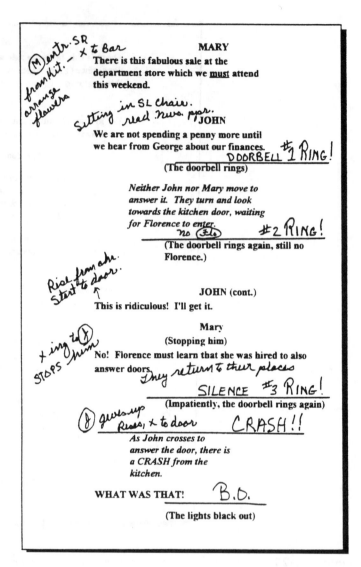

Figure 11-26 The same scene as in Figure 11-25, after the director has blocked the scene. In addition to being specific about the placement of cues, the SM has now added the blocking notes to the script.

can quickly remove the old pages and have the tabs remain in their proper place.

Inserting the SM's Personal Floor Plans

In addition to tabbing each scene in the rehearsal/blocking script, the SM should insert a copy of the personal floor plan for that particular scene. On it the SM can note prop and furniture placement and the initial placement of the actors as they begin the scene.

Script Changes

Before computers and copying machines were readily available, the task of doing rewrites could be a time-consuming job sometimes requiring late hours after rehearsals. Script changing can be done in various ways, with varying numbers of people involved. Sometimes it is privately done between the director and writer. Other times the producer and assistant director are included. On occasion, the SM may be there, but mostly in a secretarial capacity.

First comes the creative session to make the changes. Then the task to get the rewrites entered into the computer, printed out, copied, and made ready for distribution for the next day's rehearsal. The SM may be left to do this work alone or may be aided by the ASM or the PA. If the SM is really fortunate, the assistant director will take full responsibility for the entire matter and have the changes ready and distributed each time changes are made.

The Script on Computer

With a new show or a show in which the SM knows there will be some or many rewrites, it is wise to have entered into a file on the laptop a copy of the entire script. This will be a time-consuming job for someone—possibly the SM—but it will, in the long run, be very helpful in the process of making script changes.

Revised Pages

Some directors or production companies like to print up the new pages of the script in different colors for easy identification. This method is especially popular in films and television. It is not always necessary in theatre, depending on the extent of the rewrites. If the SM is responsible for making up the new pages, he or she should check to see what the director or production company prefers.

Marking Revised Pages

As each script change takes place, there should appear on each revised page, at the top right corner, a note identifying the page as a revision, just as the SM does with all charts, plots, plans, and lists when they are revised. The note should contain the word *revised* and the date. It is also a good idea for the SM to put a person's initials following the date. This could be either the person who originated the change, such as the author or director, or it could be the SM's initials: **REVISED: (6-28-99) sj.** This identifying mark becomes very important to ensure that everyone is working from the same script. It is the SM's job to see that everyone who needs to have these changes receives them.

Keeping Script Changes on File

First, it is important that the SM always have on file extra copies of the script changes for distribution. Next, on a new show or a show with a lot of script changes, it is wise for the SM to keep three file folders for script changes. One should be marked *Current*

Script Changes, another should be marked *Last Script Changes*, and the third, *Past Script Changes*. There is no predicting or outguessing what the writers or director will do next and in which direction they will travel. The SM needs to be ready to provide them with whatever they want.

FOLLOWING SCRIPT

Prompting, being on book, cueing the actors, following script—these are all terms that describe another important job the SM must do to keep the rehearsals running smoothly and efficiently. Both the director and actors expect one of the SMs to be on book at all times when they are rehearsing. When scenes are being blocked for the first time, everyone has scripts in hand, reading their dialogue and jotting down their blocking as it is created. However, once the blocking has been set and the actors are somewhat confident about knowing their lines and blocking, they will go off book and expect the SM to be on book, follow script, and feed them a line or piece of blocking should they forget.

Following Script for the Director

In following script, the SM must first serve and please the director. The director expects the SM to be ever present and ready, following the script line by line, moment for moment. The director does not want rehearsal time lost while the SM looks in the script for the line an actor has forgotten, nor does the director want to wait while the SM tries to decipher blocking notes. In some extreme cases, the director requires the actors to say every word as written in the script and do the blocking exactly as set, and expects the SM to correct the actors if they are the least bit off. Most directors allow a greater latitude in this area, but nonetheless expect the SM to correct the actors if they go too far astray.

Following Script for the Actors

Following script for the actors can sometimes be a challenge. It is the SM's job to be on script, ready to feed an actor a line or recite a piece of the blocking. Most actors, when they forget, are very good in asking the SM. There are some, however, who stumble and grope, trying to jog their memory, or become silent as they search internally. Sometimes these actors want help from the SM, but for whatever reason, do not ask. This can leave the SM uncertain, because actors in rehearsal will also grope, stumble, or become silent when they are in a moment of discovery, or taking a dramatic pause. If the SM decides the actor has forgotten the line and delivers it, and if indeed the actor was in a dramatic moment, the actor can become very upset, first because the moment was broken and possibly lost, and second, because with the delivery of the line from the SM, it appeared that the actor did not know the dialogue.

To avoid this uncertainty and to prevent the wrath of an actor who might be misunderstood, the SM tells the cast and director that he or she will feed lines and give blocking only when asked. It helps if the SM briefly explains why it is best to work in this way, so the actors and director will understand and be more willing to make this part of their way of working.

Calling out Lines

In calling out a line, the SM gives only the first part of the line. Sometimes only the first two or three words are necessary—just enough information to jog the actors' memory. The actors know their lines and usually hearing the first few words is all they need. For the SM to give more usually is an intrusion and becomes an annoyance. In addition, the SM simply reads the words from the page and does not deliver them with any sort of acting or interpretation.

CALLING TECHNICAL CUES IN REHEARSALS

When following a script that has written into it technical effects with a direct effect on the scene or the actor's timing, it is the SM's job in rehearsals to call out such cues each time the scene is rehearsed. Calling out technical effects such as lightning, a doorbell, a telephone, a loud noise, a gun being fired, or scenery being moved during the scene, aids the actors during rehearsals, giving them a greater sense of being in a performance. To call out technical cues that don't have a direct effect on the moment being rehearsed is a distraction, an intrusion, and is annoying!

The SM's Delivery Technique

In the delivery of technical cues or special effects, the SM vocally interjects them at the correct time saying,

"The telephone rings," or "Lightning," or says in a clear and audible voice, "The gun is fired." The SM may choose to imitate some sound effect cues. This is acceptable as long as it is not laughable or distracting. If, according to the script, the gun is fired unexpectedly, the SM might call out in an explosive manner, "Bang!!!" maybe even slamming a hand on the worktable to enhance the effect and perhaps jar the actor. There are, however, some things better said than imitated. It is enough to say, "The car starts" or "Footsteps are heard approaching."

When having to give an action with some detail, the SM needs to keep it simple and to the point, choosing adjectives that best fit the action and mood:

"The car starts with a 'choke' and 'gasp,' followed by a puff of black smoke."

"The rain starts falling gently on the roof."

"The sound of footsteps of a woman wearing high heels is heard coming down the hall—stopping from time to time as the steps draw near."

Sometimes, before the scene begins, it helps to set the mood and get the scene started if the SM is a little more poetic in this presentation:

"As the curtain rises, brilliant sunlight beams through the downstage window, and the song of morning birds fills the air."

"As the lights in the room fade to black, we hear footsteps approaching. Suddenly they stop! In a burst, the door swings open. There silhouetted against the hall light is the slight figure of a little man. The curtain slowly comes in."

Each SM develops his or her own approach in following script, giving lines, and calling out technical cues. The SM who is selective and keeps it simple will be highly successful and become even more valued as an SM.

TIMING SCENES, ACTS, AND THE WHOLE SHOW

Throughout the rehearsal period the SM will need to time some or all parts of the show. Some directors are greatly concerned with the length of scenes and ultimately the whole show. Some directors will from the very first reading ask the SM to take a timing. Certainly once a scene is blocked, the SM should periodically take timings. This is particularly important with a new show. With each timing, the SM notes the results on the rehearsal script at the beginning of the scene, in the left-hand margin, along with the date of the particular timing. This information is then readily available for the director, and comparisons can be made with other timings.

PROPS

Props, too, hold an important place in the SM's job during rehearsals. Props, which include hand props and furniture, require the same intensity of attention as do the other parts of the SM's work. Of all the technical departments, the SM is most involved and most knowledgeable of the props used in the show. The SM is there in the rehearsal hall when they are introduced into the play and starts the prop list from the first readings of the play. The SM knows their placement, and each day in rehearsals (if there is no prop person working the rehearsals) sees that the props are set for each scene being rehearsed.

With a brand new show or a heavy prop show, the head prop person is often hired to start working at the rehearsal hall on the first day of rehearsals. With some shows, producers are able to hold off until the last week at the rehearsal hall. On many revivals or shows being produced in regional theatre, producers will sometimes hold off on bringing in the union prop person until the show gets into the theatre for technical rehearsals. This leaves the SM in charge of the props until then.

Detailing the Props

With the SM being the key and pivotal person in creating the prop list, it is important that the SM be organized, specific, and detailed in noting the props. During rehearsals as each prop is introduced into the show, the SM needs to observe and seek out from the director and actors what they want, what they need, how the prop is used, whether it needs to be real or can be fake, and then convey that information verbally and on a list to the person gathering the props.

Red Flag Props

As each prop is introduced into the show, it is important for the SM to visualize the prop and *think*

around it. That is, the SM not only sees the prop mentally, but also sees other props that might be generated because of this one prop. Neither the director nor actors will think of these additional or secondary props until they get on the stage with the real prop. It is the SM's job to think ahead and add the secondary props to the prop list. For example, if the actor in the rehearsal is told by the director that the character lights up a cigarette, a red flag must go up in the SM's mind. Smoking a cigarette on stage means more than noting cigarettes on the prop list; matches are needed and an ash tray with a slight amount of water in the ashtray to ensure that when the cigarette is put out, it goes out completely. In addition, the SM might also ask the actor if a particular brand of cigarettes is preferred.

Red flag props are props that generate other props. As soon as food is mentioned in rehearsals, a giant red flag should go up in the SM's mind. Food items require the SM to think around the item in great detail:

- Is the food real, fake, or a substitute food used for the real thing?
- Do the actors eat the food?
- Can the food be easily eaten during the performance so the actor can continue to speak or sing?
- Are dishes and/or utensils, napkins, towels needed?
- Is the food perishable? If so, is a refrigerator needed?
- Does the food need to be cooked or prepared in some way?
- How much food is needed for each performance?
- What clean-up items are necessary?

The same is true when making and drinking drinks on stage. When this prop is introduced during rehearsals, another red flag must be raised and the SM must think around it.

The Metamorphosis of the Prop List

Stage 1 of the list begins with the SM's first readings of the play as the SM hand-writes on separate pieces of paper for each scene, the props inherent to the script. Included on this list are also *set dressing* props—items that need to be on the stage, but are not handled or used by the actors, props that have been specified in the author's notes, or have come out of the dialogue. From this list, and in talking with the director, the SM creates a rehearsal prop list for the person who will be procuring the rehearsal props.

Stage 2 starts once the rehearsals begin. During this stage the SM's hand-written list grows daily in size and detail, still being written on separate pages for each scene.

Stage 3 starts early in the rehearsals when the SM has meetings with the person procuring the props to discuss what is needed. At each meeting the SM provides the prop person with a clean and organized list, noting in detail specific needs and descriptions of the props. The list grows as the director and actors work on the show, and the information is given to the prop person at the next meeting. Having these meetings early and giving the information in bits and pieces is the only way the SM and the prop person can work and still be ready for the first day of technical rehearsals at the theatre. Throughout this time, the SM continues to work with the handwritten sheets.

Stage 4 is the final stage of the prop list. Toward the end of the rehearsal period, no later than the last week of rehearsals at the rehearsal hall, the SM transposes the hand-written prop list into the laptop, creating the prop list as presented in Chapter 6. Note on this final list that all of the information describing the props and how they are used has been eliminated. Note also that each scene is no longer kept on a separate page. The prop list is now condensed with each scene following consecutively, still having the placement of the props, but now presented more in list form. From this point, the prop list remains the same in form. The only changes made will be whatever props the director, actors, or designers add or take away.

The Performance-Preset Prop List

The *performance-preset prop list* could be considered the fifth and final step in the metamorphosis of the prop list. However, the performance-preset prop list is strictly for the SM's use when the show gets into its performance stage—be it for dress rehearsals, preview performance, or the run of the show. The props listed on the performance-preset prop list are listed according to their placement backstage and on stage, before the performance begins. This enables the SM to check the preset placement of all props. The SM can start in one area, let's say the backstage on stage right, then work toward the stage right wings, on to the stage, across the stage, into the stage left wings, and into the backstage areas on stage left, checking all along the way the placement of the props. The creation of the performance-preset prop list usually is assigned to the ASM, whose job it is to check the props for each performance after the prop person has finished setting them.

IN CLOSING

During rehearsals, as well as during all times throughout the production, the SM must be careful not to get into the position of doing work that is not part of the job, especially work that takes the SM away from the rehearsal hall. The rehearsal period is the center of action, change, development, and growth. As much as possible the SM needs to be at that center.

Each SM's experience of rehearsals will be unique, depending on the show and the people working on it. Throughout the rehearsal period the SM must be focused and concentrated on all parts of the production. It is the SM's job to oversee, observe, and keep the rehearsals running smoothly. In addition, the SM must note the blocking for the show in the rehearsal script, keeping it updated along with all charts, plots, plans, and lists. The SM must keep the lines of communication opened to all departments, seeing that all changes are properly noted and distributed. While doing all of this, the SM is also thinking ahead or reflecting back, anticipating problems or heading them off. If the SM falls short in any one area and things go wrong, people will be quick to place the blame on the SM: *Whenever possible, the buck and the blame stop at the SM's desk!*

There is still more to the rehearsal period at the rehearsal hall—the last part of rehearsal, the closing part. Primarily this part takes place in the last week of rehearsals at the rehearsal hall. In a rehearsal period of ten or seven days, this last part will be in the last two or three days. The things that happen in the last week or last few days include information enough for another chapter. So without further delay, turn to the next chapter and let's see what things need to be done to close out the rehearsal period.

12

The Last Week of Rehearsals

To say this is the last week of rehearsals is misleading, for there are still the technical rehearsals. For the SM, this chapter would be more appropriately named The Last Week of Rehearsals at the Rehearsal Hall. For the director and actors, this is the last week in which the time is strictly devoted to doing just their work. Once the show gets into technical rehearsals, the time and work becomes divided, with greater focus on technically putting the show together.

THE SHIFT IN WORK

As the rehearsals move into this final week, there comes a shift in direction of work and a new energy as everyone gets closer to the opening of the show. For the actors and director, it is time to finish experimentation and development on their parts and start bringing their work to performance level. In bits and pieces, the producer has seen the dream materialize. The producer has had many meetings and consultations with the director, watched rehearsals from the side lines, and has intervened and expressed personal feelings and opinions when necessary. The plans and designs of the technical elements have been reviewed and approved, and the producer may even have visited some of the shops and studios where these things are being produced. Now in this last week, the producer's attention is most likely directed toward the opening, perhaps planning a gala event, and surely stepping up the publicity and advertisements.

The heads of the various technical departments also are becoming more active. From time to time throughout this last week, some may stop in at the rehearsal hall to see a run-through of the show and collect any revised charts, plots, plans, lists, or schedules the SM might have. On most productions, the prop person is now working full-time and has taken over the props during the rehearsals.

For the SMs this last week becomes a time of duality—somewhat like rubbing their bellies and patting their heads. On the one hand, the SM's thoughts and work must be directed toward moving the company to the theatre, and at the same time rehearsals must keep going full speed ahead, scheduling and working the actors and director up to the last hour of the last day.

This last week is a transition week for everyone in the company. For the technical departments, it is time to be finishing construction, putting the final touches on things, gathering, buying, or renting the equipment necessary for the show, and just generally preparing to be ready for the technical rehearsals in the following week. The SM has little control over these departments. If they are delinquent in any way, the SM cannot be responsible; the SM's job was to supply them with schedules, feed them information, inform them of changes, be alert to any deficiencies, and anticipate or head off problems by having conversations first with the head of the department, then to the director and producer if things did not improve. If an SM takes on any more, it will involve taking on work and responsibility which is not part of the job and it will drain the SM of time and energy—time and energy that is badly needed in this last week of rehearsals and in the technical rehearsals to come.

On the other hand, the SM does have more control and effect over the cast and director in seeing that they are prepared and ready to move into the theatre without problems. Even then, the SM can be limited and handicapped by a director if the director has used rehearsal time poorly and ignored the SM's efforts to keep the work on schedule.

MEETINGS

Meetings become an important part of the work in this last week. With a new show or a show that is being made over, a final production meeting is most beneficial. Just as important are small meetings with individual departments along with the director and SM where the different departments can report their accomplishments, present their problems, and assure their readiness. For all meetings, the SM once again needs to be fully prepared, going over schedules, handing out revisions, and anticipating problems.

Lighting Meeting

One of the more important meetings must take place with the lighting designer and assistant. The importance of this meeting is reflected in the fact that it was scheduled on the block calendar back in the early days of the SM's production week at the production office. This meeting in the last week is for the lighting designer to see one or two run-throughs of the show. During that time the lighting designer will mark the placement of cues in the script. If the lighting designer has not been given a clean and updated script by this time, the SM sees to it that one is presented in time for this meeting.

The SM's Meeting with the Lighting Designer

After the lighting designer has viewed the show and has gotten the placement of the cues, the SM needs to have a meeting with the lighting designer to get the placement of the lights written into the rehearsal script. It is important that the SM get this information before technical rehearsals begin, because it needs to be written into the SM's new script, the cueing script (we'll learn more about the cueing script in the next chapter). The SM should not wait until technical rehearsals, but must be prepared and have done as much work in advance as is possible.

In academic and community theatre, the numbering and placement of the cues may be left up to the SM. Never in professional theatre where there is a lighting designer does this happen. The lighting designer dictates the cues and the SM notes them on the script.

Spotlight Cues

For musical shows where spotlights are used, the meeting the SM has with the lighting designer does not include noting spotlight cues. Spotlight cues will be set during technical rehearsals as the designer works through the show confirming and permanently setting all light cues.

Sometimes the SM is responsible for calling spotlight cues during performances and will need to note them on the cueing script as they are set. Other times, there is a lead spotlight person who is responsible for calling all spotlight cues. In a technically difficult show and a show where the SM must call a large number of light cues and set change cues, having a lead spotlight person call the spotlight cues is a welcome relief.

Set Moves/Scene Changes Meeting (Paper Tech)

In shows where there are major set/scenery changes, such as in musicals, it is important that the SM set up during this last week a meeting with the technical director, the head carpenter, the head fly person, and the head of props. The purpose is to get written into the SM's rehearsal script the cues for the scenery moves. At this time the SM's personal floor plans are highly useful. Often, this meeting is called a *paper tech*—that is, the set/scenery moves are envisioned and written down without benefit of having the actual pieces of scenery present to aid everyone in the decisions. Later in technical rehearsals whatever changes need to be made will be made as each set change is worked for the first time.

Sometimes the scenery changes are involved and technically difficult. The department heads may want to wait until they get into the theatre where they will have the actual pieces of scenery from which to work. As much as possible and within reason, the SM should push to have this paper tech meeting. It gets everyone thinking about a part of the show that is often put off until the last moment. If the SM must wait until the scenery is set up in the theatre, it is important to have this paper tech meeting before the actors, director, producer, and other staff members arrive to begin technical rehearsals. Time is limited in technical rehearsals and there will be unexpected delays. Patience will run thin quickly. No one wants to wait while the SM and crew first work out the set moves. By the first day of technical rehearsals, the crew and SM should be ready to start refining their work in this area.

Sound Cues Meeting

From the start of rehearsals the SM has established with the sound department the goal for having the sound effects tape or CD edited and ready for use in this last week of rehearsals. In a show where sound or music effect cues are important to the show, the SM does the show a great service by having this tape or CD ready. It is one of the things that aid the process of getting the actors up to performance level while still in rehearsals. Some directors will insist on having such a tape or CD available as soon as possible.

The purpose of this meeting between the sound department and SM is to finalize the placement of sound effect and music cues in the SM's rehearsal script. This will be a relatively easy and short meeting. For the most part, the sound department has already noted in its script the placement of all cues. Remember, this department also needs to have the most recent and updated script. This meeting is to confirm placement of cues and to see that the SM and sound person executing the cues during performance are coordinated and working with the same information.

As stated in Chapter 7, Profiles and Working Relationships, the SM is interested only in the sound effect and music cues. During the performance, the SM is not responsible for calling cues that bring up microphones and the level at which they are set. Only in very special cases will a mic cue be written in the SM's cueing script to be called during performance. If body mics are being used in the production and if the SM has not already given the sound person a copy of the Scene/Character Tracking Chart, this would be a good time. This chart will aid the sound person in creating the mic tracking chart.

Costumes/Wardrobe and Hair Meetings

The SM should talk with the heads of costume/wardrobe and hair mostly as a formality to go over the schedule for technical rehearsals and to get assurances that all will be ready for the costume parade or dress rehearsals. The SM will begin conversations on dressing room assignments, quick changes, and entrances and exits of the performers that will affect costume changes, but this part of the work will be finalized once everyone gets into the theatre.

Meeting with the Music Department

This will also be a meeting more of formality than for exchange of last-minute information. The SM and musical director have been in daily communication and have exchanged information and worked out problems as they arose. As with all of the other departments, the SM needs assurance that all is well with this department and that it is ready for the technical rehearsals. Perhaps the most important part of this meeting is for the SM to remind the music director and assistant to have drawn and submitted to the head of props a schematic drawing of the layout and placement of instruments in the orchestra pit. During technical rehearsals, a day or two before the orchestra begins working with the cast, the prop department is responsible for setting up the chairs, music stands, lights for the stands, risers for the conductor's podium, and the podium itself.

If the show is a new musical or the revival of an old one with new music arrangements and orchestrations, the SM should also ask if the new music has been sent to the arrangers, and if the various parts for the different instruments will be copied and ready for the first orchestra rehearsal. Once again, this is merely a formality and point of assurance for the SM, because 99.9 percent of the time the music director has dealt with this matter well in advance and is confident about being ready.

Set Designer/Construction Shop Meetings

Prior to the final week, perhaps on the Thursday or Friday before, the SM should talk with the set designer and visit the scenic shop where the set is being constructed, taking the director along if time and schedule permits. If the set is a rental, a phone call to the rental house is all that is necessary, asking them to double-check to see that all parts of the set have been gathered and that the set is ready for delivery on the time, date, and place as prearranged by the producer or technical director.

ADVICE TO THE SM

For one reason or another, departments sometimes start running behind in their work. While doing all the other work the SM must do, it is also the SM's job to observe the various departments from the sidelines as they progress in their work. It is true the SM has very little power and control over the various technical departments—it is the SM's job to let the professionals hired to do the job succeed or fail on their own. However, when the SM sees a situation that will negatively affect the show, the company, or the smooth running of the operation, these concerns must be expressed immediately, first to the head of the department, then to the producer and director if there is no change. This may make the SM appear to be a nervous individual, a person who worries unnecessarily. Some department heads, especially those who are falling behind or have a tendency to put off their work to the last minute, may express their annoyance about the SM. It is better for the SM to appear to be nervous or a worrier than to let matters reach problem status. The SM observes and oversees, lends support, gives advice, and presents alternatives. The SM's attention in all areas is on behalf of the producer, director, and show, looking out for their best interest. If a potential problem arises, the SM is obligated to step in and generate conversation on the matter. The SM's position of authority is well established and although the SM's power is sometimes limited, a good SM learns to use whatever power is available to effect change. In educational and community theatre, the SM has more direct control in all areas and is taught and expected to jump in and help wherever possible.

The SM must also learn self-protection. All of the people in the company, from their own positions, have certain expectations of the SM. The SM learns these different expectations and meets them by providing service, doing the job, and leaving each person responsible for his or her own work.

THE ASM

We have talked very little of the ASM's work during this rehearsal period. As stated early in this book, the ASM is ever present, just as is the PSM. The ASM takes up the slack, supporting the PSM by doing what the PSM cannot do, doing what the PSM may or may not want to do, or doing what the PSM may be incapable of doing. The ASM does this work quietly and without fanfare. The ASM's presence needs to be as strong as the PSM's, but from a secondary position. The ASM gets to shine and take center stage by working as well as any PSM. A good ASM is an underrated PSM. In this last week, the ASM gets the opportunity to step into a more prominent position, for while the PSM is off meeting with the different departments and preparing for the technical week ahead, the ASM is working closely with the director and actors, keeping the rehearsals running smoothly

and productively, and doing all the things the PSM would be doing.

BIRTH OF THE CUEING OR CALLING SCRIPT

Toward the end of this last week, once the SM has gathered all the information needed from the various departments, the SM must pull out a clean and updated script, go off to some quiet place, and neatly transpose all of the notes from the rehearsal script into cues. This is the birth of the *cueing* script or, as some people say, the *calling* script. This script will grow and develop during the technical rehearsals, and the SM will use it in each performance to call the cues for the show. Often the quiet place to which the SM should steal to create this cueing script is after hours at the office, at home, or early in the morning before the telephone starts ringing or actors start arriving for the day's rehearsal. This cueing script needs to be ready on the first day of technical rehearsals. To begin creating the cueing script during technical rehearsals is too late! The process of creating the cueing script requires time to think, time to envision the changes and plan ahead. There will be no time for this kind of work during technical rehearsals. A lot more on this subject is in the next chapter. Also, while off in this quiet place creating the cueing script, the SM is *learning the show*—learning the order of the cues, the set changes, and scene transitions. To not have this cueing script ready is gross negligence and could be professional suicide on the part of any SM.

RUN-THROUGHS OF THE SHOW

In theatre jargon, the process of rehearsing the show nonstop, as if it were a performance, is called a run-through, abbreviated as run-thru. In fact, the SM will abbreviate the word *through* in most of the writing for schedules, blocking notes, and notices posted on the callboard.

The Director's Obligation to Have Run-Thrus

By this last week in rehearsals, the director should be well past the blocking stages, unless the show is new and scenes are being changed, added, or rewritten. Even then, the director must do double-duty work by blocking the new scenes and at the same time allowing time for run-thrus of the entire show.

The SM as Watchdog

From the start and throughout the rehearsals, the SM has been vigilant in seeing that the director worked productively and stayed on schedule. The SM does not let a director get to this last week in rehearsals without being prepared to have run-thrus. However, being a watchdog over a delinquent director can be hazardous to the SM. It can cause ill feelings between the director and SM, affect their working relationship, and could mean the SM will never again be hired by this director. From the start, the SM must handle this matter delicately and with great diplomacy. It is really a matter that should be handled by the producer. If the SM's efforts to change the delinquent director fail, the SM should speak to the producer and let the producer work things out. For the SM to take on this problem alone, will become a loosing situation.

The SM's Contributions to the Run-Thrus

During run-thrus of the show in this last week of rehearsals, it is now the SM's job to do more than just follow script:

1. Without being distracting, annoying, or laughable, the SM calls out more of the cues that provide the technical elements of the show and give the actors and director a feeling of being in a performance. The SM verbally fills in the elements of the production that are not present at the rehearsal hall.
2. By this time in the rehearsals, both the PSM and the ASM are highly knowledgeable of the placement of props and furniture. They are coordinated and organized in shifting things from one scene to the other smoothly and quickly, further enhancing the feeling of being in a performance.
3. If the sound cues tape or CD is ready, the SM sees to it that the sound cues are executed at their proper times, often actually operating the tape machine or CD player.
4. During these run-thrus, the SM continues to follow dialogue, being ready to give a line upon request from the actor. There should be no delays in the delivery or lines, which would slow down the pace and flow even further.
5. This is also a good time for the SM to time the scenes and acts. The results of each timing should continue to be noted in the left-hand margin of the rehearsal script so they can be used in reference and comparison at a later time.

Invited Guests for Run-Thrus

Often within the last day or two of rehearsals at the rehearsal hall, the director might invite people to come and see a run-thru. These guests may be staff members, colleagues, or a limited number of friends and relatives of the cast. Having guests present helps shift the actors into working at performance level. It gets their energy up and provides greater motivation to perform. It is also good closure to the rehearsal hall period. Not all directors do this, however. When the suggestion of having invited guests is made, the SM needs to orchestrate and restrict the number of guests attending. There must not be more guests than the room is capable of holding.

Setting the Rehearsal Room for Invited Guests

When there is an invited audience, it becomes the SM's job to set up the room for the viewing audience. The SM must now rearrange the rehearsal room to accommodate the number of guests.

1. Scale down both the director's and SM's work tables. Keep the director's table at the center of the viewing area as it has been throughout the rehearsal period and perhaps place some VIP chairs next to the director, putting reserved signs or the names of the individuals on them.
2. The SM then sets the SM's table further back and off to the side where both the SM and the ASM can see the show and move freely to and from the stage area without disturbing the audience, to set props and change scenes.
3. If the show is a musical, the SM also sets the music director and pianist further back and off to the side, but where the music director can see and conduct the cast and pianist, and the performers can see the music director.
4. This being done, the SM can now set up the number of chairs needed for the guests.
5. Before the guests arrive, the SM sets the stage/performing area, putting all the props and rehearsal furniture in order as they will be used in the show and as they might be set if they were in a theatre doing a real performance.

Arrival of the Guests

The room and the stage should be set and ready before the guests arrive. It is poor form for the SMs to be racing about doing work that could have been done in advance. Besides, as the guests arrive, the SMs now need to act as hosts, welcoming the guests and giving whatever instructions and direction are necessary to maintain order and see that the event runs smoothly and begins on time. If the SMs are so inclined, there might be music playing as the guests arrive, but not so loud that it will be distracting. The producer and director may choose to make the occasion even more elaborate with food and drink. The SMs will coordinate this part of the setup, too, but should have help.

During the time the guests arrive and before the performance begins, the rehearsal room will echo with joyous sounds of friends seeing friends and people meeting people. The SMs, of course, will become part of this social affair, but not so much as to forget the time and the schedule. With the director's approval, the SM allows a ten- or fifteen-minute grace period for guests arriving late. At fifteen minutes before the performance is to begin, the SM announces generally to the cast and guests present, a fifteen-minute call. At the five-minute mark the SM asks the audience to take their seats, and asks the cast to either leave the room or go off to some corner where they can focus in on the rehearsal and prepare themselves for the performance.

Just before the performance begins, either the producer, director, or PSM might formally greet the guests and set up the performance by giving a brief description of the technical elements, namely the set. Showing the set designer's renderings, sketches, or a scale model makes the presentation quicker and easier.

During the intermission portion of this rehearsal, the SM announces there will be a fifteen-minute intermission. Once again the SM gives a call, first at the ten-minute mark, then at five. On completion of the performance, the SM allows a short period of time for congratulations and well-wishing, but then gently and kindly begins asking the guests to leave so the director can continue the rehearsal.

PREPARING THE CAST FOR THE CHANGEOVER

In the last week of rehearsals at the rehearsal hall, the cast, and to some extent, the director, should feel very little of the work and preparations the SM is doing. They should feel that this last week is just another phase in their rehearsal process—that of cleaning up

scenes and having run-thrus. The transition from the rehearsal hall to the theatre and into technical rehearsals needs to feel smooth, effortless, and if the director and SM have done their jobs throughout the rehearsal period, the actors and director should feel prepared and ready.

Halfway through this last week, the SM starts making general announcements to the cast, making sure the director also hears. The SM starts by telling everyone that they must make a greater effort in focusing in on their work, because once the cast gets into technical rehearsals there will be limited time for cleaning and working scenes. The SM keeps these words focused on the work they must do now, and not on the monumental task of technically mounting the show. A feeling of excitement should be built around this move. Then on the last day of rehearsals, the SM schedules one or two hours for the company manager, the director, and the SM to collectively or individually lay out the things that must be done to make the move from the rehearsal hall to the theatre organized, smooth, and on schedule.

From the SM's point of view, the following points are important to discuss with the cast, making sure the director, choreographer, and music director are also part of this meeting:

1. The actors who might be going into technical rehearsals for the first time need to be advised of the extended hours, work, energy, effort, concentration, and professional discipline needed to meet the schedule and get the show opened. The old timers need to be reminded of their past experiences with technical rehearsals and asked to draw on the good things that helped them make it through, and avoid those things that made the process difficult. They also need to be reminded to take care of themselves—to eat properly, continue their daily regimen of exercise, get plenty of rest, and allow just enough social time for relief from the show, but not so much as to interfere with what is professionally required of them. For convenience and safety, the SM might suggest the actors car pool whenever possible, and travel in groups on the way to their cars or taking public transportation at night after late rehearsals

2. If the rehearsals have been pleasant and all have worked in the expected professional manner, an expression of thanks and appreciation from the SM is endearing and affirms the good work that

has been done. If the rehearsals have been somewhat troubled or stormy, this is a good time for the SM to try and create a new beginning, asking everyone to put aside the things of the past and move forward to completing the next part of the rehearsal without incident.

3. The cast needs to be reminded that they are now sharing their rehearsal time with the crew and eventually with the members of the orchestra. Being on time becomes even more important because now more people are involved and greater amounts of time and money can be lost. Also, the schedule is not easily altered or changed to accommodate individuals (unless, of course, it is the star of the show). The SM needs to ask the cast to have patience and be helpful to the crew when possible. For the crew, working technical rehearsals will be the first time they are seeing the show, and they have little to no knowledge of the things done during the rehearsals.

4. From experience, the SM knows that for the actors, the change from working in the rehearsal room to working on the stage can be disorienting. Even the most experienced actors need a day or two to become acclimated. First, they are now performing out to the big black hole of the audience seats. Second, there are now the walls and doors of the set where once there were only taped lines on the floor. The space around them, which was open and free, now seems small and confined. On occasion, some of the actors will proclaim the construction people made the set smaller, or that the SM put the wrong measurements on the floor in the rehearsal room. Also, using the real props and furniture adds to the disorientation, not to mention the glaring stage lights and strange figures of crew people moving in the wings or staring out at them as they perform. Some actors are not aware of the true nature of their discomfort, but will just become frustrated and irritable. Others may lash out in ways that will be unbecoming and unprofessional.

   During the meeting with the cast on this last day of rehearsals, the SM might express an understanding of what they may experience and might suggest when they first get to the theatre they spend time on the stage moving about the set and handling the props until things become

familiar and comfortable. The SM might also suggest that when the rehearsal stops to deal with a technical matter, the actors use the time to make themselves more at home on the stage/set.

5. This meeting with the cast is also a good time to bring up the fact that once the actors get into technical rehearsals and especially during performance, there will be no one on book to throw them a line should they forget. For those who might be insecure in their lines, this can be an awful revelation. The SM is, of course, on book during the show and if there is a dialogue problem during performance will do everything possible to save and rectify the moment. The SM does not, however, tell the cast this. At this moment the SM is like the mother bird that pushes the youngling out of the nest to make it fly. The SM explains to the cast that they cannot depend on the SM for help because during performance the SM is calling cues and may be busy setting up cues or dealing with a technical matter when an actor needs help.

6. No matter how experienced the actors might be in the company, it is wise for the SM to go over some of the backstage rules and practices:

   • Remain quiet backstage while others are working on stage.
   • At the end of working on a scene in technical rehearsals, do not leave the immediate backstage area until the director has moved on to the next scene. Then once beyond the limits of the immediate backstage area, remain within earshot of the PA and video monitors to know what is happening on stage. If the director has agreed that the cast can sit in the audience while scenes are being technically rehearsed, it is the actors' responsibility to get backstage in plenty of time for their next scene. However, once the show is technically set and the director begins having run-thrus and dress rehearsals, the SM must insist that all cast members remain backstage as they will during performance.
   • While standing backstage waiting for their next scene, the actors must be aware of the crew working and the scenery being moved. Whenever possible, they should stand off to the side and out of harm's way.

• The cast should be reminded not to wander off, not to leave the theatre without letting the SM know and getting approval, and not to leave the theatre at the end of the workday without knowing the schedule for the next day.

7. Technical rehearsals mean extended work hours for everyone. As agreed on by Equity, the actors' workday will be twelve hours long. Ten hours will be devoted to rehearsal time, and two hours for a meal break, given no later than the fifth hour of the workday. After the twelve hours, the cast goes into overtime. This time schedule is commonly called "Ten out of twelve." In addition, at whatever time the cast is released at the end of the day, the *turn around time* must be twelve hours—that is, the cast cannot be called back to rehearsals before having a twelve-hour break.

8. Give the cast a list of the phone numbers for the backstage areas: the company manager's office, the SM's office, and the backstage public phone. Impress upon the cast the importance of calling at the least hint of being late or with any problem that might hold up a rehearsal or affect a performance.

9. Remind the cast to check the callboard in the theatre. The callboard will also have the sign-in sheet posted. Signing in becomes even more important once the cast is in the theatre. The area of the theatre is bigger than in the rehearsal hall and there are more places where an actor might be found. The SM cannot spend time looking through the theatre to see who is present, but will look at the sign-in sheet and if the block for that particular time is not initialed, the SM will assume the actor is not at the theatre and follow through on the little red box procedure.

Many of the things listed here are common sense things—things most of the actors in the company know and have experienced time and time again. For whatever reasons, the actors need to have them reviewed. Having this conversation with the cast eliminates most excuses that begin with "I didn't know!" It also reestablishes the SM as a center point of structure and order. It shows the SM's care and concern is not only for the show, but also for the individuals. It

carries everyone gently and lovingly into the technical rehearsals and reiterates once again the SM's professional expectations of discipline, behavior, and work practices.

SUPPLEMENTARY REHEARSAL SPACE

In most working situations, once the cast gets into the theatre, the director likes having a rehearsal space where either the director, the choreographer, or the music director can go to rehearse while technical work is being done on stage. If the show is new and is being produced for the first time, having supplementary rehearsal space is a necessity, for the rehearsal process will continue well into previews and past the opening performance, if necessary. Many theatres will have some kind of rehearsal space within the building. For those that don't, the SM needs to see that the production office makes arrangements for supplementary rehearsal space nearby.

The SM deals with this matter at least halfway through the rehearsal period, and certainly before this last week of rehearsals. The SM first talks with the director to see if the director needs to have this space. Most directors will say yes, but the SM must then check with the producer to see if the producer is willing to spend the money. Finding rehearsal space is one of those jobs everyone expects the SM to do. If the SM knows of a place, the SM might go through the process of booking the space alone. If finding this space is going to be time consuming, the SM needs to know the limitations of time and set priorities. For the most part, the SM should leave this work to the production office.

The most preferred rehearsal space is within the theatre building. If this is not possible, something nearby from which the cast and staff can travel quickly and freely is best. In situations where no rehearsal space is available, directors have accepted working in the lobby or foyer of the theatre.

In this new rehearsal space (except for a lobby or foyer), the SM may be expected to tape out on the floor some of the dimensions of the stage and even part of the set. The details will not be as extensive, because the cast now has the real set in the theatre by which to judge. The SM may also be expected to have some rehearsal furniture and props that are intricately used or are important to the action and scene.

CLOSING OUT THE REHEARSAL HALL

Closing out the rehearsal hall is the easiest part of all. The SM has made arrangements for the rehearsal props to be moved after the rehearsals on this last day. Some of these props may go to the new rehearsal hall. Those that are not needed and have been borrowed or rented will be returned. Others that are usable for another time and show may be put in storage.

Once the cast is finished and is ready to leave on the last day, the SM sees that the actors take with them all personal items—all comfort things they have brought to the rehearsal hall to make themselves feel at home. The SM removes all signs and things from the walls, including the callboard, and most important, removes the tape of the set from the floor. By this time the tape may be shredded to bits and pieces from wear and tear. This is where the use of cloth tape becomes most important. Anything other than cloth tape will require laborious scraping, and could take up to an hour or two to remove. With cloth tape, no matter how shredded it may be, the tape is easily pulled up by hand. A solicitous SM might get some of the cast members to help. On occasion, the volunteers might make the event into a playful, childlike game, completing the task quickly and with fun.

Sometime toward the end of this last day, the SM returns all keys to the managers of the rehearsal hall and accepts all bills they might present, making sure these bills get to the producer's office or accountant. If the space has worked out well and the service has been good, the SM might express thanks and appreciation, offering to recommend the space to other producers and SMs. It is good PR for the SM to express genuine feelings because the SM never knows when he or she might be required to find rehearsal space, need space on short notice, or work with this management again.

The SM is often the last person to leave the rehearsal hall on this last day. As a final professional gesture, the SM checks to see that the rooms are left in respectable order with the trash being picked up and the tables and chairs being stacked or stored away. With this last bit of business, the SM closes out a major part of what it takes to put on a show. Like all other parts of putting together a production, the phase just being finished is quickly set aside and the next becomes the most important. So it is as we leave the rehearsal hall and move to the theatre for technical rehearsals.

13

The Cueing Script

Before moving our discussion into technical rehearsals, we must take time in this chapter to create the cueing script. Remember, the cueing script must be put together and ready to use on the first day of technical rehearsals; trying to put it together during technical rehearsals is a grave disservice to the SM. In doing the initial work on the cueing script, the SM needs quiet time, time to think and envision the cues as they are transposed from the rehearsal script to the new cueing script.

Yes, the cueing script can be put together during technical rehearsals. In some working situations, it may be the only time in which the SM can get this job done. However, with the short amount of time allowed for technical rehearsals and with the amount of work that needs to be done, the SM is better off having begun work earlier on this script, and then as each cue is worked on during the technical rehearsal, the SM can devote energy to refining the cues rather than having to first write them down. In addition, neither the director nor the producer is willing to wait for the SM to do this work, which could have been done earlier.

THE SM's MASTER PLAN OR CONDUCTING SCORE

By any other name (the *calling script*, *prompt book*, or *production book*), the cueing script is the SM's master plan and guide to the timing and execution of all the technical elements in the show. Noted on the pages in the cueing script are the cues with the exact timing for the movement of lights, scenery, props, sound, or effects, as created by the designers and set by the director. For each performance the SM is responsible for calling all the cues from the cueing script. The cueing script is to the SM as the score of a musical show is to the conductor. Through the SM's leadership and timing, the stagehands and technicians execute the same cues.

When the cues are called and executed at the correct timing, they support and enhance the play. Cues are what keep the play moving from scene to scene, providing visual and audio effects and taking the audience to times and places imagined by the author. Like the score to a musical, the cues in a show help create a mood, a feeling, an environment, or an atmosphere. They help bring a sense of reality and believability to what otherwise would be just painted scenery, costumes worn by actors, and make-believe on a stage. When combined with the actor's work, the cues noted in the cueing script help create the magic of theatre and heighten the quality of the entertainment.

With such importance placed on the cueing script, great care and detail should be given in creating it, noting it, and keeping it up to date. The cueing script must be neat, clean, orderly, legible, thorough in the information it provides, and concise. It should always be kept in a safe place, with an extra copy also put away for safekeeping.

PREPARING THE CUEING SCRIPT

Noting cues begins with the SM's second and third reading of the play. As demonstrated in Chapter 11, The Rehearsal Script, all cues, such as a doorbell, a car horn, lights being turned on and off in a room, or streaks of lightening that momentarily light up the stage, are noted in the right-hand margin of the rehearsal script. It makes sense to note cues in this margin, as opposed to the left margin, because in our culture we read from left to right. Cues are called and executed in the same way. The dialogue or action takes place, then the cue is called and executed.

Manuscript Size

In most working situations, the scripts given to the SM at the beginning of the show are manuscript size: 8½ x 11 inches. If by chance the SM was handed a play book (5 x 7), it was suggested in Chapter 11, The Rehearsal Script, that the SM make enlarged copies, with one copy to become the rehearsal script and another set aside to become the cueing script. We have now reached the point when the SM pulls out that second copy, making sure it is updated with any and all script changes that have taken place during the rehearsal period.

Cutting and Pasting Ends of Scenes

Before entering any cues to this new cueing script, the SM checks to see that *each scene ends on one page, and then the next scene begins at the top of the next page.* In many play books and in some manuscripts, the publisher leaves only a few lines of space before starting the text for the next scene. This is not a workable situation for the SM. Almost always, the end of a scene is where the SM has the greatest amount of cues to note in the cueing script. This will require more room than the publisher generally provides.

Whenever an SM is given such a script, he will need to do some cutting and pasting, allowing plenty of blank space at the ends of scenes to write in cues. This space is especially important when doing musical shows, where there is more of everything—cues to change the lights at the end of the scene, cues to change the scenery, maybe a sound cue, possibly a projection cue, and then another cue to bring up the lights for the next scene.

Additional Pages

With the cutting and pasting, an additional page may have to be created. The SM simply numbers this page with an additional "a". For example, if page 47 is the original page, the additional page would be marked as page 47a.

Everyone Working from the Same Script

If the SM has done this cutting and pasting when work first began on the show during the production week, additional copies of the revised script should be made for the director, lead actors, the lighting designer, and the head of sound. If the budget does not permit this

expense, the SM need only make copies for the SM and an assistant, but keep in mind that when talking about page numbers in the script, only the SM and assistant have the additional "a" pages.

Tabbing the Cueing Script

Some SMs choose to tab their cueing script, either by the numbers of the scenes or the names of the scene. Other SMs by this time have learned the sequence of scenes in the show and prefer not to have their cueing script tabbed. Tabbing the cueing script is an option that can be useful depending on the SM and the show.

CUE GATHERING

Throughout the rehearsal period the SM continues to gather cues for the show. Some cues will come from the design of the set and floor plans, as laid out in the blueprint drawings, some will be given by the director, and some the SM will note from experience. In Chapter 12, The Last Week of Rehearsals, it was noted that the SM gathers the greatest amount of information on cues in the meetings in the last week of rehearsals with the different technical departments. During these meetings, the SM notes and records the cues as they are dictated. Once again, in professional theatre, the SM does not set or dictate cues in any of the technical departments. It is, however, the smart and wise SM who keeps a watchful eye as these people give out their information. The SM interjects and makes suggestions only when one piece of information is in conflict with another, when in the SM's opinion the person dictating has gone astray, or when they have run short of ideas.

The information given by the different departments is delivered with only their own cues in mind. It is the SM's job to combine and group the cues into an order in which they are to be called to give the desired timing and effect on stage. The SM's artistic contribution in this matter of cues comes during the performance, when the SM is calling the cues with impeccable timing.

NOTING THE CUES

Noting cues on the cueing script is a simple matter. Once again, a shorthand in writing is needed because the space in the right-hand margin is limited, and because the more briefly and concisely the information is noted, the quicker the SM can scan it and call the cue with the correct timing. We already have a vast collection of abbreviations and symbols that are used in noting blocking, so we need only to learn a few more that pertain directly to the noting and calling of cues. The only demand put upon the SM is that the cues be noted neatly, legibly, with concise information, with the correct timing, and that the information can be read and understood in a single glance. All SMs have their own abbreviations and variations on how to note cues, but the differences are not so great that an SM cannot pick up another SM's cueing script and understand the cues written.

Whatever group of symbols, abbreviations, or way of noting an SM adopts must be used consistently in all terms, signs, abbreviations, and hand-printed notes in the parentheses. Noting cues in a cueing script and then reading them must be a second language in which the SM does not have to think, but merely sees the information and reacts. When the SM gets into the heat of calling a show, no matter how experienced the SM may be, there is no time to think about or decipher the written cue.

Electric Cues

In every show, the light cues are the most prominent. In beginning to lay in cues in the new cueing script, it is best to begin with the light cues and build the other cues around the lights. In noting electric or lighting cues, some SMs use the prefix EQ or LQ, followed by the number of the cue, for example, EQ10 or LQ10. In Europe, it seems a common practice for SMs to use the letters LX. It is all a matter of choice, preference, and how the SM was initially taught.

> *Note:* I was taught by the first PSM I assisted in a professional show to simply use the letter Q. He believed the electric cue did not need to be distinguished further with an additional letter. I acquiesced and have followed that way ever since. This is how we will note all electric cues in this book. It is up to every SM to choose a method, but then be consistent throughout the script and possibly throughout an entire career.

Abbreviations for Noting Cues

The following list of abbreviations for noting cues will allow any SM to note clearly and distinctively all cues that must be entered in the cueing script.

Q = Light cues or electric cues (Q1, Q2, etc.)

SQ = Sound cues (SQ1, SQ2, etc.)

Q-Lites = Cue-lights are free-hanging light bulbs, usually red, amber, or blue. They are strategically placed backstage, for easy viewing in the stagehands' work area. They are placed to warn and tell the stagehands when to execute a cue. They are used mostly for the carpenters and grips working on the deck of the stage—the people moving the set pieces on and off stage. These lights are turned on and off by the SM from a panel of switches, usually placed at the SM's console. Each cue-light is numbered, usually starting on the stage right side. Each switch at the SM's console is numbered too, in consecutive order, and corresponds to the number of the cue-light hanging backstage.

During the performance and according to the cues to be executed at a particular moment, the SM may need to use one or more of these cue-lights. As a warning to the stagehands, the SM flips whatever switches are appropriate to the "on" position, and the cue-lights in those areas light up. When the stagehands see the light go on, they know it is time to stand by to execute their next cue. When it is time for the cue to be executed, the SM flips the switches to the "off" position, the cue-light in the stagehand's area goes off, and the stagehand executes the cue(s). To enter this information on the cueing script, the SM writes in *Q-Lites,* and then follows this notation with the number of the cue-lights being used in the cue (for example, Q-Lites 2–3 & 7–8).

RAIL = Cues pertaining to drops, curtains, set pieces, and items that fly in and out on the stage during the performance are noted as rail cues, RAIL-Q. Sometimes rail cues are numbered (RAIL-Q1, RAIL-Q2, etc.). Other times rail cues are simply noted as RAIL, followed by written information describing what is to be done in the particular cue. When the cues are written in this way, the SM during the performance speaks through the headset, telling the person on the rail what is to take place in the cue: "Stand by on the rail for the sky drop to go out and the office drop to come in."

TT = Turntable. In some shows the design of the set may use a turntable for which the SM is required to call cues as part of the scene changes. Turntables can turn clockwise or counterclockwise. There is no need for the SM to note the clockwise moves, because that is standard movement. However, it is wise for the SM to note in the script whenever the turntable turns counterclockwise. This reverse movement is simply noted in lower case letters as cc.

Wnch = Winch(s). Some shows, especially musicals, use as part of the set design winches that glide props and set units on and off stage. In a large show there can be as many as six winches. They can be operated manually, electrically, or by computer. They can be numbered or named by their placement backstage. The SM decides with the TD how they are to be named or numbered and then notes them accordingly in the cueing script (for example, SR-Wnch, SL-Wnch, or Wnch#1, Wnch#2, etc).

Sld# = Slide cues are cues that involve a slide projector.

Proj or **PjQ** = Motion picture projection cues.

Vd, Vid, or **Vdo** = These are the different ways to note video projection cues or video cues to be played on a TV monitor.

SPOT, SPT, SP, or **Sp** = Spotlight cues. In a large musical, there can be two or more spotlights. They would be noted as SPOT#1, SPOT#2, and so on. As a general rule, spot-cues are not numbered. If the SM calls spot-cues during the performance, the SM notes the spot number and then writes next to it what takes place with that particular spot. When it is time for the cue to be executed, the SM clearly identifies the spotlight by its number (#1, #2, etc.), and then relates to the operator what is to be done.

WARN = Warning. When calling cues for a show, the SM must first warn the technicians of the next cue. This warning gives the stagehands time to set up and prepare for their next cue.

In a large show with major scene shifts and transitions, such as a musical, there is often a large number of cues to be called and executed within one sequence or group of cues. To make sure the SM remembers all the cues and warns the technical departments involved, the SM writes "WARN:" on one or two pages before the cues actually take place, then lists all the cues coming up. During the performance the SM reads off this list, alerting and warning everyone involved.

As the use of technology grows in the theatre, the SM will add and create new abbreviations to note cues that use computers or remote controls:

Cmptr, Cptr, or **Com.** = Computer

Rmot, or **Rmt.** = Remote

Color Coding

To further aid the SM in noting and calling cues and to further distinguish one cue from the other, many SMs color code their cues. Early in their training or careers they choose a color for each department and continue to use that color throughout. When color coding, the SM should stay away from light colors, pastel colors, or colors that are similar to ones already being used, such as magenta when red is already being used, or blue-green when blue and green are already being used. The PSM for whom I first worked always used:

RED = electric cues

BLACK = rail cues

GREEN = sound cues

ORANGE = Q-lite cues

BLUE = warning cues

As I worked on more involved and technically complicated shows, I then added:

BROWN = winch cues

LIME GREEN = turntable cues

PURPLE = slide, movie, or video cues

LEAD PENCIL = spotlight cues

Color coding cues gives a second identity to the cues. After a while, when the colors for each department become implanted in the SM's mind, the SM will often recognize the cue first by its color, then by the written symbol. When calling cues for a large group of cues that are intricately timed, the colors also allow the SM to quickly scan each cue and call it with the speed needed.

The SM who color codes usually goes into technical rehearsals with the cues on the cueing script written in pencil. After the cues have been worked in technical rehearsals, the SM then takes time to rewrite the cues on clean pages of the script, color coding the script at that time. Some SMs will do this work day by day. Others will wait and do it in two or three sessions. Whatever process the SM follows, the cueing script must be color coded and ready to use by the time the SM has to call the show as if it were in a performance, such as in a dress rehearsal or preview.

PRACTICAL APPLICATION IN NOTING CUES

Let us start with an example (see Figure 13-1) from the script of the musical *Man of La Mancha*. It is the climactic scene of "The Knight of the Mirrors," in which Don Quixote is forced to face the image of his true self. The scene takes place in the last few pages of the play. In this particular production the cue numbers at this point were in the sixties. These were the cues as they were given by the lighting designer to the SM in their meeting in the last week of rehearsals at the rehearsal hall. This is how the SM's cueing script looked when going into technical rehearsals.

In Figure 13-1, the information is simple and straightforward. The numbers of the cues were decided upon by the lighting designer and the placement or time at which the cues were to happen on stage was decided upon by both the lighting designer and director.

The Caret

Calling cues and having them happen on stage is critical to the design and flow of the show. The little symbol noted in the example in Figure 13-1—the arrowhead or *caret* at the end of the lines of dialogue—is instrumental in guiding the SM to calling the cues with the correct timing. The caret marks the spot. If the timing of the cue needs to be changed, the SM moves the caret. Remember this symbol. It is the SM's guide to calling a well-timed show.

Note in Figure 13-1 that in Q67 the caret is placed not at the end of the line or on a word of dialogue, but within a note the SM has hand-printed along with the cue. Evidently, the lighting designer or the director has already decided that they want the lights in Q67 to come up as the judges appear at the top of the bridge.

Making Changes and Refining Timing

Once the show gets into technical rehearsals and once the lighting designer and director see the light cues on stage, they may add cues, take away cues, make changes, or refine those cues that have already been established. The SM notes all changes in the cueing script and places the caret in the right place, which assures that the SM will call the cues with the correct timing (see Figure 13-2).

Color Coding Figure 13-2

In addition to making all the changes and refinements requested by the lighting designer and director, the SM also color codes the cues in Figure 13-2. The SM is now ready to work with this page of cues the next time the rehearsal returns to this part of the show. The wise SM does not wait until later to color code. There may be more changes made in this section, but usually they are not as extensive. If they are, the SM will note the changes and rewrite the page of cues.

Color coding the cues shown in Figure 13-2 is simple. There are only three different types of cues to be color coded: the electric cues should be noted in red, the rail cue should be noted in black, and the winch cue should be noted in brown. Once again, color coding distinguishes the different cues and makes each cue on the page stand out.

> For a fuller experience and to see a color-coded version of this particular page of cues, along with other such pages that will be discussed in this chapter, please visit the Focal Press companions website: www.focalpress.com/companions.

> *Tip:* Before discussing the changes and new symbols entered in Figure 13-2, notice the neatness and clarity of the cues. It is important that every SM cultivate a clear and neat way of noting cues because the SM will be using this script time after time, eight performances a week, for however long the show runs. Each cue is critical to the show, regardless of how small or inconsequential it may seem. Many things can happen during a performance that will require the SM's attention. With a neat and orderly script, the SM can return to the script, find the correct place, and not miss a cue or lose the timing.

Point Cues

The first change evident in Figure 13-2 is an added cue, a *point cue*, Q62.5, which is placed between Q62 and Q63. Most times, point cues are cues that are added. Instead of numbering this added cue in its next consecutive order and then having to change all the cue numbers following, the designer made this added cue a point cue. In a situation where there are two light cues that follow each other very closely, a designer might number the second cue as a point cue. Point cues became a standard way of noting added cues with the advent and use of computer light boards. (Prior to this use, added cues were numbered with an *a, b, c,* etc.; thus, Q62.5 in Figure 13-2 would have been noted as

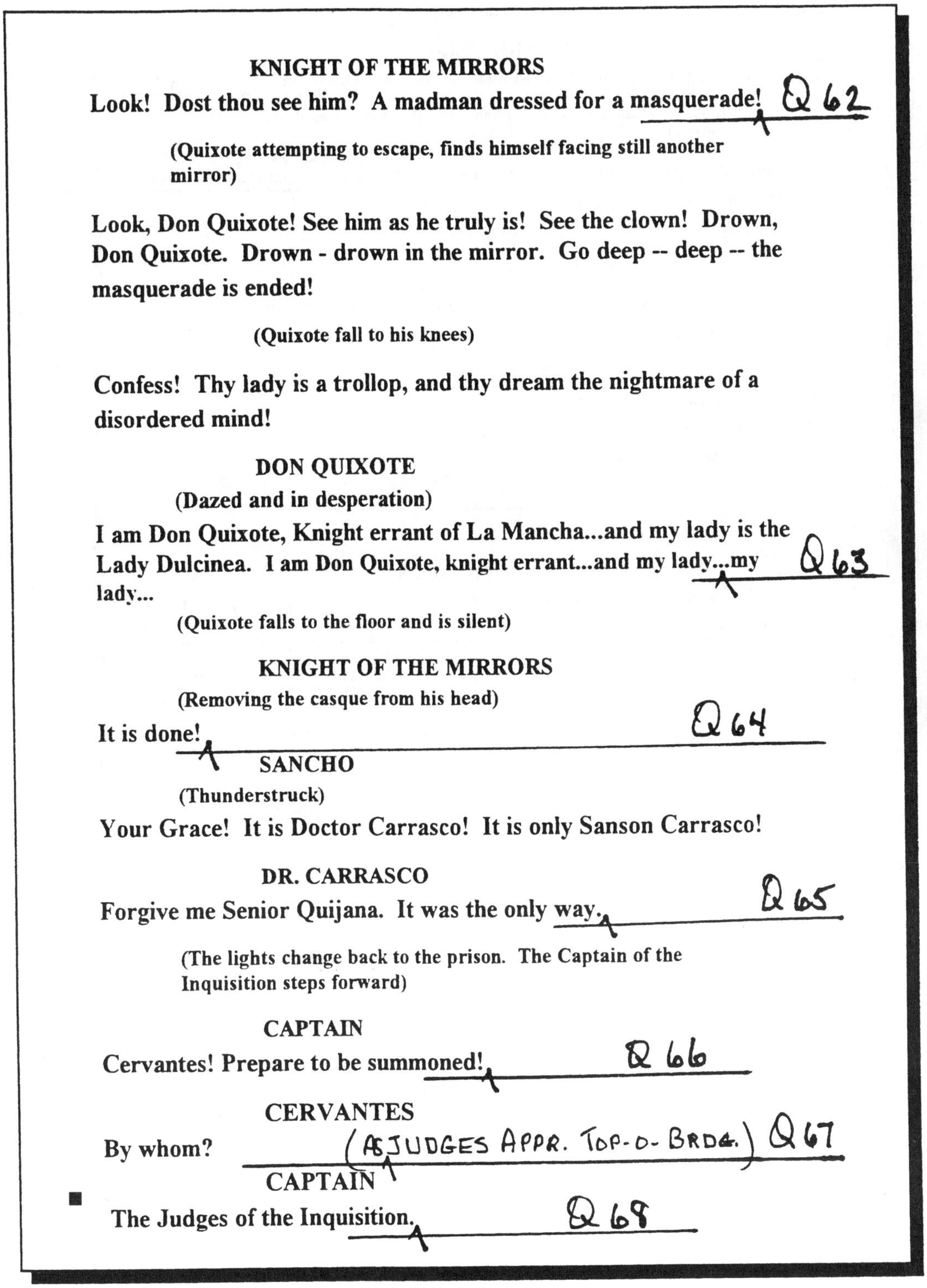

KNIGHT OF THE MIRRORS

Look! Dost thou see him? A madman dressed for a masquerade! Q 62

(Quixote attempting to escape, finds himself facing still another mirror)

Look, Don Quixote! See him as he truly is! See the clown! Drown, Don Quixote. Drown - drown in the mirror. Go deep -- deep -- the masquerade is ended!

(Quixote fall to his knees)

Confess! Thy lady is a trollop, and thy dream the nightmare of a disordered mind!

DON QUIXOTE

(Dazed and in desperation)

I am Don Quixote, Knight errant of La Mancha...and my lady is the Lady Dulcinea. I am Don Quixote, knight errant...and my lady...my lady... Q 63

(Quixote falls to the floor and is silent)

KNIGHT OF THE MIRRORS

(Removing the casque from his head)

It is done! Q 64

SANCHO

(Thunderstruck)

Your Grace! It is Doctor Carrasco! It is only Sanson Carrasco!

DR. CARRASCO

Forgive me Senior Quijana. It was the only way. Q 65

(The lights change back to the prison. The Captain of the Inquisition steps forward)

CAPTAIN

Cervantes! Prepare to be summoned! Q 66

CERVANTES

By whom? (AS JUDGES APPR. TOP-O-BRDG.) Q 67

CAPTAIN

The Judges of the Inquisition. Q 68

Figure 13-1 A scene taken from the musical *Man of La Mancha*, the "Knight of the Mirrors." The technical cues (light cues) noted as they were given to the SM during the meeting with the lighting designer and when they first went into technical rehearsals. (From *Man of La Mancha*, by author's permission. ©1966 by Dale Wasserman.)

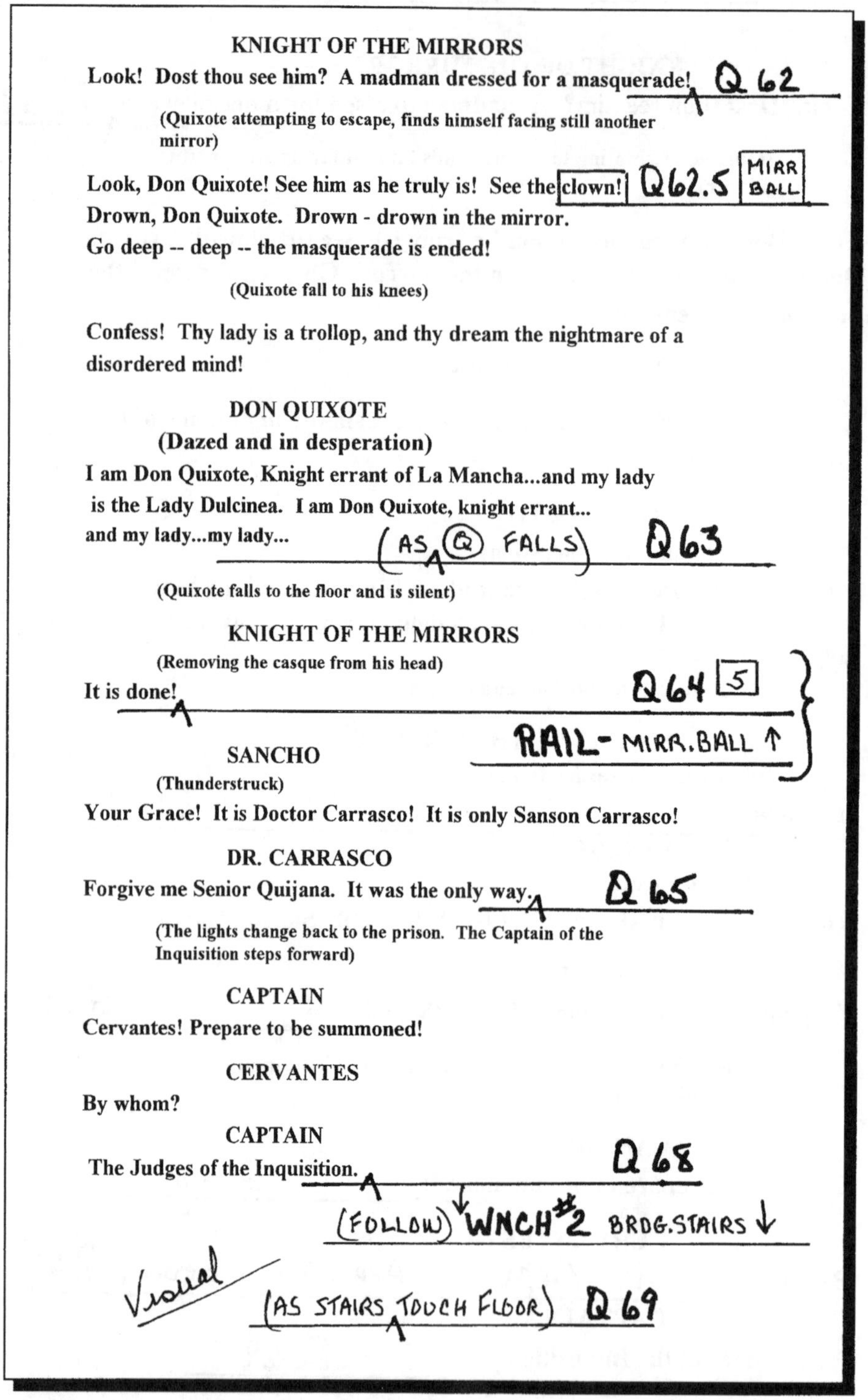

KNIGHT OF THE MIRRORS

Look! Dost thou see him? A madman dressed for a masquerade! *Q 62*

(Quixote attempting to escape, finds himself facing still another mirror)

Look, Don Quixote! See him as he truly is! See the clown! *Q62.5* *MIRR BALL*
Drown, Don Quixote. Drown - drown in the mirror.
Go deep -- deep -- the masquerade is ended!

(Quixote fall to his knees)

Confess! Thy lady is a trollop, and thy dream the nightmare of a disordered mind!

DON QUIXOTE

(Dazed and in desperation)

I am Don Quixote, Knight errant of La Mancha...and my lady
is the Lady Dulcinea. I am Don Quixote, knight errant...
and my lady...my lady...   (AS Q FALLS) *Q63*

(Quixote falls to the floor and is silent)

KNIGHT OF THE MIRRORS

(Removing the casque from his head)

It is done!   *Q64* *5*
                RAIL - MIRR.BALL ↑

SANCHO

(Thunderstruck)

Your Grace! It is Doctor Carrasco! It is only Sanson Carrasco!

DR. CARRASCO

Forgive me Senior Quijana. It was the only way. *Q 65*

(The lights change back to the prison. The Captain of the Inquisition steps forward)

CAPTAIN

Cervantes! Prepare to be summoned!

CERVANTES

By whom?

CAPTAIN

The Judges of the Inquisition.   *Q 68*

          (FOLLOW) *WNCH #2* BRDG.STAIRS ↓

Visual   (AS STAIRS TOUCH FLOOR) *Q 69*

Figure 13-2   The same scene as in Figure 13-1 (*Man of La Mancha,* "Knight of the Mirrors"). In this figure the cues have been refined or changed by the lighting designer and director, and the SM has noted the changes accordingly. In addition, the SM should color code the cues, using red for the electric cues, black for the rail cue, and brown for the winch cue. For a full color version, visit the Focal Press companions website: www.focalpress.com/companions. (From *Man of La Mancha,* by author's permission. © 1966 by Dale Wasserman.)

Q62a.) Light designers and light board operators found that allowing a nine-point range on the computer provided ample space for adding cues. In Figure 13-2, the lighting designer chose to insert the cue between Q62 and Q63 at "point five" (.5). This puts the point cue in the middle range of cues that can be added, leaving plenty of room to add cues on either side of Q62.5.

Boxed Information

Direct your attention now to the boxed in information the SM has noted just after Q62.5 in Figure 13-2, Mirr Ball (mirror ball). This note tells the SM that this cue brings up the lights on the mirror ball. This information does not help the SM in calling the cues at the correct time, but it is information that tells the SM what is supposed to be happening on the stage. After calling the cue, the SM can look toward the stage to see if the light has come up, and can take steps to correct the error if the light has not come up.

Here are some standard abbreviations used in box information after a cue. These abbreviations further aid the SM in knowing the nature of the cue:

B.O. = This cue instantly blacks out the lights on the stage.

BMP = Directors and lighting designers commonly call this a bump cue. A *bump cue* either "pops" the lights on from darkness or, if the lights are already on, pops the lights "up" or "down" to a brighter or lower intensity. A B.O. cue is a form of a bump cue that pops the light off. Bump cues are commonly used in musicals at the end of musical numbers. Either on or after the last note of music, the director or designer will have the lights bump up to an even greater intensity to emphasize the end of the number. Other times, when an actor on stage pretends to turn on a lamp or light switch, the stage lights will bump on as if the lamp or lights had been turned on.

LTNG = The information in this box tells the SM that this is a lightning cue.

FD to BLK = With the execution of this cue, the lights on stage fade out or fade to black.

RSTOR = A restore cue. The abbreviation "rstor" tells the SM that with the execution of this cue, the lights on stage will return to an original setting. An example of this is in *Man of La Mancha*, in the scene where Don Quixote sees a windmill in the distance. The stage is brightly lit with Q18, as if in sun-

shine. Quixote mistakes this windmill for a dragon, and when he goes off stage to fight the dragon, the lighting designer changes the lighting to a more colorful and fantasy-like setting, Q19. As Quixote returns to the stage, the next cue, Q20, restores the stage to the original bright, sunshine setting that was in Q18. Thus, Q20 is a restore cue.

The Count of the Light Cue

Notice in Figure 13-2 that there is also boxed information following Q64. This time there is a number. Every light cue has a *count* or duration as to how long it takes for the cue to happen—that is, how long it takes from the moment the cue is executed to the moment the cue has ended and is completed on stage. Some cues fade up or fade out slowly, as in a ten count. Each count is about one second long. A sunrise or sunset effect may be set to happen in a thirty count. Other cues happen more quickly, as in a two count, or in a blackout (BO), which is a no count. Once again, this boxed information is noted to aid the SM in calling the show. If the SM knows the count, he or she can then check the stage to see if the lights are being executed correctly.

At one time, before computer light boards were used in theatre, having the light counts noted in the SM's cueing script was very important, because the lights were manually operated by stagehands, and their sense of a count or second in time could vary. Back then it was the SM's job to look out on the stage after calling cues to see if the lights were happening with the correct speed and timing. Today, with the timing programmed into the computer, that is no longer necessary, but it is still good practice for the SM to look out on the stage after calling a cue or group of cues.

In Place of the Caret

Note with Q62.5 (Figure 13-2) there is no caret. Instead the word "clown" in the dialogue has been boxed in. Sometimes when a cue is to be called on a word within a line of dialogue, the caret becomes difficult for the SM to see at a quick glance. For easy detection of the word, some SMs boldly box in the cue word, as it has been done in Q62.5. For consistency, the SM should always use the caret and only used the boxed in cue word when necessary.

Key Notes in Parentheses

In Q63 (Figure 13-2) the SM has hand-printed in parentheses key information given by the director, information that instructs the SM to call the cue as Don Quixote falls. Notice the SM has placed the caret between the word "as" and the symbol for Don Quixote's name. Being this specific in the placement of the caret aids in calling the cue accurately. If the director changes this cue and wants it to happen earlier or later by a few seconds, or even a fraction of a second, the SM will place the caret accordingly.

Bracketed Cues

Direct your attention now to Q64 and the RAIL cue in Figure 13-2. Both cues have been bracketed together. The bracket tells the SM that these cues are to be called together. Note the caret is placed immediately following the word "done"—the place where the SM is to call these two cues.

The Rail Cue

Notice also that the rail cue does not have a number. However, there is the SM's hand-printed note, Mirr Ball, followed by an arrow pointing upwards. This tells the SM in very abbreviated terms that the rail is to take out the mirror ball. Even if this rail cue had a number, the SM would still print in this information.

Cues Cut from the Show

Notice in Figure 13-2 that cues 66 and 67 are missing: the cues jump from 65 to 68. When the lighting designer first gave the cues to the SM in Figure 13-1, cues 66 and 67 were written in. For whatever reasons, the designer or director has cut these cues. Because Q65 and Q68 are so close to each other the SM does not have to make a note that cues 66 and 67 are cut. If Q65 and Q68 were separated and Q68 appeared one or more pages later, the SM might make a note in the cueing script near Q68 saying that cues 66 and 67 had been cut.

A Group of Cues

At the end of Figure 13-2 there is a group of cues—Q68, a winch (Wnch) cue, and Q69—which evidently was added by the designer after giving the cues to the SM in Figure 13-1. Any SM who calls cues for a show will run into such groupings. Some will be as simple as the one presented here, but others will be busy, complicated, and intimidating. Let's work with this easy one first.

Arrow of Immediacy

The importance and placement of the caret has been stressed time and time again. When working with a group of cues, there is an *arrow of immediacy* that also becomes instrumental in aiding the SM in timing. Notice just under Q68 in Figure 13-2, there is an arrow pointing downward, leading the SM's eye to the word "follow" in the next cue. This is the arrow of immediacy. As soon as the SM sees this arrow, he or she wastes no time in directing attention to the next cue, which in this case is the winch cue.

Follow Cues

In the winch cue, the word "follow," encased in parentheses, is a key word for the SM. As soon as the SM sees this word, the SM knows this next cue must be called immediately following, letting no more than a *beat* or one second in time pass. This is what lighting designers, directors and stagehands call a *follow cue*. In setting up the cues for the grouping at the end of our example, either the director or lighting designer told the SM to make the winch cue a follow cue. This is how the SM noted it to give the desired timing and effect on stage. The beat or second in time between a cue may seem small and inconsequential, but that second is extremely important, sometimes for a desired effect or feeling on stage, sometimes for the safety of the movement of the scenery, and sometimes for the stagehands and actors who might be nearby as the cue is being executed.

Notice that the winch is numbered, #2, and the SM has hand-printed a note "Brdg.Stairs," with an arrow pointing downward. This tells the SM that this winch operates the bridge stairs and the stairs are to move downward, to the stage. Notice also that Q69 is somewhat removed from the first part of this group of cues. There is no arrow of immediacy leading from the winch cue to Q69, so the SM knows there is a moment before Q69 must be called. The SM does, however, have the word "visual" heading Q69, which tells the SM to look out on the stage to know when to call this cue. In addition, the note in the parentheses, "as stairs touch floor," and the placement of the caret, tells the SM exactly what to look for to call this cue.

Noting Spotlight Cues

As stated earlier, in some productions, especially in musicals in which there are two or more spotlights, the SM may not be responsible for calling the spotlight cues. In all such cases, the head spotlight operator is brought in on the first day of technical rehearsals, and the spotlight operator notes those cues and calls them to the other spotlight operators during the performance. However, in the shows for which the SM is responsible, the SM notes all spotlight cues in the cueing script along with the other technical cues. Spotlight cues are seldom numbered. There are usually too many. It becomes easier for the SM to identify the spotlight by number (#1, #2, etc.) and hand-print information after the spot number, telling the operator what should happen in the cue (see Figure 13-3). Seeing these notes in the script, the SM would say through the headset to the spotlight operators, "Spot number one, pick-up Mary as she enters from the stage left wing number two, and spot number two blackout on John as I call cue ten, then fade up on George standing stage right center, as he begins to sing."

A Complicated Sequence or Grouping of Cues

A complicated sequence or grouping of cues usually comes at the end of a scene that leads into the next scene of the play. We will start off with an easy and simple example. Let's return to our imaginary play of *John and Mary*. We will note the cues that end Scene One and lead into Scene Two.

In the last week of rehearsals at the rehearsal hall, after the lighting designer had come to see a run-thru of *John and Mary*, the SM met with the lighting designer to put in the rehearsal script the light cues for the play. The director was also present at this meeting. Together the designer and director decided that at the end of Scene One, Q13 would blackout the stage at the end of Mary's last line. Then, after John and

Mary clear stage and George takes his place at the light switch, Q14 would be executed, bringing up the lights for the beginning of Scene Two. Figure 13-4 shows how this was noted in the SM's cueing script, and this is how it looked when the SM went into technical rehearsals on the first day.

The information noted in this example is simple and straightforward. The placement of the caret for Q13 tells the SM when to call this cue. The downward arrow of immediacy under Q13 leads the SM's eye to the information in parentheses for the next cue. This information tells the SM what is to happen before Q14 can be executed. The placement of the caret for Q14 aids the SM further in this timing. Note how the information for each part of this group is concise, legible, and can be seen in a single glance. Once again, notice the abbreviations and symbols, which by now should be a little more familiar. As a further aid to calling the cues, the SM might make a heading note to Q14 with the term "visual," as in Figure 13-5.

Later on in technical rehearsals, the lighting designer and director decided to heighten the dramatic effect and emotional impact of the end of this scene. They decided that after the blackout with Q13, and after John and Mary clear the stage, the light from a flash of lightning would streak through the patio window, Q13.3. In addition to the lightning effect, the director wants a sound effect of thunder, SQ2. (Figure 13-6 shows the sequence of cues as it gets progressively more complicated.) In real life the sound of thunder usually follows lightning by one or more seconds. Knowing this, the SM asks the director if the thunder cue should be a follow cue. The director is pleased to be reminded, but decides to take some theatrical license and have both the lightning and sound of thunder come together to make the visual as well as the audio effect immediate and startling to the audi-

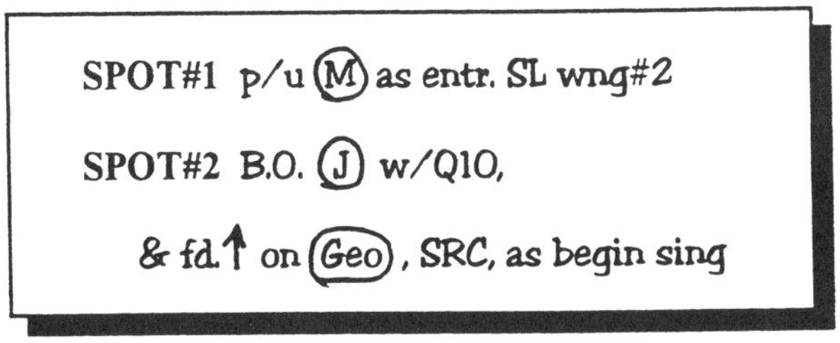

SPOT#1 p/u (M) as entr. SL wng#2

SPOT#2 B.O. (J) w/Q10,

    & fd.↑ on (Geo), SRC, as begin sing

Figure 13-3   An example of how the SM might note cues for the spotlights.

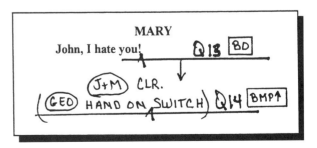

Figure 13-4   Simple cues noted at the end of the imaginary play *John and Mary*.

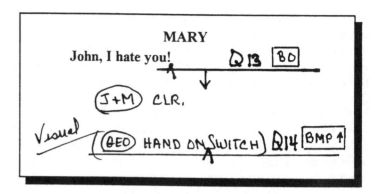

Figure 13-5 The same simple cues noted at the end of the imaginary play *John and Mary*, but with the term "visual" added to aid the SM in calling Q14.

ence. In this case the SM brackets together the light cue for the lightning and the sound cue.

In completing this sequence of cues, the director becomes more detailed and intricate in the timing and effects desired on stage and says to the SM that on the tail end of the thunder, the lights from Q13.7 should start fading in. This cue fills the room with a blue light of night and at the same time brings up some dim lights behind the scrim wall on stage left, which is the hallway leading into the apartment. Through this scrim, George will be seen entering the hallway, then with a key, letting himself into the apartment. As George enters and places his hand on the light switch, the SM will need to call Q14, which brings up the lights for the scene.

Color Coding Figure 13-6

After the SM notes the changes made by the lighting designer and director, as shown in Figure 13-6, the SM should also color code the cues in this part of the cueing script. The SM should color code the electric cues in red, while noting the sound cue in green. Once again, for a fuller experience and a color-coded version of this page, please see the Focal Press companions website: www.focalpress.com/companions.

> *Note:* The SM has separated Q14 from the other cues. The first three light cues and the sound cue are all timed close together, so an arrow of immediacy has led the SM from one cue to the next. With Q14, the SM has time for George to enter the stage, walk

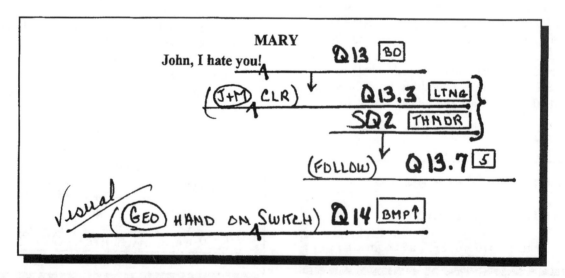

Figure 13-6 A more complicated sequence of cues, using the same scene noted in Figure 13-5 from the imaginary play *John and Mary*. The director has added a lightning cue (Q13.3) and the sound of thunder (SQ2). In addition, the SM should color code the cues, using red for the electric cues and green for the sound cue. For a full color view, visit the Focal Press companions website: www.focalpress.com/companions.

the hallway, open the door, enter the apartment and put his hand on the light switch. Though this action takes only a matter of a few seconds, in the world of calling intricately timed cues, these few seconds are plenty of time for the SM to take a breath and get into position to clearly see George as he puts his hand on the light switch.

Keeping Q14 separate from the others makes the first part of this group of cues seem less congested and possibly less intimidating, especially to the beginning SM. Whenever possible in noting a large and complicated sequence of cues, the SM should make smaller groupings. It is a tremendous help in timing and pacing for calling cues.

A Granddaddy Cue Sequence

Before leaving this conversation on complicated and intricately timed sequences and groups of cues, let me present one more example, a granddaddy of a sequence, a real humdinger! To do so, we must make our imaginary play, *John and Mary,* into a musical. Do not be deceived by the fact that the sequence of cues we are about to create is being made up from a play that does not exist. Every SM, especially an SM who calls cues for a musical, must work with one or more of these groupings.

> *Tip:* For the potential SM reading this information for the first time, don't try to master this next example. Just come for the ride. See it and know that such sequences exist. When your time comes to call a sequence like this, it will be easier. By then you will be more experienced and will have the actual set pieces and lights taking place on stage.

It is still the end of Scene One, leading into Scene Two. However, Scene Two is in a new location. It now takes place in George's office. This means the SM will also be noting cues to move the scenery. As part of the set design, there is a turntable to move part of the scenery and there are two winches, one on SR and one on SL, to glide furniture, props, and set units on and off the stage.

In the SM's meetings with the TD, the head carpenter, and the head of the rail, they tell the SM that the "apartment sky drop" from Scene One needs to fly out before the turntable can revolve. This would be cue RAIL-Q6. In addition, the "office skyline drop" for the next scene cannot come in all the way until the turntable is in place. This means a separate cue is needed, RAIL-Q7. The TD tells the SM that the SR winch, which is already on stage for Scene One, will travel off, taking with it the bar unit from John and Mary's apartment. In addition, the SL winch would

bring on the desk unit for George's office. The head carpenter suggests that the winches and the turntable cues be called together to facilitate the move and make the change happen faster. However, the SM sees that for even tighter timing, the winch cues can be bracketed with RAIL-Q6 and called together.

To aid the SM in calling some of the scenery cues, cue-lights are set up backstage at the rail, turntable, and winches. This means the SM must also write in the numbers of the switches which turn on and off the different cue-lights. As for the lights, Q13 remains as a BO for the end of the scene. Q13.3 remains as the lightning cue. Q13.7 is still a follow cue that fills the room with blue light and brings up a dim light behind the hallway scrim, and Q14 remains as the bump cue for turning on the lights.

To make this change even more involved, let's add two more elements: spotlight cues for SPOT#1 and SPOT#2, and a slide projection cue of clouds to come up on the office skyline drop. Given all this information, the SM notes this group of cues in the cueing script accordingly. Are you ready? Figure 13-7 shows the cueing script for this magnum opus of cueing.

Color Coding Figure 13-7

With this granddaddy sequence and variety of cues, color coding becomes even more important for the SM. By now we are quite familiar with the fact that all electric cues are noted in red, while the rail cue is in black, the winch cue is in brown, and the sound cue is in green. Appearing in this group is also a turntable cue (TT), which should be noted in lime-green, a slide cue (Sld#4), which should be noted in purple, and spolight cues (Spot#1 & Spot#2), which should be noted in lead pencil. For a full color view of Figure 13-7, visit the Focal Press companions website: www.focalpress.com/companions.

> *Note:* The SM has created separate groupings of cues. This not only helps in the timing but psychologically makes the entire transition feel easier to call. One cue seems easier to call than a group of cues. Several small groups of cues seem easier to call than one large group.

Noting WARN: Cues

Having experienced the series of cues in Figure 13-7, this might be a good time to talk about putting the WARN: cues in the cueing script. In a simple show where cues are mostly individual, paired together, or

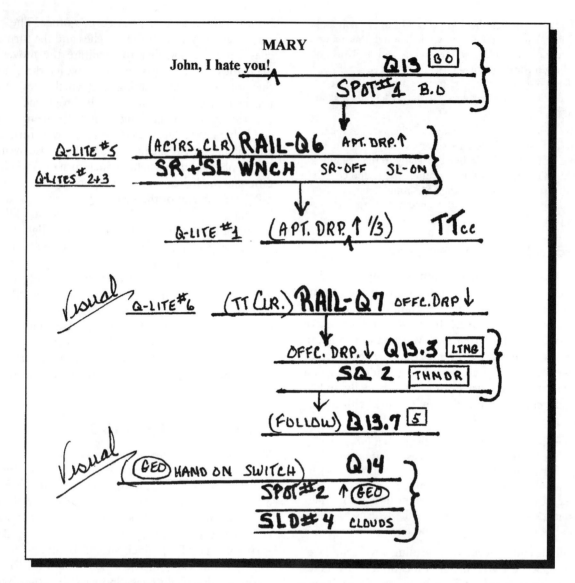

Figure 13-7 A granddaddy sequence of cues for the musical version of the imaginary play John and Mary, showing the end of Scene One ("The Apartment"), going into Scene Two ("George's Office"). The SM should color code the cues, using red for the electric cues, black for the rail cues, brown for the winch cue, green for the sound cue, lime-green for the turntable move, purple for the slide cue, and lead pencil for the spotlight cues. For a full color view, visit the Focal Press companions website: www.focalpress.com/companions.

in small groups, writing in the WARN: cues is not always necessary. As the show is being performed, the SM is following script, from time to time looking ahead to see when the next cue is coming. A page or two before the next cue is to be called, the SM verbally warns the technical departments involved, giving the warning as the SM reads from the page on which the cue is written. However, for musicals and shows with complicated groups of cues, it is best if the SM writes in the WARN: cues. The WARN: cues are designed to alert the people/technical departments involved in the next cue or set of cues, and are written one or two pages before the cues are to be called. The WARN: cues are written as a list and color coded in blue, making them stand out for the SM as he or she moves through the script during the performance (Figure 13-8).

The cues listed in the warning are not written or

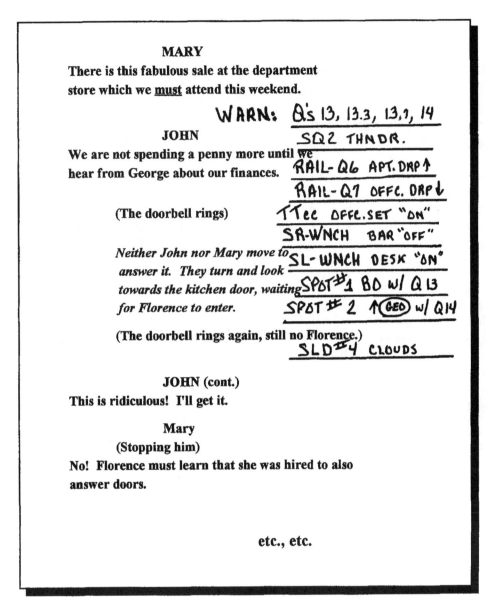

MARY

There is this fabulous sale at the department
store which we **must** attend this weekend.

WARN: Q's 13, 13.3, 13.7, 14

JOHN

SQ2 THNDR.

We are not spending a penny more until we
hear from George about our finances.

RAIL-Q6 APT. DRP↑

RAIL-Q7 OFFC. DRP↓

(The doorbell rings)

TTee OFFC.SET "ON"

SR-WNCH BAR "OFF"

Neither John nor Mary move to SL-WNCH DESK "ON"
answer it. They turn and look
towards the kitchen door, waiting SPOT#1 BO w/ Q13
for Florence to enter. SPOT#2 ↑GEO w/ Q14

(The doorbell rings again, still no Florence.)

SLD#4 CLOUDS

JOHN (cont.)

This is ridiculous! I'll get it.

Mary
(Stopping him)

No! Florence must learn that she was hired to also
answer doors.

etc., etc.

Figure 13-8   A list of WARN: cues. The cues demonstrated in Figure 13-7 are first listed as WARN: cues in the SM's cueing script, one or two pages before the actual cues are written. The SM should color code this entire list in blue. For a full color view, visit the Focal Press companions website: www.focalpress.com/companions.

read off in the order in which they are to be called. For the purpose of clarity and organization, the SM groups the cues into their technical departments. It is clearer and easier for each department to hear its cues being read off in a group rather than hearing them separately, between cues for other departments.

Except for the light cues, all the other warnings include just enough information to remind the SM what is taking place in each cue. The SM reads off each cue and also reads off this information at the same time. Doing it this way ensures that everyone is coordinated and working with the same cues. Reading off this list also acts as a review for the SM to get set up and prepared for the calling of the cues.

The SM waits to write the WARN: cues on the cueing script until almost the end of the technical rehearsals, just before going into dress rehearsals. This saves time and work, because prior to dress rehearsals, the director and designers are still making changes. With each change, the SM must rewrite and clean up the pages on which the changes have been made. Around dress rehearsal time, changes become fewer and less radical.

NOTING CUES FOR THE OPENING OF THE SHOW

Before leaving the art of noting cues and moving on to the art of calling cues, it is important to have some discussion on noting cues at the beginning of the cueing script to lead the SM through the half-hour call before the show begins, then into the opening cues which lower the house lights, raise the curtain, and start the show. To note this starting information, the SM must first insert into the cueing script two blank pieces of paper, placing them just before the first page of dialogue that starts the play. The SM starts by having a blank page on the left and a blank on the right. The notes to be written in this section begin at the top of the left-hand page.

Thirty Minutes Before Show Time

Three things happen thirty minutes before every Equity performance:

1. The house is to be opened to let the audience in.
2. The cast, by Equity rule, is obligated to be at the theatre and signed in.
3. The SM is to announce over the backstage public address system (PA), that the half-hour has begun.

Before the half-hour mark, the SM checks first with the technical staff to see that they are finished with their work—that is, the work that would be seen by the audience or the work that can disturb the audience once they are allowed to enter and take their seats. Having gotten clearance from the different technical departments, the SM checks to see that the house curtain or the show curtain is down and in place. That being done, the SM checks to see that the *preset* or *curtain warmers* are on—dim lights that pleasingly and attractively light the curtain and stage as the audience enters. Being assured all is in place and ready, the SM alerts the front-of-the-house staff, informing the house manager or head usher that the backstage is ready and the house can be opened. During the

half-hour backstage, before the show is to begin, the crew is putting the finishing touches on the technical setup of the show, while the cast is in their dressing rooms, getting into costume, makeup, hair, and doing whatever work actors need to do to be ready to perform.

Noting the Half-Hour Call in the Cueing Script

At the beginning of the half-hour, the SM announces to everyone over the PA system that the half-hour has begun. At fifteen minutes before curtain time the SM announces that there are fifteen minutes left to curtain time. At twenty-five minutes into the half-hour, the SM announces that there are five minutes to curtain. After making this announcement, the SM checks to see that all technical departments are ready. With all departments being ready, the SM gets in touch with the house manager to see if the show can be started on time. If the house manager feels more time is needed to seat the audience, the manager will ask the SM to hold off from starting the show for however long is necessary. The SM of course agrees, and at two or three minutes before the new starting time, the SM announces to the cast and crew to take their places.

These calls are standard procedure with all Equity productions. After having done several shows, this process becomes ingrained in every SM's head. However, it is good form for the SM to note this information in the cueing script at the top of the left corner of the two blank pages that were placed in the front of the cueing script (see Figure 13-9).

Head Count

After the SM has called places and while the actors who begin the play are getting in place, the SM sits at the console, puts on the headset, and checks to see that all the technical people to whom the SM will be calling cues are in place—a *head count*. Though it may not seem necessary, the ordered and structured SM makes a list in the cueing script of the departments and the names of the people with whom he or she will be communicating. It is best to have this information written in because much can and does happen at this moment when beginning the show. The SM's thoughts and concentration can be pulled away as things come up to be dealt with. For quick recovery, the SM can return to the script and not forget any other part of the procedures that follow.

<u>*BEFORE Half Hour*</u>
    Chk: TECH. DEPTS. - Ready open house
    Chk: CURT. & PRESET
    Call: FOH - Open house

<u>*@ HALF-HOUR*</u>
    @ 30 min. = ½ hr. call
    @ 15 min. = 15 min. call
    @ 5 min. = 5 min. call
        Call orchestra to the pit
        Chk: TECH. DEPTS. - Ready?
        Call: Hs. MGR. Ready to begin show?

    @ 3 min. = Call conductor to the pit

    @ 2 min. = call PLACES

Figure 13-9   An example of how the SM might note at the beginning of the cueing script the things to do within the half-hour before the show begins.

After taking a head count of the technical departments, the SM checks to see that the actors who begin the play are in place. It is wise to list their names, too, just to be reminded and do the check.

Putting in the First Set of WARN:s

Following the list of actors who start the show, the SM notes, in blue, the first set of warnings for the cues that start the show.

Pre-Show

The first set of cues the SM calls at the beginning of the show, are not always cues to bring the audience into the play, but rather to begin preliminary proceedings, such as the playing of a recorded announcement, the singing of the national anthem, or perhaps the producer or director stepping out on to the stage to talk to the audience.

In a simpler, more conventional situation, the first set of cues are for the house lights to go down, the curtain warmers to go out, the curtain to rise, perhaps a sound effect of birds chirping or rain falling,

and some electric cues to bring up the lights on the first scene. Whatever the working situation, the SM has noted and color coded all of this information on the two blank pages inserted at the beginning of the cueing script.

Example

For the full professional experience, Figure 13-10 is an actual example of the opening cues from a production of *Man of La Mancha*. Due to the number of cues, the SM has used all four sides of the two inserted blank pages. On the first side, the side not produced in this example, appears the notes for the half-hour call and the technical head count. Using this space for this information allows the SM more room on the two blank pages facing each other, for the notes that lead to the opening of the show.

In addition to noting the cues for the opening of the show in this way, the SM uses this format to note the cues that take the production from the intermission into Act Two and also when noting cues for the curtain bows. In fact, the SM uses this format whenever there is no dialogue from which to note and call cues.

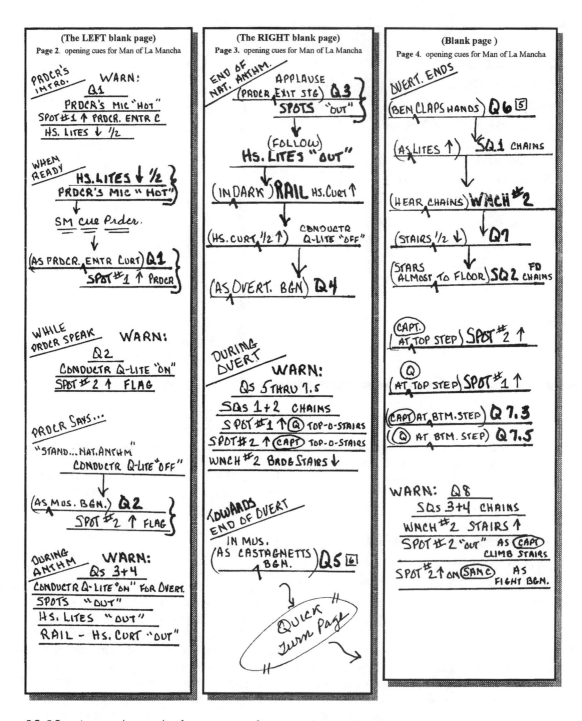

Figure 13-10 An actual example of *opening cues* from a production of *Man of La Mancha*, showing a way to note cues when there is no dialogue to use for reference points. The figure includes three pages of cues the SM had to insert at the beginning of the cueing script to get the show started. Again, color coding of cues is important: WARN: cues should be noted in blue, electric cues in red, sound cues in green, spotlight cues in lead pencil, rail cues in black, and the winch cue in brown. For a full color view, visit the Focal Press companions website: www.focalpress.com/companions.

Mastering Figure 13-10

At first glance, Figure 13-10 is overpowering and appears as a jungle of cues. There are four things that can aid SMs in mastering sections like this and overcoming their first impression.

1. The headings that are written on an angle and underlined, dividing the cues into sections.
2. The WARN: cues will be color coded to create blocks of blue writing.
3. All other individual cues will also be color coded, giving greater visual separation.
4. The SM's ability to zero in on the distinct elements in these pages and see the cues section by section, rather than as a confusing whole.

Color Coding Figure 13-10

The WARN: cues should be noted in blue, electric cues in red, sound cues in green, spotlight cues in lead pencil, rail cues in black, and the winch cue in brown. For the experience of seeing this example in color, please visit the Focal Press companions website: www.focalpress.com/companions.

CALLING THE CUES

The cues have been noted. The cueing script can stand as a masterpiece in that it is organized, neat, clean, orderly, concise, color coded, and has noted in it all the information the SM needs. However, the job is only half done. The SM must now sit at the console and, like the conductor of a musical score, lead the technicians through the technical movements for the show. Like the musicians, the technicians have noted on paper their parts, but it is the SM who, from the console, coordinates all the parts, keeping things together and in the order they have been set, seeing that all things work in harmony, with the proper timing, and are done safely. In addition, the SM keeps a watchful eye for any mistakes, correcting them as they happen, or better still, anticipating them before they happen. When an SM does the job well, calling the show with impeccable timing, no one is aware of this work. Often people will forget the SM's presence and the part the SM plays in creating the magic of theatre for each performance.

As we have gone through the process of noting cues, we have had no choice but to also discuss some of the aspects of calling cues. Noting cues and calling cues go hand and hand. The form, layout, abbreviations, and symbols used in noting cues not only inform the SM, but also become the dialogue the SM speaks in calling the cues.

Reaction Time

The most important part of calling any cue is to call it so the cue happens on the stage at the correct time—at the timing the designers and director have chosen. In calling a cue, the SM never calls it at the moment it is to happen on the stage, but calls it a second or a fraction of a second before. This difference in time is called *reaction time*—that is, *the time it takes from the moment the SM calls the cue to the time it takes for the technician to react, execute the cue, and for the cue to be seen on the stage.*

During technical rehearsals and dress rehearsals the SM learns the reaction time for each cue. Some cues require more reaction before their effects can be seen on the stage and others take less. In noting the cues, the SM places the caret in the spot that will lead to correct calling of the cues for every performance (see Figure 13-11).

In this example the SM has placed the caret just after the exclamation mark. This means the SM will call this blackout cue just after the actress finishes saying the word "you." From the audience, the director can expect to see on the stage a moment, beat, or a second in time before the lights blackout. If this is what the director wants, the SM keeps the caret in this place and moves on to the next cues. However, if the director wants the cue to happen sooner, he or she

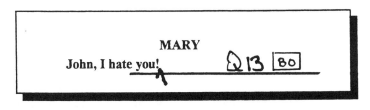

Figure 13-11 Placement of the caret, the symbol the SM uses to call the cues at the required timing.

will ask the SM to call the cue sooner. Some directors might explain to the SM their reasoning and artistic choice. They might even go into the effect they want on stage and the feeling they want to generate in the audience. In the world of calling cues, this is a bonus for the SM.

The reaction time for Q13 to be executed and happen on the stage is very short; it is only a matter of the light board operator punching a key on the computer keyboard. Also, the light board operator knows that blackouts need to be crisp and happen instantaneously, so is sitting in anticipation of executing this cue. Knowing this, the SM may move the caret to perhaps the middle of the word "you" or maybe just under the "y." The next time the SM calls this cue, the directors see if this provides the desired effect on the stage.

Feeling at Home at the SM's Console

You wouldn't think it, but feeling at home and comfortable at the SM's console is a very important factor in the mix of calling well-timed cues. With each new show, production company, or theatre the SM works, the SM may also have to work at a new console. It is important for the SM to be familiar with the way the console is set up. Calling cues requires the SM's complete attention and focus. In moments of complicated transitions, during times of mistakes, or in cases of emergency, the SM needs to react and act. Throughout the performance, as the SM sets up the cues and then calls them, the SM is reaching for switches, looking at monitors, often is tethered by a headset cable, peering out onto the stage, taking visual cues, or aiding a stagehand or actor in a moment of need. While doing all these things, the SM does not have time to think about or look for where things are on the console.

The Basic Setup

In most working situations, the SM's console is placed backstage, just off the SR wing #1. More than likely it will have only a partial view of the stage, with either curtains or scenery obstructing the rest of the view. The SM's console is seldom new and equipped with the latest technical equipment. They usually have been put together piece by piece, adding technical equipment or devices as they were needed for a particular show.

As part of the basic setup, the most stripped-down model will have some kind of a shelf or desktop on which the SM can place the calling script. This desktop usually is built into the unit at a height higher than the top of a normal desk. At this height, the SM can stand comfortably at the console and still read from the script. With the desktop being high, the SM needs to have a medium-size or tall stool on which to sit. The SM also needs a light at the console, preferably a shaded lamp that directs the light down on the script and confines the light to the general area of the desktop. The SM also needs a headset to communicate with the different technical departments while calling the cues for the show. If the show requires, there may be a panel of cue-light switches. This panel needs to be placed somewhere within arm's reach, and near enough so the SM can remain at the console with fingers on the switches and still read the cues from the cueing script.

Many consoles are now equipped with TV monitors, sometime even two or three. The primary camera usually is placed at balcony level, which provides a wide view of the stage. In some musical shows, there may also be a camera trained on the conductor for the backstage pit singers to watch, and for the SM to take musical cues.

The Experienced SM's Needs

With the experience of calling different shows and working at different consoles, all SMs learn the things they like to have at the console to make them feel comfortable and at home. They do not always have control over the equipment available and how the console is set up, but are assertive in trying to get what they want, and work with what they get.

Placement of the SM's Console Many times the placement of the SM's console has been made with little consideration for the view the SM might have of the stage. In each new working situation, the SM needs to see what the view of the stage is going to be. If the show requires the SM to take visual cues from the stage while at the console, it may be necessary to ask the technical director to set the console to provide a better view. For any number of reasons, the SM may get resistance on this matter, usually because the SM has to have this conversation with the TD when the TD is very busy setting up the show and preparing it for technical rehearsals.

The Headset In almost every working situation, the SM needs to have a headset with only one earpiece or muff; with the free ear, the SM needs to hear the dialogue through the sound monitors and hear the backstage activity. The experienced SM has also learned on which ear he or she prefers wearing the earpiece or muff. On major productions or when working in a theatre with state-of-the-art equipment, the headsets may be wireless with only a battery pack to attach to the SM's belt. However, until the time when all theatres are equipped with wireless headsets, SMs will continue to work with headsets that have wires attached, keeping them tethered to the console.

In arranging for a headset, there is a list of things the SM must request:

- One earpiece or muff
- Specify whether the piece or muff is going to be worn on the right or the left side of the SM's head
- The headset unit must have a volume control knob, to adjust the sound coming in or going out, and an "on" and "off" switch, so that the SM can have conversations during the performance that are not broadcast to everyone wearing a headset. These controls should be located on the headset or on a portable pack that can be attached to the SM in some way.
- The headset must have two channels of communication, one for the SM to use to communicate to all departments, and one for the stagehands and technical departments to use when communicating with each other
- If the headset is not wireless, the attaching cable needs to be long enough so the SM can move from the console, travel upstage to the third wing on the SM's side of the stage, as well as peer out on the stage from the first wing.

In making these requests, the SM needs to be clear and specific, otherwise the SM will get any number of combinations, none of which will make him feel comfortable or at home.

A Show Monitor   SMs discover quickly they need to have at the console a small *show monitor*—a speaker through which they can hear the dialogue, or if the show is a musical, the singing on stage and the music from the orchestra pit. The show monitor must also have a volume control knob. With the common use of microphones on stage and in the orchestra pit, and with the plentiful use of speakers throughout the stage and theatre, setting up a show monitor for the SM is not a difficult task for the sound department.

Most times they merely have to dig out of their equipment box an extra sound cable, run it to the SM's console, and attach the monitor. However, some lesser technician, one who might not be willing to put out the extra effort, may suggest the SM simply tilt the above-head show monitors toward the SM's console, or pump the sound in through the SM's headset. This is absolutely not acceptable! Those choices are only a last alternative in the poorest situation, when nothing else can be done. For many reasons, throughout the performance the SM will need the control and separation of the show monitor sound.

A Light   This is an item SMs seldom consider and never give thought to in terms of calling cues, yet it plays an important part in calling cues. The rays of the unit need to light up the desktop portion of the console where the SM reads the cueing script, and spill just enough onto the panel of cue-light switches, but not spill out everywhere else, especially out onto the stage during a blackout.

The light unit also needs to have some kind of dimmer control so the SM can make the light brighter or dimmer at will. SMs should learn to read their scripts in a dim setting so that when there is a blackout and the SM must look out to the darkened stage for the timing of the next cue, the SM is not blinded. A dim light at the console will require less time for the SM's eyes to adjust from the light on the console to the darkness of the stage.

The SM should never use a colored bulb or a gel to lower the intensity of the light. This will be the first choice most lighting technicians will offer when an SM asks for a low-wattage bulb or dimming device to be attached to the light on the console. Remember, the SM's cueing script is color coded. Colored bulbs and gels wash out whatever colors they are, and sometimes make it difficult to read the other colors. Only a neutral density gel or what technicians sometimes call a chocolate gel might be acceptable.

The SM's Stool   Some SMs are comfortable standing throughout the show, while others like to sit. Most SMs do a combination. Certainly one of the greater creature comforts is a device for sitting. Enter the SM's stool. Most theatres have stools scattered about. One of them may even be designated as the SM's stool. However, SM's stools have a way of disappearing, either being buried behind crates and boxes, or being confiscated by a stagehand to use at a workstation. One of the first things an SM must do on the first day at the theatre is to round up a stool to suit the SM's size and comfort, and clearly and boldly mark it "stage manager."

Other Items   The items listed so far are ideal, should be standard, and should be what the SM has at the console on all jobs. Any other devices, inventions, or pieces of equipment that are available should also be used to aid the SM in calling cues for the show. A microphone, permanently placed at the SM console for the SM to make an announcement to the audience is a good idea, but not a necessity. TV monitors are, of course, a great help and should be used to the maximum. In making the console comfortable, functional, and workable, the SM should also have items which aid the SM in doing the job during the show: pencils, note paper, a stop watch, a clock, the show reports, and drinking water. In both subtle and assertive ways, the SM needs to establish the console and a small space around it as the SM's area, almost a home, which is not to be used by others without permission.

Having a Backup Plan

There is a danger, however, for the SM to become dependant on all this helpful equipment. They can and most assuredly will break down at one time or another throughout an SM's career. What is an SM to do? The show must go on. Only when the show becomes disabled beyond anyone's control and possibly a danger in some way will the SM stop the show. So the SM needs a backup or to have worked out a plan. Having an extra light bulb at the console for the lamp is the simplest thing to do. Having a second amplification unit into which to plug the headset should the communication system go out, or an extra headset should the original one go out, may also come in handy. The SM must find an alternate way of calling visual cues should the TV monitor go out. The SM needs to imagine each item at the console, evaluate the chances of it not working during the performance, and devise a way to work without it. When a technical department is involved, the SM might collaborate with the different heads on how they will work should something happen.

Backstage Versus Back of the House

In some theatres the SM's console will be in a booth at the back of the house. For a small comedy or drama and with a good ASM backstage, this can be a welcome occasion for the PSM. It affords the SM a better view of the performance, visual cues will be easier to call, and the SM is better able to judge the performance, keeping the show as it was set by the director. However, if given a choice, the SM should always choose to be backstage where the cast and crew are more aware of the SM's presence and the SM has more direct contact with them. From this vantage point, the SM has greater control over the show, can be more effective in correcting mistakes, and just generally keep a hand on the pulse of the company. Sometimes the events and drama backstage can be as involved and complicated as the performance on stage.

Three Parts to Calling Cues

The three parts of every cue are:

1. The **WARN:**
2. The **STAND BY**
3. The **GO!**

The WARN: and STAND BY set up the cue, while the GO!, stands by itself and is the most critical in timing.

The WARN:

We have already discussed in detail the list-like form in noting the WARN: cues. We said that the entire WARN: section is color coded in blue, that the WARN: cues for each department are listed together, and that the WARN:s are written on one or two pages of dialogue before the cues are to be called. Also, we said that with each cue (except for the light cues) the SM has written, in symbols and abbreviated terms, just enough information to remind the technicians what is taking place in a particular cue. As a general rule of thumb, warnings are given to the technicians a minute or two before the cues are to actually happen. The WARN: is geared to allow the technicians time to prepare and be ready to execute the cue.

The example in Figure 13-12 shows a list of written warning cues that would be read by the SM through the headset as follows: "Warning, electric cues, five through seven point five. Warning, sound cues, one and two, chains effect. Warning, winch number two, lower bridge stairs to the stage floor. Warning, spot number one, come up on Quixote as he gets to the top of the stairs. Warning, spot number two, come up on the Captain as he gets to the top of the stairs."

Eliminating the WARN: When calling cues for a simple show, a show where most of the cues are in single form or in small and uncomplicated groups, the SM can eliminate the WARN: part, both verbally

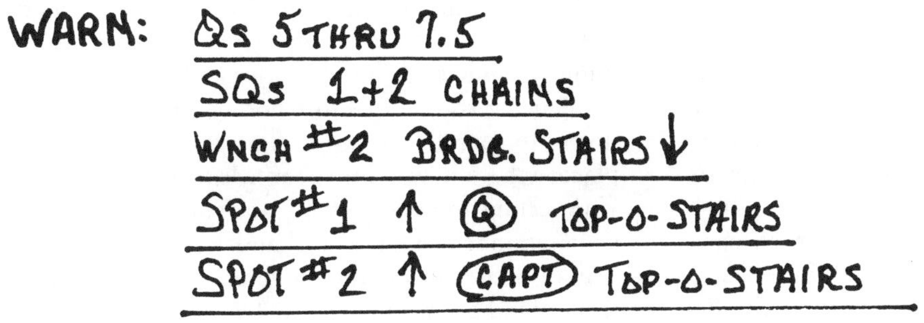

WARN: Qs 5 THRU 7.5
        SQs 1+2 CHAINS
        WNCH #2 BRDG. STAIRS ↓
        SPOT #1 ↑ (Q) TOP-O-STAIRS
        SPOT #2 ↑ (CAPT) TOP-O-STAIRS

Figure 13-12   A list of warning cues.

and in writing on the cueing script. The SM merely asks the technical department to STAND BY and when it is time, gives the GO!.

With the use of computers to work the lights, move turntables and winches, and fly things in and out, the technicians' preparation or setup time for a cue is already programmed. In most cases, the technician has merely to highlight the cue with the cursor, then hit the execute key. Whatever preparation the technician needs to do can be done when the SM gives the STAND BY. With such high-tech shows, the SM finds it simpler to eliminate the WARN: part altogether. Before doing so, however, the SM should inform all the technicians working cues, then be consistent when calling cues, giving only the STAND BY and the GO!

The STAND BY

The STAND BY tells the technicians to finish their preparation, be focused on the cues to be executed, and be ready to execute the cue on the SM's GO! command. The stand by part for calling cues is not written in the script. By this time, the dialogue in the play has progressed to the page on which the cues are written. Fifteen or twenty seconds before the cues are to be called, the SM looks at the color coded cues on the page and says into the headset: "Stand by, electric cues, five through seven point five. Stand by, sound cues, one and two. Stand by, winch number two, stairs in. Stand by, spot number one on Quixote, spot number two on the Captain."

The GO!

This is the part of calling cues that separates the good SMs from the not so good. This is the part in which the SM demonstrates a talent for timing and makes the greatest artistic contribution to the show. This is the part in which the SM reigns supreme. Nothing happens until the SM says, "GO!" It is written in stone and honored, as the Ten Commandments or golden rule might be honored, that everyone backstage taking a cue from the SM must wait and not execute the cue until the SM says, "GO!"

There are two parts in calling the GO! First the setup: "Electric cue five. . . ." Then the SM pauses, waiting for the precise time to call the cue as it is noted and careted in the calling script, and then says, "GO!"

Calling Spotlight Cues

In shows where the SM is required to call spotlight cues, after about a week of working the show, the spotlight operators learn the cues and need less description as to what they must do in each cue. When the SM is certain the spotlight operators know the cues and have good timing, the SM can become more abbreviated in delivering the information for each spot cue. After setting up the cue, the SM can also tell the operators to take the cue on their own. Working in this way expresses from the SM a vote of confidence. In addition, it gives the operators a sense of being in control of their jobs and contributing to the show. It also frees the SM to concentrate on the timing of the other cues that must be called at the same time.

QUICK, Turn Page, More Cues

On occasion, after a group of cues on one page, there may be a cue coming up quickly on the next page. To remind the SM not to delay, the SM might make a note just after the group of cues, "QUICK—turn page," and might circle this note and draw an arrow pointing to the edge of the page. The SM does whatever will help in calling a mistake-free, well-timed show.

Calling Cues with Clarity

It is not only important for the SM to be clear in speech and diction in calling the cues over the headset, but also to be clear, concise, and orderly in conveying the information for each cue. In setting up cues, the SM needs to keep each department separate and alert each by name before giving them their cues. It is also important that when reading off the list of warning cues the SM be consistent and list the departments in the same order each time. Because the electric cues are the most prominent and dominant they should be first, then the sound cues, followed by the rail and set move cues, and so on. This sets up a rhythm and pattern that become familiar to the technicians.

The SM's Pattern and Rhythm

The pattern in calling cues is created by the SM listing and calling off the cues to the stagehands in the same way every time. The rhythm is created by the amount of time the SM leaves between putting in the WARN:, giving the STAND BY, and going with the GO! The SM keeps the rhythm the same by giving the WARN: one or two pages before the cues are to be executed (which is approximately one or two minutes in time), then by giving the STAND BY fifteen to twenty seconds before the GO! part is called. To do these steps in a shorter or longer period of time can be troublesome; the shorter time does not allow the technicians to assimilate the information, prepare, and stand by to execute the cue, and the longer time leaves the technicians waiting, allowing time for their minds to wander, and possibly forget what they are about to do. Many SMs do not analyze this part of calling cues. They call the cues from instinct, and they do it well. For the beginning SM and for the PSM who many times must coach an assistant in the art of calling cues, understanding pattern and rhythm can be most helpful.

Vocal Inflection

In times past, before the use of computers, the timing at which the lights changed and the speed at which set pieces moved and things flew in and out were dependent entirely on the stagehands who were manually executing the cue. Today, wherever computerized or electronic equipment is used, the timing, speed, and movement of things are programmed and the cues are executed according to that information. The human element has been removed.

During the time before computers, SMs learned not only to call cues with clarity and order, but in places where it was important, learned to call a cue with feeling and vocal inflection. This inflection acted as a reminder to the stagehands and was the SM's way of orchestrating the movement of cues, assuring they would be executed as set by the designer and director. For example, Q13, the cue at the end of Scene One in our imaginary play, is noted as a blackout. In calling this cue, the SM might the give the "GO!" sharply, crisply, and perhaps clipped off. Even if the light board operator is working with a computer light board, calling the cue in this way induces the operator to react and execute this light cue with the same sharpness and crispness. If this same cue were a slow, ten-count fadeout, the SM might call the GO! with a soft and drawn out lilt, perhaps with the voice ending in an upward swing. The SM does not do this type of thing with all cues—it would be laughable and distracting—but is selective and uses this approach only on those cues that are manually executed by a person, and those cues that bring a certain feeling and dramatic impact to a particular moment in the show.

Watching the Stage

When the SM is first learning to call the cues for the show, especially when calling a series of cues for a transition, the SM stays mostly with eyes peeled to the page, reading off what needs to be called at the moment, and then looking ahead to see what the next cue is. However, as soon as possible, the SM must begin to look at the stage to see what is happening, to see if the cues being called have been executed and are happening with the correct timing.

Night Vision

The aspect of vision that allows each person to see in the dark is called *night vision*. People naturally and instinctively use this ability without even thinking about it, and SMs are often called upon to look out on a darkened stage to see an action or particular thing before calling the next cue. Night vision works when we peer out into the darkness, looking generally in the direction of the object we want to see, but not staring directly at it. This allows the night vision cones in the eyes to pick up the image and send it to the brain. However, with the pressure of calling cues perfectly for a show, some SMs will stare hard at the thing they need to see, thus preventing their night vision from working naturally.

Tight and Flowing

When calling a group of cues, such as the ones demonstrated in some of the previous examples, the SM must keep the cues tight and flowing. Any second in time, or even a fraction of a second, that can be saved or trimmed off in the calling of cues is very important to the overall flow and feeling of the show. No time should be wasted or lost. Wherever it is safe to do so, the SM must tighten up the space between the different cues. In some cases the SM might make the next cue a follow cue, or combine one cue with another with a bracket and call the cues together. For example, in the musical version of our imaginary play, *John and Mary*, the TD told the SM that in the scenery change from the first scene to the next, the apartment backdrop had to fly out before the turntable could start moving, otherwise the scenery on the turntable would rip through the drop. In calling these two cues, the SM calls the rail cue first to bring out the apartment drop. However, to keep the transition tight and flowing, the SM does not wait until the drop is completely up in the flys before calling the turntable cue. Instead, the SM watches the stage and, as soon as the apartment drop has cleared the highest piece of scenery on the turntable, calls the turntable cue. In the same vein, the SM knows that the drop for the next scene, the office skyline drop, has to come in. To help make this transition tight and flowing, the SM has set up with the head of the rail that as the apartment drop is being taken out, one of the stagehands is bringing in the office skyline drop, but only two-thirds of the way. As the transition is coming to an end and the turntable with the scenery for the office is coming into place, the SM does not wait for the turntable to stop before calling the cue for the skyline drop to come in the rest of the way. Instead, once again the SM watches. As soon as the office scenery clears and the skyline drops, the SM calls the rail cue. Thus, a few seconds of time has been saved and the drop is just touching down on the floor of the stage as the turntable is coming to a stop. If the scene change is taking place in view of the audience, this last movement is pleasing and attractive.

Visualizing Scene Changes and Transitions

For each performance, when calling a series of cues for a scene change or transition, the SM should know what is happening with each cue and have a strong visual picture in mind. The SM needs to visualize the lights changing, the things that fly in and out, the turntable as it revolves, and the winches as they glide things on and off stage. As an exercise and practice, it is a good idea for the SM to sit at the console at a time that should be free of disturbances (usually at a meal break), script open, and go over each scene change and transition. The SM should put on the headset, verbally set up the cues, turn on and off whatever switches are required, and while calling the GO! part for each cue, visualize what is taking place in that cue. Once the SM has done this and is familiar and comfortable with the transition, the SM should then mentally stand on stage, standing down center, facing away from the audience and looking upstage at the scenery, and again go over the GO! part of the cues, this time seeing the stage from this center position, imagining the flow and movement of things.

With this kind of practice, the SM will see how to perfect the timing in calling cues and if at anytime during a performance something should go wrong, the SM will be able to correct the problem and remain in control. The SM cannot keep mistakes from happening, but with such familiarity, can quickly correct them.

Giving Hand Cues

There are times in calling cues for a show when it is necessary for the SM to give a stagehand or actor a *hand cue*—a hand gesture to tell the person when to GO! In all such situations, when giving the WARN: and STAND BY, the SM makes eye contact with the person who is to execute the cue. If possible, the SM verbally communicates with the person, giving the WARN:, STAND BY, and GO! If it is not possible to communicate verbally, pantomime hand gestures are acceptable.

The most important part in giving a hand cue comes when the SM gives the STAND BY. The SM raises a hand high in the air so the person can clearly see the SM's position. When it is time for the person to GO! and execute the cue, the SM sharply lowers the arm in a clear and definitive manner. There should be no doubt, uncertainty, or tentativeness in making this gesture.

Working in a Congenial, Pleasant, and Businesslike Manner

When working on the headset, the SM should remain congenial and pleasant. When the SM first gets on the headset at the beginning of the show and does a head count of the technical crew, the SM greets the crew in a pleasant manner and offers some pleasant commentary if the occasion warrants. When calling cues for the show, the SM needs to be businesslike, not allowing general conversation or joking over the headsets. If departments need to communicate with each other, the SM should ask them to do it on the other channel, so the SM cannot hear what they are saying and be distracted.

> *Note:* At the end of every performance the SM should in some way acknowledge the crew for their work: "Ladies and gentlemen, once again a good show, my mother thanks you, my father thanks you, I thank you, and most of all our producer thanks you." If the show did not go particularly well due to some technical problems or an error the SM might have made, the SM acknowledges this too: "Ladies and gentlemen, I thank you for your good work despite the botched-up scene change when going into Scene 3, and the late light cue I called at the top of Act II."

When calling cues for the show, the SM should not bring into this part of the work any negative feelings or attitudes that might have developed or taken place within the half-hour before the show or within the day. If the time preceding the show has been particularly difficult, the SM needs to take a moment to set aside any negative thoughts and feelings, focus in on calling the cues for the show, and remember that during this time there is nothing more the SM can do about anything except call the cues for the performance.

Calling cues for the show requires the SM's complete attention. Any distraction can lead to missing a cue or calling it with the wrong timing. The SM needs to establish with the cast and crew, especially those standing around the console during the performance, the need to be quiet and be concentrated on the show. Everyone should also be reminded not to approach the SM at the console during the performance, unless it has to do directly with the performance or is business that needs the SM's immediate attention. To

steal from Shakespeare and paraphrase his words to suite the SM, "The show's the thing, and therein lies the concentration of the SM."

IN CLOSING

Creating a cueing script and calling cues for a show can be for the SM very satisfying and fulfilling. This is the one opportunity the SM has to make an artistic contribution to the show. It is, however, a contribution sometimes overlooked or underestimated by the SM's peers and superiors. The audience should never be aware of the SM's work. They have come to be entertained and swept into the magic of theatre. It is right that the SM's work is lost to them. The SM who looks for glory and praise for the work done in calling a good show looks to a barren field, an empty room, a house with no occupants. The experienced SM knows the importance of this work and its contribution to the show. Whatever praise or glory the SM needs usually must come from inside, but occasionally someone will recognize the SM's efforts and value the continuous good work done in calling a good show.

Learning how to note cues in a cueing script and learning how to call cues for a show is not something that can be learned in one chapter or in one semester of study. This is an art and craft that is perfected by experience and by observing others, then by doing it over and over again and again. It is learned by calling a bad show, by making mistakes, learning from those mistakes, then moving on, perfecting and improving with each performance and each production.

THE PROFESSIONAL EXPERIENCE

At this moment I can think of two nightmares an SM does not dwell on, but which are horrifying if they happen. One is to call the cues wrong in a major scene change during a performance and have the scenery crashing together and possibly causing injury to someone. The other is losing the calling script and not having a backup copy. Fortunately, in my worst calling of a scene change, I was able to salvage the moment by not destroying the scenery or injuring anyone. However, I did once lose the SM's calling script when it was the only copy.

Lost and Never Found: An SM's Nightmare

I was working for a production company where we produced four star vehicle musicals a year. For each production, we had only two weeks of rehearsals and seven days for techs. Needless to say, getting the shows on was always an intense period. As the PSM I had to learn to do only the charts, plots, plans, or lists absolutely necessary. The staff and crew heads usually were the same people on each of the productions and they worked as efficiently and economically. For each show, I was assigned an apprentice assistant, which handicapped the situation somewhat but the apprentice was anxious to learn and put in the time. The sets and props were rented and most times were from the original productions. Usually the star had already done the show, either on Broadway or in some other production. If not, the star worked before the rehearsals began, learning the songs and dialogue. We worked like a well-oiled machine. The experience was often likened to working summer stock.

One of the important things I delayed in doing my work was making a copy of the cueing script. Many times, up to the opening moments of the show the director was changing cues, and I knew that the next day at rehearsals he would have more. We would open the show on Thursday night, have a rehearsal the next day, performance that night, and have a matinee and evening performance on Saturday and Sunday. By Sunday night we were exhausted. I had learned to put off making a copy of the script until Monday, our day off. On Monday, I would clean up the script, and then at the production office make two copies, leaving one at the office and one at the theatre.

Actually, the one copy of the script I had was not lost, it was inadvertently stolen. It was in my SM's bag. The bag was leather and that is what attracted the thief. I was not aware of the bag being missing until Monday afternoon when I was ready to go to the office to make the copies of the cueing script. I cannot begin to tell you the feelings I experienced at the moment of discovery.

Fortunately, it was Monday and we did not have a performance until Tuesday night. I reported the bag missing to the police and scoured the neighborhood, hoping the thief emptied the contents of the bag in some garbage dumpster, but my time was running out. I needed to have the script for the Tuesday night performance. It was already late afternoon and if I acted now I could recreate the cueing script within the next twenty-four hours. The two major areas of cues were the light cues and the set moves. I called the lighting director, but he had gone to his home in the mountains. His daughter called him. He was just leaving to go upstream to do some fishing. He had his master script with him and he said he would leave it in the cabin for me. He gave me directions. It was a ninety-minute trip each way—three hours of valuable time. Before leaving, I called the TD, set up an early meeting for Tuesday morning with him, and asked if the head carpenter and the flyman could also be there. He was most accommodating and sympathetic. He expressed his thanks to God that it was not him who had to recreate the script.

Having read through the chapter on creating and noting the cueing script, you know what would be involved in recreating the cueing script. Once the lost information was gathered, it then had to be color coded and put into readable form. By five-thirty on Tuesday afternoon, I completed the script. Word of my having lost the script had spread throughout the company. Everyone was a little worried that night. After 123 light cues, 36 sound cues, 13 major scene shifts and a dozen assorted other cues, I missed only one cue in the recreation. It was one of those point cues that had been written in during technical rehearsals and which the lighting designer had not written into his script. The experience was a lesson well learned—one I wish I had not gone through.

Having read Chapter 5, Tools, Supplies, and Equipment, you know the SM's bag does more than just carry a script, a few pieces of paper, some snack food, and possibly a change of underwear. It is an office. It took several weeks before I remembered everything I had in the bag and was able to replace it.

14

Technical Rehearsals

When Stephen Sondheim wrote the lyric in his musical play, *Sunday in the Park with George*, "Dot by dot . . . putting it together . . .," he was writing about the way the renowned artist George Seurat worked in creating his impressionistic masterpieces with dots of paint rather than stokes from the brush. However, Mr. Sondheim could have also been writing of the way technical rehearsals work, "cue by cue . . . putting it together." Cue by cue the technical elements of the show are joined together with the work and artistry created by the actors and director in the rehearsal hall. The stage is the canvas on which the technical elements give the play mood, color, feeling, texture, environment, and movement.

THE PSM AND ASM

It was stated in the first chapter in this book that the ASM must be capable of doing all that the PSM does and that the information, though seemingly directed to the head SM, includes the ASM as well. Only when there has been a clear separation of work duties have the terms PSM and ASM been used. This rule remains even more steadfast when discussing the work to be done by the SMs in techs. Whatever work duties are prescribed for the SM in this chapter, either both SMs will share the job or while one is busy doing something, the other will take up and do another. Again, when there is a separation of work, that will be clearly defined.

NO REST FOR THE SM

On the last day of rehearsals at the rehearsal hall the SM closes out everything having to do with the rehearsal hall and, in most working situations, is at the theatre on the next day. Depending on the show and

the technical setup, the crew may have already been working at the theatre for one or more days. They may have some or all of the scenery set up, and they may be finishing with focusing lights and putting in the last pieces of sound equipment. In other working situations, the crew may be just starting their work—the drag-in or load-in.

THE CAST'S WORK SCHEDULE

Most times the cast is given one or two days off before starting technical rehearsals. In an Equity production contract, this can be their last day off for two weeks. According to an Equity agreement, the producer can work the cast for fourteen days straight without giving them a day off and without having to pay overtime. In addition, the producer can work the cast each day for ten hours—two five-hour periods—providing they have a two-hour meal break in between. This makes the workday twelve hours long and gives rise to the expression "ten out of twelve." As a third part to this work agreement, there is a twelve-hour *turnaround clause*—that is, whatever time the cast is dismissed at the end of one day, twelve hours of time off must pass before the cast can be called in for rehearsals on the next day. The SM must know each part of this rule by heart and schedule rehearsals accordingly, or the SM will cause the producer a great expense in overtime payments.

THE NATURE OF TECHNICAL REHEARSALS

Going into technical rehearsals can be like going into an Olympic event; the participants must be ready and prepared and there is no room for mistake or hesitation. Working at performance peak is the only acceptable level. Every department and person in the production must stand strong, deliver, contribute their expertise, and remain responsible for themselves and their work.

For someone who does not know all that goes into technical rehearsals, fourteen days sounds more than adequate to put a show together. For a small comedy or drama, half the time usually is enough. Even when doing a musical, if all goes smoothly, two weeks is sufficient. However, technical rehearsals seldom take place without problems, setbacks, or delays. It is the nature of the beast—there are just too many layers, too many departments, too many new parts being put together for the first time. Technical rehearsals bring together the creators, designers, and artists with the theatre, stage, craftspeople, technicians, sets, props, costumes, lights, sound, and so on. In technical rehearsals, the show becomes the main event. Even the actors, who up to this time have felt themselves to be the center of the production, must now step aside while the different parts of the production are put together.

Technical rehearsals are a time where things can go wrong, and often do. No matter how talented or experienced everyone may be, problems arise. There will be differences of opinion. Creative and artistic minds may clash. The patience factor can crash, and confidence can plummet. People can become emotionally spent. In addition, there is the ever-present enemy—time. Relentlessly, time moves forward without regard for people, problems, or situations. To some degree, all technical rehearsals have these things.

THE SM ENTERING TECHS

Of all the participants in techs, the SM must be in top form, both in body and spirit. Technical rehearsals will test any SM's endurance, skill, and performance ability. The SM will need to be confident and assured; stand strong, silent, and centered; keep a clear head; and not get caught in the drama when others may be ranting, raving, or going over the edge. An SM is best prepared for technical rehearsals by experiences from past technical rehearsals and by putting into application all the things we have discussed in this book thus far. Being ready for techs starts on the first day of the job, during the SM's production week. If the SM has faltered or lagged behind in any part of the job up to this point, it can come back to haunt the SM, especially in technical rehearsals.

The SM's work in techs is wide, diverse, and aggressive. The SM appears to be focused only on the cueing script and learning to call the cues, but in truth, continues working with the cast, serving the director, looking out for the producer's interest, and being available to the technicians to answer questions and feed them information. The SM creates a realistic daily schedule, seeing that everyone continues to work in a productive capacity and speaks up if time is being abused or is slipping away. SMs must think on their feet and facilitate whatever changes the producer, director, or designers present. SMs keep a watchful and critical eye for potential problems, circumventing those that can be circumvented and resolving others with dispatch. While working in the present, the SM is continually looking ahead, anticipating what must be done next. In short, the SM is the clockwork master backstage during technical rehearsals, the mainspring that keeps other wheels, sometimes wheels bigger than the SM, moving.

During techs, the SM works quietly and carries a big stick, keeping a low profile, but being assertive and aggressive when it is needed and appropriate. The SM is not, however, confrontational or combative. Technical rehearsals are a time when the SM must apply "people" skills to an even greater intensity. The SM is quick to evaluate and accept the responsibility of the jobs and problems that go with the SM job, but is just as quick to give to others the responsibilities of their own jobs and problems. Above all things, for technical rehearsals an SM must be ready! The SM should not be doing in techs anything that could have been done prior to going into techs. All of the above applies to the ASM as well as the PSM.

THE SM's WORK IN TECHS

The PSM and ASM arrive early on their first day of technical rehearsals. More than likely the crew is already there doing their work. The SMs' entrance should go unnoticed. As much as possible, they should remain understated. From the start, the crewmembers will be observing them, sizing them up. Though the SMs will not be their bosses, the crew is anxious to know about the SMs—to see what kind of people they are. The SMs should go around seeing the technicians with whom they have worked, and introducing themselves to department heads with whom they have not yet met. Conversations should be kept light, saving impending business for a little later in the morning.

First Business of the Day

The SM's Console

While the PSM is backstage meeting and greeting, it might be a good time to take a moment to check the location and placement of the SM's console. If the console is already a permanent part of the theatre setup there is little the PSM can do except see what devices and conveniences are already set up on the console. It is too early on this first day to discuss what the SM needs and wants for the console. The PSM will have to save this conversation for the end of the day or for the beginning of the next day, when the TD is ready to deal with this part of the setup. If the SM's console is being brought in by the production company, the SM might approach the TD at this time and ask where the TD thinks the console might be placed. This often opens conversation for the SM to determine the placement of the console and bring up any needs and wants.

Tour of the Theatre

Assuming both SMs have not previously worked the theatre or performance site, this is the best time to go on a tour. Sometimes the tour is guided by the house person. Most times the SMs do it on their own. The house person is different from the house manager; the house manager takes care of the front of the theatre (the box office, the ushers, the seating, etc.), while the house person oversees the technical elements of the backstage and the theatre in general.

To be effective in their jobs and in cases of emergency, it is important that both SMs know the layout of the facility and where things are placed. The SMs should come to know the theatre as well as they know their homes.

- They should follow the halls, corridors, and passage ways, open doors, find the different staircases which lead to other levels, and ride the freight or passenger elevator if there is one.
- They should know where the different technical departments are set up and have their offices or gathering places. See the layout of the dressing rooms and begin formulating dressing room assignments for the cast. If the rooms are locked, the ASM should find the house person and ask that they be opened as soon as possible. The SMs will need to see the sizes of the rooms and

determine the number of people who can be placed in each room. They need to see if there is a place where the cast can gather and rest, such as a green room. Check bathrooms and showers. See that the dressing rooms, the bathrooms and showers are clean. If they are not, the SMs need to inform the house person as soon as possible and ask that they be cleaned before the cast arrives.

- If there isn't already office space set aside for the SMs, the SMs need to decide on a space convenient to the stage and near the cast, which in many cases will be one of the dressing rooms.
- It is also good that the SMs take a trip down to the basement and under the stage, which many times is the way to the orchestra pit and sometimes the only crossover for the actors to get from one side of the stage to the other.
- In the last week of rehearsals at the rehearsal hall, the SMs more than likely inquired about a rehearsal room in the theatre and made arrangements for the company to use it. If up to this point the SMs have not seen the room, they need to take this time now to look it over. If rehearsal props were to have been delivered, check to see if they are there. If a piano had been requested, see if the piano is there and reasonably tuned.
- Next the SMs should journey to the artists' entrance or the place backstage where the actors will enter each time they come to the theatre. If there is a security guard or door person, the SMs introduce themselves and see if there is a dressing room key policy. They need to decide at this time if signs are needed, directing the company members to the dressing rooms and backstage areas. While on this part of the tour, the SMs also need to decide the best location for the company callboard.

Touring the Front of the House   Having covered all parts of the backstage, even places which have not been mentioned above, the SMs now need to explore the front of the house (FOH). First, they need to locate the door or passageway that leads from the backstage area out to the audience and FOH. This door is not necessarily for public use, but is often put in for convenience for easy access for the people who work in the theatre. The SMs will find this door extremely useful when they need to go out to the box office, perhaps to the administrative offices, maybe to rehearse in the lobby during the day, go out to watch a performance, or after a performance need to bring special guests to the backstage area.

Walking Through the Audience   Walking through the audience and viewing the stage from different parts of the house should be standard procedure for the SMs. They should first walk across the front part near the orchestra pit, checking sight lines. To get a good feeling of the house, the SMs should sit at the center of the house, at the back, and up in the balconies. In each position they should imagine the relationship between the show and the audience.

Touring the Box Office and Administrative Office, Meeting the House Manager and Staff   It is important for the SMs to make contact with the FOH staff and begin a working relationship, regardless of how limited this relationship usually is. During the initial meeting with the house manager, the PSM discusses the process of communication to be used with the FOH in getting the show started for each performance. At this time the SM also arranges for the placement of the Equity cast board. This is a board that is provided by the producer's office and lists in alphabetical order the names of all the Equity performers in the show. By Equity rule, this board is to be placed in the lobby, in clear view for the patrons to see as they enter the theatre. Often the theatre will provide an easel on which the board can be placed.

The SM's Office

Before the SMs can do anything else on this first morning, they must set up their office. If a space has not already been set aside, the SMs will need to find space for themselves. While touring the facility and seeing the dressing rooms, the SMs were able to assess which space or area they might use for their office. If at all possible, the place should be on the same level as the stage and in easy access to the stage. It should be located at the edge or at the far end of where the cast is generally situated. If at all possible, it should not be in the middle of the actors' living space; neither the SM nor the performers want to be in such close proximity to each other.

Cast Dressing Room Assignments

Once the SMs' office is set up and in operation, the next important order of business is the dressing room assignments. At first glance this appears to be an easy task. However, once the SMs get in the middle of this job, they find a great amount of consideration, input,

and craft must go into the assignments. No later than the last week of rehearsals at the rehearsal hall, the SM begins conversation with the production office, head of wardrobe, and director on this matter. In assigning dressing rooms there are the stars, the principal players, the supporting actors, and the ensemble performers to be considered. There is a professional protocol and order to follow. There are contractual agreements that must be honored, requests from the actors, handicaps, disabilities, age, and even ego to think about. When two or more people have to share a room, the craft is in putting people in compatible groupings. No matter how much consideration the SMs give this matter, there will be one or two cast members who are unhappy about their assignment. It is with these individuals, especially, that producers and directors like having the SM responsible for assigning the dressing rooms.

Consulting Wardrobe and Quick Changes   Before the SMs assign any dressing rooms on this first day of techs, they must consult once again with the head of wardrobe. Certain elaborate or difficult costumes, or some quick changes, may dictate which room is assigned to whom. While talking with the head of wardrobe about the dressing room assignments, this would also be a good time for the SM to discuss quick costume changes which need to be done backstage, as close to the set as possible. Together they can go backstage to find the best locations. If the scenery is in place and the crew's physical work areas backstage are defined, the SM and head of wardrobe can consult with the TD as to where the quick change booths can be placed. This is a matter that is easily put off to the last minute, sometimes not being remembered until the first dress rehearsal. It is part of the wardrobe department's job to establish the quick change areas they need. However, it is the SM's job to see that they are in place by the time the costumes are first used. The producer and director will hold the SM responsible for this.

The SM completes the business of having the quick change booths set up by talking next with the prop department, giving them the locations of the quick change booths and reminding them to furnish each with a mirror, some hooks, possibly a small table and chair, and some carpeting, if available. The electric department is also informed and reminded to put in some lighting, usually two small, clamp-on lights. Each light needs a hood that directs the light to desired areas in the booth and prevents the light from spilling into parts of the darkened backstage during the performance.

Even after initiating this part of the setup and informing the different departments, the SM in the next day or two will need to check to see that the booths get set up and are supplied. In times when the different departments are running behind in their work, setting up and furnishing quick change booths is a low priority. They will put off this task and may even forget about it.

Name Plates   While assigning each dressing room, it is helpful to everyone to have the actors' names placed outside of each dressing room. Traditionally the names are placed on the doors, but it is more practical to place them on the wall next to the door so the names remain visible when the doors are left open. Some production offices may provide professionally made name plates. Other times, the SM will have to make them up. Before the age of computers, the SM hand-printed them as neatly and professionally as possible. Today, with the use of the laptop, the SM can print out the names in the fanciest or simplest font, equal to any professional printing job. This is also a good time to make up name plates for the SMs' office, the wardrobe department, the company manager (if there is one with the show), and other designated areas for the cast and company's use.

Having the names at each door is helpful to the wardrobe department, crew, staff, and visitors who come backstage, and at the same time makes the actors feel good. If doing a musical, rather than placing signs that state only MEN'S CHORUS or FEMALE ENSEMBLE, it is more ingratiating and worth the SM's time to also list, in alphabetical order, the names of each ensemble performer assigned to the room.

Schematic Drawing of Dressing Room Assignments
The SM can, either in freehand or on the computer, make up a simple, one-page schematic drawing of the layout of the dressing rooms on each floor and write in the names of the actors assigned to the different dressing rooms. A drawing is a greater visual aid than simply making a list with the room numbers. For the first few days of techs, this drawing should be prominently placed on the callboard. Then once everyone is familiar with the layout of the rooms and the assignments, it can be moved to a far corner of the callboard and remain there for the run.

The Company Callboard

Next in importance is setting up the callboard. This is not only an item that is necessary, but it is also mandated by Equity rule. Most theatres already have one permanently in place, but this may not be the best placement for the SM's and cast's use. Sometimes it is best for the SM to establish and set up a different callboard area. Choosing a location is very important. It must be in a central place, convenient for the cast and SM, a place where the cast first enters the backstage area to go to their dressing rooms, a place they have no choice but to pass.

The SM can create a callboard area on any free wall in a hallway or corridor. Framed corked, felt, or softwood particleboard can be purchased very inexpensively. A board of 36-by-28 inches works well if the SM uses the space on the board economically. If the show is going to remain in one theatre for its run, a larger size is more desirable. If the show is touring, the smaller one will be easier to pack away and travel. The board should be lightweight, and with some strong electrician's tape it can be neatly mounted on any wall. Once in place, the board is ready to be divided into sections with the followings headings printed from the laptop and whatever other headings the SM chooses or finds important to the production:

- (Name of show) CALLBOARD
- SIGN-IN PLEASE
- DAILY SCHEDULE
- CURRENT NOTICE
- LAST NOTICE
- PAST NOTICES
- PERFORMANCE NOTES

From the start, the SM establishes that the company callboard is for official use only. Anything posted on the board by anyone else must first be approved by the SM. In addition, the SM must make it clear to the entire company that the documents appearing on the board should not be written on, altered, or mutilated in any way. Whenever possible, the SM should set aside a place adjacent to the callboard, clearly marked, where the cast, crew, and staff members can put up their own notices. The SM should keep the company callboard neat, consistent in the placement of things, up to date, and clear of outdated information. In addition to the headings listed previously, the SM needs space on the company callboard for:

- The Equity special and mandatory notices
- The dressing room assignments
- The Block Calendar schedule
- Important telephone numbers
- Performance notes from the director, producer, or SM
- Instructions of any kind, maps, etc.
- Information about parking, show tickets/house seats, places to eat
- Forms to make medical insurance claims
- Forms important to the company for organizing and administrating

With so much to be posted, the SM can hang information from the bottom part of the frame if that becomes necessary, while less important information can be taped on the wall on either side of the board.

Directional Signs

If getting from the artists' entrance to the backstage and dressing rooms is difficult, the SM needs to put up a network of signs to direct the company. Once again, professional-looking signs can be printed from the SM's laptop. They can be simple, with the company's or show's name, and possibly have a graphic of a large blackened arrow or hand pointing the way.

No Let Up for the SM

From the SM's first day of work on a production (the SM's production week), the SM must not let up on what must be done each day. In other words, don't put off until tomorrow what you can do today. The SM follows this work ethic through the rehearsal period and now, more than ever, through technical rehearsals. On this first day of technical rehearsals, the SM should not let up until most, if not all, of the work we have discussed is done:

- Meet the crew
- Start setup of SM's console
- Tour the theatre
- Talk to the FOH (discuss placement of Equity list of performers, and communication procedure to begin each show)
- Set up SM's office
- Assign dressing rooms (keys, name plates, quick change booths, schematic drawing of room assignments)
- Set up callboard
- Post directional signs

There is no time to waste. Socializing and schmoozing must be kept to a minimum. Extended lunches are for other people. Tomorrow will have it's own list of things to do.

The SM's Second Day of Techs

Once again the SMs arrive early. More than likely, the crew is already at work. If the SMs were able to complete their list of things to do on the first day, today will be easier. The PSM will work more in an advisory capacity to the crew, answering questions which will aid them in completing their work before the director, staff, and cast arrive to begin the heart of techs. If the SMs have work left over from the day before, they will need to complete that work in addition to what must be done on this day.

Departments Ready

In many work situations, on this second day, the director, producer, staff, and cast will be coming in by noon. At that time, the crew will go to lunch for an hour, while the cast becomes acclimated to the theatre. By 1:00 P.M., the heart of the technical rehearsals will begin.

With the staff and cast arriving on this second day, the SMs' morning is even fuller; the PSM needs to see that the console is set up and operating, while the ASM reminds the crew of the quick change booths and, if the show is a musical, checks the orchestra pit to see if the pianos or keyboards are in place, the conductor's podium is set up for the music director, and something has been set up to amplify the sound of the piano from the pit to the stage.

Around 10:00 A.M. that morning, the SMs need to check with each technical department, asking for assurance that the department will have its work completed and be ready without delay, by 1:00 P.M. It is the nature of technical rehearsals that there is never enough time. Many times when the SM approaches the different department heads looking for assurance and reminding them of the schedule, they complain and say they will not be ready. The SM listens to their circumstances and complaints and can sometimes help by recommending priorities, pointing out what can be set aside and what should be completed before the rest of the company arrives. Other times there is nothing the SM can do but remind the person of the schedule and say that when the producer and director arrive, the SM will inform them of the delay. In most situations, the department that complained is miraculously ready to function at the scheduled time.

At around 11:00 A.M., the SM checks to see that the backstage areas are reasonably clean and things are cleared away. If they are not, either SM must remind the TD of this work and the need to have it done before they go to lunch and the cast arrives.

The Production Table

On the day the staff and cast arrives, the SM also needs to see that a production table is set up midway in the theatre in the orchestra seating. This is often a board or table top that is large enough for the lighting designer and assistant, the director, and producer to sit at and spread out their scripts, blueprints, and laptops. This board or table top is laid over the top of some of the seats and is rigged to be level or lay flat. Also needed at this table is electrical power with enough outlets to plug in reading lamps and the laptops. The prop department places the table top, while the electric department brings in the power, and the sound department sets up headsets for the director and lighting designer to communicate with the SM and different technical departments backstage. In addition, the sound department provides a microphone that the director can use in giving directions to the performers and other people on stage who are not on headsets. In theatre parlance, this microphone is referred to as a *god-mic*. It is so named because when the director speaks through the mic, the voice comes booming out from the darkened theatre and sounds like the voice of God.

Setting up the production table is another one of those things that can be put off or forgotten. On the day of the arrival of the staff and cast, the SM should, as one of the first things in the morning, remind the different departments of this setup.

White Tape and Glow Tape

Next, if the carpentry department is reasonably ready, the SM might ask the TD or the head of carpentry to put white tape and glow tape on things and in places backstage that can be hazardous when the cast and crew are walking and working in the dimly lit areas backstage. Stairs are especially hazardous, as are the edges of platforms. Pathways or walkways might need to be taped off, to direct people and keep everyone out of harm's way. Glow tape is especially effective on the edge of scenery and in places where even the white tape cannot be seen in the dark. If the carpentry department is behind in its work and cannot do this job before the arrival of the staff and cast, the SMs might take on this job, taping the most important or hazardous places.

The Dance/Blocking Numbers

With all these things being done, the SMs can now take time to lay in the dance/blocking numbers across the foot of the stage. These numbers are easily obtained at any stationery store. They need to be white, possibly glow in the dark, have peel-off sticky backs, be no smaller than two inches, but not so large as to be readily seen by the audience.

Some stages are shallow and the edge of the stage comes right at the proscenium line. Others may have a large apron before dropping off into the orchestra. On those stages where the edge is at the proscenium line, the SM places the numbers at the edge of the stage. For those stages where the apron is larger, the director and lighting designer establish how much of the apron is going to be used as the performance area. The lighting designer will focus the lights to shine at the lowest point down stage. It is there, just within the beginning glow of that light, that the SMs lay in the numbers.

Whatever the situation, before placing the numbers, the SMs first lay in a strip of white tape at the foot of the performance area running across the width of the stage. Then, as the SMs stand at center stage looking out at the audience and facing the tape, they start laying in the numbers just below the line (in theatre terms, that would be up stage of the line). The SMs start by placing a zero at center. Two feet away on each side of zero, they place the number "1." From there on, and traveling off to their respective sides, the numbers build numerically. Laying in these numbers is done mostly for musical shows. However, directors and actors are asking for them more often even when doing a drama or comedy.

THE SM's PSYCHOLOGY OF GOOD TIMING

Early on in a career, the SM learns when to approach the technicians to remind them of things or to have something done. In the examples of setting up the quick change booths, putting the production table in place, or clearing the backstage before the cast arrives, it would have been futile for the SMs to have mentioned these things any sooner than an hour or two before they were needed. Previous to this time, the technicians were more than likely consumed with getting other things done—things which, in their minds, had greater priority. When the SM asks for something earlier than its hour of need, some technicians may assure the SM they will do it, but then possibly forget. Some might even become annoyed with the SM feeling that the SM is unduly worried or is not allowing them to freely do their jobs.

In working harmoniously with crewmembers, the SM learns the best psychological time to approach technicians on matters when there is urgency and need for immediacy. At the same time, the SM must allow the technicians enough time to get the job done. Otherwise, they will accuse the SM of asking too late. If the producer and director have to wait while a particular thing gets done, many times they will turn to the SM, holding the SM responsible for the delay. All of a sudden, what was clearly someone else's job and responsibility has now become the SM's.

GREY RESPONSIBILITIES

Throughout this book it is a continual theme that in the professional world the SM gives to associates, peers, and coworkers the responsibility of their own jobs. This is indeed a standard by which every SM must work. However, in the world of reality, the SM learns what parts of other people's responsibilities the SM must take on. *Grey responsibilities* are work that is the responsibility of others, but that the SM takes on to check and double-check to see that it will be done. If this work is not done, the blame can easily be placed on the SM. Such things as the quick change booths and the production table are prime examples.

IN THE LINE OF FIRE, MAGNIFIED

It has also been a reoccurring theme in this book that the nature of the SM's position, often places the SM in the middle of skirmishes or battles within the company. This fact is exemplified and magnified during technical rehearsals. In techs, when the cast, crew, and staff are working to put the show together, the SM becomes the central figure. The SM is the agent between the staff working out front in the darkened theatre and the cast and crew working backstage. When things are going well, the SM's work goes unnoticed and is taken for granted. However, when patience is running short, tempers are beginning to flare, frustration is running high, and time is running out, people look for a place to hang their feelings and put the blame. Sometimes it becomes easier or safer to use the SM. Such terms as *whipping boy* and *scapegoat* can be applied. Producers and directors can be most guilty of such behavior toward the SM.

For the SM's well-being, it is important that the SM knows the parts of the job and the things for which the SM is responsible. Then, during the times when it looks as if the SM is going to fall victim, the SM can clearly set the record straight and state what is the SM's responsibility and what belongs to others.

THE CREW'S EXPECTATIONS OF THE SM

At every turn in our discussion about the working relationship between the SM and the crew, the SM's limited involvement with the crew becomes more evident. In technical rehearsals, it is the SM's job to be ever watchful of all that is going on, yet not be intrusive in these observations of the crew. During techs, if the SM sees something wrong or something that needs to be changed, the SM goes to the TD or the head of that department to express these opinions or concerns. In doing so, the SM uses a careful approach and presentation to avoid putting the technician on the defensive. It is an established fact that the SM stays out of union stagehands' work. What the crew expects and needs from the SMs is that the SMs remain available to answer questions, maybe ask a limited amount of questions, know when to step in to voice their opinions, and create schedules that keep the technical rehearsals coordinated and running smoothly.

CAST AND CREW COMING TOGETHER

There is an interaction and exchange between the cast and crew that every alert, observant, and aware SM experiences over and over when the cast and crew come together for the first time. This interaction is seldom, if ever, discussed or acknowledged. By the time the cast walks into the theatre, the crew has already put in a good amount of time and work in setting up the scenery and getting the technical elements into place. They have quickly made the theatre and backstage their home, and the physical part of the show their own. The cast, on the other hand, from the work they have done in the rehearsal hall, has also made the show their own. Upon coming together, each group, in its own way, can feel invaded by the other. These feelings can become even greater with a musical show, where there can be thirty or more cast members. The cast, often in an enthusiastic and demonstrative way, comes swarming into the theatre on their first day to investigate and make this new space their own. Some crewmembers become protective of their territory. Depending on the nature of the individuals and the chemistry of the two groups, this initial meeting and feeling quickly passes and the two groups bond, create a working relationship, and easily become friends. Other times, matters can go from bad to worse with tension mounting and many complaints given to the SM from each group, and on occasion little riffs erupt, which the SM must tend to and resolve immediately.

Preventative Measures

It is important for the SM to be aware of such dynamics between the two groups. With this knowledge, the SM can better deal with the situation should it arise or, better still, take some subtle preventive steps. This work can be done mostly with the cast. In the last week of rehearsals at the rehearsal hall, as part of the transition speech to the cast, the SM can ask the cast to be aware and sensitive to the crew and the work they do and can remind them that the crew's work is as important to the show as is theirs. The SM can ask the cast to extend the same patience and courtesies to the crew as they did to each other when they were first learning the show. To help the cast better understand and if so inclined, the SM might point out the casts' feelings and attachment to the show and how the crew has developed its own feelings and attachments.

The SM Sets the Example

From the moment SMs walk in on their first day at the theatre, the crew is looking them over. They see how the SMs dress; being too trendy, funky, or conservative can leave a negative impression. They will watch the SMs' manner, demeanor, behavior, and way of working. The crew will listen to the SMs' tone of voice, see their attitude, and the way they exert their position and power. The crew formulates opinions quickly, and it will take a lot to change them.

The SMs cannot have the same conversation with the crewmembers as they did with the cast, but from the start SMs show respect, interest, understanding, and appreciation for the crew's work and their contribution to the show. The greatest impression an SM can make on the first day of techs is to be low keyed. When beginning the work for the day, the SMs need only to show that they are organized, efficient, and know the show. The SMs' strength and power comes from knowing their job and doing it well. An SM will impress by being a good listener, being understanding and appreciative of the crew's work, making reasonable and fair decisions, and by doing the work without drama, fanfare, or ego. Being assertive and asking questions is okay, but stepping over into aggression is destructive. A softer, gentler way gains respect and maintains control.

THE DAILY TECH SCHEDULE

For a better overview of what a technical rehearsal day is like, it might be good to go over a typical schedule. Technical rehearsals can last from one day to fourteen. Musical productions can take up the fourteen days, while a simple one-set comedy or drama can take seven or fewer. By all standards, the technical rehearsal day is long. The actors work ten hours out of twelve, with the usual breaks. The crew too has union rules governing the number of hours they can work and the breaks they must have. However, because of the workload and the limited time the crew has to do their work during techs, their workday is often long, with their hours being extended and the producer paying overtime.

By Equity rule, the SM comes under the same agreement as the actors. However, the SM's hours are not monitored and the SM puts in whatever hours it takes to get the job done. The SM seldom gets paid overtime unless the cast members go into an overtime situation. Perhaps Equity justifies the SM's long hours by the fact that during the rehearsal period, while the actors are on a rehearsal salary, the SM is being paid a full salary.

A typical schedule for technical rehearsals follows:

8:00 A.M.: Each technical department begins work. (Depending on the work the SM must do before the director and cast come in, the SM comes in around 10:00 A.M.)

12:00 Noon: The crew goes to lunch. The cast arrives to begin their day. The cast has an hour to work before the crew returns from lunch. During this hour, the director might give notes or rehearse the cast on the stage. If the director and actors work on stage, they cannot have any of the working technical elements, unless the producer is willing to pay a skeleton crew overtime and provide them with a lunch.

1:00 P.M.: Everyone works on teching the show—putting the technical elements together—cue by cue, working their way to run-thrus, dress rehearsals, and preview performances.

5:00 P.M.: Everyone has a dinner break. (The SM may or may not go to dinner, depending on what needs to be done before the cast and crew return. Many times the SM will have food brought in and will continue to work.)

7:00 P.M.: Everyone is back from dinner and continues teching the show.

12: 00 A.M.: Everyone is dismissed.

With this as a basis, the SM can create a good working schedule for techs. The only other factor to keep in mind is the turn-around time—twelve hours for the cast and eight hours for the crew.

DIVISION OF LABOR

Most labor unions, such as the stagehands' union (I.A.T.S.E.), have some well-defined lines for the division of labor and distinctions between the work of one technical department and another. It is important for the SM to learn which department does what things. With this knowledge, the SM knows what to expect from each department and where to bring any questions, comments, suggestions, changes, or corrections. This division of labor is learned as a beginning SM works on shows as an assistant. Sometimes the new SM learns quickly because the stagehands themselves will be the first to direct and set straight any SM who goes to the wrong department.

Along these same lines, it is also important that the SM knows not to do any of the work that is deemed stagehand's work. If some small job must be done—something as simple as moving a hand prop,

taping a spike mark, opening a curtain, or sweeping up some litter—the SM must call for a stagehand from the correct department. An SM who decides to go ahead and do the work can be reprimanded, with the matter being taken to the stagehand's union and to the producer. The only exception might be in an emergency, in a moment of danger, or to prevent an accident or injury. During such times, the SM should have no hesitation to jump in and lend a helping hand.

THE WORKING RELATIONSHIPS OF TECHS

When all is going well with technical rehearsals, it is theatre working at its best. The show magically comes together, joining the creative, craft, artistic, and technical parts, everything fitting together as everyone had designed and envisioned. For the SM, technical rehearsals can be a time of excitement and accomplishment. This is the time when the SM makes an artistic contribution to the show by calling impeccably well-timed cues. It is also a time when the SM is given more of the responsibility and care for the show and company. Life, however, does not always afford such perfection without some struggle or conflict. In fact, an SM may experience in a career more of the darker colors of techs than the broad colorful strokes so often idealized in books.

Technical rehearsals are a complicated network of technical things and people. With the technical elements being designed and assembled separately, then coming together at the theatre for the first time, there are bound to be problems. For the SM, the technical problems are the least troublesome. Professional men and women have been hired to do the job. They know their craft and usually can handle whatever problems come up or make whatever changes are presented. It is the pressure of the limited time and the conflicts that can sometimes develop between people that are wearing and destructive to the overall process. No matter how much time is allowed for technical rehearsals, there is never enough. People seem to work under the same pressure and intensity whether given one day to do the work or ten days. In technical rehearsals, Murphy's Law prevails—that is, if something can go wrong, it will! In the worst scenario, as problems mount people become insecure, protective or defensive, tempers flare, or their egos become hurt or inflated. People will look outside themselves to find fault or to place blame.

It is through these elements that things can fall apart and working relationships change in techs. This is another one of those subjects seldom discussed in preparing an SM for the job. Ignorance can be bliss, but not for an SM working a technical rehearsal. If and when technical rehearsals become less than picture perfect, it is important the SM know more about the key people with whom he or she must work and how they may act and behave under adverse conditions.

The SM

Let us start with the SM. We have already said the SM needs to have done all parts of the job with as much perfection as possible. At all times in technical rehearsals, the SM needs to be focused and concentrated on the work at hand and not putting attention on things that should have been done previously. The SM must keep a clear and open mind and remain calm and level-headed. Of all the people working techs, the SM is expected to remain sane and secure. While all others are going over the edge, the SM must be the rock on which people can place some stability. The SM needs to be ready to handle the tasks and problems at hand, and there will be plenty without the SM creating more. It is the SM's job to keep the technical rehearsals moving forward, even if at times they move at a snail's pace. The SM needs to have his or her area working and running like a well-oiled, well-tuned machine to avoid becoming enmeshed in a labyrinth of problems and blame from which it may be difficult to escape.

The Director

Techs are a time when the director must relinquish some control to the SM. The director is placed in the darkened theatre, separated from the cast and crew. It is not practical to be running backstage to direct every bit of work that needs to be done, and the director must trust the SM to do it. Some directors are able to let go and allow the SM to be in control and lead. Some directors are technically smart. They know how to communicate with the different departments. They understand the technicians' work, appreciate their contribution to the show, and know the time it takes to do things and make changes. With those directors, the SM's life during techs is made pleasant. Some directors use the period of technical

rehearsals wisely. They know how to push and prod, when to apply pressure, exert their power, wield their authority, and when to back off. Then there are those directors who are inexperienced or have very little interest or knowledge of technical rehearsals. During these times the SM takes up the slack and contributes what the director lacks.

Most frightening of all for a director during technical rehearsals is when the world gets turned upside down—when everything that can go wrong, goes wrong, when nothing seems to fit, it seems the artistry is gone and the director's vision is lost. At these times some directors abandon the technical part of the show and start redirecting. The experienced SM cannot allow this to happen. In working in the best interest of the producer, the SM needs to confer with the producer and director, suggesting compromise and a change in schedule—one in which the director can work and at the same time technical rehearsals can continue, getting done all that needs to be done before the first previews or opening performance.

The SM, Producer, and Director

During some of the more difficult technical rehearsals, the producer's or director's working relationship with the SM can be affected. Some producers or directors will use the SM's position as a place where they can vent. Some will verbally berate the SM, using the SM as a sounding board to get their point across to others. Other times, producers or directors in their frustration and anger over something else, may unfairly place the blame on the SM. The position of the SM is an easy place to go with matters or problems that producers or directors do not want to handle or cannot handle. Once again, this is when it is important that the SM know the job, know the SM's responsibilities, and the responsibilities of others. Being used can be acceptable to an SM as long as the producer, director, and SM know the game being played. Being berated or verbally abused is not acceptable. If the SM feels uncertain about any treatment, he or she should approach the producer or director privately to find the truth of the matter. SMs need to take care of themselves.

The Cast

This is a time of great adjustment for the actors. They are now having to deal with walls, stairs, and platforms which were only taped lines on the rehearsal room floor. The props will feel different, the furniture may be smaller or larger than they anticipated. Parts of costumes may be missing or not fit properly. The blocking will feel wrong and the sense of performance they once had in the rehearsal room is now gone. What was once safe and secure now appears to be lost. In addition, they are no longer the center of the day's work. Everyone is concentrated on the technical matters, and that is how it should be, but on occasion even the most experienced actors may feel abandoned.

During this time some actors will change. Some of the changes will be small and subtle with only the SM taking notice. Others will be broad and overt, for everyone working in the theatre to see. A star or a lead performer who was the very model of a professional in rehearsals may become intense, insistent, or demanding, wanting to change everything until the star once again feels safe and secure. The ensemble players too, who once worked as a team, may begin quibbling among themselves, complaining to the SM about the least little thing, or while on stage, stumbling over each other, forgetting their blocking, and becoming unsure of their entrances and exits.

Not for a moment can the SM neglect or forget the work with the cast during technical rehearsals, no matter how demanding the rest of the work becomes. The SM must continue to attend to their needs. However, in moving from the rehearsal hall to the theatre and into techs, the SM, in the talk with the cast on the last day at the rehearsal hall, changed the working relationship with them. During rehearsals, the SM was more parental and more of a caretaker. Now in technical rehearsals, the cast members need to take the responsibility for tending to their smaller needs. The SM assures the cast that he or she will still be present and available to communicate, support, and serve them, but more in their important and immediate needs. The SM leads the cast into a more mature working relationship. Like a parent whose child has grown up, the SM gives the actors the freedom and responsibility for their own professional life and work, while the SM continues to love and care for them.

The SM's greatest opportunity to communicate and assure the cast of this continued interest and work comes during talks with them over the PA system. The SM thanks them for their good work during the rehearsal day and in a caring and loving way leads them, instructs them, and keeps them informed. The SM asks if there is anything the backstage staff and crew can do to support them in small ways; do they need someone to shine a flashlight as they come off the stage, or want a prop placed differently? The SM might even assure an actor who is left in the dark on stage at the end of a scene, that the scenery will not start moving until the SM sees that the actor is clear and safe.

The Crew

Technical rehearsals are the time for the crew to learn their parts for the show. However, the crew is not afforded the same luxury in time and patience as the actors were allowed in rehearsals. This factor can be especially significant when a nervous, impatient, or inexperienced director sits out in the house, calling over the god-mic for speed and perfection. The SM must be aware of and sensitive to this factor and at the least indication of impatience or lack of tolerance in allowing the crew time to do their work or learn the show, the SM needs to become an intermediary, speaking on the crew's behalf. In a nonconfrontational way, the SM must express to the director the crews' efforts and need for time to learn or complete the task. At the same time, the SM assures the director that the SM is keeping a watchful eye and running a tight ship backstage.

No matter how diplomatically, professionally, or psychologically handled, if the crew does not deliver and the director becomes unhappy, the SM can be placed in the middle and the responsibility for the delay or problem can fall on the SM. The best an SM can do in approaching such situations is to keep the director informed as to what is going on backstage. The SM needs to create a clear picture as to the problem at hand and the placement of responsibility.

In working with the crew, the SM builds a working relationship slowly. The SM cannot be as direct and demonstrative with the crew as with the cast. Whatever personal relationships are cultivated with crew members come within time. The SM's bond with them builds on the merits of the SM's good work, the way the SM works with them, and the SM's appreciation and understanding of their work and contribution to the show.

LET THE TECHS BEGIN

For some of what has been said about techs thus far, the picture painted appears bleak and grim. Sadly, it sometimes is that way. However, no one goes into techs expecting things to be bad. They just know that technical rehearsals are a fragile and intense time. All go in with the hope and expectation that this will be a good time, and many turn out that way. Some of the darker colors have been presented to make the SM aware and to equip the SM with information and knowledge to use in the worst of times.

Most times, on the first day when the cast, crew, and staff get together to begin techs, the crew has already been working at the theatre since early morning. By the time the cast and staff are called in, it is time for the crew to go on a lunch break. Meanwhile, the cast and staff come to the theatre to settle in. The SM is there to greet and lead everyone around and get them ready to begin the technical work when the crew returns. Upon arrival of the crew, it is the SM's intent to get the rehearsal started at the scheduled time. Seldom does it work out that way. There is always some delay. A thirty-minute delay is expected and manageable. Anything longer than thirty minutes and the people who are left waiting become irritable. For the SM this is no way to begin technical rehearsals. At the start of any delay, the SM must investigate, know the cause, find out how long it will take before the rehearsals can begin, and then report it to the producer and director. To use the time of the delay effectively, the director or SM might have the cast work on the stage, perhaps running some blocking, or having the choreographer work with the cast on one of the dance numbers.

THE HEART OF TECHS

The SM is seated at the console and the ASM is left free to roam the backstage areas, to observe and troubleshoot wherever needed. The technicians are at their workstations. The actors are in place. The director, lighting designer, their assistants, and possibly the producer are seated in the audience at the production table. The stage is set for Act I, Scene 1. The curtain is down and the curtain warmers/preset is on.

If all has been working in textbook fashion, the SM already has the cues for the opening of the show written in the cueing script. If not, it is at this point the SM receives over the headset, from the director or lighting designer, the cues and their timing. The SM notes them quickly in the script and then over the headset puts in the warnings to the crew. The SM gives the stand bys and, when ready, calls the GO! cues that take out the house lights, raise the curtain, bring up the lights for the first scene, and tell the actors to begin acting. If the timing and execution of these cues are not as the director and lighting designer

wish, they will stop the rehearsal to make changes or corrections. The changes or corrections may have to do with one or more departments. Each department makes its own notes, as does the SM with the notes that pertain to the SM. Thus the technical rehearsals begin and continue—cue by cue, stopping and starting.

LAYING IN SPIKE MARKS

Some shows require many things to be *spiked*—that requires putting small pieces of tape on the stage floor to mark the corner of set units, furniture, or even marks where an actor must stand to be in a special light. The placement of these things on stage becomes established as each scene is worked and teched. For the most part, either the prop or carpentry department handles this job. As the techs continue, some of the marks may be changed as the director moves things around and adjusts the stage picture. When this happens, most directors do not want to stop the rehearsal, and ask that the change be done later. Doing this task later is often too late. The prop or set piece gets moved, or everyone forgets. Experience teaches the SM to do this job immediately, either by having a crewmember do it as the scene continues, or by having the SM do it. This is one of those jobs the union members won't complain about if sometimes the SM does it, as long as it doesn't appear that the crew is not doing their job.

To aid the SM in this very small but important task, the SM has near the console a roll of white, quarter-inch tape, which usually is the size for spiking. Sometimes, depending on the show, the SM may need different colors or larger sizes. To meet all occasions and circumstances, the experienced SM has collected a number of rolls of tape for this purpose. For convenience and to have this tape at hand at all times, the SM may loop these rolls on a rope or chain and hang it next to the console. Then when the director calls for a spike mark, the SM or a crewmember can quickly go out on stage with this collection of tape rolls and place the mark while the actors continue with the rehearsal.

CHANGES AND CLEANING UP THE CUEING SCRIPT

In technical rehearsals change is a fact of life for an SM. It is the only constant on which the SM can depend. From the moment the actors step on the stage with the scenery and props, there will be change. From the moment the director and lighting designer see the cues they have set, there will be change. Change is an ongoing process from which the SM is never freed. There is no particular place or moment in the production of a show when the changes stop. Once the show opens and gets into its run, changes in the show take a new direction. The actors begin to improve on their performances and make changes. Even the SM makes changes, improving the timing in calling the cues for the performance.

To make changes in the cueing script, the SM must have at all times a pencil at hand and a large smudge-proof eraser. Whatever changes the SM makes must be made quickly, with little delay, so the SM can lead the stagehands in executing the changes with the timing and perfection expected. By the end of each day, especially when doing a musical, the pages on which the cues have been written are often readable only to the SM. The SM must get these pages cleaned up and must do this while the cues are still fresh in the SM's mind. The SM may be called on by the director on the very next day, or several days later, to go back in review to execute these cues. In the worst of situations, the SM may not get back to these cues until dress rehearsal or even opening night. It is for these times that the SM must have the cueing script color coded and ready for performance, even if the SM knows there will be more changes. This means that at the end of the day or sometime during the day, the SM must steal off to get the cueing script up to date.

To aid the SM in cleaning and updating the cueing script, it is extremely helpful to have an extra copy of the script from which to take clean pages. In addition, it is extremely helpful that the SM have multiple copies of the pages on which a large number of cues appear. Chances are great that whatever changes the director or lighting designer make will be on these pages. With these multiple copies, the SM will already have clean pages without having to first go to the copy machine.

THE NEXT PHASE OF TECHS

Once the cues for the show have been set and all the technical kinks have been worked out, the techs move into the next phase. This move is not extreme, but is a natural progression of working and running the show. It is a time to refine and make more changes, blending the work of the actors and crew, bringing all elements to performance level. There is still, however, one more technical element to be added—the costumes. They will come at the tail end of this phase.

It is also during this part of techs that the SM learns the cues and refines the timing in calling them. Not only must the SM have the cueing script performance-ready, but the SM must also be performance-ready. Waiting until dress rehearsals or preview performances is too late. By that time the producer, director, and everyone else is expecting the SM to call the show as if the SM had been doing it for a year.

ACTORS' ENTRANCES

One of the greater sins an actor can commit is to miss an entrance. It would be erroneous to say that during performance the SM is responsible for getting the actors in place to make their entrances. The only times the SM calls the actors to their places is at the top of the show and after intermission, just before Act Two begins. From those points on, the actors are responsible for their own entrances. In rehearsals at the rehearsal hall the SM was more of a caretaker and would seek out actors if they were not standing by to make an entrance. This, of course, is not possible in techs and certainly not in performance. The SM starts early in techs to make the actors responsible for their entrances.

Having said this and having established this way of working with the cast, the SM still owes a responsibility to the show. It is the SM's job to do whatever it takes to see that each performance runs smoothly and without problems. The SM does not abandon entirely the responsibility for actors making entrances, but instead becomes an observer—a monitor. Whenever possible throughout the performance, the SM checks to see if an actor is in place, ready to make an entrance. The SM cannot monitor all entrances, especially those out of sight and certainly those made on the opposite side of the stage from the console. The SM takes on this responsibility, but in no way communicates this to the actors. As soon as they know, some actors will relieve themselves of their responsibility and depend on the SM to do it for them.

To aid the SM in monitoring entrances, the SM marks in the left-hand margin of the cueing script (not in the right-hand margin, where the cues are noted) the character's name and surrounds this information with a box to make it stand out. Then, as part of looking ahead in the script for the next cues, the SM sees this information and checks to see if the actor is in place. In a musical, the SM tracks only the entrances of the principal and supporting performers, and not the entrances of the ensemble.

Nipping It in the Bud

During this second phase in techs, the PSM and ASM become militaristic in checking to see if the actors are in place, ready to make their entrances. Their purpose? To learn early which actors have a propensity to be late or which actors have a tendency to get in place at the last minute. Before bad habits develop, either the PSM or ASM asks the offending actors to be in place earlier. Also during this period in techs, if the SMs see that an actor is about to miss an entrance, they allow it to happen. There is no greater embarrassment, lesson learned, or impression made than when the rehearsals must stop while the SMs seek out an actor who has missed an entrance.

TIMING THE SHOW, OR THE RUNNING TIME

As the technical rehearsals become less stop-and-go and more of a run-thru, the SM starts getting timings on the scenes and acts. The PSM usually does this job while calling the cues for the run-thru. However, if the show is busy with cues, the PSM might have the ASM do it. Only one or two timings are necessary at this point, just to give the director an idea of how long things are now running with the technical elements added. The SM notes this information in the left-hand margin of the cueing script along with the date of the timing. The SM already has noted in the rehearsal script the timings taken during rehearsals at the rehearsal hall, and the SM or the director can at any time compare those timings with the ones now in the cueing script.

SHOW RUNDOWN SHEETS

Once the cues have been set, the backstage becomes more organized and arranged to suit the run of the performance. All unnecessary things are packed away, the prop tables are set up, the workstations for the different technical departments become more defined, and the crewmembers settle into their space. At this point the SMs can post the Show Rundown Sheets as presented in Chapter 6, Hard Copy. Re-

member, this list of scenes needs to be simple, easy to read at a glance, done in large print, and be placed where people are working or passing. This would include hallways, corridors, staircases, the different work stations for the crew, on the back walls of the set, in quick change rooms, at the SM's console, in places where entrances and exits are made, and in each dressing room. Show Rundown Sheets are mandatory for musical shows, but the SM also should make it a habit to post them even for a one-set comedy or drama.

DRY TECHS

In any technically difficult show where there might be a lot of scenery and scene changes, it is in the best interest for the crew and SM to have one or several *dry techs*—that is, a rehearsal the SM has with the crew without the cast being present. During a dry tech, the SM sits at the console while the crewmembers take their places at their workstations. Together, as if in a performance, they run the more technically difficult cues, stopping to correct any mistakes. This kind of rehearsal is often done in the morning hours before the cast and other staff members come in to do their work.

SCENERY PLOT AND FLY PLOT

In many academic and community situations, the SM may be required to make up a scenery moves plot and a fly moves plot. In professional theatre with union stagehands working the show, the SM is not required to do this work. The heads of each department will create their own working plots or lists to aid them in executing their cues during the performance. At the end of the run of the show, however, the SM may want to create a scenery plot and fly plot for the production book that will be turned in to the production office. These plots are not mandatory, however, because all this information is noted in the cueing script, which the SM also turns in.

CHECKING SIGHT LINES

Just before the start of dress rehearsals and preview performances, it is a good idea for the SM to check the sight lines from both the backstage as well as from the audience. From the perspective of being backstage, the SM needs to stand in each wing or opening of the set and mark on the floor with white tape the closest point at which a person can stand or a piece of scenery can be placed without being seen by any member of the audience. From the perspective of being in the audience, the SM sits in the seats at the far ends of the rows closest to the stage to see that all openings on the stage that can reveal the backstage are sufficiently covered with curtains or flats.

This task, though seemingly unimportant in relationship to all the other things to be done in techs, is nonetheless important. For audience members, seeing actors or scenery waiting in the wings is distracting, spoils whatever illusion of reality might have been created, and hurts the magic of theatre. By taking the time to do this one little thing, the SM contributes to the artistic integrity of the show. It is, however, another one of those jobs the SM does that is often taken for granted and receives little recognition. The SM does it anyway, out of care for the excellence of the production.

THE BLUE WORK LIGHTS

Once the backstage area is organized, the crew's work stations are established, and everyone is familiar with what they must do during the performance, the SM should ask that the overhead work lights backstage be turned off. As soon as possible, the SM needs to get everyone backstage working under the same conditions they will be working in during performances. Of course, people cannot work in the dark. They must have some light at their work stations, light reflecting on the prop tables, and some general lighting so they can move about safely. Some theatres will have lighting instruments with blue gels already set up. If not, the electric department with the show needs to set them up. On the list of things the electric department must do during techs, the blue work lights are a low priority. If the SM does not ask for them and show they are a priority on the SM's list, the blue work lights can be put off to as late as an hour before dress rehearsal. Having the blue lights up and functioning becomes, for the SM, another one of those things that must be approached with good timing. In the poorest of situations, the SM may have to push and be assertive in getting this to happen sooner.

Through experience, SMs and technicians have found that the color blue is the best choice for these lights, possibly because blue is more like the light of night and people are comfortable with it psychologically. Green and red feel unnatural while amber can be too bright, even when at a low intensity.

CRUCIAL CUES

Also toward the end of this second phase in techs, the SM might go through the cueing script looking for cues that are so integral to the show that if they do not take place, the plot, storyline, or action will be hurt—their absence might even stop the show. With each crucial cue, the SM must decide what the SM, the cast, and the crew can do to quickly rectify a mistake or how to continue the performance without it. They must discuss an alternative plan for each crucial cue. Simple examples of such things might be a telephone that does not ring, a gun that misfires or jams, a door that won't open, or a special effect that goes wrong or does not happen. An alternative plan is excellent insurance for the show. Even with a high probability that the problem will not occur, the SM should take such measures. It is worth the time and effort.

COSTUMES, HAIR, AND MAKEUP

Just about the time in techs when the show is being run almost nonstop, the costumes are added to the show—the frosting and decoration on the already delicious cake. Each director, producer, or production company does this part of techs differently. The differences also depend on the type of show. A six-character, one-set comedy or drama will be quite different from a full-scale musical.

Some directors or producers want a formal dress parade in which the actors individually come out on stage, under the stage lighting, to display or model each of their costumes while the director, producer, designer, and their assistants sit at the production table, making notes. Other producers and directors may introduce the costumes slowly to the show, by having the actors wear only bits and pieces, or having the actors wear the costumes for only one particular scene. Often, due to the lack of tech time, all the costumes are introduced in an afternoon rehearsal, and then for the rest of the day the rehearsals are devoted to whatever problems might surround the costumes. Usually by the next day or no later than the day after, the costume problems have been resolved and the actors have adjusted quickly, welcoming the final touch to their characters. Makeup and hair may also be introduced at the same time as the costumes, or the director may have the actors add makeup and hair after the costumes have been reviewed and the problems resolved.

On the positive side, adding costumes, makeup, and hair is fun, exciting, and is a final touch to the actors' characters and the show in general. However, adding these things can also be upsetting, especially if they are of a different period or are fantastic in design. First, there is the problem of getting used to the feel and the fit. Then there is the part of doing the blocking and stage business with whatever problems the costumes might present. Also, up to this point when the actors came off stage in the rehearsal, they had leisure time before the next entrance. With the addition of the costumes, makeup, and hair, they must now be concerned with these things to be ready for the next entrance, especially if the change is quick. There are also those actors who just do not like what has been designed for them.

During the introduction of costumes, makeup, and hair, the SM needs to be alert to the problems and feelings some of the actors might have. The SM needs to trouble shoot wherever possible, calming a person who might be upset, assuring another that the problems will be heard and resolved. The SM reports to the wardrobe or hair departments all the problems they can handle, and keeps the director and designer informed of the problems that might not yet have reached them.

MUSICALS: THE ORCHESTRA

As has been stated over and over in this book, with musicals there is more of everything: more people, more scenery, more cues, more scheduling, more costumes, more problems. At this point in our discussion of working techs, the only element left for a musical is the music part of the show—the orchestra.

Scheduling the Orchestra

Time needs to be scheduled during techs for the orchestra to rehearse with the music director and conductor, and then with the cast. Once the musicians are brought in, they become a permanent part of the show and the payroll. This is a large expense in the producer's budget, so producers hold off as long as

possible before bringing in the musicians. This means they are brought in either the day before the first dress rehearsal or sometimes on the same day.

The music director works out the schedule for the rehearsals and all the particulars having to do with the orchestra, working closely with the musicians' union. The SM needs only to get the information, put it on the schedule, and see that the cast is informed and attends their part of the rehearsal.

Rehearsal Space for the Orchestra

In most working situations it is not practical for the orchestra to set up and work in the pit. Because the show is a musical, chances are the techs are running behind schedule and everyone needs all the time on the stage they can get to complete their work. The crew needs stage time in the morning before the cast and director come in. The director, along with the cast and crew, needs the afternoon and evening times. The orchestra rehearsing in the pit while others are working on the stage is annoying and disturbs the others' work. No one is willing to give up stage time. The only resolution is to put the orchestra somewhere else. It is common practice, while the orchestra is rehearsing for the first time and while the cast is having their first rehearsal with the orchestra, that the orchestra rehearses somewhere else. If the theatre has a large enough rehearsal room, the orchestra will be set up there. If not, a rehearsal room somewhere else will need to be rented and set up. To save that expense, and if the lobby or vestibule of the theatre is large enough, producers will have the orchestra set up there. Actually, working in the lobby is a good second choice. It is convenient for everyone.

Setting Up the Rehearsal Space

To set up the orchestra someplace other than the orchestra pit, the music director and SM coordinate with the TD. The prop department sets up the music stands and chairs. Electrics brings in whatever power is needed and sets the clip-on lights on the music stands. The carpentry department sets up the conductor's podium and whatever platforms might be needed, and the sound department sets up the mics and whatever amplification of sound is needed. The SM has little to do with this project other than to check with the music director to see if all is scheduled and going according to plan, and to remind the crew about the setup on the day before the rehearsal.

The SM's Responsibility to the Orchestra Rehearsal

Most times an SM is not needed to be present during the entire time of the orchestra rehearsal. On the day of the rehearsal, the SM is there at the beginning to see that the rehearsal gets started without delay and to handle any problems. Once the rehearsal is underway, the SM is free to go about some other business, but returns from time to time to see if all is still going well. Later in the rehearsal, after the orchestra has learned their parts, the SM checks again to see that the cast members are arriving according to their scheduled times.

BEFORE THE ARRIVAL OF THE FIRE MARSHAL

Sometime at the end of this second phase of techs or at the beginning of the next phase, it is wise for the SM to approach the TD and ask if everything that needs to be fire proofed or sprayed with fire retardant chemicals has been done, or is going to be done. Also, the SM needs to check all fire exits and fire lanes to see if they are cleared, or if they are going to be cleared before the fire marshal comes. The SM should also remind the TD of the fire extinguishers, asking if they are up to date and accessibly placed. If the techs have been particularly difficult and are running behind schedule, or if the TD has forgotten, the TD may respond defensively or be thankful for the SM's reminder. An SM can only do the job, prepared for either response.

THE FIRE MARSHAL'S ARRIVAL

The fire marshal always arrives unannounced. The fire marshal may come one or two days before the first public performance, be it a dress rehearsal or preview performance or may come as late as the afternoon of the opening performance. The fire marshal appears backstage, saying very little to anyone. The fire marshal knows what to look for and freely moves about the stage and backstage areas. The TD or SM will be asked if there are any open flames or pyro effects in the show and the fire marshal will want to see all licenses and permits. If things are not according to the law or meet the fire marshal's approval, this person has the power to prevent the show from performing for an audience until those things in violation are corrected.

Another Grey Responsibility

With the fire marshal coming at such a late date, if there is a major problem there usually is a mad scramble to get corrected whatever needs to be done. The things having to do with the fire marshal are not the job and responsibility of the SM, but the experienced SM takes on another grey responsibility, knowing the problem that can be created in the worst-case scenario. Once again the SM is there to protect the producer and look out for the best interest of the show.

THE FINAL PHASE OF TECHS

In this final phase of techs at least one dress rehearsal is scheduled. Before the opening performance the producer may also schedule one or more preview performances. If there are no preview performances, on the day of the opening there may be a dress rehearsal in the afternoon with the opening performance at night. In other cases, if all has gone well, the director may call a short rehearsal in the afternoon, giving the cast and crew the time off to rest and prepare for the opening performance that night.

Collecting and Returning Valuables

It is mandated by Equity that once the show gets into dress rehearsals or when the actors are required to wear costumes and can no longer keep their personal valuables on their person for safe keeping, the SM must collect valuables and management must provide a safe place until the SM returns them. As soon as the company gets into the theatre for techs, the SM will accept valuables from performers who choose to have certain items locked up. However, the SM will put the practice of collecting valuables into full swing on the first day when everyone is required to wear costumes. For the sake of order, for keeping individuals' items separate, and for quick return, many SMs provide each actor with a large, plastic zip-lock bag with the actor's name clearly printed on it. The SM makes it a standard practice that, immediately after giving the half-hour call before a dress rehearsal or performance, one of the SMs goes around collecting the items. Most SMs prefer going around to each dressing room to collect the items instead of having the actors bring their items to the SM. This gives the SM the opportunity to see and talk with the actors and gives another opportunity to keep a finger on the pulse of the company.

The SM walks through the halls and corridors calling out, "VALUABLES!!!" When approaching a dressing room door, the SM knocks and calls out again, "Valuables!" and then waits for a reply. Some people will come to the door with a bulging bag of valuables, while others will have in their plastic bag only a ring, maybe a clip of money, or perhaps a watch. When the SM reaches an ensemble dressing room of the opposite gender, every effort should be made to respect the modesty of the occupants. After knocking, calling out, and having the door opened, the SM can give the valuables container to the person answering, and have that person collect the valuables in that room while the SM waits outside.

Some SMs prefer having the cast members come to them while they wait at a designated place backstage or at the SM's console. The problem with this approach is that the actors will come at their own timing. This means an SM must be at the receiving point until the SM is sure everyone who chooses to has turned in their valuables. With the limited time of the half-hour before a performance and all the things an SM must do during that time, it is more efficient for the SM to go around, complete the business, and be off to do other things.

In returning the packets and bags of personal valuables after the performance, the SM must be as responsible and conscientious as was the case in collecting them. The SM must personally see that all bags are returned to the correct individuals.

Techs Continue

Although the technical elements have been set and worked out by this time in techs, there is always some refining and tweaking to be done in all parts of the show. Technical rehearsals are never officially over until after the opening performance. Even then, within the week following the opening, the director may continue to rehearse the cast and make technical changes in the afternoons and perform the show in the evenings.

Performance Level

In dress rehearsals and certainly in the preview performances all the technical elements, including costume, hair, makeup, and orchestra are used. If the director agrees, the SM should remind the cast and crew before a dress rehearsal that the rehearsal is to be performed as it will be for an audience. The SM reminds them that there will be no stopping unless it is a matter of safety or at the word of the director or SM. This is certainly to be the case for preview performances, even if the producer or director announces to the audience beforehand that the show could be stopped for a technical problem.

THE DIRECTOR GIVING NOTES

Sometimes immediately after a dress rehearsal or preview performance the director will give notes. Other times this will be done just before the next run-thru or performance. The notes are mostly for the cast members, but one of the SMs always attends the note sessions, and sometimes the heads of the different technical departments will attend.

Important Information for the SM

Notes from the director are very important to the SM. Aside from getting notes about calling the cues for the show, the SM must know what the actors are being told and how they are being directed. With this information the SM can maintain the director's intent and integrity, and can later transfer this information to the understudies and replacement actors. Also, if neither the TD nor the technical heads are present at the note session, it is the SM's job to take their notes and later relay the information to them.

PERFORMANCE SHOW REPORTS

Once the show gets into dress rehearsals and preview performances, the SM starts filling out for each performance a show report sheet, as presented in Chapter 6, Hard Copy. An important part of this report is noting the timing of each act. By dress rehearsals and previews the timing of the acts and the overall show is closer to what it will be throughout the run of the show. This is usable information for anyone who seeks it from the SM. It is especially useful to the house manager, who needs to prepare the staff for intermission and the end of the show. Also, the box office likes having this information to tell the patrons who might ask.

Detailed Timing Forms

After the show is in its run and the timings for each act on the show reports become consistent, the PSM will do from time to time detailed timings of the show, timing the individual scenes as well as the overall acts. The information from these timings is noted on the Performance Running Time Chart, as presented in Chapter 6, then it is placed in the front part of the cueing script for reference.

PRODUCTION PHOTOS OR VIDEOS

Often in this final phase of techs the producer and publicity department want a photo session to get production stills and video. Having a photo call at this time should be no surprise to anyone. It more than likely was placed on the block calendar that was handed out during the first week of rehearsals. Once again, if all has gone well in techs, the cast, crew, and staff are ready for this part of techs. If not, all are a little resentful at having to use precious tech time to do this work.

Some picture calls, for both still photos and video, can be simple and uninvolved. The photographers may do their work standing on the apron of the stage or moving about in the orchestra of the empty theatre. Some sessions may involve only the principal performers, while others, as with a musical show, may require the entire cast. With other photos call, the publicity department may want to set up and stage the pictures, using additional lights specifically for the camera. These events can take up as much as two rehearsals in a day, sometimes flowing over into the next day.

Picture calls are governed by Equity rule. It is important that the SM refer to the Equity handbook and know the details, especially when it comes to videotaping. If things are not done according to Equity agreement, the session can end up costing the producer a good amount of money—money the producer is neither prepared nor willing to spend.

It is the SM's job to find out the type of photo session, the needs of the producer, what the publicity department might want, and then coordinate the event accordingly. Some producers, directors, and even textbooks say the SM is in full charge of the photo shoot. The truth is, on the day of the shoot, the SM takes more of a secondary position, assisting and doing whatever the director, producer, publicity people, and even the photographer wants. The SM is there to facilitate, organize, keep order, work out logistics, keep the event moving, make suggestions that can make things easier and save time, put together the list of pictures as dictated to the SM, tell the crew when to change the scenery or lights, and see that the actors who are not being used on stage are getting into their costumes and are ready for the next picture to be taken. On some occasions, when the SM might have the producer's and director's confidence, the SM might be called on to run the entire affair. At those times the SM draws on any artistic experience as well as the experience gained from doing other photo shoots.

News Coverage and Interviews

News coverage takes less time and is not as involved as a photo session might be. Usually one or several TV stations are invited to bring in their cameras during a dress rehearsal. Sometimes the camera is handheld while the cameraperson moves about the apron of the stage. Other times the camera is placed on a tripod and set either on the stage at the far side of the apron, or in the audience. Between the existing stage lights and a light that may be attached to the camera, little time is needed to set up this equipment. For news coverage, the cameras are there to shoot only parts of the show—at the most a scene, not an entire act and certainly not the whole play. Once again, Equity rules in this matter and the SM needs to know the details beforehand and not after the fact.

Interviews with the performers can be done on camera or for the printed press, sometimes both at the same time. On many occasions, a still photographer is included. The SM usually has even less to do with these sessions. The SM is informed by the publicity department and they usually handle everything else. The SM needs only to find out where the interview is going to be held and check the schedule to see that the interview does not conflict with anything having to do with the show, the theatre, or the company. If the interview is to be done on stage with the set and stage lighting, the SM arranges to have some crewmembers there to set up the scenery and turn on the lights. Stagehands get paid for doing this work, so the SM needs to check to see that the producer is agreeable to this expense.

PIANO TUNING

One of the last things to be done before preview performances or opening night is to have the piano in the orchestra tuned. Today, electronic keyboards are mostly used and they require no tuning. However, in large musical shows with detailed instrumentation, a piano is often used as part of the instrumentation and musical arrangement. The music director is responsible for having the tuning done and usually makes the arrangements through the production office. Sometimes the music director might ask the SM to set it up. It is natural that the piano tuner prefers doing this work in a quiet theatre. Whenever possible, the tuner is scheduled early in the morning before everyone arrives, or during lunch time when everyone is gone. If the piano tuner can come only during the day when the crew needs to be working on the stage, the SM will have to arrange with the TD to keep the pounding and running of electrical tools down to a minimum. It is best to have the piano tuner come to do this work in the morning. Then if there is a problem and the piano cannot be used, there is still time to bring in another.

MORE ON THE SM's WORKING RELATIONSHIPS

Once again we come across a grey responsibility for the SM. Even though piano tuning is not the SM's responsibility, the SM checks to see that this work has been done or will be done. Remember, it is the SM's job to do whatever must be done to have the company and rehearsal running smoothly and without delays.

Sometimes, however, when the SM inquires about something that is someone else's responsibility, three things may happen: the people being asked may thank the SM for inquiring or reminding them; the people may become defensive because they are in some way delinquent in this part of their job; or the people mistakenly think the SM is stepping in to do the job. Some less responsible people may try to pass their work on to the SM. It is important for the SM to know human behavior and the people with whom the SM is working. When inquiring about a thing or a job that belongs to someone else, the SM needs to approach in a nonthreatening and nonconfrontational way, assuring them that the SM is there to help and not to criticize, complain, point an accusing finger, and most of all not to take over the responsibility of the job.

A NEW BEGINNING

In many working situations, the final dress rehearsal or last preview performance marks the end of techs. For a new show or the makeover of a show that has been previously produced, rehearsals after the opening—rehearsals resembling techs—may continue until the artistic staff is satisfied. When techs finally end and the show is about to go in its run, a heavy sigh of relief and pleasure can be taken by all. Technical rehearsals are a monumental task and a lot has been done in a very short time. For the producer, techs are an expensive period of time. The producer is now anxious to get the show in performance with the hopes of recouping the initial investment, and then making a small fortune. The director and the actors too are pleased and relieved, but there is no time to savor the moment. With the opening performance comes the reviews, critically acclaiming or disclaiming the performances, the show, or the director's work.

The SM too can take a moment to enjoy the accomplishment of techs, and possibly reflect on a job well done. The SM cannot rest on any laurels, though, but must move swiftly into the next part of the job. If the show is new and possibly headed to Broadway, changes, rehearsing, and teching will continue, sometimes in bits and pieces and other times with whole scenes or acts. This will continue until the show opens on Broadway and goes into its run. Once the show goes into its run the SM's work will becomes less intense; hours will become more normal and the SM will be able to have more of a personal life. However, the demands on the job will remain the same—the SM will need to focus attention and energy to caring for the company and maintaining the show as set by the director.

THE PROFESSIONAL EXPERIENCE: AN SM OVERWHELMED

Just at a time in my career when my resume had some good credits and I thought I had done it all, I got a production of the musical *My One and Only*. It was a West Coast production and I was thrilled to get the show because a good friend was directing and starring in it. The rehearsal period was one of the best I had experienced. I worked well with my friend and he allowed me more artistic contribution than any director had previously. I had no concerns about the technical rehearsals. I had worked in the theatre in which we were performing and knew most of the crew. I was aware that the show had some technically difficult places by the number of cues I had accumulated in the cueing script. I knew I was going to be one busy SM during the performance, especially for the opening sequence, which ran nonstop for twenty-two minutes. No problem! I had behind me the experience of burning Atlanta every night for twenty weeks in the musical production of *Gone With The Wind*. How bad could anything else be? I had no idea of what I was about to embark upon.

The opening had many parts with musical numbers and quick dialogue scenes. First there was a rainstorm with small flats of painted clouds flying in and out and across the stage. A combination of a real rain curtain and a lightning effect created the illusion of stormy weather. Of course there were flashes of lightning cues and sound effect cues of thunder. There was a bevy of tap dancing girls with umbrellas and slickers, dancing everywhere. At one point the rain stopped, the clouds parted, the sun came out (all requiring cues), and the handsome lead aviator character Billy "Buck" Chandler entered from above, hanging from a parachute. He was lowered to the stage, released from his harness, and as all lead aviator characters do, he sang and danced with the girls.

To give the female lead of the show, the lovely Edythe Herbert, channel swimmer and aquacade star, an equally impressive entrance, the scenery changed before the audience's eyes. We were now at a train station as a train unit was cued to roll out on the stage, with many blasts of CO_2. The door to the train was cued to slide open and out came more tapping beauties—the same dancers as seen in the slickers, but now in colorful bathing suits of the period. They of course tapped their hearts out before Edythe slinks

in place at the train door. The lights changed to focus on Edythe while many flashes of lights filled the stage, as if from hundreds of news pictures being taken. The flashes were outrageously out of proportion to what the three or four photographers on stage could possibly shoot in that moment.

With Edythe's entrance there was more singing and dancing. Other principal characters appeared with special light cues to point out their entrances. Then in a moment in time, the lights changed and the stage picture froze. Billy and Edythe's paths crossed. They saw each other. They were drawn to each other but never left their frozen positions. It was magical. The moment was brief. The lights were restored to their original setting and the soon-to-be lovers continued on their way. The opening sequence finally came to an end, but all is not over for the SM, because in the dark he must now cue a life-size propeller plane to be brought on stage before bringing up the lights. This, of course, must be done quickly so that the momentum of the opening and the pace of the show is not lost. When the lights come up, the sight of the plane is impressive and the audience reacts, first verbally, and then with applause.

It took us all afternoon and evening to set the cues for this sequence and then we tried running it. The director, who was also playing Billy, remained in the audience while his understudy ran the part of Billy on stage. Running the sequence was highly problematic for me. There were just too many cues, too many elements. The timing was outrageously fast. There wasn't enough time for me to read the cues in the script and then look up on the stage to take the visual cues. My timing was off. Also, with scenery and performers moving on the stage at the same time, there was an element of danger. With the least little thing being cued at the wrong time, someone could be injured.

I was overwhelmed. At first I would not admit defeat. I had worked with hard groups of cues before, but now I could not reach the accuracy and perfection the director and lighting designer were expecting in such a short time. In my desire to please, I put even greater demands and pressure upon myself. Each time we had to stop the rehearsals, I could feel the annoyance from everyone around. I could hear expletives of disapproval over the headset coming from the lighting designer, and at one point I heard the director make a comment that showed his lack of understanding and support for me. It was not meant for my ears and it was said out of his frustration, but nonetheless, I heard it. I was hurt and at the same time baffled. This was supposed to be my friend. He knew my capabilities. He knew how difficult the sequence was. I became defensive and felt a great need to confront the director. One of my weaknesses as an SM was my inability to let pass abuse directed at me. SMs need to have a great tolerance for abuse, but I never reached such a level. I said over the headset, "I heard what you said and I think it very unfair of you not to allow me the time to learn my job as you have allowed others when they were first learning their parts." The director was contrite and apologized. Fortunately, I still had enough sense about myself to ask if we could leave this segment and move on. The director agreed and I felt a sense of relief, as did everyone around.

I went home that night, broken in spirit. I had never been so defeated. I could only sleep a few hours. When I awoke, I was compelled to study my script. I was becoming more familiar with the placement of the cues, but I could only perfect my timing by actually calling the cues and seeing the action on stage. I tried playing the original cast album, but in many places the arrangement was different.

On the afternoon of rehearsals that day, we did not go back to the opening sequence. I was thrilled to have the reprieve and have another day to study. While everyone went on dinner break, I stayed behind. I sat at my console and practiced calling the cues. It was a great help to be at the console, talking through the headset, turning on and off cue-light switches, and looking at my script and then at the stage seeing in my mind's eye the action. I felt comfortable and at home.

When everyone returned from dinner, I was certain we would continue rehearsing from where we left off. Instead the director asked that the stage be set up for the opening. My heart sank and I broke out in a mild cold sweat, while visibly maintaining composure and giving an air of confidence. Despite all my study, I had improved only a little. It was progress, but still not enough for everyone else. At one point the director said over the headset, "What is the problem? What should we do? Should we have the ASM take some of the cues? Maybe we can have the stagehands take some of the cues on their own." "NO!!!"

I insisted. "The stage manager is supposed to call all the cues for the show. He is responsible for the timing. Give me a little more time. I know I can get it. The stage manager on Broadway called all the cues for this sequence, and from what I understand he had more." Perhaps it was my ego speaking, but I was insistent enough to convince the director. He said he would not get back to the opening until Friday.

The heat was on. I was now burdened with the fact that by Friday night, I HAD TO DELIVER! I knew I had to do something more to learn this sequence—change my way of studying. The answer was simple. I needed to make a cassette recording of the opening as we were performing it. The ideal thing would be to have the sound person record the opening as the cast performed it on stage. To do this, I would need a chunk of time out of the rehearsal (at least a half-hour) and the services of many. This was not practical in the tight schedule of working techs. It then occurred to me that except for some of the dialogue moments, the entire opening was filled with music. I simply needed to get with the rehearsal pianist and have her play the music while I recorded it. On the first five-minute break we had that night, I cornered the rehearsal pianist in the orchestra pit, and with the offer of a bribe, I begged her to aid me in my hour of need. Without hesitation she agreed. She said she would come in an hour before the rehearsal on the next day and we could record it in the pit while the crew was at lunch and the theatre was quiet. Perfect! And so we did!

After the recording session and for the next two days, with every chance I got, which was usually in the morning before the cast arrived and during the midday meal break, I sat at the SM's console with my cassette player and rehearsed the sequence. I even did "head" rehearsals, like the athletes—seeing myself calling the cues perfectly and successfully, while visualizing the scenery, lights, props, and actors moving about the stage. By Friday I triumphed. I was 98 percent improved. The few mistakes I made were negligible. At the end of the opening sequence and when the lights came up for the next scene with the propeller airplane perfectly in place, the cast and crew cheered and applauded me. It was my Tony-winning performance, a moment I have remembered and treasured ever since.

15

Opening Performance

People working in theatre will go through many opening performances in their careers. Academically and in the tradition of theater, there should be no difference between the work being done during rehearsals, especially in the final day of techs, and the work one does during performance. It is expected that everyone works at performance peak at all times.

In theory, by opening performance, the cast, crew, and SMs should have had the full experience of the show. There should be no differences, no surprises between what took place in dress rehearsals and what will happen in the opening performance. For the SM and stagehands, when techs have gone smoothly and according to schedule, this is often the case. The same should be true for the actors.

However, some actors are not inspired or motivated to give a full performance until they are faced with their audience. Some performers even believe they need to save their performance to keep it fresh. While this approach works well for the individual, it can be a disservice to all others. It is the director's job to lead the actors into giving a performance during all parts of the rehearsals, and when the show gets into techs, it becomes the SM's job to expect the same and generally ask the actors to continue the process. The only difference that should take place once an audience is in attendance is that the quality of the performances gets even better.

THE EVENT OF AN OPENING PERFORMANCE

Despite all the dress rehearsals and preview performances, an opening performance remains special. It is filled with excitement, high energy, nervousness, tension, tradition, and sometimes fear and anxiety.

Producers will often make opening performances special by inviting guests and dignitaries from the community. The presence of family, friends, and peers can add to the feelings. Flowers and telegrams of success and best wishes flood the backstage. The performers themselves make the night special by giving token gifts to each other. On many occasions the producer, director, or SMs might have a tray or basket of edible goodies brought in as an expression of thanks and appreciation. In addition, the press and critics are usually in the audience that night, making their judgments and formulating their commentaries, which can make or break a performance or the entire show. Then after the performance, to cap the event, there may be an opening night party at which the guests and company members dress in their most stylish fashions.

The build-up to this moment is tremendous. Opening performance belongs to the artists of the production, the creators, writers, designers, actors, choreographer, musical director, producer, and director. The SM should not miss participating in the festivities, but should not get caught in the frenzy. If by the opening performance all the kinks and problems of techs have been worked out and the SM has been working at performance peak, the SM should have nothing to worry about, nothing over which to become nervous. The SM's greatest feelings should be excitement and exhilaration. The opening performance should be only a transition to the next phase of the job, the performances and the run of the show.

As the excitement grows on opening day, it is the SM who sometimes must keep everyone grounded and focused on the show. The SM does not try to take away the fun or the feelings, but as the time gets closer to the performance, leads everyone to a more stable place where their attention and energies are directed toward the show and their performances.

HELLISH OPENINGS

If everything in life worked according to textbook, this book would be half its size. A knowledgeable and well-rounded SM is one who sails through the good times with appreciation and thanks, and in the bad times is able to cope, working with the people in his or her care to get through with some kind of success and sanity. Unfortunately, in any SM's career, there will be some opening performance that can easily be labeled hellish. The techs may have been problematic, the schedule was all but abandoned—which included not having a dress rehearsal—and the opening performance was the first time everyone had the opportunity to run the show without stopping to fix things. During such an opening performance, nerves and fears dominate.

The SM will experience a particular set of feelings. The SM's greatest concern might be with some or many of the cues that must be called during the performance that have not been dealt with since the time they were first set in the early part of techs. Despite whatever might be going on, the SM cannot let personal feelings rule. More than ever, the SM is needed to generate among the cast and crew some kind of assurance and, if possible, a sense of security. The SM cannot be Pollyanna-ish or cheerleader-like in approach. There is a greater chance of success in being direct. Acknowledge the situation, but move on by first thanking everyone for their hard work, then appeal to them to draw from their craft and professional experience. The SM asks them to become focused, concentrated, do the best they can, and assures them that nothing more can be expected of them. To help further, the SM asks if there is anything that can be simplified or changed, just to get everyone through this opening performance. The SM might suggest:

To the prop department: "Don't worry about getting the potted palms on the stage for this performance. Placement of the table and chairs is more important. If anybody complains, tell them to talk with me."

To the carpenters and scenery departments: "Do the best you can without putting yourselves or anyone else in danger. I will be watching and will not take the next cues until I see things are in place. It's okay for the next few performances if we take a little longer in making this change."

To wardrobe and dressers: "Don't worry about the hat for now. It's more important the performer gets zipped and hooked and is feeling comfortable. If there isn't enough time, save the jacket for last and the actor can be putting it on as he enters the scene."

To the actors: "Don't worry about finding your way backstage. I'll have a dresser waiting and as soon as you get off stage, she will lead you to where you need to go. You just concentrate on your performance."

To the crew and actors: "With the short time we have had to put all this together, you cannot expect to do it perfectly. I am expecting in places the timing will not be right. I expect there will be mistakes. Just remain alert. Together we have enough experience to handle any situation that might come up in the performance."

When wielding such authority and making what seems like small changes, the SM must be careful not to do anything that interferes with the play, the plot, the action, the business, or the characters. Most of all, the SM must be certain that the changes are simple and easy for the actors to assimilate and will not affect their performances. The actors must be informed of all changes, even the ones that do not directly concern them. For example, even though the potted palms are on the stage just as set dressing, the SM must warn the actors that the potted palms may or may not appear on stage for the performance.

The SM must also be ready to take full responsibility for disapproval of the changes from the producer, director, or designers. In addition, the SM must know that if anything goes wrong in or around these suggested changes, the blame will be placed on SM, even if the mistake is not directly connected with the change.

Through experience and knowledge of human behavior, the SM knows that people's fears are often greater than what is likely to happen in reality. Armed with this knowledge and the ability to lead, the SM can rest easy and trust that with most opening performances that are not quite ready, everyone will pull through. By all rights, the opening should be a disaster. However, either through divine intervention or some professional miracle, the cast and crew pull together and the show is performed remarkably well, sometimes flawlessly. Of course everyone else is thrilled and thankful.

With miracle openings, everyone is lulled into a sense of security and believes they are now home free. The SM, however, cannot be led down this path and allow everyone to rest on their laurels. Before each of the next few performances, the SM must pull the cast and crew back to reality, forewarning that if they do not put in the same focus, concentration, and effort as they did for the opening, the next performance could be the disaster they feared for the opening.

THE SUPREME POWER AND RIGHTS OF THE SM

At curtain time on opening night, the producer and director have no choice but to relinquish control of the show to the SM. It is at this point in any production the SM is in full charge. There is nothing more the producer or director can say or do. If something isn't right during the performance, they cannot stop the show to correct it. It is up to the SM to keep the ship sailing through calm as well as troubled waters. If there are any nerves to be felt on opening night for the SM, the thought of having full responsibility could be a triggering factor. The SM cannot give in to such thoughts and feelings. If up to this point the SM has done the work as suggested throughout this book, the SM has a great foundation of confidence to draw upon.

One Voice

For the sake of order, clarity, organization, safety, and timing backstage during a performance, there must be one voice controlling and calling the cues. It is a well-established fact that the SM is this solitary voice and that everyone backstage takes cues from the SM. No change or thing can be done differently in a performance without first informing the SM and getting the SM's approval and clearance. Also, it is an established fact that the producer and director stay out of the backstage during the performance. If they choose to be backstage during the performance, they remain quiet and out of the way. They should not be giving directions, making changes, or giving notes. They must save that for intermission time or after the performance. The SM has the right to ask both the producer and director to adhere to this policy, and if they don't the SM can ask them to leave the backstage until the performance is over.

With such power and authority comes supreme responsibility. The SM is expected to have a perfectly run show for every performance. With anything that goes wrong, the producer and director turn first to the SM for answers. In most instances, they hold the SM responsible and expect assurances that the problem is fixed and will not happen again.

This supreme power and authority belongs to every SM during performance. All SMs should hold it dear and call anyone to task who stands in violation—producers and directors included! Once again however, SMs take care in how they exert this authority. They must remember that this supreme rein is limited to the time of the performance and once the show is over their peers and superiors resume their power and authority, and will exert it if they did not like the way the SMs conducted themselves.

CURTAIN BOWS

In many working situations, there will be a rehearsal on the afternoon of the opening performance. If there have been no preview performances, more than likely the director has put off setting the curtain bows until this last rehearsal before opening. Some directors make it a tradition to set the bows on the day of opening. Some superstitiously believe that if they do it any earlier, it will jinx the show. There are also those directors who have been so busy with the rest of the show that they have either forgotten the bows or have avoided them.

Last Minute Cue Noting

Whatever the reasons directors have for setting curtain bows at the last moment, the SM ends up having to write curtain bow cues in the cueing script sometime in the late afternoon of opening performance. After having written an entire cueing script for the show, adding curtain bow cues is no major task. However, having to make these notes at this late date does add a little pressure to the day's work.

While the cues are being set, the SM writes them in pencil, allowing for changes. Afterwards, the SM finds time to rewrite the cues and color code them. The curtain bow cues for a small comedy or drama show are usually simple and easy to note and call. With a musical, the bows can be choreographed, done while singing some of the songs from the show, broken into many segments, and can become technically complicated. In most cases, because there are no pages of dialogue on which the cues for the curtain bow can be written, the SM notes these cues in the same way the cues to open the show were noted (see Chapter 13).

Encore Bows

Sometimes encore bows are set and made to look as if they are spontaneous due to the great amount of applause. Other times the director will leave encore bows to the SM. There are different schools of thought on encore bows and how many should be taken. Some believe that encore bows should be taken only when the demand is so great that the SM can feel it backstage from the console—then give only one or two. Other schools, such as the one from which most performers come, say give as many bows as the audience demands.

When the director leaves the encore bows up to the SM, the SM should always find out from what school of encore bows the director comes. It is then the SM's job to do what the director prefers. Ultimately, once the show gets into its run, the SM learns the intensity of the audience response and the number of encore bows to give, if any. It is always better to give a little less, because it is awkward and embarrassing for the cast to come out for another bow just as the applause is dying out and the audience is beginning to leave. It is also awkward for the audience, because they feel obligated to applaud, and some feel put out by having to give more.

Encore bows should be blocked and rehearsed the same as the regular bows. If the director has not done this, the SM should. The first thing the SM does is establish with the cast and crew that after the final bow of the regular bows, everyone stands by for possible encore bows. The SM works out with the performers whatever blocking is needed, works out with the lighting department (the light board operator) whatever light cues are needed, and has the technicians on the rail stand by to bring the curtain in and out on command. If the show is a musical, the SM also needs to work out a plan with the conductor. The SM usually makes the decision to have encore bows as the final bow of the regular bows is being taken or during the time it takes for the curtain to touch down on the stage. Once the SM has decided there will be encore bows, there is no time to lose. Everyone must go into immediate action. The encore bows need to look just as professional as the regular bows.

ARRIVAL OF CONGRATULATORY ITEMS

On the day of the opening performance, the backstage area can become filled with many congratulatory items such as flowers, telegrams, stuffed animals, candy, gift baskets, and even champagne. If there isn't a doorperson to accept these items, it becomes the SM's job to sign for them and see they are distributed to the right people and places. If the show is still in rehearsals, it is the SM's job to see these items do not distract and draw the performers' attention away from the rehearsal. The SM should either put the items in the performer's dressing room or in a place where they are out of view, and distribute them after the rehearsal. Traditionally, there is always an opening performance congratulatory letter or telegram from Equity. It is often addressed to the SM and cast and it is the responsibility of the SM to post this document on the callboard in a place for all to see.

WORKING THE PA SYSTEM

If an SM is not used to communicating over a PA system, there are some things to learn to be more effective. The SM needs to be clear in speech, sometimes repetitive, have all thoughts well organized, deliver the information to create a picture, and be brief. Each time the SM begins talking over the PA, an effort should be made to first get everyone's attention. This is best achieved by prefacing information with an attention-getter such as, "Good evening company and welcome back!" or "Cast, may I have your attention, please!"

The Half-Hour Call

Starting with the half-hour call for each performance, the quickest and most immediate way for the SM to communicate with the cast members is over the backstage public address system. The crew, on the other hand, is not always within earshot of the speakers to hear the PA, so after giving the half-hour call over the PA to the actors, one of the SMs goes around the backstage area, calling out, "Half-hour! This is your half-hour call, please!" and making sure that the rest of the company is informed. If there is some specific information the SM has to communicate to the crew, the SM must go to the different department heads.

Remember also, immediately after making the half-hour call, one of the SMs must go around to collect the actors' personal valuables. The SM has provided each actor with a large plastic food-storage bag that zips closed at the top and has each person's name clearly printed on it. It is the SM's responsibility to gather up the valuables before each performance, put them in a safe place, and personally see that they are returned to the correct individuals.

Use of the Terms *Company* and *Cast*

As part of the SM's clarity in communicating, when there is information to impart to everyone, the SM uses the term *company* in the attention-getter. When the information is only for the cast, clearly use the term *cast*.

Repetitive Information

There is some information that is important and bears repeating. When the cast and crew first come to the theatre for a performance, the green room or ensemble dressing rooms can be more like a social hall and the occupants can miss hearing the SM's call or the information being announced. Knowing this, the SM gets everyone's attention, first with the attention-getter, then by repeating the important information that should not be missed. Making the half-hour call is one of those moments: "Company! This is your half-hour call! Half-hour, please. Half hour!" The first time, the listeners might not hear it. The second time, it registers. On the third time, there is no doubt the SM has given the half-hour call. Sometimes when people fall behind in being ready for the start of the show, they will use the excuse that they did not hear the SM's half-hour call or fifteen-minute call. If the SM has been clear and repetitive, the individuals cannot use the SM as their excuse.

Giving Notes, Instructions, or Directions to the Cast

Often, after making the half-hour call, the SM may have some information or instructions to deliver—giving a general acting note, or instituting a change. The SM cannot repeat everything three times, so before delivering this information says: "Cast! Listen up! We have some changes that will affect you!" or

"Cast! Listen closely, I will not be repeating this information!" Once again, the SM should be selective and to the point. If the SM feels the information bears repeating, capsulize it or repeat the information in outline form. Never give information or notes to individuals over the PA; seek them out and talk to them privately.

Giving Directions and Being in Control

In giving directions or instructions to the cast, the SM, once again, must be clear, specific, and cover all possible questions that might be asked surrounding the particular subject at hand. The SM cannot assume or believe a thing is reasonably implied. Some listeners will come up with their own interpretation, unless the information is clearly stated.

An example of this might take place on opening night. Traditionally, just before the curtain goes up on Act One, some producers or directors like to meet with the cast. The producer or director asks the SM to have the cast on stage at the five-minute call. In doing so, the SM must consider how this affects not only the cast, but everyone working the show. The SM informs the crew and staff so they can be finished with whatever work they would normally be doing at the five-minute call, and then announces to the cast: "Cast! May I have your attention for a moment please! At the five-minute call this evening, the director wants to meet with the cast and crew, on stage." For the SM to leave the message at that will surely create concern and confusion, bring up questions, leave room for individual interpretation and assumption, and possibly create disorder. The SM must anticipate the cast's needs and questions, and continue the announcement by saying: "Cast! This meeting will cut into your preparation time. Please know that you must be in costume and makeup by the five-minute call. Directly from the meeting we will be taking our places for the start of the show. We will not have time to return to the dressing rooms to finish getting ready." The SM was clear, specific, and to the point. The cast now knows the procedure and what is expected of them. Some of the cast members may not like having their preparatory time taken away. If there are any problems around this plan, they will need to inform the SM immediately.

Normally, out of consideration for the cast and crew, the SM might suggest at the end of the instructions that if there are any problems, the individual should come to the SM. If the problem is important enough, the individual will come forward.

Half-Hour: The Cast's Time

The SM must know the cast uses the half-hour before the show to focus in and prepare for the show and should not be breaking into this time every few minutes with some announcement or delivery of information. As much as possible, the SM should deliver such information when making the half-hour call, or at the fifteen-minute call. By tradition and practice the cast knows that the SM will be talking to them throughout the half-hour. They are ready to receive information and assimilate it, but they don't want it taxing in content or delivered in long orations.

The Fifteen-Minute Call

At the fifteen-minute call, the SM once again repeats this information three times. Also in this announcement, the SM is careful and specific in the choice of wording: "Company, this is your fifteen-minute call to curtain time. Fifteen minutes to curtain, please. Fifteen minutes." The key phrase here is "to curtain." Beginning performers, and sometimes even the most seasoned performers, confuse their time, believing they have a full fifteen minutes before the next call, which is the five-minute call. In truth, when the fifteen-minute call is made, there is only ten minutes before the SM makes the next call, the five-minute call. Similarly, after the five-minute call, the actors actually have only three minutes to prepare, because the SM calls for places two minutes before the curtain is scheduled to go up.

For SMs' Use Only

The SM needs to establish from the start that the PA is for the SMs' use only. The PA should be used for official announcements, given only by the SMs, and not become a party line for anyone to use. Any social messages should be given by the stage manager or have the stage manager's approval and clearance. Everyone should know that when a voice comes over the PA backstage important information is going to be delivered and that they must listen. In the delivery of announcements, the SM can be pleasant, informal, and have a sense of humor, but not so much so as to make the PA a forum for entertainment of the troops.

The Human Side

Having established such formality and rigid use of the PA, there are times when it is appropriate for the SM to allow the PA system to be used for fun and games. Such events help keep the spirit of the company running high and the bonds strong. If the SM allows this kind of use only when the event has merit, is controlled, brief, and does not intrude on the cast or their time.

The SM can also use the medium of the PA to express thanks, give praise, offer congratulations, and show appreciation to individuals, groups, or to the company as a whole. If at one time or another the SM has made a mistake that involves a large part of the cast or the company as a whole, it is endearing and appreciated when the SM publicly acknowledges the error over the PA. Not only is it humbling for the SM, but it also gains the respect of others.

The Five-Minute Call

When the SM gives the five-minute call, it must once again be carefully and specifically worded, including the phrase "to curtain": "Company, this is your five-minute call to curtain time. Five minutes to curtain, please. Five minutes."

Even if the front of the house has asked the SM to hold the curtain for a few minutes, the SM goes ahead and gives the five-minute call. For this short amount of time, it is better if the SM has everybody ready and waiting in their places for the few minutes. If the delay is going to be longer, at the five-minute call the SM announces the delay, asking the cast to be ready anyway, because the next call will be for places.

Delays in the Starting Time of the Show

Whenever the show is delayed in starting, the SM records on the performance show report the reason. Some producers find starting the show late a grievous thing to do. They view it as someone not doing their job. No one wants to be noted as being the reason, so when house managers ask for a delay, they make an effort to get the people seated as quickly as possible. On many occasions the house manager will complete this work in a shorter time than requested. As soon as everyone is seated, the house manager calls the SM to begin the show and the ball is then in the SM's court. This is why it is advisable for the SM to have the cast dressed and ready, rather than run the risk of becoming the reason why the show was started even later than was necessary.

Star Courtesy and Consideration

After the SM gives the five-minute call, and before the call for places, the SM should check with the stars or lead performers to see if they are ready. To do this at the fifteen-minute mark is too early—something can easily delay them in the next ten minutes before the five-minute call.

Late Performers

Some stars and principal performers always need more time. The SM graciously accepts the delay, but asks and negotiates a time when the star will be ready. With performers who are late, the SM reinforces the need to start the show on time by displaying urgency in voice and manner. Before leaving the dressing room the SM asks to be informed if the person is ready any sooner. If the star or performer is not ready at the negotiated time, the SM is at the person's dressing room door, inquiring.

PROMPT AND CONSISTENT

It is an important part of the SM's job to be prompt and consistent in making the time calls during the half-hour before each performance. Everyone backstage comes to depend on these calls. No matter what business the SM is doing within the half-hour, the SM must continually keep in mind the time frames and call them. Some SMs use a digital stopwatch with an alarm set for each call to be made. If the SM should happen to be late in making one of the calls, the SM informs everyone: "Company, my apologies to you! This is a late fifteen-minute call. We are now at twelve minutes to curtain. Twelve minutes, please, Twelve minutes."

APPLAUSE AND ACKNOWLEDGMENT

It is the primary nature of all people to need, want, and desire praise, thanks, recognition, acknowledgement, and appreciation not only of themselves, but for the work they do and their accomplishments. In theater and with a successful product, the creative and artistic side—the actors, directors, producers, creators, and designers—continually get this attention from the audience, their peers, the news media, through awards, and sometimes from the world at large. The down side to being in such a spotlight is that these same people are also open to criticism and

have their failures equally recognized. At the end of a successful opening performance, the applause is immediate and gratifying. The backstage becomes filled with well-wishers and praise givers, flocking to the performers' dressing rooms or surrounding the producer, director, and whatever creators and designers might be present.

In addition to working their talent and craft, many people who have come to the entertainment world have come with an especially great and strong need for praise and appreciation. SMs and technicians too come with the same need and intensity. However, because the SMs' and technicians' work must remain subliminal, the audience remains aware of only the artists' and the creators' work. It is to the artists and creators that they flock to shower their praise and appreciation after a performance. This is the way it is. It is a fact of life not only in the entertainment field but also in other industries and professions. However, after a particularly difficult tech period, and after a successful opening performance that should have been a technical disaster, when people come backstage to give their praise, the SM and technician can feel somewhat left out.

Through years of experience, the SM grows to accept this fact and receives applause and acknowledgement in a different way. It comes quietly, in bits and pieces. The SM is not flooded with it and momentarily placed at a pinnacle. SMs know they have done a good job by calling a perfectly timed and smooth-running show and judge their success by the intensity of the activity and excitement backstage after the performance—by the pleasure the producer, director, and others display, even if they don't express it directly to the SMs. Later on, rewards, thanks, and appreciation come in the form of being hired again by the same producer or director, or when the SM is highly recommended to another producer and director.

The technicians also learn to accept their position. Some present a tough exterior, declaring and rejecting their need for all that stuff. Despite the display, it is important that the SM recognizes how hard the crew works to do their jobs and to make the show successful. It is important that the SM give to the technicians what others might forget to give. After a successful opening performance, and for that matter throughout the run of the show, the SM should shower on the crew the praise, thanks, acknowledgment, and appreciation they so richly deserve.

CURTAIN UP!

With the call of places and the rise of the curtain for the opening performance, the run of the play begins. This is the moment to which this entire book, thus far, has been dedicated. It gives one pause, is somewhat overwhelming and startling to see all that must be done to get to this moment. The SM's job, however, is not yet ended. There is still the run of the show, a possible tour, and closing out the show—each demanding the SM's continuous focus, concentration, and dedication to the job.

THE PROFESSIONAL EXPERIENCE

This is one of those theatrical stories that people tell at parties to bring a laugh to the crowd, but at the time was important SM's business. We have talked about the responsibility of the SM starting the show on time and how some performers have a tendency to be late.

The Scarlet Primper-Nell

On this one particular show, I had a star performer who was not in the lead role, but was an important name in a supporting role. She had initially made her fame in movies as a red-haired, raving beauty, with a list of very impressive film credits. In the days I worked with her, she was in less demand for films, but had brought her talents to the stage, commanding the same attention and ticket sales as she did when doing films. Our star performer was now in her sixties (some speculated older), but from the stage, with her flaming hair, with the correct lighting, and with her gorgeous figure, she was as stunning as ever.

She was a delight to work with. She was always at the theater long before everyone else, preparing for the performance. She was charming, had an excellent sense of humor, was highly professional, and always on time—that is, until we got into performance. All of a sudden it was like a dentist pulling teeth to get her out of her dressing room. I complained to the dresser, "What on earth is going on in there? She comes in early and still I have to hold the curtain until she is ready!" "I can't get her away from the mirror," the dresser cried in frustration. "She's all ready, then she sits and primps and touches up her hair and makeup for hours. Then just when you think she's

getting up to leave, she catches a look at herself from another angle in the mirror and starts primping again. If it's not her makeup or hair, it's her costume."

Between the dresser and me, we decided that after I called places, I would come to the dressing room to personally escort the star out to her place in the backstage area. This worked well because on my entrance into the dressing room, the star was distracted away from the mirror long enough for the dresser to lead the star out by the arm, as I held the door open. What we had not counted on was that just outside the star's dressing room was a six-foot wide, full-length mirror the dancers and other performers used as a final check before entering the backstage area. Upon seeing her image, our star would stop, taking poses she took on stage. We had to spend another five minutes getting her pulled away as she primped and posed from all angles.

After having this happen several times, I asked the costume people if they could store one of the performance costume racks in front of the mirror so we could get our star past. Having worked with other performers who had an obsession with mirrors, the costume people understood perfectly. The idea was a good one, but it did not work as we had expected. Our star merely rolled the rack to one side and started checking and primping again.

Tenacity being one of an SM's attributes, I was not going to be defeated in this matter. I had a show to get started on time. I also had a working relationship to maintain with the star. I tried impressing on her how important it was to me, to the producer, and to the audience to get the show started on time. She agreed wholeheartedly and promised she'd be ready. It was that damn mirror in the hall that caused her to abandon all her professional promises and values. If I could have had it removed, I would have. But it was a permanent part of the wall.

Then, during one performance in the second week of the run, after my assistant learned to call the show, I decided to stay backstage to see how things ran during the performance. I noticed one particular piece of scenery that was moved from place to place. It was a piece that was not used until the third scene in the Second Act. Due to the limited space backstage, there was no one place this piece could remain. Suddenly it hit me! You've guessed it! I begged the head carpenter to store the piece in front of the mirror. It was inconvenient for him to put it there. The space was just outside the backstage area and he and some of his crew guys carried it through double doors. I pointed out it couldn't be any more inconvenient than moving it around several times during the performance. He agreed, and this orphan piece of scenery found a home at last.

At the next performance, our star was quite annoyed. She tried moving the piece, but it was too large and too heavy for her. She ordered me to have it removed. I said I would talk to the carpenters. She was quite upset and felt very insecure as we led her to her place and she asked her dresser several times, "How do I look? Do I look alright?"

At the next performance the piece of scenery was still there. Our star turned to me abruptly, "Have you talked with the carpenters about this?" "Yes," I replied with helplessness, "but they said this is the only place they can keep it." "Where'd they have it before?" she inquired with an edge. I had to think quickly, "Uh, I think it was outside in the alley, but they are afraid the weather will ruin it or vandals." Our star said nothing more and left on her own, unescorted, to take her place backstage.

We played out the rest of the week with the piece of scenery stored in front of the mirror. Nothing more was said and I decided we were finished with the matter. The show was dark on Monday, which was our day off. On Tuesday evening as the dresser and I were escorting our star to her place for the beginning of the show, we saw that the piece of scenery was not in place. Our star, without missing a beat, stopped in front of the mirror to do her posing and primping. I looked at the dresser and she looked at me. As soon as I could I went to the head carpenter. He told me the producer's secretary called him and told him to remove the scenery—to find some other place to store it.

I needed no further information. I had a clear picture of what had taken place. Several days later the producer's secretary confirmed what I believed. She would only say that our star and her manager had come to see the producer on that Monday. Need I say more?

16

Run of the Show

It is now the day after the opening performance. The show last night went exceptionally well for everyone. From the audience's reception, the show is a hit. However, the first reviews in the morning papers were mixed and not encouraging. The producers have faith in the show. The publicity campaign is strong and they know that word of mouth will sell the show. Already, ticket sales are up at the box office.

REVIEWS AND TICKET SALES

Regardless of how good or bad the reviews, how great or poor ticket sales, the SM's work remains the same. These things have no bearing on the work the SM does during the run of the show. In talking to the cast over the PA or in meetings, the SM does not deal in terms of ticket sales or reviews. In fact, the SM does not need to post reviews on the callboard. There is always someone in the cast who follows reviews and ticket sales and brings that news to the company. If the cast chooses, they may post a review on the section of the callboard set aside for them and their social business. The impact of negative reviews or poor ticket sales that are demoralizing and destructive to the cast and show can be greater than that of good reviews or sold out performances that boost the morale of the company and make the show better.

A NEW SHOW

If the show is new and is perhaps heading to Broadway, a wave of intensive work still lies ahead. The workday will become a double-duty event with a rehearsal and changes made in the afternoon and a performance at night. There will be eight performances a week, performed in six consecutive days, with the seventh day being the day off. This means that two of the performance days will have matinee performances in addition to the evening performances. This sort of schedule for a work week is carefully guided and ruled by Equity, with time frames for rehearsing, breaks, and performances. The SM must know the breakdowns and particulars of these rules, schedule things accordingly, and see that the producer and director follow the guidelines, or they will have to pay overtime or penalty fees.

Also, if the show is heading to Broadway, it more than likely will be playing out of town, perhaps playing in different cities. Touring a show adds still another layer and dimension of work for everyone. We'll talk more about touring shows in the next chapter. If the show is the revival of a play that has been previously produced for Broadway and plans to play only in one place, there may be rehearsals for a few more days, after which the show is left to play out its run.

A SHIFT IN WORK

The Show is Frozen

Whether performing on Broadway or in just one city, once the show gets into its run, rehearsing stops. There are no more changes. The director leaves and the producer's attention goes to selling and promoting the show or to another project. At this point the show is considered *frozen*—that is, the show is now to be performed each time as set and agreed on by the director, actors, and producer.

Company Manager and SM Left in Charge

If there is a company manager with the show, the SM and company manager take over, running the show and the company. For the most part, the company manager runs the business of the company, being concerned with the daily finances, overall budget, and administration of the company. The SM takes full charge, maintaining the performance level, artistic integrity, and generally caring for the members of the company, seeing that their needs are met and their problems are resolved. With the absence of a company manager, the production office handles most of the company manager's work with the SM aiding and assisting.

If the show is an easy one and the company is cohesive, performing well together, and maybe behaving like an extended family, on most days the SM's work can be easy. It can be as simple as going to the theatre, performing the show, having some social time with the cast and crew after the show, and going home. With a musical, a show that is technically involved, or with a large cast or a cast that is problematic, the SM's days can be filled with the business of the show and continue to be long.

THE SM's WORK AND RESPONSIBILITIES

Whatever the working situation of the show or the company, there are some very specific things an SM must do as the person in charge while the show is in its run. These duties are clearly defined:

1. Calling cues for each performance: We have discussed at length how important it is for the SM to call an impeccably well-timed show for each performance.

2. Keeping the show at performance level: This subject too has been frequently brought up in various parts of our conversations. In short, the SM sees that the show continues to perform with the same integrity and intention as created by the combined efforts of the actors, director, producer, creators, and designers. This means keeping a watchful eye on the level of performance, changes the performers make to the show, and deciding if the changes are an enhancement or detraction.

3. Caring for the company: In many ways the SM has already been performing this job. Now the SM has full responsibility and is the person to whom the company members turn with their

problems, concerns, suggestions, and so on. It is the SM's job to handle as many matters as possible, or point the company member in the right direction to resolve a problem the SM can't handle. The decisions the SM makes, the advice the SM gives, or the directions the SM expresses in leading and guiding the company are on behalf of the producer and the director. By this time, the SM should know the producer and director well enough to formulate and adjudicate as they would. If the SM is uncertain on a particular matter, a conference with the producer and director is appropriate to get their input. The SM also uses Equity and the Equity rules as an aid. This is another time when it is important the SM be a scholar and aficionado of the Equity rulebook and work closely with the Equity deputies.

As part of the SM's caring for the company, the SM tries to anticipate problems and head them off, or see that adverse situations and conflicts do not escalate and become blown out of proportion. In addition, now that the SM has established a way of working and what is professionally expected from everyone, the SM can encourage and support small activities and little events that are fun, do not hurt the show, do not detract from the performances, and at the same time bring the company closer together in bond and relationship.

4. Keeping the producer and director appraised and informed: Depending on the working situation and what is set up between the producer and director, the SM may be in communication with the producer and director daily or on a need-to-know basis. All behavioral problems are to be handled by the SM. The only time the producer wants to be brought in is when the problems may have a direct effect on the show or hurt the producer's pocketbook in some way. The director's primary interest is in the artistic integrity of the show, and although the director may lend a sympathetic ear to the SM who must work with a problematic cast or company, the director is glad to be removed from the problems and have the SM keep full responsibility.

5. Keeping a log book or journal: If the SM has not started the SM's log book from the start of rehearsals, this process definitely needs to start now. Keeping the log book should have started

with the dress rehearsals and preview performance. Once the show goes into performance, the SM notes the running time of each performance, pertinent or important business of the day having to do with the show and company, all events that are unscheduled or unexpected, the audience's reaction and reception to the performance, the behavior of the company members, and when a problem is approaching or in full bloom, notes any observations about the problem as well as what is being done to head off the problem or has been done to resolve it. If desired, the SM can also make personal commentary. More on the subject of the log book in a moment.

6. Understudy rehearsals and actor replacements: It is the SM's job to have the understudies prepared and ready to perform at a moment's notice. If the show has stand-by performers, the SM keeps them up on their roles. If the show requires replacement performers, it is the SM's job to do so whenever the producer or director dictates.

THE SM's LOG BOOK

Discussion of this subject has been delayed until now. The SM's log book can be a 5-by-7-inch loose-leaf notebook, a hardbound book with blank pages, or entries in a file on the SM's laptop. The SM's log book can become at any time a legal document in an Equity arbitration that can be summoned by the producer or subpoenaed in a court of law. The entries need to be noted with clarity—information should be detailed but concise, factual, and truthful. The SM must be careful to note the information in an unbiased and journalistic way, more as an historian. If at any time the SM chooses to express a professional opinion, experience, observations, suggestions, judgments, or chooses to editorialize, this should be clearly noted in the log.

Keeping a log book is not mandated by Equity rule. It is a practice and tradition that is encouraged and passed down from SM to SM. Most SMs learn it from SMs whom they have assisted and see its value and use. Some SMs will start the log book in their preproduction week, while others will start it with the first dress rehearsals and into the run of the show.

If the SM starts the log book during the rehearsals, it is not necessary to note the schedule—that is documented with the daily schedule and a copy is kept in the SM's files for reference. However, throughout the rehearsal day, the SM might make notes on a yellow pad or on the list of things to do, then make entries in the log book at the end of the day when there is time. Figure 16-1 shows a list of things that might be noted in an SM's log book.

During performances the SM keeps a yellow note pad on the console just under the cueing script, ready to slip it out to make notes. The SM will note the starting times and ending times of each act and calculate the running time of the whole performance; make notes on performances that are exceptionally good or not up to par; comment on audience reactions, encore curtain bows, and standing ovations, if any; note lost lines or dialogue, cues missed, mistakes made, mistakes almost made, and incidents or near incidents. The SM notes joyous times, sad times, noise backstage if it becomes excessive, late entrances or near-late entrances, infractions of rules, shoddy work, conflicts and confrontations, unprofessional behavior, or anything that could be used as a reference for a later date. Seemingly small and unimportant notes written in today's entry can become tomorrow's valuable information.

After the performance, the SM transcribes these notes into the log book. The SM writes in the log book every day and never postpones making entries until another day. When the run of the show ends and the show closes, the log book remains with the SM. It does not go to the producer along with the final production book.

Sample Entries in a Log Book

The following example is an actual account of a show produced in Los Angeles. It was a musical production of *Snow White and the Seven Dwarfs*. The log book was originally hand written by the SM in a blank-page hardbound book. However, the version presented here has been edited and recreated, singling out days that were particularly interesting, and displays some of the things an SM might write. The original log book contained names and personal information which was not meant for publication. The show starred several prominent performers of the Hollywood and Broadway communities. The seven dwarfs were played by real dwarfs who instructed

- *Reh. Rm. Flooded, (roof leaked from storm) reported to building mgr.*

- *Beth Williams, to costumes, 10:30-12:noon.*

- *Dave Thompkins, late, after meal break, 5 min.*

- *Propman still has not delivered rehearsal props!*

- *Pete Rawlins, doing poorly, director said may have to release from contract. Reported this info. to producer.*

- *Surprise birthday, during break for Rhonda James.*

- *3:20, set designer came with changes.*

Figure 16-1   A list of things an SM might note in the log book.

everyone to call them little people. This show was targeted for adults as well as children, and was planned to play throughout the spring season for the Easter holiday and spring vacation.

As you read the SM's entries for this particular show, keep in mind that this was an exceptionally problematic situation, due mostly to the producer and his behavior. In most other shows, the SM's log entries are pedestrian, and not filled with so much conflict and drama.

(PERSONAL)
Stg.Mgr's
LOG BOOK
Snow White and the Seven Dwarfs
(A Musical Stage Version)
PSM: Sarah Johnston
ASM: Dan Porter
Beverly-Wilshire Theatre - Spring Break - Easter Vacation
Los Angeles, CA, March–April 1996
    Producer:
    Director:

List Star Performers Names:
List Cast Members Names:

Saturday, Mar. 23, 1996
First day of rehearsals, on stage, at the Beverly-Wilshire Theatre.
10:00 A.M., Equity business: WHAT A MESS!!! Producer's office did not have contracts ready. Equity field rep refused to let rehearsals begin without contracts being signed.
Finished Equity business 11:00 A.M. (extra hour becomes part of producer's rehearsal time).
12:00 Noon–3:00 P.M.: Little people sent on meal break.
End of Day:
Producer wants to keep performers past 6:30 P.M. (past 8½ consecutive hours) without paying overtime. He complains the Equity business robbed him of an hour rehearsal time. I pointed out the use of the extra hour for Equity business was due to his office not having contracts ready. He retorted that Equity could have bent the rules and let him rehearse today and he would have had the contracts ready on Monday. Reluctantly, he let everyone go home at 6:30 P.M.

SM's Commentary:
Producer seems to blame Equity for his bad day, and because I am aligned with Equity and make him stick to the rules, he seems to pass the blame on to me, too. In the short time I have been dealing with this producer, I feel disaster coming. This producer is a "wheeler-dealer." Always looking to break the rules—get a special deal. Money comes above any other consideration. Experience has taught me to look out for bad checks from this guy.
Sarah J

Monday, Mar. 25, 1996
Good day today. Schedule followed, much accomplished.
First time principal performers worked together. Good Ensemble feeling. FUN!
Director too, good mood. Pleasant. Not so nervous or angry.
Sarah J

Wednesday, Mar. 27, 1996
11:15 A.M., producer walks in w/CBS news crew - NO NOTICE!!!!
Performers upset. Want time to fix hair, put on makeup.
Checked Equity rulebook—24 hrs. notice for press/publicity required.
Equity deputy called Equity office. They said to go ahead, and they will settle matter with producer.
Today was little people's day off. Producer called each of them personally, last night, and asked them to come in to rehearse—to VOLUNTEER their time. Four showed up: Terri Rivers, Jack Hammer, Andrea Neville, Jane Roberts.
Equity deputy reprimanded the four who came in and handled the matter with Equity. SM informed producer of Equity's disapproval in this matter and will be talking to him soon.
Marie Lee, late (5 min.) this morning. This is her second time, but I don't think she has a problem in this area.
7:30 P.M., Production Meeting - Beverly Hotel:
Chaotic and disorderly. Could not keep producer on one subject long enough to complete things.
Designers and technical dept. heads not getting money from producer or checks are bouncing.
Producer says money people back east shifted funds, left Snow White account dry. He assures matter will be resolved by Friday so checks will be here in LA next Monday.
Personal Note:
Today I overheard the producer on the phone backstage talking to his wife, "I can't fire her. I'll have to give her two weeks' pay and where do I get another

stage manager? We open next week." After he got off the phone he approached me and accused me of going to Equity about his rule infractions (it was in fact the deputy and some of the performers, but I did not tell him that). I assured him I had not yet been to Equity on any matter, but used this opportunity to state my position and responsibility to Equity. He became angry. He told me that he was paying my salary, and that all the stage managers he worked with back in New York showed their allegiance to the person who was writing the checks.
Sarah J

Thursday, April 4, 1996
Two shows today:
11:00 A.M.–12:15 P.M. - Entire cast called in to put the horse in more scenes. Horse is getting great reaction from the audience. Producer wants the horse to appear more in show.
Changed entrances of dwarfs in 3rd scn., and cleaned choreog.
NO BREAK for performers between rehearsals and half-hour for Show #1: Producer was made aware of OVERTIME and PENALTY to be paid.
Producer happy today. Show got good notices and we are playing to 95% capacity audience.
SHOW #1
    Act I, 2:08–2:45:37 min.
    Intermission:18 min.
    Act II, 3:03–3:38:35 min.
Terrible audience—kids threw things on stage.
SHOW #2
    Act I, 4:19–4:56:37 min.
    Intermission:22 min.
    Act II, 5:18 –5:53:35 min.
A good performance. Audience reaction great. Horse stealing scenes.
MORE OVERTIME to be paid for end of day (see report turned in to Equity and copy to producer).
Sheila Fuerst paged me. Check for star's (witch's) nails. BOUNCED!
Sarah J

Saturday, April 6, 1996
THREE SHOWS TODAY!!
SHOW #1:
    Half-hour call, 1:15
    Act I, 1:49–2:25:36 min.
    Intermission:16 min.
    Act II, 2:41–3:16:35 min.
Our star forgot to bring on stage her witch's comb. Prop man was not there to remind her to pick it up from the prop table. Actress ad-libbed lines about returning to her castle to get it. Actress disappeared from view, got comb from prop man who was now standing

in the wings, and reappeared within a second. Actress ad-libbed about what a tiring journey it was. Got great laugh. Audience applauded, actress continued to ad-lib few more lines.

Light board operator executed Q16 late. Was an obvious mistake to audience.

SM missed calling Q38. Audience was not aware but broke actor's concentration.

Final curtain nearly hit Snow White again! She was told several times to step back after her bow—fast curtain coming in! I placed white spike mark where she should stand. If she misses mark again, I asked Prince Charming to step forward and lead her back.

SHOW #2:

Act I & II, 4:20–5:30:1 hr. 10 min. Producer took out intermission so he won't have to pay actors overtime. Show works better w/o intermission. Producer still able to sell merchandise before and after.

5:30 P.M.–6:30 P.M., Dinner break

Half-hour call for Show #3, 6:30 P.M.

SHOW #3

Act I & II, 7:15–8:25:1 hr. 10 min.

Show started late due to latecomers. Traffic and parking problems.

Excellent performance. Actors had fun w/show and so did audience.

Sarah J

This example is to show the type of information an SM might enter in the log book. There is no particular form to follow. The SM must, however, keep in mind that once the information is written, this book is used for reference. With this in mind, the SM groups and separates the information for easy extraction. Sometimes key words or phrases will be in uppercase letters to draw attention.

Our discussions in parts of this book have talked of no more than two performances in a day. With this production of *Snow White*, on some days there were three performances. The difference had been worked out and agreed on between Equity and the producer. More than likely, Equity took into consideration the short playing time of the show as well as the number of hours the actors would be putting in for the day, then made adjustments that were equitable to both the producer and the actors.

ACTOR CHANGES AND IMPROVEMENTS

One would think with all the work done in rehearsals and the changes made in techs, this subject of making

changes would be exhausted, but there remains still one more installment: the changes the actors bring to the show once they get into the run. These changes are sometimes jokingly referred to as *improvements*, and the SM, in trying to maintain the director's work and intention, might say to the cast, "Take out the improvements."

First there are the changes actors make as they grow in their parts, fine-tuning, working moments, perfecting timing, filling in characters with color, finding more depth and meaning, enhancing and making things richer. In short, the actors are taking wing and soaring in their parts. This can be exciting for the SM to watch as the characters mature.

The next part of change does not always come out of growth and development but rather in a search for perfection—to improve on the improvements. This often comes from the performers trying to make the parts new and exciting for themselves as well as for the audience. These kinds of changes can be borderline and sometimes questionable. The SM must make a judgment and get the actors to return to what is more acceptable if the changes are determined to be unacceptable. If the SM is uncertain about a change an actor makes, the SM may want to talk first with the actor, expressing any feelings, opinions, or concerns. If the actor feels the change is valid and is unwilling to change back, and it remains questionable in the SM's mind, the SM then needs the advice and consent of the director.

Knowing Acting and Directing

For the SM to do this part of the job well, it is helpful to have worked closely with the director and actors during the rehearsal period, watching the show come together and the characters develop. The SM also must be intimately familiar with the script—the plot, action, and the storyline—and needs to know the director's intent, interpretation, and direction. In addition to all of this, it is extremely helpful if the SM has a working knowledge of directing and acting. The more the SM knows in this area, the better the SM can make judgments, maintain what the director wants, and communicate and work with the actors.

Giving Actors Performance Notes

With changes comes another part of the SM's job—giving acting notes. Even when a change is good, the SM should comment, expressing pleasure and approval. Now that the director is gone, it is an established fact that the SM will take over in monitoring the show, watching the acting and maintaining the director's work, but the cast needs to be reminded of this.

For the SM, giving actors notes can be like stepping from the frying pan into the fire. This is a highly subjective and personal area for the actors. For actors to do a good job, they personalize and draw from within themselves. To have someone make comment on their work can set off any number of reactions, some of which can be protective, defensive, guarded, angry, and possibly filled with ego. Up to this point in the production, the director has been the only person licensed to enter this arena. For the SM to be accepted, the SM needs to display knowledge in this area. The SM must also be guarded in the approach to performance notes. If the actor feels the SM knows what he or she is talking about, the actor willingly and openly accepts the notes the SM has to give.

Before continuing further with some of the things an SM must do to be successful in giving acting notes, it might be a good time to return to Chapter 7 on working relationships and review the parts covering the SM's working relationship with actors and star performers. Having in mind some of the ways actors work and may react will allow greater success in giving acting notes. Following are some guidelines to use in giving performance notes.

1. First and foremost, the SM must approach totally ego-less. If the SM has any personal agenda or need to fulfill, it will reveal itself, get in the way, and weaken credibility with the actor.

2. Before approaching an actor with a note, the SM needs to be prepared. If the acting note is questioned or challenged by the actor, the SM must be ready to talk intelligently about the script, the action, the plot, the blocking, the director's choices, and all the other parts of the director's work. There should be no uncertainty in the SM's mind about the things surrounding a particular note the SM has given. Upon being questioned or challenged, the SM cannot be defensive or protective, but must be clear and decisive in communicating any thoughts, observations, and what changes the SM wants the actor to make. The SM needs to have full conviction of what is being presented and have a strong foundation of support for the judgment and direction being given.

3. Next, the stage manager must be certain not to step into the directing arena. It is important to establish this with the actors and remember that the SM is there as the director's representative—there to maintain, not change. The SM must stay out of telling actors how to act and how to do things—that is their craft. The SM cannot become involved with their characterization, interpretation, or manner of delivery, or ask the actors to do things that are the SM's choice and not the director's. If there is any question in the SM's mind about a particular note stepping over directing boundaries, the SM should not give the note until after having talked with the director.

4. In the approach to the actor the SM must come as an emissary, an ambassador, and not as a figure of authority who has come to judge, criticize, blame, and demand change.

5. After giving a note, the SM needs to step back to see the actor's reaction. Some will graciously take the note, even thank the SM, and act on the note for the next performance. Others will take the note silently and leave without a reaction. The SM will have to wait until the next performance to see if the note had any effect. Others, to varying degrees, will be more vocal and expressive, either in generating conversation or in challenging. The SM needs to listen carefully not only to what the actors are saying but how they are saying it—the intensity or verve of the delivery. The SM must keep in mind that each actor is the ultimate source of his or her craft, performance, and the character being played.

6. With the actors who are more extreme in their reaction and resistant in taking a note, the SM does not need to win but needs to do what is best for the show. If having further conversation with the actor will bring a resolution, then the SM can follow that course. If not, the SM momentarily sets the note aside, and once again confers with the director.

Varying Performances

Most actors will improve, enhance, and embellish upon their performance, but will remain within the original structure, intent, and direction. Some actors are highly structured in their work. Once they find what works for them, they perform it the same for every performance. Others appear to be more spontaneous; however, upon a closer look, they too work within the structure that is part of the original design and plan—they just perform it differently each time. Then there are the performers who seem to be driven to wander and experiment, even after they have improved, enhanced, and embellished their work. They may be bored or need excitement and stimulation to get them through the performance. With this kind of performer, the SM's work becomes intensified and the application of all of the suggestions on giving acting notes are put to their greatest use.

The SM's Transition in Giving Performance Notes

In giving performance notes to actors, the SM must start by taking it slowly and must build a performance note–giving relationship. This relationship begins in rehearsals and escalates during techs when the SM gives notes concerning technical matters. From there, the SM can transition into giving acting notes, first by giving positive and complimentary notes. By the time it becomes the SM's responsibility to give actors notes during the run of the show, it is possible to transition into giving the less favorable notes without much resistance.

Giving Stars Performance Notes

For the most part, the SM should play a limited role in giving star notes. To have gotten where they are, most star performers have perfected their craft or at least know what they must do to maintain their star status. If there is a question in the SM's mind about what a star is doing in a performance, the SM should first confer with the director or, if the director is not available, with the producer. Star performers have created a certain style and persona. In most cases this is what the audience has come to see, and this is what the star will give to them. It is often this style and persona that makes the star perfect for the part and unique in playing the role.

There come, however, in every SM's life, times when a star must be given a performance note. The SM's experience will be wide and varied. Most stars have respect for the SM's work and appreciate the SM's care and concern for the show. On occasion, a star performer may even ask the SM to watch a particular thing in the show and give an opinion. Other times, a star's reception to an SM's acting note can be

silent, cold, and possibly painful to the SM. The best an SM can do is follow the suggestions listed previously for giving acting notes, and guard against giving notes that work against the star's style, persona, or way of working.

A Greater Latitude for Star Performers

The American Declaration of Independence proclaims that all people are created equal. In theatre, this is an ideal all SMs would like to follow with the people in their care and charge. However, the truth is there is a chain of command—an order in which people are considered and treated according to their position and status. Among the cast members, this fact holds especially true for the star performers. The producer, director, and SM allow stars a greater latitude and degree of freedom for change and expression than they allow other performers in the show. In extreme cases, they will allow a star performer to do something in a performance that they would not allow another performer. By all ideal standards, this is unfair, sets up a double standard, and perhaps places the SM and the others in authority in a hypocritical light. The beginning SM who detests this notion and vows not to play such favoritism eventually succumbs. In efforts to treat star performers the same as everyone else, the SM may end up standing alone, unsupported, and may not work again for either that star, producer, or director.

Delivering Other People's Performance Notes

For any number of reasons, either the producer or director will have the SM deliver performance notes that should actually be delivered by the producer or director. Whenever the SM is put in this position, and the SM knows there could be a volatile or explosive reaction from the performer, the SM needs to take some steps before doing this job. If the note was not dictated in friendly or positive terms, the SM should edit and clean it up—taking out the things that might be inflammatory. In this editing, however, the SM cannot lose the note's content or its meaning and intent. Upon delivery, the SM needs to make it clear from the start who the message is from and that the SM is only the messenger. This point cannot be stressed enough. On hearing the contents of the note, the actor may become upset and filled with feelings that lead to forgetting who is the originator of the message and taking out these feelings on the SM—the deliverer.

A Final Step: Follow-Up

There remains still another step for the SM in giving performance notes. The SM must follow up on the note by watching to see if the actor has, in any way, responded to the acting note and made the desired change. If the actor has changed and all meets the SM's approval, either after that performance or before the next the SM should have a follow-up conversation with the actor to thank the actor, express the SM's appreciation for the actor's work, and ask if the actor was comfortable with the change.

If the SM sees the actor has responded to the acting note but the actor's performance is still not what the SM thinks it should be, the SM first expresses thanks and appreciation, then has further conversation to lead the actor into the desired change. The SM will, once again, need to be specific and clear in what is being asked.

If after giving an acting note the SM does not see any change in the next performance, the SM should wait one or two more performances. If by that time the actor still has not made any attempt to change, the SM needs to approach the actor, generating further conversation on the acting note.

It will be easy to follow up and thank the actors who have accepted the acting note and have made the change. It will be more difficult with the actors who do not. In not acting on the note, the actor may have forgotten, may be demonstrating resistance, or may be trying to turn the moment into a power play with the SM. The SM does not know which until approaching the actor again and initiating further conversation. The SM must follow through and do this final step on all the acting notes given.

THE ASM TAKES STAGE

It has been stated several times throughout this book that the ASM must be knowledgeable and capable of doing all of the work of the PSM. With such aptitude and to be a successful ASM, the ASM must work in the shadow of the PSM. It is the ASM's job to aid and support the PSM, do the work the PSM dictates, to fill in where the PSM is weak, or do the work the PSM chooses not to do. When the show gets into its run, it is time for the ASM to stand alone and display

some of his or her talents and abilities. It is time for the ASM to start calling the cues for the performance.

During technical rehearsals, the PSM was very careful not to have the ASM tied up with work duties that needed to be done for each performance. During technical rehearsals the ASM's job was to move from area to area, wherever someone was temporarily needed, and work as a trouble-shooter or facilitator. The ASM was in places where the PSM could not go and became an extra pair of eyes to see things the PSM could not see.

The ASM Prepares

Usually by the end of the first week of the run and into the second week, the cast and crew have worked out whatever problems they might have had in performing and the show is running smoothly. The ASM is not needed as much backstage, which leaves the ASM free to start calling the cues for the show. By the time this moment comes, a good ASM has already begun preparing for this part of the job.

- The ASM has gotten approval from the PSM to sit out front to watch one or two performances.
- After seeing the show, the ASM may want to spend one or two performances looking over the PSM's shoulder as the PSM calls the show.
- During techs and during the first week of the run, the ASM has watched the scene changes, getting a good visual image of the scenery as it moves and the lights as they change.
- The ASM has made arrangements to take home the PSM's calling script, or comes in early for several days, to create a separate color-coded calling cue script. The ASM's way of noting a cueing script is ideally not greatly different from the PSM's. Ideally, the ASM's copy should be a carbon copy of the PSM's script.
- Once the ASM has a calling script completed, for one or two performances the ASM might sit with a headset on and follow along with the script as the PSM calls the show. This will help the ASM in learning the timing of the different cues. In addition, the ASM sees how the PSM calls the show and, wherever possible, can do the same.

In other words, when the time comes for the ASM to start working with the PSM to learn the show, the ASM is prepared and has already begun the learning process. The ASM should not be just starting to learn the show.

The ASM's Working Disadvantage

It is important that there is little difference between the PSM and ASM when calling the cues for the show. It is the ASM's job, as much as possible, to duplicate and recreate the timing and calling of the cues as the PSM calls them. Unfortunately for the ASM, the crew has learned the show with the PSM calling cues and their timing is dictated by the PSM's timing.

A second working disadvantage for the ASM is that while the PSM had the luxury of learning the show and making mistakes in techs, the ASM has no room for mistakes. The ASM is learning and calling the show during a performance, when the audience expects to see a perfect and professional show. It is important that as the ASM learns to call the show, the PSM stands at the ASM's side with a headset on, and is ready to correct any mistake or avert any possible disaster. Even after the PSM feels the ASM is able to go it alone, the PSM should remain close by for one or two more performances.

Musical Shows

When doing a musical, to make it easier for the ASM who is first learning, it is a good idea for the ASM to do the first act for one performance, the second act for the next performance, and on the third performance, do the entire show. This gives the ASM time to assimilate the enormous number of cues for each act that usually accompany a musical. By the end of the second week of the show's run, the ASM should be navigating the ship as expertly as the PSM, creating the same theatrical magic.

Show Insurance: The Show Must Go On

Having the ASM call the show ensures that the show will go on should the PSM, for any reason, become unable to call the show. With the ASM calling the show, the PSM is free to go out front to watch performances or stay backstage to do company business and keep the show organized and running smoothly.

Updating the Blocking

One of the first things the PSM must do after the ASM has learned calling the cues for the show is return to the rehearsal script and bring all the blocking up to date. If you recall, when the SMs go into technical rehearsals, the PSM sets aside the rehearsal/blocking script and the cueing script becomes the important book from which to work. Meanwhile, during techs and even after the show opens, more changes are made in the blocking. With techs being as they are, the PSM does not have time to note the changes made in the blocking and instead sets this part of the job aside with the promise that, once the show goes into its run, the PSM will return to bring the blocking up-to-date. This is now that time. The PSM might update the blocking either while sitting out front at the back of the theatre, as long as nearby audience members are not disturbed, or from one of the wings, as long as the cast and crew are not hampered.

At this point, the rehearsal/blocking script has been marked and erased many times and has gathered many other notes during rehearsals. It is strongly recommended that the PSM transfer the updated blocking notes into a clean script, which can then be used in understudy rehearsals and turned in to the producer at the end of the show as part of the production notebook.

If the blocking has changed radically, the PSM might want to start from scratch with a clean script and follow each character during the performance, noting the blocking. For further assistance, the PSM might go over the blocking notes with the understudy or even the performer. However, this is time consuming and can be taxing for the actors. The blocking has become so mechanical and ingrained in the actors that too much time may be spent jogging their memories.

DAYS OFF AND MATINEE DAYS

According to Equity agreement with producers, the work week starts on Monday and ends on Sunday. Equity rule states that after six consecutive days of work, the actors must have the entire seventh day off or be paid overtime. It further states that on the day after the day off, the actors cannot be called in to work any earlier than the half-hour call before the performance, unless the producer pays overtime and possibly a penalty fee. This gives the actors a sense of having had two days off. It is also agreed between Equity and producers that the actors will perform eight shows within the six-day period of work. Any more than eight performances in a work week, and the producer is obligated to pay overtime. Any fewer than eight performances means that the producer still pays the full salary, unless a different agreement has been reached with Equity.

Traditionally, theatres are dark on Mondays, which becomes the company's day off. For any variations or deviation from this work week, the producer works out the differences with Equity. Rarely will a producer choose to have a performance on the seventh day. The cost can be too great.

Matinee Performances

Traditionally, matinee performances were on Thursday and Saturday. With the expansion of regional theatre and civic groups producing shows, some producers found it was more convenient for their patrons, and they could draw a larger matinee audience, if they had matinee performances on other days. Some have chosen to have their matinee performances on Saturday and Sunday. The advantage to this schedule is the company has its days free throughout the week, but starting with Friday night's performance, the company performs five shows within a two-and-a-half day period. If the show is busy, difficult, or is a musical, this can be a grueling work schedule.

REHEARSALS DURING THE RUN OF THE SHOW

What! More rehearsals? Yes. Brush-up rehearsals, line rehearsals, understudy rehearsals, rehearsals for new actors, stand-by performers rehearsals, and put-in rehearsals all happen during the run of the show. As part of the different Equity contracts with producers, producers can call in the cast for a limited number of hours for rehearsals each week without having to pay them for this time.

Brush-Up Rehearsals

Having rehearsal time once the show opens allows the director time to make changes or clean up things during any part of the run of a show. Also, once the show is left in the SM's hands, if the SM feels the show or a particular part of the show has fallen below performance level, the SM too can call a brush-up rehearsal. For the SM, brush-up rehearsals are not

to redirect or make changes, but to get everyone back to the original direction.

Brush-up rehearsals can be as simple as having the cast sit in the green room to run lines, or as involved as having the performers up on their feet, on stage, and doing the blocking along with the lines. Brush-up rehearsals usually involve just the actors. If some of the technical elements of the show are needed during a brush-up rehearsal, the SM must get clearance from the producer to have a skeleton crew come in and pay for their time. For any rehearsal held on stage, whether using technical elements or not, the SM must know the policy of the particular theatre. Some theatres require a paid union stagehand to be present, even if it is only to turn on the work lights.

Line Rehearsals

If the cast has been away from the show for a period of time longer than the normal day off, the SM might choose, or even be asked by the director or producer, to have a brush-up rehearsal. If the show is not complicated and the SM is confident the actors remember their blocking, the SM might choose to have only a *line rehearsal*—a rehearsal where the actors sit around in the green room or out on the stage and run their lines. A good line rehearsal exercise which helps get the actors to remember their lines, is to have the actors say their lines at double speed or as fast as they can and still be heard, remain intelligible, and maintain the meaning. This sort of exercise is jarring, taxing, gets the adrenaline flowing, and quickly brings the lines back to conscious memory.

Understudy Rehearsals

Enter another important part of the SM's job. Equity rule requires that the producer assign and pay Equity actors to understudy (U/S) certain featured roles within the show. Consideration for U/Ss starts as early as the audition period when the producer, director, and casting director choose actors for smaller roles with the thought of having these actors also U/S the larger roles—the principal roles. However, once the choices are made, the contracts are signed, and rehearsals to put the show together begin, very little work is done with the U/Ss until after the show opens. Then, all of a sudden, the producer and director realize that if the U/Ss are not ready and if one of the principal performers becomes unable to perform, the show will not go on. There now comes a rush to have the U/Ss ready.

Often, the job of preparing the U/Ss is left to the SM. Sometimes the director will play a major role in preparing them. Neither the director nor the SM should have to spend a lot of time teaching the roles to the U/Ss. Throughout the rehearsal period, the actors contracted to U/S must, in addition to doing their regular parts in the show, also be working on their own, learning their U/S parts. It is the U/S's responsibility to learn the lines, learn the songs (if the show is a musical), take down the blocking, and keep all changes up to date before they come to the first official U/S rehearsal with the director or SM.

The ASM should also be required to be at all U/S rehearsals to follow script, read in the parts without understudies, help set up whatever rehearsal furniture and props are being used, and use this time to further learn the show, as directed by the director.

The SM Must Be Prepared
Regardless of the U/S's responsibility for being ready for the first U/S rehearsal, the SM must also be ready to work by having the blocking for the show up to date and having a good working knowledge of the script, the action, the character development, and so on. In addition, the SM must know the director's work—the director's intent, meaning, and interpretation. The SM also must be ready to work with an actor who has come unprepared. In U/S rehearsals it is the SM's job to convey the director's work to the actors who have either missed getting it themselves, or who have not yet incorporated it into their performance.

Restrictive Guidelines
To work the U/S rehearsals effectively, the SM steps into the directing arena, but in a limited way:

- The SM does not *direct* the U/Ss, only *prepares* them. The SM leads them to giving performances in keeping with the director's work and similar to the way the principal performer is performing the role. The directing has already been done by the director. The SM only mimics the director's work. Whatever directing techniques the SM might use are only to get good performances from the U/Ss.
- Neither the SM nor U/S is allowed to change the blocking, bits of business, or interpret the role in such a way that it is removed from the director's

work, or is so different that it will cause the other actors on stage to become distracted and possibly thrown in performing their parts.

The Soul of Understudy Work
With such restrictions, the art and craft of the U/Ss' work comes in duplicating the roles (staying within the bounds and framework of the director's and principal performers' work), and at the same time making the roles their own, performing them as if the roles had been tailored and directed just for them. It is important that the SM know this of U/S work to be able to better prepare the U/Ss and lead them into giving good performances, thus ensuring the show goes on and the artistic integrity of the show is maintained.

An Assortment of Understudies
SMs will work with an assortment of U/Ss during their careers. Some will know exactly what to do as an U/S, staying within the bounds and framework or the role and yet making the role their own. They will come fully prepared and will require little to no direction from the SM. Others will be young, inexperienced, and on occasion, were chosen by the producer or director just to fill the requirements of Equity. With these U/Ss, the SM must know all about preparing U/Ss and apply that knowledge.

The Understudy Who Will Never Go On
To add to the assortment, the SM will work with those actors who are U/Sing the star role in a star vehicle. Either the star has the reputation of never missing a performance, or without the star's performance the show will not go on anyway. Knowing this, some actors U/Sing a star role may slack off, putting little effort into learning the parts. With these U/Ss the SM must appeal to their professional senses, asking them to meet the responsibility for which they are receiving additional pay, and at the same time, aid the other U/S performers in rehearsing their parts during U/S rehearsals.

No Performance During Understudy Rehearsals
Every now and then an SM will work with actors who refuse to give a performance during U/S rehearsals. If the director were present, these actors would work at full capacity—for the SM they feel less motivated. Seeing this, the SM must ask the U/S to give some kind of performance during U/S rehearsal. A standard and stock reply is often, "Don't worry! When I get into performance, I'll do it." This is unac-

ceptable. The SM must know that the actors can perform the roles before they go on in their part. If the SM accepts this excuse and it turns out the U/S cannot deliver, not only will the show suffer, but the actor's poor work will reflect on the SM as not having done the job well. When an SM comes across an U/S who refuses to perform in rehearsals, the SM must be adamant in getting the actor to give some sort of performance.

In the same light, an SM may work with actors who have understudied the role before, or even performed it in another production. The first problem the SM may encounter is the U/S may want to perform the role as it was done in the other production. Another problem might be the actor may not want to put in the time each week at U/S rehearsals. Once again, the SM must be strong and insistent, working the U/S rehearsals to serve both the show and the other U/Ss.

The Understudy's First Performance

No matter how prepared an U/S might be, when it comes time for the U/S to go on in the part, the event becomes highly charged for most everyone. It usually comes on short notice and sometimes as the result of backstage drama. Often the U/S's first performance is done with a lot of nervousness, excitement, anxiety, and adrenaline—somewhat similar to the feelings experienced for an opening performance. This is another one of those times when the company pulls together to help the U/S and keep the show at performance level.

For the first performance of a U/S the SM tries to redirect the charged energy to confidence and assurance. Over the PA, the SM officially announces to the company the U/S's performance and asks for everyone's attention and alertness during the performance, reminding them that if something is different they should go on with the show and that it will be corrected after the performance. Either the PSM or the ASM should be left free backstage for the U/S's first performance. The SM needs to watch to evaluate the U/S's performance and, at the same time, be ready to handle or avert any problems that might take place.

If the U/S should go on for a second performance, the SM must be aware of the possible letdown that sometimes takes place. After the first performance the U/S may become too confident, may be more relaxed, resting on the laurels and the success of the first performance. In anticipation of a possible letdown, the SM should talk privately with the U/S and to everyone over the PA. First the SM thanks them for their good work, then warns them of the possible letdown, and asks that they once again become focused, alert, and concentrated.

Whether there is a second U/S performance or not, the SM should, on behalf of the producer and director, publicly thank the U/S. The SM should also privately express personal, sincere, and heartfelt thanks for the work the U/S has done, not only in the performance, but in preparation for the role and throughout the U/S rehearsals.

Being a U/S is often a thankless job. Lots of time, energy, and good work is put in with little to no payoff. Those fantastic and wonderful stories about a U/S going on and becoming a star overnight happens only on rare occasions. Only in movies and plays such as *All About Eve* does such magic appear to be an everyday occurrence. The reality in most cases is that the principal performer returns and the U/S's performance becomes a faded memory of a moment in time.

Scheduling Understudy Rehearsals

Equity has regulated the number of hours that can be devoted to U/S rehearsals each week during the run of the show. It also states that rehearsals for U/Ss must be posted in advance. Once again, the SM must know the Equity rulebook. The smallest error in timing or posting the notice can cost the producer money.

In the first weeks of U/S rehearsals the SM should use all the time allotted by Equity for U/S rehearsals. Once all the U/Ss are up on their parts and the SM is confident they can perform their roles in a moment's notice, the SM can reduce the rehearsals to once a week or to every other week, but cannot stop U/S rehearsals entirely.

Often, with posting of the first notice for U/S rehearsals, there comes a series of moans and groans. Even within the first week of performances, the actors have quickly adjusted to having the daytime off before going to the theatre to perform at night. In consideration of the actors, many SMs will schedule U/S rehearsals in the latter part of the day. This gives the U/S performers the whole morning and part of the afternoon free before they have to be at the theatre to rehearse. Then once they get to the theatre to rehearse, they are also there for the evening performance. However, in scheduling in this way, the SM must also allow time for the actors to have a meal break after the U/S rehearsal, and to be at the theatre in time for the half-hour call.

Whenever possible, and without expense to the producer, the SM should have the U/S rehearsal on the stage, hopefully with some or all of the scenery and props. However in most professional situations, to have some or all of the technical elements requires having at least one union stagehand present. The most an SM can hope for is a bare stage with work lights. In other situations, the SM will hold U/S rehearsals in a rehearsal room, providing a minimum of props, sometimes only tables and chairs. Not having the props and scenery is not a great handicap to the U/S actors. They can see these things being used at each performance, and if they need to, they can come in early before a performance and work with the particular item. Perhaps one time during the run of the show, the SM might get the producer to agree to having a skeleton crew come in so the U/Ss can have a chance to work with the set, props, and lights at least one time before they have to go on or before the run of the show ends. On occasion, especially when on the road with touring a show, U/S rehearsals will be conducted wherever there is space—if not at the theatre or in a rehearsal room, perhaps in a hotel ballroom, conference room, deserted foyer or lobby, or even an abandoned restaurant or night club.

Understudies Watching from the Wings

Throughout the run of the show, the SM should encourage all U/Ss to watch the principal performers from the wings during the performances. In doing so, however, the SM opens the door to a number of potential problems. The SM should ask the U/Ss to be certain to stay out of the sight lines of the audience and, as much as possible, stay out of view of the actors on stage. In standing in the wings, the U/S must also remain aware of entrances, exits, and scene changes, stepping off to the side until all is clear. These things are common sense, things the SM expects every actor working in theatre to know. However, actors often forget as they stand there, concentrating and studying their parts. On occasion, some U/Ss may become even less aware. They might mouth their lines or say the words in a soft whisper. For a performer on stage to see their U/S standing in the wings and hearing their lines being echoed is distracting, disconcerting, upsetting, and unsettling.

Understudy Rehearsals for Musicals

With musical shows, the SM's work for U/S rehearsals usually is doubled. Not only is there more of everything, but the SM must also schedule and coor-

dinate rehearsal time with the dance captain and musical director or conductor. In addition, the SM must have at the rehearsal space a piano. If the SM cannot use the stage to hold the U/S rehearsal and cannot get a piano in the rehearsal space, it is possible to have the actors sing the songs a capella, and then for another time schedule a music rehearsal with a piano. Another choice is to have the show pianist put the music on audiocassette or CD and use the recording as the source of music for the U/S rehearsal. It is, however, always the SM's first choice to have the actors do their music with a live piano.

Stand-By Performers

Stand-by performers usually are performers who are not in the show, but who are standing by, fully prepared to step into a role at any given moment. Stand-by performers many times are performers who are known to be excellent performers in the business—performers who are capable of carrying this particular show, or perhaps any other show. Stand-by performers are chosen for the main principal or starring role. Sometimes they have performed the role in another production and are celebrities in their own right. They have been chosen by the producer for their box office draw, should the original actor or star become unable to perform the show. Today, stand-by performers are not used as frequently, and can be found mostly standing by for a major show on Broadway.

There is no one particular policy followed when working with a stand-by performer. It is whatever the producer and director decide and set up. Sometimes the stand-by is required to come to the theatre for each performance and stand by. Some are allowed to leave just before the last scene. In more liberal situations, the stand-by may be able to leave by intermission, or may not be required to come to the theatre at all, but have with them a pager or cell phone where they can be reached and get to the theatre in a short time.

Most times the director works with the stand-by, while the SM is brought in to give the blocking notes and read the other parts. Sometimes it becomes wholly the SM's job. On those occasions, the SM might have some of the U/Ss join the rehearsal to do their parts, to aid and support the stand-by. Stand-by performers are usually extended more freedom in performing the role than is allowed a U/S—especially if the stand-by has some star status. It is the SM's job to observe, evaluate, and if the differences are great, try to lead the stand-by performer closer to what the director wants, or to confer with the director.

If the stand-by performer's entry into the show is not on short notice, almost always the director or SM will hold a put-in rehearsal, calling in the cast and crew, and using all the technical elements. If the stand-by performer has made any changes in the part, everyone will get to see them at this time.

Replacement Performers

Usually with a principal role or star performer's role, the director is instrumental in putting in the replacement actor. With lesser roles, it is often left up to the SM. When called on to do this job, the SM once again must apply all the SM knows about the show and the director's work. The SM must, however, be careful not to try to make the replacement actor a copy of the original actor. The SM must allow the replacement performer freedom, but watch to see that the new actor's approach and choices are not extremely different or in opposition to what the director wants. If, after working with the replacement actor and trying to lead the performance in the direction the director wants, the replacement actor remains resistant to change, the SM must consult with the director and possibly have the director come in to work with the actor. On occasion, the SM may even be in charge of auditioning and casting the replacement actor.

PROMPTING OR FEEDING ACTORS LINES

We have discussed this subject on other occasions in this book, but it bears repeating. The SM should never feed actors lines on stage during a performance, or lead them in any way to believe that this will happen. Some plays and movies depict the SM as standing in the wings throwing lines to actors. If the SM ever does this, it is in the most extreme cases or situations. Starting with the first dress rehearsal, the SM reminds the cast of their responsibility for their own dialogue, and assures them that the SM can no longer be available to save them by throwing lines as was done in rehearsals.

To feed actors lines with promptness and accuracy, the SM must follow the script 100 percent of the time. During the performance, the SM needs to be free to set up cues, call cues, watch the show, and handle any immediate problems that might affect the show. Even with a simple comedy or drama where the cues might be far and few between, the actors cannot be dependent on the SM. Just when they need the SM most, the SM will be doing some other part of the job during the performance and will not be watching their dialogue.

CREATING CLOSE FRIENDSHIPS

Now that the show is in its run, the SM has more time to relate in a social way and perhaps cultivate and develop some friendships within the company. This, however, is not always an easy thing to do, especially among the cast. By this point in time, the cast has bonded among themselves, creating pairs or little groups. In addition, the position of the SM is considered management, and there remains that gulf between the two working groups. Cast members sometimes feel restricted in what they can say or do when the SM is around. They welcome the SM in group social events, but when it comes time to go off and have a close and sharing friendship, the SM is not always an ideal choice.

It is sometimes easier for the SM to cultivate friendships among the crewmembers. As we have seen, the SM's rule and jurisdiction over the crew is minimal, so there is less fear or stigma for a crew member to be seen chumming around with the SM. In having to work so closely together, the PSM and ASM will often bond and become good friends.

THE PROFESSIONAL EXPERIENCE

The work the SM does during the run of the show is similar from show to show. These experiences will be wide and varied, depending on the cast, crew, producer, director, and often, the star. Any person who makes working in theatre a career cannot escape having at least one or two backstage experiences or stories to tell. SMs collect more than their share. Here are a few.

Star Power: Box Office Power

I worked with a well-known Broadway star who had originally created the lead role in a very famous Broadway show. He was now doing a West Coast production of the show and I, fortunately, was hired as the SM. The star performer was notorious for stopping the show whenever the spirit moved him. He would break character, step to the apron, and talk directly to the audience. The audience loved it. As soon as it happened in a performance, word spread quickly throughout the backstage and the ensemble performers would gather in the wings to watch. The man was clever, witty, endearing, and very good at ad-libbing or improvising. As the SM, I showed disdain and disapproval each time he did this, but secretly I enjoyed it and looked forward to when it might happen. However, as the SM, I felt it was my job to maintain the artistic integrity of the show. I approached the star and expressed my position and opinion. He complimented me for doing such a fine job, but told me directly to leave his performance up to him. I talked with the producer about this matter and he agreed with me, adding, "A nightclub is one thing, but not a Broadway book show!" I thought for sure he would have a talk with the star, but in the next weeks, the star continued. Box office receipts were up, so I can only guess that was reason enough to leave things alone. Another possibility might be that the producer did talk to the star performer, and the star performer told the producer what he told me.

Walking in Elephant's Shoes

In another show, a star performer who had not acted in fifteen years was cast in a supporting role. This actor made his mark as a star performer in the first part of his career, then left the theatre to become a golf pro. After being absent from the theatre for well over a decade, it was quite a coup for the producer to have gotten this star.

It was obvious from the first day of rehearsals that the performer had become rusty in his craft and skills as an actor. He was stiff in his movements, had great trouble remembering his lines, his delivery was flat and meaningless, and he did not listen to the other actors in the scene—he would cut them off before they were finished saying their lines. We wondered if the producer had made a mistake. The director spent an inordinate amount of time with this actor, but with little result. One day, out of frustration and anger, the director sent me off to another rehearsal room to work with this star performer and the two other actors in the scene, saying, "Drill him over and over until he learns the lines and listens to what the other characters are saying."

We ran the scene several times. Each time I took a different approach, trying to get the actor back to the basics of acting. He could take direction and do a thing one time, but he was unable to repeat it. This would have been fine if we were doing a movie. We would have filmed the scene and sent him on his way. This, however, was theatre; the actor needed to repeat his work over and over, first in rehearsals and then in performance.

I could see the star was struggling and suffering from many feelings. I had great empathy for him and tried to make the rehearsal easier. I complimented him on the improvements, I put some of my attention and focus on the other actors, and I tried to keep the atmosphere light and not filled with a sense of its importance. At one point in the rehearsal, after the star performer continually cut off the other actor's lines, I said in a lighthearted manner, "Let's run the scene again, and this time allow your fellow actors to finish their lines." I then added jokingly, "You know how actors are, they want to say every word they have coming to them." The two actors working with us chuckled, but not our star performer. He took major offense. He came at me with such voracity, such intent, fury, and venom, that I remained stunned and pinned in my chair. I dare not repeat his words, but in essence, he told me I was no director, and how dare I tell him how to act. He reminded me of his London experience, having worked with Sir Laurence Olivier, and of his Tony nomination. He said that I was a mouse trying to walk in elephant's shoes. From his point of view, he was right, for this man had worked with some of the top theatre directors. His fury was great and he had not yet spent his feelings. He attacked further, becoming more personal. In the ten years of my experience up to that time, I had never experienced such an attack and I was not prepared for it. I had been criticized, condemned for mistakes, even ostracized by the cast for a choice or decision, but my self-esteem always remained intact. I lost my composure. I rose from my chair and strongly suggested the actor leave the room before I told him what I thought of him. I too was ready to attack personally, and I had plenty of ammunition stored in my arsenal. This of course provoked the star performer further and he came nose to nose with me, challenging and daring me to speak. The two actors looking on separated us. The one with the star performer led him out of the room.

I was now mostly upset with myself for having taken this direction and course of action. It was obvious the star performer's words, expression, and feelings were not actually about me, even though the words were. Once again, the position of the SM came in the line of fire and this time it was in some other war. I asked for the room to be cleared and spent some time regrouping my thoughts and feelings.

Meanwhile, the star performer went to the director and told him he was leaving, without giving an explanation. The two actors were able to fill in the director. When I returned to the rehearsal room, the director continued to work and said nothing. I had now become paranoid, and felt even worse. I saw the director's silence as an indication of his disapproval for my actions, and in my mind his silence confirmed that I was wrong. I lived with that feeling for the rest of the day and into the next.

Next day at rehearsals our star returned. At first we kept our distance, barely acknowledging each other. However, I knew I needed to mend the relationship if we were to continue working together. I had hoped he would have approached me first to make it easier, but he didn't. Finally, as we passed in the hallway, I took the moment to speak. I apologized for my behavior. I assured him I would never step beyond the bounds of SMing with him again. He too apologized or said what appeared to be an apology. He was not direct in his words and spent most of his time telling me what I did wrong. At the end we shook hands. We continued to work civilly together, but I could see I was not one of his favorite people. Ashamedly, I must also admit that he was not one of mine.

The Reluctant Star Understudy

On occasion a producer or director will hire someone knowing the individual will be a problem, but to serve themselves or the show, they go ahead anyway, knowing the SM will have to deal mostly with the problem person. In this particular case, an actor of some star stature was hired to play a lesser principal role. The performer wanted the lead because he had done it on Broadway as one of the replacement actors before the show closed. The producer of our show, however, chose another actor to play the lead part, one who was younger and more known to the public through his television and film work. As a backup, however, the producer wanted the star actor to U/S the lead role, a cruel twist of fate that sometimes happens in the entertainment business. The star actor reluctantly agreed and signed the contract. Our troubles with this actor began early in rehearsals when he started telling the director how to direct the show and how it had been done on Broadway.

In U/S rehearsals he became worse. He refused to do the role as the director had directed it, and after the first rehearsal he refused to come to the U/S re-

hearsals. The producer had to have a talk with him. This actor tried my patience further by complaining that the director did not come to U/S rehearsals to work with him personally. He also wanted to rehearse on stage with the scenery and props. Most of all, he was annoyed with me for asking him to turn in some kind of performance in rehearsals. I did this not to see if he was capable of turning in a performance, but to help the other U/Ss in working their parts. He argued that everyone in the business knew what he was capable of and the performance he could turn in.

One day in U/S rehearsals, I said out of frustration, "If I can get the producer to agree to let us work on the stage with set and props for two rehearsals, will you give an all-out performance?" "Sure," my star U/S replied without hesitation or a blink of the eye. I was taken aback. What had I gotten myself into? No producer would go to such an expense for even one rehearsal, let alone two. I was desperate enough to approach the producer. I was surprised again when the producer agreed without hesitation.

What I did not know at the time was that the star U/S had already been to the producer on this very matter and been turned down. So when I presented my idea of working on stage with the set and props, the star U/S already knew it was not going to happen and agreed to strike the bargain with me. However, between the time the star U/S had spoken to the producer and the time I approached the producer, there had been a major change. The actor playing the lead was exercising the clause in his contract that allowed him to leave the show to do a movie. He would be gone for four weeks, but then would return for the last week in L.A. and the run in San Francisco. So now the producer was ready to pay the money to have the U/S rehearse on stage with props, lights, and scenery.

The producer did not, however, want word of this getting out. There were still two weeks before the lead actor left to do the movie. The producer did not want a rush at the box office in the next two weeks, and then have sales drop for the next four weeks. In addition, he was in the middle of his campaign for next year's season subscribers and did not want anything negative to affect a subscriber's decision in buying tickets, so he asked that I not say anything. Also, the producer wanted to keep this entire matter from the star U/S until the week before he was to go on. He did not want the U/S's publicity people getting out the word. Meanwhile, the producer wanted me to rehearse the U/S with as many hours as I had allotted to me by Equity. When I told the actor we would be having U/S rehearsals on stage for the next two weeks, he too was surprised and regretted having made the bargain with me. He performed with some reservation in the first week. In the second week, when he was told of his going on in the part, he was more than willing to give a performance during U/S rehearsals.

Through the years I have remained friends with this reluctant U/S. One time when reminiscing, I told him of my deception. He forgave me and then confessed that at the time, he was just being a jerk. It seems he was having personal and financial problems and had taken the job as the understudy because he needed the money. He was hoping to do as little work as possible, thinking he would never go on.

17

The Touring Show

Touring shows have various names but are always touring shows; they just come in different Equity packages with varying pay scales and working agreements. Traveling with a touring show can be like a double-edged sword. On the one side, it can be exciting and adventuresome: on the other, it is difficult and tiring. On the exciting and adventuresome side, people with a touring show may go to cities and countries they might not have otherwise visited on their own. They get to meet and live among the people in different places, see the local landmarks and attractions, and make new friends. On the other hand, traveling with a show can be wearisome, moving from city to city, living out of a suitcase, being away from home, family, and friends. In addition, while paying the inflated prices of living out on the road, each person often has the continued expense of maintaining a permanent residence. The added expense of being on the road has been taken into consideration when Equity negotiated the touring salary, but the scale is often not enough and lags behind the rate of inflation. While on the road, company members must live sensibly or they will find their paychecks being consumed by expenses.

TYPES OF TOURING SHOWS

Some people love the change of being on the road while others merely bear it, doing it only for the work and pay. With the difference in pay scale and working agreements, some tours are more preferred than others. In order of preference they are:

1. **THE NATIONAL TOUR**
   This is probably the most coveted of tours, for the pay and the long number of weeks playing in one place. A national tour is a show that

travels throughout the United States, playing in most major cities. This usually is a new show or a revised show that has just completed a successful run on Broadway. Some national tours are scheduled and booked in each city for only a certain number of weeks. Once the engagement is finished, regardless of ticket sales, the show closes and moves on to the next city.

In recent years producers have started putting together one or two more additional companies of the same production before the original production on Broadway has played itself out. These companies are placed in cities where they are not in competition with the Broadway production or with each other, such as in San Francisco, Los Angeles, Houston, or Chicago. They are booked with an open-end run and remain until ticket sales drop. For the sake of the budget, the producers hire mostly local actors to play the smaller or lesser roles. By doing this, the producers do not have to pay for the housing of these actors, and do not have to pay the touring pay scale. Sometimes in the second production the producers will feature the original star performer from Broadway, or the producers will hire another performer of equal stature and acclaim. On many occasions the PSM from the Broadway production will temporarily fill the position with the second company, with the intention of having the ASM take over for the run.

These additional companies are not a national tour in the truest sense. Depending on the agreement the producers have made with Equity, only the few who have been brought in from out of town fall under the terms of a touring contract. After the show has played itself out, either on Broadway or in one of the additional cities, the producers create a national touring company and travel the show to the other cities in the rest of the United States.

2. **THE INTERNATIONAL TOUR**

This tour is similar to a national tour, but the show travels to different cities in different countries. The tour may be extensive, traveling to many countries and cities, or it may be limited, playing only one country and just a few cities.

3. **OUT-OF-TOWN TRYOUTS OR A PRE-BROADWAY RUN**

Traditionally, a new show destined for Broadway was produced in New York. Before its run on Broadway, the show had tryout performances in one or more nearby cities: Boston, New Haven, and Hartford were some of the popular choices. In recent times, some new shows have been put together in Los Angeles, San Francisco, San Diego, or even Canada, and have done a pre-Broadway run as a national tour, making their way to New York City. If the show proves to be successful on the road, the producers will follow through in bringing it to Broadway.

Regardless of the show's origin, being with a new show and going into tryouts or a pre-Broadway run is not an easy job. Once the show gets on the road, the workday becomes more full and more intense with rehearsals in the afternoons, making changes and revisions. Some of the changes may be simple and painless, but others can involve a complete makeover of a scene or an entire act. On some occasions, scrapping the entire show and sending everyone home is the only remaining option. The work is hard, but the reward is great if the show gets to Broadway and has a successful run.

4. **REGIONAL TOURS**

Regional tours are similar to national tours, but they play a specific area in one part of the country, such as New England, the Southeast, the Midwest, or the West Coast. Most of these shows are produced by a regional theatre or production company and started out to play in just one city, but due to the success of the production, the producers decide to tour it to nearby cities and towns. The play dates in each town are usually short, sometimes only one or two weeks in one place. The more frequently the show moves from one place to the next, the harder it is for the entire company. The pay scale for an Equity regional touring contract is not as high as a

national tour. On occasion, if the show proves to be extremely successful on the regional tour, the producers might consider taking it to Broadway.

5. **SUMMER STOCK**

Working in summer stock is not touring in the traditional sense of moving from place to place. The members of a summer stock company are removed from their homes, friends, and family, but once they travel to the town where the production is based, they remain there for the entire season—usually from June to September, Memorial Day to Labor Day. Summer stock companies are almost always located in summer tourist or resort towns. In some respects working summer stock can feel like a vacation, with the members of the company participating in some of the local color and festivities, meeting new and interesting people. On the other hand, the pay is middle of the road and summer stock companies usually do a series of plays, or a repertoire of plays. This means rehearsing and mounting new productions during the day and performing at night.

Traditionally, summertime is a slow time of the year for people who work in theatre. Producers both in N.Y. and in other cities usually finish producing their shows in April, or early May at the latest. They do not start up again until late summer or early fall. Despite the pay and intensity of the work in summer stock, people who work in theatre and do not have a job for the summer welcome having a summer stock job.

6. **BUS AND TRUCK**

Bus and truck is just as it says—the company travels by bus and the technical parts of the show travel by trucks. The show usually is booked in a place for one or two weeks before it moves on. The living accommodations, though monitored by Equity, are less plush and more utilitarian. The transition time between the final performance in one town and the opening performance in the next usually is short, most times two days. If the show is simple and can be set up quickly, the transition can be limited to one day. The next town usually is a day's trip away—sometimes only a few hours, other times, twelve or fourteen hours. On many occasions, this travel day is also the cast's day off.

7. **SPLIT WEEK TOUR**

This is a whirlwind tour of traveling, setting up the show, and performing. Everyone and everything travels by bus and truck. The distance between each town is short. The show may arrive in a town on Sunday and by Monday night it is set up and ready for performance. The final performance may be on Wednesday night. That night the show is taken down, traveled to the next town, and once again is made ready by the second day.

To move so swiftly and set up in such a short time, the show has to be simple. The set, props and costumes are minimal, and the technical setup has to be no more than six to eight hours. This kind of a tour is extremely difficult and tiring for all. The members of the company literally live out of their suitcases.

8. **ONE-NIGHT STANDS**

A split week can seem like an eternity of time to play in one town when comparing it to a tour of one-night stands. The most practical show to do with this kind of a tour is a show that is done as a *reading*—a show in which the actors sit on stools, possibly reading their parts from scripts. The stage may be dressed with black curtains, the lighting limited to areas and specials, and for the different scenes the actors may arrange and rearrange their stools. The members of this kind of tour barely get the lids to their suitcases open before they are closing them and traveling to the next town.

9. **ROAD SHOW**

The term *road show* is generic for any show that travels. Many times a show that travels on a tour is cut down or streamlined from its original production. On occasion, scenes or dances may be cut from the show or cut down to be less strenuous. The scenery, lighting, and sound are almost always simplified.

EQUITY CARE

Through the work of Equity, some very high standards for working conditions have been established for the actors and SMs of touring shows. There was a time when actors went out on the road and were at the mercy of the producer. Some producers were very honorable and caring, but others treated the actors as second-class citizens, having very little concern or consideration for their needs or working conditions. Today, Actor's Equity monitors carefully every tour-ing show under its jurisdiction, seeing that pay scales are met, working conditions remain in accordance to contractual agreement, and that the members are cared for in whatever events or circumstances come up while on the tour.

THE COMPANY MANAGER, TOURING MANAGER, AND SM

Only on a large show with a big budget will there be both a company manager and a touring manager. Whenever possible, producers will have only a company manager. In many ways, the parts of each job are similar. When both managers are traveling with a show, the company manager is generally in charge of the company, making travel arrangements, setting up housing in each city, and caring for the daily expenses and general budget. The tour manager, on the other hand, deals mostly with the crew and technical parts of the show, making the arrangements to transport the equipment, dealing with the local union and crew, and often traveling to the next city two or three days in advance to see if the next performance site is prepared to receive the show. The company manager works closely with Equity, knowing the rules and regulations, while the touring manager works closely with I.A.T.S.E., knowing their rules and regulations. In the absence of a tour manager, the company manager also does the tour manager's work.

With the presence of both a company manager and tour manager, the SM's job is made easier. The SM's attention and efforts may be focused on maintaining the show and giving more personal attention to the cast. If there is only a company manager, the SM may be called on to aid the company manager in whatever way the company manager asks. In the absence of a touring and company manager, the work of these positions is divided among the production office, the TD, and the SMs.

THE WEAR AND TEAR OF TOURING

Touring shows, especially ones that play in towns for short periods of time, move frequently, and have one or two days' transition time from one city to the next, from one setup to the other—are hard on everyone involved.

The Road Crew

The road crew consists of the heads of the various technical departments and their assistants. Moving the show from one place to the other is toughest on the road crew who travels with the show—the *roadies*, as they are affectionately called. From the moment the curtain goes down on the final performance in one city and rises on the opening performance in the next, their work is continuous, stopping only to eat and get some sleep. They must strike the show, get the technical elements and equipment securely and safely packed for travel, travel to the new location, set up the show, and have it ready for the opening performance.

The SMs

For the SMs too, each move is a major event. Not only must they pack out their part of the show, but they must oversee the travel day for the cast. Once they are in the new town, they must set up shop at the new facility and see that the show is ready for the first performance. No less than two weeks in a town is a welcome schedule for the SMs as well as everyone else in the company. With a two-week engagement, the cast and crew can have the following weekend for rest and personal time.

The Actors

Actors probably have it easiest in touring. After the final performance at a location, they are responsible for clearing out their dressing rooms, taking their personal belongings, and seeing that dressing rooms are left clean and in respectable order. Most touring shows will travel the actors' makeup kits for them. It is the actors' responsibility to clearly mark their cases with their names and put them in the travel container provided. The prop department becomes responsible for traveling the makeup kits. Once the actors' work is done after the final performance in a town, they can return to their living quarters to get some rest and be ready to travel to the next town.

THE PARTS AND PHASES OF TOURING

We will now discuss the major parts and phases of touring:

- Part One: Closing Out the Show and Packing
  Phase One: Preparation
  Phase Two: Striking and Packing
- Part Two: Traveling
- Part Three: Setting Up and Being Ready for the First Performance

Part One: Closing Out the Show and Packing

It might seem more natural to have traveling as the first part of touring a show. However, once a show is on the road, the cycle of moving the show and company from one place to the other begins with closing out the show. Closing out the show and packing to move it to the next town is different from closing out the show permanently at the end of its run, which we will discuss in the next chapter. Closing out a show on the road means taking things apart, keeping every nut and bolt, every costume and prop, and every scrap of administrative paper, and packing them away neatly and safely so they can be traveled, set up, and used in the next place.

The Producer's Transition Time

The transition time between the final performance in one city and the opening performance in the next is expensive time for the producer, not to mention the box office down time. In concern for budget and costs, the producer keeps the transition as short as possible. The time the producer allows for this is often ideal time and not realistic time. The producer allows only for a perfect experience with no problems or setbacks. Whenever possible, and with Equity's consent, the producer will travel the cast on their day off. This saves the producer from loosing still another day. The SM can give the actors some compensation for this personal time lost by delaying their rehearsal call at the new theatre until the last moment possible, which is usually in early or midafternoon on the day of the opening performance.

Two Phases to Closing Out a Touring Show

There are two phases in closing out a show while out on the road: the preparation and striking the show and packing. In the preparation, each department does whatever it needs to do in advance to ensure that once the strike and packing begins things will go smoothly, quickly, and safely. There will be no time for anything else. For the most part, preparations for the move begin in the last week of the run in a particular town, and get finalized in the last two or three days before the final performance. In some situations, the company manager begins preparation work for the next location even earlier.

The SM's Preparations

In the final week in a city, preferably at the beginning of that week, the SM publishes, posts, and passes out a schedule, along with pertinent information such as addresses, phone numbers, flight information, and procedures to be followed for the new location. This schedule is produced in conjunction with the company manager plans, reservations, and arrangements. The SM confers with the company manager and gets approval before the schedule is posted and passed out.

Next, the SM consults with the company manager, checking to see that all advance, follow-up, or confirmation calls for travel and housing have been made for the next town. If there is no company manager with the show, the production office usually handles this business. In such cases, the SM confers with the production office. When the production office is handling this business, it is wise that the SM also call to confirm things; it is more assuring if the SM has direct conversation with the people with whom the SM will be dealing in the next town, checking to see if everyone is coordinated, working in the same time frame, and has the correct arrangements and information.

Another important matter in preparation to moving is to see that a housing list for the next town is put up in enough time for the members of the company to sign up. Once again, the company manager handles this business, but in the company manager's absence, the SM does it. Equity has some very specific requirements, restrictions, and rules governing housing. The SM needs to be familiar with the details and see that they are followed.

Last on the SM's list of preparatory things to do is something small and, at first glance, unimportant. Sometime before the final day in a city, and certainly before the final curtain, the SM should ask the prop department or carpentry department to dig out from storage the crates and boxes which will carry the SM's equipment and materials to the next town. These crates and boxes should be put somewhere out of the way and yet accessible for the SM to get to after the final performance. To wait and ask for these things after the final curtain and after the crew

has begun striking the show becomes an inconvenience, because by then the crew heads and stagehands are busy striking and packing their own areas.

The Last Performance

Often on the day of the last performance the feeling backstage is charged with a different energy. The SM feels it, not only from the performers, but from the crew, too. Perhaps it is the excitement of moving to a new city, or maybe it is the anticipation of the whirlwind and marathon work of striking the show, packing, traveling, setting up in the new town, and having the show ready for the first performance. On occasion the feeling can be one of sadness for leaving a place where the company has felt most welcomed and made new friends.

Advance Packing

It is unwritten but strongly believed that the last performance should be delivered with the same focus, attention, and energy as the opening performance. It is everyone's intention to give their best. However, in anticipation of the move, people's thoughts, especially the crewmembers', slip into striking, packing, and the travel ahead. With any task that is difficult and tiring, it is natural for people to want to make the job easier. The crew has found that one of the ways to lighten the load is to start packing in advance. The prop and costume departments especially will start packing things during the last performance—things that have been used and are no longer needed for the rest of the performance. There is nothing wrong with the practice, and those who do it should be commended for their conscientious work and forethought. However, this practice should be of concern to the SM. Two things can happen. Invariably, something gets packed away that is needed later in the show and on occasion the people doing this work tend to concentrate more on packing than on the performance. Sometimes they are late for a cue or miss it entirely. It happens, and every SM who has the experience quickly learns to make it a standard practice to announce at the half-hour call before the final performance that everyone must remain focused and concentrated on the show and not drift off to thoughts of packing and moving.

Let the Packing Begin

Phase Two of closing out the show begins with the fall of the final curtain—the backstage becomes transformed into a metropolis of action, movement, and activity. The crew becomes a high-powered, fine-tuned, well-oiled working machine with all its parts performing efficiently and with speed.

The Company Manager and Touring Manager.   At least two or three days before the final show, the touring manager's office is packed away and the touring manager is off to the next town, making arrangements for the arrival of the company and show. The company manager, on the other hand, will often begin packing on the day of the final performance and can have the office closed out and packed away within an hour of the final curtain. Once the company manager's work is done, and he or she is no longer needed at the theatre that night, the company manager can return to the hotel to get some sleep and be ready to transport the cast, usually on the next day. It goes without saying that until the show is packed out of the theatre and the crew is either back at their living quarters or on the way to the new location, the company manager is on call.

The SMs.   With the fall of the final curtain, the SMs too become a whirling dervish of action in packing. More than likely, while one SM was calling cues for the final performance, the other was beginning the process of packing. The real work cannot begin until after the final curtain falls. The SMs are responsible for clearing and packing away the callboard and having their office packed into the travel containers provided. They are also responsible to begin packing some of the things on the SM's console, saving the more technical equipment for the sound and lighting departments. Once the lighting and sound departments complete packing the console, the prop department takes over and becomes responsible for moving the console and the SM's stool, seeing that they get put on the truck and arrive safely at the next location. For assurance that the SM's stool does not get left behind or picked up and used by someone else, the SM should have the stool clearly marked "STG.MGR."

At some point in the SM's pack-out, one of the SMs needs to go out to the FOH to retrieve the Equity cast list, which was placed in the lobby when the company first arrived. The SMs are also responsible for seeing that the actors have left the dressing rooms and their general living spaces backstage in neat order, cleared of garbage, and have left nothing behind. In addition, they check to see that no pieces of costumes are left behind, and they make a note of those

rooms or actors who left their dressing rooms in unsatisfactory condition.

Once the SM's things are packed, the boxes and crates need to be securely closed with tape or locks. The boxes and crates also need to be clearly and boldly marked "STAGE MANAGER." The prop department is responsible for traveling the SMs' things. Upon completion of packing, the SMs check with the head of the prop department, asking where they should pile their boxes and crates so they will not be forgotten or left behind. Also, in thinking ahead to the arrival at the new theatre, the experienced SM has learned to remind the prop person that when the SMs' boxes and crates are unloaded from the truck, they should be placed where the SMs can easily retrieve them. The SM knows these things can easily end up in some corner, buried, behind pieces of scenery or other crates.

There continues to prevail the myth that the SMs must stay at the theatre on strike night until the last piece of equipment is packed and on its way. That is the job of the TD or head carpenter. In a professional situation, the SMs are not permitted to do any work that is done by union stagehands. If they stay until the strike and drag-out is completed, they will just be standing around watching. It is better for the SMs to return to their living quarters to get some sleep. More than likely the next day will be filled with the business of traveling the cast to the new city.

Before leaving the theatre that night, the SMs check with the company manager, the TD, and department heads to see if anything more is needed of them. Seldom are the SMs needed at this time. However, like the company manager, the SM's are on call for any matter that might need their attention.

Once the SMs know they are free to go, out of politeness, professional courtesy, and good politics, they go around to the house crew and local crewmembers to extend their thanks, appreciation, and to say goodbye. This particular evening may be made of goodbyes, but chances are the SM who works a lot will be saying hello at another time.

Part Two: Traveling

It is the goal and objective of everyone in the touring company to move, set up, and have the show ready for the first scheduled performance in the new city. Almost always, the technical portion of the show travels by truck. Depending on the budget of the show, the distance to be traveled, and the type of tour, the company members may travel by bus, van, or airplane. Traveling has its degree of wear and tear on everyone. At best it is tiring. The most welcomed part is arriving at the next location, being set up in the new living quarters, and being back into the performances.

It is important to get the road crew to the next location as quickly as possible, to give them some time to sleep and be at the new theatre early to begin setup. In many cases the producer will fly the crew while the rest of the company travels by bus or van. If the company manager is not needed in the next town early, he or she may travel with the cast, along with the SMs. At least one if not both SMs always travels with the cast. If the company manager is present, the SM aids and shares in the duties. If not, the SM takes full responsibility.

Traveling the Cast

Either the company manager or the production office makes the arrangements and handles the business for transportation and the new living accommodations for the company. It is the SM's job to be in communication with the company manager or production office and get from them whatever information is needed to create a schedule and lay out instructions pertinent to the particular move. A lot can go wrong, even on a short trip. In creating the schedule and writing out instructions, the SM must be detailed, specific, clear, and answer questions before they are asked. The information is posted on the callboard and copies are given to everyone in the company—the right hand must know what the left hand is doing (see Figures 17-1 and 17-2). During the move, each group within the company is working within its own time frames, but at one point on the day of the first performance the SM must bring everyone together to get the show working for the first performance at the new location. In creating the different time frames for the schedule, the SM is wise to schedule more time than is actually needed. This allows for emergencies, latecomers, or unexpected problems.

Establishing Promptness

If the SM has been with the show since its rehearsals, the SM's expectations for people being on time are well established. Being on time remains as important in traveling as it does in all parts of working in theatre. Neither the plane schedule, the time to travel from one place to another, nor the opening performance in the new town can be delayed or changed. At

the meeting with the company just before starting out on the tour, the SM reminds everyone about being on time and adds as a statement of policy that the ground transportation will leave exactly at the scheduled time and those who are not present at that time will have to find their own transportation, be it to the airport or to the next city.

Having established this rule the SM follows through on it. However, without letting anyone know, the SM also allows ten or even fifteen minutes for delayed time. At five minutes before the scheduled time to leave, the SM does a role call. If someone is not present, this grace period is used to locate the missing person(s). The SM's first concern is for their well-being. Being assured they are safe and well, the SM then finds out if they can make the bus in the next few minutes. If so, the departure is delayed. If not, the SM reminds them of finding their own transportation.

After locating the missing individuals and after having decided whether the departure can be delayed a little longer, the SM returns to the waiting company. To those who have been waiting, the delay in time has appeared to be time the SM used to locate the missing person(s), and not a grace period. If the SM has decided to wait for the individual, this waiting time might be used to restate the SM's position and feelings on this matter of being late. If the SM has decided that the late individuals will find their own transportation, the SM might just return to the waiting company without comment and order the driver to leave. The effect of saying nothing and leaving everyone uninformed can be unsettling, but it leaves a great impression! It reinforces the SM's commitment to leaving on time and displays that the SM is a person of his or her word.

Persons Traveling on Their Own

Some members of the company may have made arrangements with the production office or company manager to travel to the various cities on their own. In all such cases, the SM instructs these people that before leaving each city, they are responsible to have their car in good running condition, if possible should have a cellular phone with them, have the schedule, be on time for all scheduled events in the next town, and if there is any problem or delay, must call both the company manager and SM on their cellular phone. The SM must also make it clear that calling does not relieve the individuals of their responsibility of being at the new location and/or being

TRAVEL INFORMATION

LUGGAGE / BAGGAGE

Because of the length of the tour and the different climates in which we will be traveling, the producer is allowing each company member an extra suitcase or footlocker-sized piece of luggage, in addition to the two suitcases which will travel with you. This extra piece will not travel with you when traveling by plane, unless you are willing to pay the fee for the extra luggage. Instead, this extra piece will travel with the show and the prop department. Carry-on bags are separate and not counted as the two pieces of luggage allowed. Remember, your carry-ons must be small enough to place one of them under the seat in front of you and one of them above in the overhead bin.

Starting with traveling from our first city, and with every city thereafter, you will be required to have your extra piece of luggage at the theatre, no later than your arrival time for the first performance of the last day.

Once we are in the new city, this luggage will be delivered to you on the morning after the opening performance. Please pack it with things you will not need for a day or two. If you wish to retrieve this luggage sooner, you can come to the theatre on the morning of the opening performance to get it. However neither the staff nor the crew will be able to assist you, other than leading you to where the luggage is stored.

If something is not clear or if you have any questions, please see me!

Thanks,

Sarah J.

Figure 17-1   Travel information to the cast telling them some of the procedures to follow and what to expect as they embark on touring with the show.

on time. Calling is just to inform management, so they do not worry and use their time trying to locate the missing individuals.

Luggage and Baggage Handling

The SM takes as much care and concern for the handling and moving of the luggage as for the members of the company. For the people traveling, the contents of their suitcases are their life support—the necessities and comforts for living. For performers out on the road, the suitcase is their home away from home—the items that make them feel at home no matter where they hang their hats and set out their makeup cases.

Tagging Each Piece. All luggage and carry-on pieces must be clearly and identifiably marked and tagged so if a piece is separated from the group, it can be quickly be recovered. The production company often provides tags or stickers with the name of the

Schedule

DEPARTURE, from Chicago to Denver

Sunday, June 27.

All extra baggage traveling on the prop truck must be at the theatre before the matinee performance today. **REMEMBER: *There is <u>no</u> evening performance!***

Monday, June 28.

6:30 AM, all baggage traveling on the airlines, must be in the Stranton Hotel lobby.

Cast members not staying at the Stranton, if you choose, you can bring your luggage the night before. We have made arrangements with the concierge to lock them up in a separate closet. HOWEVER, when dropping off your luggage, personally see that it gets locked up.

8:15 AM, bus pick-up at the Miller Apts.

8:30 AM, bus pick-up at the Hilltop Hotel

9:00 AM, EVERYONE, meet in Stranton lobby for *head count. **Please be on time!!!*** Bus departs for the airport, **PROMPTLY**, at **9:15AM** (Have breakfast before this time. There will be no time to stop and eat.)

11:05 AM, American Airlines
  Flight # 117
  Departs Chicago, O'Hare Airport 11:05 AM
  Arrives Denver, 12:42 PM

(REMEMBER: *Time Zone Change* - ONE HOUR)

UPON ARRIVAL:

- EVERYONE, meet at baggage claim for baggage pick-up and head count.
- Bus will travel to the various hotels from the airport.
- Settle in, get rest (tomorrow's call, earlier than normal)

TUESDAY, June 29.

12:00 PM, All ensemble performers meet in theater lobby for rehearsal with orchestra.

1:30 PM, All Principals meet in lobby for rehearsal with orchestra. All ensemble performers meet with Dance Captain in rehearsal room, backstage, at theater.

3:00 PM, Settle into dressing rooms and be ready for tech rehearsal.

3:30 PM, Cue to Cue Tech with new crew.

5:00 PM, BREAK for DINNER

7:30 PM, HALF-HOUR CALL

8:00 PM, OPENING PERFORMANCE, Denver

Figure 17-2 Schedule for the cast traveling from Denver to Chicago, detailing the times they must meet and the procedures they must follow from June 27th to June 29th.

show. In addition, the SM sees that each piece is marked with the person's name and two telephone numbers: the number of the production office and a personal number of the individual. The personal number should be a place where the company member can retrieve a message, such as an answering machine, family member, or friend. If a piece is lost, the owner can check with the numbers listed to see if someone has found the missing luggage and has called. Written along with the phone numbers should be a note asking the finder to call one or both numbers and leave a message. The SM should instruct the company members not to put their home address or city. It is best to have the luggage remain where it was found. This allows greater control in retrieving it and cuts down on the time the lost piece is separated from its owner. If the SM provides the tags to the company members, it is most helpful at the baggage claim to have them in a bright fluorescent color.

Baggage Check-In. When traveling with a large company there can be well over a hundred pieces of luggage. Whether traveling by ground transportation or by air, the SM leaves all people responsible for their own luggage. It is their job to see that their pieces get loaded on the bus or truck. If they are traveling by air, they continue to be responsible for their pieces once they are at the air terminal, seeing that each piece gets properly tagged with the correct destination information and is sent off to be loaded on the plane.

Once again the SM facilitates and oversees—seeing that all do their part and that the bags get safely loaded on the ground transportation and none get left behind. If the company is traveling by air, at the air terminal the SM has the luggage unloaded at curb side and checks to see if the luggage can be checked in at this point. If it can, the individual bags are tagged as a group, but each person is still responsible to see that their bags are properly tagged and sent off. As a double-check, the SM also keeps an eye out, seeing that the porters tag the bags with the correct destination and send the bags off to be loaded on the plane. If the bags must be processed inside and cannot be checked in as a group, the SM directs the group to the inside and sees that each person checks in his or her own bags.

Baggage Claim. When at the baggage claim in the new city, each person in the company continues to be responsible for retrieving their own luggage. This is when the colorful tags help as the different pieces come around on the conveyor belt. Meanwhile, one SM seeks out several porters with carts to help move the luggage, while the other SM checks and makes contact with the drivers of the ground transportation. Often, the drivers are at the baggage claim and make themselves known. After the luggage is retrieved and a head count is taken, the SM has the porters take the baggage to the ground transportation vehicles that take the company members to their new living quarters.

The Partner or Buddy System

With a large number of company members traveling, the SM uses any devices possible to aid in keeping organized and have control. Another effective tool is to incorporate the partner or buddy system. That is, whenever the group is traveling, each person within the group is assigned and paired off with another person in the company. They are not required to sit together when traveling or be best friends. On the day of travel they call each other, checking to see that each knows the schedule and is on time. Then when on the bus or at the airport just before departure or boarding the plane, each person looks around, checking to see if their partner or buddy is present. If not, they notify the SM or company manager.

When traveling by ground transportation and traveling long distances, there will be frequent stops throughout the day. It can be time-consuming for the SM to do a role call each time the members of the company load on to the transportation. The SM merely reminds the travelers to check to see if their buddies are present before moving on. There is, however, a flaw in this way of working: if both people of a partnership are absent from the point of departure, there is no one to report their absence. For assurance and as a failsafe device, the SM can implement this system by assigning to each pair another pair of buddies Their only job is at the time of boarding or departure, when each person of each pair looks around, first for the individual buddy, then for the pair to which they have been assigned. Now there are four people checking on each other. The SM has reduced the odds of no one being present to report on the others and can work with greater assurance, efficiency, and control.

Part Three: Setting Up and Being Ready for the First Performance

On-the-Road Living

When arriving in each new town, the first thing to be done is for all to get situated and set up in their new living quarters—the SM, too, even before going to the theatre to begin working at the new venue. Between the time of arrival in a new place and the opening performance, everyone will be putting in a long day at the theatre. At the end of such a day, everyone should be able to return to the lodgings to rest, without first having to unpack and settle in.

Making Yourself at Home. An important key to living on the road is to not live out of the suitcase—unpack, especially when living in a hotel or motel room. Even if it is for only a week, use the drawer space, hang things in the closet, set toilet articles out on the counter, create a kitchen area for snacks, set up your music, move the TV for best viewing, and set up the desk for your books, writing material, and laptop. In fact, after the suitcases have been emptied, put them away. As for split-week engagements or one-night stands, there is no choice but to live out of the suitcase. Even then, living can be made tolerable and convenient by packing neatly and putting things in departmental groups. Then, in a matter of a few minutes you can place your luggage on counter tops and about the room.

Living Accommodations. The living accommodations, though monitored and regulated by Equity, vary greatly. Some places might be upscale and swanky, while others, though nice, are very basic. Most will be at hotels or motels, usually single rooms, but if they are available and members of the company choose, they can share an apartment. At times, the entire company will stay in one establishment and other times they might be split up, living in two or three different places. Information for living accommodations usually is posted on the callboard several weeks in advance of each city, allowing enough time for the cast members to sign up and for the company manager or production office to make the arrangements and confirm the reservations. Once the company gets to each city, it is up to the company manager or SM to keep track of who is staying where, and create a list of room and phone numbers where each person can be reached.

A Temporary Callboard

From the start of the tour, the SM establishes with the company members that for the first few days at each new city, a temporary callboard will be set up in the lobby or entrance area to the living accommodations. This board will be whatever the hotel can provide and will contain only the most immediate informa-

tion needed for the cast. The company members are responsible for checking this board until the official callboard is set up in the theatre and everyone is settled in and performing.

The New Performance Site

Sometimes the theatre is located just around the corner or a few blocks away from the living accommodations. Other times it may require transportation to get there. By Equity rule, the producer must provide transportation if the theatre is over a certain distance away from where the cast members are living. The producer may pay for use of the public transportation in the city or may provide a bus or van that will pick up the company members each day. In a big-budget show, the SMs may be fortunate to have a car at their disposal, which is for staff use and has been rented by the company.

Also, each theatre will be unique. Some will be brand new with state of the art equipment and spacious dressing rooms for individuals as well as ensemble performers. Others may be historical landmarks, with a raked stage, sumptuous decor, and dressing rooms going up three or four flights of stairs. There will be one or two theatres that are just downright old and almost unusable, forcing everyone in the company to do what they can to set up the show and live in the backstage space.

The Show Crew, House Crew, and Local Crew

We have already met the *show crew*—the heads of the different technical departments that travel with the show, also called the roadies. When the show arrives at a performance site, the show crew meets up with the *house crew*—the stagehands hired by the performance site to head the backstage technical departments. These two groups join forces to set up the show, work the performances, and strike the show at the end of its run in that particular city. However, with most shows the show crew and the house crew are not enough to do the job. More stagehands are needed. It would be extremely costly for the producer to travel a full crew. Instead, the additional crewmembers are picked up in each town—the *local crew*. The producer's office, tour manager, company manager, or TD handles this business, making the arrangements for the additional crew members through the I.A.T.S.E. office in each town. Only in rare instances does the SM have anything to do with this work.

For the most part, stage crews are the same the country over. Only the accents or colloquial expressions may differ. They are glad to have the show in town and glad for the work. Time permitting, they will guide the company members to some of their landmarks, local color, and brand of hospitality.

A Mini-Tech

Yes, it is back into technical rehearsals! To one degree or another, everyone traveling with the show repeats the work done in technical rehearsals when the show was first being put together. The difference is, the technical kinks have been worked out and everyone is more experienced in the setup. It is now a matter of working with the new crew, teaching them what to do during performance, and resolving any problems that might come up in putting the show in this particular venue. With the transition time being so short from one city to the next, the pressure and urgency in this mini-tech can be great, and the hours for the crew and SM, just as long as in the original techs.

The SM

The work procedure for the SM in setting up at the new theatre is just as it was laid out and described in Chapter 14 on technical rehearsals. For review, this might be a good time to turn back and scan that part of the chapter, but following is a checklist of the things the SM must do:

- Meet the local house crew and house person
- Start set up of the SM's console
- Tour the theatre
- Talk to the people working the front of the house, set up the cast/Equity name board, and discuss the procedure to be followed to begin each performance
- Walk the audience areas, checking for sight lines and the feeling of the house in relationship to the show
- Set up the SM's office
- Assign dressing rooms (keys, name plates, and make schematic drawing of the room assignments)
- Set up the callboard
- Post directional signs (if needed)
- Check to see that quick change areas are set up
- Post show rundowns throughout the backstage areas
- Lay in white tape backstage for sight lines and places where it is needed for safety

Putting it Together

On the afternoon of the performance, the SM uses this time to once again put the show together. If the show is technically simple, the SM has a dry tech to teach the new members of the crew the show. If the show is technically difficult or a musical, the SM will more than likely have a cue-to-cue tech with the cast and crew.

The Cast.   With each new performance site, the cast needs time on stage. With a musical show or a show with difficult blocking, the performers need to go over the spacing and sight lines for the new stage. They may need to run certain scenes and most definitely one or two of the dance numbers. They will also need to do a sound check.

The Orchestra.   If the show is a musical, the producer will more than likely bring with the show only the conductor or music director and certain key musicians: the assistant conductor, who usually is the lead keyboard person; maybe a base player, a trumpet player, or lead violinist, if their particular instrument is important to the score; more than likely a drummer, and if the show requires, a percussionist. The rest of the musicians are picked up locally. Again, the production office, the company manager, or the conductor handles this business and makes the arrangements with the local musicians' union.

The orchestra is brought in on the day of the performance. Sometimes they work in the orchestra pit while the conductor runs them through the music. Other times, they will work in the morning in some other place and come to the theatre in the late afternoon to work in the pit, working with the cast and doing a sound check.

Making Changes.   Each new performance site brings its own set of problems—some simple, some more complex, each affecting the show in some way. Sometimes it means cutting down the set or changing blocking, perhaps adding or eliminating cues. Remember, the TD is responsible for handling all technical problems and changes. The TD advises and apprises the SM of the changes, while the SM envisions how the changes might affect the show. The SM, along with the dance captain (if the show is a musical), will make whatever changes are needed on the stage with the actors.

Another Opening

No matter how many opening performances the company goes through while touring a show, each takes on an excitement similar to the first opening performance. The excitement is often generated by the presence of the local press, dignitaries, and special guests, perhaps people dressed in formal wear, and possibly a gala gathering after the performance at which the cast becomes the honored guests. For the SM, this opening performance excitement or keyed-up feeling may be due more to the fact that the local crew is new to the show and has had very little time to learn their parts.

The ASM

For the first two or three performances in a new city with a new crew, the PSM calls the cues to the show while the ASM remains free backstage to move about and troubleshoot any problems that might occur during the performance.

ADDITIONAL WORK FOR THE TOURING SM

Spike Marks and Taping

Practically every show has spike marks to which the SM must attend at each new performance site. They might be to mark the placement of a set unit, to tell the prop department where to put a piece of furniture, or to mark the center of a special light where an actor must stand. If there are only a few spike marks, as in a small straight play, the SM may have the spike mark locations committed to memory. If there are many, as in a musical, the SM should have them noted on a set of the personal floor plans that were created for the show.

Many shows today, especially musicals, travel with their own floors. For the purpose of traveling and easy installment at each theatre, the flooring is made in 4-by-8-foot sections, and the sections are numbered. When the flooring is taken up at one performance site, the spike marks and dance/blocking numbers along the edge of the apron remain and travel with the different sections. When the floor is installed in its numerical order at the new theatre, the spike marks and dance/blocking numbers are in place. It is then the SM's job to see if the marks are suitable for the particular house in which the show is now going to perform. If they are not, the SM changes them.

Additional Conversation with the FOH

During the time the SM meets and talks with the house manager and maybe even meets those in charge of the box office, the SM needs to check on performance times and matinee days. The SM should ask to see a copy of the playbill the theatre will be giving to its patrons, and take a stroll out front to check the marquee for names, spelling, and billing. The company manager usually does this business, but if there is no company manager, it is important that the SM take up the slack. In addition the SM will need to talk with the box office about cashing checks for the company members, how to handle the use of house seats, and talk about complimentary seats.

The SM may also have to locate the administrative offices for the theatre. If the show is not traveling with its own copy machine, the SM will need to make arrangements to use the theatre's machine, offering to pay for whatever copies are made. If the company has not made arrangements to have its own phone line put in backstage, the SM will also need to make arrangements to use the theatre's phones.

Focusing the Show Lights

Another job an SM might be required to do while out on the road is to assist the lighting department in focusing the lights at each new venue. The ASM may be assigned this job or on a big show both SMs may be needed. Once the lighting instruments are hung and the set and furniture is in place, the lighting department then needs to adjust each lighting instrument to shine on the stage as dictated by the lighting design and plot. This job requires two people—one who climbs up to each lighting instrument to adjust the lamp and one who stands on the stage in the center of where the light is to shine. As the person above moves the lamp into position, the person on the deck looks up into the light, telling the person above to stop when the brightest part of the light (the hot spot) is shining in the eyes of the person on stage. The person above then locks the lamp into place, shutters off the excess light from spilling into another area, checks to see that the safety chain or safety line is securely in place, and moves on to the next lighting instrument. This is a time-consuming job and with both SMs assisting the job can be done in half the time. For the SMs, this is work in addition to all they must do when moving into a new facility. SMs must learn to budget their time, doing all things with the same concern and efficiency.

Spotlight Cues

In shows where there are many spotlight cues and more than one spotlight is used, the assistant to the head electrician traveling with the show usually doubles as the head spotlight operator. The assistant finishes helping in setting up the lights on the stage, and then retires to the spotlight booth with the new operators, who have been hired as part of the local crew. The assistant teaches the new operators the cues and in performance calls the cues.

In the more economical, tightly budgeted touring shows, or in shows where the SM is required to call all spotlight cues during the performance, the SM is given the dubious honor of teaching the new spotlight operators their cues. With the transition time from one city to the next being as short as it usually is, the SM seldom has enough time to go over all cues with the new operators, and instead gives them a crash course. The SM explains the more difficult cues, familiarizes them with the preferred method and style of calling the spotlight cues, and assures them that the other cues are easy and that the SM will talk them through those cues during the performance. They will also have a chance in the mini-tech to become a little more familiar with the show.

Local Actors

With some touring shows local actors are hired as extras or to play in small roles. In most cases the preliminary work for finding and hiring these actors has been done by the production office, tour manager, or company manager. However, once the company gets in town and while the show is being set up, it is the SM's job to rehearse these new people and work them into the show. With a musical show, the SM has the help of the dance captain and the music director or conductor. Even with their assistance, this becomes additional work for the SM and consumes time in a schedule already filled with things to do.

ANOTHER SM MYTH

It is generally believed that when a show is planning to go out as a touring show, the SM is responsible for making cuts or alterations to the technical part of the show to make the show easier to travel and set up at the different venues. In a professional company, the producer, designers, and director are in charge of making changes. The SM may sit in on their meetings and may make suggestions, but for the most part changes are dictated to the SM. Once the changes have been made, the SM returns to the charts, plots, plans, lists, and cueing script, revising them to reflect the touring show.

ON THE ROAD RELATIONSHIPS AND BEHAVIOR

We said in Chapter 16, Run of the Show, that although the position and authority of the producer and director are ever present and omnipotent, once the show gets into its run and the producer and director have gone on to other things, the company manager, the tour manager, and the SM become the lead positions of authority. While out on the road, although the producer and director are but a phone call, E-mail, or fax away, the company manager, tour manager, and SM become even more supreme in their authority.

LIVING TOGETHER

When the show was rehearsing and playing at home base, there were many days in which everyone spent at least nine hours together. For the most part, everyone was on their best professional behavior and some of their more annoying habits or ways of living were either not as prominent or did not have the opportunity to display themselves. Now that everyone is together, traveling, living, working, and socializing throughout every day, people become more revealing, and there is greater chance for differences and possible conflict. In addition, people out on the road will sometimes act in ways they normally do not act when at their home base. Things that were acceptable or of little concern to them at home sometimes become more important while on the road. Some may miss being at home, or even resent being away. Others find a new freedom and sometimes act in ways that are different, unbecoming, unprofessional, or unacceptable.

The more extreme cases are easy for the SM to identify and deal with. It is the subtle ones, in which a person begins to complain a little more, becomes a little more demanding, or is agitated and irritable, that are difficult to deal with. None of these things are excuses or justification for poor or unprofessional behavior, but the SM who is aware of and understands how being on the road can affect people, can more effectively serve and deal with the affected company members.

The Actors

The tone or tenor of the company will change once a show gets on the road. Most times the change is gradual and subtle, with little shifts in relationships. At first, being on the road is fun, like a holiday—the honeymoon period. Gradually, the company members gravitate to each other, forming little groups, often pairing up as friends, lovers, companions, or for purely economic reasons. The romanticized view of being on the road with a show begins to wear thin, while the more strident difficulties of traveling and individual personalities become pronounced. As in life, sometimes the relationships created last the entire tour and beyond. Sometimes the relationships end when the tour ends. For others, a relationship may end abruptly at any time during the tour. Most times the relationship ends quietly, but other times it can be drawn out and cause a disturbance in the company.

During the time the relationships are developing and flourishing the SM watches quietly. In an effort to keep the company in a positive light, the SM, either through request or through observations, weaves these relationships into the fabric of the company. The SM sees that certain individuals travel together, sit at the same banquet table, are assigned to the same dressing room, or puts their names together to share the same living quarters. When breakups or separations occur, the SM acts quickly and quietly, making changes and arrangements not only for the general tenor of the company, but for the show as well.

The Crew

The individuals of the crew appear to be the more seasoned and experienced in traveling with a show and living on the road. They demand equal consideration and care, but require much less maintenance from the SM or company manager. They seem to be more accepting of the hardships, complain less, carry less baggage, and require fewer gadgets and creature comforts to make them happy.

Cast and Crew

In other parts of this book we have discussed the relationship, dynamics, and separation that can exist between the cast and crew members due to the nature of their jobs. If the cast and crew are very different, perhaps incompatible on many levels, the relationship can take a turn and become strained. Being on the road can magnify matters. During the times when the show is moving from one city to the next, the crew becomes separated from the cast, being totally consumed with striking, traveling, and setting up the show, with little time to eat, sleep, and do personal hygiene. The cast, on the other hand, has only to travel to the next place, set up in their new living quarters, perhaps explore the local neighborhood, and be ready to rehearse on the afternoon of the day of the opening performance. If both groups are not aware of the other's work, such a working situation can put more strain on the relationship. If the engagements in each town are short and the transition time between one city to the next is tight, the cast and crew have even less time together.

Despite the gulf and drawbacks, most cast and crewmembers overcome their differences, often times striking up friendly and sometimes personal relationships. From time to time an SM will have a cast and crew who remain apart and separate despite any effort to bridge the gap. The reassuring part of such a relationship is that it never affects the performance. The atmosphere backstage, however, can be sterile. The SM will continually get complaints from each group about the other. An SM cannot prevent such a relationship from taking place, but can deal with each group to keep things from escalating and perhaps affecting the show.

The reverse of a troubled relationship between the cast and crew, though welcomed, can create a new set of problems for the SM. They are now too friendly and sometime during a performance they may forget about the show and become focused more on fun and good conversation.

The SM

The SM also feels and suffers all the highs and lows of touring the other company members experience. With each tour the SM should get better at stabilizing these personal feelings, living less at the extremes and more in the middle.

The SM's working relationship with the crew, technical heads, and assistants remains the same whether out on the road or at home. While out on the road, the SM needs to give more care and attention to the company and more specifically to the actors than would be normal when performing at the home base. The SM needs to be even more accessible, listening to the complaints, problems, and concerns of the individuals no matter how small or insignificant they might appear. The SM takes an active part in helping to resolve situations and problems which could affect the show or company, but at the same time is careful not to become a caretaker. The SM does not take away an individual's responsibility to be an adult, a professional, and in charge of his or her own life and actions. Some people want a caretaker or parent figure and will seek out anyone in the company who in the least way displays an inclination toward this kind of a relationship.

It is disheartening and destructive to the company and to the show to have a group of actors, stagehands, and staff members who can't wait for the tour to end. This feeling is infectious and highly contagious. All that is needed is for one or two people to become afflicted and it can spread. It is also foolish for the SM to think that the company will remain joyous and harmonious, free from conflict and strife. The SM needs to remain alert in the good times as well as the bad. The SM should see that as the different groups or couples form they do not operate to the exclusion of others or to the company as a whole. The SM must also be alert and take care not to get pulled into the different factions and special interest groups. The SM takes everyone's interest into consideration.

THE PERFORMANCE ON THE ROAD

In all the time a show spends out on the road, the performance is least changed or affected. Only in extreme cases will actors take their problems out on the stage and let it affect their performance. Once the show has been tailored to travel, the show remains virtually the same. This is due in part to everyone being professional and the work the SM does to maintain the performance and artistic integrity. It is also due to the fact that once the scenery and props are in place, the audience is seated, and the lights on the stage come up, the real world momentarily disappears, while the imaginary world of the play and theatre takes over.

THE PROFESSIONAL EXPERIENCE

The following diary account was a photocopy left on my console while I was traveling on the road with a show. To this day I do not know who left it there. No one ever came forward to ask, "Did you read the ar-

ticle I left you?" No one responded when I thanked the person over the PA system. This diary account, though written in a lighthearted spirit, conveys what an SM can experience in the course of a day while out on the road.

The article had been copied directly from a newsletter published by the Stage Manager's Association in New York. At the bottom of the first page, separated from the text of the article was the following information: Anne Sullivan was the recipient of the second annual Del Hughes Award for Lifetime Achievement in the Art of Stage Management.

As I read the article, I chuckled, laughed out loud, and one or two times even cried out, "Oh! Ain't that the truth!" I quickly bonded with Anne. It was as if she had walked in my shoes, and I in hers. It was also a relief to hear another SM make the same comments, have the same complaints, express the same feelings that I had. Being an SM is sometimes an isolating experience; as things happen with a show, there is only you and your assistant. There are times when you need to have the view and opinion of another SM, and share your experiences.

Here is that article.

On the Road with a Major Musical, by Anne Sullivan

MONDAY, 6:35 A.M.: Arrive Nigends City via (bless the Company Manager) limousine after 2½-hour ride from Nadaville. Dropped at Hotel Lataque. Given key to small dark room smelling of cigarette smoke. Windows won't open. Dog starts coughing. Complain to front desk. Told to take it or leave; choicer selection of rooms might occur after 2 P.M. Breakfast in coffee shoppe: bacon, scrambled eggs, toast, tea.

7:40 A.M.: Walk to theatre carrying heavy briefcase and urging sleepy dog along. Can't find stage door. Look for trucks. Can't find trucks. Have a sudden and piercing fear that am in wrong city. See one truck skidding along icy street. Finally sight all trucks except one—doubtless truck with deck and hanging goods. Follow truck to circular building without doors. Walk all around building. Dog shivering. Briefcase growing leaden. Tears freeze on face.

7:58 A.M.: Still can't find stage door. Enter by loading door. Boost dog and briefcase up. See stage. Stage left looks enormous. Stage right which is prompt side barely exists. Look at house. Cavernous. Balcony rail fully 90 miles away. No rational position for box booms. Seats taken out for sound man all the way over audience lift where he will be able to see little of second act. Orchestra pit presumably works on elevator. Is all the way down and completely out of sight now. Greet Advance Carpenter and Advance Electrician. Summon up big smiles and handshake as have not seen them for whole week. Advance Elec. says must use house fronts run off house boards. Ask where office is and if phones are in. Both look embarrassed and introduce House Carpenter who almost breaks hand with his shake. Ask who is House Propman. Old man drinking coffee in corner pointed out. Introduce self and dog. Ask where dressing rooms are and if phones in. Follow him on tour of dressing rooms. Find office. Phone is in. Pick it up. Phone not working. Breakfast for our crew provided by promoter: eat danish and wash down with canned o.j.

8:15 A.M.: Loading doors opened and unloading starts. Arctic wind fills backstage. Settle dog on packing blanket in office and go around all dressing rooms with assistants, Tillie and Spike. Tillie actually located stage door. Figure out assignment of dressing rooms, wardrobe room, hair room, and offstage quick change rooms. Note washer and dryer have been rented by theatre and hooked up. Only choice for pit singers is damp and dismal location in basement. Locate Company Manager's office. Check their phone. Doesn't work. Find place where orchestra rehearses. See our Propman and tell him where orchestra rehearses and where wardrobe and offices located. Show Sound Man pit singers' hole and dressing rooms.

9:05 A.M.: Stop on stage on way out front. Trucks are still unloading. Stage right totally covered up by scenery and crates. Electricians hanging upstage pipes. Carpenters screwing in deck downstage. Much shouting from flyfloor as local flyman evidently deaf. Head out front. Very dark. Follow trail of old popcorn to front of house. Box office closed. Find cleaner and ask location of House Manager's office. Go upstairs. House Manager not in but secretary is. Ask about phones. She says phone man coming. When? Soon. Ask for list of doctors. Coming soon. Find out where Xerox machine is. Ask for mail.

9:46 A.M.: Check to see that musical instruments and music trunk on way to rehearsal room. Deck is down. Carpenters hanging downstage. Trucks still unloading. Stage left now filling up with crates. Musicians

trickling in. Local wardrobe people arrive for 10 o'clock call. Tell them call is at 1 P.M. Says so right on Yellow Card. Walk dog. Spike goes to orchestra rehearsal to make sure it starts without problems.

10:20 A.M.: Trucks all unloaded and doors closed. Take off parka. Coffee and donuts served to crew. Have chocolate-covered donut and tea. Read mail. Try not to be distressed by bills which haven't caught up. Tillie and Spike sort mail and distribute to our crew, put up name signs on dressing room doors, type out dressing room list with copies for stage door person, wardrobe, and hair. Find House Electrician and ask how he wants cue sheets for fronts written up. Start writing according to his specifications.

11:12 A.M.: House Manager appears backstage. Very pleasant. Complain to him about phones. Says he will call phone company again. Give him sheet of paper with times of acts, late seating policy. Give him duplicate for Head Usher. Tell him we take 15 minute intermission. He wants 20 minutes for bar business. Compromise on 17 minutes. Discuss starting times and who rings bells. He says they always start promptly at 8. Bug him about doctor list. Ask about restaurants close to theatre and if anything open after show. Nothing is. Check stage again. See uneaten sugar donut. Eat it. Tillie and Spike unpack office and set it up. Wardrobe Supervisor arrives. Show him dressing rooms and washer and dryer. He nods sourly.

11:56 A.M.: Phone man arrives. Walk dog. Feed dog. Go to McDonald's with Tillie and Spike. Have Big Mac, french fries, choc. shake.

1:01 P.M.: Return to theatre. Phones functioning. Advance Electrician talking to infant daughter on ours. Advance Carpenter smoking large cigar in office. Dog coughing. Work resumes on stage. Units being put together. Electricians hang downstage pipes. Spike shops for stationery and first aid supplies, peanuts and tea. Tillie setting up callboard and posting dressing room list, Stage Managers' and Company Managers' phone numbers, doctor list (Xeroxed with copies for all SMs and Co. Ms). Write out rehearsal schedule for week and post.

2:12 P.M.: Send Tillie to hotel to try and change all our rooms. Discover office phone numbers completely different from those given out. Call N.Y. office with new numbers. Type up stage manager reports for last week.

2:49 P.M.: Phone rings. Equity man wanting to know why cannot give vacation to chorus girl from company who is crying in his office. Explain that two other people already on vacation that week. Equity man not satisfied. Says she's crying. Tell Equity man I can cry louder.

2:56 P.M.: Phone rings. It's Star wanting phone number of doctor as feeling horrible. Get flyfloor cue-sheets and write-in changes for this theatre. Also write changes in prompt book.

3:06 P.M.: Bandage finger of local grip who bleeds over typed SM reports.

3:15 P.M.: Coffee and donuts again for crew. Eat cinnamon donut. Company managers arrive with tales of travel with cast. Commiserate and show them to their office.

4:37 P.M.: Electrician wants to know where SM desk is going. Go out and look at stage right. Though now cleared of crates still no room anywhere. Call Advance Carpenter. Ask him through clenched teeth where am I supposed to be. Advance Carpenter smiles sadly and shakes head and suggests I cue show from out front. No way. Advance Carpenter says I can't use desk and that Electrician will have to make up board with cue lights. Electrician swears. Have desk moved to office. Walk dog to calm rage. Feed dog. Chomp on peanuts that Spike has returned with. Wardrobe Supervisor bursts into office with news that washer has overflowed. Go out front to tell House Manager who swears.

5:25 P.M.: Cleaners appear backstage with mops for flood already mopped up by dressers.

6:00 P.M.: Eat dinner at Holiday Inn with Tillie and Spike. Have overdone and overpriced filet mignon, baked potato, salad, pie.

6:59 P.M.: Return to theatre. Freezing. All heat off. House Carpenter laughs and says it is practice of management. Look for House Manager. His office locked. Get his number from ancient Propman who makes me swear not to reveal source. Call House Mgr. and order heat turned on. House Mgr. no longer pleasant. Go out on stage and start making focusing marks with chalk. Mark every 2 feet left and right and every foot going U.S. from portal line. Electrician brings walkie-talkie and asks if am ready to focus. Say yes and focus fronts with local electricians who are very good. Nine instruments lampless but all plugged correctly so must count blessings.

Sound man plays Willie Nelson loudly to test speakers.

9:33 P.M.: Break for tea and three Pepperidge Farm cookies scrounged by Tillie. Spike changes trunk list after 3 actors call to report change of hotels, gives list to our Propman and then walks dog.

10:48 P.M.: Initiate discussions with our crew heads on whether to work until midnight or stop at 11 because all so tired. Everything in good shape so decide to stop at 11.

11:01 P.M.: Walk to hotel. Tillie has changed me to larger room with real air. Unpack clock, tea, oatmeal cookies, mug and dog food and clean shirt for tomorrow. Bed.

TUESDAY, 6:30 A.M.: Wake. Wonder where am, take shower, make tea, eat oatmeal cookies. Feed dog.

7:45 A.M.: Walk to theatre. Enter victoriously by stage door. Theatre nice and warm.

8:02 A.M.: Start focusing pipes and booms. Local truck delivering trunks.

10:09 A.M.: Coffee and donuts for crew. Eat glazed donut. Ask Tillie to phone star at 11 and ask about his health. Continue focusing. Wardrobe Supervisor says washer not fixed yet and how is he to do laundry. Ask Spike to bug House Manager and also to inform our Company Mgr. Tillie goes over SM cue lights with electrician.

11:29 A.M.: Have to replug 8th pipe. Walk dog. Phone rings. Local police. Someone has reported seeing a trunk fall off a truck on Main Street. Tell Spike, who turns pale and rushes out. Tillie says Star hoarse and feverish but will go on.

12:00 Noon: Lunch. McDonald's. Repeat yesterday. Sound department making pink noise on stage.

12:46 P.M.: Return to theatre. Ask Wardrobe Supr. if washer functioning. Answer yes but dryer doesn't heat properly. Ask Tillie to follow up with House Manager. Spike goes to Xerox spec sheets for next 3 towns turned in by Advance men. Makes enough copies for all crew heads. Tillie put cast sign out front and sticks names in alphabetical order. Sound men putting up stage speakers, moved #1 booms.

1:10 P.M.: Finish focusing 8th pipe and specials. Refocus #1 booms.

2:22 P.M.: Set winch limits with Winch Man. Wardrobe department setting up quick change off-stage.

2:24 P.M.: Prop department moves refractory table and 5 chairs into space set up by wardrobe dept. Loud altercation into which Tillie steps. Compromise agreed upon and hated by both departments.

3:09 P.M.: Start getting ready for Tech rehearsal. Ask Tillie and Spike if all actors who didn't travel with the company have called to check in. All accounted for except Principal Deputy. Spike calls Principal Deputy who is in hotel room and gives sass.

3:28 P.M.: Tech rehearsal begins. Do all flyfloor cues and winch setups. Look at light cues for each set. DSR winch grazes own legs whenever goes by. Tell Advance Carpenter. Tell Carpenter. Tell House Carpenter. Finally devise dance movement to avoid being hit by winch.

3:58 P.M.: Orchestra starts to move into pit. Discover pit elevator won't work. Our electrician fixes. Raging Wardrobe Supervisor comes on stage. Washer overflowed again. Tillie leads him off.

4:07 P.M.: Orchestra starts to play. Loudly. Territorial dispute S.L. between Props, Carpenters, and Assistant Wardrobe Supervisor. Spike settles by screaming louder than any of them. Tech. rehearsal continues.

4:48 P.M.: Tech. rehearsal ends. Ask to see act curtain.

5:00 P.M.: Crew knocks off. Orchestra plays on loudly. Walk crossover. Tillie puts up signs with arrows. Check for hazards. Check set for hazards. Spike walks all over deck and marks screws coming up. Propman mops deck. Spike remarks loose screws. Walk dog. Gather thought about what to tell actors. Tillie and Spike test paging system from each dressing room. Catch up on catastrophes. Spike goes to McDonald's for food for all SMs. Go over problems with Dance Captain. Eat Big Mac, fries, choc. shake.

5:59 P.M.: Orchestra stops. Actors start arriving. Can't find dressing room, stage, offices, anything. Tillie and Spike lead them around. Chat with Star who can only whisper.

6:30 P.M.: All actors here. Yell at Principal Deputy for not reporting arrival. Call actors on stage. Show them x-over and quick change areas, tell them curtain is guillotine and works slowly, remind to check all costumes and props and let us know any change of address. Show pit singers their hole. Dance Captain plays piano and eats sandwich at same time. Sound man gets levels on wireless mics with principals. Also levels on pit singers' mikes. Actors rehearse quick changes with local dressers.

6:43 P.M.: Singers' Deputy complains about safe and sanitary conditions in pit singers' hole. Wardrobe Supervisor complains that actor spoke sharply to local dresser. Hairdresser complains that ingenue not ready for appointment. Head Usher wants to know times of each act. Hand him another copy of sheet given to House Manager. Sound man complains one pit singer too close to mike. Male pit singer complains that female pit singer using perfume and he can't sing under such circumstances. Sniff female pit singer. Found to be clear of perfume and only smelling of soap. Star complains that dressing room too hot. Actor who changed hotel and told no one complains he didn't receive trunk. Tell Spike.

7:30 P.M.: Spike calls half-hour, collects valuables. Crew returns, brings act curtain in, fixes screws on deck, rehearses fly cues involving actors. Check cue lights and all stations on headset again. Chorus dancer brings piece of birthday cake. Eat it. Crew makes opening setup.

8:00 P.M.: Call places. Send conductor to pit. Conductor calls to say pit lights all out. House electrician unable to be found anywhere. Our electrician fixes pit lights. House Manager comes back and says hold curtain 20 minutes. Promoter's wife and two cousins and their wives materialize stage left. Tillie ejects them.

8:08 P.M.: House lights out and curtain up. Say Hail Mary. Get through show without flyfloor falling or hurting anyone. Audience laughs in right places. Only hit by winch 3 times. No bad opening night.

10:28 P.M.: Final curtain in. Say thank you to crew. Youngest dancer says thank you for good show. Producer comes back with 4 pages of notes. Promoter comes back with complaint about harsh treatment given his relations.

11:16 P.M.: Go to party. Only place in town to eat. Wonder why party dress getting tight.

1:54 A.M.: Walk dog. Bed. Don't set alarm.

18

Closing the Show

A show closes for two reasons: it is either at the end of its scheduled run, or box office receipts are down and financially, it is no longer feasible for the producer to keep the show running.

THE CLOSING NOTICE

It all starts with the official two-week-closing notice from the producer, which is posted on the callboard. A producer can close a show at any time, giving no notice. The producer is, however, bound by Equity agreement to either post a two-week notice or pay the actors two weeks' salary. A similar agreement exists between the producer and the stagehands' union, I.A.T.S.E.

FEELINGS

For every opening of a show there comes a closing. The opening was joyous, and for the most part the closing is sad. No matter how seasoned people working in theatre become, no matter how many shows they might do, when it comes time to close a show (or to leave it), there is always sadness. With a show, whether it was successful or not, the members of the company have bonded—sometimes as a group and extended family, other times between individuals. Some will remain in touch with each other regardless of the separation. With others, their paths may cross either at an audition or with some other show. For many, this will be the last time in seeing anyone from the group. In addition to the sadness come feelings of worry, fear, and loss: loss of friends, loss of having a steady job, and loss of a weekly paycheck. Now it's fear and worry that the next job will not come before the money runs out or one has to take another one of those temporary jobs.

There are those few occasions when the closing of a show for some or all of the members of the company is a joyous occasion. SMs especially will find throughout their careers one show, if not several, where the closing is at least a relief, if not joyous.

THE SM's OBLIGATION TO THE END

In the tradition of theatre, the show must go on, and the final performances must be performed and delivered with the same spirit and energy as were the first. An SM cannot prevent the members of the company from having their feelings, but can prevent their feelings from affecting the show and taking away from the last performances. The SM cannot allow the company to abandon the show—close it before its time. The SM has an obligation to the producer, to the artists and creators who put the show together, and to the members of the company, in spite of their feelings. Most of all, the SM and the company have their professional obligation to the last audiences who have paid the price and expect the same values as were given to the first audiences.

The SM too is open and vulnerable to feelings. While keeping the show together, SMs must keep their feelings in check and not allow them to get in the way of doing their job to full capacity and to the very end.

A FINAL SM MYTH

For the SM, the easiest part of working a production is closing out the show. To dispel a final myth, the professional SM has only to close out the SM's part of the show and not the entire production, as might happen in waiver, community, or academic theatre. The heads of each technical department take responsibility for closing out their own areas. Upon striking the show for the last time, the lighting and sound departments pack and return the equipment to the rental house from where it came. The head carpenter and crew are in charge of dismantling the set. In some cases, the set was built specifically for the production and is the property of the producer. At the close of the show, the producer puts the set in storage for future use, sells it to a company who buys used sets, gives it away to a school or local college, or destroys it. The props are often a combination of rentals and purchases. What was rented is of course returned, and what was bought usually goes with the set. Sometimes the costumes are rented, sometimes they are made specifically for the show, and other times they are a combination of both. Those that were rented are returned, and those belonging to the production company are either put in storage or sold to a costume house, which in turn rents the costumes for other productions.

THE SILENT PREPARATIONS

On notice of the show closing, the production office, company manager, tour manager, SMs, and heads of the various technical departments must begin their preparatory work. Each person must think and plan ahead, because when that final curtain falls there will be no time to think of anything but striking the show, packing the equipment into trucks, and getting out of the theatre. For the producer this is once again a matter of money. The producer cannot afford to stretch the strike and disperse the equipment over several days. The quicker the better. The preparatory work needs to be absolute and complete.

As the preparatory work is being done, there should be little fanfare or change backstage. As much as possible, things should remain as they have been for the run of the show. There should be no change in work procedures and the placement and order of things. The cast and crew should see, hear, or feel very little of the preparations and not continually be reminded of the pending closing.

THE SM's PREPARATORY WORK

The SM's preparatory work to close the show is minimal. If the SM has been complete and thorough in creating hard copy—the plots, charts, plans, lists, cueing script, blocking script—and has kept them up to date, the only thing the SM will need to do upon notice of the show closing, is return to the files, start pulling information, and begin duplicating it for the production book—the book that will be given to the producer at the close of the show.

THE PRODUCTION BOOK

Putting this book together is by far the most important work the SM does in closing out a show. The production book is the bible of the show and company. It is a three-ring binder (sometimes two or three binders) holding a copy of the cueing script, a copy of the blocking script, copies of the old script pages (if script changes were made), and all the charts, plots, plans, lists, and pertinent information the SM created and collected for the show. Accompanying this book will also be whatever drawings, sketches, or pictures the SM has collected, along with any audiotapes or CDs, videotapes or DVDs, and floppies containing the information the SM has kept on the laptop. The production book should be divided and tabbed into sections for easy reference.

With the easy access and use of copy machines, computer printouts, and other duplicating devices, the task of creating this book should be simple, possibly even joyous, giving a sense of pride and accomplishment, and might bring closure to the show for the SM. If the SM has been delinquent in keeping good files and keeping the information up to date, the task ahead will be monumental, overwhelming, and the production book will probably end up being incomplete and of little value to the producer, archives, or future productions.

State of the Production Book

Disregarding the caliber of the show, the prestige or lack of prestige of the production company, and setting aside the size of the show, company, or its success, the SM should submit to the producers some sort of a production book. There are some factors and situations that dictate to the SM how detailed, accurate, and all-inclusive the information in the production book should be.

If the show was new, never having been produced before on Broadway, regional, or local theatre, or if the show was a revival, but an all-new production which was intended for touring or Broadway, it is the

SM's job and responsibility to have a production book that is complete and filled with detail. In addition, the SM should include in the production book copies of things as they were changed, as the show grew and developed, a primary example being the script changes. The SM is not responsible for gathering and including detailed information for each technical department. The SM submits only the information that was gathered about a department to allow the future SM to do his or her job. The heads of the other departments remain responsible to the producer and will submit their own information. The SM must realize that the information gathered and turned in will be of tremendous value for the history of the show, for future productions, and whatever publication of the script might occur.

When preparing a production book for a show that was the recreation of a show that had already been produced on Broadway, and was perhaps intended to play only in one place, the SM still submits all that was gathered and kept on file, but can be less detailed and concerned in putting the production book together. Some producers, regardless of how small or limited their production, want the maximum an SM can give in putting together the production book. Others are less interested, and are satisfied with whatever the SM turns in.

The SM's Personal Library

Every SM should create a personal library and file for every show worked on. While putting together a production book for the producer, SMs should also assemble one for themselves. Not only will this copy act as a backup copy, but can be used later for reference. There will be several times in an SM's career where the producer or director of a show will call the SM to regain information they lost or neglected to gather and keep. Eventually, the SM's library can be given to a group, school, or organization that can use the information to teach or recreate its own productions.

The Cueing Script

It is not important that the producer or production company get the original copy of the color-coded cueing script. In referring back to this script, a person would be interested only in the placement of the cues. The color coding was for the SM's working ease. This being the case, the SM can keep the color-coded cueing script as part of the SM's library and submit to the producer or production office the extra copy (the security copy) the SM has kept in a safe place.

The Blocking Script

When assembling the production book, the SM does not need to include the original blocking script, which if you recall, was the SM's rehearsal script. Instead, the SM can turn in a copy of the rehearsal/blocking script and keep the original for his or her library. Better still, if the SM has transferred the blocking notes to a clear script, as was suggested in Chapter 16, Run of the Show, a copy of this script can be turned in to the producer, while the SM keeps the original.

Much to Do About Nothing

In spite of all the attention paid to the production book and the promise of it being used as a reference in the future, in many cases it ends up sitting on the shelf. When doing another production of a show, the producer, director, artists, and craftspeople, want to make their own statement, express their own creative values, bring life to the show in their own way. Many times these people make it a point not to look back and be influenced by someone else's work. Only on occasion might a director check back to see what another director did with a particular scene, effect, or difficult moment in the show. The producer is more apt to refer back to old budgets and expenses. Even for the SM, it is easier to create new charts, plots, plans, and lists, rather than take what was done by some other SM. Then why all this fuss and attention in putting a production book together? It is for the archives, posterity, historical value, and for those few times when someone wants to look back.

A Production Book for the Director?

Only if the director asks for it! Keep in mind, every chart, plot, plan, or list the SM made was already given to the director. Most directors keep the information given to them and in some way create and keep their own production book. By the time the show goes into its run and the director leaves the show, the director probably has created a production book and has it sitting on the shelf in the director's own personal library. Any additional information the SM might provide at the close of the show will be a supplement or update to what the director already has.

THE LOG BOOK

As discussed earlier, the SM's log book stays with the SM. It becomes part of the SM's personal copy of the production book.

The Final Address List

Just when SMs thinks their list-making days are over, there comes one more list to be made—the *final address list*. In it's simplest form, this list can be made up with only the cast members' names and addresses. For a more comprehensive list, the SM often includes the technical heads and the immediate staff members with the company. To be all inclusive, the SM might assemble the names and address of all the people associated with the show—the artists, creators, office production staff, even the craftsmen, vendors, and rental houses. The SM already has most, if not all, of this information on the laptop. Now it is only a matter of seeing that the information is correct and put into form on a list. In addition to listing the person's current address, the SM might also include a more permanent phone number or address, perhaps that of a family member or good friend—a place where the person can be reached regardless of any moves, travels, or jobs.

Once again, this information is strictly for the producer, production book, and the director. It is not for general distribution. If the cast wants a final address list, the SM either has the cast members create their own, or creates an additional one just for them. However, before doing so, the SM has the people who choose to be on this list sign up to give their approval. At the head of this sign-up list, the SM includes a statement reminding everyone that the list will be released for general distribution throughout the company. The SM makes a copy of the signed approval list, keeping the original and including the copy in the production book given to the producer or production company.

COLLECTING SCRIPTS

On shows where the scripts must be returned to the publishing company or to the producer at the end of the run, the SM must now go around and start collecting these scripts. The SM accepts scripts any time throughout the run, but once the closing notice goes up must start an active campaign to collect all scripts. Some actors, out of superstition, will insist on keeping their scripts until the final curtain. Others, as part of their warm-up and ritual before each performance, go over their scripts. With the people who refuse to relinquish their scripts, after the fall of the final curtain, the SM must go to them or they will forget, leaving the theatre and taking the scripts with them.

If you recall, upon passing out scripts—especially those that had to be returned—the SM created a list, noting the script numbers, to whom each script had been given, and had the actors sign for them. This is the time to take out that list. As each script is returned, the SM checks to see that the script is in reasonably good condition and that all the individual's blocking notes have been erased. If the script's condition is acceptable, it is good practice for the SM to have each actor initial the list once again, this time for having returned the script. Any script in poor condition or not returned must be paid for by the performer. When the scripts were first handed out, the actors were told to make their blocking notes in pencil and that they would have to pay for them if at the end of the run the scripts were lost or in poor condition. Most people will fulfill their professional obligation and return the scripts in good condition, but there will always be one or two who have been irresponsible or neglectful. Without malice or an accusatory tone, the SM informs the person of the amount to be paid. The SM must be firm and not let the matter linger. More than likely there is less than two weeks left before the show closes. If the performer delays in paying, the SM will need to report this matter to the production office and have them deal with it, by possibly deducting the amount of the script from the person's final paycheck.

PERSONAL PROPS

There are two kinds of personal props: the props an actor brings to the show to use during the performance, and the kind that are gathered by the prop department but are specifically for the actor to use. Both are usually small and personal items, perhaps a pocket watch, a handkerchief, a piece of jewelry, or a pair of eyeglasses. Each is left in the actor's care throughout the run, and the actor remains responsible for bringing it on stage or having it in place to use during the performance.

At the close of the show, the props that belong to the show must be returned. In all respects, it is the prop person's responsibility to collect the item upon the final curtain. Personal props, however, are items easily forgotten. The SM does everyone a service if upon the closing notice the SM reminds first the prop person of the personal props, and then the actors of the items left in their care and responsibility. Once again, when the final curtain falls, the actor will more than likely forget to turn in the props. While the SM is making rounds to return the actor's personal valuables and to collect the last of the scripts, the SM can also collect the personal props belonging to the show.

THE LAST PERFORMANCE

There is one last thing that happens when a show is closing. It happens in the very last performance and can be unsettling for the SM who has cared for the show as his or her own. Some actors make it a tradition to play little jokes or pranks on their fellow performers during the last performance. The SM who wishes to maintain the show to the very end must take a stand against this happening, even if the SM privately thinks the jokes are funny and are not harmful to the show. At the half-hour call of the final performance, the SM must express disapproval of this practice and remind the cast and the company of their professional obligations for performing the show as it has been set and as it has been playing throughout the run.

These little jokes and pranks start out simple. They are funny mostly among the cast members. For the most part they do not hurt the show, nor is the audience aware of them, but these things have a tendency to grow and escalate. People have a great inclination toward wanting to top the last joke, making the next one bigger and funnier. In its most outrageous form, some actors will forget about the show, the character they are playing, the audience, and direct the thrust of their performance toward the joke and entertaining their fellow actors.

The SM cannot prevent the actors from doing as they choose, but this little speech prohibiting jokes often diminishes the severity of the jokes and pranks. If the cast is particularly difficult or unruly, and it seems that things might get out of control, the SM

might remind everyone that there will be other shows on which the SM will be working and in which they might want to perform. It is not necessary to say any more than that. They will get the picture. (See the account written at the end of this chapter under The Professional Experience.)

THE EQUITY BOND

Upon signing an agreement with Equity and before anyone can be hired, the producer must put up a bond—the amount of which is determined by Equity. The bond is held until the show closes and is delayed in being returned to the producer until Equity is assured the producer has met all financial obligations to the contract and to the membership. Whatever money remains outstanding or that the producer neglects to pay, that amount is taken out of the bond. The SM has no dealing with this matter other than to report to the Equity deputy or the Equity office all the payments the SM knows of that are delinquent or remain outstanding.

DEPARTURE AND GOODBYES

Every show an SM works becomes an indelible part of that SM's life. In most cases, the work, responsibility, and obligation of the job became the center of the SM's life to the exclusion of some or all social life and relationships. No matter how hard an SM tries to keep a balance, the job and the show usually dominate. The SM who wants to be successful usually gives in. Good or bad, joyous or sorrowful, love-filled or hate-filled, the show and the company become the SM's child. Now it is time to close it and set it aside. Never again will this production, the performances, the relationships, and the feelings be duplicated. Most of the memories will fade, leaving in mind only the more extreme experiences.

People will depart and separate from the SM's life, perhaps never to work together again or see each other. Others will pop up unexpectedly. Still others will be like perennial flowers and show up in several shows on which the SM works. Some friendships will remain long after the production while others will be strong and flourishing only as long as the show lasts.

For the most part, the SM should keep goodbyes simple and personal, going to those people to whom the SM particularly wants to express sentiments. However, as a professional gesture or social grace, the SM should express general thanks and appreciation either over the PA system or in posting a note on the callboard. With a group that has been particularly near and dear, the SM might bring in a basket or tray of goodies, or some parting champagne for toasting and extending best wishes.

No show is a casual or passing event to an SM. Each and every show becomes a part of the SM's soul. Some shows go on to become history and that SM's name will forever be connected with that event. Some shows are like being with a family, while others are like being off to war. Some stage managers will continue their work in teaching, or perhaps write a book. Some stage managers will decide when they have had enough and will choose the time to stop, while others will have the time chosen for them. Some will be saddened by their departure from the work, while others will be glad to have only their memories.

THE PROFESSIONAL EXPERIENCE

I worked a touring show with a group of young professional actors. I had heard that for the last performance elaborate plans were being made to play jokes on each other. Throughout the time I was with the show, the cast displayed little respect toward the standards or codes of theatre and what was expected of them as professionals. This included a lack of respect for the position of the SM.

In hearing about the jokes that were being planned for the last performance, I became greatly concerned. From what I had experienced of this particular cast, I knew they were quite capable of great impropriety on the stage. I knew I could not stop them, but I took a strong stand and was very clear about my disapproval.

During the performance, things escalated. To top each other, the humor turned blue. One performer, who was playing a lead role, thought it would be funny to drop his pants and display his rear to the actress playing opposite him. He was wearing tights, so his act was not as revealing as one would think, but his intentions were lewd and not in the remotest way in character. I was extremely upset with this person. This was the final straw in our working relationship. Throughout our time together, he had been unruly, disrespectful, and uncontrollable. He had little regard for anything but himself, his immediate gratification, and drawing attention to himself, whether on stage or in his everyday life.

Immediately after the performance, and despite the fact that this was the last performance, I called the actor into my office. I told him I was making a report of his actions. I said I would also include in this report my experiences with him during the time we worked together. I said I was sending the report to Equity, with a copy being sent to the producer, and a copy being kept in my files. He was unimpressed and freely showed his disdain. I stated further that at any time I had the opportunity, I would freely, without solicitation, tell any producer, director, or casting person of his actions and my experience of him.

Only one time did I have the opportunity to tell of this actor's behavior, but it had no effect. He was hired anyway because he was fast becoming a performer who could sell tickets at the box office. This actor moved over to films and television, taking with him the same attitude and behaviors. He became one of Hollywood's bad boys, professionally as well as in his personal life. Eventually, his way of living and working caught up with him, and as soon as his name was no longer a draw on the marquee, producers were no longer willing to put up with him. When last heard of, he was playing dinner theatre and summer stock. Perhaps he has changed, or perhaps he has not, and is inflicting himself on some other SM.

19

In the Line of Fire

This chapter is included to give a complete picture of the professional experience. This story is based on one SM's experiences, but also includes a compilation of experiences from other shows. The details may be unique to this story and this SM, but the experiences can happen to any SM. Names of the people have been changed, and in most cases, things are described in general terms to keep this tale from sounding like tabloid journalism. As you travel through this adventure, take note not only of the things this SM goes through, but what things he may have contributed to the conflict.

PROLOGUE

Unlike in the Dickens tale—"It was the best of times. It was the worst of times"—for me, it was only the best of times. For five years I had been working for a top producing company with important talents from theater, film, and television. I had only one direction to travel and that was to Broadway. Up to this time, Broadway had eluded me. Every show that promised to take me there was either stillborn or died as we traveled the country in tryouts.

GETTING THE JOB

It was late February. I read in the trade papers that the producing company for which I had been stage managing was doing a remake of a very famous musical show which was originally produced on Broadway in the mid 1940s, and that Gaylord Channing was directing and choreographing and Vera Darling was starring. The article said the show would have a complete makeover, it would have a West Coast run, and then make its way across the country to Broadway. On reading such news, my heart raced with excitement. That was quickly followed with grave concern. Why had I not heard from the production company? In past years, by this time I had already talked to the office and

was assigned the shows I would be doing for the season. Some of my fears kicked in. Rather than stay with my feelings for too long, I decided to call the production office. I had a good relationship with Connie, the producer's secretary. She would fill me in.

Connie said I was on the producer's list for him to call, but in his usual fashion he was late and doing things at the last minute, or when they reached near crisis. Connie said she would have called me herself, but the producer made a point of wanting to talk with me personally. This concerned me even more, because in the past whatever conversations the producer needed to have with me were done through Connie. Connie put me on hold to see if the producer could talk to me now. She returned and said to wait by my phone, that he would get right back to me. I knew he wouldn't and he didn't. It wasn't until the first week in March that I heard from him.

By this time my desire to have the job was even greater and my anxiety level was rising. When I received the call it was Connie wanting to set up an appointment for the next day. I canceled or postponed whatever I had scheduled and made myself available.

From the start of our meeting I could see the producer was preoccupied. My heart sank. He was direct and his very first words were that he could not offer me the job of the Production Stage Manager, the PSM, on the Channing–Darling show. He said he had to give it to another stage manager who had been working for him for a much longer time. That was understandable. The person he chose was a friend and had been my mentor when I first started working for this producer. Before I could comment, the producer quickly went into a color commentary on the show, making it sound even more special, important, and enticing. He also said that because the show was going to be completely made over and because Mr. Channing and Miss Darling were known to be somewhat difficult and demanding, and because the show was heading to Broadway, he wanted to have his two strongest stage managers on the show. He wanted the ASM to be as experienced and capable as the PSM . . . and would I be interested in the ASM position?

Would I be interested? YES, I would be interested! I would have taken a job sweeping floors, if that's all there was. I of course did not respond with such candor and juvenile expression. I maintained my composure. I expressed my desire to work on the show and said that I would love working with my friend and mentor again. "There's only one problem," the producer interjected. There came another sinking of my heart. It seemed Mr. Channing had his own choice for the stage manager. He wanted his person as the PSM, but the producer was adamant in having a PSM he knew and trusted, someone who had worked for him before and knew would be loyal to him. Well, if Mr. Channing could not get his man on the show as the PSM, he was now insisting this person be hired as the ASM. The producer wanted double indemnity, having trust and loyalty from the ASM too. There came a stalemate and test of wills between Mr. Channing and the producer. However, the producer had a plan that had already begun even before I had accepted the ASM position.

Mr. Channing's man was in New York and the producer had purposely held off making a decision on him. Auditions were only five days away. The producer had conveniently sent his man (the PSM) out of town to troubleshoot on a show in San Francisco. It was not practical to bring out Gaylord's man at such short notice. The producer apologized to Mr. Channing for not making a decision sooner on the ASM position, but promised he would within the week. Meanwhile, he told Mr. Channing that I would temporarily take over and handle the auditions. The idea behind this maneuvering and posturing was to give Mr. Channing a chance to meet me, know me, and see how I worked. Well, it worked. I did my usual bang-up job. By the end of the auditions Mr. Channing had warmed up to my presence, was comfortable, and stopped hawking his man as the ASM. The office quickly signed me to the contract. I got the job and that ended that.

THE HONEYMOON

The stage management was told over and over by the production office that this was not going to be an easy show—that rehearsals would be four weeks of hell. I did not find it that way. While everyone around me complained, I was energized. Each day the rehearsals began at 10:00 A.M. The PSM and I usually got to the rehearsal hall by 9:00 A.M. Almost always, Gaylord and his assistant were already there working before any of the cast members arrived. Because Gaylord was both the choreographer and director, he had to divide his time between working on the dances and working on the scenes. The plan was to have the dancers come in at 10:00 A.M. and work with them until 1:30 P.M. At 1:30

P.M. the dancers were excused for an hour-and-a-half lunch while the principal performers came in to begin their work day. According to union agreement, the actors' work day was 8½ hours long. This meant that by 6:30 P.M. the people who had come in at 10:00 A.M. had to be excused, and the people who came in at 1:30 P.M. had to be excused for the day by 10:00 P.M.

With this kind of a schedule, our day was very long. Gaylord often missed lunch entirely or had his assistant get him a sandwich from the catering truck. The PSM and I brown-bagged our lunches. We staggered our breaks so someone was always with Gaylord, and went off into an empty rehearsal room or down to the office lounge. I never took more than a half-hour, because I was anxious to get back to watch Gaylord work. For our dinner break we either brown-bagged it again or had the PA bring in something. Gaylord did take the time for dinner. For us, there were always things to do. We welcomed the quiet time and usually got lots of quality work done.

By the time the actors were released at 10:00 P.M. and the by time we met with Gaylord and closed up the rehearsal hall, it was at least an hour later. Fortunately, I lived close to the rehearsal hall, so by midnight I was showered and in bed. I had no trouble sleeping.

The PSM and I dared not divide or stagger the time we came in each day so our workday could be shorter. We agreed, and the office encouraged, that we should both be at the rehearsal hall at all times. Gaylord was a man of many whims, needs, and changing moods. When he wanted something, he wanted it NOW! Within a moment, without any warning, he would change the rehearsal schedule, sometimes deciding to do something that had not even been scheduled. He would have the stage management call up performers and insist they come to the rehearsal within the hour—sooner, if possible.

In the first week of the rehearsals, Gaylord complained to the office that he was very dissatisfied with the stage managers; he hated the idea that one time the PSM worked the rehearsal room, then another time I worked it. The reason the PSM and I chose to work this way was so we could both learn the show, both have the experience of working directly with Gaylord, and if the truth be known, both have relief from the extreme tension of working the rehearsal room. Gaylord wanted only one SM to work the rehearsal room at all times. To look over at the SM's table and see a different face disturbed him, it broke his concentration. He told the production office that he wanted me to remain in the rehearsal hall, and have the PSM running around taking care of the business of the show and the company. The PSM was mortified at such a suggestion and refused, saying it was insanity to work in this way. All the points he argued seem to fall on deaf ears. The producer said he had to give Mr. Channing the best possible working environment he could, and if this was how Mr. Channing wanted to work, this was how it would be. This was one of those moments of defeat every stage manager experiences in a career. As for myself, I was secretly thrilled. I wanted to be with Gaylord, having a front row seat as he created, spun his brand of theatre magic, and exercised the genius for which he had received several Tony Awards. I of course concealed my delight. The PSM felt Gaylord favored me and that he was being treated as the assistant.

Working with Gaylord was like being on one of those loop-de-loop roller coaster rides for fourteen hours each day. I was younger then, resilient, eager to experience all that being a stage manager had to offer. On the other hand, the PSM was not as anxious to take that kind of a ride again. Each day after seeing the hoops through which I had to jump to do the job and keep Gaylord happy, he quickly become happy with the working arrangement. I was the perfect candidate to be with Gaylord. I worked very hard at being the perfect stage manager he wanted. I worked in textbook fashion. I was flexible and accommodating. I became quite adept at anticipating Gaylord's every need and mood. I kept the rehearsal room quiet and orderly, fending off any outside disturbances. I kept the actors in another room, having only those actors with whom Gaylord was working in the main rehearsal room. Without realizing it, I had stepped well past the bounds of giving service and became a servant. I was praised and commended for my work. Gaylord was pleased, too. In a rare moment of expression to the producer he said, "Those two guys you got down there are dynamite." The stage managers became the fair-haired boys and heroes of the production office.

ENTER MISS DARLING

Miss Darling was unable to be with us for the first three weeks of rehearsals because she was still out on the road doing another show. You would think Gaylord would have been upset not to have the star at rehearsals from the start. Instead he was quite pleased. One day when I expressed concern for Miss Darling's absence and all the work that had to be done with her in the last week of rehearsals, Gaylord laughed, "Don't worry about Vera Darling. She'll have it down quicker than you can write it in your script." Then he added in confidence, "I'd just as soon get her in the last week, than have her in my hair all this time while working on the show." I was taken back by the change in his tone of voice.

Because of Vera's absence, the book part of the show suffered greatly. Gaylord spent hardly any time on the script, devoting most of his time to the choreography and staging of musical numbers. Vera's under-

study filled in. "We'll concentrate on the book after Vera gets here," Gaylord promised. Many of the principal performers expressed among themselves and to the stage management their annoyance at Miss Darling's absence. They were careful, however, not to reveal their feelings to Gaylord.

It was Monday, the beginning of the fourth week of rehearsals. Miss Darling was expected at noon to meet everyone, get settled in, and be ready to begin work with Gaylord at 1:30 P.M., while the dancers were at lunch. This was the day we had all waited for with great excitement and anticipation; that is, everyone except Gaylord, who said earlier that morning, "The whole morning's gonna be lost with her taking over and distracting everyone."

We had heard some inside, industry nightmare stories about Miss Darling. The production office kept saying to the stage managers, "Be sure you guys are pulled together. Have as much done as possible. If you think Gaylord Channing is a handful, wait until Vera Darling gets here!"

By this time, a second assistant stage manager had been chosen. She had been hired as a pit singer, so she had enough free time to aid us in our work. Both the PSM and I had worked with her before and we were glad to have her. The producer quickly gave his blessings for our choice. He felt Miss Darling would be pleased to have a female representative on the stage management staff.

Gaylord too was concerned about Vera. He had us set aside a rehearsal room just for her. "Put her someplace where she can hold court," he said with disdain. He also ordered that when he was not working with her, we had to keep her out of the rehearsal room and keep her busy working with other things. "Have a phone put in her room and under no circumstances is she to use the production phone in the rehearsal room. In fact hide it! Put it in your briefcase if you have to."

By 12:20 P.M. Vera had not yet arrived. The PSM called her at home. Her secretary said they were running late and were just leaving. Gaylord was not at all surprised and kept rehearsing. By 1:30 P.M. she still had not arrived. The dancers were excused for lunch and we began work with the principal performers.

At about 1:55 P.M. I accidentally ran into Vera and her entourage as they were wandering the halls, looking for the rehearsal hall. Six of them, all carrying packages, bags, and bundles. At first I did not know it was she. She was unrecognizably dressed in a turban, dark sun glasses, tailored slacks, a rag-like scarf wrapped several times around to protect her throat, and a tattered, green, bulky knit, cardigan sweater, revealing years of use. She carried a Gucci shopping bag that also showed years of use, a personal-size Igloo ice cooler, and a brown paper sack with snacks and goodies from a local supermarket. Over her shoulder was a tote bag containing Tiger, a miniature breed dog with lots of hair.

I recognized first the flaming red wig on the wig-block, dressed in the famous Vera Darling style. It was being carried, carefully, and ceremoniously, by her hair dresser, Daisy. Daisy was a large, buxom, impressive woman whose rolling walk demanded you step aside, unless you were willing to be trampled. "Miss Darling?" I said with a giant question mark, and then introduced myself. She was glad to see me and without delay or formality, unloaded her baggage onto me— Tiger remained with her. As we traveled down the hall she chatted as if we had been friends for a long time. Once in her personal rehearsal room, she was pleased with many of the comforts and perks the producer had set up for her. Within a short time of meeting Vera, I was charmed and enchanted. I was certain that whatever nightmare stories I had heard were just theatre stories blown out of proportion.

Vera was anxious to see Gaylord and the "kids" as she called them. She wanted to "pop" into the rehearsal room. "NO," I said with alarm, but then calmly added, "Gaylord's in the middle of working on one of the numbers in the show. Everyone's anxious to see you and meet you. If you walk in now everyone will loose concentration. You know how Gaylord is about rehearsals." "You're absolutely right," Vera said as she touched my arm warmly in a friendly gesture. "Don't tell me about Gaylord! I know him all too well." "Why don't you get settled in and when Gaylord is finished, we'll come to get you," I said as I was leaving the room. "Great," she called out.

I left Vera and entered the main rehearsal room. Gaylord looked up angrily, as he always did whenever someone entered the room. As I passed him, he said half under his breath and from out of the corner of his mouth, "Is she here yet?" "Yes," I responded in somewhat the same under-the-breath manner, and Gaylord continued to rehearse. On several occasions, when it was apparent Gaylord was through with a segment of his work, I asked if I should go and get Vera. "No!" he would reply and continue to work, going to something new. Meanwhile, Vera was becoming inpatient. She sent in Daisy several times to find out what was taking so long.

This sort of thing went on for over three hours. Finally at 5:45 P.M., Gaylord turned to me and said, "Go get her," and he left the room for what I thought was one of his many trips to the bathroom. I sent the second ASM to get Miss Darling. The assistant returned and we sat and waited. Just when our waiting was becoming awkward and our patience began running short, the doors to the rehearsal room flung open and in walked Vera! She made a Western-type cattle call, "YEEEEE-HA!!!!!", threw the short end of her scarf over her shoulder, took a cheesecake pose, and said in

her best Zsa Zsa Gabor impersonation, "Darlings!" She was as clownish and crazy as we had all seen her on TV and in the movies. It was a thrill to see her in person and performing for us. We roared with laughter and applauded as she now dipped and strutted across the floor like Norma Desmond in *Sunset Boulevard*, stopping in the middle of the rehearsal room where she held court. Vera knew her audience and how to work the room. She disappointed no one. She greeted everyone and personalized her conversation with a comment, joke, or quick story. She charmed and captivated us all.

About a half-hour later, Gaylord returned in just enough time to perform his greeting and reunion with Vera. Gaylord also knew how to work his audience. He was witty, charming, and had impeccable timing in his dialogue and delivery. This was a side of him we seldom saw in rehearsals. My PSM friend was most amused as he watched. "A play within a play," he said. "Isn't it interesting how Gaylord waited until forty-five minutes before sending the dancer's home before he had Vera come in? And isn't it interesting how he disappeared for her entrance, but then made one of his own? I guarantee you there will be more to come." None of this was apparent to me. I felt my friend was jaded in his observations. I did not hear his words coming from wisdom and experience.

THE HONEYMOON IS OVER

Little by little, all that the PSM, myself, and the second ASM had built in our working relationship with Gaylord slowly disintegrated. It was a process of which we were not aware until we were in the middle of it all. The last week of rehearsals became harder than the first three weeks combined. There was just too much to do and the pressure was on to get it done, because in the following week we were scheduled to move into the theatre to start technical rehearsals. Gaylord tried postponing techs, but the producer held fast. The producer stood to lose too much money if the delay was even for a day. Fortunately, the technical rehearsals were scheduled for two full weeks and not the abbreviated ten days that producers prefer having.

The production office was right. Vera was a handful. All three stage managers were like acrobats and jugglers, trying to keep both her and Gaylord serviced and happy. The script was a major problem for Gaylord. Now that Vera was at rehearsals and they were working on it full-time, Gaylord felt the dialogue was antiquated, and he continually arranged and rearranged scenes and their order. This created a lot of work for the stage management, but fortunately, Gaylord's assistant helped, too.

Vera, just by being Vera, could set off Gaylord into moods or fits of anger. On one of the day's rehearsals, it was Vera's birthday. At different times, she had no less than three cakes brought in to the rehearsal room as a surprise to her. Upon arrival of the third cake, I insisted it be brought into her room and she be surprised there, but Daisy intervened and said Vera would be very upset if she couldn't share this cake too with everyone. Upon entry of this cake, Gaylord angrily looked over at me, holding me responsible for the interruption. He threw his hands up in the air and left.

Vera loved having long, drawn-out conversations about character, motivation, dialogue, or the timing of acting moments. This drove Gaylord mad. His patience and temper grew even shorter. He attacked whoever happened to be in his line of sight. His assistant caught the brunt of most things. Once or twice I came in the line of fire, and when it happened my confidence was shaken. Thanks to the PSM and the production office, I was reassured and sent back into combat.

In this last week at the rehearsal hall, and especially in the last two or three days, people's tempers in all departments were beginning to flare. They needed to have information, and wanted answers so they could be prepared for the technical rehearsals—answers that only Gaylord could give. Gaylord continually put them off saying that if he didn't get this part of the show done, there would be no show at all.

The costume people needed to have Vera for fittings, but Gaylord would not release her from the rehearsals. He wanted her to go after hours. Vera refused. She was too tired after rehearsals. We had the costume people set up a little alteration shop in a storage closet down the hall from the rehearsal room, and every chance they got, they had Vera in with them stitching, pinning, fitting, and even redesigning.

You could feel the tension and fear from the production office, too. One morning, just as we were beginning rehearsals, the producer came down to the rehearsal room, something he never did. He stuck his head in the door and motioned for me to join him in the hallway. He spent the next few minutes telling me how I needed to be more in charge and take greater control of the rehearsal. He said that whenever I saw Gaylord and Vera getting into one of their drawn-out conversations or about to get into some conflict, I needed to step in and get the rehearsal back on track. As a stage manager, I had learned to do that, and in other shows I did it. Gaylord and Vera were something else. The few times I tried getting the rehearsal back on track, they glared at me, then continued as they chose. I felt highly responsible to the producer, but felt helpless in doing as he instructed. I also felt it was unfair of him to transfer the responsibility for Gaylord's and Vera's behavior to the stage manager. They were professionals and should have remained responsible for

their own actions. That sense of enjoyment and pleasure I once had for working on this show and working with Gaylord and Vera was fading fast.

TECHNICAL REHEARSALS

Technical rehearsals came much too soon. We needed at least another week. Before I knew it, we were closing out the rehearsal hall, and I was driving up to San Francisco where we would do our techs, have previews, and have a tryout run before returning to L.A. Fortunately, the PSM was on top of all that needed to be done in leaving the rehearsal hall, while I continued to work with Gaylord without interruption. From our perspective, the stage managers were prepared. The same could not be said for some of the technical departments. Once we got into techs, I felt a sense of relief. The PSM was now in full charge, and I was there as the ASM.

The show was technically very difficult. The set was new and innovative in design. It had many mechanical kinks to work out. The opening scene alone took a great amount of time. The scene started with an empty stage, with just a backdrop and some portals. Then as the show began, the stage grew and filled with sets, props, lights, and people. It was a signature trademark of Gaylord's directing and staging. The cues were monumental for the PSM and I was glad just to be the ASM. I knew, however, later I would have to learn to call this sequence. I watched as it developed and was set.

In addition to all our internal problems, the theatre at which we were working had just been renovated from a movie house to a legitimate theatre. We were the first show to perform there. There were problems with some of the equipment installed in the backstage, which caused further delay or setbacks.

The stage manager's console was set up on stage right. The PSM instructed me to work from stage left and remain free to troubleshoot and facilitate wherever I was needed and most of all to keep him informed and apprised of all things. Whenever there was a problem on stage, I was the SM to step out on the stage to oversee and facilitate. This increased my visibility to Gaylord, who sat in the darkened theatre at the production table, and put me in the direct line of fire. Whenever Gaylord became dissatisfied or unhappy about something on stage he would call out my name over the god-mic, his voice resounding throughout the theatre. At first I did not mind being put in this position because I was being very helpful to the PSM. As I took care of the problems on stage the PSM was able to use the time to put cues in his cueing script and rewrite some of the ones that had already been set. However, as time grew short in the techs, Gaylord's fears turned into anger, and I became the object of all his ill feelings. He was merciless, attacking with ferocity, vengeance, venom, anything he could use to get out his frustrations.

For the most part, stage managers learn to develop a thick skin, ignoring this kind of behavior from directors, and taking the abuse. I did quite well—for a while. While I was growing up I learned to be highly assertive and express whatever was bothering me. I sometimes did it aggressively, so I had to learn to keep that in check. In addition to all that I was experiencing from Gaylord, I was also feeling alone. The producer and PSM had their own problems, worries, and insecurities. They no longer had time to acknowledge my work or assure me my work still pleased them.

My skin was only so thick and the control I maintained over my aggressive behavior could hold out for only so long. With the next outburst and tirade aimed at me from Gaylord, I stood my ground at the apron of the stage, and told him exactly what I thought. When I was through I felt justified and relieved. I left the theatre for a while to clear my head. As my anger subsided, a new set of thoughts and feelings settled in. What I had just done was not the thing to do. I felt I had broken a rule or code of being a stage manager. When I returned, I felt even more alone. No one came to console me. Some looked away, others talked of other things. The PSM didn't even ask where I had been for the past hour. In that moment of outburst at Gaylord, I had weakened myself as an SM. My action had no effect on Gaylord. He continued to work as he had been, finding someone to receive his abusive behavior. I did not, however, learn the lesson of this experience until after I left the show and had time to reflect more clearly.

That evening after rehearsals, at the local bar just outside the theatre, I did have a moment of consolation. It was what I needed and it came from Vera herself. "Sweetie, don't let Gaylord get to you. He thrives on that kind of stuff. It gives him power over you. He likes to find peoples' weaknesses, then see them squirm. The man's under a lot of pressure right now. He hasn't had a hit in years, and this show's gotta do it for him. Me, if it doesn't work, I can go back on the road." Then she added in confidence, "You know, I was the one who got him this job. No one would hire him. He's the right person for this show and I wouldn't do it unless he directed it. He's brilliant, but he's a nutcase. I just let him rage and carry on. Then when he's through, I do what I want anyway." I could not have been more consoled, and having it come from Vera Darling herself had even greater impact. We had a drink together and began a social friendship.

The closer we got to preview performance the stormier techs became. Battles and skirmishes flared up everywhere. There wasn't one person or one department who did not come under Gaylord's fire. During the quiet times, when everyone was out on meal break and the PSM and I remained to complete work, we would see Gaylord pensively walking the stage, solemn and glum. Darkness hung over him. His eyes were at times filled with storm and fury. Other times they were sorrowful and filled with fear. He would move about the set or sit on the prop bench. Sometimes he would do a step from one of the dances he had created, and other times he would measure out the performance space by taking long strides and counting the steps he took.

One could not help but feel for the man. Usually I went about my business and gave him his private time. One time, however, I tried making contact. I wanted to try and get back some of what we'd had in early days of rehearsals. I approached him and clumsily expressed myself. He listened and with dark eyes he stared at me. Then with hardness and powerful directness, he said, "Have more concern for your job and you'll be better off in this business." His words were crushing. I retreated like a wounded child. Later that evening after rehearsals, I was able to bounce back with more support from Vera over drinks. What I did not know at the time was that Gaylord's words were words of great wisdom and advice. I believe he was expressing the nature of the business and how as an SM I could be eaten alive if I didn't take care of myself. Instead, I took his words at face value, in the context of our present relationship.

THE SAN FRANCISCO TRYOUT

As expected, the technical rehearsal time was not nearly enough. The preview performances were upon us. Everyone swore it could not be done and predicted disaster for that first performance. It was amazing how smoothly everything went. There were glitches, but few were revealed to the audience. In preparation for any possible mistakes, just before the rise of the curtain for each preview performance, Vera would slip out on the apron of the stage to greet the audience. Within seconds she had them all charmed. Then, just before she left the stage, she would remind the audience that this was a preview by making a joke about the discounted prices they paid for their tickets, and how she needed the money. She'd add that the show was still being prepared for Broadway and that we were a work in progress, which allowed us to make mistakes or even stop the show if we had to. Of course we never stopped the show and with each performance the mistakes were fewer and fewer.

We were indeed a work in progress. The show changed daily. We'd rehearse all day, then perform the show at night with the changes. As stage managers, our day began at the theatre at 10:00 A.M. and lasted to about midnight, sometimes until 1:00 A.M., especially when we had to meet with Gaylord after the show. My day started even earlier. Most mornings, I would meet Vera and a small contingency of her entourage at the coffee shop to have breakfast and go over schedule, script changes, or just generally socialize—which really consisted of Vera telling old show-biz war stories.

The show finally opened. The evening was a gala event. It was heavily covered by the San Francisco press. The press, however, was asked not to review the show until the second or third week of our run. They were most accommodating and waited. They wrote articles on us, repeating Vera's words that we were a work in progress. Gaylord stayed with us for one more week, then left us for three weeks. His plan was to give everyone a rest, let the show play, and then when he returned he would make whatever changes were necessary.

Normally, within the second week of any show, the ASM begins learning and calling the cues for the show. With this show, the PSM decided it would be best if we waited until after we opened in L.A. "Let's not give Gaylord anything more to pick on," he said. It was okay with me! We had a long run ahead of us and there would be plenty of time to call the show. Besides, I was still busy backstage overseeing and troubleshooting.

THE PSM's TURN

In the third week Gaylord returned. Surprisingly, it was nice to have him back. He was rested and a lot more civil—for a few days anyway. The changes he made in the show were neither as many nor as great as we thought they would be. Once again, we rehearsed every day and performed every night. On matinee days he had the cast come in an hour earlier just to give notes.

Each night before the cast leaves the theatre, and if there is to be a rehearsal for the next day, the stage manager is required by Equity to have posted the rehearsal call. Management is required to give the cast twelve hours' notice. If the rehearsal is being called by the director, it is a common practice for the stage manager to get the schedule from the director during intermission and post the notice sometime during the second act. Sometimes we'd see Gaylord during intermission and he would give us the schedule, but other times he would not show up backstage until after the performance. During the times we did not see him, the cast would have to wait until we got the information. Of course we preferred getting and posting the information early and not making the cast wait.

On one particular evening the PSM saw Gaylord backstage during intermission, giving the actors notes.

For whatever reason, Gaylord was in one of his moods. When the PSM asked him for the rehearsal schedule, Gaylord snapped, "How can I give you a the rehearsal call when I haven't seen the rest of the show?" The PSM, caught off guard, retorted, "The same as you have any other night since previews. You know the Equity rule!" With a few profane expletives, Gaylord told us what he thought of Equity and disappeared somewhere backstage.

To keep the cast informed, to prepare them to wait after the performance, and to keep them from coming to us and asking what the schedule was, before the intermission was over, the PSM posted a notice on the callboard saying there would be a rehearsal for the next day, but we would get the information after the performance. The PSM posted the notice, called places and was ready to start the second act, when all of a sudden we saw Gaylord coming across the stage toward the stage manager's console at a very quick pace. He had crumpled in his hand the PSM's notice. "How dare you overstep my authority! I had already told the kids there would be no rehearsal tomorrow!" The PSM, being a person of greater presence and experience than myself, allowed Gaylord to rave. When the PSM decided he'd had all he could take, he asked Gaylord to leave the backstage so that he could start the show. Gaylord became even more enraged. The PSM ignored him and went about his business. Gaylord left. Before the PSM brought up the curtain for the second act, he called me over to his console and said, "Stand by me and start learning the show. By the end of this week, I am out of here!"

The PSM turned in his notice that very night. Next morning I was called early and told to be in the producer's office at 9:00 sharp. I was worried. As much as I liked being a PSM, I did not want to be one on this show. To my great relief, the producer talked the PSM out of quitting. He thanked us both for doing a job above and beyond what a stage manager should endure. He jokingly added, "I told you it was going to be hell. That's why I wanted you two guys."

VERA'S MADNESS

The reviews came out. Generally they complimented Gaylord's work but were extremely hard on Vera. Their greatest complaint was that she was too old for the part. Vera swore she did not read reviews, but from that point, she changed. The critics hit a tender spot. Vera loved being the senior member of the group she had gathered around her. It was okay for her to make jokes about her age, but she got angry when someone else even approached the subject. On official documents she only included the month and day of her birth, never the year.

By the time the reviews came out, Gaylord was back in New York, scheduled to return the week before we were to go to Los Angeles. During this time Vera became isolated from everyone except for Daisy and Frank, Vera's hairdresser and driver. They were now her constant companions. Practically everyone had to go through them to get to Vera. My breakfast meetings with Vera were cut off. Daisy said Miss Darling was tired and wanted to sleep in mornings.

Vera found fault with everything. She complained that the ensemble performers were unprofessional. They upstaged and distracted her. Her costumes, which were once acceptable, were now wretched and she wanted all new ones. The designer had to be flown in to appease her and redo many of them. Vera said some of the principal performers had changed their parts and wanted the stage management to rehearse them back to the way Gaylord had directed them. When we watched the performances, when we approached the actors, and when we checked our blocking notes, very little change had occurred—certainly not enough to call a rehearsal. We reported our findings to Vera and she became irate. She lashed out at the PSM, "Don't tell me what I see on stage. I didn't start in this business yesterday!" Any messages Vera had for the stage managers were now verbally delivered by Daisy. Before each performance we'd see Daisy steam rolling across the stage. We nicknamed her The Sherman Tank. Daisy thrived on this part of her job. She delivered the messages with relish, great authority, and with a righteous air.

No area went untouched by Vera. She now set her sights on the lighting of the show. In a note to the stage managers, which was of course delivered by Daisy, Vera said the blue night lights in the night scene made her look sick and haggard. She wanted more pink light on stage. Adding pink light would destroy the night effect the lighting designer had created and the director wanted. The PSM went to Vera's dressing room and assured her that although the lights on stage were blue, she was in a soft lavender spotlight and the brightness of the spotlight overrode the blue lights on stage. Again she attacked. "Blue lights and green lights are murder on flesh tones. I don't care how many lavender spotlights you have on me!" Her suggestion was that the stage manager have some of the ensemble performers come on stage with lanterns, which would give a reason to bring up more pink light on stage. The PSM brought the suggestion to the lighting designer and the designer refused. However, in a few days we saw the prop man coming in with six lanterns and the head electrician informed the PSM that by order of the producer, a new light cue, bringing up pink light, had been added to the show.

The conductor of the orchestra was next to come under fire. During one of the performances, as sometimes happens, the conductor accelerated the speed and tempo of the big dance number in the second act, which ran almost eight minutes and in which Vera danced almost all of that time. Even the dancers came off huffing and puffing that night. The conductor acknowledged his mistake and before the next performance he went around to everyone and personally apologized. The man was an experienced and excellent conductor, having conducted many shows on Broadway, and he was usually very consistent in his work. When he approached Vera's dressing room, she refused to see him, saying she had to get ready for the show. Within a few days the conductor was gone and a music director with whom Vera had worked on other shows took over.

Vera was on a mission. She was determined to save the show and insisted on many changes. She changed her part considerably, much of which was in direct opposition to Gaylord's direction. By this time the producer had returned to Los Angeles, but the PSM kept him informed with daily calls. Generally, there seemed to be a lack of response to anything the PSM reported to the production office. It was as if someone had proclaimed a hands-off policy, and Vera was free to do as she chose.

LAST WEEK IN SAN FRANCISCO

Once again, as planned, Gaylord returned in the last week of San Francisco to prepare us for our run in Los Angeles. On the first evening of his return he saw the performance. We did not see him at intermission. When he came backstage after the performance he passed the stage manager's console without stopping, but saying on the run, "Take out all those ridiculous lanterns in the night scene and put the lights back to the way I had them!" He streaked across the stage, going directly to Vera's dressing room. He ordered everyone out, even Vera's guests who had come to see the performance that night. For the next two hours he and Vera went at it, head to head. We could not hear what was being said, but there was a lot of yelling. Daisy stayed glued to the door, straining to hear. At one point she tried entering the room and we heard Gaylord yell, "GET OUT!" Daisy sent the rest of the entourage home. Only she and Frank remained. The PSM and I stayed a while longer, but then we left, too. Next day we got a full account from the doorman who said he ended up leaving at 1:00 A.M. after everyone left.

Next day was matinee day, so there was no rehearsal, but for the rest of the week, on every day we could, we rehearsed. Each day Gaylord had the principal performers come in along with Vera's understudy. He would make his changes, usually bringing the show back to the way he had directed it. Then around

4:00 P.M. he had Vera come in. Between the understudy and the stage managers, Vera was given the changes, while Gaylord disappeared during that time. He would return with just enough time to run Vera and the actors through the changes and disappear again, leaving Vera and the cast to the stage managers to dismiss.

THE LOS ANGELES RUN

Moving the show to Los Angeles was like starting technical rehearsals all over, but only in a more consolidated fashion. Gaylord rehearsed the cast at the rehearsal hall while the crew set up the show at the theatre. Once all the technical elements were set up, the cast moved to the theatre and we went into technical rehearsals for two days.

The opening in L.A. was gala, but not the event it was in S.F. Generally, the show received better reviews. Vera was complimented on parts of her performance, but her age continued to be an issue. However, we did not think the opening performance would even take place. Vera came in that afternoon wrapped in a winter coat, speaking in hushed tones and whispers, pantomiming much of her conversation, and practically turned her dressing room into a hospital. She said, or rather Daisy said, that Vera had a throat infection and she was under the doctor's care. Gaylord was the only one who showed little concern, "I've yet to see Miss Vera miss a performance, let alone an opening night." An hour before the half-hour call, the doctor came with his magic medicine, and shortly after he left Daisy came out to announce that Vera would be performing that night but that before the overture began, Vera wanted to make a curtain speech to the audience.

Vera was simple and effective. She told the audience she had been sick all day and that if in the musical numbers she brayed like a mule to please forgive her. In her sincerest voice, with perhaps a tear in her eye, she said that she had never missed a performance, and she didn't want to disappoint the wonderful people who had come tonight (she got generous applause). She thanked the audience for their support and added, "If you are dissatisfied, PLEASE, tell the lovely people at the box office, and your money will be refunded or you can come back another time as my personal guest" (bigger applause, with a few whistles and a catcall of, "Thata girl, Vera!").

In the truest tradition of the theatre, the show went on. Vera performed beautifully. In her first song she was shaky, just enough to make us all nervous. In the reprise, she cracked, but went on to the big finish. By the third song, the symptoms of her illness were all but gone. In the big dance number in the second act, she sang and danced with magnificent energy and spirit. At the end of the scene, the audience cheered and applauded longer than they ever had for this number. Backstage, the cast members surrounded Vera, congratulating her as Daisy intervened and whisked Vera off for her costume for the final scene.

During the last scene of the performance that night, whoever was not on stage, watched from the wings. This was the stuff of which drama was made. The applause that night warranted six extra curtain bows. We were all certain we had a hit on our hands and we were ready to settle in for an extended tour across the country, then a long run on Broadway. The opening night party was the most exciting I had ever attended. Vera, being fashionably late, made an entrance more grand and more spectacular than I had ever seen. Gaylord did not attend.

The next day the story of Vera's illness was in the trade papers and in all the city newspapers. Even the tabloids, within the week, carried a twisted and somewhat perverted story on the event. That evening, Vera once again came to the theatre wrapped in winter clothing and was back to whispering. Once again the good doctor came, and once again after the doctor left Daisy announced to the stage managers that Miss Darling would perform, adding that Miss Darling wanted to give her curtain speech again. Almost word for word, Vera repeated her speech from the night before. In fact she repeated her whole performance. She was shaky in her first song, cracked in the reprise, and went on to the big finish. She was as spirited in the big dance number in the second act, but this time for the final scene, there weren't as many people backstage watching from the wings. Vera continued for almost a week making her preshow curtain speech, even after the doctor stopped coming and she no longer had to whisper when she talked.

SPIRALING DOWNWARD

After the opening in LA, the quality of life backstage became less stormy. Gaylord was back in New York and whatever problems Vera had, the producer was close at hand and dealt with them daily. All their business was done behind closed doors and that was a relief to the rest of the company. We knew there was unrest with our star, but we all slipped into complacency, secretly hoping the past was behind us and it would be smooth sailing from here on. Well, it wasn't! Problems in every area popped up. The stage management had its share.

Throughout my career, I have experienced that the stage manager is expected to be perfect in the job in all ways and at all times. I don't believe I have imagined this about stage managers. I got this view from the way peers, associates, and superiors reacted each time a stage manager made a mistake. They seemed intolerant, showed little forgiveness, or displayed little understanding or compassion.

In a less-complicated production, the stage manager's continuous perfection is easily achieved. In a show, especially in a musical, or in a musical Gaylord directs, expectations for sustained perfection are unreasonable and are not humanly possible. The stage manager is going to make mistakes. However, in my drive to do my best, I did not take into account the degree of difficulty of the show. When I started calling the cues for the performances, my expectations for perfection were even higher than others expected of me. That became a calling card for unhappiness and eventually disaster. I had my share of imperfection.

THE HA! CUE

Being a master at his craft and art, and creative and innovative too, Gaylord knew how to create magic and illusion in the theatre. Being a choreographer, he was very much aware of timing, counts, and intricate moves. He loved doing set changes in view of the audience. He loved building the stage from nothing into something, as he did with the opening. For a stage manager, calling cues for one of Gaylord's shows was like conducting a symphony. It demanded perfect timing and most times any mistakes became magnified and glaring.

In the first big dance number of the show, Gaylord once again started with an empty stage. Vera, as the character she was portraying, was alone on the stage silhouetted against a cyc, which was lit in blue and filled the back part of the stage. From behind the stage right proscenium a hand pops out (spotlight pickup), and a finger beckons Vera. Vera takes the hand and for the next thirty-seven counts of music a line of dancers appears, one by one, dressed in characters that were in the mind of Vera's character and imagination. The number built beautifully, and was a major contribution to this new version of the show. From the start all of us in the company loved the number. I was thrilled to see it being created, growing, and developing before my very eyes in rehearsals. I was certain I was witnessing theatre history. We were all sure it would become as famous as the "mirror" dance in *A Chorus Line*, the "small house of Uncle Thomas" production number from *The King and I*, or the "dance at the gym" in *West Side Story*.

On the thirty-seventh count, when all the dancers/characters were out on the stage, everyone was directed to say "Ha!" in a soft whisper, and at the same time the stage manager was directed to call a light cue that popped on a change of lights. For everyone this became the "Ha! Cue." Simple enough? Sounds like it should be, but it wasn't. Both the PSM and myself had

a very difficult time calling this cue with the perfection and timing Gaylord wanted. Without going into a lot of explanation and excuse making, let it be sufficient to say that the cue was problematic for the stage managers and a sore point for both Gaylord and Vera. One day Vera asked me, "Are you ever going to get the 'Ha Cue' right?" I apologized and tried to explain. She was not open to anything I had to say. Her only comment was, "Well, it certainly does not help the show." I felt even worse than I had. It wasn't until the second week in our L.A. run that I finally stumbled upon the right timing. When it happened and the light on stage popped on at the perfect moment, Vera did one of her famous, clownish double-takes. The audience laughed and applauded. Each performance thereafter, Vera reacted to the light coming on, but it never played as spontaneously or got nearly the same audience reaction.

THE CURTAIN BOWS

While in preview performances in S.F., it was decided that if there were to be additional curtain bows after those that had been set by Gaylord, Vera would be in control (and not the stage managers as is usually the case). Vera was to signal the stage manager to bring up the curtain for the additional bows. Although this was an established plan, it was never executed because the bows set by Gaylord were extensive, and after they were taken the applause did not warrant more bows. Generally the plan was forgotten. However, on one particular night, one or two days after Vera and Gaylord had their big blowout in her dressing room, Vera decided to exercise her option to take additional bows.

Unfortunately, I was calling the show that evening. The applause was barely strong enough to carry through the bows Gaylord had set, let alone any extra bows. After I called what I thought was our final bow, I called the cue for the house curtain to come in and for the house lights to come up. Seeing the house lights was the conductor's cue to begin the exit music. On this night Vera signaled to me for the extra bows. I did not see her and was already making notes in the stage manager's log. When Vera heard the music, she came storming off stage to the stage manager's console. "Didn't you see me signal you for extra bows?" "No. In all this time we have never taken extra bows. Truthfully, I had forgotten all about it!" "You're supposed to be a professional. You're suppose to do what the director sets, not what you decide," and she stormed off to her dressing room, with Daisy close behind. About ten minutes later, Gaylord came storming across the stage toward the stage manager's console. Even before he reached me at the console, he started shouting, "DON'T YOU EVER change something that I have set. When a star of Miss Darling's standing wants to take an extra curtain bow, YOU GIVE IT TO HER!" and he too stormed away.

There I stood, totally perplexed. I thought to myself, "Have I gone mad? Where did I go wrong? How did this become my fault?" I told the PSM of the incident. I was left with the impression he was glad it did not happen to him. He gave no support or consolation. He just warned me to watch for Vera's signal. From that evening on, Vera never again signaled to take extra bows, even on opening night in Los Angeles.

Several years later while on a sound stage in Hollywood, I was visiting one of the principal performers who had been in the show. He was now starring in his own TV series. As we recalled the incident, he said, "Don't you know what was going on back then? You were a pawn in a vicious fight between Vera and Gaylord. If you remember, that was right after Gaylord and Vera had their big blowout. Vera was now getting back at Gaylord. This was one of the ways she could show him that she was still in control, by taking extra bows." "But why did Gaylord come down so hard on me? I would have thought he would have at least understood," I asked with the same perplexed feelings I had back then. My friend smiled and said, "Foolish boy! His reaction was all for show. To make things look better between him and Vera and to show he still supported her."

THE PORTRAIT CUE

For this next incident I take full responsibility. I had become distracted at the moment the cue should have been called. There is a Murphy-like law for stage managers when calling cues during an extended run of a show: The cues that are easy become hard, and the hard cues become easy. The hard cues become easy because the SM studies them and becomes concentrated and stays focused when they come up in the performance. With an easy cue, the stage manager is confident from the start and during the run of the show becomes too comfortable. Thus the cue can be missed. The portrait cue was one of those cues for me.

The portrait cue came in that part of the show where Vera stood under a ten-foot portrait of her character and sang a very moving and poignant song. The number was simply staged. The lights were dimmed part way with a glow on the portrait, while Vera stood in a soft pink spotlight.

Just prior to the cue, I had become momentarily distracted. When I looked out on the stage, I wondered why the stage felt and looked so different. Then it hit me—THE LIGHTS! THE CUE! My heart sank. My mind raced wildly. What should I do? Should I have the light board operator manually bring up the cue

slowly. No, that would distract Vera. Leave it alone—keep it simple. The cue being missing does not hurt the play. The audience will never know there was supposed to be a light change there. So I made the decision not to have the cue executed, and said to the light board operators over my headset, "Guys, I missed the cue. We won't bring it up now, we'll just move on to the next cue when the time comes."

The missing light cue did not seem to affect Vera or her performance. I had hoped she might not have been aware of it what with the bright spotlight shining in her eyes. I should have known better. During intermission, Daisy came steamrolling across the stage. She delivered the message full out. She made no effort to temper her words or the feelings she expressed on Vera's behalf. I felt absolutely awful. I didn't want this to ruin the rest of Vera's performance. I thought if I went to her and apologized now, instead of waiting until after the show, it would relieve some of her anger. I went to Vera's dressing room. Daisy raced ahead of me. She opened the door to warn Vera. "I don't want to talk to him!" I heard Vera yell out. "How dare he come in the middle of my performance to talk about this. Isn't it bad enough he ruined the scene?"

THE CHICKEN CAPER

While in the middle of each event, each skirmish with Vera, it was like living through an earthquake. Things happened quickly and without warning. One moment I was going along doing my job perfectly, next moment my world was turned upside down. All I could do was try to get myself to a protected place and hold on. This next event had to do with a chicken's head.

In the play, Vera's character is required to shoot off the head of a metal, weathervane chicken, placed high above a set piece over on stage left. Of course we used blank ammunition, and of course the chicken's head was rigged to pop off, and of course this was a critical cue for the stage manager. It required exact timing to create the illusion that the chicken's head had indeed been shot off.

To get my best timing, each performance at this point in the show I would stand in the stage right wing to call this cue. From this vantage point, Vera was standing in profile to me and very close to the stage right wing. I could see clearly as she pulled the trigger. Just as she squeezed, I'd call the GO! part of the cue. This allowed enough time for the electrician to react, push the button that activated the solenoid, which in turned popped off the chicken's head. It was a fun moment for both me and the audience: for me, because I had perfect timing in calling this cue, and for the audience, because the illusion was so good. Of course Vera made the laugh even greater by her comic antics.

On this particular night, I stood in the wing as usual. As Vera squeezed the trigger, I called the GO!. The rifle fired, but the chicken's head did not pop off. All we could hear was the electrical buzzing sound of the solenoid, trying to free itself to make the chicken's head pop off. Vera, never expecting this to happen, gave a double-take. The audience went into hysterics. Both Vera and I were surprised. Of course Vera took full advantage of the moment and began ad-libbing as she cocked her rifle. The empty cartridge ejected from the rifle and landed on the stage floor. As Vera took aim, I warned the electrician to stand by to execute the cue again. Vera squeezed the trigger, and I called the GO!. The rifle fired, but still the chicken's head did not pop off. There was just the buzzing sound of the solenoid. This time Vera, as her character, pretended to be angry and determined to shoot the head off of this chicken. She shuffled her feet as a bull would just before he is ready to attack. She planted herself squarely into position and cocked the rifle. Another empty cartridge ejected onto the stage floor. She took aim, squeezed, and once again I called the GO! Still, the chicken's head did not pop off. Out of frustration and anger as the character, Vera threw her rifle aside, picked an empty cartridge from the stage floor, and threw it at the chicken. Just at that moment the chicken's head popped off. The show was stopped. Vera spent the next three or four minutes working the audience. At one point she came to the wing in which I was standing and pulled me out on to the stage, headset and all. In pantomime she indicated that it was my fault the chicken's head did not pop off. The audience loved this and applauded. Then with an Italian gesture of brushing the finger tips under her chin, which loosely translated means good-for-nothing, Vera sent me back off stage. It was taken in good fun and I thought nothing more of it.

Next morning in both of the trade papers and in the city newspapers, there was a story praising Vera's genius improvisation, and discrediting "a very forgetful stage manager." I didn't know it at the time, but Vera's manager had called the different papers, getting out the story for the publicity. I was annoyed that it made me look incompetent, but was not concerned because I was not mentioned by name, and the people who mattered, like my bosses, knew the real story. Two days later, in a radio interview, Vera told this story to the interviewer, but at the end she said, "The stage manager said that it was a mechanical error, but I think he forgot his cue."

I was flabbergasted, shocked, hurt, and angry. How could she possibly think that! The most inexperienced person in theatre would know that it was a mechanical error. I went to the theatre early that night to allow time to talk with Vera. When I questioned her on the matter she looked me directly in the eyes and coldly said, "Well honey, didn't you forget?" I was shocked even more. I asked if she saw me in the wing that night. I reasoned with her, saying, "Yes, I could have missed it one time, but certainly not a second and third time!" I asked if she heard the solenoid buzzing. None of that seemed to matter. Vera was convinced that the chicken's head not popping off was my mistake. Even sending the electrician to her dressing room made no difference. I could not understand her unreasonable behavior. I should have known at that time I was history. That Italian gesture meant more than good-for-nothing—it was "la bacca morte," "the kiss of death." I had two more scenes to play out before the fatal day.

THE PSM AND I

Things also happened when the PSM called the show. With the show being so technically difficult and the timing so critical, the PSM and I were always thankful to get through a performance without error. If there had to be error, we prayed it was hidden from both the audience and Vera.

Vera attacked the PSM, too, but she didn't seem to hold his mistakes against him with the same voracity. Also, it appeared that I made more mistakes because I called most of the shows during the week. Normally the PSM and the ASM share more equally the number of shows each calls during the week. On this show, once I learned the cues, the PSM only called one of the shows on the matinee days. This meant I was calling a show every day—six shows to the PSM's two. This of course gave me greater visibility to Vera and increased the chances that if an error was to take place, I was the stage manager doing the job.

THE FLOOD OF BLUE LIGHTS

This next episode was spread over three performances. To set up this next incident, we must go back to the night scene and those blue lights that Vera hated. At one point in the scene Vera goes through a door and behind a flat of scenery, as if she had gone into her bedroom. She continues the scene by yelling out dialogue from behind the flat, or popping her head through a cutout window in the flat. While doing all of this, Daisy and two dressers are also behind the flat, hidden from view of the audience, helping Vera to change into a formal and an elaborately dressed and styled wig for the next scene, the big dance number in the second act.

During each performance, when Vera left to go behind the scenery, I'd call, Cue #65. With this cue, whatever white light was on stage became lower, more blue night light was added, and the light around the window became brighter (yes, pink light), drawing the audience's attention to Vera as she popped her head in and out.

On this particular night, as the lights changed to Cue #65, the area just behind the flat, where Vera was getting dressed, became flooded with blue light. That would have not been so bad, because Vera was not modest. She had no problem if the crew or cast members saw her when she stripped down to her bra and pants, as she had to do in one other change in the wings during the show. This time, however, parts of the audience could see her—those who sat on the extreme sides. She had to huddle close to the back of the scenery so as not to be seen and at the same time continue her dialogue and get dressed.

These were the days before computer-operated light boards were used. This was a time when we were still using those large dimmer boards backstage, which required several stagehands to run. Chances of an extra switch, lever, or dimmer being brought up with a cue were greater, and in every long-running show, it happened at least once if not several times. This is part of the reason why stage managers make it a habit to watch the lights on stage as a light cue is being executed.

On this night, I saw the blue lights come up on Vera. Immediately, I called through my headset to the head electrician on the light board, "BLUE LIGHTS! You got some extra blue lights on the stage and they're flooding behind the flat where Vera is getting dressed!" The electrician checked all the settings of the dimmers and reported back, "We got no extra dimmers up back here. Every dimmer up, is supposed to be up!" Meanwhile, Vera, Daisy, and the dressers were waving their arms furiously to get my attention and pointing to the blue lights. I acknowledged them with a wave and continued my conversation with the head electrician. "I'm telling you, either you or one of your men has an extra dimmer up and Vera is having a fit!" The electrician checked again and again he reported back that he could find nothing out of place. By this time Vera was nearly dressed. The worst was over and it was time to call the cues to change the lights and the scenery into the next scene, which was done in view of the audience.

Within seconds of the scene ending and as the scenery changed Daisy was at my console wanting to know what happened and was telling me how mad Vera was, and that if she could have, Vera would have come right off the stage and slapped me in the face. I thought that to be strange professional behavior and passed it off as what Daisy was saying and not Vera. Finally I said, "Daisy, I have a show to run! I'll talk to Vera after the show." At the end of the show, no sooner did the curtain fall than Daisy was steaming across the stage towards me. "Vera wants to see you. NOW!"

Vera was blazing mad—madder than I had ever seen her before. Her eyes bulged. She allowed me no space to speak and explain. She said that she was sick and tired of my excuses—that it was my job as the stage manager to see that these things didn't happen—and if they did, I was to correct them right away. She accused me of ignoring her and the dressers as they tried to get my attention. Now the fires within me flamed, but she would not hear anything I had to say. She blocked her ears and screamed, "I don't want to hear anymore about this!!!" Daisy came running to her rescue and pulled me out of the room.

I was so angry, so frustrated, so confused that all I could do was go to some secluded stairwell and let out an exasperated yell—several of them. It felt good. The sound echoed up and down the stairs and I'm sure reverberated into the building. I didn't care. However, I did not sleep most of that night. My instincts told me to go to the production office in the morning and quit, but I didn't. I didn't want to give up the job, the weekly salary, the long run, and the chance to work on Broadway. Next day was matinee day, and I went in to work, determined this would be the beginning of a new day. I would set my feelings aside and do the job without error. That in itself was a mistake. Perfection on this show was impossible, and yet that was the standard I set for myself. Was I working toward my own demise? I was!

During that afternoon in calling the cues for the performance, I was doing quite well—not one mistake, not one glitch in timing. I was achieving my goal of perfection. I had no concerns about cue 65. I was certain one of the stagehands working the boards had made a mistake and perhaps the head electrician was covering for his man, especially because of Vera's reaction. But, I'll be damned, those blue lights came up again, and again Vera squirmed and pressed against the scenery. In addition, Vera yelled out at me, in a very loud stage whisper, some descriptive and profane adjectives, in reference to my character and my work as a stage manager. Over the headset, I ordered the head electrician to leave the boards and come into the wings where I was standing. He did and we looked. He could not see any extra blue lights lit other than the ones above our heads in the stage right wing which were supposed to be lit. I dreaded the coming of the end of the performance, but after the curtain fell, I heard nothing from Vera's encampment. Daisy did not descend upon me.

Being a matinee day, immediately following the performance, everyone went to dinner and did not have to be back until the half-hour call. Without discussing it with or getting approval from the PSM, I ordered the TD and the crew to stay after the show, cutting into their meal time. I asked for the scenery for the night scene to be set up along with the lights for cue 65. I didn't care if it would cost the producer overtime and penalty. The crew was annoyed with me. They felt I was overreacting. They promised they would check the matter at half-hour, but that was too late for me. By then the audience would be coming in and if the blue lights out front needed to be adjusted, they couldn't without raising the curtain and revealing the stage to the audience.

With great reluctance they did as I asked. I buckled somewhat under their feelings when the TD said that we didn't need to fly in the flat behind which Vera stood to get dressed. He said we knew where on the stage the piece landed and that we could just stand there in its place. We did, and there shining in our eyes were blue lights coming from the stage right wing. I said, "It's those blue lights hanging on the light tree." The electrician checked his cue sheet and reported that those lights were supposed to be on. "Maybe they got moved and are now out of focus," I suggested. "That's not possible," the electrician said. "They're locked off. Nothing flies past them from the flys, and we don't have scenery going in and out of the wings that goes up that high." I deferred my instincts to his experience, assumed I was wrong, and we all went to dinner.

That night, the PSM, the head electrician, and I stood in the wings and as I called cue 65, we watched the blue lights come up and flood on Vera. This time Vera pushed the dressers away and without regard for the audience, called out to the PSM, sotto-voce, "Is that... (she used the same profane and descriptive adjectives in reference to me) ever gonna get this cue right?"

The next day the crew was brought in to set up the scenery and refocus the blue lights. The problem was resolved. The PSM and TD explained to Vera and spoke on my behalf. She listened but she didn't seem to hear. Her only comment was, "I've had other problems with him. Problems only seem to happen when he's calling the show!"

EPILOGUE TO THE BLUE LIGHTS

There is a tag or epilogue to this incident. It does not, however, change the course of my fate at the time. During a performance about a week later I was standing in the wing. I called cue 65. The lights came up. Everything was as it should be except there was strong blue light hitting the edge of the flat behind which Vera was standing and it was just beginning to spill over behind the flat. I need not tell you the fear that came over me. I stepped back to look up at the blue lights above my head in the stage right wing. As I did, several dancers moved into the wing to get ready for the next scene. As

part of keeping their bodies warm and limber while they waited, they continued to stretch and bend. As I looked up, I saw the light units that projected the blue lights on the stage shake. When I looked among the dancers, there was one dancer holding on to the pole of the light tree with both hands doing deep knee bends. With each movement he made, the blue lights above vibrated and shook.

I called the cues for the scenery to change into the next scene. Then while everyone was on stage, I went to the pole of the light tree. First I shook it. Naturally, the lights above shook and vibrated. Then I placed both of my hands on the pole, as I had seen the dancer do, and I twisted. The pole moved ever so slightly. So slightly, in fact, that I was not sure it had moved at all. I tried it again and again. Each time the pole moved a fraction of an inch. I gasped. I was shocked and at the same time elated. So this was how the blue lights had been knocked out of focus and flooded behind the flat and on Vera! In that moment I felt relieved and vindicated. After the performance, I announced my discovery to the world. No one seemed to be impressed. The PSM put up a notice on the callboard asking everyone not to touch the poles to the light trees and the incident was forgotten. I had hoped this new information would change Vera's mind about me. It didn't, and it didn't stop what was to happen next.

MECHANICAL FAILURE

When the axe fell, it was swift and final. It came in the scene in which Vera was placed on a trapeze at center stage by some of the ensemble performers. They'd spin the trapeze around and at the same time I'd call cues for the trapeze to be raised up to a thirteen-foot level above the stage, and for the lights to change. With the change of lights, the stage was plummeted into darkness, with only a very bright pool of light (pink) coming from above.

Once the trapeze reached high trim, Vera took out a six shooter that she wore in a holster at her side and would shoot upstage toward a black backdrop. With each shot, a giant star lit up on the backdrop. For the climax to this spectacle, Vera took out another six shooter, and as she fired shots in rapid succession, I called cues that sent the stars spinning and the lights chasing.

After Vera's final gun shot, I called a series of other cues that brought the trapeze down to stage level, changed the lights, and started the scenery changing. As this was happening, the ensemble performers were directed to enter stage from all directions, help Vera off the trapeze, lift her onto their shoulders, and carry her off to stage left in celebration and jubilation. This scene change and transition was not as involved as some of the others, but it was dangerous because of the number of performers on stage. If a cue for the scenery to move on and off stage was called at the wrong timing, someone could be injured.

On this particular ill-fated night, after the trapeze was spun around I called the cues for both the trapeze to ascend and for the lights to change. The trapeze started upwards, the stage plummeted into darkness, but there was no bright pool of pink light coming from above. Vera was left in total darkness as she ascended to a high point, while twirling around on the trapeze. All my greatest fears and worst nightmares as a stage manager came full blown. I yelled into the headset, "John, bring up the pink special above Vera!!!" He yelled back, "I did!" I yelled back, "It's not on—she's in the dark!"

Through the headset I could hear John scuffling, turning on and off the switch that brought up the pool of pink light. "I think it's broken," he yelled out. "I'll have to patch it in to something else!!" Meanwhile, I could hear Vera yelling out things at me in full voice. I was panicked. "John, bring up some light—any light!" Vera started shooting. "Forget the stage lights! Start bringing up the stars!"

Vera was now silhouetted against the lighted stars, and if I added any other light to the stage, it would have revealed the black drop on which the stars were mounted and would have spoiled the illusion of the stars being suspended. I didn't notice that night, but someone told me later, that when Vera shot her gun, she didn't aim it at the backdrop as she normally did, but rather shot off into the wing where I stood at the stage manager's console.

On Vera's final shot, I called the cues for the trapeze to come down to stage level and for the lights to change. This time, however, Vera did not allow the ensemble performers to pick her up onto their shoulders, to carry her off stage left. Instead, she pushed them aside and made a beeline to stage right, directly toward me. The ensemble performers were confused and uncertain. They were now scattered all over the stage and standing in places where the scenery was coming in. Some followed Vera off, others drifted into different wings. I had all I could do to watch and see that no one got hurt. Meanwhile, in my peripheral vision, I could see Vera coming at me. When she reached me, she began beating on me and kicking, using abusive language fit only for a barroom brawl. I held up one arm to protect myself and I must confess my language became equally abusive as I tried to ward off Vera and make the set change at the same time.

Upon completion of the set change, I lost all control and my senses. I ripped off my headset and dove into the group that by now had surrounded Vera. It was the only time in my life I felt murder in my heart. Fortunately, it was too late. Daisy had pulled Vera back, and three stagehands grabbed me and took me from out of the backstage area. I cannot tell you what happened for the rest of the performance. The PSM took over calling the show, and I was sent home.

Next morning, I was called and ordered to be in the producer's office by 9:00 A.M. When I arrived, no time was wasted. The producer and his associate told me I was being taken off the show, to which I felt great relief. They said I was being paid two weeks' salary, and that I would no longer be working for the production company. Ever again. I sincerely thought the last part of their statement was a joke. I smiled, but they were serious. The producer and his associate felt that I was incapable of working as a stage manager. They said I was combative and prone to emotional outbursts. They preached how a stage manager, under any conditions, must maintain composure, propriety, and calmness. I then spent the next hour trying to understand the producer's reversal toward me and my work. Did my past work record not count for anything? Did they not take into account the people with whom I was working and how they themselves said that this would be a difficult job? No, they didn't. Their responses were vague and evasive. They said Vera had written in her contract approval of everyone who worked on the show and that they had to let me go. I understood that part, but why would they not hire me to work on other shows? They remained cold and distant, returning to how I had behaved with Gaylord during techs and now with Vera. They continued to say I was no longer fit to be a stage manager. This of course was devastating.

On the second day after the incident, the entire story was in the trade paper. Vera's manager was once again at work, getting as much publicity out for the show as he could. The story, as told to the newspapers, was written to make Vera a victim of an incompetent stage manager, whom they now named. They made Vera look like a hero for surviving the ordeal high on the trapeze. By the end of the week the local papers had picked up the story, the tabloids reworked it to make it even more sensational, and two months later, a friend working in London read about it in a British published magazine.

Needless to say, the time that followed was not the best of times. I felt a range of many things. I looked to Actor's Equity for help, but they were limited in what they could do. I was told this would pass and that it was not the end of my career. They were right, but at that time I could not see it that way. There were no other producing companies in town that produced the same caliber and quality of shows. The only thing I seemed to have left was to go back to working at the things I did when I was in between jobs, waiting for the next big show.

Vera and the show never made it to Broadway. It toured in a few cities, but then closed. There was a part of me that was glad. Two years later, the producing company that had fired me went out of business. I was saddened, but at the same time relieved, because each time I read in the papers about their next production, I went into a state of depression. Shortly afterwards, the associate producer who was present when I was fired called and offered me the PSM position in a show he was independently producing. I was flabbergasted. He never offered information on what had happened with the Vera incident and we never talked about it. I worked for him on this production and at the end he gave me a bonus check for the good work I had done. We became good friends, working associates, and our families have gathered on many social outings since then.

IN CLOSING

My experiences as a stage manger have been growth filled and maturing. They have taught me things about being in show business, about the behavior of people in theatre, and about being a stage manager that I was never able to read in a book. I had to live the experiences to learn.

As an SM you will have your own experiences and learn your own lessons. If, however, you find yourself on the same path as the one I have traveled and are about to cross the same muddy waters, I hope you can learn your lesson from my experience and cross the bridge I have built over such turbulent waters. If not, then by all means bypass the bridge and have the experience for yourself.

Glossary: The SM's Working Vocabulary

The vocabulary in some professions can be like another language. Fortunately, most terms in theatre are familiar. It is a matter of learning how they are used within the context and framework of a production.

Do not try to read this section in one sitting, and above all, do not feel that you must master each term. Your initial contact is the most important part. Later, as you continue to read this book and as you work and grow, these terms will have relevance.

Each term is defined for the SM and delivered from this point of view. For many definitions, additional information is given to create a greater picture and understanding. In some definitions, technical details have been simplified or left out. Also, in some definitions, other theatrical terms are used to help define their meaning. These terms have been italicized and can be cross-referenced. Similarly, at the end of many definitions (noted in parentheses) there are still other terms that are related or have the same meaning. They too can be cross-referenced.

For definitions of the different positions in the production staff, acting company, and technical staff, see Chapter 3, The Stage Manager's Chain of Command List.

Above   Aside from the usual meaning of something being higher or over something else, directors will use this term when giving directions, asking an actor to, "cross above the sofa" or asking a prop man to place the chair "above the table." In each case, the director is asking to have the action or the placement take place further up stage, away from the audience.

Act curtain   Also called the *front curtain*, the *main curtain*, the *grand drape*, the *house curtain*, the *show curtain*, and, in slang or colloquial terms, *the rag*. This is the curtain that hangs at the front of the stage and covers the opening through which the audience views the performance. When raised or parted, it reveals to the audience the scenery and performers.

Acting notes   Critiquing a performer: a producer, director, or SM telling actors something complimentary or critical about their work/performance. Acting notes reinforce the performer's good work, or ask the performer to change something that is not acceptable or desirable either for the show, for the director, or the producer.

Action

1. The physical movement on stage as seen by the audience during the performance. The action seen on stage comes from the storyline and in some places is suggested by the author. However, for the most part, the action is created and set by the director and performers. (See also **Blocking.**)
2. The action may also be the course or direction in which the plot and storyline moves—the progression and order of the scenes and events. It is the things that motivate and move the characters into doing the things they do.

Actor's Equity Association (A.E.A.)   Commonly called "Equity": the union to which professional actors and SMs belong when working in live theatre, performing plays, or doing Broadway musical–type shows.

Actor's measurements   See **Measurements.**

Ad-lib   An ad-lib is dialogue, music, or action performed on stage that is not written into the script or score, or has not been set by the director. It can also mean to *improvise*, to perform extemporaneously, without having planned or rehearsed.

Amateur   By standards used in this book, a professional is a member of an established actor's, stagehand's, or craftsmen's work union, while an amateur/nonprofessional has not achieved such membership and status.

1. In general terms, amateurs are people who may be just beginning to learn and work in their chosen profession. They have yet to achieve the degree of knowledge, artistry, and craftsmanship that makes them desirable to be hired by people in professional standing.
2. Sometimes the difference between professional and amateur is defined by whether or not one is being paid for the work.

3. On some occasions, the term *amateur* can be used negatively, either in a snobbish way or to be critical of a person's work, performance, or behavior.

Amber   A yellowish-orange or golden-orange color often used in creating a sunrise or sunset lighting effect on stage. Its warm glow can be the reflection of a fire, or general lighting for a remembered scene from the past.

Amphitheatre   A theatre with a bowl-like seating arrangement—successive rows of seats are raised on a somewhat steep incline to afford each person a good viewing position. Ancient amphitheatres include the open, outdoor structures in which the Greeks performed their plays and the circular Roman Coliseum. The Hollywood Bowl and Rose Bowl are examples of modern amphitheatres.

Anticipate   To be ready and focused, waiting for a particular thing or event to take place during a performance. An SM is often required to anticipate calling a cue on a particular word or action to achieve perfect timing or a desired effect as prescribed by the director. By anticipating, the SM calls the cue precisely at the moment needed. For the same reasons, actors also may be asked to anticipate saying a line of dialogue or doing a particular action.

Anti-pros   The area in front of the proscenium above the heads of the audience who sit in the first few rows. This is where some of the lighting instruments and other technical equipment can be hung. Sometimes the anti-pros is simply a steel pipe suspended from the ceiling, in full view of the audience, on which the equipment is hung. Other times it is built into the ceiling, concealing the equipment. When built into the ceiling, the space may be just large enough for a technician to crawl on hands and knees to hang the equipment and adjust the lights or large enough for a technician to stand and even operate a spotlight. When built into the ceiling, this space may also be called the ceiling beam. (See also **Bridge, catwalk; Truss**)

Apron   The forward part of the stage floor and performing area. When the house or main curtain is in place, the apron is that clearly defined area of the stage just in front of the curtain.

Arbor   The metal framework that houses the ropes, pulleys, and steel-bar counter-weights of the *fly* or rail system. This structure is placed backstage on one side or the other of the stage. It is designed to make the work easier for the stagehands to fly the drops, curtains, or pieces of scenery in and out.

Area lighting   A section of stage generally lit by two or more lighting instruments. Lighting designers break up the stage into areas, using as many areas of light as needed to cover the entire stage. These areas are usually numbered. They can be operated independently, creating isolated areas on the stage, or used in combination, creating larger areas or lighting the entire stage.

Arena stage   An acting/performance area surrounded on all sides by the audience. Sometimes circular, square, or rectangular in form. Aisles dividing the audience into sections also permit the actors to make their entrances and exits on and off stage. (See also **Horseshoe stage; Thrust stage**)

Artist's entrance   The entrance to the theatre used by members of the company. This entrance is separate from the public entrance. It is usually off to the side or at the back of the building and most often leads directly to the backstage area.

Asbestos curtain   See **Fire curtain**

Aside   A line of dialogue that is delivered directly to the audience by the actor. (See also **Breaking the fourth wall; Fourth wall**)

Atmosphere people   Performers appearing in a show who have no lines of dialogue: people used in scenes to do minor tasks or background action. Sometimes they are used simply to dress the stage as attendants or guards.

At the top, from the top   A phrase used mostly by directors and SMs in rehearsals, instructing the actors to start at the beginning of whatever section of the play they may be working on at the time.

Austrian curtain   A curtain, when hanging across the stage or in the closed position, with pleats or folds like a normal curtain. At the back of the curtain there is a series of ropes traveling from the bottom to the top that divide the curtain into vertical sections. When operated, the ropes travel upward, causing the curtain to rise horizontally. From the audience's point of view, the curtain rises from the bottom upwards. As it rises, the material of the curtain gathers at the bottom, creating scallop or *bunting* folds in each divided, roped section.

Backdrop   A large flat piece of *muslin* or canvas material with scenery or designs painted on it that is stretched across the entire back part of the stage. These drops help complete the illusion of a particular *setting* in the play and separate the backstage area from the onstage area.

Backers   The people who invest their money in the show to get it started and subsidize it until the show becomes successful and returns a profit.

Backers' audition   The presentation of the play to a group of potential investors. The presentation can be done simply with the actors sitting and reading the play from scripts, be a fully produced production, or be presented somewhere in between.

Backing

1. Financial support by investors to get a show produced and started in performances.
2. Flats or pieces of scenery that are placed on the set behind windows or where doors open to help create the illusion that there is something more beyond the boundaries of the setting on stage. Backings prevent the audience from seeing through to the activity backstage.

Back lighting   Lighting instruments on stage hung from above and further upstage. These lights are turned to shine down on the backs of the performers. They usually are hidden from the audience by a *boarder* or *teaser*. This technique in lighting helps give greater depth to the stage by making the performers stand out from their background. This design started in films and television and carried over into theatre. Today every lighting design and plot includes some kind of back lighting.

Balcony lights   Lighting instruments placed on the front part of the balcony and hung low enough to be out of view of people sitting in the balcony. These lights are best used as *fill lights* or *washes* to generally light the stage. (See also **Balcony rail; Front lights**)

Balcony rail

1. A rail placed at the front of the balcony to help prevent audience members from accidentally falling over the balcony and into the orchestra.
2. The balcony rail with which the SM will have the most interaction is a steel pipe placed in front of the balcony and out of view of the audience, where lighting instruments are hung. With the addition of electricity to light the stage, designers found the balcony to be an excellent position and eventually the balcony rail became a permanent part of lighting design and theatre construction.

Band   A small group of musicians, as in a rock band. In a more classical sense, a band is a group whose instruments consist mostly of wind, horn, and percussion instruments, as in a marching band, dance band, or jazz band. (See also **Orchestra**)

Barn doors   A metal unit placed at the front end of a lighting instrument. It has two or four adjustable flaps that help block light from spilling into unwanted places on the stage. Barn doors aid greatly in *focusing lights*. (See also **Focus**)

Batten   A length of wood 3 to 4 inches wide and 6 to 10 feet long on which curtains, flats, and small set pieces are tied or lighting instruments are hung. Battens are often used to hang the curtains that create the *wings* on each side of the stage. In most theatres today, the wood batten has been replaced with a steel pipe.

Beat

1. In music, a beat is the drive behind the music, the unit of time or accent within a measure.
2. In acting and directing, a beat is a moment of time—usually a second and usually a rest or moment of silence. Directors will often ask actors to take a beat before saying their next line or performing their next bit of *business*.

Being thrown   This expression is commonly used when a performer is distracted during a performance, becoming momentarily lost or confused, not remembering the next line of dialogue, or forgetting a piece of business.

Biography, bio   A written paragraph printed in the program, briefly telling interesting facts, listing awards, and giving past credits of the actors, director, producer, and some of the main designers. On occasion, a bio on the SM may be included. The term *bio* is more commonly used. At some time during every rehearsal period on a show, the SM will receive word from the publicity department to gather bios.

Biscuit monitors   Small speakers placed throughout the backstage areas at various technical stations, through which stagehands can hear the SM call the cues for the performance. Many biscuit monitors have been replaced by wireless headsets, but on a large show in which several stagehands are executing cues, headsets for each person is either not practical or not financially feasible and biscuits continue to be used. Each biscuit has its own volume control knob, which should be adjusted so that the SM's voice calling the cues does not resound throughout the backstage area.

Bit   A small section of *action* or *business* performed by an actor as part of the performance. Usually a bit is a physical and comical thing. Sometimes a bit is invented by the actor or director to create a greater illusion of reality, to add color to the character, or heighten the drama or comedy. (See also **Blocking; Stage business**)

Bit part, walk-on part   A small role in a play or musical. The actor is usually on-stage for a very short time and can have few to no lines of dialogue. ASMs are sometimes given these parts.

Black   A term used by directors, technicians, and SMs to describe the stage when it is totally dark: "Bring the stage to black." "Start the scene change in the black." "When you are ready, go to black."

Blacks   These are the black curtains on stage that create the *wings*, dress the back part of the stage, and make up the *boarders* or *travelers*.

Blacklight, ultraviolet light (UV light)   A deep purple light that gives off invisible ultraviolet rays. When directed against black curtains and with no other lights present, blacklight gives the appearance that the stage is in darkness. Only white objects, strongly bleached objects (such as clothes or hair), or objects dyed or painted in special iridescent fluorescent colors are vividly reflected by this light and appear to glow in the dark. All other colors are reflected to a much lesser degree, appearing very muted or almost black.

Blackout (BO)   A blackout is when all the lights on-stage are turned out at the same time, plunging the stage into darkness.

Block and tackle   The block and tackle is designed to hoist into the air extremely heavy objects or payloads. The rope is laced through and around two or more wheels or pulleys, which makes it possible for one person to operate. The block and tackle allows the operator to stop and rest or change hand positions while the object remains suspended in the air at whatever level it was stopped. Today most block and tackles are motorized and use chains in place of ropes.

Blocking   The placement and movement of actors as they perform their parts during a performance. The blocking is created by the director and actors during rehearsals. The SM notes the blocking in the rehearsal script. The blocking is set and subsequently repeated for each performance. Blocking is the *action*, *movement*, *bits* of *stage business*, and *timing* performed on the stage.

Blocking notes, blocking script   The notes actors, directors, and SMs write in their scripts to remind themselves of the movement, placement, business, action, and timing of the characters on-stage. Blocking notes are written in a theatrical shorthand, using abbreviations, symbols, initials, and stick figure diagrams with arrows. For SMs, making a blocking script with detailed notations is a major part of the job during rehearsals, and is very important later for understudy rehearsals, putting in replacement actors, reminding actors who forget or change their performance, for publication of the play, or for the producer's archives. (See also **Action; Blocking; Block the show; Stage business; Stage directions**)

Block the show   To block the show is to move the actors around the stage as they say their lines. Blocking is creating action, movement, bits of business, and working out timing. This is the first stage of rehearsals.

Blueprints, blueprint drawings   These are mechanical drawings done in half-inch or one-inch scale. They are made by the designer and detail the design of the set. The various pages of a set of blueprints note the size of the stage and the layout and floor plan of the set, and give construction specifications, measurements, and dimensions of the individual pieces of scenery. (See also **Drawn to scale; Elevations, elevation drawings; Scale drawings**)

Boarder lights, strip lights, teaser lights, bank of lights
These are long units or strips of lights. Each unit is divided into many sections or slots of equal size, and within each slot a light bulb is placed. These units are usually hung above the stage and behind the *boarder* or teaser. They are often *focused* to project their light straight down onto the floor of the stage. When lit, they flood a wide strip of light in their immediate area and do not cover the entire stage.

Within each unit, the light bulbs are divided into three or four circuits. The bulbs for a circuit are placed apart from each other in every third or fourth space, depending on the number of circuits involved. Each bulb within the same circuit is covered over with the same colored *gel*. Each circuit has a different-colored gel placed over it, so that when a particular circuit is lit that same color of light appears across the stage. Each circuit can be operated separately or in combination with the others.

These same lighting units can be placed on the floor with their lights directed upwards. When placed on the *apron* of the stage they become *footlights*. When placed at the back of the stage with their light projected onto *backdrops* or the *cyclorama (cyc)*, they are called a *ground row* or *cyc lights*.

Boarders, teasers, valance   Short curtains or narrow flats hung at intervals across the top of the stage and running the full length of the stage. They are used to conceal from the audience the unsightly lighting instruments, electrical wiring, and other technical things that are hung above in the flys and are not part of the set design or overall view of the stage. Sometimes these boarders are painted, designed, and cut out to be part of the scenery, completing and complementing the overall look of the stage; at other times they are made of black material or painted black. (See also **Tormentors**)

Boards   A colloquial expression used by people in theatre when referring to the stage. Most stages are made of tightly fitted pieces of wood or boards. An actor who has been out of work but is now performing in a show may say, "It's good to be back on the boards."

Body microphone (body mic), body pack, radio pack   A body mic is a miniature microphone head with a transistor body pack which is hidden under the actor's costume and goes virtually unseen by the audience. The microphone is placed either near the throat, over the ear, or on the forehead near the hairline. The body pack is no bigger than a pocket calculator. It is placed in a cotton pouch and strapped on the actor, either at the waist, with the bulky part placed in the small of the back, or on some other part of the body where it is comfortable and at the same time cannot be seen by the audience. The only wire with which the actor must contend is the one traveling from the microphone head to the body pack. The body pack is battery operated. It transmits the sound signals to a radio receiver, which is usually somewhere backstage. The receiver sends the signal to the amplifier, which in turn broadcasts the signal through speakers to the audience.

Body mics are also called wireless mics, radial mics, or radio mics. The cotton pouch is used to absorb perspiration. If a performer becomes wet during the performance or has a tendency to perspire heavily, the sound person will first place the body pack in a plastic baggie or condom to prevent the unit from shorting out.

Book   This term is used mostly when talking about a musical play. It refers specifically to the script—the dialogue, plot, and storyline of the play.

Booking flats, two-fold or three-fold   Two or three 10-by-4-foot flats, hinged together. They are usually free-standing units that are convenient for stagehands and SMs to use in many situations backstage. They are especially good for setting up *quick change* dressing rooms in some out-of-the-way corner backstage or just behind the set.

Book show   A musical show that has a script with a storyline, dialogue, and a plot. The songs in a book show are character driven—they come from the storyline, and are integrated to help move the play along. The storyline does not stop to let characters sing or perform their specialty, as often happens in a variety or vaudeville show. The characters in a book show sing because their feelings can no longer be expressed in dialogue and are best expressed in song and music.

Box booms, boom lights   Box booms are areas in the audience off to each side and close to the stage where the *box seats* are traditionally placed. With the advent of electrical lighting and sophisticated lighting design, in many theaters the box seats were removed and pipes were set up and rigged to hang lighting instruments. Because of their extreme angle, these lights make excellent *side lighting*. When box boom lights are used in combination with other lights on stage, they give depth to things on the stage that might appear to be flat if lit only from the front. When box boom lights are used by themselves they create dramatic highlights and shadows.

Box office, ticket office   The place at the front of the theatre from which the patrons purchase their tickets for the various performances.

Box office receipts   The number of tickets sold for a performance for a day, a week, or the entire run of the show: the amount of money made.

Box seats   Seats at the extreme sides of the theatre and close to the stage, probably the most famous being the one in which President Lincoln sat at Ford's Theatre in Washington, D.C. At one time these were prestigious seats reserved for royalty, dignitaries, or the rich. They are not the best seats in the theatre for viewing a performance, but were in great demand among the aristocracy so they could be on display and be seen by the other members of the audience.

With the advent of electrical lighting and sophisticated lighting design, the box seats were replaced with pipes and rigging to hang lighting instruments and became known to people working in the theatre as the *box booms*. For a long time theatres were built without box seats, but they have had a resurgence. For SMs these seats present an almost unsolvable *sight-line* problem.

Box set   A simple, three-sided set, usually the interior of a room for a drama or comedy. The *fourth wall* of this room is an imaginary wall through which the audience views the play.

Breakaway   Anything that is designed and constructed to pull away or apart. This can be a prop, a piece of scenery, or a costume.

Breaking character   This is something performers do when they stop speaking or acting as the character— when they do something that is not true to the character. (See also **Breaking the fourth wall**)

Breaking the fourth wall   Actors break the illusion of the fourth wall when they look at people in the audience, acknowledging their presence, or speak directly to them. Sometimes the fourth wall is broken simply by the actor crossing too far down stage onto the *apron* of the stage, breaking the illusion of the boundaries of the setting or room in which the characters are supposed to be living. (See also **Fourth wall**)

Bridge, catwalk   A long, narrow walkway that runs above and across the top of the stage. It is in the fly space, hidden behind the *boarders* or teasers. Technicians use the bridge or catwalk for better access to hang and focus lights or to operate special effects. Sometimes actors use this space to make a special or unusual entrance or exit.

Sometimes a bridge or catwalk is concealed in the ceiling of the theatre just above the heads of the people who sit in the first few rows of the audience. This bridge serves the same purpose as the walkway built in the fly space on stage. Technicians will also refer to this bridge above the audience's heads as the ceiling beam or the *anti-pros*.

Bring up the lights   A direction given most often to the technician operating the light board or to the SM, asking that some light be brought up on stage, be it for rehearsals, for performance, or in the audience at the end of the show. Most times the lights are on a dimmer, thus the expression, "bring up the lights."

Brush-up rehearsal   A rehearsal the director or SM might hold after the show has opened and is in performance. Brush-up rehearsals are often called when the actors or the company have had more time off from performing than just the usual time allowed for the day off.

   An SM will call a brush-up rehearsal if, during the run, the actors have become sloppy in their performance or have made unacceptable changes in their performance or in the show.

Bump, bump-up   An abrupt or popping movement of lights on stage from a lower intensity to a brighter one. Commonly used at the end of musical numbers with big endings to emphasize and heighten the emotional feeling for the audience. The opposite of a bump would be a *blackout*.

Bump cue   A lighting cue that pops the lights up to a brighter intensity. When this term is used among lighting designers, technicians, directors, and SMs, everyone understands the expected action of the lights and the effect that should appear on the stage. (See also **Bump, bump-up**)

Bunting   A piece of material or drapery folded and hung in scallop or swag fashion. Bunting-type folds are often seen at the top part of curtains or grand drapes for a decorative and detailed look. Bunting is commonly seen in red, white, and blue, and is hung on grandstands or anything having to do with an American holiday or event.

Business, stage business   The movement and action of the actors as they perform their parts. Lighting a cigarette or crossing to the door are simple forms of stage business. (See also **Blocking**)

The business, the biz   Sometimes used to refer to show business.

Buttons

1. In musical terms, a button is additional music played immediately following the end of a song or instrumental number. It can be as brief as one note or a single chord, or it can be extended to a series of notes and chords. Its purpose is to punctuate, emphasize, or finalize the ending.

2. Broader usage of this term by directors and actors means much the same thing; their buttons, however, may be a gesture or a look just before exiting or ending a scene. The sound of the door slamming behind an actor can be a button. (See also **Tag**)

Call

1. This term pertains mostly to scheduling—telling the actors when and where they should be, be it for a rehearsal, a performance, or meeting a bus to go to the airport. Each day the SM gives the actors their call for the next day.

2. "Call the actors." Throughout rehearsals, the SM will hear this direction many times from the director. The director is asking that the actors be assembled in one place. Calling the actors can simply be calling them from one rehearsal room to the other or getting them from their dressing rooms to the stage, or it can literally mean calling them on the phone. (See also **Half-hour call**)

Callback auditions, callbacks   The audition(s) after the first audition. If a performer's initial audition seems to provide what a producer, director, or casting people want, the performer is asked to return for a second audition—a *callback* audition. These auditions often take place on another day. There are fewer people in competition, but the performer is up against the best of the competition. Callbacks give the casting people an opportunity to view the talent once again and, if they choose, put individuals together in pairs or in groups.

Callboard   The official bulletin board for the actors. It is the place where all important information, official notices, Equity notices, and schedules are posted. It is required by Equity that a callboard be set up, in clear view, and be accessible wherever the performers report daily. This is not a community board for everyone's use; anything placed on this board must first be cleared by the SM.

Calling cues, calling the show   During each performance, the SM sits at a console using the cueing script to follow the dialogue. Either over a headset or using visual signals, the SM communicates to the various technical departments when to execute their particular cues.

   There are three steps an SM must follow in calling cues. A minute or so before a cue or group of cues is to be executed, the SM gives the *warning*, telling which cues are to be executed. About fifteen seconds before the execution, the SM gives the *stand by*, which tells all those involved to be ready and alert. At the appropriate time, the SM then gives the *GO! cue* (See also **Timing**)

Calling places   See **Places, places please**

Calling script, cueing script   This is a script void of all SM's notes except those dealing directly with the cues for the show during the performance. This script may also be called the *prompt book* or the *prompt script*.

Cameo, cameo role   A role not large enough to be considered a supporting role, although it might be important, significant, or pivotal to the play in some way. A cameo may be merely a walk-on appearance with few to no lines, or it can be larger, possibly involving several scenes and a good amount of dialogue. On occasion, these roles are played by prominent performers with name value, which also helps to generate *box office receipts*.

Candle power A term used by lighting technicians, carried over from the days when candles and gas lamps were used for lighting the stage. Today candle power is a unit of measurement for the amount of illumination or intensity given off by the lamp in a stage lighting instrument.

Carbon arc spotlight Two carbon rods are clamped into a lighting instrument called a spotlight: one rod is negatively charged, the other positive. The ends of the rods are placed opposite each other with a small space left between. An electrical current is sent through the rods and an intense and blinding arc of light is created within the small space between the rods. This light is reflected onto the stage from a mirror and through a lens, creating a circular area of light brighter than most lighting instruments on the stage. The carbon arc spotlight is commonly used in musical and variety shows.

 The carbon arc is inconvenient to use during a performance because the carbons burn down and need to be changed. With improved technology, carbon arc spotlights are being replaced by lighting instruments that use lamps that give off a brighter intensity of light, such as the Xenon (pronounced *zee-non*) spotlight. Spotlights are often simply called "spots." (See also **Follow spot; Limelight**)

Card stock Lightweight cardboard, three or four times the weight and thickness of typing paper, but not as thick as poster board. Good for making small signs or nameplates for dressing room doors.

Cast The group of actors chosen to perform in the show, from the starring and/or lead role to the smallest walk-on part.

Casters Wheels under platforms and set units that allow the units to be rolled on and off stage. There are *swivel casters*, sometimes called *smart casters*, which allow a unit to be pushed and moved in any direction, and there are *directional casters* or *fixed casters*, which limit the unit's movement to a straight line or a single plane.

Casting The process of choosing actors to play the various roles in the play.

Cast party A social event in which the cast gets together to celebrate the opening of a show, the success of a show, or the closing of a show. Most times the cast party is for the entire company, including friends, relatives, and guests. Only on rare occasions is it limited to only cast members. A cast party may take place in the green room of the theatre, in someone's apartment or home, or in a hall or grand ballroom.

Caterer A food service business that prepares, delivers, or sets up food at any location requested. The catering may be a truck—a kitchen on wheels which parks outside the rehearsal hall—or simply having a platter of cold cuts and potato salad delivered. On a grander scale, the caterer may serve a banquet for the entire company at a cast party.

Cattle call See **Open auditions**

Catwalk See **Bridge**

Ceiling beam See **Anti-pros; Bridge**

Characters The individual people within the play who have been created by the author and whom the plot and storyline revolve around.

Characterization An actor's portrayal and realization of a character. The actor finds the feelings and drives—the force and impetus that make the character act, behave, and respond as it does. The actor uses these things to make the character come alive as a real, unique individual.

Chit Noting on a small piece of paper an amount of money spent, along with the date and the reason for which the money was spent. Chits can be used by the SM as receipts as long as they are not for large sums of money. Chits are used for receipts that have been lost or for money spent where receipts are not given, such as public phones, parking meters, and vending machines.

Choreographer The artist who creates the physical and emotional movement, arrangement, and order of steps within a dance.

Choreography The physical and emotional movement of a dance created by the choreographer.

Circuit

1. In terms of stage lighting, a circuit is the flow of electrical current to a single light instrument or to a group of lighting instruments. There are many circuits of lights within the lighting design and light plot of a play. Circuits can be operated individually or in combination with each other.
2. In terms of business and theatre talk, a circuit is a group of theaters or performance sites to which a show can travel and perform. Sometimes the circuit is regional, such as the Florida circuit or the Borscht circuit, but it may also be national, such as the old Orphium circuit. A circuit may also be a chain of theaters owned by one managing company, such as the Schubert theaters.

Claques, shills People placed in the audience to applaud, laugh, react, or take part in the show. Shills pretend to be normal audience members.

Clean entrance or exit When a director or SM asks an actor to make a clean entrance, they are asking that while the actor waits to enter, he or she should stand back far enough to avoid being seen by the audience. Another element in making a clean entrance or exit is that the actor enters the stage, in a direct approach, without being hesitant or tentative, unless that kind of entrance or exit is by design. Most of all, when asking an actor to make a clean entrance the director or SM is asking the actor to be in character, be at performance level, and give the impression that the character is entering with a purpose or intent and has just come from another place or location.

Cleaning, cleaning a scene   The director and/or actors refining their work—be it just a moment in the play or an entire scene. Actors perfecting their parts in character, motivation, and delivery and directors working on timing, pace, tempo, stage business, stage pictures, or making whatever changes they feel will improve the play. (See also **Clean-up rehearsal**)

Clean-up rehearsal   After a scene, an act, or the entire play has been *set* with the *blocking, bits* of *business, timing,* and *characterizations,* a director will have clean-up rehearsals to improve, retime, rework, or change the performance. Throughout the run of a show, if the actors become sloppy in their performance or if the actors make changes that do not meet with the approval of the director, producer, or SM, a clean-up rehearsal might be called to get the show back to the way it was originally set.

Clear!

1. A statement or call of warning made backstage by stagehands and SM, asking people to move and clear an area. The expression "Clear, please!" is a courteous yet firm way of asking people to move quickly. In situations of safety, the tone of voice used tells the people of urgency or eminent danger.
2. "Clear!" is also a statement or call telling others that it is safe to proceed with their work or next move.
3. "Clear" is used after something on stage has moved and is either out of the way or safely in place.
4. In still another subtle use of the word, "clear" is exchanged backstage when scenery is being moved and there is clear space above the piece as well as on the sides, making it safe to move the piece without damage. (See also **Clearance; Head high; Heads!, heads up**)

Clearance   Backstage, clearance is the amount of space between one thing and another. During *set changes,* stagehands look for the clearance on the sides and above as they move the set pieces on and off stage. The stagehands working the *flys* are always concerned with clearance, for many of the drops, *flats,*

curtains, etc., are hung with only six inches of clearance on either side.

Click (clique) track   Mixing prerecorded music with live music being played on the stage or from the orchestra pit. On the tape or CD of prerecorded music, there is an additional track that includes an electronic metronome beat set to the recorded music. This track is broadcast only to the conductor who, during the performance, wears a headset to hear both the prerecorded music and the click track. The click track enables the conductor to keep the live music synchronized with the recorded music.

Closed rehearsal   Generally speaking, a closed rehearsal is one in which no one outside the company is allowed to attend or enter the room while the rehearsal is in progress. A more restrictive closed rehearsal limits severely who can be present and/or enter the room. An even more restricted closed rehearsal allows no one except the director, SMs, and the actors who are rehearsing to be present.

Cold reading   Sometimes at an audition an actor is given a script and is asked to read a scene without preparation as part of the audition. The actor may be given some information on the scene or the character(s) in the scene, but little else.

Collating   Putting together in order or sequence the pages of scripts or packets of information. Before the advent of copying machines with a collating feature, ASMs spent a lot of time doing this process by hand, especially when working a show with major script changes or rewrites.

Comedy of manners   A style of plays performed in the nineteenth century dealing mostly with human weakness as the central theme, as in the penny-pinching miser from the play *The Miser.*

Company   The company consists of the entire group of people who have been hired to work on a particular show. The producer, director, creators, designers, SMs, performers, technicians, production assistants, and administrative staff make up the company.

Company bow   The entire cast of performers on stage at the end of the show bow together. During the *curtain call,* bows begin with the individual performers playing the smaller roles, then build up to the lead and starring roles. Finally, the entire cast takes the company bow.

Company doctor   Each show has a doctor on call for anyone in the company. This doctor gives general care and advice, functioning like a family doctor. Any condition requiring more serious care is turned over to a specialist.

Comps, comp tickets, being comped   The term comp is an abbreviation for the word complementary. Being comped means to receive tickets to see a performance without having to pay for the tickets.

Computer light board   See **Light board; Light board operator**

Conductor   The person who leads the musicians/orchestra during a performance.

Conductor's podium   A podium that has a larger than normal top for musical scores or large sheets of manuscript music. The podium is traditionally placed in the center of the orchestra pit on a raised platform. From this position the conductor can see the musicians as well as the performers on stage, and can also be seen by them.

Construction shop   The place where the set/scenery is built and painted. This may be a commercial place that specializes in such work, or it may be part of the backstage area set up to do this work. This place may also be called the scene shop, or simply the shop.

Costume   The clothing, accessories, and undergarments each performer wears during the performance while appearing on stage. This can range from today's street wear bought directly off the racks in department stores, to elaborate period and specialty pieces designed and constructed specifically for a particular show.

Costume construction   The making or construction of a costume—from the designer's and artist's conception on paper, to cutting out the pattern and assembling the pieces, to fitting and altering the costume for the performer.

Costumer   The individual or company who provides the costumes for the show.

Costume shop   The place where the costumes for a show can be made, purchased, or rented. Most costume shops have in stock a variety of costumes that cover periods past, present, and future. Some of the costumes are new, but most have been used in other shows. When a producer decides to use ready-made costumes, the costumes are pulled from the racks, fitted, and altered to each performer.

Costume sketches   Drawings or renderings the costume designer makes to show the designs of the costumes being created for the show. Sometimes these sketches are done in black and white in pencil, ink, or charcoal, other times, in full color renderings. Almost always, the designer attaches swatches of material that will be used to make the costume.

Counter, make a counter-move   This term is most commonly used among actors, directors, and SMs when blocking the show. Counter-moves are secondary moves made by one or more actors in response to a primary move made by another actor. A counter-move is made to change the composition of the stage picture and to direct the attention or focus to where the director wants it to be. A counter-move can be as simple as a turn of the head, a twist of the body, or a shift in weight from one leg to the other or as large as a complete body turn to face another direction or move to another position on the stage.

Counter-weights, counter-weight system   The counter-weight system is part of the rail or *fly system*. It is designed to counter the weight of a drop, curtain, or piece of scenery that is being pulled in and out (on and off the stage). Without a counter-weight system, the stagehand pulling a rope would be pulling the total weight of the item being flown, and it could take up to four stagehands to pull one rope, depending on the weight of the item.

Today, large steel bricks are used as counter-weights. When placed in the cradles between each rope, they make it possible for one stagehand to operate the rope with ease. The first counter-weights in theatre were flour sacks or canvas bags filled with sand (thus the term *sandbags*). A good counter-weight system is especially important when doing musical shows where the fly system can be an intricate part of the scene changes. (See also **Flys**)

Crash box   A box made for the purpose of creating a crash sound effect off stage. These boxes are made by the prop department, and usually are made of wood for durability and repeated use. The crash box is often filled with broken glass or junk pieces of metal, and nailed shut. During the performance, at the appropriate time and on cue, the box is either dropped, rattled, rolled, or a combination of all three, depending on the desired effect.

Crew   In professional situations, the crew is a group of union stagehands hired to head, work, operate and maintain the various technical elements of a show. During the performance, the crew works and runs all the technical elements of the show.

Critic   See **Reviewer, critic; Reviews, notices**

Cross lighting

1. Lighting instruments hung from the extreme sides of the stage with their beams of light projected across the stage. Lights hung in the *box booms* or from the wings on *light trees* are used as cross lighting. (See also **Kickers, shin busters**)
2. In terms of *lighting design*, lighting instruments that light an area or a particular thing are often hung from different sides of the stage. When the lights are focused on the area or on the item, they cross from the different sides. This assures that the area is lit well and gives greater dimension to things in the area or to the particular item.

Crossover   The space backstage where the performers and crewmembers can cross over from one side of the stage to the other without being seen by the audience. A crossover usually is behind the set, a drop, or a curtain. On occasion, due to the lack of space backstage, the crossover may be down the stairs, through the basement, and up the stairs to the other side of the stage.

Cue   A cue is something done during a performance at a precise time. Cues are the threads and stitches woven into the tapestry of a performance. Some cues are designed to provide technical support; others to help create illusion, move the show at an entertaining pace, or generate the magic of seeing a live performance.

1. For the SM, cues are sections of information that were set during technical rehearsals and noted in the cueing script to allow them to be called out during each performance with impeccable timing. During the performance, the SM sits at a console with the cueing script, and through a headset or with visual gestures, tells the various technical departments, and sometimes the actors, when to execute their cues. (See also **Calling cues, calling the show; Cueing script, calling script, prompt book**)

2. For the actors a cue may be a word, a line of dialogue, or an action that tells them when to speak, do their next bit of business, or make an entrance or exit. During rehearsals, actors may also use this term when they have forgotten their next line of dialogue; they may simply ask the SM, "Cue?" (See also **Line?, line please?**)

3. When actors are first learning lines or need to be refreshed on their lines, the SM or some other person may sit to cue them by reading from the script all the other character's lines as the actors recite their lines from memorization. (See also **Cue line**)

Cueing script, calling script, prompt book   Whatever the name of this book, it is the SM's bible in running the show. In it is noted all the technical cues that are to be executed during each and every performance, and the precise timing of each. The cueing script is created during technical rehearsals and is written by the SM as the cues and timing are given by the director and technical heads. The cueing script is kept separate from the rehearsal script and the production notebook.

Cue line   The last line of dialogue a character speaks just before the next character speaks. The cue line is the line of dialogue actors listen for to know that another actor's speech is ending and their speech should begin.

Cue to cue tech rehearsal   A rehearsal that takes place in the theatre just after the technical elements have been added to the show. This rehearsal is directed toward

working and running the technical cues. Instead of having the actors recite all their dialogue, the SM moves the rehearsal along and keeps it focused on the technical parts by having the actors start their dialogue a line or two before a technical cue is to take place. After the cue has been executed, the SM stops performers and tells them where to start the dialogue for the next technical cue.

Curtain!   An expression often called out by an SM or director during rehearsals to create the image of the curtain opening or closing to signify the beginning or ending of a scene, an act, or the entire play.

Curtain   The soft cloth items that hang on stage to create performing areas, to cover the lighting instruments and other technical equipment hanging above the stage, to block the audience's view of the distracting backstage activity, or to create wings from which the performers can make entrances and exits. A primary example is the curtain that is draped across the front of the stage, covering the *proscenium opening*, which is not raised or opened until the show is ready to be presented and seen by the audience. (See also **Act curtain**)

Curtain bows, curtain calls   Bows the actors take at the end of the performance. These terms are used interchangeably; however, curtain bows pertain mostly to the bows the director sets, while curtain calls pertain mostly to the additional bows the performers take due to the continued applause of the audience. (See also **Encore**)

Curtain line   An imaginary line across the stage where a curtain touches down or travels across the stage floor. Most times the curtain line refers to where the main house curtain stands, which is usually just behind the *proscenium* arch. When this curtain is being lowered, it is important that SMs and actors remain aware of the curtain line to prevent curtain collisions with actors or damage to props or pieces of scenery that might be standing on the line.

Curtain speech   A speech by someone who goes on stage, either before or after the performance, and talks with the audience. This usually is done by the producer, director, or star. On occasion, for some special reason, the SM may be called upon to do this. Recorded announcements or announcements made to the audience from a backstage mic are not considered curtain speeches.

Curtain warmers, warmers, the preset   These are the lights projected on the house curtain as the audience enters to be seated. These lights are usually set at a low intensity to give color, add interest, or perhaps set a mood for the show. They are turned on by the show electrician before the audience enters and disappear on the SM's cue as the show is about to begin. When no house curtain is used and the stage is left open for the audience to see as they enter, the lights set on the stage are also called curtain warmers.

Cut-out drop   A canvas or muslin drop with cut-out openings that are part of the design. Through the cut-out design, the audience can see beyond to another drop or pieces of scenery. Cut-out drops aid greatly in the illusion of depth. They create a reality for both the scene and scenery. A good example would be in a garden setting where a cut-out drop might have the trunks of trees, leaves hanging from above, and a rose-covered trellis. As the actors enter or exit from behind this drop, they can be seen by the audience.

Cutting and taping, cutting and pasting   A quick and on-the-spot way for the SM to make changes in the script by first cutting the pages to rearrange dialogue, insert new dialogue, or change cues, then taping the information together in the new order. Later, when the SM has time and does not need to be attentive to the director, actors, or the rehearsal, the changes can be made on a laptop, and revised pages distributed.

Cyc lights   This is a general term used for any lights that are focused or flooded on the cyc (cyclorama). The lights being projected on the cyc from above are almost always *boarder lights*. These same units, when placed on the floor with their light flooded up onto the cyc, are called *ground row* lights.

Cyclorama (cyc)   The cyc is a large, seamless, white or off-white drop, which is stretched and pulled to be perfectly smooth. This drop is almost always the last drop at the back of the stage. It stretches across the entire length of the stage and is usually permanently in place. When lit with theatrical lighting or with projected images, this drop dramatically changes the look of the stage, creating full-stage silhouettes, sunrises or sunsets, cloudy skies, a skyline of buildings, or simply color and design for any desired mood, feeling, or effect.

Dance numbers

1. The dances in a musical show.
2. In a more literal sense and as used by the director, choreographer, dancers, or SM, these are large numbers placed across the entire edge or *apron* of the stage. They are set at two-foot intervals and are used by the dancers to help them maintain their placement and spacing on stage during the dances. The actors will also use these numbers in their *blocking*. A zero is placed at center stage, and then two feet away on each side of zero, the number one is placed. From there and traveling out to the respective sides of the stage, the numbers build numerically.

Dark

1. A term used to describe the stage when there is not enough lighting on the stage.
2. A lighting designer or director might ask the SM to "Go to dark," which means they want all the lights on the stage to go out.
3. The mood or humor of a play or particular character that is filled with negative feelings and emotions. Shakespeare's *Hamlet* and *Othello* are examples of dark plays and dark characters.
4. The theatre is dark when there are no performances due to the cast's day off or when the theatre is closed with no show set up and performing in it.

Dead spot   A dark or dimly lit spot on stage.

Deck   The stage floor. This term was brought to the theatre when sailors were brought in as stagehands to work the *flys*.

Delivery   The way in which an actor says lines. The presentation of the actor's performance.

Device   In terms of acting and directing, a device is something an actor or director may add to enhance a performance or a character, such as a limp, a mannerism, a way of speaking, a smile, or even the use of a prop or costume. (See also **Handle**)

Dimmer board/Dimmer pack   See **Light board**

Directional casters   See **Casters**

Doctor   See **Company doctor; Scene doctor, play doctor**

Dolly, truck   A device with wheels used backstage, to aid in moving heavy or awkward items.

1. A hand truck or hand dolly stands upright with wheels or rubber tires at the bottom. There are one or two handles at the top to help direct and control the dolly. At the bottom and in front of the wheels is a large lip or metal shelf. The shelf is tucked under the cargo and then the payload is tilted back and wheeled to its new destination.
2. A flatbed dolly is a wooden or steel platform on wheels. Either a rope or a steel handlebar is attached at one end for pushing or pulling. Many items can be loaded on the flatbed at one time, or a very large and awkward thing can be loaded on and held by one person while another pushes or pulls.

Double take   A comic bit of *business* in which the actor does at least two looks in rapid succession. The actor first looks at something or someone, then looks away and quickly looks back. Some performers have perfected this bit of business using several looks or takes. This business or routine was worked and perfected in vaudeville and burlesque and it has carried over into the present with performers doing their own variations and getting big laughs.

Douser A shutterlike device built into most spotlights that allows the operator to instantly *blackout* the light falling on stage, without having to turn off the electricity to the spotlight.

Down stage

1. The area on the stage closest to the audience.
2. For a performer or anyone standing on stage, this term is used to describe a movement toward the audience. When blocking the show, the director may ask an actor to move down stage.
3. The SM notes this direction in the *blocking script* as DS.

Dragging For SMs, directors, and actors, when something is dragging, it means the timing or delivery is too slow. (See also **Timing**)

Drag-in, drag-out Drag-in and drag-out are slang or colloquial expressions used mostly by stagehands. Drag-in describes the act of bringing into a theatre or performance site the technical equipment of a show and setting it up for a performance. Conversely, the drag-out is taking out of the theatre or performance site the technical equipment. The terms load-in and load-out are also used.

Drama critics See **Reviewer, critic; Reviews, notices**

Drawing-room comedies High-spirited comedy plays, often lapsing into complete and utter farce, which were written and performed in the mid to late nineteenth century. The setting and action of these plays usually took place in a salon, bedroom, or drawing room of a wealthy and sometimes extremely eccentric individual. The subject matter dealt with love, romance, wealth, fidelity, and adultery. The plays often became bawdy, challenged the intellect, and questioned the social and moral fabric of the day. Many times, one of the characters was afflicted with lunacy, madness, or idiocy—sometimes all three—which often drove the plot and storyline to greater farce.

Drawings

1. Technicians and designers sometimes use this term as a short version for blueprint drawings.
2. This term may also refer to the designer's artistic drawing of the sets and costumes, also called *sketches* or *renderings*.

Drawn to scale To document on paper the scenery and floor plan of the stage and performing area, the dimensions for both the stage and scenery must be downsized so the entire stage and set can be drawn on a piece of paper of reasonable size, as in *blueprint drawings*. The scale for blueprint drawings usually is one inch (sometimes a half inch) for every foot of actual space the set and floor plan take. The scale of each blueprint drawing is noted in the bottom right-hand corner of the page. Knowing the scale, the SM can determine with a ruler the actual size of any part of the set or performing area and relay that information on request. (See also **Elevations, elevation drawings; Scale drawings**)

Dresser A person hired to work backstage in the costume department. Dressers assist in the care and maintenance of the costumes and aid the performers in getting dressed in costume pieces that may be difficult to put on alone. Dressers are an essential factor in quick costume changes. The star dresser usually works only with the star and is more accommodating in providing personal service.

Dressing the set See **Set dressing, set decorating**

Dress parade The dress parade takes place during the *technical rehearsals*. After the scenery, sound, lights, and props have been put together with the actors' performance, the costumes are added so they may be viewed by the director and designers against the set and under the lights. A dress parade usually includes makeup and hairstyles. Sometimes the dress parade is formally presented with each performer coming forward in parade fashion. Other times, the performers will wear their costumes and makeup for the different scenes as they continue to rehearse.

Dress rehearsal A performance-like rehearsal done in the theatre with full costume, makeup, hair styles, and all the technical elements of the show. Dress rehearsals come in the last week or last few days of *technical rehearsals*. Dress rehearsals are designed to give the cast, crew, and SM the experience of performing the show as if an audience were present. (See also **Final dress**)

Dry tech A technical rehearsal in the theatre with only the crew, SM, and sometimes with the director and designers present. Running and working the technical cues and technical elements of the show without the actors present and performing their parts.

Dutchman A strip of material, usually black, that is placed over the space where two flats or pieces of scenery meet. A dutchman prevents the audience from seeing through to the distracting backstage activity, thus maintaining the illusion that walls are real and solid in their construction.

Duvetyn, velour, velveteen These materials are all similar in appearance and are used to make up the curtains that dress the stage. They are velvet-like cotton materials, usually black, more durable than real velvet, and less expensive. Pieces of these materials are often draped or stapled around the bottoms of platforms, large props, or set pieces to cover unsightly construction. When these items are set on the stage with curtains made of the same material and color, and when the stage is properly lit, the covered areas can virtually disappear from view.

Eight-by-ten (8" x 10") glossy   See **Head shots**

Electrics   A backstage expression for lighting and anything having to do with the electrical department.

Elevations, elevation drawings   Elevation drawings are part of the *blueprint drawings,* and are drawn in the same scale as the *floor plans* page of the blueprints. While the floor plans give a flat perspective of the set looking down from above, the elevation drawings give a flat perspective of the set looking straight ahead at eye level. Elevation drawings detail the height of all things within the set and design. The elevations page is the brother to the floor plan page. When the elevations page is placed under the floor plan page so both pages can be seen at the same time, the measurements of the set design on each page line up. The reader needs only to run a finger from one page to the other to get the different perspectives. (See also **Scale drawings**)

Eleven o'clock number, eleventh hour number   This term originates from the early days of musicals. At the time, shows started between 8:30 and 8:45 in the evening and could finish as late as midnight. By eleven o'clock a good strong song and/or dance number was needed to keep the audience's interest and enthusiasm, which would then carry them through to the end of the show. Today, shows start earlier in the evening and are shorter in length. The term "eleventh hour number" has remained in use but the eleventh hour number now comes within the tenth hour of the evening. The "Hello Dolly" song and dance in *Hello Dolly is* the eleventh hour number for that show.

Encore

1. To return to the stage and perform further for the audience. A singer or musician performing in concert might return to perform additional numbers due to the audience's generous, appreciative, and continuous applause.
2. Encore bows. When the applause is generous, appreciative, and continuous, the SM might have the performers come out for additional or encore bows.
3. Encore performance. A star performer might do an encore performance by repeating a performance at another time, due to popular demand.
4. Built-in encores. Today, concert performers will build in an encore by doing a number that the audience believes is the last one. At the end of the number the performer will take the bows, leave the stage, return, take more bows, and then do one or more numbers that were planned, rehearsed, and are part of the show. Some directors of musical

plays make it a practice to build into their *curtain bows* an encore by reprising the songs and dances in the show.

Ensemble, ensemble performers   Usually in musical shows. The group of performers who make up the singers, dancers, and extras. While the star(s), principal performers, and supporting actors stand out as individuals, the members of the ensemble remain anonymous, doing their work as a group.

Entr'acte   (Pronounced *on-teract*) In a musical play, the overture is played before the curtain rises and the play begins. The entr'acte is the music played leading from the intermission into the second act.

Epilogue   The epilogue is a scene that follows the final scene of a play. The epilogue is like a *tag* or *button* to the play; it brings greater resolve or closure, ties up loose ends, and gives additional information to the audience, telling how the plot, characters, or action continues in the future. The opposite of the epilogue is the *prologue,* which appears at the beginning of the play. (See also **Prologue**)

Equity   See **Actor's Equity Association**

Fade-in, fade-out   A transition of light, either fading from darkness to light, or fading from light to darkness. (See also **Fade to black**)

Fade to black, go to black   Directors, designers, technicians, and SMs use this term when asking that the lights on stage fade out all the way to a dark or *black* stage.

False proscenium, show portal   The false proscenium or show portal is a *flat* placed just behind the permanent proscenium arch of the stage. Many times false prosceniums and show portals are designed and decorated to complement the theme or scenery of the show. A false proscenium or show portal makes the opening to the stage smaller. Designers use this to their advantage when designing a small or intimate play, or when a small show must perform in a theatre with a large proscenium opening. (See also **Proscenium**)

Feedback

1. That squealing sound heard when a microphone comes too close to a speaker, or when the volume of the sound (the *gain*), is turned up too high. Technically speaking, feedback is the same sound waves amplifying themselves over and over.
2. When performers ask for feedback on their performance, they are asking for conformation on doing a good job, or looking for constructive commentary with suggestions for improvement. The director should be the only person giving actors feedback on their performance. When an SM is in the position of having to give feedback, it must be

given with care and concern for the performer and the show.

Female plug At one end of an electric cable or extension cord there is always a female plug—a plug that accepts the two or three prongs of the *male plug*. The female plug is always the source of power, while the male plug taps into that power and carries it to a lighting instrument, appliance, or apparatus that requires electricity to function.

Fill light Fill lights are part of the light design to make a more even pattern of light, either in a specific area or across the entire stage. Fill lights fill in the dark spots on stage that usually occur between the different areas of light across the stage. Fill lights reduce deep shadows. Fill lights enhance the light already present on stage, but when lit by themselves, are flat and uninteresting.

Final dress The last *dress rehearsal* before *previews* or *opening night*. Many times the producer will open the final dress to invited guests to give the cast and crew the experience of performing the show for an audience.

Find your light This statement is made to actors on stage, asking them to stand in the brightest part of the light in the area in which they are performing. As part of their craft, performers learn to feel or sense the brightest part of a light (*hot spot*) coming from the different lighting instruments focused on the stage. (See also **Key light**.)

Fire curtain An asbestos or highly fire-retardant drop hung in front of the main *house curtain* and set immediately behind the *proscenium arch*. In case of a fire, this drop is lowered to seal the audience part of the theatre from the stage and backstage areas. The fire curtain is designed mostly to protect the audience, because fires are more apt to start on stage and spread from there. Some fire curtains are made of steel. In times past, the fire curtain was lowered by hand by a stagehand or fire marshal who might be on duty. Today most fire curtains are automatically released, triggered similarly to the way a smoke alarm is set off. The curtain lowers at a moderate speed with the sound of a warning alarm. The alarm alerts anyone on stage who might be standing in the line or path of the curtain.

In some theaters the fire curtain has a scene or design painted on it. It is left in view as the audience enters and taken out ten or fifteen minutes before the show begins, to reveal the main house curtain or *show curtain*.

Fire laws Rules and regulations governing the prevention of fire and the safety of the people in the theatre, both backstage and in the audience. Without invitation or announcement, a day or two before the *opening night* of every show, the SM will see a city fire

marshal walking through the theatre and backstage areas. The fire marshal will be checking to see if the curtains have been flame proofed, the fire extinguishers are accessible and fully charged, all fire exits, escape routes, and pathways are left open, and all fire laws are being followed. The fire marshal will also check to see if the *fire curtain* is operational, if *open flames* are being used in the show, and that all necessary fire permits have been obtained.

Fire retardant A chemical that can be sprayed on or soaked into materials to prevent them from burning easily and causing a fire to spread quickly. (See also **Flame proof**)

Fire up An expression used by technicians and SMs when asking for electrical power to be turned on, either for the lights on stage or for some other instrument requiring power.

First electrics (second electrics, third electrics, etc.) Sections of lighting instruments that hang overhead on stage. In each section, lights are hung on a pipe along the entire width of the stage. The first electrics is the first pipe of lights, usually a foot or two away from the *proscenium arch*. Traveling up stage away from the audience, the second electrics usually is 6 to 10 feet away, depending on the depth of the stage. The third electrics follows at about the same distance still further upstage. On a large stage there can be a fourth and sometimes a fifth electrics.

These lights provide a good portion of the light needed to light the stage, scenery, and actors. Like all the other rigging and stage equipment hung overhead on stage, these lights are concealed from the audience by a teaser or *boarder*. On occasion they are left in full view as part of the stage design and scenery. These sections of lights are also referred to as the #1 electrics, #2 electrics, etc.

Fittings A term used in theatre primarily in costuming. Fittings are the beginning of the final phase in making or preparing costumes for a show. It is during this time that the performers must try on each costume to see how it fits so the costumers or wardrobe people can make alterations. Costumes sometimes are made specifically for the actor. Other times, the costumes are already made and pulled from the rack in the costume shop. In either case, the actor must go through one or more fittings.

Fix a scene The process of changing or redirecting a scene, or sometimes an entire act. This may mean reworking characterizations, changing *blocking*, rewriting the script, or all of the above. (See also **Scene doctor, play doctor**)

Fixed casters See **Casters**

Flame proof Material and items on the stage and in the backstage areas that have been treated with a *fire re-*

tardant chemical to keep them spreading fire or bursting into flames.

Flash pot   A small container, usually metal, that is hidden or disguised from the audience. It is electrically wired and capable of holding explosive flash powder or flash paper. When a current is sent to the device, the powder or paper explodes into a flash of fire and/or a puff of smoke. The use of flash pots is highly regulated by law and the fire department. In some situations, a licensed pyrotechnic operator is required.

Flat lighting   Lighting on stage that comes mostly from the front, giving no dimension or depth to the scenery or actors. Lighting with no *side lighting* or *back lighting*. A *wash* is typical of flat lighting.

Flats   Wooden frames braced at all joining corners. Flats usually are 10 feet by 4 feet and are covered with muslin or canvas. Some are covered with *velour* or *duvetyn*, depending on the intended use and purpose of the flat. Most times, flats covered with muslin are painted to become part of the scenery. An SM's favorite use of flats is as *backing* at places on the set where the audience can see through to the backstage activity. Another is to book two or more flats together, making a *quick change room* adjacent to the set or somewhere in the backstage area where it will not interfere with the moving of people or scenery.

Flood, flood light   A stage lighting instrument, a lamp, or a bulb that allows the light to spread onto the stage in a wide and undefined area.

Floor plans, ground plans   These are the drafted *blueprint drawings* of the set as viewed from above—looking down onto a flat, one-dimensional picture of lines and measurements. The floor plans are the layout, boundaries, and limits of the scenery as it is placed on the stage. It is from these drawing that the SM gets information for taping the outline of the set on the rehearsal room floor, and for relaying information about the set to the director or actors during the rehearsal period.

Flop   An unsuccessful or failed show; a financial flop, a critical flop, or both. Also called a turkey.

Fluorescent, iridescent colors   Vivid colors, usually lime, orange, or yellow. These colors are brilliantly reflected under an *ultraviolet* light when there is little to no other light present on stage.

Fly gallery   The area on either side of the backstage where the stagehands stand to pull the ropes that make drops, curtains, set pieces, or lighting equipment fly in or out, to and from the stage. In times gone by, this area usually was raised well above the floor backstage. This gave the stagehands a better view of the things they were flying in and out. With the perfection of the *fly system* and the addition of

the steel-brick *counter-weight system*, today most fly galleries are on the stage floor level.

Flymen   The stagehands who stand at the *fly rail* and pull the ropes that fly in and out the drops, curtains, set pieces, and lighting equipment that hangs overhead on the stage. (See also **Fly gallery**)

Fly rail, pin rail   In general terms, the fly rail is the place backstage where the stagehands stand to operate the ropes to the *fly system*. More specifically, the fly rail or pin rail is that part of the *fly system* where the stagehands stand to secure the ropes to ensure that the drops, scenery, etc., won't go crashing to the stage floor. Today, the apparatus to do this consists of a clamp, which holds the rope in place, and a safety ring, which ensures that the clamp won't come loose. In times past when the fly system was first introduced into the theatre, the pin rail was a wooden pole or beam set on its side, about 3 or 4 feet off the floor. Along this pole or beam were pegs or wooden pins that penetrated through to both sides—thus the term "pin rail." It was around these pegs that the ropes were tied and secured.

Flys   Any part of the system that flys in and out the drops, curtains, set pieces, or lighting equipment that hangs above the stage. (See also **Fly gallery**)

Fly space   The space or area above the stage that houses the *grid*, pulleys, *pipes*, and ropes needed to fly in and out the scenery and technical equipment that hangs above the stage.

Fly system   The structure, steel framing, mechanisms, and rigging of ropes and cables backstage that aid in flying in and out the scenery and technical equipment that hangs above the stage. (See also **Fly gallery; Counter-weights, counter-weight system**)

Focus

1. In the world of stage lighting, this means to adjust each lighting instrument so its beam of light is aimed toward the stage in a particular direction and *shuttered* so the light covers only a desired area.

2. In acting and directing, this term is used in different ways:

   Taking focus or pulling focus is when an actor in a scene draws the audience's attention. When done at the appropriate time, this is admired by all; when done inappropriately, it is soon followed with an *acting note* to the performer. (See also **Take stage**)
   Giving focus is when actors turn or position themselves to direct the audience's attention to another actor or to another part of the stage. (See also **Counter, make a counter-move**)
   Holding focus is when an actor, through presence, position on stage, attitude, energy, move-

ment, and all that comes with performing, keeps the audience's attention on himself.

Focusing lights   After the lights on the stage have been hung and the scenery/furniture is in place, two stagehands from the electric department adjust the lighting instruments that light up the different areas or places on stage. One stagehand works at the different lighting instruments, while the other remains on the floor of the stage. The stagehand above aims each lighting instrument so the beam of light shines in the prescribed place on the stage, according to the light plot and design. The stagehand on deck stands in the place where each lighting instrument is to be directed and tells the stagehand above when the hottest or brightest part of the light (the *hot spot*) is shining in his or her eyes.

This being done, the stagehand above locks the instrument into place with a wrench, *shutters* off the light so it falls only in the area it is designated to illuminate and, if needed, uses *barn doors* to block any light that falls into another area or onto another object. Finally, as a safety precaution, each instrument has a safety chain attached to it, which the stagehand above wraps around the pipe on which the instrument is hanging.

Follow cue   A follow cue is a cue that comes immediately after another. When an SM is calling cues for the show, there is only a beat in time, no more than a second long, before the follow cue is called. Follow cues are used to create the split-second timing that is sometimes needed to have technical things happen correctly on the stage and to create the illusion or magic seen in a live performance.

Follow script

1. During rehearsals, the SM or some other designated person follows the dialogue in the script as the performers do their lines from memory. If an actor forgets some dialogue, the person following script must be ready to verbally give the line upon request from the actor. The script follower must also remain alert and correct any wrong words or lines of dialogue being said.
2. During a performance the SM also follows script, but this time for the purpose of *calling cues* for the performance.

Follow spot   A lighting instrument emitting a strong and intense beam of light that usually is brighter than any of the lights *focused* on the stage. This instrument is placed on a stand that can swivel and tilt, thus enabling the person operating the light to follow the performers on stage. (See also **Carbon arc spotlight; Limelight**)

Footlights, the foots   Lights that are placed on the floor at the front edge or *apron* of the stage. In older the-

aters, these lights are built into the floor of the stage. In newer theaters, the lighting designer may choose to place strip light units in this position.

A drawback to this kind of lighting is the shadows cast across the backdrop or on the scenery as the performer moves about the stage in front of the foots. Older performers like footlights because they give them a more youthful appearance. Lighting designers seldom use footlights except for a special look or effect, or when doing a vaudeville or variety show.

Fouled

1. When a rope in the *fly system* gets kinked or tangled and prevents a drop or piece of scenery from flying in or out.
2. Similarly, stagehands will use this term when a drop or piece of scenery gets caught or hooked onto something in the flys and cannot be flown in or out. (See also **Hung up**)

Fourth wall   The *proscenium* opening, through which the audience views the play, is the fourth wall. Prior to the nineteenth century, plays were presentational in style with the performers speaking their dialogue out to the audience even if their words were being directed to another character on the stage. By the twentieth century, naturalism and realism had become the modern form of play writing and presentation. With the works of Chekhov, Stanislavski, and Eugene O'Neill the convention of the fourth wall became even more important, giving the audience the feeling that they were observing life, seeing it through the fourth wall of a room. (See also **Box set; Breaking the fourth wall**)

Four walls, four walling it   In its purest form, four walling it is when a show moves into a theatre or performance site bringing with it everything the show needs. The theatre provides only the four walls and the permanent parts of the building such as the lobby, audience seating, stage area, and a fly or rail system. The rest, including box office, ushering, parking, security, and janitorial staffs, is provided by the producing company of the show. There are, however, wide variations on this theme and most theaters today provide much more than just the four walls.

Freezing the show   The point at which the director, producer, and actors stop changing and improving the show and perform it the same way each time it is presented. Once the show has been frozen, it becomes the SM's job to keep the show at performing level, seeing that changes made are minimal, in alliance with the director's work, and within the artistic integrity of the show.

French scenes   Plays are divided into acts and scenes within the acts. French scenes are smaller scenes within each scene. They are not indicated in the script. A French scene begins when a character physically enters the stage. It ends and a new French scene begins with the entrance or exit of a character, be it the same character that just entered, a new character entering, or a character that was already on the stage. A French scene may be short, with no dialogue and only a bit of *business* before someone enters or exits the stage, or it may be many pages long, during which no one enters or exits. Dividing the play into French scenes is useful to the director and SM in setting up a rehearsal schedule.

Fresnel lamp A stage lighting instrument whose light passes through a Fresnel lens. This lens causes the light to diffuse or *flood* on the stage in a general and undefined area, without the hard edge a spotlight has.

Front curtain The curtain that hangs on the stage, just behind the *proscenium* arch, covering the opening of the stage and preventing the audience from seeing anything on stage until the curtain opens or is raised. (See also **Act curtain**)

Front lights The lights that are placed in front of the *proscenium* and out in the *house*. These are the lights in the *anti-pros*, the *box booms*, the *balcony lights*, and whatever spotlights the show might be using.

Front of the house The lobby, foyer, box office, marquee, and often where the manager's office and executive offices for the theatre are located.

Frosted gel A translucent gel placed in the front part of a lighting instrument that diffuses and softens the light falling on the stage or an actor. (See also **Gels**)

Full dress, full dress rehearsal A rehearsal done in the theatre with costume, makeup, and hairstyles after all the other technical elements have been added to the show. Full dress rehearsals take place in the last few days of *technical rehearsals,* after the *dress parade,* and just before the preview performances or *opening night.* Full dress rehearsals are performed nonstop, as if an audience were present. When it is time to have a full dress rehearsal and things are going well, the director and producer may invite guests to watch.

Gain The volume or level at which the sound is set. The intensity or decibel output of the sound. To raise or lower the gain on the speakers/monitors is to make the sound louder or softer. To raise or lower the gain on the mics is to give the mics a greater capacity to receive the sound. If the gain is set too high, it can result in *feedback.*

Gel burn out This is when the intensity of the light passing through the *gel* burns a hole in the gel, or melts it to the point where the white light of the bulb is being projected onto the stage rather than the color from the gel.

Gel frames Devices to hold the colored *gels.* A gel frame is a two-flapped metal frame hinged together like a book. A square piece of gel is placed between the flaps, the flaps are closed, and the frame is slipped into slots at the front part of a stage lighting instrument.

Gels To get the various colors of light on the stage, a clear, transparent, and colored cellophane-type material is slipped into a slot at the front part of the lighting instruments. Originally gels were made from a gelatin substance, thus the abbreviated name, *gel.* Today they are made from plastic or mylar and are able to withstand intense heat before starting to melt or burn out. (See also **Gel burn out**)

Getting the show on its feet The entire process of lifting the show from the written page to the live performance: setting the *blocking,* developing the characters, or adding the technical elements. (See also **On your feet**)

Ghosting When the lights on stage are quickly turned off, as in a *blackout,* there remains for one or two seconds more, a slight glow of light before the lamp goes out completely. During this brief moment, the audience can still see whatever is on stage. Actors, SMs, and stagehands must remain aware of this ghosting effect and wait for the stage to go completely dark before making their next moves. To see the actors scurrying to leave the stage or the stagehands starting to move props and scenery spoils whatever illusion of reality may have been created for the audience.

Ghost light The ghost light is a single light left on the stage after everyone has left the theatre— a night light. Traditionally, this light is a bare bulb placed on a pole and stand, and is set in the middle of the stage. More commonly today, the ghost light is a single light that hangs from above. Its purpose is to prevent anyone from falling off the stage and into the orchestra pit; however, superstition has it that a light must be left on for the ghosts and spirits of actors past, who have worked this theatre and come out at night to repeat their performances.

Gig Job. This term was once used strictly by jazz musicians. At first it meant a short-term job, lasting for one night or maybe a week. Eventually it was used to refer to any job a musician got. The term quickly spread and became accepted language among all musicians, including those who performed in the classics. Actors and people working in the theatre, especially those working in musical theatre, picked up the term and have made it part of their jargon.

Give a line During rehearsals the SM or some designated person *follows script.* An actor may forget a line of dialogue and ask for the line. The person following script gives the exact wording of the line.

Give stage   A performer on stage moves or turns in such a way so the central point of interest is directed to another actor or part of the stage. (See also **Take stage**)

Giving acting notes   See **Acting notes; Notes**

Giving focus   See **Focus**

Giving a line reading   See **Line reading**

Gobo   A pattern, an image, or a design cut out on a thin plate of metal or aluminum. This plate is placed into the front part of a lighting instrument (usually a *leko*). When the light passes through the cutout, it projects the image on whatever part of the stage the designer or director chooses. There are some lighting instruments designed specifically for this purpose which may also have a motor built into them to make the cutout move, such as one projecting images of clouds in the sky. Gobos are effective in creating rays of sunlight, patterns of leaves, or shadows from moonlight. Images from gobos can suggest locations such as the bars of a prison or the grid of a dungeon. Gobos can also have a subliminal effect and induce strong feeling and emotions, such as a Star of David, a Red Cross, or a swastika.

GO! cue   For the SM and anyone involved in executing a cue during performance, this is the third and final part in the SM's *calling a cue*. The SM gives the first part—the *warning*—and the second part—the *stand by*. Each part is important in preparing for the cue, but the GO! is most important. It is what governs the technical timing of the show and has a direct effect on the performance.

God mic   A microphone placed in the audience for a director, producer, or casting person to use as they speak to the performers on stage during rehearsals or auditions. Technicians and SMs quickly came to name this mic the god mic because the person speaking was often in the darkened theatre and seemed to be a disembodied voice, booming from the darkness.

Gofer, runner, production assistant   This usually is a young, energetic person, who aspires to work in show business. The gofer often has few to no credits and is looking to start somewhere. Being a gofer is the proverbial getting your foot in the door job. The term gofer is a combination of the words "go" and "for" (go for this, go for that), and while the word gofer is often used, the terms runner or production assistant are preferred. The production assistant works mostly with the producer, director, and SM, running errands and going for things.

Go up on a line   Anytime an actor forgets a line of dialogue. The most intense and terrorizing application of this phrase is when an actor goes up on a line during performance. (See also **Up**)

Green room   A designated room or place in the theatre where guests may come to meet the performers after the performance. Most times it is backstage and convenient to the dressing rooms, in which case the green room also becomes the assembling place for the actors during the performance. Company meetings are often held in this room, and it is a favorite place for the director to assemble the cast to give *notes*. Today, the green room is seldom green. Some are elaborate and beautifully decorated. Many are comfortable and homey, with old prop furniture and very distinct evidence of long use. The green room got its name from the room in Covent Garden in London, at the turn of the century, which happened to be painted green.

Grid   The framework of pipes or wooden beams built high into the ceiling of the *fly space* above the stage. From the grid hangs the network of ropes, pulleys, pipes, and cables that is part of the *fly system*. (See also **Fly gallery**)

Grip   A stagehand who moves the set pieces and units. The term has its roots in film, referring to the person who was hired specifically to move and carry lighting equipment, and sometimes props and scenery. (See also **Schlep**)

Ground cloth   A large canvas cloth that is laid out on the rehearsal room floor, having painted or taped on it the dimensions, boundaries, and limits of the set. This cloth can be folded or rolled up and taken anywhere, then laid out again so the actors can rehearse. For *one-set shows* and in situations where the rehearsals are moved from one location to another, this is a very workable idea. Today with multiset musicals, ground cloths are less practical and are seldom used. Instead, each setting of scenery is taped to the rehearsal room floor with different-colored tape, and great effort is made to secure the same rehearsal room for the entire period of rehearsals.

Ground plans   See **Floor plans**

Ground row

1. Several units of *boarder lights* or strip light units placed on the floor of the stage in a single row and at the foot of the *cyclorama*. These lights are focused up on the cyc to give it color. The best effects created by the ground row of lights are sunrises, sunsets, and full-stage silhouettes.
2. A ground row is also a strip of low, cutout scenery, placed on the floor of the stage, and at the foot of the cyc. Sometimes the cutouts are made to look like distant hills, rocks, a fence, or vegetation. This scenery helps give dimension or a finished look to

the set, but is made mostly to hide the ground row of lights, which might be just behind.

Guy line, guide line   A length of rope or *line* attached to a pipe, a large prop, or a piece of scenery that must be raised or lowered. As the item travels up or down, a stagehand holds the rope guiding the object off in one way or the other, preventing it from twisting, turning, or getting *hung up* on anything that might be nearby.

Gypsy   A familial and loving term dancers use for themselves. This term describes the style of their professional lives—traveling with touring shows, moving from town to town, and setting up a home in whatever housing is provided.

Half-hour call   The latest time a performer is allowed to arrive at the theatre for a performance. This period of time is regulated by Equity rule, and is strongly enforced by the SM. It is during the final half hour that the actors prepare for the performance by getting into costume, makeup, hair, and character. If actors require more time to prepare, they come to the theatre earlier; however, they are only responsible and accountable to the SM at half hour. At the beginning of the half-hour call the SM counts heads to ensure everyone is present for the performance. If someone is missing, the SM first alerts the *understudy, stand by actor,* swing dancer, or dance captain, then starts calling the different phone numbers on the cast address list to try and locate the missing person. If a performer arrives any later than the half-hour call, that performer is questioned, officially written up in the SM's log book and/or show report, and warned about tardiness.

Halogen lamp   A stage lighting instrument and bulb that emits a very bright and intense white light. Sometimes this instrument is used in place of the *carbon arc spotlight*, but the rays of light coming from these lamps cannot be turned on and off as in most bulbs and lamps and they also need time to warm up to reach their full intensity.

Ham   A person who enjoys performing and does so at any given opportunity, be it formally on stage or informally in private or social situations. This term can be used negatively to criticize a pretentious or overbearing performer. Other times it can be a compliment, expressing a performer's ability to be entertaining.

Hand cue   Sometimes when the SM is calling cues for a performance, it may be easier or necessary to give a hand cue instead of giving the cue verbally. Of course the person executing the cue must be within viewing range, and must be able to see the SM clearly. In all such cases, the SM still goes through the three steps

required in calling cues: the *warning*, the *stand by*, and the *GO!* For the warning the SM makes visual contact with the person. A hand over the head is the stand by cue. For the GO! the SM brings the hand down in a large gesture so there is no doubt that the GO! has been called.

Handle   In terms of acting and performing, a handle is a little extra something an actor puts into the dialogue or character. This could be a sigh, an exclamatory word, or a catch phrase— something that is not written into the script. Sometimes actors will use a handle for coloring of character, to get timing, to sound real and conversational, or just to give them time to think of their next line. SMs must watch to see that the performer does not overuse this device.

Before beginning work on the play or the character, some directors and actors need to first find something on which to base their work. They need to study and analyze the play or character, perhaps finding a premise, a motivating thread, the author's intent, or just creating something of their own. Once they find their handle, the director or actor can begin to develop the play or create the role.

Hand props   Size and ease of handling during the performance determines what is a hand prop. This rule, however, is not always clear and steadfast. A drinking glass; a large, wrapped present; food substances; or hats used in a dance are classic examples of hand props. Yet a small wooden chair or foot stool, though easily handled during a performance, is not considered a hand prop. The difference between what is a hand prop and a regular prop is not crucial to the show. The classification of hand props in a show happens at the whim and discretion of the prop person and/or SM.

Hanging lights   The act of a stagehand attaching lighting instruments to pipes and poles and plugging them into their various circuits.

Hanging the show   An all-inclusive expression that describes the act of stagehands hanging drops, set pieces, flats, curtains, and the lights for the show. Hanging the show is usually the first step in setting up a show on the stage, and is done before the set and props are put into place.

Hard edge   See **Sharp edge, hard edge, soft edge**

Hard wall, hard wall set construction   Scenery, set pieces, and flats covered with a thin veneer, masonite, or plywood. Hard wall set construction got its start in films and television. This kind of construction requires more bracing, which makes the set pieces stronger, but heavier to handle. On the other hand, the set is more durable, can withstand greater use, wear and tear, and the rigors of traveling with a touring show. Hard wall construction for interior scenes also maintains greater reality in that the walls don't flap when a door opens or closes, or when the actors go up and down stairs.

Head high   A direction given to the stagehand operating the ropes for the flys. It tells the stagehand to fly in or fly out a drop, set piece, or curtain, to about seven to eight feet above the stage floor. In rehearsals, this allows people on stage to continue working without hitting their heads. (See also **Clear!**)

Heads!, heads up!   A safety call made from backstage, warning the people on stage to look up because something is being flown in or out from the flys. Upon hearing this call, experienced people in theatre know to stop immediately, see if they are in any danger, and take themselves out of harm's way. The tone of voice used in making this safety call is an excellent indicator of the urgency and degree of danger. Even a soft drop or curtain can cause injury, because steel pipes or chains are often placed into the hems of these things.

Head shots   An 8-by-10-inch glossy photograph of a performer. Usually a close shot from the waist or shoulders up. Actors submit these pictures along with their resumes at auditions. Head shots are an important aid and tool in casting and help the casting people to remember the different performers. These are often the pictures that are included in the program or playbill.

Heavy prop show   Just as the phrase suggests, this is a show that uses a lot of props and furniture.

Hemp   The material most commonly used in the early days of theatre to make up the ropes used in the *fly system*. Today the ropes are made mostly of synthetic materials that are more durable and smoother to the hands. (See also **Hemp house**)

Hemp house   Those theaters that still use *hemp* ropes and *sandbags* as their *flys* and *counter-weight system*.

High trim   Having to do with the *fly system* and the highest point at which a drop, curtain, piece of scenery, etc., is placed on the stage during the performance. (See also **Trim**)

Hi-hat   A device that can be slipped in front of most lighting instruments. When held in the hand, this device looks like a man's top hat, worn as formal wear in the early part of the nineteenth century, but with the top cut out. When slipped in front of a lighting instrument, the hi-hat narrows the beams of light hitting the stage to a smaller and more specific area. The longer or taller the shaft of the hi-hat, the narrower the area of light projected onto the stage.

Hit your mark   For actors, hitting their mark means to cross to an established point on stage, without looking down to see if they are in the correct position.

These marks are taped or painted on the stage floor with an *X* or a *T*. These points are established by the director or choreographer, and are usually crucial for lighting, *sight lines,* or the overall picture and composition of the stage. (See also **Spike marks**)

Hold   A term mostly used backstage when the SM, director, or a stagehand wants someone to stop what they are doing, remain in place, and stand by to continue.

Hold book, be on book, be on script   See **Follow script; Give a line**

Hold the curtain   Delaying raising the curtain for the performance to begin.

Holding focus   See **Focus**

Hook   Actors and directors sometimes like to find an idea, a premise, a motivating factor, the author's intent, or just create something of their own that becomes the bases for their creative work on a character or the play. (See also **Handle**.)

Horseshoe stage   A stage surrounded on three sides by the audience. (See also **Arena stage; Thrust stage**)

Hot spot   The part of a lighting instrument that projects the brightest or most intense amount of light on the stage. Actors are often asked to find the hot spot of the light in which they are standing for better audience viewing. SMs too must learn to find hot spots. Many times when traveling with a touring show, the SM is asked to help in *focusing lights*. (See also **Focusing lights**)

House   For people working in theatre, the house is that part of the theatre where the audience sits to watch the show. (See also **Front of the house**)

House crew   The house crew includes the technical department heads and stagehands hired by the theatre to maintain the facility and work whatever shows come to that facility. (See also **Local crew**)

House curtain, main curtain   The curtain or drape hung just behind the *proscenium* arch. This curtain is a permanent part of the theatre and is used to cover the opening of the stage as the audience enters to be seated. This curtain differs from a *show curtain* in that a show curtain is brought in by the show performing at the theatre, and is often designed to complement the scenery and/or look of the show.

For the SM, the house curtain or show curtain is an item that will be dealt with at least two times during a performance, if not four or more times. This curtain can be made of plush velvet, elaborately pleated, or it can be plain and simple, made of relatively inexpensive material.

House lights   The lights that light up the theatre as the audience is entering or leaving the theatre.

House man   This term is reserved for the person who is technically in charge of the care and maintenance of the stage, theatre, and possibly the building in which the theatre is housed. The *technical director* of the show remains concerned with the care and maintenance of the show, while the house man is the person to turn to with problems having to do with the theatre itself. People in theatre may also use this term in reference to the house manager, the person in charge of the jobs and activities of the box office, the lobby, the marquee, and the ushering staff.

House right, house left   These positions are determined from the audience's point of view as they sit facing the stage. *Stage right* and *stage left* are the opposite and are determined from the actors' point of view as they face the audience. Novice performers and beginning SMs often get the two mixed up.

House seats   Prime *orchestra seats* set aside for each performance which are used as complimentary seats for VIPs or guests, or sold to members of the company for their guests, friends, or business associates. A day or two before each performance, whatever house seats remain unused usually go on sale to the general public.

House speakers   Sound speakers placed in the audience, either at the sides of the *proscenium* and/or above just in front of the proscenium. Their purpose is to enhance the audience's hearing by having broadcast through the speakers the dialogue being spoken by the actors on stage, the music being played in the orchestra pit, or the prerecorded music and sound effects played from the sound booth. (See also **Monitors**)

Hung up   Something that is caught or hooked on something else. Scenery being moved on and off stage can get hung up on the stage curtains. As items fly in and out from the flys, they sometimes get hung up on items hanging nearby. (See also **Fouled**)

Iambic pentameter   Five beats or accents within a line or section of dialogue. Dialogue that is written and delivered with five beats or accents for each grouping of words. All of Shakespeare's plays are written in iambic pentameter.

IATSE, I.A.T.S.E.   The International Alliance of Theatrical Stage Employees. The stagehands' union.

Imaginary wall   See **Fourth wall**

Improvise   To perform without benefit of script and/or rehearsal. To create dialogue, music, or action as it comes to mind rather than having it planned or mapped out ahead of time.

Ingenue, soubrette   Young lead or supporting female roles. An ingénue differs from a soubrette in that an ingénue's character is simpler and more innocent, while a soubrette is pert and more coquettish.

In one   (First see **Wings**) *In one* describes the performing area on stage closest to the audience. It starts with and includes the first *wing*. It crosses the stage to the first wing on the opposite side and goes down to the edge or *apron* of the stage. Thus anyone performing in this area is performing in one. This term has its roots in vaudeville and burlesque, where comics and small acts were placed with a curtain or drop hanging closely behind. Meanwhile, beyond the drop or curtain, props and scenery were being set up for a larger, more elaborate act or scene. This technique is especially effective in today's multiscene musical shows. Playing a scene in one creates a closer, more intimate feeling with the audience.

In sync   The term *sync*, is an abbreviation for *synchronize* or *synchronization*. Being in sync is when two or more elements of the show are working together in a compatible relationship—when the live music from the orchestra pit is playing together with the prerecorded music. For the SM, having all parts of the production performing in sync is the most meaningful and important form of this definition. (See **Lip sync; Click track**)

Iridescent colors   See **Fluorescent colors**

Iris   A mechanism built into spotlights and some stage lighting instruments that allows a stagehand to adjust the size of the circle of light coming out of the instrument and hitting the stage. (See also **Douser**)

Jumping the gun   Anticipating and executing a cue or line of dialogue before its proper time. Doing something before the time as set by the director.

Juvenile   Young lead and supporting roles.

Key light   Areas of lighting on stage are lit with two or more lighting instruments. The instrument emitting the brightest light and covering most of the area is the key light. Performers are asked to find and stand in their key light for better audience viewing. If the stage were lit with only key lights, its appearance would be flat and washed out. Other lights set at different intensities, from different angles, and from the sides give depth, dimension, and greater form to the actors, scenery, and objects that appear on stage. (See also **Back lighting; Fill light; Hot spot**)

Kickers, shin busters   These are lighting instruments, usually *lekos*, that are placed on the floor of the stage. Sometimes they are placed at the foot of the stage and off to the extreme sides. Most times they are placed in the wings with their light projecting across the stage. When used in this way, these lights create a surrealistic pattern of *cross lighting* or *side lighting*. Kickers are commonly used in ballet and dance concerts. Not only do these lights create dramatic mood, effect, color, and design, but they light the dancers' bodies for better viewing of their movements.

The terms kickers and shin busters come from the humor of stagehands, because these side lights emphasizes the dancer's legs as they move and kick. In a second and perhaps more literal meaning, these side lights give a "kick" to the lights already on stage. As a third meaning, when these lights are placed on the floor, they are easily kicked or bumped, sometimes causing a bruise or minor cut on the shins.

Kill   In theatre, the term *kill* means to stop doing or using something: "Kill the chair in the second act"; "Kill the business with the glass in the restaurant scene"; "Kill the lights on the stage left side"; "Kill the sound, please."

Lamp   This term can refer to either the entire lighting instrument or to only the bulb inside. At home we use bulbs. In theatrical lighting they are more correctly called lamps.

Lashed together   Two *flats* tied together with a thin rope or *sash cord*, which is also called *lash line*.

Lash line   A thin rope or *sash cord* that is used to tie or lash flats together.

Legit house   A theatre that presents only plays and Broadway musicals—not vaudeville, burlesque, or other types of live stage shows.

Legitimate theatre   A term that distinguishes plays and Broadway musicals from vaudeville, burlesque, or other live stage performances.

Legs, tormentors   The long curtains or tall flats that dress each side of the stage. They create the different *wings* from which the performers and pieces of scenery can enter or leave the stage. Legs and tormentors also prevent the audience from seeing into the backstage area. When flats are used, some technicians and designers may call them portals.

Leko   The brand name of a particular kind of stage lighting instrument that has became a generic term for all lighting instruments of this kind. The leko is widely used and popular because of its capabilities. Leko lights are good for throwing light from longer distances and leave a circular pattern of light on the stage which, when adjusted, can have either a *sharp* or *soft edge*. This lighting instrument is also equipped with an *iris* to make the circle of light larger or smaller, and to sharpen or defuse the edge of light. It also has a *shutter* that can be adjusted to prevent light from spilling into unwanted areas or onto things that are not to be lit.

Levels

1. Stage level is anything that is on the same floor or level as the stage. The backstage area and some dressing rooms are at stage level. The orchestra pit is below stage level.
2. Platforms or risers are structures that create different levels for the scenery and on which the actors can perform.
3. Performance level is the pitch and intensity at which an actor performs for an audience. Actors are often asked to do rehearsals at performance level.
4. Light levels are the amount of brightness or intensity of a light on stage that helps create the mood, atmosphere, or effect.
5. Sound levels are the loudness or softness of the sound—the volume, the gain.

Light board   In general terms and without technical explanation, the light board is a piece of electrical equipment—a panel or console, with switches and levers. Every light on stage is in some way plugged into the light board. During performance, when called for by the SM, every light cue in the show is executed from this board by an electrician stagehand, the *light board operator*.

In days gone by, the light board was more commonly called the dimmer board or the dimmer rack. These boards, with their *rheostat dimmers* and protruding handles, were large, usually built into one of the walls backstage, required two or more stagehands to operate, and could have only one light cue preset in advance. In the 1960s and 70s, the Eisenhower Board became state-of-the-art equipment. The rheostat dimmers were replaced by a dimmer pack and the board was capable of *presetting* many cues at one time.

With the perfection of electronic equipment, the dimmer packs have become even smaller and the computer keyboard and monitor has replaced the light board console entirely, requiring only one person to operate the whole thing. Even more revolutionary is the computer's ability to store the cues for the entire show. At any time, any cue, in any part of the show, can be brought up on the stage. In addition, all the technical information as to which lights are being used and at what intensity is displayed on the computer monitor. (See also **Light board operator**)

Light board operator   This technician is part of the electric department. During technical rehearsals he sits at the light board, which today is a computer keyboard, and sets the levels and intensities of the light cues for the show, as instructed by the lighting designer and/or director. During performance, this operator executes the light cues as they are called by the SM. In the days before computer light boards, for a large musical show, there could be as many as six stagehands, sometimes more, to operate the light board. Today it takes only one at the keyboard.

Lighting design   The selection, layout, and arrangement of all lighting instruments that light the stage, including the placement of various lighting instruments, deciding on their angle of projection and the intensity at which they will light the scenery, performing areas, and actors. Light design is also deciding on *gel* colors to be used in each scene. The lighting designer paints the stage with lights. The designer's use of lights establishes an environment, sets a mood, creates special effects, and lights the stage for audience viewing interest and pleasure. In making these choices, the designer must also complement the scenery, costumes, actors, and the play itself.

Light movement, the movement of light   The lights changing on stage during the performance and seen by the audience. Light designers and directors use the movement of light to enhance and complement the show. Each time the SM calls a light cue during a performance, the SM checks on stage to see the lights change as they move from one cue to the next. (See also **Moving lights**)

Light plot   A drafted *blueprint drawing* that notes the placement and layout of all the lighting instruments and *gel* colors that are to be used in the design of lights for a show. (See also **Lighting design**)

Light spill   Unwanted light spilling onto something or into another area.

Light towers   A flat grid of pipes welded together, on which lighting instruments are hung. These towers usually are placed backstage in the wings and hang overhead with their lights focused on the stage to create *side lighting*. Light towers can also be placed in the audience off to the far sides of the stage and become the *box boom lights*. (See also **Light tree**)

Light tree   A single, free-standing pole screwed into a heavy metal base. Along the top half of the pole stage lighting instruments are clamped. These trees usually are placed in the *wings* just behind the wing curtains or portals. They are set out of view of the audience and out of the way of the performers, as well as out of the way of the pieces of scenery that must move through the wings. Light trees are convenient to create *side lighting* or for hanging lighting instruments where there is no other way to hang them.

Limbo   A place or space on stage that has no distinctive setting or environment that relates to the play or scenery. Most times this place is off to either side of the stage, in front of the proscenium, and if used during the performance, may be lit by a *spotlight* or *pool of light*. Narrators, announcers, or characters who speak directly to the audience are often placed in such an area. Sometimes, when a set is backed by curtains or nondescript flats, the space above the set is referred to as limbo.

Limelight

1. To be *in the limelight* is a theatrical and colloquial expression meaning to be in a prominent position where a person can be seen by others, and has the focus and attention: to be highlighted, singled out, or in prominent view.

2. The term limelight comes from the first spotlights used in theatre when electricity was first used as stage lighting. Lime was placed in a metal container and when mixed with an electrical current, a bright glow was created. With the use of a mirror and lens, that glow was reflected onto the stage, creating a very intense and strong circular pattern of light, thus a *spotlight* and the term limelight. The limelight was eventually replaced by the safer, *carbon arc spotlight,* which is now in transition and being replaced by the intense *Xenon* (z-non) lamps.

Line?, Line please!   During rehearsals, an actor may ask the SM or the person *holding book* for a line of dialogue that the actor cannot remember.

Line reading

1. The way an actor says a line of dialogue. A line reading is the meaning, feeling, intent, expression, inflection, tune, tone, motivation, attitude, personal experience, and character study that influences how an actor will say a line of dialogue.

2. Giving a line reading means telling an actor how to say a line of dialogue. Most performers dislike this approach; they prefer talking about the meaning, feeling, intent, motivation, personal experience, or character study. Some directors direct by giving line readings. Others will use a line reading only as a last resort. SMs should make it a standing rule never to give line readings.

Line rehearsal   A rehearsal in which the emphasis and focus is on saying the lines of dialogue in the play, leaving out the physical action or movement of the play. Directors and SMs will have this kind of rehearsal to help the actors remember and memorize their lines. A line rehearsal is also useful in refreshing the actors' memories after they have had time off from performing the show.

Lines

1. The dialogue written in the script. The words the actors speak.

2. In the technical world of stagehands, a line is any length of rope.

Lip sync   An actor silently mouthing the words to a song that has been prerecorded, giving the impression that the actor is actually singing the song. Many times the voice on the prerecord is the performer's own voice, and the choice to lip sync instead of performing the number live may be to save the actor's voice when performing a difficult show, or to allow the actor to do a strenuous dance and sing at the same time.

Live Stagehands use this term when explaining where things are placed backstage—the place and space a thing occupies: "The prop table on stage right will live just behind the kitchen wall of the set"; "The porch unit will live in the stage left wing for the entire show, ready to be moved on and off stage when it is needed." (See also **Store**)

Load-in, load-out See **Drag-in, drag out**

Local crew The stagehands hired in each town to work a touring show. The show will travel with its own technical department heads, who are called the show crew or road crew. It is, however, more economical for the producer to hire stagehands in each town, rather than having the expense of traveling and housing all of the stagehands needed to set up the show and run it.

Long-line, short-line The *long-line* and the *short-line* are the ropes or *lines* that the stagehands operate to fly curtains, drops, etc., in and out—to and from the stage. These ropes travel through the *fly system* and are attached to pipes hanging in the *fly space* above the stage. To hold the pipes suspended above the stage and parallel to the floor, each pipe must have at least two ropes or lines attached to it. One line is at the right end of the pipe, the other at the left end— the *long-line* and the *short-line*.

Either rope can be the long-line or the short-line, depending on which side of the backstage the *fly gallery* is placed—the place where the stagehands stand to operate the ropes. The rope that travels the longest distance from the stagehand, through the fly system, across the stage, and over to the far end of the pipe is the long-line. The short-line then is the rope traveling the shortest distance and closest to the side where the stagehand is standing.

There will be times when a drop or curtain is hanging at an angle and not parallel to the stage floor. This is easily corrected by having a stagehand adjust either the long-line or the short-line until the object is straight. To communicate this quickly and effectively, it is important the SM know which line is which.

Having said all of this, with today's *counterweight system*, the long- and short-lines are permanently fixed into place with little to no chance of their becoming unadjusted. There are, however, still some theaters without upgraded fly systems. It will be in those theaters that the SM may be called on to deal with such problems and apply this knowledge of the long-line and the short-line.

Low trim Having to do with the *fly system* and the lowest point at which a drop, curtain, or piece of scenery

is placed on the stage during the performance. (See also **Trim**)

Main curtain See **Act curtain**

Male plug The two- or three-prong end of an electric cable, extension cord, or lighting instrument that is inserted into *a female plug* to get electricity. (See also **Female plug**)

Management An all-inclusive term that groups together the producing company, the producer, the company managers, and their staffs. The counterpart to management is the employee. The director remains independent, but is often considered management. Being a member of Equity, the SM is an employee and Equity expects loyalty from the SM. However, due to the nature of the SM's work, the cast members and director see the SM as management, as does the producer, who also expects the SM's loyalty.

Mark it

1. Direction given to a stagehand to record on a cue sheet the level or position of a thing, such as light intensity, sound level, or placement on stage. (See also **Spike marks**)
2. In rehearsals, the director may ask an actor to *half-perform* a scene or a moment in the play, either to conserve the actor's energy or to pass over something that may need to be changed or fixed at a later time.

Mask, masking

1. There is the kind of mask that is placed over a person's face to change, cover, conceal, or disguise the persons's identity.
2. In backstage talk, to mask something is to cover over an area or space that should not be seen by the audience: to hide from view of the audience the backstage area with a *curtain, flat,* or piece of scenery.
3. Masking is also the item or material used. Such things as *curtains, flats, boarders, teasers, portals, tormentors,* pieces of scenery, or strips of material can be used as masking. The areas that most often require masking on the set are open doorways, hallways, behind windows, the wing spaces, and the equipment and rigging hanging overhead, above the stage.

Master of ceremonies (M.C.) A person/performer who hosts a show. Most commonly used for *variety shows.* Usually a comic performer who comes out to *warm up* the audience by welcoming them, perhaps telling jokes, and ultimately introducing the different acts or various portions of the show. (See also **Warm up**)

Measurements   The primary definition of this term for the SM is in dealing with costumes. Within the first days of rehearsals, or even before, as soon as an actor has signed a contract, it is important to the *costumer* to get the actor's *measurements* so the costumer can start making the costumes or pull them from the rack at the costume shop and begin alterations.

Melodramas   Simple morality plays presented at the turn of the twentieth century, depicting one-dimensional characters: the hero and heroin (the lovers), the villain, the beleaguered or disabled parent, the child or baby, and the comic or buffoon. The acting was stylistic, broad in gesture, and presentational in dialogue. The themes were almost always of goodness and evil, purity and piety, honesty, faithfulness, devotion, or all of the above.

Mezzanine   If a theatre has more than one balcony, the first balcony is referred to as the mezzanine. If there is only one balcony and it is divided into sections, the first part may be called the mezzanine, while the rest is called the balcony and/or upper balcony.

Mic   An abbreviated term for microphones.

Mid-stage traveler   A curtain placed somewhere in the middle of the stage between the *downstage* edge of the stage and the last curtain or drop *upstage*. It is a curtain that can be opened or closed on cue. (See also **Traveler**)

Mid trim   Having to do with the *fly system*, this is the middle point or interim point at which a drop, curtain, piece of scenery, etc., stops a performance as it is traveling in or out, on or off the stage. (See also **Trim**)

Milking, milking the audience   A performer getting the most possible reaction from the audience, by extending and playing on something that brings the audience pleasure or moves them emotionally. When done well, milking can be a positive thing for the performer and the show. However, a little milking goes a long way, and performers not good in the art easily step over the line, making it a distracting and negative thing.

Mixer

1. A piece of electronic sound equipment that enables a technician or director to artistically mix, blend, and balance the sound the audience hears through the *house speakers*. The mix can be simple, mixing and balancing a few *body mics* or *stage mics* to amplifying the actors' dialogue, or it can be involved as in a musical, mixing together a full orchestra, prerecorded music, the lead singers, and perhaps a chorus.

2. The term mixer is also used when referring to the technician who operates the mixing console during the performance.

Mix sound, sound mix   To balance and control all the elements of what makes good and clear sound before it is broadcast through the speakers; to combine, through a piece of electronic equipment, the singer on the stage with the music being played from the orchestra pit so each element does not overpower the other; to artistically select what elements of the sound should dominate, blend, or be subdued. (See also **Mixer**)

Monitors

1. Sound speakers strategically placed in the audience and throughout the backstage to transmit the dialogue or music being performed on the stage. In musical shows, monitors may also be placed on the *apron* of the stage or in the *wings* facing the performers to enable them to hear the music from the orchestra, the solo singers, or hear themselves sing.

2. The sound monitors placed throughout the backstage areas are called show monitors or program monitors. They are usually smaller speakers of lesser quality and are placed in hallways, dressing rooms, the green room, at the SM's console, and in strategic places for the crew and technical heads to hear the performance. In many theatres today, video monitors have also been added to enhance the monitoring of the show. The SM also uses the sound monitors to make the *half-hour calls* and announcements to the cast and crew before the show begins. (See also **Biscuit monitors; Public address system**)

Monologue, soliloquy   A group of lines spoken by an actor/character without interruption of dialogue from another character. When spoken directly to the audience, it is called a monologue. When delivered to no one in particular (as if to oneself), representing the mind and thoughts of the character, it is called a soliloquy.

Motivation

1. The character's inner drives and feelings. As the actors discover and develop their characters, they find the things that make the characters act, behave, and respond as they do.

2. The impetus or force behind an actor's or director's work.

Mounting the show   A term used to describe the overall work of technically putting the show together; combining the sets, costumes, lights, sound, and props with the actors and the work they created at the rehearsal hall. (See also **Technical rehearsals**)

Movement

1. For the SM, movement is anything that moves on the stage: the blocking, dancing, scenery and props, or lighting changes.
2. Movement can also mean the speed, pace, and tempo at which the plot, storyline, action, or actor's performance moves.

Movement of light See **Light movement**

Moving lights Computerized electronic and motorized stage light units. The units can be programmed to change their projection of light to any part of the stage. Each unit can work independently or in combination with other such units, creating spectacular movement of light on stage. These instruments got their start in rock concerts, but quickly moved into the lighting design in *legitimate theatre* presentations. Built into many of these units is a collection of *gobo* plates that can be programmed to create an array of patterns or effects on the stage.

Mugging A performer making overly dramatic facial expressions. Only in cases where mugging is done by design is it an acceptable thing, otherwise mugging can take away from the reality and believability of a character and/or the play. If done while another actor is performing, it will pull the audience's attention and *focus* away and direct it to the person doing the mugging.

Music stands Black metal stands that are placed before each musician in the orchestra. They are made to hold music scores and sheet music. In the absence of an SM's console on which to put the *cueing script*, a music stand is ideal to use during the performance. The prop department usually is responsible for setting up the music stands in the orchestra pit, and is the source to go to when one is needed.

Muslin A cream-colored, durable, tightly woven cotton material. It is stretched and attached to the wooden frame of a *flat*, which usually is made into scenery. Before the scenic artist can apply paints, the muslin must first be stiffened and sealed with *sizing*, which also shrinks the material, pulling it even more tightly over the frame. The muslin can then be easily painted on.

Notes Telling an actor or technician something complimentary or critical about their work. A complimentary note reinforces good work. A critical note points out something that is not appropriate for the performance or show and asks for a change. As long as the director is with the show, notes come from the director. Once the director leaves, all notes must go through the SM. (See also **Acting notes**)

Notices See **Reviewer, critic; Reviews, notices**

Number one, number two, number three electrics See **First electrics**

Off book, on book Being off book is the time during rehearsals when actors know their *lines* well enough and do not need to work with the script in hand. However, when an actor gets *off book*, the SM or some designated person needs to get *on book*. The person on book must follow the script carefully and be prepared to *give a line* at any moment. (See also **Follow script**)

Olio A comic sketch used mostly in *melodramas*. They were always presented on the front part of the stage with a drop or curtain placed closely behind, called the olio drop or curtain. An olio's subject matter had nothing to do with the play. Their purpose was to keep the audience entertained while, behind the curtain or drop, the scenery and props were being changed for the next scene. (See also **Roll curtain**)

On cue, on my cue, on the GO! cue These are variations of a phrase an SM uses when instructing a stagehand or actor. This direction tells the person not to execute the cue until the SM gives a signal or tells them verbally to execute the cue—when to GO!

One nighters, one night stands Touring shows that perform in a town for one night.

On a one (two, three, etc.) count A direction given mostly to an actor, technician, or SM. A "one count" would be a *beat* or about one second long; thus a "three count" is three beats or about three seconds long. When given a direction of this kind, the person knows the length of time to take in executing a cue or an action during the show. A lighting designer or director may tell the SM to have the lights come up on a "four count." An SM may ask the actors or technicians to hold for a "count of three" after the lights go out and before they start to change the scenery.

One-set show In its purest form, a one-set show is a show in which the *action* of the entire play takes place in one location and in one setting without a shift or change of scenery. There are, however, sets that are divided into two, or sometimes three, different locations. All parts of the set remain on stage for the whole performance and the audience is moved from one location to the other by a change in lighting and the actors' movement. These sets too may be called one-set shows.

On its feet

1. A colloquial expression. In the literal sense, it is the director getting the actors up on their feet and *blocking* the show—physically placing and moving the actors on the stage.
2. In a less literal sense, this expression is used when a scene or the entire play is blocked, the actors are able to recite their lines from memory, and everyone is ready to continue rehearsals to refine

and develop their performances and the show as a whole.

On point   A dance term describing toe dancers as they rehearse or perform while standing on their toes. (See also **Toe dancer**)

On stage   From the audience's point of view, on stage is the area in which the performance takes place. This would include the backstage area. However, for all who work the show, on stage is the area and space that the audience can see, the space in which the actors perform, the space that is defined by the curtains, drops, and scenery. The backstage remains separate to people working in theatre, and they never generalize by using the term "on stage" to include the backstage area.

On your feet   Asking the actors to stand and move about the stage or rehearsal room as they say their lines of dialogue. This movement sometimes starts as improvisation, as it comes to the minds of the actors, but eventually becomes *blocking* that is formally set by the director.

Opaque   Materials and substances that are solid and do not allow light to pass though.

Open auditions, open calls, cattle calls   Auditions that are open to union and nonunion performers alike. Shows being produced under an Equity contract are required to have an open call. Open calls are designed by Equity to give its members the opportunity to audition for all roles in the show. Advertisements of these auditions inform the actors of the day, time, and place. Seldom are the auditions set up by appointments, but rather the actors show up at their convenience within the advertised time.

A standing rule for all Equity open calls is that the Equity members are auditioned first. All non-Equity actors must wait until there are no other Equity members present or until the end of the day.

Open calls for musicals and shows that are popular and promise long-term employment often turn into what actors call cattle calls. The term is derived in part from the large number of actors who show up for the audition, but comes mostly from the way the actors feel as they are herded through the audition, often at a fast pace, with their audition time and interview cut to a minimum.

Open-end run   A show that is booked into a theatre without a planned closing date. The show will perform until the box office receipts are down and the theatre and producer deem the run no longer financially viable.

Open flames   Any fire or flame appearing on stage or being used backstage that is not contained in some way to help prevent or delay the fire from spreading. The open flame of a match or candle has the potential of quickly igniting other flammable objects, while a cigarette or hurricane lantern, although just as deadly if handled carelessly, is less threatening.

Opening night   The first official performance open to the public, signaling that the show is ready to be seen and reviewed by the press. Opening nights can become gala events and are often celebrated with a party by all who have worked on the show.

Out, the out position   Anything not in view of the audience. Things that are in the wings, backstage, or up in the flys are out or in the out position. Also, to take something out of the play—to not use it in the show.

Out front   For the people backstage, out front is any part of the theatre beyond the *main curtain* and *apron* of the stage. Out front includes where the audience sits, as well as the lobby, foyer, box office, marquee, public phones, taxi stand, or passenger unloading zone.

Orchestra

1. A group of musicians who play at concerts, operas, or plays. An orchestra is distinguished by the use of violins and other string instruments. (See also **Orchestra pit**)
2. Seating on the main floor of the theatre. In ancient Greek theatre, this was the semicircular space in front of the stage where the Greek chorus performed. In Roman times, this space was reserved to seat senators and other persons of distinction. (See also **Orchestra seats**)

Orchestra pit   Generally speaking, the orchestra pit is the place in the theatre where the musicians are placed to play the music for the show. Traditionally, the orchestra pit is the area just in front of the stage between the audience and the stage. Most times the pit is sunk below the audience floor by several feet. To prevent audience members from falling into the pit and to make the movements of the musicians less distracting to the audience, the pit is usually enclosed in some way. However, the top of the pit is left open to allow the music to flow out to the audience and performers on stage, and to allow the conductor to see both the musicians and the action on stage.

Orchestra seats   The audience seats on the first floor of the theatre or seating on the same floor level as the stage. Viewing a performance from these seats puts the patron at a more natural eye level, while seats in the other parts of the theatre put a viewer at an extreme and less natural viewing angle. Orchestra seats are considered prime seating for which patrons pay a premium price.

Pace   The speed at which the show is performed or the speed at which the actors perform their individual parts. When actors are told to pick up the pace, they are being asked to perform everything that has been set by the director, but to do it more quickly, within a shorter period of time. This period of time is a matter of a few seconds, but it makes a difference in holding the audience's attention and keeping them entertained. Actors will sometimes confuse pace with *rushing*.

Page   Aside from being a sheet of paper which makes up a script, for people in the theatre, page also means having someone stand behind a curtain without being seen by the audience and pull the curtain apart or to the side. The curtain is parted or pulled aside just enough so as not to reveal too much of what is behind, but at the same time allow space for a person or piece of scenery to pass through without getting entangled or *hung up* in the curtain. An SM will often page a curtain for a speaker to get on or off stage, for a producer or director who might go out before or after a show to talk to the audience, or for a stagehand who is moving a prop or piece of scenery. (Compare this to **Walk the curtain**)

Paging system   The public address system set up backstage with speakers in hallways, corridors, and dressing rooms. The paging system enables the SM to speak to the members of the company and give the calls before the show begins and during intermission.

Pan   To severely criticize a play or piece of entertainment. A term closely associated with critics and *reviewers*. A pan review can sometimes mean the difference between the success or failure of a show. (See **Reviewer, critic; Reviews, notices**)

Paper tech   A meeting prior to *technical rehearsals* in which the SM, director, various technical department heads, and sometimes the producer gather in conference to plan, discuss, and work out on paper the technical elements of the show. This includes set changes, placement of important or large props, and entering some or all of the light and sound cues in the SM's *cueing script*.

Par cans   A stage lighting instrument that looks like a gallon can opened at one end. Placed inside is a sealed beam lamp that puts out a strong beam of light. Depending on the desired effect, the lighting designer might choose a spot seal beam that confines the light to a condensed area, or a flood that spreads and defuses the light. These lamps are good for *back lighting* or to create a general *wash* across the stage.

Passorelle   See **Ramp; Runway**

Patch, patch in   This term is used mostly in the electrical department. To patch in is to pull the plug in from a light or group of lights on stage and plug in another light or group of lights. Sometimes there are not enough circuits in the dimmer pack to hold every light or group of lights the lighting designer wants. In such cases, during the performance the lighting technician pulls the plug to one circuit and patches in an-

other. Similarly, the sound department will patch in equipment as it is needed during the performance.

Performance level   A quality and standard of work ready to be seen by an audience; an actor performing with the *intensity*, *pitch*, and *delivery* as set in rehearsals and established by the director and actor; a high level in *timing, pace,* and *tempo,* which holds the audience's interest and attention and provides the entertainment they came to experience.

Performing area, playing area   In general, this is the space on stage that includes the set and placement of props as well as the space in which the actors move and perform. More specifically, the performing or playing area is the space left over after the sets and props have been put into place—the space in which the actors can move about the stage during the performance.

Period play   A play set in another period of history, requiring costumes and setting that reflect the period.

Personal props   Any small prop that is left in the actor's care throughout the run of a show. The actor is responsible for bringing the prop on stage or having it in place to use during the performance. These include such props as a pocket watch, eyeglasses, a handkerchief, or a piece of jewelry.

Personal-size floor plans   These are the floor plans the SM creates on 8½-by-11-inch paper of the different sets for the different scenes in the show. The SM takes the information from the *blueprint drawings*, but reduces the *scale* down to ¼ inch or ⅜ inch so all the information can fit on the smaller page. Having the floor plans reduced to this size is convenient in many ways; they can be put in scripts, production notebooks, distributed to actors and technicians, and aid in setting props and in doing scene changes in a multiset musical.

Perspective drawings   Drawings made by the set designer that render a three-dimensional picture of the set and scenery, giving the height, width, and depth as seen by the audience. Most times these are freehand sketches of the designer's conception that are done in pencil, charcoal, or watercolor. Other times they are carefully drafted, drawn to *scale*, and include specific details and measurements.

Petty cash   This is a cash amount of money given to the SM from the production office to spend on miscellaneous or unexpected daily expenses. The SM is highly accountable for this money and it must be returned in the form of receipts or leftover cash.

Pink noise   At each new performance site in which the show plays, the sound department needs about an hour of quiet time in the theatre to balance or equalize the sound. During this time the sound technician broadcasts through the speakers a loud, annoying, hissing, static-like sound—pink noise. This noise contains all frequency bands and it is the sound person's job to see that all the frequencies are equal in volume. The most important information an SM needs to know about pink noise is that the sound technician needs the hour of quiet time and the SM may need to include that time on the schedule.

Pin rail The pin rail is the part of the *fly system* backstage where the stagehands tie off the ropes after having flown in or out a drop, curtain, etc. (See also **Fly rail**)

Pipes Pipes in theatre play their most important role in the *fly system*. They hang in the fly space above the stage from ropes or steel cables. In the early days, when the fly system was first used in theatre, these pipes were long lengths of wood about the size of a two-by-four and they were called *battens*. From these pipes or battens the drops, curtains, pieces of scenery, electrical instruments, and so forth, are hung.

Pipes are also slipped into the bottom hems of drops to keep the drops flat and free of wrinkles, and to help the drops fly in a straight path without the least little breeze blowing them, causing them to get *hung up* on neighboring drops or pieces of scenery as they fly in and out.

Pit See **Orchestra pit**

Pit singers Singers who sing backstage; singers in addition to the singers on stage. Producers, directors, and music directors choose to have pit singers to give a fuller sound to the chorus numbers, to do vocal backgrounds, and to support the dancers in numbers where the dancers must also sing. Most times pit singers are also contracted to play small parts in the show and/or understudy major roles.

At one time, pit singers were always placed in some corner of the orchestra pit where they could see and be led by the conductor. Today, with the use of a video camera, sound monitors, a video monitor, and microphones, the pit singers can be placed virtually anywhere backstage, even in some out of the way place or room. Having the pit singers backstage is easier and more convenient when they must also do other things in the show.

Places, places please Before the rise of the curtain during a performance or in a rehearsal, the SM calls "places, places please" to tell the actors to stand by and be ready to begin. Within a minute or two after that call, all actors are required to be standing by and ready to begin performing.

Platforms See **Risers**

Play, it doesn't play Something that does not work in the show. It is either lacking in entertainment value,

the timing is wrong, or it doesn't fit the character of the play.

Playback Sound effects or music previously recorded then played back through speakers and monitors during a performance. (See also **Prerecord**)

Playbill The program that is given to patrons, free of charge, as they enter the theatre to take their seats. This program is not to be confused with *show programs,* which are more elaborate, include production photographs, and are sold to the patrons.

Between pages of advertisements in the playbill appear the title credit page, the page that lists the characters and the actors who play the characters, the technical credits page (of which the SM(s) head the list), and pages containing pictures and short biographies of the principal and supporting performers along with the creators and designers of the show.

Play doctor See **Scene doctor**

Playing area See **Performing area**

Plug

1. The kind with which we are most familiar is the electrical plug attached to lamps, appliances, extension cords, and cables used in the electric department.
2. A plug in theatre is also a small unit or piece of scenery. It is constructed to fit into an already existing space in the scenery, such as a window, doorway or hallway. When the plug is put into place it changes the look of the set and with the rearrangement or changing of props, furniture, lighting, and with theatrical license, the audience is moved to another setting and into another scene.

Podium, speaker's podium A stand or theatrically designed piece of scenery, behind which a person can stand to address the audience. An SM will have many occasions to deal with this item: having it set on stage, lighting it, or asking the sound person to bring up the sound on the speaker's podium. There is also the *conductor's podium,* which is placed in the *orchestra pit* for the conductor.

Point cue A light cue that comes in between two consecutively numbered cues. Often, after the lighting designer has numbered the light cues in the show, the decision is made to add one or more cues between two particular cues. Instead of renumbering all the cues that follow, the lighting designer labels the added cues as point cues; for example, Q13.1, Q13.2, etc. Since the advent and use of computer-operated light boards, numbering added cues in this manner has become standard practice. Prior to the use of computers, point cues were often labeled as Q13a, Q13b, etc.

Point-of-view (POV) The SM frequently abbreviates this as POV. This is a term from film and television that describes a camera angle showing the viewing audience what the character sees. With the tremendous crossover of film, TV, and stage actors, this term has become a part of the actors' and directors' conversation during rehearsals.

Pool of light   A small, isolated area of light in which a performer can stand. Usually the rest of the stage is dimly lit or in total darkness. This pool of light can consist of one lamp or several lamps, but the light is restricted to the small area. (See also **Special**)

Portals   See **Legs; Wings**

PR   The abbreviation for *public relations.*

Practical, a practical   A prop or piece of scenery that functions as it does in real life. Something an actor can use and operate during the performance. A door that opens and closes and through which an actor can pass is a practical. A lamp on a desk or a light switch on the wall for the actor to turn a light on and off is a practical. Food that is edible is practical.

Prerecord, playback   Sound effects or music that have been previously recorded and are then played back during a performance from a cassette, CD, or reel to reel tape. Most of the time the prerecord and playback is music. When the music is used in straight plays such as comedies or dramas, it can be played as the audience enters and is being seated, during intermission, at the end as the audience leaves, or during the performance to complement or enhance the mood or a feeling.

In musicals, the prerecord and playback is used more extensively and in different ways. Sometimes it is arranged to complement the orchestra as it plays during the performance, giving it a fuller instrumental sound. Other times it is used in place of the orchestra. In other cases it is arranged to accompany performers as they sing, dance, or play a musical instrument. In still other cases, a prerecord and playback is of the performer singing, allowing the performer to *lip sync* during the actual performance.

The techniques of prerecord, playback, and lip sync have their roots in film and television. More and more, prerecord and playback are becoming accepted parts of legitimate theatre production and part of the SM's vocabulary. (See also **Click track; Lip sync**)

Preset

1. Anything that is set and put into place before the show starts and remains there ready to be used during the performance. Props are preset on the stage or off in the *wings* ready for the actors to use. Pieces of scenery are preset backstage, ready for the next scene change, and costumes are preset in the *quick change booth* ready for a quick change in a forthcoming scene.

2. The lights set on the curtain or on an open stage as the audience enters to see the play, are also called a preset. (See also **Curtain warmers**)

3. During the performance, the electricians setting up the next light cue and having it ready to be executed on the SM's command is presetting. Before the use of *computer light boards,* presetting a light cue was done manually, setting dimmers and switches. Today, putting the next light cue into preset is a matter of tapping a few keys on the keyboard.

Press   These are the writers and commentators from news media who will do articles on the show and make their critical judgments. They are often invited to see the show on the opening night or within the first week. Their work and attention can help make or break the show. (See also **Public relations; Reviewer, critic; Reviews, notices**)

Previews, preview performances   Performances of the show immediately following the technical rehearsals and before the opening performance. For the cast and crew, there is no difference between a preview performance and a performance done on opening night and thereafter. The purpose of previews is to get audience reaction and to work out problem areas within the show before the official opening and before the *press and reviewers* come to see the show. People who come to see preview performances are either invited guests or patrons who pay discounted prices for their tickets.

Production assistant (PA)   Usually a young, energetic person who aspires to work in show business. In most cases, the title of production assistant is more prestigious than *runner* or *gofer.* However, the PA does the same work as they do. If PAs have experience at the job and a good working knowledge of theatre and production work, they may be given tasks from the SM, director, or producer that might ordinarily be delegated to their assistants. (See also **Gofer**)

Production book   The SM begins assembling this book on the first day of work on a show and continues adding to it until the show closes. The production book is a compilation of all the information the SM creates and assembles on the production having to do with practically all aspects and departments. This book is divided into four specific entities:

1. Rehearsal/blocking script
2. Cueing script
3. Loose-leaf notebook (*production notebook*) in which all charts, plots, plans, drawings, lists, vendor information, CD, floppy disks, and audio tapes are kept.
4. Information kept in the SM's filing system.

At the close of the show, all parts are combined into one big book and turned over to the producer or production office. This book becomes everything anyone ever wanted to know about the production. The information in this book is important for future reference, especially if the show was new or produced on Broadway for the first time.

Production meeting   A meeting where the *production staff* gathers to discuss, plan, coordinate, schedule, work out, and report on the progress and problems of each department. The first of these meetings takes place either before rehearsals begin or within the first week. Then depending on the extent of the production, there may also be periodic production meetings. They can be short and daily with only the SM, director, and whatever department needs attention on that day, or they can take up a whole morning or afternoon with the entire production staff in attendance.

Production notebook   The SM's production notebook is a loose-leaf notebook containing all charts, plots, plans, drawings, lists, vendor information, CDs, disks, and audiotapes having to do with a particular show. The SM begins assembling this book on the first day of working on the show. During rehearsals and the run of the show, the production notebook is the SM's bible of information and it should be within arm's reach at all times for quick reference. At the close of the show, much of the information in this notebook is copied and placed into the *production book,* which the SM turns in to the producer. (See also **Production book**)

Production numbers   In a musical show, production numbers are songs and/or dances that are staged with greater *production value* than the other songs and dances. In a musical play, when a character's feelings heighten and can no longer be expressed in words, the character sings and/or dances. The same holds true for a production number. When a song or dance can no longer be expressed in just lyrics or in simple movement, the director and choreographer heighten its production values, adding more performers, creating extensive and complicated choreography, perhaps using special costumes, incorporating props, and almost always use lighting effects to support and enhance the mood and visual look.

On occasion a production number can involve only one person, such as the "Make 'Em Laugh" song and tap dance number in *Singing in the Rain.* A production number can also be soft, lovely, and lyrical, such as the dream ballet "The Carousel Waltz" in *Carousel.* Or a production number can seem simple, such as the clever and rhythmical hand-slapping, hand-clapping, toe-tapping number in *The Will*

Roger's Follies, where the performers remain seated in a row across the stage, using isolated parts of their bodies as the choreography.

Production pictures, production shots, production stills   Eight-by-ten-inch (8 x 10) photographs of the actors in various scenes from the show. Sometimes these shots are set up specifically for the camera. Other times they are taken as the actors perform their parts in a dress rehearsal or during a performance. They are used for press release, in advertisement, and as a historical record of the show.

Production staff   The creative, artistic, administrative, and technical people required to produce a show, including the producer, author/writer, director, designers, choreographer, musical director, SMs, heads of technical departments, accountants, publicity people, the production office staff, and all the assistants.

Production stage manager (PSM)   The head or lead SM. This more elaborate title got its start with musical shows where two or more SMs were needed and eventually required by Equity.

Production table   A tabletop or large piece of plywood that is laid across the seats in the middle of the theater during *technical rehearsals.* It is here that the producer, director, and designers sit to watch and give instructions through headsets as they technically set the show. It is important that this table has access to electric power with several outlets to plug in one or two desk lamps, laptops, and whatever other electrical appliances the staff sitting at this table might use. Also, there must be a microphone with an on/off switch (see **God mic**), and headphones to communicate to the different technical departments and SMs backstage.

Production values   The quality of artistic and technical support given to the show, either to the show as a whole or to particular segments, such as song and dance numbers.

Program monitors   See **Monitors**

Prologue   The prologue comes at the beginning of the play, before the first scene. Its purpose is to set up the audience for the action, plot, mood, characters, or all of the above. The prologue's counterpart is the *epilogue,* which comes at the end of the play. Examples of prologues and epilogues are easily found in Greek plays, Shakespeare's plays, and many of the plays written in the nineteenth century. (See also **Epilogue**)

Prompt

1. To give an actor a forgotten line of dialogue.
2. To sit in a rehearsal with an actor, reading the other character's lines in a play, while the actor performs lines from memory.

Prompt book, prompt script   The term prompt book originates from theatre in the nineteenth century when a person, during performance, sat with a script in the *wings* or below stage level in the center of the stage in the *apron* and followed the script. It was this person's job to be ready at any moment to give actors a line of dialogue or remind them of a bit of *business,* should they forget something. This term remains in use today, but people now use it when referring to the script the SM uses during performance to call the cues. For greater clarification, in this book the prompt script is called the *cueing script.*

Prop box   The container in which small props and hand props are placed for safe keeping when the show is not in performance. This may also be the container in which the propman keeps tools and supplies to work the job and to repair and maintain the performing condition of the different props.

Propman, prop master, property master   Terms that name the person in charge of the props or properties within a show. (See also **Props, properties**)

Props, properties   Items used by the performers in the play. Props are used to enhance the action, plot, or characterization, and to create an illusion of reality. Props are not to be confused with *set dressing* or set decoration, which are items not used by the actors, but are present merely for appearance in decoration and design. (See also **Hand props**)

Prop tables   Tables set off each side of the stage on which small props and hand props are placed in readiness for the performance. The propman sets the props on the table in the same place and in the same way for each performance, and during the performance, the actors are required to pick up and return to the table whatever props they can.

Proscenium, proscenium arch, proscenium opening   These are terms that define the frame surrounding the opening of the stage through which the audience views the show.

PSM   The abbreviation for Production Stage Manager.

Public address system (PA)   The PA system is spread throughout the entire backstage by monitor speakers. This system is used primarily by the SM to communicate with the cast and crew. During the performance, sound from the stage is *patched into* the PA system, thus making the speaker monitors also show monitors or program monitors.

Public relations (PR), publicity department   In most theatre producing companies the public relations and publicity departments are one and the same. Most often, this department consists of a desk tucked away in some corner of the production office, with one person doing the job of a full staff. It is this department's job to create or generate anything that presents the show in a favorable light and sells tickets. This is done through newspaper ads or television commercials,

creatively taking favorable quotes from reviews and publishing them, generating magazine articles, doing behind-the-scenes video, or setting up interviews and guest appearances with the stars on local radio and TV programs. One of the more successful methods is to create a poster and logo that are highly recognizable and identify the show at a single glance, such as the ones created for *Les Miserable, Cats,* or *Phantom of the Opera.*

Pulleys   In its simplest form, a pulley is a metal wheel with a hook or device that allows the pulley to be secured to a solid object, such as a wall, ceiling, or beam. One end of a rope is slipped through the pulley, over the wheel, and brought down to a stagehand at floor level. At the other end of the rope an object or payload is attached. When the stagehand pulls the loose end of the rope, the rope glides through the pulley and rides over the wheel, making it easier for the stagehand to hoist the object up into the air. If the payload is heavy and the stagehand is unable to change hand positions while pulling, two or more stagehands will be needed to hoist the object or it will come crashing to the floor. Pulleys are an important part of the *fly system.* A close relative to the pulley is the *block and tackle.*

Pulling focus   See **Focus**

Put-in rehearsal   A rehearsal held to put in an understudy or a new performer. This kind of rehearsal usually comes after the show has opened and been in its run.

Quick change   This phrase most often refers to a costume change during performance that needs to be completed in a very short time. Quick changes develop within a show when an actor in a scene leaves the stage and needs to reappear on stage dressed in another costume within a very short period of time. (See also **Dresser; Quick change room**)

Quick change room   A small, enclosed area backstage, placed close to the set, which allows an actor to come off stage, quickly change into another costume, and return to the stage for the next appearance. Often this room is created by assembling two or more stage *flats* together. Sometimes bed sheets or blankets are all that is available and are strung up with ropes. The bare essentials for a quick change room are a low-wattage light, a covering for the floor to protect the costumes from getting dirty, and a *dresser* to assist the performer in the quick change. A more elaborate setup would include hooks for clothes or a clothes rack, a mirror, a table and chair, makeup, hair supplies, and drinking water.

Radio pack   See **Body microphone**

Rag   A slang or colloquial term used by stagehands when referring to the main curtain or *house curtain.*

Rail system   See all definitions under **Fly**

Rain curtain   A network of water spouts or valves, evenly spaced, one after the other. They are placed above the stage across the entire length of the stage. When the valves are opened, water falls from above to create a wall or curtain that looks like rain falling. The water at the bottom is caught in a trough, and can either be drained away or recycled to continue the effect.

Rake   To angle or tilt a prop, piece of furniture, scenery, or any object on the stage for better viewing by the audience.

Raked stage   A stage that slants down toward the audience. A traditional design found mostly in older European theatres and theatres in America built before 1920, its purpose was to afford the audience a better view of the stage picture. However, a raked stage was unnatural for the actors to walk on, very difficult for dancing, and terrible for placing scenery and props without having to anchor down everything.

Ramp

1. A platform or walkway that starts at floor level or zero degrees, and slopes up on an angle to a higher level. An incline.
2. A second kind of ramp in theatre is a platform. It can range from 3 to 6 feet wide and is constructed for actors to walk and perform on. Some ramps are extensions of the stage, jetting straight out into the audience, such as a *runway* or *thrust stage*. Others start at the side of the stage, circle or arch around into the audience, and end up attached to the stage at the opposite side. Ramps are used mostly in musicals, burlesque, vaudeville, or variety act shows. Traditionally, ramps are used in the musical plays *Gypsy* and *Hello Dolly* as part of the set design.

Reaction time   The fraction of time it takes for a person to react after being told to execute a cue. When calling cues during a performance, every SM learns to include reaction time in the calculation of timing to increase precision and accuracy in having the cue or effect happen on stage.

Reading

1. At an audition, an actor may be asked to read a scene from the script. This is called a reading. (See also **Cold reading**)
2. A reading of the play often takes place in the first or second day of rehearsals when the cast of actors first gets together. At that time they will all sit and read the play from the script. (See also **Table read**)
3. Another type of reading of the play might happen in a more formal situation with the actors possibly sitting on stools, reading the play from their scripts for a paying or nonpaying audience, or for a group of people who are potential backers/investors.

Read through, read thru   When the cast sits and reads through a scene or the entire play without performing any of the physical action or movement of the play. This is usually done on the first day of rehearsals. (See also **Table read**)

Rehearsal furniture, rehearsal food   In its simplest and cheapest form, rehearsal furniture can be folding chairs or bridge chairs placed together side by side to make a sofa, a park bench, or the front seat of an automobile. Rehearsal furniture can be various wooden boxes that act as a coffee table, a tree stump, or a soapbox. When the chairs and boxes are combined they can become a four-poster bed, a 12-foot conference room table, or a sumptuous banquet spread.

In more elaborate form and in high-budget productions, rehearsal furniture can be old and used furniture that is close to what the actor will be using during the performance. Similarly, rehearsal food can be a slice of bread with a plastic knife and fork to represent steak being eaten at a fine restaurant, a styrofoam cup of grape juice for a fine glass of vintage wine, or carrot sticks as crunchy snack food.

Rehearsal script, blocking script   This is the script the SM uses during the rehearsal period. In it the SM notes *blocking, cues, set changes,* and any information that will be needed when technically putting the show together in the *technical rehearsals*. During technical rehearsals, the blocking script is temporarily put aside while the *cueing script* is created and used for calling cues during the performance. However, once the show opens, the SM returns to the blocking script, updates it with whatever changes were made during technical rehearsals, then uses this script for understudy rehearsals, replacing actors, and for reminding actors of the original blocking when they forget or change their blocking. When the show closes, the SM either keeps the rehearsal script or includes it in the *production book* that is given to the producer or production company.

Renderings   The designer's drawings or sketches, usually depicting the set or costumes. Some will be done in color and in great detail. Others may be pencil, ink, or charcoal sketches.

Rheostat dimmer   The type of dimmers used in the old dimmer boards. They had a coil of copper material which, when passed through a field of electricity, allowed the lights on stage to be raised or lowered in brightness or intensity.

Repertory   A group or repertoire of plays presented in a season by the same producing company and using the same group of actors. Sometimes each play is presented for a short period of time within the season and then closes. Other times the plays are alternated, presenting a different show each week, then repeating the list of shows until the season is completed. Still other times, the entire repertoire of plays may be presented within a week, sometimes one play being performed in a matinee and another in the evening.

Repertory company   A group or company of actors hired to perform in several plays that are presented within a season of plays. In one play, an actor may be cast in a lead role, playing the hero. In another, he may be the villain or have only a *walk-on part*. (See also **Resident company**)

Repertory theatre   A theatre presenting to the public a season of plays in which the same group of actors is used in the different plays.

Reprise   (pronounced *re-preeze)* In musicals, a reprise is a song or piece of music that is performed for a second time in the show, either in part or in whole. The reprise can be performed by the same character, exactly as it had been the first time, or it can be arranged differently in presentation, perhaps with new lyrics to fit the moment of the play and performed by another character.

Resident company   A group of actors hired to perform in a season of plays for a theatre or producing company. This term is freely interchanged with the *repertory company* and *repertory theatre.*

Restore cue   A lighting cue that brings the lights back or restores the lights to a previous setting.

In some plays, the writer may stop the action of the play for characters to speak their thoughts or talk directly to the audience as in a monologue or soliloquy. At this point, the lighting designer or director may choose to change the lights to give greater focus to the character who is speaking. After the monologue or soliloquy, the lights are restored to the previous setting and the action of the play continues.

This restore cue in the SM's cueing script will be numbered in the same way as all other light cues. However, in general conversation, the participants more than likely will refer to the cue as the restore cue, rather than naming it by its number.

Return   A *flat* or wall of scenery. Returns are most commonly used at the ends of a *set unit* or a *box set.* Sometimes they are painted to look like part of the scenery to give the illusion that the setting continues off stage, beyond the audience's view. Other times they are flats painted black or in a dark color, to give a finished look to the set. In practical terms, a return is used to cover the unsightly and distracting activity taking place backstage. The term return is often used interchangeably with *masking* and *tab.*

Reviewer, critic   A news media person who professionally comments, gives an opinion, or passes judgment on the merits of a play or piece of entertainment. (See also **Reviews, notices**)

Reviews, notices   Articles or commentaries presented in the news on the merits of a play or piece of entertainment. Reviews can sometimes make the difference between the success or failure of a play. There are, however, some very famous plays that have survived bad reviews, gone on to be box office successes, and become part of theatre history.

Revolve, revolving stage, turntable   A circular part of the stage floor that turns at least 180 degrees, but usually a full 360 degrees. A revolve or turntable is used mostly in musical shows. They serve to change the scene and scenery, or give the illusion of traveling from one location to another. While a scene is playing on the front half of a revolve (the part facing the audience), props, furniture, and other scenery can be placed on the back half. Then on the SM's cue, the table is turned and the new scene is quickly moved into place. This change is often done in view of the audience, creating theatre magic and requiring impeccable timing from the SM and stagehands as they execute the change. Sometimes a stage may have two or more turntables, each having different scenes appear on them. Other times the tables work in conjunction with each other, creating one big scene to fill the entire stage.

Rhythm   The combination of beats or repeated accents within a measure of music. Similarly, rhythm in acting and directing is a combination of repeated beats and silences performers use in the delivery of their words, lines of dialogue, movements, or comic bits of business.

Ring down the curtain   The action of flying in the *main curtain,* usually done quickly. Sometimes this is done for effect by choice of the director. Other times, it may be done because of fire or an accident on stage.

Risers, platforms, levels   Generally speaking, these are wooden, boxlike structures or units that are built at various heights and sizes, creating performing areas or levels higher than the stage floor. These units can be used separately for a small scene or in conjunction with each other to create different areas such as the rooms of a home. They can also be used together to create one set and location across the entire stage.

Road crew   See **Show crew**

Roadies   The stagehands or stage crewmembers who travel with a touring show.

Road show   A show that is designed and set up to travel and perform in different towns and theatres. In most situations, the scenery travels by truck while the actors travel by van, bus, or plane.

Rococo Elaborate and decorative design of swirls, twirls, frills, and flourishes from the Rococo period of architecture and design in the eighteenth century. In theatre this term is more generally used to describe the elaborate and decorative design of scenery, props, costumes, and sometimes the acting style of an actor.

Roll curtain (drop), olio curtain (drop) A roll curtain is not the traditional curtain with pleats and folds, but rather a piece of material hung flat across the stage. Instead of flying in or out or parting in the middle, this curtain rolls from the bottom as it travels upwards.

Roll curtains are most popular in melodramas and vaudeville. Most times roll curtains have a design or scene painted on them. When used at the front of the stage to cover the proscenium opening, it more than likely will be called a curtain, but when used further back on the stage to back a scene, it may be called a drop. Stagehands will use the terms interchangeably. Furthermore, when a roll curtain is used to back a comic sketch (olio), as in a melodrama, it will be called an olio drop or curtain.

Roll curtains are most effective in theatres where there is no rail system or *fly space*.

Rosin box A low-cut box containing rosin powder, usually placed in or near one of the wings for the dancers and actors to use before entering the stage. The box is big enough for the performers to stand in to accumulate the rosin powder on the soles of their shoes. This powder gives the performers better traction on the stage. To a great degree, it prevents them from slipping and becoming injured.

Rundown See **Running order**

Run a line Technician's jargon, meaning to attach a rope at one place and then bring it across or over to another place.

Run lines The actors reciting their dialogue, but doing little to none of the action or movement that usually goes along with their dialogue. Directors and SMs have the actors *run lines* to either help them memorize their lines or refresh their memories after having been away from the play for a time.

Runner See **Gofer; Production assistant**

Running order, rundown of the show The chronological order of acts and scenes within the show.

Running time The length of time it takes to perform a scene, an act, or the entire play. For each performance, the SM is responsible for noting the running time on the show report.

Run of the play, run of the show The length of time or number of performances a show performs for the public. This can be as short as one performance or it

can be for as many performances as the public will continue to purchase tickets. A run of the play is from the opening performance to its last performance. (See also **Run-of-the-play contract**)

Run-of-the-play contract A contract in which an actor or SM agrees to stay with a show for at least a year's time. Under Equity rules, the contract must be renegotiated at the end of the year's time. There are important terms included in this kind of an agreement and SMs should be familiar with the various points, not only for themselves, but to better deal with actors and producers on this matter.

Run a scene In rehearsals, the act of going through a scene. Sometimes this involves having the actors sitting around saying dialogue. Other times, it means having them on their feet also doing the blocking, possibly using props, and perhaps even wearing costumes.

Run the show

1. The SM sitting at the SM's cueing console calling cues during the performance.
2. After the producer and director turn the show over to the SM for safe keeping the SM is in charge of running the show—keeping it as it has been directed and set by its creators and designers.
3. During rehearsals, to run the show is to allow the actors to go through the entire show as if in a performance without stopping to direct, correct, fix, or clean.

Run through (run-thru) In rehearsals, the director will let the actors perform a scene, an act, or the entire play nonstop, to give them a sense of continuity and flow, to help them get their timing, and to give them the experience of performing the show.

Runway A walkway ranging from 3 to 6 feet wide which is an extension of the main part of the stage. Some runways extend straight out into the audience. Others start at one side of the stage, circle or arch around into the audience, and end on the opposite side of the stage. This arching kind is also called a passorelle. Runways are commonly used in fashion shows, burlesque shows, and in some musicals such as *Gypsy* and *Hello Dolly*. (See also **Ramp; Thrust stage**)

Rushing The tempo or speed of whatever is being performed is moving too quickly. The *timing* or *delivery* is too fast and some of the entertainment value is being lost.

Safety chain A chain attached to things that hang above the on-stage area or over the heads of the audience. It is required that each lighting instrument have a safety chain to prevent a lamp from crashing down on an actor or members of the audience.

Sandbags   Canvas bags filled with sand that were primarily used as counter-weights in the old days when the *fly system* was first used in the theatre. (See also **Counter-weights; Flys**)

Sash cord   A sturdy, thin rope, usually made of fine cotton or nylon, which is used mostly for opening or closing window curtains, window blinds, or light-weight stage curtains. Stagehands, however, will use this cord in many other ways. (See also **Ties, tie lines**)

Scale drawings   Used mostly in *blueprint drawings* detailing the design of the set, the floor plans, and the placement of the scenery. To get the full dimensions of the scenery for a scene onto a sheet of paper that is convenient to handle (as in a blueprint), the actual dimensions of the stage and set must be downsized. In the professional blueprint drawings the set designer creates, every foot of real space on the stage is noted on paper as one inch, or sometimes a half-inch. For even greater convenience, the SM might downsize the blueprint drawings even further on letter-size sheets of paper (8½ x 11), using ¼- or ⅜-inch scale. (See also **Drawn to scale**)

Scale model   A three-dimensional, scaled down miniature of the set. These models are made by the set designer and are usually preferred over the designer's sketches. Scale models are a good representation of the space used, the performing area, and the relationship of set pieces, drops, and furniture props to each other. (See also **Scale drawings; Drawn to scale**)

Scene change, scene shift, set change   Moving or changing the scenery and props on the stage. Sometimes it is only a matter of moving things to a different placement on the stage; other times, as in musicals, a scene change is taking the scenery of one scene off the stage and replacing it with different scenery for the next scene. A scene change takes the audience to another time and location. Sometimes scene changes take place in full view of the audience and sometimes they are done in the dark.

Scene dock, scene dock doors

1. The place outside the theatre, either to the side or at the back of the building, where trucks loaded with scenery, props, costumes, sound equipment, and so forth, can back up to the building and unload. In most newer theatres and civic center buildings, the scene dock doors lead into the backstage storage or work area. In older theatres, the doors may open directly into the backstage.
2. Some theatres have a backstage area in which sets can be constructed and drops painted. This is often

called the scene dock, but is also referred to as the *construction shop*, scene shop, or simply, the shop.

Scene doctor, play doctor   A director, producer, or writer who has the ability and talent to rework, fix, and save a scene or an entire show from failure after all attempts have been made by the original director, producer, or writer to fix and save the scene or show.

Scene shift   See **Scene change**

Scene stealing, stealing the scene, stole the scene/show
These are phrases with negative and positive meanings at different times, depending on the situation. They can be compliments, criticisms, or insults.

1. It is a compliment when actors do such a good job in performance that they inadvertently stand out, taking the focus and attention away from their fellow performers and their performances.
2. As a criticism or insult to the actor's work and professional integrity, to steal the scene or show is when an actor intentionally takes the focus and attention at a time when it is inappropriate, distracting, or harmful to the play and his fellow performers.

There is an old actors' adage that warns against performing with children or animals, for they will steal the scene. Scene stealing can be done intentionally through ego, or unintentionally through talent. An SM learns to recognize the difference. If the SM feels that a case of scene stealing is harmful to the show, a consultation with the producer and/or director is in order. Depending on who is committing the offense and the severity of the act, the producer or director may deal with the situation or leave it for the SM to handle.

Scene shop   See **Construction shop; Scene dock, scene dock doors**

Scenic artist   The person who paints the scenery. On occasion this is also the designer, but most times the scenic artist is an artist in painting scenery, props, and drops.

Scenic designer   The person who designs scenery for the play.

Schlep   A colorful Yiddish term that has crept into the theatre vernacular (especially on the east and west coasts) that means to carry or drag along.

Schmoozing   A colorful Yiddish term that means talking: talking done in different situations and for different reasons—fun talk, social talk, small talk, sweet talk, amorous talk, business talk, talk done with hidden meaning, or talk to manipulate or get something. SMs are witness to all kinds of schmoozing and may themselves take part in some.

Schtick, doing schtick   Doing comedic *business*—a little comic routine. Schtick is a Yiddish term that has its roots in vaudeville and burlesque. Schtick is often associated with *slapstick*, burlesque, or hokey comedy. In theatre, when schtick is used at the right time and place it is highly effective. However, when it is used to draw attention or get laughs that are not right for the moment, the character, or the play, it can be distracting and take away from the entertainment value and show in general. (See also **Stage business**)

Scrim   A gauzelike drop which, when lit from the front, appears solid and opaque. Designs or scenes may be painted on the front. However, when the lights in front of the scrim are faded out and the lights in the back of the scrim are faded up, the scrim and its paintings seem to disappear, becoming transparent and allowing the audience to see through to the scenery and action taking place behind the scrim.

Season tickets, subscription tickets   Theatre tickets sold in advance for a group of plays that a theatre company is presenting for a particular season. Patrons who purchase tickets for a season purchase them at a discounted rate and are offered preferred seating. These patrons are referred to as *subscribers*. Their tickets are distinguished from others sold at the box office as subscription tickets.

Second electrics   See **First electrics**

Set   The scenery placed on the stage.

Set change   See **Scene change, scene shift, set change**

Set dressing, set decorating   This can be furniture, curtains, rugs, pictures, lamps, knickknacks, and plants—all the things used to decorate the set to make it look more interesting. If any of these items are handled or used by the performers, they become props. It is the set dressing and decorating that creates the illusion of reality and helps bring authenticity to a certain period, time, or place.

Set piece   In most cases this term refers to a piece of the overall set: the railing to a staircase, or the latticework to a porch or garden scene. Stagehands will sometimes generalize and call a *set unit* a set piece. (See also **Set unit**)

Set the scene

1. The work a director and actors do in rehearsals, creating and developing the *movement, business,* and *action* for a scene, and creating and developing the character and interpretation. Getting the scene ready for public viewing.
2. A brief explanation or description written into the script by the author, either at the beginning of the play or at the beginning of each scene. These descriptions give just enough information about the plot, characters, action, feelings, mood, time, place, or technical effects to lead the reader into the play or scene.

3. On the first day of rehearsals, the cast traditionally reads the play together for the first time. During that reading, either the director or the SM will set the scenes by reading aloud the information at the beginning of each scene.
4. In rehearsals when the director asks the SM to set the scene, the director is asking that the rehearsal props and furniture be put into place. (See also **Set the stage**)

Set the stage   To get the scenery and props ready and into place for a rehearsal or performance.

Setting   A term used loosely and in different ways:

1. The place or location where the scene takes place.
2. The paragraph of information written in the script at the beginning of each scene. (See also **Set the scene**)
3. The placement of the scenery, props, and set dressing for a scene.

Setting lights, setting light cues   This happens in the early part of the *technical rehearsals*. The lighting designer and the director sit in the darkened theatre picking and choosing the lights, the colors, and the intensities that will be used for each scene in the play. Each group of lights chosen becomes a *cue* and is given a number. The SM enters these numbers in the *cueing script* and is told where and when in the script these cues are to be executed. Setting lights is like painting the stage with light and color. Designers and directors who are good at it are like artists applying paint to canvas.

Set unit   A piece of scenery smaller than the overall set that stands alone. Sometimes a set unit is an addition to the set, such as a gazebo in a park scene. Other times it is a piece of scenery flown in from the *flys* or rolled in on a platform, which is isolated by stage lighting and used for a small scene.

Sharp edge, hard edge, soft edge   In terms of stage lighting, some lighting instruments when focused on the stage leave a circle of light which is clearly seen and distinctively defined by a sharp or hard edge. A *leko* light is a good example of this kind of light. Other lighting instruments, such as a *fresnel lamp* or a *par can*, leave on the stage a soft and defused light edge.

Shop   See **Construction shop; Scene dock, scene dock doors**

Short-line   See **Long-line, short-line**

Show crew   The stagehands who travel with the show. This crew usually consists of the heads of each technical department. The rest of the crew is picked up locally in each town. (See also **House crew; Local crew**)

Show curtain   The show curtain is different from the *main curtain, house curtain,* or the *grand drape* that permanently hangs in the theatre, just behind the proscenium to cover the stage as the audience enters. The show curtain also hangs at the proscenium and covers the stage, but is designed specifically for the show and will be taken down when the show leaves the theatre. Stagehands, however, will sometimes call any curtain covering the stage the show curtain. For clarity in communication, the SM should be specific and not mix the terms.

Show monitors   See **Monitors**

Show portal   See **False proscenium**

Show program   A more elaborate version of the free *playbill* program that is given to the theatre patrons as they enter to take their seats. Show programs are created by the producing company of the show and are sold to the patrons. Show programs include colored *production photographs* and more detailed information about the show, its history, the creators, designers, staff, and the actors.

Show report   A document the SM fills out for each performance. On it is noted the date and place of the performance, the time each act begins and ends, any mistakes or problems that occurred during the performance, or anything different or special with the company from the time they came in at the *half-hour call*.

With some shows and producing companies, this report is to be turned in to the producer each day. With other productions, the producer may be interested in receiving the information verbally from the SM. Still other producers are selective in the information they want to receive and prefer having the information on the report kept in the SM's files until a time when it might be needed.

The information on this report is often duplicated in the SM's log book. If the producer/production company does not require a show report, the SM may eliminate it and keep the information only in the log book.

Shutter   A device built into many stage lighting instruments. There are four sides to a shutter. When each side is adjusted, the shutter cuts off part of the beam of light falling on stage. This gives the lighting designer control to cover a specific thing or area. It also allows the designer to take away light that spills into another area or on an object nearby. Adjusting the shutter becomes part of the business of *focusing lights*. (See also **Focus**)

Side   A very abbreviated form of the script containing only the scenes and dialogue of a particular character. Traditionally sides were 5 by 7 inches in size. They were commonly used until the middle of the twentieth century. With the improvement of copying machines and with the change in acting style and approach in studying for a part, actors insisted on having the entire script. Today if sides are given out they are given only to actors playing small roles, and are regular, script-size pages.

Side lighting, side lights   Any stage lighting that comes from the side. Most times this is lighting that comes from instruments hung in the *wings* or in the *box booms*. When used alone, they create dramatic highlights and shadows. When used in combination with other lights on stage, they help things on stage stand out that might otherwise appear flat if lit only from the front.

Sight lines   The line of vision each audience member has while seated and looking at the stage. The more up front and off to the sides a person sits, the worse the sight line becomes; the side of the stage closest to the person is cut off from the line of vision, blocking any action that takes place on that part of the stage. Conversely, while sitting in the same extreme side seat, the audience member is able to see very well across the stage to the opposite side. Unfortunately, while watching a musical show where *legs* or *portals* make up the wings on each side of the stage, this same audience member can often see through to the distracting activity backstage.

Actors, directors, and SMs are aware of the sight-line problems for the audience. Each time the show gets on a new stage, they check and make whatever adjustments are necessary in the *blocking*. An excellent rule of sight lines for actors to follow during performance is: *If from the corners of their eyes the actors can see the seats on the ends of the first row, they can be certain everyone in the audience can see them and that they are performing within the sight lines.*

People backstage, working or standing in the wings, must continually be aware of the sight-line problems from their point of view. If they can see any member of the audience from where they are standing, they can be sure the audience member can see them. They need to stand or work further back until they can no longer see any audience member. Every SM should frequently remind stagehands as well as cast members of this problem by saying, "If you can see any of the audience, the audience can see you."

Sitting on their hands   A phrase used to explain a lack of response, reaction, or applause from the audience.

Sizing   A paste-like mixture that is painted on muslin- or canvas-covered flats and dries to a clear and somewhat rough finish. The sizing shrinks the material, making it tighter over the frame of the flat. It also seals the material, making it stiffer and less porous. When dried, the flats are ready to be painted by the *scenic artist*.

Skeleton crew   A minimum number of stagehands and not the full complement of crewmembers that is used when setting up a show or during the performance. An SM may ask for a skeleton crew for a rehearsal being held on stage when sets, props, and possibly lights are being used.

Sketch   Aside from being an artist's rough drawing, a sketch is also a short comical scene. Sketches have their roots in vaudeville and burlesque, and have carried over into television in the variety-type shows.

Sketches, drawings, renderings   The designer's/artist's concept of what either the set or costumes will look like. Sometimes sketches are done in watercolor, other times in ink, pencil, or charcoal. Some drawings will be detailed and look very close to what they will be in real life. Others may be quick renditions, showing a general look and giving a splash of color.

Slapstick   Broad physical comedy, cultivated in the music halls of Europe, perfected in vaudeville and burlesque, and brought to an art form by Charlie Chaplin and others in films. The Three Stooges took the term literally and made slapstick more physical and outrageous.

Sneak it in, sneak it out   During performances things go wrong and mistakes are made. When an SM must make a minor correction on the stage in full view of the audience, the SM may ask the stagehand or technician to slowly take out that which is incorrect and put in that which is correct. Sneaking in or sneaking out minor mistakes such as light cues or sound cues can be done without major distraction to the play, actors, or audience. Scenery and prop mistakes, no matter how minor, are more obvious and distracting. In all such cases, it is better to leave the mistake and not try to sneak it in or out.

Snow machine, snow cradle   A device or unit hung in the *flys* above the stage and out of view of the audience. When they were first used in theatre they were usually made of cloth and hung like a sling or cradle. Within the sling or cradle was the material that, from the audience's point of view, could be interpreted as snowflakes. Throughout the cloth of the sling were holes through which small amounts of the snow material could pass. When the sling or cradle was jiggled or moved in a rolling fashion, the snow material passed through. Today snow machines are much improved. Some are still operated manually, but most are motorized. Most are enclosed cylinders with holes or slits along the surface. Inside are lightweight plastic flakes that look more like snowflakes.

Soft edge   See **Sharp edge, hard edge, soft edge**

Soft opening   When a show performs for a paying public before the official opening date and before the critics are asked to come to pass their judgment and make their commentary. Producers use this approach with difficult and expensive shows to work out problem areas and ensure critical success.

Soliloquy   See **Monologue**

Soubrette   Minor female roles—pert, coy, or coquette in character. (See also **Ingenue**)

Sound check   There are four types of sound checks:

1. The SM has little to no involvement in the first type of sound check, which is done when a show first sets up in a theatre or performance site. It is for the sound department to balance and equalize the sound. (See also **Pink noise**)

2. For a musical show, there is a sound check between the orchestra and the sound department. As the orchestra plays, the sound department adjusts the levels for the mics set up with the different instruments, and balances the sound the audience will hear during the performance.

3. The third kind is for the performers while on stage. The SM is responsible for scheduling and facilitating this event, and seeing that the actors speak their lines as they move about the stage. Depending on the production, the actors may be wearing *body microphones,* have only the use of stage mics that are strategically placed about the stage, or have a combination of the two.

4. For musicals or variety arts shows, the sound check is done in combination with the music/orchestra and the artist singing. Also during this kind of a sound check, the level of the monitor speakers on stage through which the artists can hear the music and/or their own voices is adjusted.

Sound mixer   See **Mixer**

Sound monitors   Sound speakers to amplify the dialogue, music, or sound effects during the performance. (See also **Monitors; Speakers**)

Spacing   The placement and space between people, props, and scenery on the stage. Spacing is the layout, the composition, and the overall picture as seen by the audience. Directors, choreographers, and SMs are most concerned with spacing, especially when a large number of people are on stage. To assure that the spacing and stage picture remains the same for each performance, *spike marks* may be placed on the stage and *dance numbers* are placed on the *apron* at the edge of the stage.

Speakers   Units that broadcast sound out to the audience. The terms speakers and monitors are used interchangeably, but for the SM it is best to keeps the terms separate, using *speakers* for the sound being delivered to the audience, and *monitors* for the sound being delivered to the performers on stage and the cast and crew backstage.

Special   A small area or *pool of light* on the stage to highlight or single out something. Specials usually consist of one lighting instrument or sometimes two, but seldom more. Specials can be used alone with no other lighting on stage, or in conjunction with other lights.

Speech   Several lines spoken by an actor without the interruption of another character's dialogue. A speech with more than several lines can become a *monologue*.

Spelvin, George   A fictitious name that appears in the program in place of an actor's real name. Actors will sometimes use this name when performing in a show that is not sanctioned by Equity. Producers and actors also will use this name when an actor is playing more than one role in a show, and they don't want the audience to know the real identity of the actor playing the additional role. The name George Spelvin is an inside joke among the people in theatre and its use and purpose are not commonly known to the public.

Spike marks   Pieces of tape or paint marks placed on the stage floor to mark the positions of the set, set pieces, platforms, props, furniture, and where actors are to stand. With these marks, things can be properly placed every time for every performance. (See also **Hit your mark**)

Spill, spill light   Unwanted light on stage that is falling on an object or into another area.

Spot   An abbreviated term for spotlight.

Spot lamp   A bulb or stage lighting instrument that confines and concentrates the intensity of light to a specific and small area, as opposed to flooding and distributing the light into a larger and undefined area.

Spotlight   See **Carbon arc spotlight; Follow spot; Limelight**

Spotting   A technique dancers use when doing a series of turns to help keep their balance, remain in one place on the stage, and keep from getting dizzy. The dancers choose a spot to look at and, as they turn their bodies, they try to keep their eyes focused on the spot as long possible. When it becomes physically impossible for their eyes to remain fixed on the spot, they release their gaze, whip their heads around, and return their focus to the same spot. They will repeat this action as long as they continue their turns.

SRO (standing room only)   Theatres used to be designed and constructed with a space at the back of the audience just behind the orchestra seating. This space was part of the pathway or walkway for patrons to use as they were going to their seats or leaving to go to the lobby. If a show was a sellout, producers would paste in large letters across the *three-sheet posters* in front of the theatre, "SRO," and sell more tickets, at a slightly reduced price, to patrons who were willing to stand at the back to see the show. This was permissible as long as the aisles, emergency fire-escape routes, and exits were not blocked. Today the construction of theatres has changed. There is no longer that space at the back and with the enforcement of stricter fire laws, no one is permitted to stand to watch the show regardless of what space might be available at the back of the theatre. However, people in theatre continue to use this term simply to indicate that the show is a sellout.

Stage business   An all-encompassing term that includes the *movement, action,* and *timing* of anything that happens on the stage during the performance. This is primarily the physical part of the play: the actor's *blocking,* the dancers' *choreography,* or the changing of props and scenery. Stage business comes mostly from the storyline and the inventive minds of the actors and director. It adds interest, continues the illusion of reality, and can heighten the drama or comedy.

Stage clamp, squeeze clamp   A device that operates like a pair of pliers or scissors. However, a stage clamp has great tension between the handles and requires squeezing to open rather than being easily manipulated with the fingers. A stage clamp is used to hold things firmly together. The part that is clamped onto things is designed with serrated teeth for better gripping and holding. This tool is a favorite with technicians and SMs, for it is a quick fix to hold flats together or pinch a split in a curtain that should remain closed.

Stage directions   Information included in a script in addition to the dialogue. At the beginning of an act or scene, the stage directions may give information to help set up the plot, storyline, mood, atmosphere, scenic layout, or characters. The stage directions written within the scene, in parenthesis, and between the lines of dialogue, give information dealing specifically with the character.

In an original, unproduced script, the stage directions are written by the author. In a play that has been produced and then published, much of the stage directions come from the director and actors as it was created and performed in the show.

Stage level   Anything that is placed on the same floor or level as the stage. The backstage area is, of course, on stage level. The star's dressing room may be on stage level while the others may be on floors above or below.

Stage mics   Microphones placed at the edge of the stage or hanging from above to help amplify and support the actors in projecting their dialogue out to the audience.

Stage mother, stage parent   A parent, guardian, or assigned adult who is in charge of and responsible for a child performer, or a performer who is a minor. By state law, a responsible adult is required to be with the minor at auditions, during rehearsals, and during all performances.

Stage picture   The overall look and composition of the stage as viewed from the audience. This includes both the scenery and the placement of actors.

Stage right (SR), stage left (SL)   Split the stage in half by first finding the center of the stage and then running an imaginary line from the *apron* edge up to the back. All parts of the stage that fall on either side of that line become SR and SL. However, SR and SL are always the actors' right and left as they stand facing the audience. In our Western society where we read and view things from left to right, it becomes a natural thing to view the stage in the same way, placing stage left on our left and stage right on our right. SR and SL is never determined from the audience's point of view. People first working in the theatre often become confused and it sometimes takes a while for them to make the change in concept and view. SMs must get this information fixed firmly in their minds and know it as surely as they know their names. (See also **House right, house left**)

Stage setting   The design and layout of the stage. The scenery, props, dressing, lighting, and sometimes the performers used to create the overall picture on stage.

Stage whisper   Actors saying their dialogue as if whispering, but loud enough for the patrons sitting in the last row of the audience to hear.

Staging   The arrangement and order of the physical *movement* and *action* of the play as created by the director and actors. Creating composition and design on the stage with the use of technical elements as well as the physical presence of the actors. (See also **Blocking**)

Stand by

1. To ask an actor or stagehand to remain nearby, waiting, and ready to do a part of their job.
2. For the SM *calling cues* during a performance, the phrase stand by is the second part of a three-part phase. First is the *warning*, second is the *stand by*, and third is the *GO!*
3. A stand by is also an actor who has been rehearsed in a particular role, and who remains available to step into the role at any time. Some stand-by actors are required to come to the theatre for each performance. Others are free to do as they choose as long as they remain available when called upon. Actors who accept stand-by status usually are compensated for keeping themselves available, usually are standing by for a star or lead role, and

often are themselves actors with some celebrity status.

Standing room only   See **SRO (standing room only)**

Star shows   Shows that have cast in them a star performer. Also an expression used to further categorize the type of shows on which an SM works. (See also **Star vehicle**)

Start at the top   See **At the top**

Star vehicle   A show in which a star playing the main character is pivotal and important to the storyline and action of the play. Fanny Brice in *Funny Girl* was a star vehicle for Barbra Streisand. The characters Felix and Oscar in *The Odd Couple* are star vehicles for the actors playing those roles. *Phantom of the Opera* is less of a star vehicle because the Phantom, Christina, and Raoul share the importance in storyline and action. *A Chorus Line* is not a star vehicle. (See also **Star shows**)

Step on a line, step on someone's line   To overlap and sometimes cut off another actor's speech or business before they are finished speaking. In life, people regularly cut into what other people are saying. On stage, it is the job and craft of the actor to create the illusion of real and spontaneous conversation, and at the same time not step on someone's line, *action*, or *business*.

Stills   See **Production pictures, production shots, production stills**

Stock, stock company, summer stock, stock contract   Theatre performed mostly during the summer months. Shows produced in towns that attract a tourist or vacationing crowd. Shows performed in stock usually are recreations of originals, scaled down in *production values*, and usually are produced on a smaller budget. Stock is a good source of work for actors and SMs during a time of the year when there is apt to be fewer shows being produced for Broadway or in regional theatres. (See also **Repertory theatre; Resident company**)

Stop and go rehearsals   In rehearsals as the actors *run a scene*, the director may stop the actors to clean-up or correct parts of the scene. The director will then have the actors run the change and continue with the scene until the next moment arrives that the director feels needs fixing. (See also **Work through**)

Store/storage   The places backstage where things are kept before they are brought out to be used in the performance. "The train unit will store behind the cyc until we are ready to use it in the second act." (See also **Live**)

Straight plays   An expression used to separate comedy and drama plays from musical plays.

Strike

1. To remove from the stage. To take away or clear away.
2. An aggressive action taken by actors or stage-hands, under the leadership of their unions, to not work until contract negotiations resume and dis-agreements are resolved.

Strip lights   See **Boarder lights, strip lights teaser lights, bank of lights**

Strobe light   A lighting instrument placed at the front of the stage, either on the floor or hung from above. A strobe light is designed to pulsate or flicker on and off many times per minute. This light works best on a dark stage with no other lights. As the performers move naturally under this light, they appear to move in short, choppy, or jerky movements, creating an eerie, comical, or old-time movie effect. The effect is simply done. Each time the light goes out, the audi-ence does not see the movement made in the dark. The dark moment is so brief that the brain discounts the dark and connects together only the lighted mo-ments.

Subscribers   Theatre patrons who purchase tickets for a season of plays by paying in advance. (See also **Sea-son tickets**)

Subscription tickets   See **Season tickets**

Supernumerary, super   See **Atmosphere people**

Swag, swag drapes   Anything that is hung in a rounded or looped fashion. A rope, chain, or electrical cable can be hung in a swag. More commonly, the top part of a curtain can be pulled back into a swag while the bottom part continues to hang downward. (See also **Tab curtain, tab drapes**)

Swatch of material   A small piece of material or fabric—a sample piece. Costume designers often attach to their *sketches* swatches of material to give the pro-ducer, director, performers, and even the set designer an idea of the look and color of the costumes before they are constructed.

Swivel casters   See **Casters**

Sync or synchronization   See **Click (clique) track; In sync; Lip sync**

Tab   A flat, a curtain, or a piece of material placed on the stage to block or mask the audience's view of the backstage areas. (See also **Return**)

Tab curtain, tab drapes   A certain way a curtain opens and remains hanging. As the rope is pulled to open a tab curtain, the curtain parts in the middle. The top parts of each side pull upward and off to their respec-tive sides into *swags*. As the swags are being formed, the bottom parts to each side travel along, but remain hanging downward, bunching together into pleats

and folds. On occasion, instead of the curtain parting in the middle, the tab will start at the far side of the curtain and pull into one large swag. Tab curtains and drapes are most commonly used to frame prosce-niums, windows, or archways.

Tab a curtain back   To tab a curtain back is to have a person stand behind a curtain, concealed from the au-dience's view, and at a prescribed time, pull the cur-tain back or to the side. The curtain is opened just far enough to allow someone or something to pass through without getting entangled or *hung up* in the curtain. (See also **Page**)

Table read   The cast, director, SM, and sometimes the producer and writers, all seated around a table or group of tables, usually in the rehearsal hall, to read the play for the first time. This term originated in tele-vision and then made its way to theatre.

Tab out   An expression used mostly by designers, direc-tors, stagehands, or SMs, asking that the *tab curtain* open in its normal tabbing fashion in view of the au-dience, and then disappear from the stage up into the *flys*.

Tab show   A cut-down version of a play or musical in which the actors perform only parts of the scenes. If the show is a musical, the actors do the important storyline/dialogue, then go into the songs.

Tag   Something added on to the end. A tag is a small or short addition to the main body of a scene, a song, or a piece of music. Its purpose is to punctuate, empha-size, or bring finality. In a play it can be one word, a line of dialogue, or a very short scene. In a musical a tag can be a note, a chord, or a few bars at the end of a song or instrumental number. (See also **Button; Reprise**)

Take a beat   A second in time. Actors may be told to take a beat before saying their next line or doing their next piece of business. An SM may take a beat before calling the next cue.

Take it out

1. Usually an order given to a stagehand who is working on the rail, requesting that a drop, cur-tain, piece of scenery, or something that is presently on the stage, be flown out and taken from view.
2. Take it out can also be a direction to an actor to remove something from the performance—some-thing that is not *playing* well, does not fit the char-acter, or something the performer has added that the producer, director, or SM have decided should not be in the show.

Take stage   An actor who enters the stage or scene in character and with authority. An actor who moves about the stage with ease, assurance, and comfort, commanding the audience's attention and focus. Ninety-eight percent of the time, taking stage is good and part of the actor's craft in performing. Only when it is motivated from the ego or designed to bring attention to oneself as in *mugging,* doing *schtick,* or trying to *steal the scene,* is it wrong and not wanted.

Taking focus   See **Focus**

Taping the set   This is strictly SM's work. Before the rehearsals begin, it is the SM's job to tape on the rehearsal room floor, the life-size dimensions of the set and performing area. In a *one-set show* this is a relatively easy task. For multiscene musicals with different settings, the SM must overlay each set with a different colored tape to distinguish one from the other. At times there can be as many as five different colors on the floor. However, once the rehearsal furniture is in place for a scene and the actors are told which color to follow, there are relatively few problems in this technique of taping and overlaying sets on the rehearsal room floor.

Taping the show   The word taping in this phrase refers to videotaping. For clarity in communication, it is best if the SM uses the full term videotaping. (See also **Videotaping**)

Teasers   See **Boarders, teasers, valance**

Tech   The abbreviation for *technical.*

Technical rehearsals (techs)   The period during rehearsals in which the technical elements of the show are brought together in the theatre and combined with the work done by the director and actors in the rehearsal hall. The term *mounting the show* is also used to describe this period in rehearsals.

   During the technical rehearsals the *cues* that the SM *calls* during each performance are set. Once all the technical elements have been added and the cues established, technical rehearsals become *dress rehearsals.* Technical rehearsals usually end once a show opens. However, if a show is heading to Broadway, technical rehearsals will continue intermittently to incorporate changes that affect the technical elements of the show.

Template

1. A flat cutout of an object as viewed from above. It usually is made from *card stock* or a thin plastic. SMs will make a template of a large prop, a *turntable, platform,* or *set unit* that is used in many scenes or gets moved to various positions on the stage. The SM draws and cuts out the template to scale to fit either into the *blueprint drawings,* or into the SM's own personal 8½-by-11-inch floor plans. The template can be used as a stencil or a handy tool by laying it on the floor plan and showing the actors, director, and technicians how the object fits into the various settings, or how it travels to the different positions.

2. Another kind of template shows up in the electrical department. It usually is a square piece of tin with a pattern or design cut out within the square. This tin is placed into the front part of a lighting instrument and as the light passes through the cutout, its pattern is projected onto the stage. (See also **Gobo**)

Tempo

1. The speed at which the rhythmic beat of a measure of music is played.
2. In acting, tempo is the pace or speed at which the actor performs: the pace and speed at which the actor delivers dialogue and performs the *blocking* in the various moments and scenes throughout the play.

Ten out of twelve (hours)   Normally, an actor's workday is 8½ hours long, from the time they are called in to the time they are excused to go home. This includes 7 hours for work and a 1½-hour meal break.

   When it is time to go into *technical rehearsals,* because of the amount of work that must be done during this period, the actor's union, Equity, has agreed with producers to extend the actors' workday to 10 hours with 2 hours for a meal break. The actors' workday, from the time they are called in to the time they are excused, is now 12 hours long. Thus the term "ten out of twelve."

The theatre is dark

1. This is when a theatre is closed, having no event or production performing in it.
2. For the people working in a show, the theatre goes dark on their days off—the days the cast does not perform the show. Most dark days are on Monday.

Theatrical license   A liberty taken on stage and in a play that may not be true to real life.

   The best example of theatrical license is *timing.* In many plays, the amount of time it takes for the action and storyline to be completed is shorter than the amount of time it would take in real life. An actor striking a match, putting it to wood in a fireplace, then having an electric light come on to represent the glow of the fire or perhaps a fan blowing shredded colored silks to represent the flame of a fire, is theatrical license. In most cases, the audience accepts whatever theatrical license is given to them and does not let it take away from their sense of reality or distract them from the performance or their entertainment.

Third electrics   See **First electrics**

Three-sheet poster   The large 41-by-81-inch posters placed in glass cases or on billboards outside in front of the theatre. The term three sheet comes from the fact that in times past printers had to print these posters in three separate pieces. The pieces were then pasted up in front of the theater to make one large poster. With the advancement and improvement of printing presses and reproduction of pictures and artwork, a three-sheet poster is now printed in one piece. (See also **Window cards**)

Throw it away

1. A direction given mostly to performers telling them to give less emphasis or importance to a line of dialogue, an *action,* a reaction, or piece of *business.*
2. A throw-away line is a line of dialogue that the director and/or actor decides is not important and is written into the script more for coloring or expression of character.

Throw a line   A colloquial expression used by actors, directors, and SMs. During rehearsals, actors sometimes forget a line of dialogue. Upon request from the actor or director, it is the SM's job to give (or throw) the line that cannot be remembered.

Thrust stage   A stage in which a good portion of the floor goes past the *proscenium* arch and out into the audience, covering what might have been an orchestra pit. If the thrust is not too wide and if it projects far enough out into the audience, patrons may be seated on the three sides of the thrust.

   Runways are a form of a thrust stage, but narrower. A runway, however, does not best describe a thrust stage. For clarity in communicating, the SM should keep the terms separate.

Ties, tie lines   Short lengths of sturdy, thin rope 12 to 18 inches long. Along the tops of curtains and drops are grommet eyelet openings. These lengths of tie line are knotted into each opening, leaving two loose ends of equal lengths. To hang the curtains or drops in the flys, pipes are lowered and the loose ends of the tie lines are tied to the pipes. Tie line is also important in the electric department in tying cables together or tying electric cable along pipes in the flys.

Timing

1. Having to do with the actual length in minutes of a scene or the entire play.
2. The speed, pace, and *tempo* at which a scene plays.
3. The actor's delivery. Through timing, an actor gets the most impact, value, and entertainment out of the dialogue or the business in the performance.
4. The SM's calling cues during the performance at precisely the correct time.
5. Creating the illusion of real time and yet taking *theatrical license* to keep the show moving at an entertaining pace.

Toe dancer   A classically trained ballet dancer, who with the use of special hard toe ballet slippers, dances on his or her toes.

Tormentors   Tall *flats,* pieces of scenery, or long curtains (about 8 to 10 feet wide) that are placed on each side of the stage to make up the *wings* and hide the activity of the backstage from the view of the audience. The term tormentor is also used when describing the *boarders* or *teasers* hanging overhead—the narrow flats or curtains that run across the length of the stage, covering the technical equipment hanging above.

Touring show   See **Road show**

Trades, trade papers   Newspapers, magazines, and other publications dealing with theatre, show business, or entertainment in general. In addition to articles about theatre, many of these publications list auditions for actors, talk about upcoming shows, and sometimes advertise for SMs.

Translucent   A material that allows light to pass through but cannot be seen through, such as frosted glass, some plastic materials, or thin muslin. When lit from the front, translucent materials appear solid or opaque. When lit from the back, the light passing through becomes defused, leaving a glow. When translucent material is lit from the back and a performer steps into that light, a very clear and distinctive shadow or silhouette is created. (See also **Opaque; Transparent**)

Transparent   Materials or substances that allow light to pass through so that things beyond or behind can be seen. (See also **Opaque; Translucent**)

Trap doors (traps)   A cutout in the stage floor through which performers, props, scenery, or special effects can pass, either entering or exiting the stage. When covered with the same material as the stage floor, the trap doors become barely visible to the audience. Magicians use trap doors effectively. Stagehands shorten the term to *traps.*

Traveler, traveler curtain

1. A traveler is a curtain that splits in the middle and each half glides off to its respective side. The traveler can be operated manually or by electric motor. On some occasions, a traveler curtain may start at one end of the stage and travel across the entire length to the other side. In some theatres when there is no fly space above the stage, this kind of traveler is especially useful. Drops can be hung on it and moved on and off stage when needed.
2. The term traveler refers also to the steel mechanism or rod that is above the stage and hidden from view of the audience, and on which the curtains or drops are hung.

Trim, high trim, mid trim, low trim, out position   Speaking in terms of the fly system, trim is the various levels or heights at which the drops, curtains, and so forth, are set and seen by the audience. The levels or heights are set according to the bottom line of the item hanging. When the item is hanging in the flys out of sight, the trim is in the *out position.* When needed on stage, the piece is brought to the *low trim,* which means the bottom line of the item is set down on the stage floor. The *high trim* and a *mid trim* are heights in between.

A good example of these trims takes place in the opening scene of the musical *How to Succeed in Business Without Really Trying.* The character Finch enters on a scaffold from above the stage. The scaffold starts up in the flys in the out position. Just before the performance starts, the actor gets on the scaffold. On cue from the SM, the scaffold is brought first to a high trim for the initial entrance and to begin the opening song. On further cues, the scaffold is lowered to a mid trim for the middle part of the song, then to the low trim so the actor can get off. In its final move, the scaffold is brought back up into the flys and into the out position.

For technicians, directors, designers, and SMs, trim is also seeing that the bottom line of any item hanging on stage from the *flys* is straight and parallel to the stage floor. At times an item can slip out of trim, with one end hanging higher or lower than the other. If the SM sees this problem, the SM must communicate it to a stagehand to be resolved. This is where knowledge of the *long-line* and *short-line* is most valuable. (See also **Long line, short line**)

Trip line   A rope or wire that is pulled or tugged to release a catch or hook, which in turn releases something to fall, drop, shoot out, or pop open.

Truck, hand truck   See **Dolly, truck**

Truss   A grid of aluminum tubing bars on which lighting instruments and heavy equipment such as sound speakers can be safely hung. The grid may be suspended above the stage in the flys or out in front of the *proscenium,* hanging in full view of the audience and over the heads of those sitting in the first rows of the *orchestra seating.*

Tryouts

1. This term is most commonly used today when talking about the out-of-town performances of a new show, before going to Broadway.
2. This term is also used in place of *auditions.* Used mostly by people not in theatre.

Turkey, flop   A failed show. Turkey is a more derogatory term and implies that the show was bad. A flop can sometimes be a critical success but a financial flop at the box office.

Turn-around time

1. A period of time between the end of one event and the start of another: for example, the time it takes at the end of one performance for the stage crew, SM, and actors to set up and be ready for another performance.
2. The amount of time off labor unions have established between the end of one day's work and the start of the next. For the actors, Equity has established twelve hours. For the stagehands, IATSE has made it eight. If either the group as a whole or the individual members are called in any sooner, the producer is required to pay overtime and possibly a penalty.

Turntable   See **Revolve**

Two-fold or three-fold flats, booking flats   Two or three 10-by-4-foot flats hinged or *lashed* together. Two-folds and three-folds are able to stand freely by themselves. They are convenient and useful for the SM in many ways and situations. They can be set up quickly as a backing to hide the distracting backstage activity from view of the audience, and are especially useful in setting up a *quick change* dressing area.

Two-for (pronounced *too-fer*)   A short electric cable that has two female plugs spliced in at one end, which allows two items to be plugged in at the same time. At the other end there is one male plug that is plugged into one power source, supplying power to the two female plugs.

Type casting   Choosing actors because of their physical appearance, their qualities, or characteristics. Choosing actors to play certain roles because they have successfully played them in the past. Sometimes a certain type of role is what they do best. Other times, it is the only part they can play. Still other times it is the only part producers, directors, or casting people can imagine an actor playing.

Ultraviolet light (UV)   See **Blacklight**

Understudies   Actors chosen and paid to learn the various principal roles within a show that are being performed by another actor. Understudies within a show usually are actors already hired to play a smaller role, or they are members of the *ensemble.* If for any reason the regular actor cannot perform, the understudy must be ready to perform the role at a moment's notice. Understudies are the producer's insurance policy that the show will go on. In many situations, it is the SM's job to rehearse the understudies and get them *up* on their roles. (See also **Stand by**)

Unit, set unit, wagon   A unit or set unit is a piece of scenery that fits into part of the main set or is made to stand on its own. Such units are brought on stage for smaller scenes while the lights go dark on the rest of the set. For mobility and ease in moving, a set unit can be flown in from the *flys* or built on a platform with *casters* and wheeled on and off stage. Stagehands will sometimes call platform units on casters wagons.

Unit set   A basic set that remains on the stage for the entire play. As the play progresses and scenes change, different pieces of scenery may be brought in and props and furniture may be changed to give the set a different look.

Up

1. For performers to be up on their lines, is to say the performers have the lines memorized and can recite them without laps of memory. Similarly, for performers to be up on their parts means that they are ready to perform them.
2. To say a performer went up on the lines can mean the performer either forgot lines, got them mixed up, or jumped ahead several lines or pages of dialogue.

Up on your feet   Directors and SMs use this expression in the early part of rehearsals, when placing the actors on stage, adding *movement to* the show—adding the *blocking* and *business*. Similarly, a director gets a scene or the entire play up on its feet.

Up stage (US)

1. The direction an actor travels on stage when moving away from the audience and up toward the back part of the stage. A direction given to actors as the director *blocks* the show—"Cross up stage to the sofa."
2. A different use of this term is when an actor during performance stands just slightly up stage of another to deliver dialogue. There is no problem with this positioning until the actor standing further down stage must speak lines. This actor is forced to turn up stage to say the lines, thus facing away from the audience. In most *blocking* situations, this is neither comfortable for audience viewing nor desirable to the actor who must turn up stage. In blocking the show, directors and actors are careful to avoid this.

   Standing up stage with the other actors on stage having their backs to the audience is a strong position and brings the attention and focus to the actor standing up stage. For a particular moment in a scene, a director might choose to position the actors on stage in such a manner. Sometimes, intentionally or unintentionally, during a scene of dialogue an actor may move one or two steps further up stage. If done continually, the other actors will complain bitterly to the SM, and it becomes a situation the SM must resolve without delay.

Valance   In the world of curtains and drapery, a valance is the material at the top that is separate from the rest of the curtain. A valance adds design interest and helps frame the curtain or opening in which it is hung. Sometimes the material of the valance hangs straight down in pleats or folds. Other times the valance is draped in a *bunting* or *swag* design.

Variety act   A performing artist, such as a singer, dancer, mime artist, magician, juggler, etc., who has put together a piece of entertainment that can be put into a show.

Variety show   A show in which there are various types of acts, singers, dancers, comics, jugglers, magicians, or whatever a producer and/or director might put together for an audience's entertainment.

Velour   A velvety material made of good quality cotton. (See also **Duvetyn, velour, velveteen**)

Velours   A general term used for the curtains or drapes that hang on stage and are made of *velour, duvetyn,* or *velveteen* material.

Velveteen   A material that looks and feels like velvet but is not of the same quality. (See also **Blacks; Duvetyn; Velour**)

Video monitors   Television screens placed throughout the backstage areas for the cast, crew, and SM to visually monitor the performance on stage. At present only a single-lens camera is used, giving a full view of the stage. The camera usually is placed on the *balcony rail* out of view and reach of the audience.

Videotaping   Recording on videotape a scene, parts of the show, or the entire show. The SM must be watchful for any kind of videotaping of the show or of the actors' performances. All videotaping must first be cleared by the producer, director, actors, and Equity. Otherwise, fees and penalties must be paid by the producer.

Vignette   A short scene or sketch.

Wagon   See **Unit**

Walk the curtain   To stand behind one of the ends of a curtain, out of view of the audience, and walk with the curtain as it is opening or closing, and possibly guiding it around set pieces, props, or pieces of furniture which might be placed on or near the *curtain line*. (See also **Page**)

Walk-on part   See **Bit part**

Walk-through (walk-thru)   To go through a scene, an act, or the entire show, doing everything that is done during a performance, but doing it at half the intensity or *performance level*. Directors may choose to do this with the cast to conserve their energy. An SM may do this as a refresher rehearsal, after the cast has been away from performing the show for several or more days. (See also **Read through; Run through; Work-through**)

Warm up

1. An SM or a director asks the dancers and singers to warm up by physical and vocal exercise before a rehearsal or performance so they won't injure their bodies or voices.

2. A person who steps out on stage before the show begins to talk to the audience, welcome them, put them in a good mood, and set them up for the performance they are about to see. This might be done by the producer, director, or even the star of the show; for dress rehearsals that are attended by an audience; or for preview performances. In regional theatre, where much of the audience is made up of season ticket holders, the producer or the figurehead of the organization might come out before each performance to talk to the audience. Unlike the *master of ceremonies,* the warm up person is not seen during the show and may or may not return at the end of the performance.

Warnings   For the SM, the warning is the first part of the three-part phase in *calling cues*. First is the warning, second is the *stand by*, and third is the *GO!* Warnings are important because they alert the technicians/stagehands that a cue is coming up, and allows them time to prepare to execute the cue.

Wash   General stage lighting that covers or washes across the entire stage and set. A wash is flat and uninteresting lighting. It must be used with other lights that bring color, depth, and dimension to the set and performers.

White noise, room noise   An SM may hear this term used by one of the technicians in the sound department. In simplest terms, white noise is general ambient sound or the sound that is present in a quiet room. This term has no relevance or effect on the SM's job. The term *pink noise* does. (See also **Pink noise**)

Winch   A cranking device operated from the backstage by one or two stagehands which enables a turntable to turn or set units to glide on and off stage. Winches were first made of wood and used ropes to move the objects. Later they became steel frame devices using heavy gauge steel cables. Shortly thereafter, electric motors were attached, reducing the labor to the turn of a switch. Today they remain motorized, but are controlled by computer.

Window cards   Replica copies of the show poster, but downsized to 22-by-14 inches. They are printed on heavy *card stock,* distributed to businesses and merchants. The window cards are usually placed in storefront windows or in places where the patrons of the different establishments can easily see the card. (See also **Three-sheet poster**)

Winging it   A performer working extemporaneously or by improvisation, performing without previous planning or rehearsal—sometimes without benefit of a script. In a moment of emergency, a performer may be asked to go on stage to hold the audience's attention while the problem is being resolved. Whatever the performer does during that time is called winging it.

Actors also wing it when they forget the planned/rehearsed parts of their performance, such as the blocking and dialogue, but continue to perform until they find their way back, or until someone comes to save them and lead them back.

Wings   The openings on each side of the stage through which the actors and scenery can enter or exit the stage. The wings are the spaces created by the curtains or flats hung on each side of the stage. The wings are neutral spaces between being on stage and being backstage. They are the area in which actors and scenery wait, remaining unseen by the audience. (See **In one; Legs, tormentors; Sight lines**)

Wireless   A miniature microphone actors wear during their performance. There are no visible wires leading from the microphone head or from the actor. Instead, the actor wears a *radio pack*. The radio pack transmits the sound signals to a receiver. The receiver sends the signal to the amplifier and is then broadcast through speakers. (See also **Body microphone**)

Work in progress   Creating a show in a rehearsal or workshop environment. Creative artists joining together, improvising, acting out a skeleton script, or taking a thread of an idea and building it into a scene and eventually into a show. This way of working was most effectively done in the creation of the musical, *A Chorus Line,* the script of which reflects many of the personal stories the actors brought to the workshop.

Work-through (work-thru)   Rehearsals in which the director will stop to fix, clean up, and refine all elements of the actors' performance. A work-through rehearsal will take place after the actors and director have blocked the scene, an act, or the entire play. Work-throughs are effective after the lines and blocking have been memorized and the actors have had a chance to develop and interpret their characters. A work-thru is similar to a *stop and go rehearsal.* (See also **Cleaning, cleaning a scene; Run through; Walk-through; Working the show**)

Working a scene   In rehearsals, the director and actors perform some or all of a scene, stopping and starting, refining and changing, to improve their work and the overall scene. (See also **Cleaning, cleaning a scene**)

Working drawings   Scale *blueprint drawings* created by the set designer, detailing the design, measurements, and placements of the scenery, drops, furniture, and large props. From these drawings, the artisans and craftsmen construct the set and make or gather the props and furniture. The *light plot,* although separate and not included with the blueprint drawings, serves as the working drawing for the lighting technicians.

Working the show   In rehearsals, the director and actors perform some or all of the show, stopping and starting, refining and changing, to improve their work and the overall show. (See also **Working a scene**)

Work lights

1. Lighting used on stage during rehearsals, when setting the stage with props and scenery for a performance, or when doing technical repairs.
2. The work light is also the one light, required by law, that is left lit on the stage after everyone has left the theatre. This is a safety light, sort of a night light, or as people in theatre have come to call it, the *ghost light.*

Zip cord   Household gauge electrical wire; wire used for extension cords. Zip cords are not designed to power high-wattage lighting instruments such as the ones used to light the stage. A heavier gauge wire or cable is needed and is safer for theatrical use.

Index